CRIMINOLOGY

CRIMINOLOGY

SECOND EDITION

JOHN E. CONKLIN

Tufts University

MACMILLAN PUBLISHING COMPANY
New York

Macmillan Publishing Company
866 Third Avenue, New York, New York 10022

Library of Congress Cataloging in Publication Data

Conklin, John E.
  Criminology.

  Bibliography: p.
  Includes indexes.
  1. Crime and criminals. I. Title.
HV6025.C59 1986   364   85–4980
ISBN 0–02–323790–2

Printing: 1 2 3 4 5 6 7 8   Year: 6 7 8 9 0 1 2 3 4 5

ISBN 0-02-323790-2

PREFACE
TO THE SECOND EDITION

This second edition of *Criminology* has been revised for easier reading and studying, reorganized and expanded to include a new chapter on the criminal justice system, updated to include current statistical material and research published in the five years since the first edition appeared, illustrated with photographs and cartoons, and supplemented with boxed material on crime in other societies.

To make the book easier to read, many more subheadings have been used. The shorter sections make the organization of the book clearer and material easier to locate. References now appear in the text in the style of many journals, with a bibliography and a name index at the end of the book. Important terms are italicized in the text, listed alphabetically at the end of each chapter, and defined in a glossary of important terms at the end of the book. Each chapter now has a detailed but concise summary, as well as an annotated list of suggested readings. In addition, I have carefully edited the entire book for smoother reading.

The book is now organized into four major sections: Perspectives and Methods, The Extent and Nature of Crime, The Causes of Criminal Behavior, and Reactions to Crime. Chapter 1 in the first edition has been subdivided in this edition into two chapters, Chapter 1 on The Study of Crime, and Chapter 2 on Methods of Criminological Research. Chapter 4 in the first edition has been restructured here as two chapters: Chapter 5 on Geographic and Temporal Dimensions of Crime, and Chapter 6 on Social Dimensions of Crime. This second edition includes a new chapter, 14, on The Criminal Justice System, which precedes the three chapters on Deterrence and Incapacitation, Retribution, and Rehabilitation.

This new edition makes extensive use of research that has appeared since the first edition was published in 1981. Many examples are taken from newspapers and magazines that have appeared in recent years. Statistics have been updated, with the most recent available FBI statistics and National Crime Survey victimization data being used. Students and instructors are encouraged to consult annual FBI crime reports and documents that present recent NCS data for statistics published since this book went to press.

I have selected the photographs that illustrate this second edition, and believe that they will contribute to the reader's understanding of crime and societal reactions to it.

A major feature of this second edition is the addition of seventeen boxed selections called "Cross-Cultural Perspectives." These adaptations of articles and books illustrate general points made in the body of the text with material on crime in China, the Soviet Union, Switzerland, Brazil, Greece, Argentina, Italy, India, Israel, Mexico, France, and Great Britain. These cross-cultural perspectives are integrated into the text so that readers will know when to read them and what general points they are illustrating. In addition, other cross-cultural material is presented in the body of the text.

I would like to thank the following for their comments and suggestions for this second edition: Professors David S. Alcorn, Gary Hill, Richard J. Lundman, Michael L. Radelet, and William Wilbanks. I would like to thank James D. Anker, senior editor at Macmillan while this new edition was being prepared, for his encouragement and assistance. Thanks are also due to Patricia Cabeza for her professional production work on the book, and to Joyce Rappaport for copyediting the manuscript. I would like to express my gratitude to Anne Pietropinto at Macmillan, who taught me much in the writing of *Sociology: An Introduction* (1984) that has been helpful in my work on this second edition of *Criminology*. Maureen DeVito's typing of the bibliography is greatly appreciated.

J.E.C.

AUTHOR BIOGRAPHY

John E. Conklin is Professor of Sociology and Chair of the Department of Sociology and Anthropology at Tufts University in Medford, Massachusetts.

Professor Conklin was born in Oswego, New York, in 1943, and raised in Syracuse, New York. He is the father of three children—Chris, Anne, and Lydia—and is married to Sarah Belcher.

After earning a bachelor's degree, with honors in economics, from Cornell University in 1965, Professor Conklin attended Harvard University, completing his doctorate there in 1969. He then worked for a year at Harvard Law School's Center for Criminal Justice. He started teaching at Tufts University in 1970, and now offers introductory sociology, crime and delinquency, deviant behavior and social control, and sociology of law.

Professor Conklin's first book, published in 1972, was *Robbery and the Criminal Justice System*, a study based on data gathered in Boston. In 1973, he edited a collection of papers on organized crime, *The Crime Establishment*. In 1975, Macmillan published his study of community reactions to crime, *The Impact of Crime*. An examination of white-collar crime was published in 1977, entitled *"Illegal but Not Criminal": Business Crime in America*. Macmillan published the first edition of *Criminology* in 1981 and the first edition of *Sociology: An Introduction* in 1984.

CONTENTS

4   The Costs of Crime   65

5   Geographic and Temporal Dimensions of Crime   89

6   Social Dimensions of Crime   111

THREE   THE CAUSES OF CRIMINAL BEHAVIOR   135

7   Biological and Psychological Causes of Crime   137

8   Socioeconomic Causes of Crime   167

9   Social Control and Commitment to the Law   202

10   Learning to Commit Crime

11   Opportunity and Organization to Commit Crime

12 Criminal Careers 301

FOUR REACTIONS TO CRIME 323

13 Community Reactions to Crime 325

Cross-Cultural Perspectives

CRIMINOLOGY

ONE
PERSPECTIVES AND METHODS

Chapter 1 introduces several basic concepts used in the study of crime and delinquency. We examine the social origins of the law—interest groups, public opinion, and expert evidence—and learn that crime is a social phenomenon rather than an intrinsic characteristic of behavior. The conceptual approach around which the book is organized is introduced, and an overview is provided of later chapters on criminal careers, informal and formal reactions to crime, and crime-reduction strategies.

In Chapter 2 we look at several research strategies that criminologists have used to study crime and delinquency. The advantages and disadvantages of each method are explored, and one example of criminological research in which the method has been used is discussed in detail. This chapter shows the broad variety of research methods that criminologists have used and provides some specific findings from their studies.

1

The Study of Crime

We are all interested in crime. We watch police shows on television, go to movies that deal with crime, read mystery novels, and follow crime news on television and in the newspapers. The reasons for the broad appeal of crime as drama include escape, stimulation, relaxation, and the appeal of a "good-versus-evil situation where some sort of hero wins at the end through talent and, very importantly, morality" (Richard Meyers, cited in Pace, 1982: F9).

The portrayal of crime in the mass media does not, however, accurately reflect what criminologists know about patterns and causes of crime. What sociologists, psychologists, economists, political scientists, and biologists know about crime is the product of systematic study. They gather empirical data to test their ideas, and revise these ideas to fit new information. In this book, we focus on sociological research but also draw on material from other disciplines that have studied criminals and criminal behavior.

THE NATURE OF CRIME AND DELINQUENCY

Before we define crime and delinquency, we need to become familiar with some concepts that sociologists use to describe social rules, the violations of those rules, and reactions to those violations.

Basic Concepts: Norms and Deviance, Laws and Crime

All societies have rules that govern behavior. These rules or *norms* make explicit certain social expectations about what is appropriate behavior for particular people in specific situations. Norms reflect the culture's *values*—those things that are considered worthy, desirable, or proper. For instance, the norm that we dress in our best clothes for a wedding or a funeral reflects the importance of the occasion and our desire to show respect for others. The norm against suicide reflects the value that cultures place on the preservation of human life.

Deviance, the violation of a norm, may be approved behavior (as with heroic acts during a battle) or may be disapproved behavior (as with cowardice). In other words, it is possible to deviate from a norm by "overconforming" (for instance, by turning in a hundred-page seminar paper) or by "underconforming" (for example, by turning in merely one page). Usually, however, deviance refers to underconforming or disapproved behavior.

Deviance in a disapproved direction is often met with a *sanction,* an effort to ensure future conformity to the norm and punish past nonconformity. One example would be a failing grade for a student who turned in a one-page seminar paper when a twenty-page paper was required. Another example is the sanctioning of suicide; for centuries, those who killed themselves were prohibited from being buried in consecrated ground, and often their property was confiscated by the state. Sanctions can be informal, including a critical glance or a spanking, or they may be formal, as in a military trial of a deserter or a criminal trial of an accused murderer.

Some informal social norms become legal norms. Through the political and judicial process, *laws* are passed and interpreted, and informal rules become formal laws. As a subset of norms, laws are written down and formalized by the political system. Over the last 150 years, problems once seen as private have increasingly been redefined as public matters warranting the intervention of such official agencies of the state as the police, the courts, and the prisons (Lane, 1967; Silver, 1967).

A *tort* is a civil wrong for which a plaintiff, or complaining party, can sue a defendant who is alleged to have caused the plaintiff harm. The outcome of civil cases is often monetary restitution or damages, with money paid to the victorious plaintiff by the losing defendant.

A *crime,* in contrast to a tort, is an act that violates the criminal law and is punishable by the state. A crime is considered an offense against the state rather than an act against a specific individual. This definition has its origins in medieval Great Britain, where the king replaced formal vengeance by victim against offender with sanctions by the state. Thus, today a robbery is dealt with by the courts as *State* v. *Jones* rather than as *Smith* v. *Jones.* Smith as the victim of the robbery might sue Jones, the alleged robber, in civil court to recover money for damages caused during the holdup, but this rarely happens. Instead, the offense would be dealt with in criminal court, with a prosecutor or district attorney acting on behalf of the state in bringing charges against Jones.

The Characteristics of Crime

Crime is behavior that is subject to legally defined punishment. Indeed, the French sociologist Emile Durkheim (1895, 1933) asserted in the late nineteenth century that punishment is the defining characteristic of crime and that other characteristics—such as social harm—are corollaries rather than defining traits. Punishable behavior includes a myriad of actions, from forcible rape to price fixing and from murder to pollution of the environment. Because crime includes so many diverse acts, it makes little sense to speak of "crime increasing" or "the typical criminal," without referring to specific crimes or specific criminals. However, many crimes have some common characteristics.

Crime usually involves *criminal intent,* the willed or conscious desire to commit an act that violates a criminal law. Prior to the twelfth century, the law did not include the idea of a guilty mind that formed criminal intent; guilt was then based simply on the causing of injury. Over time, the idea of intent was gradually introduced into the law, partly as a result of the influence of Christian teachings about sin and moral blame (McVisk, 1978). However, today not all acts designated as crimes involve criminal intent. Some crimes arise from negligence or recklessness. Others are strict liability offenses, meaning that there is no need to prove criminal intent in order to convict the defendant. For example, having sexual intercourse with a female under the age of consent is statutory rape, even if the male does not know the age of the female and even if he does not intend to break the law.

In most crimes, however, the law requires a causal connection among criminal intent, criminal conduct, and harm. For instance, an act that violates the law and causes harm may not be treated as a crime by the legal system if criminal intent is absent. This practice is based on the idea that punishment makes sense only if the violator of the law is responsible for his or her behavior. For intent to exist, an individual must have criminal capacity, or be in control of his or her own behavior. Capacity is lacking in people who act under duress, are legally insane, are too young to have criminal capacity (usually defined as being under the age of seven), or are not legally adults (usually defined as being between the ages of seven and seventeen or eighteen).

Juvenile Delinquency

People who violate the law but are not legally adults may be found delinquent by judges in juvenile court. Rather than being convicted of a crime, juveniles are adjudged delinquent. These delinquents may have committed an act that would be a crime if committed by an adult. The designation *juvenile delinquent* is also applied to those who commit *status offenses*, acts such as underage drinking, running away from home, or truancy that are violations only because those who engage in them are below the age of majority.

The juvenile justice system was developed in the United States late in the nineteenth century, with the first juvenile court established in Illinois in 1899. The juvenile court was a product of efforts by the *child savers*, people committed to providing delinquent adolescents with help rather than punishment. The child savers saw nineteenth-century cities as breeding grounds for crime, especially by recent immigrants, and they tried to prevent juvenile misbehavior by taking young people from the cities and placing them in reformatories in small towns and rural areas. In theory, these reformatories would have the environment of a "healthy" home, and juveniles would be cured of their deviant behavior through education and retraining in middle-class values (Platt, 1977).

Today the label "delinquent" is applied to youthful offenders under the age of nineteen in one state, to those under the age of sixteen or seventeen in twelve states, and to those under the age of eighteen in other states (*The New York Times,* December 6, 1982). However, every state has also established some conditions under which juveniles can be prosecuted and punished as adults. This is a result of a widespread, and apparently growing, belief that fifteen- and sixteen-year-olds sometimes commit serious crimes knowingly, and that the juvenile justice system provides little punishment for them. Thus, in recent years the punishment of adolescent offenders has begun to replace the types of treatment favored by the child savers. For instance, public outrage over the rape and murder of a twelve-year-old girl by two boys aged fifteen and sixteen led to a change in Vermont law that reduced from sixteen to ten the age at which defendants might be tried as adults in criminal court (*The Boston Globe,* July 12, 1982).

Nevertheless, most states place the primary emphasis on the treatment of juveniles rather than on punishment for the specific acts committed. The of-

In recent years, some critics of the juvenile justice system have called for more punishment of adolescents who commit serious crimes.

Photo by Burt Glinn © Magnum Photos, Inc. © Magnum Photos, Inc. Reprinted by permission of Magnum Photos.

fender's age is thought to confer a kind of diminished capacity. Thus, when a thirteen-year-old boy in Texas shot and killed his English teacher in the classroom, the youth became the subject of a juvenile delinquency proceeding rather than a criminal trial (*The New York Times*, May 19, 1978).

Criminal Sanctions

In its ideal form, the criminal law is specific in nature, uniform in its application, dispassionate in its enforcement, and reflective of the culture's informal norms (Sutherland and Cressey, 1978: 5–8). Criminal law provides a way to control behavior by allowing or prohibiting certain behaviors for particular individuals in specific situations. Thus, in some circumstances a police officer can use lethal force to stop an escaping felon, but a private citizen generally is not permitted to kill an escaping felon. The same act is treated differently because each individual occupies a different status. The law is also specific to the situation. A victim who fears for his or her life during a crime may use lethal force in self-protection and have the action treated as justifiable homicide. However, people are not generally allowed to use lethal force to prevent a simple theft without having to face a charge of murder or manslaughter.

The criminal justice system imposes formal sanctions on those convicted of violating the law. The consequences of these formal sanctions differ from those of such informal sanctions as criticism or banishment from a group. Formal criminal sanctions include the loss of property through a fine, the restriction of freedom through probation, the loss of liberty through imprisonment or incarceration, and even the loss of life through execution. Informal norms are commonly cast in terms of a positive goal; for example, a term paper must be completed for a course. Legal norms are more often stated in terms of kinds of behavior to avoid; people are told not to kill or to steal property.

Formal Laws and Informal Norms

Critical to the functioning of the criminal law is the consistency between formal laws and informal norms. In complex societies such as the United States, where many groups with different norms live side by side, it is inevitable that some laws will not be supported by the norms of all groups. Thus a significant proportion of the American public favors the legalization of marijuana, but most people continue to support existing laws that punish those who possess, sell, or use the drug. Even punishment for crimes that involve serious harm may not be fully supported by informal norms. For instance, A Yemeni immigrant in California shot to death a fourteen-year-old boy found under the bed of his fifteen-year-old daughter, apparently because the boy had violated the father's strict moral code of Islam (*The Boston Globe*, June 19, 1980). Here the law conflicted with an informal norm about when it was acceptable to take another person's life. See the Cross-Cultural Perspective for a description of a similar situation in contemporary Greece.

In simple tribal societies, informal norms often overlap to a great extent with the law. In these societies there is general agreement between popular attitudes toward right and wrong and the legal definition of crime. This makes for a stable society, even if it is one also characterized by stagnation and unresponsiveness to externally induced change. In such a society, the rights of individuals may be jeopardized because the few are forced to conform to the will of the many.

In complex industrial societies, such as the United States, there is less overlap between the law and informal norms. If the lack of consistency between the two becomes too great, the government may resort to harsh sanctions against those whose actions conflict with the law. This conflict between the law and informal norms may undermine popular support for the government, but it can also keep a society flexible and responsive to change and new ideas.

The law is most likely to reflect informal norms in a society that has a "rule of law," a system in which the law is made through specified channels, announced to the public, and enforced consistently (Selznick, 1969: 11–18; Sutherland and Cressey, 1978: 4–12). Institutions that permit or encourage

A Cross-Cultural Perspective: "Crimes of Honor" in Greece

Conflict between informal norms and the law often characterizes societies undergoing social change. Industrialization and urbanization can divide a country between traditional rural areas and modern urban centers. A modern way of life involves greater reliance on a formal legal system, and the law sometimes conflicts with the standards of behavior in more traditional communities.

In Greece, a society that has a relatively low crime rate, about two-thirds of all murders involve the protection of "family honor." For instance, in a village coffee shop in front of a number of friends and relatives, a fifty-year-old waiter shot and killed a young man who was to have become his son-in-law. The victim had abandoned the waiter's daughter just before the wedding, claiming that her dowry, a furnished apartment, was inadequate. The waiter denied being a murderer, saying he had simply done his duty to protect his family's honor.

A Greek professor of criminology explains these "crimes of honor" as follows:

> The feeling of being insulted is compounded by norms of a restricted society, where the prestige of the family is usually the key to public esteem and where the anonymity or broadmindedness of urban centers is lacking. Resort to murder is the last attempt to regain respect in the eyes of the local community by showing that the offended person would stop at nothing to prove his righteousness. Under these circumstances cold-blooded murder becomes an honor.

The professor also points out that few Greeks adhere to these justifications for murder, and he attributes these crimes to "outdated and distorted values, . . . narrow-mindedness and lack of education." He states that these traits characterize the "least developed parts of Greek rural society," where most of the crimes of honor occur.

Greek law does not exempt these killings from punishment. However, the courts often take informal norms into account when these offenses are tried. One official in Greece's Justice Ministry describes the criminal justice system's effort to resolve differences between the law and informal norms as follows:

> Premeditated murder is murder and cannot justify different legislation, whatever provokes it. But in practice Greek courts unofficially take such traditionally established sentiments into consideration and can be lenient if the culprit has been provoked to extremes.

SOURCE: Based on " 'Crimes of Honor' Still the Pattern in Rural Greece," *The New York Times,* February 10, 1980, p. 22.

popular communication with lawmakers increase the consistency between informal norms and the law. Consistency is also greater when laws are effectively communicated to the public by lawmakers, either through the schools or the press; this socializes citizens in the law and encourages conformity to legal standards.

SOCIAL ORIGINS OF THE CRIMINAL LAW

A detailed examination of all of the factors that influence the criminal law would require a massive book. Here we look at the social sources of the criminal law to which sociologists have paid particular attention.

Crime As a Social Phenomenon

Criminal law is a social phenomenon, and crime itself is a social product. Behavior defined as crime in one society may occur in a different society but not be regarded as suitable for punishment by the state.

We can see the social nature of crime by looking at variations in the legal definition of theft in different societies. Although most societies define theft of property as a crime, there are significant differences in the way this behavior is treated. In Norway, petty theft from a relative with whom the thief lives is not treated as a crime. In Colombia, thieves are exempted from criminal sanctions if they can show that they or their family had a pressing need for food or clothing, that there was no legal way to meet those needs, that no violence was used to perpetrate the theft, and that no more was taken than was necessary (Radzinowicz and King, 1977). The Soviet Union distinguishes between the theft of private property and the theft of socialist property, a distinction based on state ownership of land and the means of production (Chalidze, 1977; Shelley, 1981b; Simis, 1982). Variations in the definition of theft and in sanctions against it also exist *within* the United States. Some states define the cutoff point between petty and grand larceny, for which there are significantly different penalties, as $50, and other states draw the line at $75 or $100. In industrial societies, taking a neighbor's property for personal use is generally regarded as a crime, but in some tribal societies one may actually be expected to take and use a neighbor's property in time of need. Understanding why one society permits such behavior while another condemns it as crime requires a careful study of the social structure, values, and level of economic development of each society.

Theoretical Perspectives on the Criminal Law

Two important theories of the development of the criminal law are the *conflict* perspective and the *consensus* perspective. Both emphasize the political and social nature of the law, but conflict theorists claim that the law benefits some groups to the detriment of others, and consensus theorists regard the law more as a reflection of popular agreement on standards of behavior.

THE CONFLICT PERSPECTIVE

The *conflict perspective* sees criminal law as closely intertwined with the distribution of political power and economic resources in a society (Quinney, 1970; Gordon, 1973; Taylor, Walton, and Young, 1973, 1975a; Krisberg, 1975; Balkan, Berger, and Schmidt, 1980; Inciardi, 1980b; Platt and Takagi, 1981; Bernard, 1981). Conflict theorists argue that only certain behavior is legally defined as crime, and that the people who control power and resources determine which kinds of behavior will be defined as crime and which kinds will be permitted. The criminal law in a capitalist system thus reflects the will of the economic elite, and behavior that threatens the interests of that elite—such as theft and violence by the poor—will be harshly sanctioned (Reiman, 1984).

Some conflict theorists assert that criminologists should link the study of crime to the pursuit of social justice and the liberation of oppressed people (Krisberg, 1975; Taylor, Walton, and Young, 1975a; Schwendinger and Schwendinger, 1975). This view denies the "objective" nature of criminal behavior and regards offenders as victims of oppression. Property crime, for instance, is regarded as an effort to accumulate property as rapidly as possible, a goal highly valued in capitalist systems. These conflict theorists believe that criminology should be "normatively committed to the abolition of inequalities in wealth and power"; it should not try to find those factors that distinguish offenders from nonoffenders or seek ways to change people who violate the law (Taylor, Walton, and Young, 1975b: 44).

The conflict perspective claims that the criminal justice system in capitalist societies is biased against those who are disadvantaged by class or minority-group status. Conflict theorists argue that lower-class people are more likely than middle-class people to be watched by the police, arrested in suspicious circumstances, held in jail rather than released on bail, tried in court, found guilty, and receive harsh sentences (Chambliss, 1969; Reiman, 1984).

The conflict perspective directs attention to the origin of the criminal law. Its critical approach forces criminologists to reexamine their premises and their conclusions. This perspective has also shifted attention from the "conventional crimes" of murder, rape, and robbery to white-collar crime and government corruption, even though conflict theorists have produced relatively few empirical studies of these offenses. Instead, they have either drawn on selected case studies to buttress their arguments, or have relied on research by other criminologists.

The conflict perspective does not explain why capitalist systems such as Japan sometimes have low crime rates, whereas socialist societies such as the Soviet Union seem to have significant amounts of crime (Clifford, 1976; Chalidze, 1977; Simis, 1982). Even if socialist nations did have low crimes rates, this might be accounted for by the oppressive social control that exists in some totalitarian socialist states, rather than by the greater amount of social justice and lesser amount of economic inequality.

THE CONSENSUS PERSPECTIVE

In contrast to the conflict perspective stands the *consensus perspective*. This position claims that the criminal law in any society represents social consensus or agreement about which kinds of behavior should be punished by the state. Consensus theorists propose that the law reflects shared values and norms held by all members of the society, rather than the norms and values of a particular group. Consensus is derived from discussion and compromise by elected lawmakers, rather than imposed on society by a group that controls political power or economic resources (Durkheim, 1895, 1933: 70–110).

Consensus theorists see crime as behavior that exceeds the society's limits of tolerance. In this view, crime is behavior detrimental to the public interest, rather than behavior detrimental to the narrow interests of organized groups that are able to influence the law. For the consensus theorist, the critical question becomes why some people do not share consensual values and thus violate the law, rather than why the law defines their behavior as criminal.

USING THE CONFLICT AND CONSENSUS PERSPECTIVES

Probably the best way to view the criminal law is to examine the degree of consensus and the degree of conflict involved in the passage of a law, as well as the extent of public support for the existing law. Some laws reflect a widespread social consensus; for example, murder and rape are almost universally regarded as harmful acts that ought to be punished (Brown, 1952; Clifford, 1978). Other laws reflect the outcome of social conflict among groups; for instance, an antitrust law in the United States was the result of a victory by small businesses, labor, and farmers over large corporations (Quinney, 1970).

Conflict over a particular law can give rise to consensus about that law over time (Glaser, 1978: 15). For example, laws about predatory acts such as crimes against property and crimes of violence may be initiated through social conflict but perpetuated through consensus. Laws against nonpredatory acts such as gambling and consensual homosexual behavior often stem from the actions of people who think that their own way of life is being threatened by others.

Social Sources of the Law

One important source of the criminal law is conflict between organized interest groups. A second source is public opinion, which can produce changes in the law as that opinion shifts over time. A third influence is expert evidence that points to the need for different criminal sanctions.

INTEREST GROUPS

Interest groups, or people who organize to further their shared economic, political, or moral goals, are often able to use resources such as money and political power to translate their interests into law. Interest groups may be social classes or may be based on a shared economic goal, but often they have a moral rather than economic basis.

Some interest groups base themselves on "moral indignation," a sense that those who "do wrong" should be punished for the sake of justice or for their own good. Sometimes moral indignation is aroused and organized by *moral entrepreneurs,* people who promote the idea that certain behavior is harmful and should be punished (Becker, 1973). Often these "mobilizers of bias" lack direct contact with the groups they condemn (Chambliss, 1974: 20–25). Moral entrepreneurship is relatively uncommon for conventional offenses such as murder, rape, and robbery—crimes that have obvious victims and pose clear threats to the security of person and property—but other kinds of behavior have attracted the attention of moral entrepreneurs. One example was Anita Bryant's campaign to prevent and overturn local laws that guaranteed gays the same legal rights as heterosexuals. Support for this antihomosexual movement came from people seeking to protect a particular way of life and set of values from those they felt were threatening it; the supporters' interests were not primarily economic in nature.

One law that was influenced in a relatively minor way by economic interests was the Prohibition Amendment that was in effect from 1920 to 1933. The most important support for making the sale of alcoholic beverages illegal came from temperance forces who sought to protect "the American way of life" from immigrants who supposedly drank and threatened that way of life. The advocates of prohibition sought to protect their position as exemplars of a particular life style, rather than to augment their economic well-being. Several factors led to the repeal of the Prohibition Amendment, including a lack of resources for enforcing the law and the absence of popular support. Another reason for repeal was economic: New jobs and additional tax revenue that the liquor industry could provide appealed to a nation in the throes of the Great Depression.

Interest groups sometimes succeed in having a law enacted but then fail to get it enforced. The resources and influence of a group may be expended at the enactment stage so that there are no means left to press for enforcement once the law is passed. This was one reason for the failure of Prohibition; the "drys" were able to get the amendment passed but were unable to secure adequate funding, committed agents, and public support for the Prohibition Bureau (Gusfield, 1963).

PUBLIC OPINION

Another important influence on the criminal law is public opinion. For example, popular response to brutal attacks on elderly victims by young robbers led the New York state legislature to consider a special law under which offenders who assaulted and robbed the elderly would be given more severe penalties than criminals who attacked younger victims. A new category of crime defined by the age of the victim would have been created. The proposed law passed the state Senate and Assembly, but was vetoed by the governor in 1977 (Fishman, 1978).

Popular opinion has kept laws against the use, sale, and possession of marijuana on the books, but in recent years in many states the moderation of public sentiments has led to a reduction in penalties for these offenses. The very definition of certain drugs as illegal is largely a result of ideological positions and moral attitudes held by the public. For example, alcohol and cigarettes are legal substances under most circumstances, even though their harmful effects have been demonstrated more clearly than have those of marijuana. Still, marijuana is seen by a majority of the public as a harmful drug that should be kept illegal, and alcohol and cigarettes are seen as substances that should be free of criminal sanctions.

EXPERT EVIDENCE

Evidence collected and presented by experts who have a recognized claim to objectivity may, on occasion, influence the law. For example, research by Harvey Wiley between 1902 and 1906 on the harmful effects of food preservatives on people led to passage of the Federal Food and Drug Act of 1906, which established the Food and Drug Administration (Anderson, 1958). Another influence on this law was the scandal created by Upton Sinclair's novel *The Jungle* (1906, 1960), which revealed the filth that characterized meatpacking plants. Public opinion and interest groups also played a part in the passage of this law, but research evidence and a vivid, thinly fictionalized account of the consequences of no regulation convinced lawmakers to establish federal regulation of food and drugs.

Evidence presented by experts was also used to create a special category of criminal offender known as the sexual psychopath. In most states in which laws against these offenders were passed, a series of dramatic sex crimes had aroused public demand for punishment and treatment of offenders. Psychiatrists were often influential members of commissions that considered changes in the law, and they provided what was widely regarded as objective evidence on which to base laws that defined sex offenders as a group distinct from other criminals (Sutherland, 1950).

The Legalistic Definition of Crime

We have seen that the criminal law is affected by social influences such as interest groups, public opinion, and expert evidence. No behavior is intrinsically criminal; it must be defined as crime by the law. In this sense, both crime and the criminal law are social in origin.

Some criminologists would prefer that criminology focus primarily on the process by which criminal laws are created. For the most part, their work pays little attention to the content of criminal behavior or its causes (Quinney, 1970). In this book, we will spend more time examining the content and causes of criminal behavior than we do exploring the origin of criminal laws, while still recognizing that those laws are social in origin. This position treats crime in a legalistic way, beginning with the law's definition of crime and studying behavior that violates the law, rather than regarding the development of the law as the primary topic of study.

Some criminologists have criticized this legalistic approach, claiming that it implies an acceptance of the values of those who make the law (Becker, 1973; Platt, 1975). This is not necessarily the case, however, for it is certainly possible to recognize the existence of a body of criminal law and examine the content and causes of behavior that breaks that law, without at the same time giving one's moral support to that body of law or personally condemning behavior that violates it.

Sociologists who have sought to replace a legalistic definition of crime with one that is sociological or personal have encountered problems, for crime is by definition a violation of a legal norm rather than a violation of an informal norm, a "conduct norm," or a "human right" (Sellin, 1938; Schwendinger and Schwendinger, 1975; Platt, 1975). Nonlegal norms are less stable and certainly less easy to define than are criminal laws. Abandoning the study of violations of legal norms for the study of violations of informal norms leads either to the general study of deviant behavior or to a study of behavior that the individual sociologist happens to believe is wrong or immoral.

CRIMINOLOGY: THE STUDY OF CRIMINAL BEHAVIOR

Criminology is a discipline that gathers and analyzes empirical data in order to explain violations of the criminal law and societal reactions to those violations. Because crime includes so many kinds of behavior, some criminologists have developed *typologies,* or sets of categories of crimes and criminal careers. Another approach is to develop a conceptual approach to the study of law-violating behavior and apply that approach to different kinds of crime.

Typologies of Criminals

Criminologists have developed several typologies of criminals in an effort to understand better the similarities and differences among various kinds of violations of the law. One influential typology is Don C. Gibbons's (1982) classification of criminal role careers, including the "professional thief role career," the "embezzler role career," and the "opiate addict role career." Gibbons bases his typology on the assumption that much criminal behavior is patterned in a limited number of ways and that a typology can accurately describe offender types. Another useful typology is Daniel Glaser's (1978) categorization of crimes: predatory crimes such as murder and robbery, illegal performance offenses such as public drunkenness, illegal selling offenses such as the sale of narcotics, illegal consumption offenses such as drug use, disloyalty offenses such as treason, and illegal status offenses such as truancy by juveniles.

There are important reasons to distinguish among crimes and criminal careers. An explanation of why one person commits armed robbery may be very different from an explanation of why another person embezzles funds from an employer. However, concepts and theories can help to explain both acts. For instance, the robber and the embezzler may both justify their actions by claiming a lack of responsibility for their behavior or a lack of serious harm to the victim. To use an analogy, the education of medical students does not focus directly on types of diseases, but rather on more general conceptual knowledge that can be applied to the understanding of different diseases. Medical students take courses in anatomy, histology, and pathology, rather than on cancer, high blood pressure, and pulmonary diseases. Criminological theories are not as well developed as medical theories, but there are empirical findings and theoretical ideas available to help us to understand the causes of crime and to develop strategies to reduce the crime problem.

A Conceptual Approach to Criminology

Rather than develop an elaborate typology in this book, we will emphasize the concepts and theories that criminologists have developed, and use those concepts and theories to explain different kinds of crime. For instance, robbery and price fixing are clearly different kinds of behavior, but both offenses might be explained by the concept of relative deprivation, the idea that people commit crimes when they feel they have less than others with whom they compare themselves and when they feel they are rightfully entitled to more than they have.

The conceptual approach used in this book focuses on four factors: the needs and motivations of offenders, the way that potential offenders reduce their commitment to the law, the way that specific skills and motivations to commit crime are learned, and the way that opportunities for crime are found. Let us look briefly at each factor.

NEEDS AND MOTIVATIONS

The needs and motivations of people who engage in crime may be biological in origin, psychological in nature, or socially induced. Thus, a murder may be committed by one person because a brain tumor led to violence, by another person because of delusions about persecution by others, or by a member of a juvenile gang who is trying to impress a peer group by being tough.

REDUCING COMMITMENT TO THE LAW

Having certain needs, desires, or motivations is a necessary but not sufficient reason to commit a crime. Because all people to some extent learn that they should abide by the law, potential offenders must reduce their commitment to the law before they violate it. The critical question becomes, "Why, in a society in which such actions are widely known to be criminal and severely punishable, are they committed?" (Walker, 1974: 61–62). People who violate the law are often only weakly attached to it and to people and institutions that support the law, including parents, teachers, and peers. Being unconcerned about the opinion of others who are committed to a conventional way of life makes it easier to neutralize the constraints of the law. People also neutralize the law by using rationalizations to justify their violations; for instance, they may claim that their circumstances make it acceptable for them to commit a crime.

LEARNING SKILLS TO COMMIT CRIME

Another factor critical to the perpetration of many crimes is the learning of skills needed to commit a crime. This learning may be from the general culture, from the mass media, from other criminals, or from noncriminals who convey values conducive to crime. Safecrackers must learn how to "blow" a safe or pick a lock. Armed robbers have less to learn, because holding a pistol and demanding money require few specific skills. Some offenders use specialized skills that they have employed for legitimate purposes to commit a crime; one example is an accountant who uses bookkeeping skills to embezzle funds from a company by manipulating the books.

OPPORTUNITIES TO VIOLATE THE LAW

Given the need or desire to commit a crime, the reduction in commitment to the law, and the learning of the requisite skills, another factor needed before a crime can be committed is the opportunity to violate the law. Crime is sometimes situational in nature; that is, people who might not otherwise think of breaking the law may commit a crime if they are confronted with a tempting opportunity to make an illicit gain with little risk. Others systematically seek opportunities to commit profitable crimes, planning their offenses in advance and organizing a group of criminals to carry out illegal acts. Social change can increase opportunities for crime. For example, bank robberies have increased with the development of suburban branches that lack good security, and auto thefts have increased as the number of cars available to be stolen has grown.

One aspect of the opportunity to commit crime that we give special attention to is the relationship between offenders and victims. A careful investigation of the interaction between offenders and victims—and the physical and social environment within which they interact—is needed to make sense of criminal behavior and to design effective crime-prevention strategies (Lewis, 1981: 11).

Criminal Careers

Our conceptual scheme can help us to understand the reasons that people commit criminal acts. When individual acts of crime by an offender accumulate over time, we speak of a *criminal career,* a sequence of criminal acts that may lead an offender to change his or her self-concept, behavior, and commitment to a life of crime. An understanding of criminal behavior requires knowledge of the factors that give rise to individual acts that violate the law, but it also requires detailed information about the way that those acts add up to a criminal career.

Reactions to Crime

Society responds to crime in many ways. Some of these are institutional; for instance, the criminal justice system responds by punishing those who are convicted of violating the law. Other responses are less formal, such as the reaction of a bystander to a crime or community action against drug dealers.

COMMUNITY REACTIONS TO CRIME

A community's social structure influences its amount of crime. Tightly knit neighborhoods are often able to keep the crime rate low by maintaining informal social control in an area. Public surveillance of the streets and willingness to call the police can deter potential offenders from violating the law, or cause them to commit their offenses elsewhere.

Later we look at informal social control as one response to crime, and as a factor involved in the causation of crime. We examine the social conditions conducive to bystander intervention in a crime, and collective reactions to crime such as citizen patrols and community action groups. The direct response of people to convicted offenders is also examined, with particular attention to the way that the social isolation of offenders makes their reintegration into society difficult and pushes them back into a life of crime.

THE CRIMINAL JUSTICE SYSTEM

A full understanding of the nature of crime requires attention to the criminal justice system: the police, the courts, and the prisons. What criminals do and how criminal careers develop are influenced by the agents of criminal justice (Pepinsky, 1980). We look at the way that the exercise of police discretion influences who is arrested and who is not. We look at the way that race and sex play a part in the processing of suspects.

The reactions of the criminal justice system to suspected offenders can push them into criminal careers, or deter them from further crimes. However, there is much to learn about crime without limiting the analysis to the behavior of those who are found guilty in court. For instance, we can learn much about robbery by studying police reports of robberies that do not lead to arrest, and we can learn much from interviews with the victims of those robberies.

IDEOLOGICAL JUSTIFICATIONS FOR PUNISHMENT

The formal responses of the criminal justice system to crime are based on several ideological justifications for punishment. These justifications reflect ideas about why offenders should be punished and what might be accomplished by punishing them.

Deterrence and incapacitation   The "first line of defense" against crime is deterrence, the use of sanctions to prevent crime by raising the cost of crime to offenders. We will look at the assumptions that underlie the deterrence model and examine research on the effects of severity, certainty, and promptness of punishment on the deterrence of crime.

We also examine a rationale for punishment closely related to deterrence: incapacitation. Some people believe that crime can be prevented if offenders are locked up for longer periods; keeping them off the streets is seen as a way to keep them from victimizing the public.

Retribution   When the threat of sanctions fails to deter crime, a second rationale for punishment usually enters the picture: retribution. This rationale does not suggest that punishment should try to reduce crime, but only that those who do wrong ought to suffer in return. Moreover, this philosophy of retribution states that suffering should be in proportion to the seriousness of the harm produced and the blameworthiness of the offender.

Rehabilitation   Throughout most of the twentieth century, the rationale for punishment that has dominated American penology is rehabilitation, the idea that convicted offenders should be reformed so that they will not commit crime again. Recently, this model has lost some favor because considerable research has shown that treatment programs have been ineffective in changing offenders. We will look at the way the police, the courts, and the prisons have been influenced by the idea of rehabilitation, and we will evaluate the various treatment methods that have been tried.

Solving the Crime Problem

Conservatives, liberals, and radicals have proposed different ways to solve the crime problem, but in recent years most American political leaders have focused on reform of the criminal justice system as the best way to reduce crime. A second approach to crime reduction that has received less attention from politicians is situational crime prevention, the policy of making it more difficult for offenders to victimize people and property. A third approach, eradicating the causes of crime, has also received little attention from political leaders recently, but it may be the only effective way to reduce crime in the long run.

Ideally, criminology should begin with a description of criminal behavior, using criminal statistics and interviews with offenders. It should then proceed to theories that explain the causes of crime, and conclude with policies derived from those descriptions and theories. Much criminological work does not take this form. It is either descriptive, nontheoretical, and lacking in policy analysis; or it is theoretical without empirical evidence or policy implications; or it prescribes policies but lacks supporting evidence and theoretical justification. The effort in this book is to integrate all three approaches—the descriptive, the theoretical, and the prescriptive.

SUMMARY

Criminology is the systematic study of violations of the criminal law (a set of formal norms that label certain behaviors legally punishable). Criminology also focuses on societal reactions to those violations of the law.

Crime includes a diversity of behavior, but most offenses are characterized by criminal intent that leads to behavior defined as socially harmful. People who are not thought capable of forming criminal intent, such as the legally insane, are not punished with criminal sanctions. One important group that fits this criterion is the juvenile delinquent, who in this century has been subjected to treatment rather than punishment for violating social and legal norms.

Crime and the criminal law are social phenomena, for behavior is socially defined as punishable rather than intrinsically criminal. This accounts for differences in the law from one society to another, and even from one jurisdiction to another within a society. Conflict theorists point to the criminal law as the social product of the domination of one group by another one that has more economic resources and political power. Consensus theorists see the law as the outcome of compromise and agreement among various groups. Both perspectives provide useful ways of looking at crime and the criminal law.

The law has several social sources. One is interest groups, which are sometimes based on economic and political goals, and sometimes based on the moral beliefs of an organized constituency. Moral entrepreneurs may work to get laws that support their own views written and enforced. In democracies, public opinion is another important source of the law. Occasionally, the expert evidence of specialists such as psychiatrists is used to write and interpret the law.

This book takes as a starting point the law's definition of crime; it does not define crime in terms of "conduct norms" or "human rights." This position acknowledges the inequality of power among groups in getting the law written and enforced as they wish, and it does not imply moral support for the criminal law.

One approach to criminology is to examine different types of crimes or criminal careers. Instead of using such a typological approach, this book employs a conceptual scheme, applying theories and ideas about crime to specific offenses. The conceptual approach used in this book focuses first on needs and motivations to commit crime, and then on the ways that offenders reduce their commitment to the law before violating it. Offenders learn criminal motives and skills before violating the law, and they must find the opportunities to commit crime. When these factors lead to multiple crimes by the same person over time, we speak of a criminal career.

Reactions to crime can be informal or formal. Communities respond to crime with civilian patrol groups and citizen groups to improve the neighborhood, and bystanders may or may not respond to a crime they see in progress. The criminal justice system responds to crime in a formal way, and in doing so influences the behavior of offenders in various ways. Punishment has been justified as a way to prevent crime through threat (deterrence) or by locking up offenders (incapacitation), as a way to mete out penalties that are deserved (retribution), and as a way to reform offenders (rehabilitation).

Conservatives, liberals, and radicals have proposed different solutions to the crime problem. Over the last two decades, American political leaders have attacked the crime problem by trying to change the criminal justice system. Other approaches that would probably be more effective focus on situational crime prevention and the eradication of the causes of crime.

IMPORTANT TERMS

child savers	criminology	norm
conflict perspective	deviance	sanction
consensus perspective	interest group	status offense
crime	juvenile delinquent	tort
criminal career	law	typology
criminal intent	moral entrepreneurs	value

SUGGESTED READINGS

JOSEPH R. GUSFIELD. *Symbolic Crusade: Status Politics and the American Temperance Movement.* Urbana, Ill.: University of Illinois Press, 1963. A sociological analysis of how an interest group based on moral beliefs changed the law to prohibit the sale of alcoholic beverages in the United States.

ANTHONY M. PLATT. *The Child Savers: The Invention of Delinquency,* 2nd ed. Chicago: University of Chicago Press, 1977. A sociological and historical study of the development of the juvenile justice system in the United States.

———— AND PAUL TAKAGI, ED. *Crime and Social Justice.* London: Macmillan Press, 1981. A collection of recent essays by radical criminologists.

JAMES Q. WILSON. *Thinking about Crime,* rev. ed. New York: Basic Books, 1983. An influential collection of essays by a conservative political scientist.

2

Methods of Criminological Research

Criminologists have used different research strategies to study crime. Some offenses have posed knotty problems. For instance, criminologists have had a difficult time gaining access to people who engage in white-collar crime. As a result, "[p]rivate enterprise remains extraordinarily private. . . . We know more about the motives, habits, and most intimate arcana of primitive peoples in New Guinea . . . than we do of the denizens of executive suites in Unilever, Citroen, or General Electric" (Lewis and Stewart, 1961: 111–112). However, in recent years criminologists have devised ways to study white-collar crime. They have used court records, data from regulatory agencies, autobiographical accounts, interviews with the few white-collar offenders in prison, and interviews with retired corporate executives (see, e.g., Clinard and Yeager, 1980; Clinard, 1983).

Even though the personal values of criminologists may influence the kinds of crime they decide to study and their research methods, it is possible to be relatively detached in the collection and interpretation of data. Stating a hypothesis and gathering data that might support or refute that hypothesis help to increase objectivity, even if the selection of the problem for study—for example, robbery or white-collar crime—reflects personal values. In this chapter, we look briefly at several studies that have employed different research strategies; this will provide us with an idea of what criminologists study and how they go about their work.

COMPARATIVE AND HISTORICAL RESEARCH

One way to illuminate the problem of crime causation is to study violations of the law in other societies and at other times. This process allows us to gain insight into the relationship between crime and factors such as level of economic development and rate of urbanization. *Comparative research* can be used to evaluate whether a theory of crime developed in one society also explains crime in other societies, that is, whether a theory is universally true or limited in scope. The comparative approach also helps to generate theory, for differences in crime from one society to another must fit a general theory of criminal behavior (Bennett, 1980).

Comparative research of this sort is uncommon. Crime has been studied in countries other than the United States, but researchers rarely collect data simultaneously in different countries so that they can make direct comparisons

(Beirne, 1983). Methodological problems with crime statistics gathered by the police, the courts, or the prisons also make comparisons difficult (Johnson and Barak-Glantz, 1983). Comparative research is hampered, too, by geographical, political, and linguistic barriers, by the lack of funding, and by the absence of a research tradition in some societies (Clifford, 1978; Kaiser, 1978). Moreover, criminologists from one society sometimes approach the study of crime in another nation with an ethnocentric bias or a theoretical preference that distorts their interpretation of the data (Johnson and Barak-Glantz, 1983).

Similar in some ways to comparative research in contemporary societies is *historical research*, which examines the same society at different times and looks at the ways that crime has changed with economic and social development. Historical research often requires reliance on nonstatistical material, although historical researchers have used official statistics from the past and have quantified material from historical documents. Frequently, these researchers use accounts by observers of the time, records of legislative hearings, narrative material from court files, and other documentary evidence to learn about crime in the past.

Historical studies put contemporary crime in perspective, show how people have reacted to crime in the past, and suggest problems that may be encountered by nations now undergoing social and economic change. For example, one review of historical research concludes that the recent upsurge of violent crime in Western societies is a deviation from a decline in violence that has been going on for more than a century (Gurr, 1981). A study of public reactions to crime in nineteenth-century Paris shows that the "law-and-order" movement in the United States during the late 1960s and early 1970s was not unique (Chevalier, 1973). One historical study that illuminates the nature of crime in today's developing societies is J. J. Tobias's *Crime and Industrial Society in the 19th Century* (1967).

Tobias's Study of Crime in Nineteenth-Century England

J. J. Tobias's study of crime in industrializing England found that the criminal statistics of that period were practically worthless for systematic study. Changes in crime statistics during the nineteenth century revealed more about the development of the police force than they did about the amount of crime being committed. As a result, Tobias had to rely on parliamentary reports and contemporary accounts to piece together a picture of crime during this era.

Using documentary material, Tobias gathered information on criminal careers in the nineteenth century. He shows the needs that were met by criminal activity and the ways that society generated those needs. He helps us to understand why some people felt little commitment to abide by the law, and how new recruits to a life of crime learned skills and motives conducive to violating the law. He also shows how opportunities for crime changed during the century.

Tobias finds that crime rates were high early in the century because social institutions had failed to respond to a sizeable increase in population; more specifically, there was a growth in the number of young people in the country, but no commensurate growth in employment opportunities. Migration from rural areas and small towns to larger towns and cities proved unsettling to many people, and these larger towns and cities provided ample opportunities for crime and anonymity, which reduced the risk of arrest.

During the nineteenth century, crime decreased as the social environment became more settled. Economic development increased job opportunities and raised incomes, and government resources were used to introduce social services for the disadvantaged. The police and the courts also changed over the course of the century, from a system that had a low rate of detection and severe penalties for the few offenders who were convicted, to one that had more lenient sentences but a higher rate of detection. Tobias argues that this change enhanced the deterrent effect of the law and contributed to the decline in the crime rate.

It is difficult to support Tobias's interpretation of these historical changes with precise data, but he provides convincing documentary evidence of the social changes that accompanied the long-term decline in the crime rate. His conclusions are also consistent with evidence about the changing nature of crime in societies that are now undergoing social and economic change.

OBSERVATION

One method that has rarely been employed to study criminal behavior is *observation.* This method involves the social scientist in the careful and systematic watching of behavior. Ideally, interaction between an offender and a victim would be observed while it is occurring, and the observer's presence would not affect the behavior of the participants in the crime.

Observational methods are especially useful in uncovering information that might be missed by asking offenders or victims questions about their behavior after it has occurred. Observation of behavior can raise questions that might not otherwise occur to social scientists, such as why juvenile gangs encourage experimentation with drugs but discourage addiction to drugs. Unexpected findings from observation can lead to the development of new theories, the reformulation of old theories, or additional research to test ideas in a more formal way.

Observation has many advantages, but it also has important drawbacks. It is difficult to know if the incidents or individuals observed are representative of all incidents or individuals. For instance, if we analyzed observational data on how bank robberies are committed by studying the films taken by cameras in banks, we would still not know if the behavior of robbers who hold up grocery stores, taxicabs, or gas stations is the same as the behavior of bank robbers.

One difficulty encountered in some observational research involves the problem of confidentiality. Data collected by social scientists can be subpoenaed and used in court against people who have been observed committing crimes. Thus, promises of confidentiality made by researchers to offenders have no legal basis, and criminals may be threatened by the information collected by researchers.

Another problem with observational methods is that the behavior of the people who are being observed may be influenced by the presence of the researcher. For instance, the police may be less likely to engage in brutality against citizens if an observer is recording the interaction (Reiss, 1968). Similarly, most criminals are unlikely to break the law if witnesses are present. Burglars make sure that no one is watching before they enter a building, robbers search for a victim who is alone on the street, and drug dealers do not want witnesses when they transact their business. Even if observers could become "flies on the wall," they would find that few crimes occur in their field of vision, for crime is a statistically rare occurrence. Even the police, who are trained to look for crime where it is most likely to occur, do not come across a crime in progress very often.

In spite of the drawbacks of the observational method, some crimes have been studied in this way. Francis A. J. Ianni (1972) spent more than two years observing the activities of an organized crime "family." Sociologists have observed the behavior of juvenile gangs (Miller, 1974; Horowitz, 1983). A controversial use of the observational method is reported in Laud Humphreys' book, *Tearoom Trade: Impersonal Sex in Public Places* (1975).

Humphreys' Study of Tearoom Trade

Humphreys used the observational method to study a violation of the law: homosexual acts by men in public restrooms (called "tearooms" in the slang of the gay subculture). Most of the arrests for homosexual behavior in the United States involve acts in public places, even in states that have legalized homosexual acts between consenting adults in private.

Typically a tearoom encounter includes two participants in the sexual act and a "watchqueen," a third man who acts as a lookout to ensure privacy and warn the participants of intruders. The watchqueen often takes voyeuristic pleasure from the sexual act. Acting as a watchqueen in order to gather data, Humphreys systematically observed and recorded information on fifty homosexual encounters. He allowed the other participants to think that he was just another watchqueen, rather than a sociologist gathering data, but he did not need to lie to the men about the reason he was present because most encounters occurred in silence.

Humphreys learned that the interaction leading to sex usually involves little or no talking by the participants. Agreement to have sex is reached on the basis of glances, body positioning, and nonverbal signals. This elaborate nonverbal process prevents participants from approaching men who are not interested in sex, and thus helps to protect those who are involved in the "trade" from the anger of unsuspecting outsiders. Humphreys concluded that because outsiders are screened out of the tearoom activity, this behavior poses no serious threat to straight society.

Humphreys' use of deception to observe the tearoom trade was criticized, but there was even harsher criticism of the second phase of his study, in which he traced the addresses of the men from their license plate numbers and then interviewed them (while he was in disguise) in their homes. Humphreys protected the potentially harmful information that he had gathered, but his critics contend that the men's reputations were threatened by the very existence of that information. Humphreys and his supporters claim that the men gave up their right to privacy when they chose to engage in sex in a public place, but Humphreys later expressed reservations about this aspect of his research.

By interviewing the men in their homes, Humphreys was able to show that about half of them were married; some also had children. Compared to their neighbors, these men were more politically conservative, had higher incomes, and worked more hours each week. Their homes, cars, and clothing were especially neat. Humphreys suggests that the men were trying to convey the impression that they were highly respectable in order to hide "the discreditable nature of their secret behavior" (Humphreys, 1975: 135).

Humphreys' observational research uncovered some information that could not have been discovered by asking questions of a sample of men from the general population or even by interviewing a sample of gays. Had he told the men in the tearoom that he was a sociologist observing their behavior, they probably would have left the restroom, and so his deception may have been necessary to gather the data. However, his research raises serious ethical issues and posed a threat to the men he studied.

BIOGRAPHIES

A fruitful way to study the sources of criminal behavior and the development of criminal careers is to examine in detail the experiences of a single offender. This *biographical method* reveals the needs and motivations of the offender, the way that commitment to the law is reduced, the way that criminal skills are learned, the obstacles encountered in pursuing a legitimate career and an illegitimate life style, the pattern of criminal activity over a lifetime, and the consequences of contact with the criminal justice system (Rettig, Torres, and Garrett, 1977).

One problem with the biographical method is that the criminal who is studied may not be representative of all offenders. Separating an offender's experiences into those that are idiosyncratic and those that are common to other offenders is a difficult undertaking that requires more information than can be provided by one criminal's biography. The richness of the account of one offender's life in crime thus sacrifices the representativeness provided by research on a sample of offenders, even though the biographical method often yields hypotheses that can be tested on a cross section of offenders.

Another problem with the biographical method is that offenders may intentionally or unintentionally distort their experiences. They may do this because of faulty memories, because they view the past in light of their present circumstances, or because they want to glorify and romanticize themselves to the interviewer (Rettig, Torres, and Garrett, 1977). This problem of distortion can be minimized by double-checking the accuracy of the account with the offender at different times or by interviewing friends and relatives of the offender (Klockars, 1974).

An early example of the biographical technique is Edwin H. Sutherland's (1937) study of "Chic Conwell," a professional thief who recounted his life of crime in great detail. William J. Chambliss (King and Chambliss, 1984) used a similar approach to study "Harry King," a "box man" or safecracker. Another valuable biographical study is the story of a heroin addict and thief named Manny (Rettig, Torres, and Garrett, 1977). The biographical method has also been used to good advantage by Carl B. Klockars in his study, *The Professional Fence* (1974).

Klockars's Study of a Professional Fence

Klockars began to study the fence, who is a middleman between thieves who steal property and members of the public who buy stolen goods, by immersing himself in the literature on fencing. This helped him to frame questions for his interviews with a professional fence named "Vincent Swaggi," who was recommended to him by a thief as an ideal subject. Klockars wrote to Vincent about his proposed research, and, after promising the fence anonymity, Klockars began an interviewing process that took about four hundred hours over fifteen months.

Klockars's account provides insight into the early stages of Vincent's criminal career. While still in the eighth grade, Vincent learned from two uncles how to "hustle" inferior pens at high prices. Vincent was drawn to this and other illegitimate activities by the excitement of "scoring," the financial rewards, his family's needs, and his boredom with school. Although not all fences are drawn into a criminal career in this way, Vincent's early experiences with crime probably have something in common with those of other fences.

Vincent later moved into the business of supplying other hustlers with merchandise, such as furs and sweaters. He found that he could make money by packaging flashy but inexpensive items in attractive boxes with high price tags. Vincent next began to operate as a fence; he bought stolen goods from thieves, who were often truck drivers, and sold the merchandise to the public at a price that was below retail.

To maximize his profits, Vincent learned and developed several techniques to pay thieves as little as possible for the goods they offered to sell him. He would tell them that the stolen merchandise was incomplete, useless, out-of-fashion, or of poor quality. He profited from the thieves' lack of knowledge about the actual value of some of the items, and made it his business to know the value of those items. Vincent also learned that he could offer less to thieves who were desperate for money, especially heroin addicts in need of money for a quick fix.

A major contribution of this biographical study is evidence on the way that Vincent rationalized his involvement in a criminal career. He had an elaborate system of justifications: He had never stolen anything, there is an important distinction between theft and receiving stolen goods, the criminal receiving of stolen goods would continue even if he stopped, he did not cause the theft of goods, and the victims of many thefts were wealthy corporations that could afford the loss. Vincent also justified his behavior by a "metaphor of the ledger"—a balancing of the good he had done against the evil he had done—that came out strongly in his favor. He also claimed that many "upright citizens" are morally flawed, and that they often buy goods from him that they suspect are "hot." Later in this book we will see that this process of justifying violations of the law is an important aspect of the development of criminal behavior.

ANALYTIC INDUCTION

One way to develop an explanation of a particular kind of crime is to interview several people who have committed that crime. From those interviews a researcher can develop a tentative explanation for the crime, and that explanation can then be tested with a different group of offenders. The second set of interviews may suggest modifications of the original explanation. The revised explanation can then be tested with additional interviews and reformulated further if necessary. Through this process of *analytic induction*, the criminologist can eventually arrive at a general explanation of the crime.

When this method is carefully applied to a clearly defined crime, it can be a useful way to study the causes of criminal behavior. It provides insight into the offender's perceived needs, the way that criminal skills are learned, and the way that opportunities to engage in crime are found. Because this method requires attention to an offender's past experiences and present behavior, it also illuminates the nature of the criminal act and the criminal career.

In spite of these advantages, analytic induction has not been used much by criminologists. Critics of the technique claim that it produces no more than a good working definition of the problem (Morris and Hawkins, 1970: 47). Others suggest that the conclusions reached by those who have used this method must be tested by other criminologists who have less commitment to the theoretical explanation on which the original research was based. This method has also been attacked for its failure to use standard data collection instruments such as questionnaires, and for failing to compare the offenders who are interviewed with a control group from the general population who did not violate the law (Glaser, 1974: 70–72).

One of the few examples of the use of analytic induction is reported in Donald R. Cressey's *Other People's Money: A Study in the Social Psychology of Embezzlement* (1953, 1971).

Cressey's Study of Embezzlement

Cressey's research is based on interviews with 133 men who had embezzled money from people who had entrusted them with the control of funds. In his study, Cressey sought an explanation that would fit all cases of criminal violation of financial trust, which he defined as a situation in which an offender initially accepted a position of trust in good faith, rather than to perpetrate a crime, and later violated that trust by stealing funds.

Cressey began with a hypothesis to explain trust violation. He later revised that explanation on the basis of successive interviews, until he arrived at a general explanation of embezzlement. He spent about fifteen hours with each embezzler, searching for cases that would require him to reformulate his original hypothesis. His first hypothesis was that "positions of financial trust are violated when the incumbent has learned in connection [with] the business or profession in which he is employed that some forms of trust violation are merely technical violations and are not really 'illegal' or 'wrong,' and, on the negative side, that they are not violated if this kind of definition of behavior has not been learned" (Cressey, 1953, 1971: 27). This hypothesis was based on Sutherland's research on white-collar crime, but it was soon abandoned because Cressey found that some trust violators knew that their behavior was wrong and said they had only "kidded themselves" by saying that their conduct was not illegal or wrong. In addition, several trust violators did not know anyone in the profession who had engaged in theft from whom they might have learned justifications for their own crimes.

Cressey's second explanation of trust violation was that "positions of trust are violated when the incumbent defines a need for extra funds or extended use of property as an 'emergency' which cannot be met by legal means, and that if such an emergency does not take place trust violation will not occur" (Cressey, 1953, 1971: 27–28). This reformulation had to be revised because some violators said that although they had faced an emergency at the time of their embezzlement, they had also faced similar emergencies at other times and had not violated the law. Moreover, some embezzlers said that they had not faced any financial emergency at the time of their embezzlement, but had committed the crime because of antagonism toward their employer.

Cressey's third formulation was that "persons become trust violators when they conceive of themselves as having incurred financial obligations which are considered as nonsocially sanctionable and which, consequently, must be satisfied by a private or secret means" (Cressey, 1953, 1971: 28). In reexamining his interview notes, Cressey found that in some instances there was no financial obligation or debt for which the offender felt responsible at the time of the crime. In addition, some offenders had had such obligations in the past but had not violated the law. At this point, Cressey realized that trust violation would have to be explained by a combination of factors rather than by a single cause.

Cressey's fourth hypothesis did not emphasize nonshareable financial obligations, but rather nonshareable financial problems (Cressey, 1953, 1971: 29). This meant that the financial difficulty faced by the trust violator did not have to be an obligation, but might simply be a discrepancy between current income and current expenditures. Cressey suggested that a trust violator had to be aware of the financial problem, and know that it could be solved through the violation of trust, in addition to having the technical skill to commit the crime. However, some embezzlers met all these requirements, but reported that their ideas of right and wrong had kept them from violating the law.

With this information, Cressey developed his final explanation: "Trusted persons become trust violators when they conceive of themselves as having a financial problem which is nonshareable, are aware that this problem can be secretly resolved by violation of the position of financial trust, and are able to apply to their own conduct in that situation verbalizations which enable them to adjust their conceptions of themselves as users of the entrusted funds or property" (Cressey, 1953, 1971: 30). All elements are critical to the violation of trust; if any one is absent, embezzlement will not occur.

A study of six cases of large-scale trust violation in Canada suggests that Cressey's explanation may be incomplete (Nettler, 1974). This Canadian study found that embezzlement sometimes occurs when there is no nonshareable problem; greed rather than need to solve a specific nonshareable problem may motivate some embezzlers. This evidence would suggest that Cressey's explanation of trust violation needs to be revised rather than abandoned.

PATTERNS OF CRIME

Another way to study crime is to look at it as a social phenomenon with a specific form or structure. This study of *patterns of crime* often involves the use of police statistics to determine where crime is committed, who commits it, who is victimized, and what are the major dimensions of the criminal act. Research of this kind looks at the spatial distribution of crime in a city, the social background of offenders and victims, relationships between offenders and victims, and the social processes that lead to crime.

This patterns-of-crime approach assumes that police records can provide a comprehensive and valid description of crime and its participants. However, as we will see later in the book, police statistics may not be very representative of all of the crime that occurs in a community. For instance, police records in Philadelphia, where this method has often been used, contain many details about crimes reported to and recorded by the police, but there is evidence that a smaller proportion of all crimes that actually occur in Philadelphia are reported and recorded than is true for other large American cities (Skogan,

1976b: 111–112). Thus, Philadelphia crime statistics may not reflect the actual nature of crime in that city very well.

Patterns-of-crime studies are useful in describing the criminal act and in providing information on the prior arrest records of offenders and victims. However, they usually do not deal with the issue of crime causation in much depth. These studies do not tell us much about how offenders reduce their commitment to the law, learn criminal skills, or find opportunities to commit crime. The failure to interview offenders as a part of the study of patterns of crime is a major shortcoming of this research technique. In crimes such as homicide, where a high proportion of offenders are caught and convicted, much could be learned from interviews that cannot be discovered in police reports.

The patterns-of-crime approach has been used extensively at the University of Pennsylvania's Center for Studies in Criminology and Criminal Law, where Marvin E. Wolfgang pioneered the approach in his *Patterns in Criminal Homicide* (1958). Robbery and rape have also been studied using the same approach (Normandeau, 1968; Amir, 1971). A national study of four violent crimes in seventeen cities used a similar research strategy (Curtis, 1974).

Wolfgang's Study of Homicide

Wolfgang used police records on homicide from 1948 through 1952 in Philadelphia to analyze the race, sex, and age of homicide offenders and victims, the methods and weapons used to commit murder, the temporal and spatial patterns of homicide, the presence of alcohol in the offender and the victim at the time of the crime, the previous criminal records of offenders and victims, and the motives of offenders. He also explored the interpersonal relationships of offenders and victims, homicides committed during other crimes, and the extent to which victims contributed to their own murders. He looked at the solution of homicide cases by the police and at the court's disposition of charges against suspects.

One important finding that emerged from Wolfgang's research was that offenders and victims in homicide cases are often intimately associated with each other. For instance, about one-fourth of the homicides involved an offender and a victim who were relatives, and an additional 28.2 per cent involved offenders and victims who were close friends. Homicides between strangers were relatively rare, accounting for only one-eighth of the cases. This finding helped to focus criminologists' attention on the interpersonal dynamics of intimate relationships as a factor that can lead to lethal violence.

Another important conclusion was that homicides frequently occur in a context that includes the use of alcohol. Alcohol was absent in the homicide situation in only 36.4 per cent of the cases. In 43.5 per cent of the murders, both the offender and the victim had been drinking, in 9.2 per cent of the cases only the victim had been drinking, and in 10.9 per cent of the cases only the offender had been drinking.

Wolfgang's study of homicide provides many other important findings. For example, he showed that most murders occur between an offender and a victim of the same race; murders of whites by blacks or of blacks by whites are relatively rare. He also found that murder rates were highest among young black males, a finding he later used to support his theory of a subculture of violence. In spite of the limitations of police statistics, they can provide us with useful data on the patterns of crime in society.

THE COHORT STUDY

One problem with some research techniques is the lack of a time dimension; that is, little attention is paid to the way that a criminal career develops over time or the way that crime rates increase or decrease. One strategy that introduces a time dimension follows a carefully defined group of people who are in a common situation over a period of time. Such a group is called a *cohort*. A cohort of all of the individuals born in a given year will experience similar events over their lifetimes, even though they may be affected differently by those events. For instance, all people born in 1915 experienced the Great Depression during their adolescence, although some were exposed to abject poverty during that era and others were relatively insulated from its effects.

The ideal way to carry out a cohort study is to begin to collect data at an early age for the members of a cohort, and then follow them through adolescence and into adulthood. Such a study might take as long as twenty-five years to complete, if we assume that little crime is committed before the age of ten and that most offenders stop their criminal activities by the age of thirty-five. This kind of study would not have to rely solely on official records of delinquency or crime, but could use questionnaires to measure violations of the law. Interviews could be done periodically to measure changes in the individual's social situation—for example, adjustment to school or family income—that might be associated with violation of the law. This long-term cohort study would yield much information on the causes of criminal behavior and the development of criminal careers that we cannot get from other kinds of criminological research.

Cohort studies do have several drawbacks. They are expensive to conduct, because they take so long to complete, and thus researchers may have difficulty getting funding for such projects. Pressure on academic researchers to publish scholarly work may inhibit them from undertaking cohort studies that will not yield data for years. In addition, interviewing cohort members on a regular basis may interfere with the normal process of growing up.

In spite of the difficulties with cohort studies, several such projects have been done. An important early cohort study was the Cambridge-Somerville Youth Study (Powers and Witmer, 1951; McCord and McCord, 1959; McCord, 1978, 1979, 1981). Another major cohort study has been carried out in England (West, 1969, 1982; West and Farrington, 1973, 1977), and a study of the relationship between juvenile delinquency and adult criminal careers has been done in Wisconsin (Shannon, 1982; Lab, 1984). One cohort study that has received much attention is reported in Marvin E. Wolfgang, Robert M. Figlio, and Thorsten Sellin's *Delinquency in a Birth Cohort* (1972).

Wolfgang, Figlio, and Sellin's Cohort Study of Delinquency

Wolfgang, Figlio, and Sellin studied a cohort of all males born in 1945 who lived in Philadelphia continuously from the age of ten (the first age at which there were a significant number of arrests) until the age of eighteen (the age at which juveniles became adults). The researchers studied only boys because of "the greater incidence, frequency, heterogeneity, seriousness, and persistency of male delinquency" (Wolfgang, Figlio, and Sellin, 1972: 30). Records kept by the schools, draft boards, the police, and the juvenile courts were examined for all 9,945 boys in the cohort. All police contacts that resulted in a written report about a delinquent act were examined. A study of the experiences of some of those boys as adults has also been done (Wolfgang, 1974).

Wolfgang, Figlio, and Sellin looked at the characteristics that distinguished boys who had had contact with the police from boys who had had no such contact. Thirty-five per cent of the boys had at least one contact with the police as a juvenile, but a mere 6 per cent of the boys accounted for 52 per cent of all of the police contacts in the cohort. This suggests that a policy that could keep this small group of chronic offenders from engaging in delinquency would have a major impact on the overall rate of juvenile delinquency.

Blacks and lower-class boys were more apt to have police contacts than were whites and middle-class boys. In fact, the likelihood that a black middle-class boy would have contact with the police was the same as the chance that a white lower-class boy would have. The cohort technique permitted such conclusions because nonoffenders as well as offenders were included in the study. Conclusions of this sort are not possible when the research strategy includes only people who have committed crimes.

COMBINING RESEARCH STRATEGIES

Criminologists sometimes combine several approaches in their study of crime. This enables them to maximize the advantages and minimize the disadvantages of each method. Information that cannot be found in police records, such as how crime is planned, may be uncovered in interviews with offenders. Material that cannot be gathered by interviewing offenders, such as the overall distribution of crime in a city, can be found in police records.

In this chapter we have looked at some studies in which sociologists have combined research strategies. Klockars (1974) relied mainly on the biographical method in his study of the professional fence, but he also examined police arrest records, observed a fence at work, and read historical documents on fencing. Humphreys (1975) supplemented his observations of homosexual acts in public restrooms by interviewing the men in their homes. Another study that investigated one kind of crime by using several sources of data is this author's *Robbery and the Criminal Justice System* (1972).

Conklin's Robbery Study

The first step in this study was a careful examination of Boston's police records on robbery. To study possible changes in robbery over time, crime reports were studied for two periods, the first six months of 1964 and the first six months of 1968. About the same proportion of robberies in each period were street robberies, purse snatches, and commercial robberies, but for each type of robbery more money was stolen in 1968 than in 1964. The police data were used to describe patterns of robbery and to explore several hypotheses about the dramatic increase in robbery rates during the 1960s.

A second aspect was to follow robbery suspects through the criminal justice system. Suspects were followed from arrest by the police through the final disposition of their case in court. Collecting information in this way made it possible to determine which characteristics of the defendants and which aspects of the crimes with which they were charged affected the court's disposition of the case. For instance, the study found no clear-cut pattern of racial discrimination in the determination of guilt or in the sentencing of convicted offenders.

Interviews were also conducted with sixty-seven imprisoned robbery offenders. These interviews did not yield enough information to use the analytic induction method to explain all robberies, but they produced information that could not be found in police or court records. The motives of the robbers were examined, the way they planned their crimes was investigated, and their criminal acts were studied in detail. Interviews provided evidence for classifying robbers as professionals, opportunists, addicts, or alcoholics.

To supplement the interviews with the robbers, ninety robbery victims were also questioned. These victims said that they had been selected by the robber because they had been alone or outnumbered, appeared to have money, or were in an isolated area. After their victimization, these people reported that they took more precautions in handling money, became more suspicious of strangers, and stayed home at night. These interviews provided a different perspective on robbery from the one gained by questioning offenders, and both sets of interviews supplemented the data gathered from police and court records.

OTHER STRATEGIES OF CRIMINOLOGICAL RESEARCH

This chapter has not covered every strategy for studying crime and the criminal justice system. Other methods that we will look at in the following chapters include surveys, experiments, and the use of records kept by organizations other than the criminal justice system.

The police, the courts, and the correctional system are not the only useful sources of data for criminologists. For instance, department store records have been used to study shoplifting, a crime that often is not reported to the police by store managers (Cameron, 1964). In recent years, private security forces have patrolled private and public spaces to an increasing degree, and the records of these firms may prove to be an important source of information for criminologists in the future.

Surveys are studies in which samples of people who are representative of a larger population are asked a series of prepared questions. In Chapter 3, we will see that surveys have been used to measure the extent of crime in two ways, by asking people about their experiences as victims of crime and by asking them about their own involvement in criminal activity. Surveys have also been used to test theories of crime and delinquency, as we will see, in Chapter 9 when we examine Travis Hirschi's (1969) use of survey data to test the control theory of delinquency.

Experiments are controlled studies in which people are treated in different ways to determine the effects of that treatment on their attitudes and behavior. One experiment created a "mock prison" and assigned subjects to be "inmates" or "guards"; this study contributed to our understanding of the social structure of prisons (Zimbardo, 1971, 1972; Zimbardo et al., 1973; Haney, Banks, and Zimbardo, 1973). Experiments have been used to evaluate the effectiveness of rehabilitation programs; one such study assessed the impact on inmates of group counseling (Kassebaum, Ward, and Wilner, 1971). A series of experiments conducted by Bibb Latané and John M. Darley (1970) has helped us to understand why bystanders often fail to come to the assistance of victims of crime. Another important experiment tested the impact on ex-convicts' criminal behavior of providing them with financial assistance after they were released from prison (Rossi, Berk, and Lenihan, 1980).

A recent innovation in the study of crime is the use of mathematical models and econometric techniques. These are abstract formulations of the relationships among variables and are evaluated with data gathered from the police, the courts, and the prisons (Hellman, 1980; Phillips and Votey, 1981; Fox, 1981a, 1981b). These methods have been used to study the deterrent effect of punishment, including the death penalty, and to examine the relationship between crime and unemployment.

Criminologists have used many different strategies to study the criminal justice system's reaction to crime. They have observed interaction between the police and suspects on the street (Piliavin and Briar, 1964; Reiss, 1971; Skolnick, 1975; Black, 1980). They have observed the operation of the courts, including the process of plea bargaining (Rosett and Cressey, 1976; Blumberg, 1979). Others have used the records produced by criminal justice agencies to study issues such as racial discrimination in sentencing and the factors used by parole boards to determine when to release an inmate.

In this chapter, we have looked at some of the ways that criminologists systematically study criminal behavior and responses to it by the criminal justice system. Each strategy of research can provide useful information if properly used, but none by itself can give us a complete picture of crime and the institutions that deal with it. As a result, in the following chapters we rely on research that has employed many different methods to study crime.

SUMMARY

Criminologists use many research strategies. Some employ the comparative method, looking at crime in two or more societies to test or develop theories. Comparative research often encounters obstacles such as language problems, lack of official crime data, and the ethnocentric biases of researchers. Historical work is a kind of comparative research, for it compares the past with the present, either explicitly or implicitly. Tobias's study of crime in nineteenth-century England uncovered information about crime that may be relevant to today's developing countries.

Observation is a method that criminologists use on occasion, but the desire of most offenders to keep their crimes secret means that researchers often face problems when they try to watch crimes in progress. Observational methods have been used to study the police and the courts, and sometimes to study crime, as Laud Humphreys did in his study of homosexual encounters in public restrooms.

Another useful method is the biographical approach. This method will not tell us how representative a particular offender is of all criminals, but it provides a richness of detail often missing from research based on official statistics or the survey method. Klockars contributed to our understanding of the crime of fencing in his fascinating biography of Vincent Swaggi.

Analytic induction tests a hypothesis with interviews with several offenders, revises the hypothesis to take new data into account, tests the reformulated hypothesis, and continues in this way until an explanation for all crimes of a particular kind is developed. Cressey used this method in his study of embezzlement or trust violation.

Another method is the patterns-of-crime approach, one that uses police data to investigate the distribution of crime in time and space and to study offenders and victims. Wolfgang used this strategy to study homicide, and others have applied it to robbery and rape.

A very productive, but expensive and time-consuming, strategy is the cohort study. People who have a common characteristic—usually the same year of birth—are studied over time, allowing for the collection of data on criminal careers. Wolfgang, Figlio, and Sellin used this method to study delinquency.

Criminologists often combine research strategies, interviewing offenders and victims, analyzing police data, and tracing defendants through the courts. Each method casts a somewhat different light on crime and adds a piece to the overall picture of behavior that violates the law. The author of this book used several methods to study robbery and reactions to it by the criminal justice system.

Many other research strategies have contributed to our knowledge of crime, as we will see in the following chapters. Unofficial records of crime, such as those kept on shoplifters by department stores, have been used by researchers. Surveys have been used to study victimization and self-reported crime, enhancing our knowledge of the nature and extent of crime beyond what official statistics can tell us. Experiments have been used to evaluate the effects on offenders of prison treatment programs and financial assistance. Sociologists and economists have used mathematical models and econometric techniques to study crime in recent years. Many of these methods have been used to study the operation of the criminal justice system, as well as the criminal behavior with which it deals.

IMPORTANT TERMS

analytic induction	comparative research	observation
biographical method	experiment	patterns of crime
cohort	historical research	survey

SUGGESTED READINGS

TRAVIS HIRSCHI AND HANAN C. SELVIN. *Principles of Survey Analysis.* New York: Free Press, 1973. This book, originally entitled *Delinquency Research*, takes a critical look at the use of survey research to study juvenile delinquency.

LAUD HUMPHREYS. *Tearoom Trade: Impersonal Sex in Public Places*, enlarged ed. Chicago: Aldine, 1975. The last sixty-five pages include several articles that deal with ethical issues confronted by sociological researchers, especially those who study deviants and criminals.

CARL B. KLOCKARS. *The Professional Fence.* New York: Free Press, 1974. Chapter 8, "The Biography of a Research Project," is a useful account of how Klockars employed several strategies to understand the professional fence.

TWO

THE EXTENT AND NATURE OF CRIME

n Chapter 3 we look at the development of modern criminology. We then examine three measures of crime. Official crime statistics provide us with information about crimes reported to the police and suspects arrested by the police. Victimization data gathered in surveys show that much crime is not reported to the police; these data can be used to construct a more complete picture. Crime is also measured by self-reports, which are questionnaires filled out by people who admit to their own violations of the law.

The costs of crime are examined in Chapter 4. We look at the financial costs, including the exorbitant cost of white-collar crime, the expense of maintaining the criminal justice system, and losses to the victims of conventional property crimes. We investigate the physical harm caused by crimes of violence and by white-collar crimes. Finally, we examine the social costs, including the corrosive effects of white-collar crime and government corruption and the reactions of people to the threat of conventional crime.

Chapter 5 explores some of the variations in crime rates that theories of crime must explain. The crime problem in Japan, China, and Canada is examined and compared to the crime problem in the United States. Regional variations within the United States are investigated, as are variations in rates by size of community. We look at the distribution of crime within metropolitan areas and at the relationship of crime to migration and population density. Temporal variations in crime rates, such as changes over the years, are also explored.

In Chapter 6 we look at variations in crime rates by four social characteristics: sex, age, race, and class. We examine male-female differences in both juvenile delinquency and adult crime, and the way that female involvement in crime and delinquency has changed in recent years. We investigate variations in crime rates by age, and the way that a society's crime rate is affected by the age distribution of its population. We explore black-white differences in crime rates. The complex relationship between class and both adult crime and juvenile delinquency is examined, using both official arrest data and self-report studies. In addition to studying the way that sex, age, race, and class are related to violation of the law, we look at differences in victimization rates for people with these characteristics.

3
Measuring Crime

The scientific study of criminal behavior originated in Europe in the nineteenth century. Until then, there had been much speculation about crime, but it was abstract and not based on empirical research. Early ideas about the causes of crime have generally proved inaccurate or incomplete, but the history of these ideas is important for understanding the emergence of modern criminology.

THE EMERGENCE OF MODERN CRIMINOLOGY

From 1500 until about 1750, philosophers who investigated the problem of crime usually proposed that people freely chose how to act. This assumption of "free will" implies that people are responsible for the consequences of their behavior. Another implication is that people can be controlled through fear, especially the fear of pain. Punishment by the state, an institution based on a "social contract" among its citizens to live together in peace, thus becomes the primary means to instill fear and prevent criminal behavior.

Classical Criminology

These ideas were the basis of the *classical school* of criminology. This approach developed during the Enlightenment, an eighteenth-century movement in European thought that emphasized progress, individualism, the use of reason, the questioning of tradition, and the use of empirical data to test abstract ideas.

The major proponent of the classical school was an Italian, Cesare Beccaria (1738–1794), who sharply criticized the criminal justice system, especially judges who imposed arbitrary and harsh punishments. Along with earlier philosophers, Beccaria believed that punishment was needed to prevent people from violating the law. He thought that people were motivated by pain and pleasure, that they exercised free will, and that rationality and responsibility characterized human action. According to Beccaria, fear of punishment would lead people to conform to the law.

Beccaria claimed that punishment should be based on the harm that the criminal act did to society, rather than on the harm incurred by the victim. Harm was to be judged by the consequences of the act rather than by the intentions of the offender. Marxist critics have argued that this approach contains a basic flaw: In capitalist societies, social harm will inevitably be defined in a way that protects the interests of capitalists from interference by other classes (Taylor, Walton, and Young, 1973: 3).

Beccaria hoped that making punishment proportional to social harm would limit the arbitrary punishment meted out by judges. Implicit in his theory is the notion that similar crimes should be punished similarly, an idea violated by the judges of his time as well as those of today. This idea, basic to the theory of retribution or "just deserts," suggests that an offender's characteristics and the circumstances of the crime should not be taken into account in meting out punishment.

Beccaria's ideas were the basis of the 1791 criminal code of France, but problems arose in implementing that code. The code ignored differences among offenders and differences in the circumstances of crimes. It treated first offenders and repeat offenders alike when they were convicted of similar offenses, and it gave no special attention to offenders who were minors, insane, or retarded.

The revised French criminal code of 1819 provided for somewhat more judicial discretion, allowing judges to consider the circumstances of the crime but not the offender's intent. The underlying assumption was that the idea of free will was valid, but that individual responsibility could be influenced by pathology, incompetence, or insanity. The notion of premeditation—the consideration of one's behavior prior to acting—developed as a measure of free will (Vold, 1979). Age, mental capacity, and the circumstances of the crime were accepted as factors that could mitigate punishment, for these factors were thought to reduce personal responsibility. This led to the use of testimony by experts to help the courts decide on the extent to which defendants could be held responsible and punished for their actions.

The idea implicit in the 1819 code was that sentences had different effects on different kinds of offenders. This was the beginning of the rehabilitation rationale for punishment, the idea that the goal of punishment is to change offenders so that they will not commit crime again. Individual choice of behavior was the basis of the 1819 code, but choice was increasingly seen as influenced by social and psychological factors (Taylor, Walton, and Young, 1973: 9).

Cartography

Some European nations had been gathering official data on crime since the sixteenth century, but it was not until the nineteenth century that scholars began to use these statistics to understand crime. Their approach has been called *cartography*, because it involves the use of data to map or chart patterns of crime.

Important studies using this approach were published in 1833 by Guerry, a French lawyer, and in 1838 by Quetelet, a Belgian mathematician. These two cartographers worked independently, but came to similar conclusions from their studies of national crime data. Both found that the annual total of crime recorded in a country remains fairly constant over time, and that each kind of crime remains about the same proportion of the total over time. They concluded that officially recorded crime is "a regular feature of social activity" that is better explained by social conditions than by individual predispositions (Taylor, Walton, and Young, 1973: 37).

The cartographic approach was used to great advantage in a ground-breaking study of suicide by Emile Durkheim (1858–1917), one of the founders of sociology. In his writings on crime, Durkheim (1895, 1938) shared with Guerry and Quetelet the idea that crime is a normal feature of social life. He did not mean that crime was good or to be encouraged, but rather that crime exists in all societies and therefore must be studied in its relationship to the social structure. Durkheim did suggest that crime has some positive functions, or consequences, for society: It delineates what behavior is acceptable to the members of society, it draws official attention to the social conditions that cause crime, and it can create social solidarity in opposition to people who violate important social standards.

Positivism

Modern scientific criminology grew out of the work of three Italian students of crime—Cesare Lombroso, Enrico Ferri, and Raffaele Garofalo. They saw the proper course of criminology as "the systematic elimination of the free will 'metaphysics' of the classical school" (Taylor, Walton, and Young, 1973: 10). Rather than try to reduce crime by relying on the criminal justice system, as did the classical criminologists, they sought to learn the causes of crime and then eliminate the conditions that produce it. Modern criminology has been dominated by this perspective, but the criminal justice system has been dominated by classical thinking during the twentieth century.

This perspective, which is called *positivism*, relies on the scientific method, quantifying and measuring behavior and the social conditions associated with that behavior. Positivists claim that scientific neutrality is possible in the study of crime, and that criminologists should focus on criminal behavior rather than on the criminal law. Positivists see themselves as relatively objective in their work, but critics allege that a positivist approach implicitly supports the existing legal system by adopting the state's definition of crime. However, positivists do have a legitimate claim to objectivity, for compared to the work done by scholars who argue that scientific neutrality is impossible, positivists have generally produced more reliable results—that is, results that different scholars would also get if they applied the same scientific methods to the same data.

Positivists claim that human behavior is subject to causal laws. This assertion that behavior is determined, or at least influenced, by forces outside the control of individuals contradicts the classical position that people are rational beings who exercise free will and determine their own behavior. Positivism sometimes goes too far in denying individual freedom to choose how to behave, but it lends itself well to the study of social, psychological, economic, political, and biological influences. Research by positivists can thus generate recommendations for policies to reduce crime—for instance, by strengthening the family or by cutting poverty.

CESARE LOMBROSO

Cesare Lombroso (1835–1909) was the first influential proponent of the positivist approach to criminology. He has been called the "father of criminology" because he was able to direct the study of crime away from questions of free will and personal responsibility to a more scientific basis. Although Lombroso's ideas about the biological origins of crime have proved erroneous, and sometimes even ludicrous, his work did mark an important turning point in criminology. By stressing measurable characteristics, even if they were the wrong ones, Lombroso made it possible to determine which factors actually are related to criminal behavior. In the early editions of his textbook on the criminal offender, Lombroso attributed crime primarily to biological factors, but his research led him to downplay the significance of these factors and give greater emphasis to insanity, poor education, and social background in later editions of his book. This change in his views on crime causation is testimony to the positivist method, for by focusing on measurable factors Lombroso was able to test his ideas about the causes of crime and then modify his theory in light of new evidence.

BEYOND LOMBROSO

Enrico Ferri (1856–1929) and Raffaele Garofalo (1852–1934) were two positivists who went beyond Lombroso in the study of the causes of crime. Ferri focused on causes such as climate, age, race, sex, psychology, population density, and political and economic conditions. His work has been criticized for failing to specify the relative importance of each factor in the causation of crime. Garofalo shared some of Lombroso's ideas on crime causation, but his work focused on psychological factors such as the lack of compassion among offenders. Positivism is not necessarily associated with any particular theory of crime, but is instead a method that can be used to assess the influence of many different factors on criminal behavior.

By 1900 the seeds of modern criminology had been sown. The emphasis on measurement, scientific neutrality, and the testing of hypotheses with empirical data was a major advance over the speculative work of the classical school. Even if the early positivists' explanations were often inaccurate or incomplete, they did provide criminologists with the methods to determine whether explanations are right or wrong. The positivist approach offers the possibility that ultimately a theory of crime supported by research will be developed. Positivists generate theories to explain their research findings, and then test those theories with more research, modifying their explanations to fit new evidence. Before a theory supported by research can be developed, however, it is necessary to collect data on the dimensions of crime that must be explained by a theory. In the rest of this chapter we look at several methods for gathering data on crime.

OFFICIAL CRIME STATISTICS

Criminologists often use measures of crime produced by law-enforcement agencies to study criminal behavior and offenders. Because students of crime frequently use statistics they do not collect, they must have a thorough knowledge of how those statistics are produced (Black, 1970). Changes in law-enforcement practices over time may alter the way that crime statistics are gathered; when this happens, a change in crime rates may reflect a change in enforcement activity rather than a real increase or decrease in the amount of criminal activity (see, e.g., Tobias, 1967).

History of Crime Statistics in the United States

Before 1870, little attention was paid to the measurement of crime in the United States. In that year, a federal law was passed that required the attorney general to report annually to Congress on the amount of crime in the country; this law was largely ignored. In the following year, an organization that was the forerunner of today's International Association of Chiefs of Police (IACP) called for the collection of national crime data, but a committee to deal with that task was not formed until 1927. Two years later a manual for reporting crime statistics was distributed to police departments around the country and the collection of data began. There was some disagreement over whether the Federal Bureau of Investigation (FBI) or the Bureau of the Census should gather the data and issue a report. In 1930, the FBI began compiling crime statistics, and later that year Congress passed a law authorizing the FBI to continue collecting crime data (Maltz, 1977; Inciardi, 1980). These statistics are now published in an annual volume, *Crime in the United States: Uniform Crime Reports.*

In 1931, Thorsten Sellin stated that "the value of a crime for index purposes decreases as the distance from the crime itself in terms of procedure increases" (p. 346). This view was widely shared and led the FBI to focus on crimes reported to and recorded by the police, rather than on data on arrested suspects, defendants in court, or prison inmates. The farther we move from the report of the crime, the more likely we are to get a distorted picture of it. For example, research shows that systematic distortion in the arresting of drug suspects does not allow us to measure crime trends with arrest data (DeFleur, 1975). This is because changes in arrests over time are related to changes in the perceived seriousness of drug law violations and changes in patterns of law enforcement.

Ideally, national crime statistics would include police data on reported crimes and arrested suspects. Suspects would then be followed through the criminal justice system, and information would be recorded on the disposition of cases and the sentences meted out to convicted offenders. Maintaining such records would be costly and difficult, but it would give us a more complete picture of crime than we now have. In 1981, the Bureau of Justice Statistics in the United States Department of Justice, with the assistance of seven states, began to collect data on arrested suspects and the criminal justice system's processing of them. Three states dropped out of this study because of budgetary constraints and other problems, but four states provided some preliminary offender-based transaction statistics (OBTS) (Bureau of Justice Statistics, November 1983b).

FBI Crime Statistics

The FBI has achieved nearly complete coverage of the country in its collection of data from the police. It now gathers statistics from nearly 16,000 city, county, and state law-enforcement agencies, which cover about 97 per cent of the country's population. Coverage is best for major metropolitan areas, where 98 per cent of the population is covered, and worst for rural areas, where 90 per cent of the population is covered. In 1983, forty-one states had crime-reporting programs that gathered statistics from local police departments and forwarded them to the FBI; the FBI collects data directly from local police departments in the other states. What the FBI misses, however, are crimes reported to agencies and institutions other than the police. For instance, statistics on crimes recorded by campus police forces often fail to get into the FBI's annual crime reports.

The FBI presents detailed data on eight crimes, the Part I offenses that together constitute the *crime index.* The FBI presents much less information on twenty-one Part II crimes. Table 3.1 defines the eight Part I and the twenty-

Table 3.1: Offenses in the FBI's Uniform Crime Reporting System

PART I (INDEX) OFFENSES

Murder and nonnegligent manslaughter: the willful killing of one human being by another.

Forcible rape: carnal knowledge of a female forcibly and against her will, including attempts.

Robbery: taking or attempting to take anything of value from another person by force or threat of force.

Aggravated assault: unlawful attack by one person upon another for the purpose of inflicting severe or aggravated bodily injury, usually accompanied by the use of a weapon.

Burglary—breaking or entering: unlawful entry of a structure to commit a felony or a theft.

Larceny—theft: unlawful taking, carrying, leading, or riding away of property from the possession of another; excluding motor vehicle theft, embezzlement, con games, and forgery.

Motor vehicle theft: theft or attempted theft of a motor vehicle.

Arson: willful or malicious burning, or attempt to burn, with or without intent to defraud, of a house, public building, motor vehicle or aircraft, or personal property of another.

PART II OFFENSES

Other assaults (simple): assaults and attempted assaults where no weapon is used and that do not result in serious injury to the victim.

Forgery and counterfeiting: Making, altering, uttering, or possessing, with intent to defraud, anything false that is made to appear true.

Fraud: fraudulent conversion and obtaining money or property by false pretenses.

Embezzlement: misappropriation or misapplication of money or property entrusted to one's care, custody, or control.

Stolen property; buying, receiving, possessing: buying, receiving, and possessing stolen property, including attempts.

Vandalism: willful or malicious destruction, injury, disfigurement, or defacement of any public or private property, real or personal, without consent of the owner or persons having custody or control.

Weapons: carrying, possessing, etc.: all violations of regulations or statutes controlling the carrying, using, possessing, furnishing, and manufacturing of deadly weapons or silencers.

Prostitution and commercialized vice: sex offenses of a commercialized nature, such as prostitution, keeping a bawdy house, procuring, or transporting women for immoral purposes.

Sex offenses (except forcible rape, prostitution and commercialized vice): statutory rape and offenses against chastity, common decency, morals, and the like.

Drug abuse violations: state and local offenses relating to narcotic drugs, such as unlawful possession, sale, use, growing, and manufacturing of narcotic drugs.

Gambling: promoting, permitting, or engaging in illegal gambling.

Offenses against the family and children: nonsupport, neglect, desertion, or abuse of family and children.

Driving under the influence: driving or operating any vehicle or common carrier while drunk or under the influence of liquor or narcotics.

Liquor laws: state or local liquor law violations, except drunkenness and driving under the influence; federal violations are excluded.

Drunkenness: drunkenness or intoxication, excluding driving under the influence.

Disorderly conduct: breach of the peace.

Vagrancy: vagabondage, begging, loitering, etc.

All other offenses: all violations of state or local laws, except the preceding offenses and traffic offenses.

Suspicion: No specific offense; suspect released without formal charges being placed.

Curfew and loitering laws: offenses relating to violations of local curfew or loitering ordinances where such laws exist.

Runaways: limited to juveniles taken into protective custody under provisions of local statutes.

SOURCE: Adapted from William H. Webster, *Crime in the United States, 1983: Uniform Crime Reports.* Washington, D.C.: U.S. Government Printing Office, 1984, pp. 342–343.

one Part II crimes. The FBI justifies its presentation of more detail on the Part I offenses by claiming that these crimes

- are regarded by the public as very serious,
- are relatively frequent in occurrence, and
- often come to the attention of the police.

CRITICISMS OF FBI STATISTICS
Critics claim that the public may regard Part I offenses as serious because the FBI gives them the most attention. In other words, the FBI's choice of what to include in Part I conveys to the public a particular image of "the crime problem," one that for the most part consists of crimes against persons and property by people who have low incomes or who are members of minority groups (Reiman, 1984).

The FBI's crime report pays little attention to white-collar crime. Of the eight Part I offenses, only arson is sometimes a white-collar crime. White-collar crimes such as price fixing and government corruption fit the FBI's criterion of being relatively frequent, but no mention is made of those offenses in its crime report. Some of the Part II crimes are white-collar offenses, such as embezzlement and fraud. However, the FBI does not indicate that white-collar crimes inflict much greater financial losses on the American public than do all the crimes in Part I of the report (see Chapter 4). Local law-enforcement agencies rarely learn of white-collar crimes because of their complexity, because the public thinks that the police will not deal with such offenses, and because corporate victims of white-collar crime keep some of those offenses secret so as not to harm their public image. As a result, FBI crime reports convey the impression that white-collar crime is of little consequence in American society.

FBI reports are also deficient in failing to indicate the pervasive involvement of organized crime in criminal activities in the United States. Data on arrests for gambling, narcotics, and commercialized vice appear in Part II of the FBI's reports, but these statistics do not show gangsters' involvement in these offenses, nor are any data presented on loan sharking (usury), a major source of revenue for organized crime.

Crime Rates

The FBI Uniform Crime Report gives the absolute number of crimes and the crime rates for the index offenses, except for arson for which data are incomplete. The FBI calculates national *crime rates* by dividing the number of reported crimes by the number of people in the country, and then expressing the result as a rate of crimes per 100,000 people. For instance, in 1983 there were 19,308 recorded cases of murder and nonnegligent manslaughter in the United States. The estimate of the nation's population in 1983 was 233,981,000. The murder rate per 100,000 is thus calculated as follows:

$$\frac{19,308}{233,981,000} \times 100,000 = 8.3 \text{ per } 100,000$$

Expressing the crime rate in this way makes more sense than simply stating how many homicides occurred in 1983. For example, if the United States had 19,308 murders in a year in the past when its population was exactly half as large as its 1983 population, the murder rate in that earlier year would have been twice as high as it was in 1983, or 16.6 per 100,000 people.

The failure to look at crime in terms of rates led to one particularly absurd effort to explain crime. Prince Peter Kropotkin asserted that there was a fixed relationship between the average temperature in a country, the degree of humidity in that country, and the absolute number of murders that occurred in that nation, a formulation that makes no sense because it does not take into account the size of the country's population (Mannheim, 1965: 204). Kropotkin's "law" would suggest that two countries with the same climate should have equal numbers of murders each year, even if one nation had ten times as many people as the other.

Crime rates, rather than the absolute number of crimes, are the appropriate measure for comparing countries, states, or cities. In the following excerpt from an advice column in *The Boston Globe,* the letter-writer asks a question about crime rates in the correct way, but the newspaper provides an inappropriate response:

> Q. I have to make a job choice between New York City and Houston. Can you tell me how the crime rates for these cities compare—V.P., Burlington [Mass.]
>
> A. The latest available annual (1977) FBI major crime statistics for New York City and Houston are as follows: New York—1,553 murders; 3,899 rapes, 74,404 robberies; 42,056 assaults; 178,907 burglaries; 214,838 larcenies; and 94,420 motor vehicle thefts. Houston—376 murders; 965 rapes; 6,153 robberies; 1,810 assaults; 33,419 burglaries; 60,839 larcenies; and 13,726 motor vehicle thefts (*The Boston Globe,* May 7, 1980, p. 86).

Here the newspaper gives the total number of crimes in each city, making it impossible for the letter-writer to compare the crime rates of the cities without looking up their populations. The letter-writer wanted to compare risks of victimization in the two cities, and crime rates are needed to do that. FBI reports do not give city-by-city crime rates, but these rates can be calculated by using Census data on the populations of the cities and FBI data on numbers of crimes in the cities. Let us see what happens when we calculate murder rates for New York City and Houston:

	NUMBER OF MURDERS (1977)	POPULATION (1977)	MURDER RATE PER 100,000 PEOPLE
New York City	1,553	7,298,000	21.3
Houston	376	1,555,000	24.2

New York City had many more murders than Houston in 1977, but it also had a much larger population. When we calculate murder rates per 100,000 people—a measure of the risk that a person such as the letter-writer will be killed in a given year—we find that the homicide rate per 100,000 people was actually higher in Houston, by 24.2 to 21.3. Based on the faulty answer by *The Boston Globe,* the letter-writer would have moved to Houston, even though the risk of being murdered there was greater than in New York City.

Sociological criminology often focuses on crime rates. Rather than examining and explaining each and every criminal act, it makes more sense to look at rates of crime and seek explanations for variations in crime rates among different social groups. For instance, if men have a higher murder rate than women, this has implications for the explanation of murder and for the development of policies to reduce murder. Explanations of the difference might focus on biological, psychological, or social differences between men and women that predispose men to be more violent. If differences in the upbringing of boys and girls were found to be linked to differences in murder rates by adult men and women, policies might be developed to change the way that parents treat their children.

RATES OF CRIMES AGAINST THE PERSON
Throughout the FBI reports, rates of crime per 100,000 people are presented. This way of calculating rates makes sense for crimes against the person such as murder, aggravated assault, forcible rape, and robbery, because in these crimes of violence it is individuals who are at risk. As we will see, rates per 100,000 people make somewhat less sense for crimes against property. FBI rates for the index offenses are shown in Table 3.2.

Table 3.2: Rates of Crime per 100,000 People, United States, 1983

CRIME	RATE PER 100,000 PEOPLE
Murder and nonnegligent manslaughter	8.3
Forcible rape	33.7
Robbery	213.9
Aggravated assault	273.3
Burglary	1,333.8
Larceny—theft	2,866.5
Motor vehicle theft	429.3
Arson	*
Crime index total	5,158.6

* Sufficient data are not available to estimate the crime rate.

SOURCE: William H. Webster, *Crime in the United States, 1983: Uniform Crime Reports.* Washington, D.C.: U.S. Government Printing Office, 1984, p. 43.

Murder and aggravated assault For both murder and aggravated assault, the FBI divides the total number of crimes by the total population, to arrive at a rate per 100,000 people. Because any person in the population can be the victim of these crimes, this method of calculating rates makes sense. One difficulty with aggravated assault rates, however, is that individual police officers may differ in their judgment about how serious an assault must be to be classified as an aggravated assault—a Part I offense—rather than as a simple assault that would be a Part II offense.

Forcible rape According to the FBI's definition, forcible rape can only involve female victims, even though some states now define rape in sex-neutral terms. Because the FBI presents forcible rape statistics only for sexual assaults that involve women as victims, it makes no sense for it to present rates of forcible rape per 100,000 people in the country, because nearly half of the people in the denominator used to calculate the rate are men. For instance, the 1983 FBI rate of forcible rape was 33.7 recorded rapes per 100,000 people (women and men). The rate of forcible rape would be better expressed by dividing the number of rapes (78,918) by the number of women in the country (120,267,000), a rate of 65.6 rapes per 100,000 women. This rate gives us a better idea of the risk of rape faced by women, although calculating the rate in this way means that it cannot be compared to rates of murder or robbery that are calculated per 100,000 people (both men and women).

Robbery Rates of robbery make sense when calculated per 100,000 people in the country, because any individual can have money or property taken by force or threat of force. However, robbery rates would provide even more information if they were presented as rates for individuals working in commercial establishments such as banks and stores, and rates for individuals in noncommercial roles. As we will see later in this chapter, victimization surveys make this distinction between commercial robbery and robbery from the person. Because robbery involves theft, calculating rates in terms of how much property is available to be stolen would also be useful.

RATES OF CRIMES AGAINST PROPERTY
Motor vehicle theft, larceny, burglary, and arson are crimes against property, even though it is people who own the stolen or burned property. The FBI calculates crime rates for these offenses by dividing the number of incidents by the number of people in the country, and expressing the rates as offenses per 100,000 people. Rates calculated in terms of number of offenses per amount of property available to be stolen or burned would provide more useful information.

Motor vehicle theft Rates of auto theft that are calculated in terms of thefts per 100,000 people conceal more information than they provide. For instance, in 1883 the rate of motor vehicle theft was of course 0 per 100,000 people, for the simple reason that there were no cars to be stolen; the first reported auto theft was not until 1905. In 1983 the rate of car theft was 429.3 per 100,000 people. Comparing this rate with the rate a century earlier means little unless we know how many cars were available to be stolen in each year. Thus, the rate of auto thefts per number of cars in the country would make more sense than the rate of auto thefts per capita that the FBI presents. Some of the increase in car thefts in recent years is attributable to the fact that the number of cars in the country has grown faster than the number of people, and there are thus more cars to be stolen. We need to remove the effects of changes in the opportunities available for this crime to see the real meaning of changes in crime rates (Sparks, 1980a).

Larceny Unlike robbery, larceny does not necessarily involve theft from an individual. Many kinds of larceny—for example, pickpocketing, purse snatching, and bicycle theft—do involve the theft of property that belongs to an individual, but other types of larceny do not—for example, theft from pay telephones or parking meters, shoplifting from stores, and theft of public property.
   Rates of larceny increase as the affluence of a country grows, and so it might be better to calculate larceny rates as the proportion of the Gross National Product (GNP) that is stolen each year, rather than as the number of

larceny incidents per 100,000 people. In the nineteenth century, Filippo Poletti suggested looking at theft in this way. He recommended that the amount of crime in a country be compared with the amount of honest economic activity in that country, rather than with the number of people in the country. Poletti saw increases in property crime as a by-product of increases in available property and economic transactions (Radzinowicz and King, 1977: 78). The increase in the property available to be stolen is a major reason that rates of property crime grow dramatically during economic development (Clinard and Abbott, 1973; Shelley, 1981a).

Burglary   Rates of burglary might also be expressed in terms different from the FBI's rates of burglaries per 100,000 people. The presence of more physical structures means more opportunities for burglary, and it is those structures rather than the people living in them that are the targets of burglars. In one community there might be 1,000 people living in 250 housing units, and in another community there might be 1,000 people living in 500 units. In the first community, 5 burglaries would translate into a rate of 500 burglaries per 100,000 people; the per capita rate would be the same in the second community. However, if the rates were calculated in terms of targets available for burglary in each community, the rate in the first community would be 2,000 burglaries per 100,000 housing units, and the rate in the second community would be only 1,000 burglaries per 100,000 housing units. This second way of calculating burglary rates would indicate that the first community was a higher risk area for burglary, because any given housing unit had twice as great a chance of being burglarized.

Arson   Incomplete data made it impossible for the FBI to calculate an arson rate in 1983. If statistics were available, the FBI would provide a rate of arson incidents per 100,000 people. A better method would be to give a rate of dollars in property lost through arson per dollar value of property in the country. Another way would be to calculate rates in terms of arson incidents per number of buildings in the country. Because arson is a property crime, rates should reflect the risk of loss through this crime. This information might be supplemented with per capita rates of lives lost or injuries sustained in crimes of arson.

THE FBI CRIME INDEX
In calculating an overall rate of Part I crimes, the FBI adds the reported number of seven crimes (omitting arson because of incomplete data) and divides by the number of people in the country to get a rate of index crimes per 100,000 people. In 1983 the crime index rate was 5,158.6 per 100,000 people.

The FBI does not attempt to weight the index crimes by their relative seriousness. Obviously a homicide is more serious than the theft of a quarter, but the FBI treats both the same in calculating the crime index rate. The FBI also treats all motor vehicle thefts as index crimes, even though most auto thefts are for "joy riding" rather than for resale of the car or its parts. A theft in which the car is shipped out of the country for resale would seem to be more serious than a theft in which teen-agers abandon a car unharmed after it runs out of gasoline.

Until 1972 the FBI distinguished between the theft of property worth more than $50 (an index offense) and the theft of property worth less than that amount (not an index offense) in an effort to count only the most serious thefts in the crime index. Critics attacked the use of the arbitrary cutoff of $50, especially because the figure was not increased over the years in spite of inflation. Rather than try to adjust the cutoff point for defining serious theft, the FBI in 1973 simply dropped the distinction between serious theft and petty theft and began to report all cases of larceny together.

If the FBI systematically applied a measure of the relative seriousness of various crimes to police crime reports, the informational value of the crime index rate would be improved. However, a seriousness scale might magnify some of the problems with FBI statistics. Thus, weighting crimes would mean that robberies would count more than simple larcenies, but white-collar crimes would still be omitted from the overall crime rate. Nevertheless, some consideration of the relative seriousness of the different index crimes would provide better information than is now available from the crime index rate (Wolfgang, 1968: 281). For instance, the overall crime index rate might remain the same for two consecutive years, even if a decline of 10,000 murders were offset by an increase of 10,000 larcenies from one year to the next. Clearly crime in the second year would be less serious because of the reduction in murders, but the FBI crime index rate would not reveal that change in the composition of the crime rate.

Gathering Crime Statistics

To ensure uniformity in the reporting of crime by local police departments and state reporting programs, the FBI circulates a *Uniform Crime Reporting Handbook* to tell the police how to record crimes. Still, crimes may be counted

A police arson squad officer stands in front of burned-out buildings in the Bronx, New York.

Photo by William E. Sauro. Reprinted by permission of the New York Times.

somewhat differently by local police departments. For instance, some departments may record an auto theft the instant a car is reported missing, and other departments may put such a report aside for a few hours to make sure that the owner does not call back to say that someone in the family had just borrowed the car. The FBI is aware of such differences among police departments and cautions readers of its reports "against comparing statistical data of individual reporting units," in part because of different "administrative and investigative emphases of law enforcement" (Webster, 1984: v). However, if we cannot compare the crime rates of various communities, then we cannot add the crime rates of those different communities to get a national crime rate, and the FBI does that every year.

Sometimes multiple offenses are committed during the same crime incident. Thus, if an offender threatens a couple with a knife, forces them into their car, tells them to drive him somewhere, and then steals their money before riding off in their car, he has committed two simple assaults, two kidnappings, one auto theft, and one robbery. In this case, the FBI says to count only the most serious offense, or one robbery. Some might consider kidnapping a more serious crime than robbery, but the FBI does not treat kidnapping as an index offense, probably because it occurs relatively infrequently. Information is lost because the FBI ignores some offenses and records only the most serious crime in a series of offenses, but recording each different violation of the law would overstate the extent of crime.

CRIME REPORTING

Because the police can cover only a limited territory and do not have easy access to private places, they learn of many crimes from citizens, usually victims or witnesses. Sometimes people call the police switchboard to report a crime, and other times they report crimes directly to officers on the street or in patrol cars. About 95 per cent of all recorded robberies are reported to the police by the public, rather than discovered in progress by the police (Conklin, 1972).

Some citizen complaints to the police are not officially recorded as crime. One study found that only two-thirds of all complaints to the police produced an official crime report (Black, 1970). Another study found that most robberies that citizens report to interviewers in a survey are not reported to the police and recorded by the police as "founded" (or verified) crime incidents (Block and Block, 1980).

In contrast to *reactive police work* in which officers respond to a citizen's report of a crime, some police work is *proactive,* or the result of efforts by the police to discover and deal with crime on their own initiative (Reiss and Bordua, 1968; Reiss, 1971). Arrests for prostitution and narcotics offenses rarely result from complaints by the public, but are typically the result of efforts by the police, especially the vice or narcotics squad. In crimes such as these, the number of recorded violations may tell us more about the size of the vice or narcotics squad than about the frequency with which the offenses occur. External pressure from political officials, the FBI, or crime commissions can also affect the level of proactive police work. For instance, after the Wolfenden Report, which dealt sympathetically with homosexuality, was issued in Great Britain in 1957, there was a decline in arrests for homosexual acts, even though there was no change in the law itself (Walker, 1971: 27). Because the rate of arrests for "vice" offenses fluctuates wildly with changes in the social climate and changes in law-enforcement practices, the FBI does not include them in Part I of its Uniform Crime Report.

Reasons for nonreporting   People fail to report crimes to the police for many reasons, the most significant of which have to do with the nature of the crime incident itself. Victims are least likely to report offenses that are attempted rather than completed, offenses in which there is little or no financial loss or physical injury, offenses that do not threaten their sense of personal security, offenses that do not seem serious to them, and offenses in which no firearm is used (Hindelang, 1976; Skogan, 1976b, 1984; Block and Block, 1980). We can see from Table 3.3 that the reasons for not reporting an offense to the police vary significantly from one crime to another.

Many victims who do not report crimes to the police say that they think there is little or nothing the police can do to catch the offender or retrieve the lost property. This view is supported by police statistics, which show that the police indeed are least likely to arrest suspects in those crimes that the public feels the police can do little about (Skogan, 1976a: 547–549).

Some victims do not report crimes to the police because they believe that the offense is not very important. This may occur, for instance, when an inexpensive item is stolen, or when no real harm is done in an assault. Victims may think that the police will be annoyed with trivial complaints, and indeed in the past the police may have been unresponsive when called to deal with a minor matter. The increased ownership of theft insurance—including automobile insurance—leads many victims to report crimes to the police even when they have little hope that their property will be recovered, for insurance companies often require notification of the police as proof that a theft occurred. State programs that compensate victims for their losses may also increase crime reporting.

Some crimes are not reported because the victim is afraid of what the police might discover if they investigate the crime. Thus, a drug dealer who is robbed by another dealer may not report the crime. Other victims do not report crimes because they do not want to cause trouble for the offender. A related reason is the fear that the offender might take reprisals against the victim for reporting the crime, especially if the victim and offender are known to each other.

Victims are often unwilling to report crimes to the police because they see the offense as a private or personal matter. Rape victims may avoid the police because they feel stigmatized by the sexual attack. Assault victims may not report the crime because the attack was by a spouse or a parent. Police statistics in developing countries probably undercount assaults to a great extent, because there is often a tradition in local villages of dealing with crime— especially assaults between people who know each other—in an informal way, rather than by bringing in the police (Clinard and Abbott, 1973: 219–228).

Some victims do not report crime to the police because they think that calling the police is too much trouble, especially if a suspect is arrested and they have to testify in court. Inconvenience is also a reason that many crimes are not reported to the police in developing nations; the police in these societies are often located in distant towns that are not connected to villages by telephone or transportation (Clinard and Abbott, 1973: 23–24). Witnesses, as well as victims, may not report crimes because of inconvenience. A study in which "shoplifters"—who were actually participants in an experiment—tried to gain the attention of other shoppers in order to determine how many shoppers would report their thefts found that only 28 per cent of all shoppers even said they had seen the "crime." Of those who admitted to seeing the shoplifting, only 28 per cent reported it to store personnel. Many of the witnesses said

Table 3.3: Reasons for Not Reporting Crimes

PERCENTAGE OF VICTIMIZATIONS NOT REPORTED TO THE POLICE, BY REASON FOR NOT REPORTING

CRIME	Private/ Personal Matter	Nothing Could Be Done/Lack of Proof	Not Important Enough	Reported to Some- one Else	Police Wouldn't Want to Be Bothered	Too Incon- venient	Fear of Reprisal	All Other Reasons	Not Given
Crimes of violence									
Rape	35	18	4	8	*	2	16	42	2
Robbery	15	21	15	9	9	6	7	39	5
Aggravated assault	31	10	22	11	7	3	5	22	4
Simple assault	32	8	30	14	7	2	3	14	3
Crimes of theft									
Burglary	9	23	23	7	10	2	1	44	2
Larceny	8	23	39	3	10	2	1	32	2
Motor vehicle theft	12	18	16	8	8	3	*	52	1

Note: Percentages add to more than 100 per cent for each type of crime because some people gave more than one reason for not reporting.

* 0 or less than 0.5 per cent.

SOURCE: 1981 Bureau of Justice Statistics National Crime Survey; table from Bureau of Justice Statistics, *Report to the Nation on Crime and Justice: The Data.* Washington, D.C.: U.S. Department of Justice, October 1983, p. 25.

that reporting the crime would have been inconvenient or troublesome (Gelfand et al., 1973).

Sometimes victims or witnesses tell others such as a security guard, a friend, or a relative to report the crime. They may also report the crime to a federal or state regulatory agency, a local district attorney, the military police, or the campus police; in these cases, the local police may never learn of the crime.

Crimes that lack victims, or more accurately crimes that lack complainants—such as prostitution and gambling—may not be reported to the police because the participants see the behavior as a private and consensual exchange over which the law should have no jurisdiction, and because no participant believes that any harm was done.

Cross-national surveys have found that crime reporting is not closely associated with attitudes toward the police; in other words, people who are hostile toward the police seem to be as likely to report crime as people who are friendly toward the police. In addition, demographic variables such as race and income do not seem to be closely related to whether a victim will report a crime. Females are slightly more likely than men to report crimes, according to cross-national surveys, and the elderly are more likely than younger people to report crimes (Skogan, 1984). For the most part, however, it seems to be the seriousness of the incident and the type of the offense, rather than social characteristics or attitudes toward the police, that determine whether a victim or a witness will report a crime.

POLICE RECORDING PRACTICES

Aside from being incomplete because of nonreporting, police crime statistics have other problems (Lejins, 1966; Chilton, 1968; Wolfgang, 1968; Weis, 1983). Because politicians and the public sometimes attribute rising crime rates to police ineffectiveness, the police may not record all of the crimes about which they learn.

The organization and guiding philosophy of a police department can influence the accuracy of its crime statistics (Kitsuse and Cicourel, 1963). A legalistic department may see the failure to arrest a suspect as a weakness of the officer, but a service-oriented department may stress the solution of problems without formal arrest; the first department would probably record more interpersonal conflicts as crimes and produce more arrests (Wilson, 1968: 172–226). If a department assigns the collection of crime statistics to precinct captains, and rewards them for low crime rates in their precincts, the captains will have an incentive to omit crimes from their official reports. With centralized crime reporting through a switchboard in headquarters, with greater professionalism, and with greater departmental resources, a police department will probably record crime more accurately and more completely, and thereby provide a more valid picture of the crime problem, even though this may mean a higher official crime rate than if some crimes were omitted from the department's reports (Skogan, 1976b: 110–114; McCleary, Nienstedt, and Erven, 1982).

Sometimes the police record a crime that is reported to them, but classify it as a less serious crime than it really is. This will reduce the rate of serious crimes but inflate the rate of minor offenses; because most public attention is focused on the index offenses, this will make the police look better to outsiders. For instance, forcible rape may be classified as simple assault, and thefts in which force is used may be called larcenies rather than robberies. One example of this downgrading of offenses occurred in 1972 when a Vassar College student was assaulted by a thief and robbed of her purse. The police officer to whom she reported the crime recorded it as a larceny, an index offense but one that is less serious than robbery. The following exchange took place when the student spoke with the officer:

> POLICEMAN: Over here we're considered a Harlem precinct . . . and that's a very bad connotation. So as a result, what they try to do is knock down everything they can. Like if you were robbed and there was no force involved, they make it grand larceny.
>
> STUDENT: I see.
>
> POLICEMAN: Because of the fact that this way the number of robberies looks very bad for this area. . . . So, like say that your bag was snatched, then they try to make it "loss of property" just to knock everything down. Because at the end of the year the Commissioner comes out with this thing about we knocked down crime (Sibley, 1972: 1, 40).

POLITICAL USE OF CRIME STATISTICS

Police statistics have been used for political purposes at both the local and national levels (Seidman and Couzens, 1974; Cronin, Cronin, and Milakovich, 1981). Rising crime rates have been used to justify higher police salaries and increases in police personnel, although police chiefs often acknowledge that police efficiency cannot be evaluated by crime data or arrest statistics (*The Boston Globe*, February 14, 1983). J. Edgar Hoover was a master at using rising crime rates to argue for increased FBI appropriations from Congress. However, he also argued for more funds when crime rates dropped, claiming that the crime problem was finally being solved and that it was no time to reduce support for the fight against crime.

Politicians sometimes use rising crime rates to attack their opponents as "soft on crime." They may claim that reductions in the crime rate during their own time in office show that they have successfully battled crime, even if they cannot demonstrate exactly how they did so. An interesting twist on this argument was heard during Richard M. Nixon's administration, when he asserted that even though he had not actually reduced the crime rate during his first term in office, he had managed to reduce the rate at which crime rates were increasing. Public opinion polls after both the 1968 and 1972 elections showed that the crime issue was a major reason that traditional Democrats "crossed over" and voted for the Republican Nixon.

CLEARANCE AND ARREST STATISTICS

When the police are satisfied that they know who committed a crime, they classify the crime as "cleared" or solved. Most but not all cleared crimes lead to an arrest, and when someone is arrested the police provide information on the suspect to the FBI. In 1983, 20.6 per cent of all index offenses were cleared by arrest; 46.5 per cent of all violent crimes (murder, forcible rape, robbery, and aggravated assault) were cleared, but only 17.7 per cent of all property crimes (burglary, larceny, and auto theft) and only 17.3 per cent of arson cases were solved.

A 1984 study by the Police Foundation (Lawrence W. Sherman and Barry D. Glick, cited in Burnham, 1984a) found that police departments define arrest in different ways, in spite of the FBI's efforts to standardize the definition. As a result, the probability that a citizen will end up with an arrest record depends on the jurisdiction in which an arrest is made. Because of improper and inconsistent recording practices, the use of arrest data to evaluate police departments or to assess the characteristics of offenders is risky.

One problem raised by the use of FBI arrest data is how representative arrested suspects are of all people who commit crime. Some criminals are arrested repeatedly, and others are rarely arrested. It is quite likely that an offender will eventually be arrested if he or she commits many crimes, but some offenders are more likely than others to be arrested for any given crime. Some studies indicate that younger offenders are less likely than older ones to be arrested if they commit a crime, but other research finds that younger offenders are more likely than older offenders to be arrested for any given crime (Goldman, 1963; Conklin, 1972; Boland and Wilson, 1978). Arrest data probably distort the distribution of the ages of all actual offenders, but the nature of that distortion is still unclear.

The FBI has developed a system of centralized and computerized records of arrested suspects, known as the Interstate Identification Index. Supporters of this program justify it in the name of more efficient crime prevention, but the program also threatens the privacy of Americans (Laudon, 1981). Perhaps 36 million Americans—about 30 per cent of the work force—have a record of a criminal conviction, and even more have been arrested and acquitted. In black ghettoes, as many as 90 per cent of young males may have arrest records (Radzinowicz and King, 1977: 314). Gathering detailed information on all these people means that centralized files will exist on a substantial portion of the American population. This poses a threat to people who are arrested mistakenly and later acquitted, but whose arrest records may remain on file with the FBI. Congressional researchers once found that nearly half of a sample of criminal records on file with the FBI were incomplete or inaccurate (Burnham, 1982). Mistakes in these records could keep people from getting jobs or securing government benefits, and this might push a person deeper into a life of crime (Schwartz and Skolnick, 1962; Erickson and Goodstadt, 1979). Moreover, critics allege that the FBI's national criminal history file will have little if any effect on crime rates, because "well over 90 per cent of violent street crime is committed by local criminals who are already known to cities' and states' computerized systems" (Laudon, 1981: A27).

Using FBI Data for Criminological Research

FBI crime data are of limited usefulness for criminologists, even though they provide an indicator of the level of police activity in the nation. These statistics have also been used to get a reading on how crime rates change over time, but rising crime rates can result from more complete reporting and recording of crime as well as from increases in the actual amount of crime. For instance, surveys indicate that the actual amount of crime declined somewhat from 1973 to 1983, even though FBI statistics indicate that crime increased during that time.

The way that the FBI gathers its statistics does not allow criminologists to do much additional analysis of the data. If the FBI collected information on each crime incident recorded by the police, criminologists could use those data to explore certain aspects of crime, such as the relationship between the age of the offender and the use of firearms. However, the FBI gathers only summaries of the number of crimes recorded by local police departments, and then adds the figures from those summary reports to produce the tables in its annual report. This report thus tells us how many murders occurred in each year; how many murders occurred in each region of the country; and the sex, race, and age of arrested murder suspects. There is no way, however, to analyze the FBI data beyond the tables presented in the report. For instance, there is no way to determine how many whites and blacks are arrested for murder in the South in comparison to how many whites and blacks are arrested for murder in the Northeast.

MEASURING CRIMINAL VICTIMIZATION

Crime rates can be calculated in several ways, and each kind of rate has both merits and drawbacks (Erickson, Gibbs, and Jensen, 1977). Using official crime statistics, we can look at rates of recorded crime per capita, rates of recorded crime per number of available crime targets, number of arrests for each kind of crime, and other rates based on crimes or suspects known to the police. Because many crimes are not reported to the police, or are not recorded by the police if they do learn of them, the rate at which people are victimized is likely to be greater than the rate of crime reported to the police.

History of Victimization Surveys

Apparently the first effort to measure crime by surveying members of households was carried out in 1720 in Denmark (Clinard, 1978: 222). However, the first large-scale, systematic effort to measure victimization by interviewing a cross section of a population was not conducted until 1966 in the United States (Ennis, 1967). This study of 10,000 American households by the National Opinion Research Center sought to determine how often people are victimized by crime. Since 1972, the federal government has done *victimization surveys* similar to the one carried out in 1966. These National Crime Surveys (NCS) question national samples to measure both personal and household victimization rates. These surveys are perhaps the most costly effort to gather crime data ever undertaken (Inciardi, 1980a; Sparks, 1982). The Cross-Cultural Perspective shows that victimization surveys have also been carried out in other countries.

Comparing NCS and FBI Data

The NCS program measures crime in a somewhat different way than does the FBI's Uniform Crime Reports (UCR) data collection program. Consequently, the results of these two efforts to measure crime are not strictly comparable. The NCS measures the offenses of rape, robbery from the person, aggravated and simple assault, household burglary, larceny from the person, larceny from the household, and motor vehicle theft. It does not measure murder and kidnapping, and for reasons of economy it stopped collecting data on commercial burglary and commercial robbery in 1977. As a result, we cannot compare NCS data on burglary and robbery with the FBI's UCR data on burglary and robbery, for the latter include burglaries and robberies of commerical establishments as well as of private households and individuals. In recording crimes against the household, the NCS and the FBI methods are the same; for instance, each counts one incident or one victimization for every burglary that is reported. However, the NCS and FBI methods of dealing with crimes against the person differ somewhat. If a robbery has two victims,

A Cross-Cultural Perspective: A Victimization Survey in Switzerland

Victimization surveys have been used to measure crime all over the world: in Great Britain, Canada, Australia, West Germany, the Netherlands, the Scandinavian countries, Japan, the Ivory Coast, and other nations. One comparison of crime rates in different countries that used victimization surveys was Marshall B. Clinard's comparison of Zürich, Switzerland; Stuttgart, West Germany; and Denver and Portland (Oregon) in the United States. All of these cities had populations between 383,000 and 630,000.

The Zürich survey used a representative sample of 248 households and questioned about 940 people aged fourteen and over. The survey was patterned after the one used by the NCS program to measure victimization in the United States, and was administered by a large Swiss public-opinion polling organization.

Because Swiss households are more closely knit than the average American household, it is likely that interviews with the head of the household in Switzerland provided more complete reporting of crimes suffered by members of the household than would be the case in the United States. Moreover, the relative infrequency of crime in Switzerland might make offenses more salient to respondents and therefore make people more likely to remember those crimes than if the crime rate were high.

The Zürich victimization survey found that neither household nor personal crime was widespread. The rate of burglaries or attempted burglaries in Zürich was about half as great as in Denver and Portland, and slightly lower than the rate in Stuttgart. The rate of larceny from the household and the rate of motor vehicle theft were also significantly lower in Zürich than in the other three cities. The rate of robbery from the person was about half as high in Zürich as in Denver, Portland, and Stuttgart. Larceny from the person was about half as common in Zürich as in Stuttgart, and much less than half as common as in the two American cities. The rate of assault was slightly more than half as high in Zürich as in Denver and Portland, but the rate of assault was somewhat greater in Zürich than in Stuttgart.

The victimization survey in Zürich confirmed the results of a cross-national comparison of official crime statistics: Switzerland has a relatively low rate of household and personal crime. For several reasons, the results of the Zürich victimization survey could not be compared with the official crime statistics for that city to determine how much crime that actually occurred there was not reported to and recorded by the police.

SOURCE: Based on Marshall B. Clinard, *Cities with Little Crime: The Case of Switzerland.* Cambridge, Engl.: Cambridge University Press, 1978, pp. 61–72.

the FBI counts only one robbery incident, but the NCS records two victimizations. NCS data are oriented to victimizations and to individuals, whereas FBI data are oriented to crime incidents and to both organizational and individual victims (Reiss, 1981). Table 3.4 outlines some of the differences and similarities of the two methods of collecting crime statistics.

The Dark Figure

Victimization surveys have uncovered a substantial *dark figure,* the number of crimes that actually occur but are not recorded by the police. The dark figure exists for many reasons, especially the failure of victims to report crimes and the failure of the police to record all reported crimes. Figure 3.1, a hypothetical example that graphically depicts the dark figure, shows an actual total crime rate that is constant over time, as represented by the horizontal line parallel to the time axis. At time 1 (t_1), some of this total amount of crime is

Table 3.4: A Comparison of FBI Uniform Crime Reports and National Crime Surveys

	FBI'S UNIFORM CRIME REPORTS (UCR)	NATIONAL CRIME SURVEY (NCS)
Offenses measured:	Homicide Rape Robbery (personal and commercial) Assault (aggravated) Burglary (commercial and household) Larceny (commercial and household) Motor vehicle theft Arson	Rape Robbery (personal) Assault (aggravated and simple) Household burglary Larceny (personal and household) Motor vehicle theft
Scope:	Crimes reported to the police in most jurisdictions; considerable flexibility in developing small-area data	Crimes both reported and not reported to police; all data are for the nation as a whole; some data are available for a few large geographic areas
Collection method:	Police department reports to FBI	Survey interviews; periodically measures the total number of crimes committed by asking a national sample of 60,000 households representing 135,000 persons over the age of 12 about their experiences as victims of crime during a specified period
Kinds of information:	In addition to offense counts, provides information on crime clearances, persons arrested, persons charged, law-enforcement officers killed and assaulted, and characteristics of homicide victims	Provides details about victims (such as age, race, sex, education, income, and whether the victim and offender were related to each other) and about crimes (such as time and place of occurrence, whether or not reported to police, use of weapons, occurrence of injury, and economic consequences)
Sponsor:	Department of Justice Federal Bureau of Investigation	Department of Justice Bureau of Justice Statistics

SOURCE: Bureau of Justice Statistics, *Report to the Nation on Crime and Justice: The Data.* Washington, D.C.: U.S. Department of Justice, October 1983, p. 6.

reported (the solid vertical line) and some of it is unreported (the dotted vertical line, which is the dark figure). By time 2 (t_2), the rate of reported crime has increased and the amount of unreported crime has decreased, but the actual total crime rate remains the same as at time 1. By time 3 (t_3), in this hypothetical case, the official crime rate and the actual total crime rate are the same; in other words, at time 3, all crime that occurs is reported to and recorded by the police. Figure 3.1 shows how the official crime rate (the slanted line) might increase over time without any increase in the actual total crime rate (the horizontal line). This would happen if people began to report crime that previously had not been reported or if the police began to record more of the crime reported to them. If this happens, official crime rates could rise without any increase in the actual total crime rate. Because NCS data and FBI statistics are not comparable, we cannot show actual changes over time in the size of the dark figure.

Figure 3.1: Hypothetical Example of Changes in Crime Rates over Time

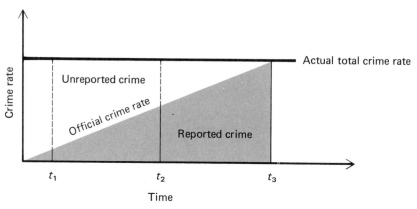

The dark figure has several important consequences. One is to keep cases, usually the least serious ones, out of the criminal justice system. As we have seen, victims are not as likely to report less serious crimes, and so those offenses that come to the attention of the police are likely to be completed crimes, to involve larger losses of property and greater personal injury, and to be committed with firearms (Skogan, 1984). Offenders who commit crimes that are not reported to the police cannot be brought to trial, reducing the deterrent effect of punishment. Police and court resources are sometimes allocated on the basis of how much crime is recorded in a community, and thus differences in crime reporting from one area to another could lead to a misallocation of resources. Victim compensation programs and insurance programs may also be affected by the failure to report and record crime, for benefits and premiums may be based on a distorted picture of how much crime occurs. FBI estimates of the financial costs of crime must also be inflated to account for crimes that are not reported or recorded. The dark figure varies from one crime to another, as we can see in Table 3.5, where the proportion of each NCS offense that is reported to the police is shown.

Table 3.5: Police Reporting Rates for Personal and Household Crimes, NCS Data, 1982

CRIME	PERCENTAGE OF VICTIMIZATIONS REPORTED TO THE POLICE
Crimes of violence	48.2
Rape	52.8
Robbery	56.2
Assault	45.9
Crimes of theft	26.9
Personal larceny with contact	32.7
Personal larceny without contact	26.7
Household crimes	
Household burglary	49.3
Household larceny	26.8
Motor vehicle theft	72.4

SOURCE: Bureau of Justice Statistics, *Criminal Victimization 1983.* Washington, D.C.: U.S. Department of Justice, June 1984, p. 4.

CRIMES AGAINST THE PERSON

The rate of murder obviously cannot be measured in a victimization survey, because the victim is no longer alive to be interviewed. However, most homicides are probably reported to and recorded by the police because of the seriousness of the offense and the difficulty of concealing the crime.

Victimization surveys indicate that forcible rape is often not reported. Recent NCS data indicate that the victimization rate for rape is about twice as high as the FBI's rate, but the ratio may be even higher because many rape victims may be unwilling to tell the strangers interviewing them that they have been raped. Since the 1960s, feminists have managed to increase the public's awareness of rape. This has increased the police's sensitivity to rape victims and has led to the establishment of rape counseling clinics in hospitals. Because rape victims today are more likely to receive support and less likely to be subjected to abuse than was the case two decades ago, we might expect that they are more likely to report their victimization today. However, many rape victims still do not report the crime, fearing insensitive treatment by the police and being wary of the ordeal of testifying in court if a suspect is arrested.

Recent NCS surveys indicate that somewhat more than half of all robberies of individuals are reported to the police. Since the NCS stopped measuring commercial robberies in 1977, comparison of FBI and NCS robbery rates has not been possible. We would expect rates of reporting for robbery to be higher than they are, because most robberies are committed by strangers and there is thus no one the victim wants to shield from arrest and prosecution. Victims apparently fail to report robberies because they believe that nothing can be done about their loss, because they do not feel the crime was important enough, or because they view it as a private or personal matter.

About 40 to 50 per cent of all aggravated assaults are reported to the police, but many assaults involving people who are known to or related to each other are not reported, and these offenses may be concealed from interviewers as well. These offenses include assaults between spouses and assaults between parents and their children.

CRIMES AGAINST PROPERTY

Slightly less than half of all burglaries are reported to the police. Larceny is reported to the police even less frequently, perhaps one-fourth or one-third of the time. Many burglaries and larcenies are not reported to the police because the losses involved are small or because the victim believes that nothing can be done about the lost property. By contrast, most car thefts are reported because cars are expensive items that are identifiable and therefore capable of being recovered by the police, and because insurance companies require reporting of the theft to the police before they will pay for the car or for damage to it.

Methodological Problems with Victimization Surveys

Victimization surveys are subject to several methodological problems (Sparks, 1981b, 1982; Brantingham and Brantingham, 1984). One problem is the issue of validity, or how well the surveys actually measure the amount of crime in a society (Booth, Johnson, and Choldin, 1977). Forgetting can lead to underestimation of the amount of crime that has actually occurred, and it makes it difficult for subjects to tell interviewers exactly when they were victimized. Respondents may also refuse to tell interviewers about crimes for similar reasons to those that keep them from calling the police: the stigma of being victimized, unwillingness to confide in a stranger, and reluctance to take the time to give details of the crime.

Another problem is that victimization surveys may overestimate the amount of crime that occurs. Respondents may incorrectly interpret some experiences—such as the loss of a wallet—and report them as crimes. Overestimation of crime rates can also occur if people report crimes that occurred prior to the period about which they are being questioned as having occurred during that period. This problem of "telescoping" may result from a faulty memory or from the respondent's wish to have something to talk about with the interviewer. This problem of telescoping may inflate victimization rates by as much as 20 per cent, leading to estimates of crime rates that are higher than actual rates (Brantingham and Brantingham, 1984). Overreporting can also be encouraged by interviewers who prod respondents to remember crimes, both to keep the interview interesting and to ferret out the "hidden crime" on which the victimization survey is predicated (Levine, 1976, 1978; Singer, 1978).

Because of these and other methodological problems, the results of victimization surveys should not be regarded as "true" measures of crime. However, they are an advance over police statistics because they measure some of the crime not reported to the police. Even though victimization surveys and police statistics reveal different amounts of crime, both measures often lead to similar conclusions about the distribution of crime in society. Sometimes, however, these two measures lead to different conclusions (Schneider, 1976; Booth, Johnson, and Choldin, 1977).

Even if they provided a valid measure of certain kinds of crime, victimization surveys have not given us a complete and balanced picture of crime. They have not been used to measure white-collar crime, organized crime, or crimes without victims such as gambling and prostitution (Johnson and Wasielewski, 1982). Victimization surveys provide little or no information on offenders, as do FBI data on arrested suspects. To develop a full picture of crime, the surveys must be supplemented with other kinds of data.

Another shortcoming of victimization surveys is that they have been used primarily to look at the amount and distribution of crime rather than to test or develop theories of criminal behavior (Johnson and Wasielewski, 1982). Victimization surveys have repeatedly shown that much crime is not reported and recorded, but they have contributed less to our understanding of the social processes that generate crime; as a result, they have contributed relatively little to the development of policies to reduce crime.

Other Measures of Victimization

One way to study victimization without using surveys is to analyze nonofficial records. Shoplifting has been studied in this way. A study of three Chicago department stores found that many cases of shoplifting known to the stores were not reported to the police; in one store, only 12 per cent of the cases were brought to official attention (Cameron, 1964).

Auditors as well as store detectives can detect theft, but much embezzlement and employee theft that auditors uncover is never reported to the police. Probably 85 per cent of all computer crime is never brought to official attention, in order to avoid adverse publicity for the victimized company, and because managers do not know how to prevent further computer crime and do not want to call attention to their vulnerability (Parker, 1976). The extent to which a company may go to prevent adverse publicity can be seen in a series of crimes that preceded the 1950 Brinks robbery in Boston. The thieves who carried out that crime stole about $400,000 from various Brinks drop-offs before the major robbery, and none of the smaller thefts was reported to the police. The company apparently preferred to absorb the losses rather than advertise that it could not guard the property entrusted to it, for this would have scared away potential customers and increased the company's insurance rates (Behn, 1977).

Victimized companies that conceal their losses from the police and the public often develop their own systems of private justice, dismissing dishonest workers or trying to get them to pay back stolen money. Those employee crimes that are reported to the police and prosecuted in court usually involve relatively large sums of money (Robin, 1970; Lundman, 1978).

MEASURING CRIME BY SELF-REPORTS

Crime can be measured by police statistics or by questioning participants in the incident through a survey. Victimization surveys ask a cross section of the population about its experiences as victims of crime during a specific period, often six months. Another way to measure crime is to interview a cross section of the population, or a more limited sample such as high school students, about their involvement in crime and delinquency as offenders. *Self-report studies* reveal that much crime that respondents will admit to in confidential interviews or on self-administered questionnaires never makes its way into police statistics.

History of Self-Report Studies

The first use of survey methods to gather self-reported information about involvement in crime and delinquency was Austin L. Porterfield's (1946) research that used this "self disclosure" method to compare college students with delinquents who had been through the juvenile court. Porterfield found that both groups had been involved in delinquency in similar ways during their adolescence. In 1947, a self-report survey of adults discovered that 99 per cent of a sample of "law-abiding" middle-class people admitted to at least one crime (Wallerstein and Wyle, 1947). These early studies showed that much self-reported crime is never detected by the police.

In 1957, James F. Short, Jr., and F. Ivan Nye (1957) developed a checklist of delinquent activities to be filled out anonymously by respondents. They found that delinquency was more evenly spread across social classes than was indicated by official crime statistics, which showed much more delinquency among the lower classes. Since this pioneering work, many researchers have used self-reports to test and refine theories of crime and delinquency and to provide a more complete picture of violation of the law than is given by official statistics (Weis, 1983). Table 3.6 shows six questions used by Travis Hirschi (1969) to gather self-report data on delinquency among California students and to test the control theory of delinquency.

Self-report studies have also been conducted with groups of offenders other than those who engage in conventional crimes and delinquent acts. For instance, in 1976 the Internal Revenue Service (IRS) mailed questionnaires to 1,200 corporations to ask about their use of illegal bribes and "slush funds."

Table 3.6: Survey Questions Measuring Self-Reported Delinquency

1. Have you ever taken little things (worth less than $2) that did not belong to you?
   A. No, never
   B. More than a year ago
   C. During the last year
   D. During the last year *and* more than a year ago

2. Have you ever taken things of some value (between $2 and $50) that did not belong to you?
   A. No, never
   B. More than a year ago
   C. During the last year
   D. During the last year *and* more than a year ago

3. Have you ever taken things of large value (worth over $50) that did not belong to you?
   A. No, never
   B. More than a year ago
   C. During the last year
   D. During the last year *and* more than a year ago

4. Have you ever taken a car for a ride without the owner's permission?
   A. No, never
   B. More than a year ago
   C. During the last year
   D. During the last year *and* more than a year ago

5. Have you ever banged up something that did not belong to you on purpose?
   A. No, never
   B. More than a year ago
   C. During the last year
   D. During the last year *and* more than a year ago

6. Not counting fights you may have had with a brother or sister, have you ever beaten up on anyone or hurt anyone on purpose?
   A. No, never
   B. More than a year ago
   C. During the last year
   D. During the last year *and* more than a year ago

SOURCE: Adapted from Travis Hirschi, *Causes of Delinquency.* Berkeley, Calif.: University of California Press, 1969, p. 256.

A total of 304 corporations did not respond, but among those that did, the IRS found 481 potentially illegal slush funds and seventy-one cases of apparent criminal fraud (Egan, 1978).

The Dark Figure

Self-report studies confirm the conclusion of victimization surveys that the dark figure, or hidden amount of crime, is large. For instance, a study that asked 180 boys, most of whom had been in trouble with the law, about their involvement in twenty-two crimes and delinquent acts found that the boys admitted to an average of 680 offenses (Erickson and Empey, 1963). A study of male heroin users that employed self-report questionnaires found that the drug users confessed to an average of 337 crimes per year (Inciardi, 1979). Research on forty-nine incarcerated robbers found that they admitted to a total of 10,505 offenses during their careers, an average of 214 crimes per offender (Petersilia, Greenwood, and Lavin, 1977). These and many other studies dramatically demonstrate that official crime statistics undercount the amount of crime.

Another conclusion from self-report studies is that nearly everyone in the general population has broken the law at some time, even though most of the violations are petty. The general population falls on a continuum from highly criminal to completely noncriminal; it is not composed of two discrete groups of criminals and noncriminals. Researchers who compare a sample of convicted offenders with a "noncriminal" sample drawn from the general population usually fail to consider that many of these "noncriminals" have in fact engaged in crimes themselves. Large numbers of people commit a few, often trivial, crimes; some commit a larger number; others commit quite a few crimes, including some serious ones; and a small proportion of the population commits many crimes, including large numbers of serious ones (Elmhorn, 1965). Researchers have found that the more often a person violates the law, the more likely that person is to commit a relatively serious crime.

Methodological Problems with Self-Report Studies

Self-report studies have several methodological shortcomings that account for their failure to provide an ideal measure of crime (Reiss, 1975; Nettler, 1984; Brantingham and Brantingham, 1984). The questionnaires used in these studies sometimes lack validity; that is, they do not measure accurately the amount of crime that respondents have committed. Subjects may fabricate behavior to impress interviewers, or they may fail to mention some offenses out of fear that the information will be passed on to the police, in spite of guarantees of anonymity. At least two studies show that some kind of external control over lying is needed to ensure the validity of self-report instruments (Clark and Tifft, 1966; Farrington, 1973).

Another problem with self-report studies is the way they have been carried out. The use of many different self-report questionnaires by researchers means that their results are often not comparable. Self-report studies would be much more useful if the same questionnaire were administered over time to national samples. This would allow us to generalize about the amount of crime in the population as a whole, and to look at changes in the amount of crime over time (Brantingham and Brantingham, 1984). We have accumulated some data of this sort on victimization experiences, but we do not yet have such information on self-reported violations of the law. In fact, we know relatively little about self-reported crime by adults, for the vast majority of self-report studies have been carried out on samples of juveniles.

Self-report studies are also flawed in that they ignore certain kinds of behavior. They rarely include questions that add to our knowledge of white-collar crime or organized crime. The way that questionnaires are written usually makes it difficult to compare the results of self-report studies with official crime statistics or with NCS data. This is partly a result of the use of self-report questionnaires with juvenile samples, for this means that respondents are asked about acts that would be crimes if they were adults as well as about juvenile status offenses such as truancy and underage drinking. Some questionnaires even ask about acts that would not get a juvenile into trouble with the law; one example is a question about masturbation.

Some self-report studies classify juveniles as delinquents if they admit to one or more delinquent acts. Questionnaires that ask about large numbers of acts are more likely to classify a high proportion of respondents as delinquents, even though many of them might be only minimally involved in trivial acts of delinquency (Reiss, 1975; Hindelang, Hirschi, and Weis, 1979). Self-report studies should emphasize the frequency of delinquency and crime and the seriousness of the acts, rather than whether an individual has ever engaged in any act that violates the law.

Because of their methodological shortcomings, self-report studies cannot be employed to assess the efficiency of official crime statistics, even though these studies do confirm that there is a large dark figure of crime (Brantingham and Brantingham, 1984). They have proved useful, however, in telling us about the characteristics of people who violate different kinds of laws with various degrees of frequency. This information can be compared to official data on arrests, convictions, and sentences to assess the fairness with which the criminal justice system treats different kinds of people (Brantingham and Brantingham, 1984).

Because of the methodological problems with each of the three major measures of crime, none provides us with a perfect measure of the "true" amount of crime. When all three measures agree on the extent and distribution of crime, we can have some confidence in the conclusions. When the three measures disagree, as they sometimes do, it is difficult to know which one to use.

SUMMARY

The classical school of criminology that developed in the eighteenth century assumed free will and individual responsibility, sought to deter offenders from crime by the threat of punishment, and emphasized punishment in proportion to the social harm caused by the criminal act. During the nineteenth century, cartographers such as Guerry and Quetelet looked for patterns of crime that appeared in official crime statistics. Positivists, reacting to the classical school's emphasis on free will, began late in the nineteenth century to use the scientific method to search for the causes of crime. Cesare Lombroso was the first to use empirical evidence to test hypotheses about why people violated the law, an approach that laid the groundwork for modern criminology.

Today criminologists use several statistical measures to study crime. Sometimes they use official statistics gathered by the police, the courts, or the prisons. The FBI began to issue Uniform Crime Reports more than fifty years ago, and these reports now provide statistics on crimes known to the police throughout the United States. The FBI provides detailed data on eight Part I crimes that together constitute the crime index, and less detailed information on twenty-one Part II offenses. The FBI's reports pay little attention to white-collar crime or organized crime, and thus present a distorted picture of the crime problem that emphasizes crimes committed by young males who are often poor and members of minority groups.

Official statistics are used to calculate crime rates, usually in terms of number of offenses per 100,000 people. This kind of rate makes sense for crimes in which people are victimized, but it makes less sense when property is the target. Careful thought should be given to the way that crime rates are calculated and to the exact meaning of those rates. Rates can be used to compare the risk of victimization in different cities or countries and to look at changes in crime over time.

Crimes come to the attention of the police when victims and witnesses report offenses and the police react, and when the police uncover crime on their own initiative through proactive work. Crimes are not reported to the police for many reasons: a sense that nothing can be done, a feeling that the offense is unimportant, a belief that the police do not want to be bothered, fear of reprisals, or definition of the crime as a private matter. The police may fail to record crimes, sometimes to keep crime rates down and make themselves look more effective. Official crime statistics have been used for political purposes, at both the local and national levels. These statistics are of limited use for criminological research because of the summary form in which the FBI collects data.

A second important measure of crime is the victimization survey. A cross section of a population is questioned in detail about their experiences as victims of crime during a given period. This method was first used on a large-scale basis in the United States in 1966, and today it is employed as part of an ongoing federal effort to measure crime. Because the methods of these NCS surveys differ from those used by the FBI to collect data, the two kinds of statistics cannot be compared easily. Victimization surveys have found a large dark figure, the amount of crime that occurs but does not make its way into police records. Because victimization surveys have methodological problems, they are not a "true" measure of how much crime there is, but they are important sources of information.

A third measure of crime is the self-report survey, a questionnaire administered anonymously to get respondents to tell about crimes they have committed. Self-report surveys were first used in the United States in 1946, and since then they have been used to measure the extent of crime and delinquency and to test theories of crime and delinquency. Self-report studies find a large dark figure, and sometimes they reach conclusions about who violates the law that differ from research based on official arrest data. Self-report studies have some problems: Most have been done with adolescents, many have asked about involvement in trivial offenses, and there are some questions about how validly they measure crime and delinquency. When self-report studies agree with official statistics and victimization surveys about the nature and extent of crime, we can have confidence in the results, but when the three measures disagree it is not clear which is the best indicator.

IMPORTANT TERMS

cartography	dark figure	reactive police work
classical school	positivism	self-report study
crime index	proactive police work	victimization survey
crime rate		

SUGGESTED READINGS

PAUL BRANTINGHAM AND PATRICIA BRANTINGHAM. *Patterns in Crime.* New York: Macmillan, 1984. Chapters 3 and 4 contain useful discussions of official crime statistics, victimization surveys, and self-report studies.

RICHARD F. SPARKS. *Research on Victims of Crime: Accomplishments, Issues, and New Directions.* Washington, D.C.: U.S. Government Printing Office, 1982. A comprehensive examination of the use of survey methods to measure criminal victimization, including methodological problems with victimization surveys and what can be learned from this method of measuring crime.

IAN TAYLOR, PAUL WALTON, AND JOCK YOUNG. *The New Criminology: For a Social Theory of Deviance.* London: Routledge and Kegan Paul, 1973. An important Marxist critique of early, as well as contemporary, theories of criminology.

GEORGE B. VOLD. *Theoretical Criminology,* 2nd ed. prepared by Thomas J. Bernard. New York: Oxford University Press, 1979. A useful textbook on theories of criminal behavior and the development of modern criminology.

WILLIAM H. WEBSTER. *Crime in the United States, 1983: Uniform Crime Reports.* Washington, D.C.: U.S. Government Printing Office, 1984. The annual FBI report presents statistics gathered from local police departments on crimes known to the police, cleared offenses, arrested persons, and law-enforcement personnel.

The Costs of Crime

The costs of crime are exorbitant. People are injured and killed, and they lose money and property. They fear strangers as potential thieves and assailants, stay home rather than venture onto unsafe streets, and criticize the police for being unable to control crime. Dishonesty by elected officials undermines faith in the political system and keeps voters home on Election Day. Corporate crime reduces public support for the economic system.

In this chapter we look at three costs of crime. First we examine the financial costs. Next we look at the physical harm that crime causes. Finally, we explore the indirect social costs to people who fear victimization. It is difficult to assess these costs of crime exactly, but we can make some estimates.

FINANCIAL COSTS OF CRIME

Estimates of the financial costs of crime often appear to be more precise than they really are. Estimates can be made only if certain assumptions and guesses are made about how much crime actually occurs in the country, a problem we considered in Chapter 3. Even if we could measure exactly how much crime occurs, it would still be difficult to estimate the cost of each offense. For instance, if a robber beats up a person and steals $25, the victim loses the money but the robber has the use of that money. Placing a monetary figure on the physical and psychological harm to the victim is nearly impossible. If the robber uses the $25 to buy heroin, we might count this expenditure as another cost of crime, even though counting both the initial theft of $25 and the use of that money for heroin might be seen as double counting. If the robber were then arrested, some part of the police budget should be allocated to the crime. The arraignment and trial also cost money, and if the offender is convicted and imprisoned there would be the additional costs of incarceration. The robber's family might have to receive welfare benefits during the offender's imprisonment. The absent parent might create a family environment in which the children are more likely to get involved in delinquency. We can see that the initial loss of $25 in the robbery might be quite a small amount when compared to all of the other costs associated with the crime.

Different Costs of Crime

One cost of crime is the *direct loss* of property. For example, arson destroys buildings, and vandalism ruins property. Both offenses reduce the stock of useful things in the world. We can also speak of direct losses from murder, although placing a monetary figure on lost lives is difficult.

A second kind of cost of crime is the *transfer of property.* The theft of a radio in a burglary and the theft of cash in a robbery transfer property from the rightful owner to the thief, and perhaps eventually to a fence and then to a new owner. The victim of the theft regards himself or herself as having lost the property, but from a societal perspective the property has been transferred from one person to another rather than made useless.

A third financial cost of crime arises from crimes of violence in which a victim is physically hurt. These *costs related to criminal violence* include the loss of productivity by incapacitated victims, unemployment compensation paid to victims, fees paid for physical and psychological therapy for victims, and social security payments and funeral expenses associated with homicides.

Yet another type of cost of crime is the expenditure of money on illegal goods and services such as narcotics, prostitution, and gambling. *Illegal expenditures* can be considered a cost of crime because they divert money from the legitimate economy and represent a loss of potential revenue for people who produce and supply legal goods and services. However, from another point of view, we might regard illegal expenditures as entertainment expenses, which are often paid for with income earned at a legitimate job. Some of these illegal expenditures do not victimize anyone, for no direct and obvious harm to another person necessarily results from spending money on narcotics, prostitution, or gambling. Indeed, expenditures on legal goods such as cigarettes and alcohol may produce more obvious harm than do expenditures on some illegal goods and services.

Enforcement costs, a fifth kind of financial cost of crime, include the money spent by various criminal justice agencies. Employees of these agencies regard their salaries as legitimate payments for services, but from another perspective crime diverts this money from other purposes. If enforcement costs are treated as a financial cost of crime, it follows that redefining some behavior that is now criminal as noncriminal would reduce the cost of crime.

A sixth financial cost of crime involves *prevention and protection costs.* This includes the millions of dollars that people spend for alarm systems, spotlights, locks, bars, and other "target-hardening" devices, as well as the money they spend on insurance premiums to cover their losses through theft.

The Costs of Crime in the United States

Because the financial costs of crime are calculated in various ways, there is no real way to calculate a total figure for all of the costs involved. Adding the amount of property destroyed in arson to the amount spent on illegal drugs and the total cost of police salaries is much like adding apples, oranges, and peaches. We can, however, assess the costs of certain kinds of crime, the costs of the criminal justice system, and other costs associated with crime.

WHITE-COLLAR CRIME

The most expensive crime in financial terms is *white-collar crime,* any illegal act, punishable by a criminal sanction, that is committed in the course of a legitimate occupation or pursuit by a corporation or by an otherwise respectable individual of high social status (Sutherland, 1949, 1983; Edelhertz, 1970; Conklin, 1977; Clinard and Yeager, 1980).

Estimating the cost of white-collar crime is not easy. Not only do we have to calculate direct losses to victims, but we must also determine how much prices rise as a result of the passing on of the companies' losses to consumers. The ramifications of a single white-collar crime are often complex and difficult to assess. For instance, when a bribe is paid by a business executive to accomplish a particular objective, neither the bribe-giver nor the recipient may feel that any loss has been incurred. However, there is a loss to the public from such transactions. Thus, the cost of a bribe paid by a construction firm to a city inspector may be passed on to the individual who has contracted to have the building erected, and the cost of the bribe might then be passed on to the building's tenants in higher rents. The fact that the tenants never learn of their losses does not make the bribe any less of a financial loss to them.

Even though it is difficult to place an exact dollar figure on the financial cost of all white-collar crime, we can state with some certainty that the cost of all such offenses far exceeds the cost of all conventional property crimes that constitute what is widely regarded as "the crime problem." The financial cost of crimes such as robbery, larceny, burglary, and motor vehicle theft does not approach the losses from bribery, kickbacks, stock fraud, embezzlement, computer crime, price fixing, and other white-collar crimes. The Joint Economic Committee of Congress estimated that in 1976 one-third of all financial costs of crime in the United States could be attributed to white-collar crime; $44 billion was lost in that kind of crime (*The New York Times*, January 2, 1977). A similar estimate of $42 billion was made by the Chamber of Commerce of the United States (1974: 6) two years earlier. The cost of white-collar crime may now be twice those estimates, but we lack good data on current costs.

About half of the losses from white-collar crime are due to consumer fraud, illegal competition, and deceptive sales practices. Consumer fraud includes the sale of defective merchandise, the misrepresentation of interest terms, and the sale of unneeded or faulty home and auto repairs. Illegal competition costs billions of dollars each year, and introducing competition where it has been absent can save consumers much money. For instance, an antitrust action against the manufacturer of the drug tetracycline reduced the price of that drug by 75 per cent (*U.S. News & World Report*, November 25, 1974). Deceptive sales practices are also costly; one estimate, now more than a decade old, placed the loss from deceptive grocery labeling alone at $14 billion (Senator Philip A. Hart, cited in McCaghy, 1976: 205).

One costly white-collar crime that involves deceptive sales practices is the sale of counterfeit merchandise. A 1984 study by the Federal Trade Commission concluded that fake merchandise annually costs American workers 131,000 jobs and causes between $6 billion and $8 billion of lost sales each year for American companies. The FTC report states the following:

> The quality difference between the real and the counterfeit products can be of particular importance in some industries to the health and safety of the consumer, as is the case for defective auto parts, ineffective or nonsterile drugs and pharmaceuticals, and ineffective agricultural chemicals (cited in Farnsworth, 1984: 4).

Forty-three nations, including the United States, were mentioned by the FTC as sources of counterfeit goods that companies try to pass off as brand-name products, but the greatest problem seemed to be in East Asia. Taiwan and Hong Kong, for instance, have produced inexpensive counterfeits of Apple computers that outsell the original product by ten to one in East Asia (Hollie, 1982). In the United States, cassettes of record albums and films have been counterfeited. In the summer of 1983, for instance, several prints of the movie *Return of the Jedi* were stolen—one at gunpoint from a theater—to copy for cassettes to be sold for home use. Estimates of annual losses to the film industry from such piracy range from $100 million to $500 million (Harmetz, 1983). Counterfeiting has also caused substantial losses for couturier houses that produce designer clothing, purses, and cosmetics. Fake goods, which often carry the symbol of the designer firm and may be made from materials similar to those used by the manufacturer of the original, are often shoddily made; this may cause customers who are dissatisfied with the counterfeit product, but who think it is an original, to avoid purchasing the original in the future. In addition to lost sales, designer firms incur the expense of legal action for copyright infringement against the manufacturers of counterfeit goods (Anderson, 1981; Lohr, 1984).

Another business crime that is very expensive, indeed probably as expensive as all conventional property crime, is stock fraud and security theft. Securities are sometimes stolen by brokerage house employees, who may deliver the securities to members of organized crime in return for cancellation of the employees' debts that arose from gambling or borrowing from loan sharks. The gangsters then transport the securities out of the country and use them as collateral for loans from foreign banks.

One costly crime that occurs in the commercial sector is employee theft and embezzlement. Estimates of annual losses from these crimes range from $1 billion to $7 billion, but a good recent estimate would probably be closer to the higher figure. In 1980, retail stores lost about $20 million per day from "inventory shrinkage," which includes employee theft, shoplifting, and bookkeeping errors. In some urban stores, the percentage of merchandise lost through such inventory shrinkage equals or exceeds profits (Barmash, 1981). Crimes of this sort are costly for victimized companies; between 15 and 30 per cent of all business failures are due to losses of this sort (*U.S. News & World Report*, October 26, 1970). Theft by employees and fraud by customers cost banks four to five times as much each year as do bank robberies (Smith, 1981). As a consequence, in the late 1970s the FBI began to focus its attention on bank frauds netting at least $100,000, and turned over the investigation of bank robberies to state and local police agencies.

An increasingly important kind of theft is computer crime. Because computers provide access to highly concentrated assets, it is often not much more difficult to steal a million dollars than to steal one dollar. In fiscal year 1979, the 1,083 computer-related bank thefts about which the FBI learned cost an average of about $500,000, compared to an average loss of only $23,000 in bank embezzlements without a computer and an average loss of only $3,000 to $4,000 for bank robberies (Smith, 1981). Between 1980 and 1983, the following large-scale computer-related crimes occurred: a bank embezzlement that netted $21 million, a securities fraud that involved the loss of $53 million, a commodities fraud that produced a loss of $50 million, and an inventory fraud of $67 million (McLellan, 1983). Losses from computer crimes and other forms of internal theft are often passed on to customers and clients in higher prices and fees, rather than deducted from profits or from dividends paid to stockholders.

TAX FRAUD

Cheating on income taxes is not generally regarded as a white-collar crime, for it is not committed during the course of a legitimate job, even though it is work-related. In addition, people of all classes can engage in tax fraud, whereas white-collar crime is limited to middle- and upper-class people. However, tax cheating may be white-collar crime if it involves corporations in the intentional underpayment of taxes.

The General Accounting Office estimates that income tax cheating cost the federal government $87 billion in 1981, an increase from $29 billion in 1973, the first year for which statistics are available (Cowan, 1982). Studies based on anonymous questionnaires have found that about one taxpayer in five cheats to some extent (*The Boston Globe*, March 25, 1985). Some underpayment results from the "tax protester" movement, in which people file returns but omit the payment of taxes in protest of government policies; the number of such returns tripled from 1978 to 1981. Compliance among other taxpayers, whether individuals or corporations, has also declined. Some simply do not report earned income, and others overstate deductions and credits. This change is probably due to a declining risk of being caught, or at least the perception that the risk has declined. Noncompliance is greatest for income about which taxpayers feel the IRS will remain ignorant. The number of IRS investigators declined in the early 1980s, even though $6 can be recovered for every $1 spent on such enforcement (Jackson, 1982). In spite of widespread noncompliance with the payment of taxes in the United States, the problem is not nearly as bad as it is in Italy, as we see in the Cross-Cultural Perspective.

A Cross-Cultural Perspective: Tax Cheating in Italy

Italy has perennially had a difficult time getting its citizens to pay taxes. One widely heard explanation is that Italians are antagonistic toward taxation because for centuries foreign invaders had imposed taxes on them. In recent years, the government has taken measures to increase compliance with the tax law.

In 1972, only two million tax returns were filed by Italians. The introduction of a full payroll deduction system in 1974 improved the situation, and 21.5 million returns were filed in 1981. The failure to file a return was greatly reduced by the 1974 measure, but there is still much underpayment of taxes.

Returns filed in 1981 showed that the average reported income was slightly less than the earnings of an average blue-collar worker, whose income is toward the bottom of the income scale. This indicates that many, perhaps most, taxpayers underreport their incomes. Cheating is especially common among the self-employed, who are not subject to the payroll deduction system.

There is much evidence of wealth in Italy—exclusive shops in large cities, many expensive cars, and enormous ransoms paid in kidnappings. However, in 1981 only 16,000 out of 24.5 million taxpayers reported incomes in excess of the American equivalent of $62,000. Many of the wealthy either underreport their incomes or simply do not file returns.

Political leaders hope that new measures introduced in 1981 and 1983 will reduce tax cheating and thereby strengthen the government's fiscal position.

SOURCE: Based on Sari Gilbert, "Tax Cheating a Way of Life for the Italian," *The Boston Globe*, April 19, 1984, p. 54.

CREDIT CARD FRAUD

An important part of the American economy is the credit card. About 70 per cent of all families have at least one card, and there are about 600 million cards in the hands of American consumers. About 30 per cent of all retail sales involve the use of credit cards (Molotsky, 1984).

The criminal abuse of these cards has grown in recent years. Losses to credit card issuers from counterfeit cards increased from $66,000 in 1977 to $15 million in 1981, and then to between $40 million and $50 million in 1982 (Block, 1983). In addition to counterfeiting, credit card abuse includes the use of stolen, lost, and altered cards and fraud in telephone orders by credit card. A deputy assistant attorney general, testifying before a Senate subcommittee, estimated that in 1982 banks alone lost $128 million due to credit card fraud (Block, 1983). As with other lucrative offenses, organized crime has entered this activity in recent years, for even one fake card can produce a high profit.

INSURANCE FRAUD

When people who face a risk insure themselves against financial loss, an opportunity for fraud exists. The American Insurance Association estimates that 15 to 20 per cent of all insurance claims in 1982 were fraudulent, up from 5 or 6 per cent a decade earlier. The $11 billion a year that is lost through insurance fraud is a result of claims for nonexistent accidents, padded doctors' bills, overpayment of claims for burglary losses, and arson-for-profit schemes (Landis, 1982). Some people pad their claims because they assume that the insurance company will pay them less than they have lost. Some claims are even more blatantly fraudulent than padded claims, as we can see from the following two examples:

> There was a traveling salesman who started off his fraud career by claiming he had gotten sick after finding a fly in a candy bar. This was rapidly followed by a fly in a bottle of soda. Then he took to chipping the same two teeth on half a dozen candy bars. Most of these claims were denied, so the salesman began slipping and falling around his sales territory. After breaking the same pair of glasses in nine separate men's room accidents, he made the mistake of taking his forged optometrist's bill to the same agent who had paid him for breaking the glasses before.

> One body shop in New York City . . . let car owners deliver their cars to the shop in the morning, and by noon the cars would be stripped of their parts. The auto bodies were rolled out on the street to be found by the police. The owners could then report their cars stolen and collect from their insurance companies. The body shop would then roll the cars back into the shop, replace the parts, and have the cars ready for delivery the same day (Landis, 1982: D2).

Arson-for-profit schemes are a major source of insurance fraud. Building owners who find their neighborhoods deteriorating and taxes and repair costs rising may burn down buildings (Maitland, 1980). In some cases, a building is overinsured or even insured more than once, and then the insurance claim may exceed the real value of the building. Insurance companies contribute to the problem of fraud by not inspecting buildings before writing policies, by settling with arsonists if the cost of investigating the fire is too great compared to the size of the claim, and by ignoring their option of forcing the owner to rebuild rather than collect the money (Maitland, 1980). One sociologist claims that arson and arson-for-profit schemes are so intrinsically a part of the capitalist economy of the United States and so closely linked to routine business decisions that they are probably beyond the control of the criminal justice system (Brady, 1982).

ARSON

In addition to being a source of insurance fraud, arson also involves the direct loss of property. The FBI estimates that the monetary value of property lost or damaged in reported cases of arson in 1983 was $795 million. Industrial and manufacturing structures suffered an average loss of $59,372 in reported cases of arson, compared to an average loss of $9,418 in cases of arson in single occupancy residences (Webster, 1984). Total losses from arson probably exceed the FBI's estimate, but we do not know how much arson is not recorded as such by local police departments, and NCS victimization studies do not ask about arson.

Fires that are deliberately set kill hundreds of people, as well as destroy millions of dollars worth of property. Communities such as the South Bronx, New York—where there were more than 30,000 suspicious fires between 1973 and 1983 (Brady, 1983b)—are destroyed, and insurance premiums are increased to cover losses.

VANDALISM

Another crime that produces direct losses of property is vandalism. Assessing the overall cost of vandalism requires us to make many assumptions. For instance, we might count as a cost of vandalism the expense of repainting a wall or a subway car every time graffiti is scribbled or painted on it; this would provide a very high estimate of the cost. In assessing the cost of vandalism, we might wish to include the aesthetic damage that vandalism causes to public and private property. Others, however, look at some graffiti not as vandalism but as "folk art." Should we then deduct from the costs of vandalism what it would cost to provide art for those public places that are adorned with "graffiti art"? Clearly, there are value judgments implicit in any calculation of the costs of vandalism, and estimating those costs is made more difficult because property may not be destroyed but simply be made to look different. For instance, broken windows in an abandoned building might be treated as vandalism, but if the building had little or no value it is not clear that we should count the cost of replacing those windows as a cost of crime.

CONVENTIONAL PROPERTY CRIMES

The kind of crime that constitutes what people see as "the crime problem" is conventional property crime, which includes robbery, burglary, larceny, and car theft. The FBI estimates that in 1983 the total reported loss from robbery—theft accompanied with force or the threat of force—was $323 million. Reported burglaries—unlawful entries into structures to commit serious crimes—accounted for $2.7 billion in losses in 1983. Larceny, which is simple theft without force or fraud, accounted for losses of $2.3 billion. Motor vehicle thefts accounted for another $4 billion, although most cars were recovered and even those that were damaged still had some market value (Webster, 1984). The total loss from conventional property crimes reported to the police in 1983 was thus $9.3 billion, much less than estimated losses from all white-collar crimes and about one-tenth of annual losses from tax cheating.

Another estimate of the cost of conventional crime was calculated from NCS victimization data for 1981. This estimate of losses of $10.9 billion for the crimes of rape, robbery, assault, personal and household larceny, burglary, and motor vehicle theft was based on the loss of cash and property, the cost of property damage, and medical expenses for victims of violent crimes (Bureau of Justice Statistics, April 1984a).

CRIMES OF VIOLENCE

Crimes of violence such as murder, rape, and aggravated assault produce financial losses. These offenses lead to lost wages, hospitalization expenses, and the costs of therapeutic services. The financial costs of murder have been calculated by adding up the total wages the victim would have earned if he or she had lived until the expected age, the cost of welfare or social security payments to the victim's survivors, and the cost of the funeral. Another kind of cost related to criminal violence is the money spent by state compensation boards to repay victims or survivors for losses suffered during a crime.

NARCOTICS

The illegal use of narcotics entails several kinds of costs: the money paid for illegal drugs, the revenue lost to the government because required taxes are not paid on those drugs, and the cost of the secondary crimes committed by drug users to get the money to pay for drugs. Counting the money spent on illegal drugs as a cost of crime reflects an assumption that these illegal expenditures divert money from legitimate expenditures. Another position is that the purchase and use of illegal drugs is a victimless crime that does no direct social harm (Schur, 1965). Secondary crimes, especially by heroin addicts, cost society money when shoplifting, burglary, robbery, and other property offenses are committed to support expensive drug habits. The cost of these secondary crimes is included in the cost of property crimes, but it can also be seen as a by-product of narcotics offenses.

Narcotics are more expensive when they are illegal than when they are legal, and the high price of illegal narcotics leads to crime to support drug use. One unintended consequence of drug enforcement efforts can be to drive the price of drugs up by cutting the supply. Users must then commit more crime to support their habits. Thus drug enforcement can increase the cost of crime in three ways. First, enforcement itself costs money; second, the transfer cost of crimes against property may increase to pay for drugs that have been made more expensive because of enforcement efforts; and third, illegal expenditures increase as the cost of drugs rises.

PROSTITUTION

In estimating the costs of prostitution, as in estimating the costs of narcotics, some have assumed that money spent on illegal services is money that otherwise might have been spent on legitimate goods and services and so is lost to the economy. However, from another perspective, it is difficult to see how money spent for sex with a prostitute is any more of a financial loss than money spent to attend a movie or a baseball game. The Joint Economic Committee of Congress estimated that in 1976 about $10 billion was spent on prostitution in the United States (*The New York Times*, January 2, 1977).

GAMBLING

It may be easier to make a case for an economic loss from illegal gambling than to make such a case for prostitution and narcotics use. Gambling with a bookie produces a loss for the economy in those states that have lotteries or other forms of legalized gambling, if people who might bet legally use their money to bet in illegal ways. Funds are diverted from the state, which would have used that money for education or other social services. This could cause taxes to be higher, or services to be fewer, than would have been the case if the money had been gambled legally. Another cost of illegal gambling is that money bet with a bookie who has links to organized crime may be used by gangsters to finance the importation of drugs or to engage in loan sharking. However, there is some evidence that many, perhaps most, bookies are not members of organized crime and that much money spent on illegal gambling does not make its way into the hands of gangsters (Reuter and Rubinstein, 1978; Reuter, 1983). In 1976, an estimated $5.9 billion was spent on illegal gambling in the United States (*The New York Times*, January 2, 1977).

MAINTAINING THE CRIMINAL JUSTICE SYSTEM

Another financial cost of crime is the expense of maintaining the criminal justice system—the police, the courts, jails and prisons, and related legal services. These institutions cost American taxpayers $26 billion in 1979.

The costs of the criminal justice system are not direct losses to victims of crime, but rather costs that result from societal decisions about how to respond to crime. Some critics claim that these decisions are not really societal at all, but are instead made by a powerful and self-perpetuating "crime industry" that consists of vested interests in the criminal justice system who ask for and receive ever-increasing resources (Blumberg, 1974: 31). Increases in the expenditures of the criminal justice system—such as raises for police officers—escalate the cost of crime in one sense, but they do not necessarily reflect greater direct losses to victims. Whether an overall reduction in crime in the United States would immediately reduce the cost of the criminal justice system is uncertain. It would probably take some time after crime rates decreased before the funds allocated to the police, the courts, jails, and prisons also declined.

In 1979 there were 1,252,229 employees of criminal justice agencies throughout the country. Over half were police officers, and police departments accounted for the largest amount of expenditures of any part of the criminal justice system, as we can see from the following breakdown of the $26 billion spent on criminal justice in 1979 (Bureau of Justice Statistics, June 1983):

Police protection	$13.9 billion
Judicial	3.4 billion
Legal services and prosecution	1.7 billion
Public defense	.6 billion
Corrections	6.0 billion
Other criminal justice agencies	.4 billion
Total expenditures	$26.0 billion

Most expenditures on criminal justice are at the local rather than state or federal level. In 1979, $15.3 billion was spent by local (city, town, or county) agencies, $7.4 billion was spent by state agencies, and $3.4 billion was spent by the federal government (Bureau of Justice Statistics, June 1983). The federal role in criminal justice was greater from 1968 to 1982 than it has been since 1982, when the Law Enforcement Assistance Administration (LEAA), an agency of the Department of Justice, was eliminated. While it was in existence, LEAA spent about $8 billion trying to reduce crime and improve the criminal justice system. LEAA may have improved the functioning of the criminal justice system, especially by encouraging planning and communication among agencies, but there is no evidence that it reduced crime, and for this reason—as well as for its cumbersomeness and wastefulness—it was disbanded in 1982 (Pear, 1980; *The New York Times*, April 12, 1982).

The high cost of the criminal justice system is attributable in part to the high crime rate of the United States in comparison to other Western industrial nations. Over the last century, there has also been an increase in the proportion of all Americans who are in prison at any given time, and today's rate of imprisonment is higher than that of any other industrial nation for which we have data (Cahalan, 1979). The high cost of corrections is also explained by the fact that it costs at least $60,000 to build a new prison cell and costs about $15,000 to maintain an inmate in prison for a year (Radzinowicz and King, 1977: 292).

At the end of 1982, there were 412,303 men and women in state and federal prisons, and another 208,000 in local jails. A total of 1,335,359 men and women were on probation—or court-imposed supervision—and 243,880 were on parole—or supervised release from jail or prison (Galvin, 1983). The high costs of imprisonment have led some critics of the criminal justice system to argue for even more use of probation and parole, which are much less costly than incarceration, but others believe that more prison cells should be built.

The costliness of a crime is different if one considers the expenses attributable to reactions to it by the criminal justice system, rather than direct financial losses to victims. For instance, conventional property crimes account for a large proportion of police, court, and correctional costs, even though losses

Table 4.1:   Some Estimates of the Financial Costs of Crime

SOURCE OF COST	ESTIMATE OF COST (BILLIONS)	YEAR	SOURCE OF ESTIMATE
White-collar crime	$44	1976	Joint Economic Committee of Congress
Tax fraud	$87	1981	General Accounting Office
Credit card fraud (bank only)	$.128	1982	U.S. Deputy Assistant Attorney General
Insurance fraud	$11	1981	American Insurance Association
Arson	$.795	1983	FBI Uniform Crime Report
Vandalism	no reliable estimate available		
Conventional property crimes	$9.3	1983	FBI Uniform Crime Report
Crimes of violence	$3.8	1976	Joint Economic Committee of Congress
Narcotics	$21.4	1976	Joint Economic Committee of Congress
Prostitution	$10	1976	Joint Economic Committee of Congress
Illegal gambling	$5.9	1976	Joint Economic Committee of Congress
Criminal justice system	$26	1979	Bureau of Justice Statistics

SOURCES: Joint Economic Committee of Congress ("That Costly White Collar Mob," *The New York Times*, January 2, 1977, Section 3, p. 15); General Accounting Office (Edward Cowan, "Your Honest Taxpayer Bears Watching," *The New York Times*, April 11, 1982, p. E4); U.S. Deputy Assistant Attorney General (Elizabeth J. Block, "Bandits Wielding Plastic," *The New York Times*, May 22, 1983, pp. F12, F13); American Insurance Association (Dylan Landis, "Insurance Fraud: Billions in Losses," *The New York Times*, July 6, 1982, pp. D1, D2); FBI Uniform Crime Report (William H. Webster, *Crime in the United States, 1983: Uniform Crime Reports*. Washington, D.C.: U.S. Government Printing Office, 1984); Bureau of Justice Statistics (Bureau of Justice Statistics, *Justice Expenditure and Employment in the U.S., 1979*. Washington, D.C.: U.S. Department of Justice, June 1983).

to victims of those property crimes are small compared to losses from white-collar crimes, which account for relatively little of the cost of maintaining the criminal justice system. In other words, the offenses on which the criminal justice system focuses its resources do not seem to be those that cost victims the most.

PHYSICAL HARM FROM CRIME

Many crimes cause physical harm to their victims. People are murdered or raped, they suffer injuries in assaults, are poisoned by contaminated food, and are hurt by defective products. Physical harm also occurs in more subtle ways. For example, by promising medical miracles, a quack doctor may prevent patients with curable diseases from seeking competent medical care until it is too late to be treated successfully.

White-Collar Crime

Many people assume that white-collar crime does not harm its victims physically. However, some victims of white-collar crimes are hurt, even though such harm is more often a result of negligence than of intent.

Physical harm from white-collar crime takes many forms. Air pollution, which sometimes involves criminal acts, causes respiratory ailments. Hazardous and often illegal working conditions result in many deaths and injuries each year. Some of the 20 million serious injuries that occur each year as a result of the use of consumer products, including some of the 110,000 cases of permanent disability and some of the 30,000 deaths, can be attributed to criminal negligence or deceptive advertising by manufacturers (Schrager and Short, 1978: 415). The Ford Motor Company was charged with reckless homicide for the deaths of three young women in Indiana in 1978; however, a jury acquitted Ford, finding that they had marketed a defective car but had not been reckless in their recall efforts (Kramer, 1982; Cullen, Maakestad, and Cavender, 1984).

In some cases, white-collar crime even involves the intentional taking of lives. For instance, in 1976, Don Bolles, a journalist who was investigating white-collar and organized crime in Phoenix, Arizona, was apparently killed by a "hit man" hired to keep illegal activities secret (Kelly, 1977; *The New York Times*, November 7, 1977).

Murder

Probably the most easily measured physical harm is the number of lives lost in murders. In 1983, 19,308 murders were reported to the FBI by local police departments, a figure very close to the estimate of 19,300 deaths by homicide made by the National Center for Health Statistics (1984). Because murders are usually reported to the police, and because the FBI gathers data from most police departments in the country, the FBI figure is a good estimate of the number of people murdered.

To get some perspective on the meaning of the number of murders that occur each year in the United States, it is instructive to compare the total to deaths that occur in other ways. The National Center for Health Statistics (1984) estimates that 29,080 people committed suicide in 1983, but the actual number of suicides may have been twice that number. In 1983, 44,600 people died in traffic accidents, about half of them in crashes in which alcohol was present. Thus, more people commit suicide and more people die in car accidents than are murdered each year, although the death toll from murder is high, especially compared to other industrial societies.

Forcible Rape

In 1983, there were 78,918 cases of forcible rape and attempted rape reported to local police departments in the United States, but there were at least twice that many actual incidents, according to NCS victimization studies (Hindelang, 1976; Bureau of Justice Statistics, November 1983a).

Rape always involves psychological damage to the victim, because by definition it does not involve consent. Rape often involves physical harm as well. A study of 646 reported rapes in Philadelphia found that 85 per cent involved some physical force by the offender. In 29 per cent of the cases there was roughness by the rapist; in 25 per cent the rapist beat the woman "in a nonbrutal fashion"; in 20 per cent the offender beat the victim brutally; in 11 per cent the offender choked the victim; and in only 15 per cent of the rapes was no physical force used (Amir, 1971: 155). Another study found that 48 per cent of rape victims were injured and 19 per cent injured seriously enough to require medical attention (Hindelang, Gottfredson, and Garofalo, 1978). In 1983, the FBI reports that about 300 murders also involved a sex offense, and many of those were rapes in which the victim was murdered.

Aggravated Assault

In 1983, there were 639,532 cases of aggravated assault reported to local police departments. This crime is defined as an unlawful attack, often with a weapon, in order to do bodily injury to the victim. Many victims of this crime are permanently incapacitated. Others suffer injuries from which they eventually recover, but they may lose wages or jobs as a result of being victimized. An eight-city study found that 35 per cent of aggravated assault victims were injured and 18 per cent injured seriously enough to need medical attention (Hindelang, Gottfredson, and Garofalo, 1978).

Much aggravated assault is never recorded by the police, and may not even be reported to interviewers in NCS studies. Victims may be reluctant to report being beaten by their spouse, and child abuse is a form of assault that is often concealed by the victim because of fear of the abusing parent. Another kind of aggravated assault that rarely comes to public attention is the illegal use of force by the police.

Robbery

There were 500,221 robberies reported in 1983. It is difficult to assess the amount of harm to robbery victims, because the FBI provides no information on this. A study of robbery in Boston found that 73 per cent of victims during the first six months of 1968 escaped without injury. Another 7 per cent suffered slight injuries, and 20 per cent required some hospitalization because of injuries sustained during the holdup (Conklin, 1972). An eight-city study found that 29 per cent of robbery victims were injured, with 12 per cent hurt seriously enough to warrant medical attention (Hindelang, Gottfredson, and Garofalo,

1978). Using the results of these two studies, we can estimate that in 1983 between 60,000 and 100,000 robbery victims required hospital treatment.

Research indicates that physical injuries during robberies are least common when an offender has a firearm, somewhat more common when a knife is used, and most likely when the offender uses no weapon at all (Conklin, 1972; Hindelang, Gottfredson, and Garofalo, 1978). Victims confronted by armed robbers are probably least likely to resist and are thus least likely to be injured. Victims who believe that they can overpower an unarmed robber are more likely to be injured while resisting.

Robberies sometimes lead to murders; these offenses would be classified as murders rather than robberies. The FBI estimates that in 1983 about 2,000 murders had robbery as the motive. Thus, about one murder in ten begins as a robbery. However, only about one robbery in every 250 results in a murder.

Narcotics

Heroin addiction has physically harmful effects. Addicts' health often deteriorates because they spend their money on drugs rather than on food, shelter, and clothing. The harmful consequences for addicts' health seem to be more a result of the high price of heroin, which in turn is due to its being illegal, rather than a result of the pharmacological effects of the drug itself.

Many heroin addicts are admitted to emergency rooms for drug overdoses or for the effects of the interaction of heroin with other drugs they have used. In the United States in 1982 there were 11,538 emergency room admissions related to heroin use and 771 heroin-related deaths (Kessler, 1983). Many of the estimated 500,000 heroin addicts and 3.5 million occasional users of heroin in the country suffer physically from their use of the drug (Kihss, 1982).

SOCIAL COSTS OF CRIME

Crime has a much greater impact on society than can be measured by the financial loss and physical harm that it causes. The social costs of crime are indirect: fear felt by citizens, suspicion of strangers, skepticism of voters at election time, and wariness of investors in the stock market. Fear of victimization by conventional or white-collar crime affects the attitudes and behavior of people in important ways that may even contribute to the crime problem.

White-Collar Crime

White-collar crime has major social costs in addition to the enormous financial losses it inflicts on the public. The President's Commission on Law Enforcement and Administration of Justice (1967a: 5) called white-collar offenses "the most threatening of all—not just because they are so expensive, but because of their corrosive effect on the moral standards by which American business is conducted." However, less than 1 per cent of the material published by this commission dealt with white-collar crime. Edwin H. Sutherland (1949, 1983), who first used the term "white-collar crime" in 1939, also believed that a major cost of this kind of crime was its harmful effect on public attitudes, especially on the public's confidence in the economy. White-collar crime may reduce the public's willingness to invest in the stock market and engage in commercial transactions, and a capitalist economy that relies on public investment is thus weakened.

Illegal campaign contributions by large corporations can lead to public cynicism toward business and government. Voters may believe that business is the "power behind the throne" and that politicians are corrupt. Bribes paid to officials of other nations can weaken foreign relations and diminish national prestige abroad. A company's interest in protecting its foreign investments may even lead to the rigging of elections or to the overthrow of a democratically elected regime that is seen as hostile to American business.

Business crime may also set an example of disobedience for the general public. Citizens who rarely see white-collar offenders prosecuted and sent to jail may become cynical about the criminal justice system. A sense of injustice may develop when they or their friends are given long sentences for crimes that cost society much less than offenses committed by wealthy corporate executives or large multinational firms.

Government Corruption and Police Brutality

Illegal activities by government officials can have widespread social consequences. Public faith is reduced by illegal campaign contributions, the abuse of privilege by officials, and tax abuse by political leaders. Such behavior can reduce the legitimacy of the government if citizens begin to question the right of political leaders to exercise power.

The many abuses of the Nixon administration helped to drive a wedge between the government and the people, as did the Vietnam War during both the Johnson and Nixon administrations. The Watergate scandal, involving both the conventional crime of burglary and the offense of obstruction of justice, was only the most obvious abuse. President Nixon also violated several court decisions that required him to spend money that Congress had appropriated for various programs. He was also found to have engaged in "tax avoidance" and was given the opportunity to pay more than $400,000 in back taxes that he had withheld improperly. Many observers, including members of Congress, felt that had he not been president at the time, he would have been charged with the crime of tax fraud. One direct effect of Nixon's tax abuse was that several judges presiding over trials of less influential people charged with tax law violations refused to send them to prison when they were convicted. In addition, some inmates serving time for conventional property offenses claimed that because President Nixon had not been prosecuted for his crime, they should be released from prison for their less serious offenses.

Police corruption and brutality can also undermine the legitimacy of the government. If those who enforce the law also violate it, citizens may feel that they do not need to abide by the law either. Exposés of police corruption and brutality create hostility toward law enforcers and the government they serve, as we can see in the following exchange between a young black man and a police chief:

"Okay man, you pretty smart. If I smack my buddy here upside the head and he files a complaint, what you gonna do?"

"Arrest you," the chief replied.

"Cool. Now let's say one of your ugly cops smacks *me* upside the head and I file a complaint—what you gonna do?"

"Investigate the complaint," the chief said. If it were true, the police would "take action" and "probably suspend" the officer.

"Well," the black rejoined, "how come we get arrested and *you* only get investigated?" (Wilson, 1983: 108–109).

Organized Crime

The activities of organized crime also have social costs. One essential element of organized crime is the corruption of public officials and police officers, who allow gangsters to operate without interference (Cressey, 1969, 1972; Conklin, 1973). Reports of corruption can undermine faith in local, state, and even federal government. People may be unwilling to discuss political matters openly for fear that all officials are linked to organized crime (Gansberg, 1970; Chambliss, 1971). The influence of organized crime with elected officials can lead to public resignation and the belief that young people would be better off pursuing careers other than politics.

Conventional Crime

Conventional crimes, such as the FBI's index crimes, also have social costs in addition to financial costs and physical harm. Indeed, the effects on daily life of robbery, rape, and burglary are probably greater than the social effects of white-collar crime and organized crime, even though the financial costs of white-collar crime and organized crime greatly exceed the monetary losses from conventional crime. Victims and witnesses may be traumatized by conventional crimes, live in fear of retaliation, or spend hours testifying in court (Conklin, 1975; Sheleff and Shichor, 1980).

FEAR OF CRIME

The public seems most afraid of unprovoked attacks in public places by strangers. Robbery is a prototype of the kind of crime most feared by the public: It usually involves theft with violence or the threat of violence by a person with whom the victim has had no previous contact, and it is usually unprovoked and unpredictable. The public fears most those crimes that occur least frequently, namely murder, rape, and robbery; "fear of crimes of violence is not a simple fear of injury or death or even of all crimes of violence, but, at bottom, a fear of strangers" (The President's Commission on Law Enforcement and Administration of Justice, 1967a: 52). This is true even though the chance of being killed by a stranger is much less than the chance of dying in a car accident or the chance of dying in an accidental fall (Silberman, 1978: 6). Many crimes of violence, particularly murder and aggravated assault, are committed by people with whom the victim is acquainted or related, rather than by strangers.

A study in Baltimore found that there was an important difference between concern with crime and fear of victimization. *Concern with crime* as a political issue was a basis of support for "law-and-order" politicians; it was also linked to antagonism toward changes in race relations. This concern with crime was most common in communities that had relatively low crime rates. On the other hand, *fear of victimization,* the perception of a high risk of becoming involved in a crime, was most widespread in communities that had relatively high crime rates (Furstenberg, 1971). A study of fear of crime in Seattle found that it was based to an extent on a realistic assessment of the threat of becoming a victim; fear of victimization was associated with perceived seriousness of crime and perceived risk of the crime occurring (Warr and Stafford, 1983).

Fear of victimization seems to be greatest among people who have been directly victimized (Biderman, 1981; Skogan and Maxfield, 1981; Baker et al., 1983). However, a relatively small percentage of adults, perhaps only 3 per cent, are injured in crimes of violence during any given year. Individual property crimes have modest effects on fear, but they may have a large cumulative effect because they are relatively common (Skogan and Maxfield, 1981).

The threat of crime seems to cause fear even in the absence of actual victimization (Skogan, 1981). Sometimes people's fear is much greater than seems warranted by the actual risk of victimization that they face. For instance, women are the victims of crime less often than are men, but they fear crime more, perhaps because of the threat of sexual assault. Likewise, many studies find a relatively low rate of victimization for the elderly, but much fear of crime among them. This may be due to their belief that they are physically vulnerable and will not recover if injured (Skogan, 1981; Skogan and Maxfield, 1981). Fear of crime among the elderly is also closely associated with their lower degree of confidence in the police (Baker et al., 1983), their greater dissatisfaction with the neighborhood in which they live, and their lower overall morale (Yin, 1982). Some research suggests that fear of crime among the elderly may have a realistic basis, because the elderly may be more susceptible to crime if we look at the amount of time that they are at risk. Elderly people are probably on the streets less often than younger people are, and this may mean that the number of crimes per number of hours that the elderly are actually at risk may be quite high (Lundquist and Duke, 1982; Stafford and Galle, 1984).

CRIME AND THE MASS MEDIA

Former Attorney General Ramsey Clark (1970: 45) has said: "Most lives in America are unmarred by serious crimes. The only meaningful impression such people can have about the incidence of crime is from the press, other communications media and the police. As crime becomes more topical, the tendency of distorted impressions to mislead increases."

Television, radio, and newspapers rapidly disperse crime news throughout the nation and inform even the residents of relatively crime-free areas of the extent of crime in the society. Not only is news of crime more readily available today than in the past, but also the national organization of the media provides more dramatic crimes to report than was true in the past when the population was smaller and news was more likely to be local. The media focus on attention-grabbing events, thereby bringing only the most sensational and bizarre crimes to public attention. As a result, people develop a distorted view of crime as inexplicably and unpredictably violent, even though petty larceny, burglary, auto theft, and commercial fraud are much more common than murder and rape.

Crime stories sell newspapers and are relatively easy to get. The crimes that appeal most to the press and their readers are those that are visible and spectacular, have sexual or political implications, can be presented in graphic—usually violent—terms, and seem to be the product of individual aberrations rather than social conditions (Chibnall, 1977). Crime news seems to be reported more as entertainment than as information.

A systematic study of televised crime based on observations of six weeks of prime-time programs in the United States in 1981 found that crime was rampant on television, with violent crime twelve times as common on television as in real life, and murder—the most common crime on television—one hundred times as frequent. After murder, the next most common crimes on television were robbery, kidnapping, and aggravated assault. The crimes most often experienced by the public—theft, burglary, car theft, and public drunkenness—showed up in television programs much less often than crimes of violence (Lichter and Lichter, 1983).

Not only are criminal acts portrayed in a distorted way on television, but those who commit crimes are also shown inaccurately. We can see from Table 4.2 that television criminals are more likely than arrested suspects to be older and to be white. Whereas 30 per cent of arrested suspects in real life are over the age of thirty, televised shows involve offenders over thirty in three-fourths of the cases. Television does portray the sex of offenders accurately, with about as many "prime-time criminals" being male and female as is the case in FBI arrest statistics. Television also pays relatively little attention to the link between poverty and crime; the characters who commit crime are often well-to-do people.

This study also found that television misrepresents the consequences of crime. The police fail to solve about four-fifths of all serious crimes, but in prime-time shows only 8 per cent of offenders get away with their crimes. About two-thirds of them are apprehended, one-fifth of the cases are left unresolved, and a few offenders vow to change their ways. Television seems to suggest that crime does not pay, but in fact most real crimes do not lead to

Table 4.2: A Comparison of Television Crime and Crime Reported to the Police

	TELEVISED CRIME*	FBI CRIME DATA**
KIND OF CRIME		
Violent crime	88%	10%
Property crime	12%	90%
Total	100%	100%
SEX OF OFFENDER		
Male	89%	84%
Female	11%	16%
Total	100%	100%
AGE OF OFFENDER		
Under 18	6%	21%
18 to 30	18%	49%
30 to 50	57%	23%
Over 50	19%	7%
Total	100%	100%
RACE OF OFFENDER		
White	88%	74%
Nonwhite	12%	26%
Total	100%	100%

* These figures are based on observations of six weeks of prime-time television shows during 1981.

** The first set of figures is based on index crimes reported to the FBI; the other three sets of figures are based on FBI arrest data.

SOURCE: Linda S. Lichter and S. Robert Lichter, *Prime Time Crime: Criminals and Law Enforcers in TV Entertainment.* Washington, D.C.: The Media Institute, 1983, pp. 16, 20–23. Reprinted by permission.

an arrest, and even fewer lead to conviction and imprisonment. Another distortion introduced by television is that private detectives and citizens solve more crimes than the police do, whereas in fact relatively few offenses are solved by people other than the police (Lichter and Lichter, 1983).

In distorting the nature of crime, the mass media may produce a higher level of anxiety among the public than would exist otherwise. Heavy watchers of television seem to be more likely than people who watch less television to see the world as violent, dangerous, and crime-ridden (Gerbner and Gross, 1977; Duffy, 1982). However, another study found that because most people have similar experiences in their exposure to media presentations of crime, that exposure is not closely associated with differences in feelings about personal safety. Instead, fear of crime seems to be, at least in part, a result of hearing about the experiences of acquaintances who have been victims of crime. As a result, crimes that occur in neighborhoods where social ties are extensive seem to have the greatest impact on residents (Skogan and Maxfield, 1981).

CONSEQUENCES OF THE FEAR OF CRIME

Fear of crime has many socially harmful consequences. Fear of crime in the schools destroys the atmosphere necessary for learning, leads students to avoid dangerous places such as restrooms, and can increase truancy. This may produce financial losses for schools if federal and state reimbursements are based on the number of students in attendance.

Fear of street crimes, particularly robberies, causes people to stay home rather than venture outdoors. People lock their doors and windows, install expensive alarm systems or bright lighting, and buy watchdogs. The purchase of protective measures might even escalate to the point that the costs of protection against crime could become greater than the losses from the crimes that those measures are designed to prevent.

When people go out, they may do so only during the daylight hours or travel only in groups. At night, they may use their cars to travel short distances or take cabs to avoid walking on unlit streets. People who are afraid may avoid certain neighborhoods, which in turn become even more deserted and dangerous. People may give up visiting the library, attending meetings, and using local parks. They may forfeit income from overtime work that would require them to return home after dark.

A few people even respond to their fear of crime by moving to communities that seem safer. A 1980 Gallup poll found that crime was the leading reason given for dissatisfaction with cities: 24 per cent of those who wanted to move from the city in which they lived cited crime as the reason, compared to 16 per cent who mentioned overcrowding and 12 per cent who mentioned the absence of job opportunities (Herbers, 1981). What is not clear is how many people actually move because of their fear of crime. For instance, one study found that flight to the suburbs was due more to the attractiveness of suburban living—part of which, of course, may be a safer environment—rather than due to an effort to escape central-city neighborhoods (Skogan and Maxfield, 1981).

Fear of rape restricts women's freedom of movement. Children and adolescents who are raped often stay out of school for some time, and may even transfer schools to avoid questions and social discomfort. Adult rape victims often need outside help in homemaking and parenting, either because of physical injury or psychological distress. Some adult victims quit their jobs or stay

Fear of crime leads people such as this woman to protect themselves by locking doors and windows, installing alarms, and buying watchdogs.

away from work for a time in order to avoid having to talk about the rape (Burgess and Holmstrom, 1976).

The fear of crime often becomes generalized to a fear of the streets, especially in communities that have high crime rates. As Jane Jacobs (1961: 30) says, "When people say that a city, or part of it, is dangerous or is a jungle what they mean primarily is that they do not feel safe on the sidewalks." The public nature of the streets and sidewalks evokes a fear of strangers who are encountered there. As one observer notes: "The street is public, and the public display of tabooed behavior threatens to make it part of daily life. Openness gives such behavior an actuality and carries the threat of public acceptance and approval" (Rhodes, 1972: 36).

Fear and trust   Social life, especially in large cities, requires a faith that others will abide by the law. Crime can reduce that trust under certain circumstances, although some research finds that fear of crime is not strongly associated with mistrust and suspicion (Skogan, 1981). Even the crime of burglary, a relatively common nonviolent offense, can create mistrust. Imagine how the couple in the following incident felt:

> It was in Briarcliffe, N.Y., where a young couple went to dinner one evening at a local restaurant, and returned to find their car apparently stolen. After reporting it to the local police, they returned to their home and the next morning were surprised to see the car in the driveway, with an envelope on the windshield.
>
> "There was an emergency and we had to borrow the car," the note read. "Please excuse the inconvenience, but perhaps these two theater tickets will make up for it." The couple, surprised but pleased, told the police that their car had been returned, and the next Saturday used the theater tickets.
>
> When they returned that night, they found that their house had been completely looted (Andelman, 1972: 49).

The burglars used the trust felt by most people to their advantage; the effect on the couple was probably to make them less trusting of strangers and maybe even of their neighbors. This crime was not a violent one; the impact on interpersonal trust could be even greater for victims of rape, robbery, or assault.

Fear of crime can lead people to react negatively even to strangers who mean well. Ex-convicts who want to quit crime often find that they must conceal their identity as a convicted offender to be accepted by others. The suspicion faced by ex-convicts often impedes their reintegration into society and pushes them back into a life of crime. In other cases, reactions to strangers sometimes go beyond rejection and suspicion. For example, in 1970 an eighteen-year-old car owner shot and killed a newspaper delivery boy early one morning because he incorrectly assumed that the boy was planning to damage or steal his car (*The New York Times*, October 18, 1970).

A dramatic example of the harmful effects of the fear of crime occurred in Atlanta, Georgia, a few years ago. Between May 1979 and July 1981, twenty-nine young blacks disappeared; all but one were later found murdered. During this time, young blacks in the city were traumatized by their fear that they would be the next victim. Tests show that children became less verbal and more withdrawn, a change that was greatest in neighborhoods where the murder victims had lived. Children became more mistrustful of strangers, and even interviewers had a difficult time approaching them. The children also suffered a decline in self-esteem and self-confidence. They became more hostile toward others, fought more at school, and even carried weapons to defend themselves. Nightmares became more common. Fear of the dark, fear of school, fear of being left alone, and fear of being outdoors all increased. Participation in sports and organized youth programs declined. Parents sometimes exacerbated these fears by being overprotective, an understandable response in the circumstance (Rawls, 1981; Prugh, 1981; Stuart, 1981). When Wayne B. Williams was arrested for some of the murders and eventually convicted of two of them, the murders stopped and tensions abated (Sheppard, 1982). Whether the reactions to the murders will have long-term effects on Atlanta's children can only be determined by follow-up studies.

One crime that did have long-term effects on the victims was a bizarre kidnapping in Chowchilla, California, in 1976. A school bus with twenty-six children was hijacked, and the children were buried underground in a truck trailer for sixteen hours; eventually, they dug their way out. Nearly five years later, these children, who were between five and fourteen when the kidnapping occurred, still showed effects. They experienced nightmares, feared ordinary things such as cars and dogs, and manifested an "on guard" mistrust of everyone. Some blamed themselves for their own victimization. They had a distorted sense of time, thought, and perception. Adults experiencing stress of this sort often use denial as a defense mechanism, but the children did not. They faced the reality of the event and the threat that it posed for them. Most of them continued to fear another kidnapping, even five years later (Timnick, 1981).

Fear and community ties   The French sociologist Emile Durkheim claimed in 1895 that crime enhances social solidarity within a community by bringing people together in opposition to an act that violates the law. A recent study of reactions to crime concluded that

> collectivities will unite and react to crime if there is a community able to identify itself as insiders and if an opposing group of outsiders (in a sociological rather than geographical sense) can be identified. [This perspective] does not argue that solidarity will be increased within a geographical area where there are few crosscutting ties and where individuals feel no sense of community (Podolefsky and Dubow, 1981: 10).

The heterogeneity of many American communities, particularly in urban centers where crime rates are the highest, and the high rate of geographic mobility of Americans mean that the conditions necessary for a unified response to crime will not exist in many communities.

Under many conditions, predatory crime "impedes and, in the extreme case, prevents the formation and maintenance of community" by disrupting social ties among neighbors (Wilson, 1983: 26). We would not expect petty thefts to have much effect on community solidarity, but murders and robberies can lead to a deterioration of street life, protective measures by residents, and even a further increase in the local crime rate.

Fear of crime sometimes reduces attachment to the community in which a person lives. People may come to fear their neighbors and see the neighborhood as a place filled with threat, even though people do tend to see their own neighborhood as less dangerous than nearby communities (The President's Commission on Law Enforcement and Administration of Justice, 1967a: 50). Residents who see their community as being in decline are the most afraid of crime; residents with strong ties to the neighborhood are generally less fearful (Skogan and Maxfield, 1981).

People want a good neighborhood in which to live, and part of what constitutes a good neighborhood is the "observance of standards of right and seemly conduct in the public places in which one lives and moves" (Wilson, 1983: 28; also, Wilson and Kelling, 1982). Perceptions of uncivil behavior on the streets of a neighborhood—including gangs of teen-agers hanging out on street corners, abandoned and burned-out buildings, drug addicts and prostitutes in doorways, and signs of vandalism such as graffiti and broken windows—increase people's fear of victimization and their concern with crime. For people to be very afraid of crime in their community, both a perception of a high rate of serious crime and a perception of incivility are needed. Fear of crime can be reduced by attacking perceptions of incivility directly, rather than by reducing the crime rate (Lewis and Maxfield, 1980). One controversial effort to do this involved using public funds to pay for vinyl decals that would stick on the window frames of burned-out buildings in the South Bronx, New York. These stickers showed windows with curtains and hanging plants, and were supposed to improve local morale by "sprucing up" the neighborhood. However, residents of the South Bronx responded with anger that the city government seemed to be more interested in making the community look prosperous than it was in rebuilding the neighborhood and providing people with jobs (McFadden, 1983; Geist, 1983).

Fear of crime can generate suspicion and mistrust in homogeneous small towns as well as in heterogeneous urban communities. For example, in his book *In Cold Blood*, Truman Capote (1965) reports that a common reaction to the brutal murder of a family of four in Holcomb, Kansas, was suspicion of long-time friends and neighbors. The woman who owned the local café remarked:

> One old man sitting here that Sunday, he put his finger right on it, the reason nobody can sleep; he said, "All we've got out here are our friends. There isn't anything else." In a way, that's the worst part of the crime. What a terrible thing when neighbors can't look at each other without kind of wondering! Yes, it's a hard fact to live with, but if they ever do find out who done it, I'm sure it'll be a bigger surprise than the murders themselves (cited in Capote, 1965: 70).

Others in the town concurred; for instance, the brother of one of the victims said, "When this is cleared up, I'll wager whoever did it was someone within ten miles of where we now stand" (cited in Capote, 1965: 88). When two outsiders to the community were apprehended, "the majority of Holcomb's population, having lived for seven weeks amid unwholesome rumors, general mistrust, and suspicion, appeared to feel disappointed at being told that the murderer was not someone among themselves" (Capote, 1965: 231). Many refused to believe that the two strangers had committed the murders. The café owner said, "Maybe they did it, these fellows. But there's more to it than that. Wait. Some day they'll get to the bottom, and when they do they'll find the one behind it. The one who wanted Clutter out of the way. The *brains*" (cited in Capote, 1965: 231; emphasis in the original).

These reactions do not suggest that people will always unite in response to crime, even in homogeneous and closely knit communities where the offenders are outsiders. Instead, dramatic crimes and persistently high crime rates seem to be more likely to breed mistrust, insecurity, and a weakened attachment to the community. In some neighborhoods, this can reduce human traffic on the streets, which weakens informal social control over potential offenders. Fewer people on the street also means less patronage of local businesses, and this may cause shopkeepers to close early or move their businesses to other neighborhoods. The threat of crime in a community may also lead corporate decision makers to locate a new plant in a different neighborhood, and this could speed the deterioration of the community by raising the local unemployment rate.

Conventional crime is a major source of fear. Fear itself is a social cost of crime, one that is enhanced by media sensationalization of bizarre crimes. Reactions to the fear of crime are also social costs. People respond to their fear of crime by staying home and avoiding strangers, mistrusting neighbors, and even moving from their community. These reactions can diminish social solidarity in a community, and this in turn can create conditions that are conducive to even higher crime rates.

SUMMARY

Crime has several kinds of financial costs. Property can be directly lost through crime, or it may be transferred from the owner to the thief. The victims of criminal violence suffer lost wages and hospital expenses. Expenditures on illegal goods and services are often considered a cost of crime because they divert money from the legitimate economy. There is also the cost of enforcing the law and the money that people spend for prevention and protection.

White-collar crime is today the most financially costly of all crimes to the American public; illegal competition, deceptive advertising, product counterfeiting, stock fraud, and price fixing are some of the crimes by "respectable" people that cost Americans billions of dollars each year. Fraud—including tax fraud, credit card fraud, and insurance fraud—probably accounts for losses even greater than the amount lost due to white-collar crimes. Arson and vandalism produce losses in the form of destroyed property and property that must be replaced or repaired. Conventional property crime, though very expensive in absolute terms, costs the American public much less than white-collar crime and fraud. The financial costs of crimes of violence are also significant. Narcotics, prostitution, and gambling, none of which usually results in complaints to the police, divert money from legitimate economic expenditures. The cost of maintaining the criminal justice system is high, but this is more a result of decisions about how to respond to crime than a direct cost of crime to victims.

Another way to measure the costs of crime is in terms of physical harm. White-collar crime causes physical harm through environmental pollution, unsafe working conditions, and defective consumer products. Often this harm is due to negligence, but sometimes it is deliberate. Physical harm from crimes of violence can be measured by the number of victims or by the actual harm suffered by victims. Analyzing the proportion of rapes and robberies that result in murder is another way to assess physical harm from crimes of violence. Narcotics use, especially heroin use in societies where it is illegal, is associated with physical harm to users and addicts, including drug overdose deaths.

Crime affects society in ways other than financial loss and physical harm; it is detrimental to social well-being in many ways. White-collar crime undermines faith in the economic system. Government corruption and police brutality reduce the legitimacy of the government, as do payoffs to politicians by members of organized crime groups. The fear that results from conventional crime is also costly, sometimes leading people to act in ways that actually increase the crime rate. The mass media contribute to the public's fear of conventional crime by exaggerating the threat of violence, distorting the frequency of different kinds of crime, and downplaying the enormous financial costs of white-collar crime. Fear of crime and perceptions of incivility in a neighborhood can reduce interpersonal trust and weaken social solidarity.

The financial cost of white-collar crime is far greater than the cost of conventional crime, but white-collar crime has less effect on people's daily behavior. This may be because its effects seem to be diffuse and because victims have a difficult time seeing how white-collar crime costs them money. White-collar crime does not cause the fear of unprovoked violence at the hands of a stranger that conventional crime does, and so people are less likely to adjust their behavior to its threat. People may think that there is little they can do to keep from becoming the victim of white-collar crime, but they do develop strategies that they believe will reduce their risk of victimization by conventional criminals. Because people are concerned with the sudden financial losses and physical injuries caused by conventional offenses such as robbery and rape, they seem to be more likely to change their behavior to prevent victimization by such offenses than they are to change their behavior to avoid the larger financial losses produced by white-collar crime.

IMPORTANT TERMS

concern with crime

costs related to criminal violence

direct loss

enforcement costs

fear of victimization

illegal expenditures

prevention and protection costs

transfer of property

white-collar crime

SUGGESTED READINGS

JOHN E. CONKLIN. *The Impact of Crime.* New York: Macmillan, 1975. A detailed look at the effects of conventional crime on community life.

CHARLES M. GRAY, ED. *The Costs of Crime.* Beverly Hills, Calif.: Sage Publications, 1979. A collection of essays by economists, dealing with the costs of crime and the costs of public and private responses to crime.

DARYL A. HELLMAN. *The Economics of Crime.* New York: St. Martin's Press, 1980. An introduction to the way that economists look at the financial costs of crime.

WESLEY G. SKOGAN AND MICHAEL G. MAXFIELD. *Coping with Crime: Individual and Neighborhood Reactions.* Beverly Hills, Calif.: Sage Publications, 1981. A report on research that examines the social consequences of crime for community life.

5

Geographic and Temporal Dimensions of Crime

n 1983 the new chief of public security for China said that his country had "quite a problem" with crime (*The New York Times*, June 24, 1983: A5). This "problem" was a rate of 71 reported crimes per 100,000 people in 1982, which compared to a rate of 5,553 index crimes per 100,000 people in the United States in the same year. There are differences in the collection of crime statistics in the two countries that make it difficult to compare crime rates, but China does seem to have a much less serious crime problem than the United States.

In this chapter, we look at differences among nations in crime rates. We also look at variations within nations, by region and by size of the community, and at variations in crime rates over time. In Chapter 6, we turn to variations in crime rates by sex, age, racial and ethnic group, and class. In these two chapters, we use statistical measures of crime and delinquency. As we have indicated earlier, each of the measures that we use—the FBI's UCR data, the NCS victimization data, and self-report data—has flaws. These drawbacks should be kept in mind as we look at the geographic, temporal, and social dimensions of crime.

Knowledge of how crime rates vary from group to group and from society to society can point the way to a theory of crime causation. Statistical variations in crime rates are facts that criminologists' theories must explain, but these variations are not, by themselves, theories of crime. For instance, knowing that men commit more murder than women does not tell us why this difference exists, but it does tell us that a theory of crime should account for this difference.

CROSS-NATIONAL VARIATIONS IN CRIME RATES

In the criminologist's ideal world, all nations would define crime and gather statistics in the same way. We could then compare the crime rates of different countries, facilitating the development of a general theory of crime causation. Unfortunately, this situation does not exist, nor is it ever likely to. There are significant cross-national variations in laws, and the law-enforcement process and the collection of crime data also differ from society to society.

Most developing nations have poor crime-reporting and record-keeping systems. The rudimentary nature of their police forces and the absence of mechanized record-keeping systems account for their lack of reliable crime data (Clinard and Abbott, 1973: 26). Fewer than a dozen countries have complete and reliable systems of crime statistics (Radzinowicz and King, 1977: 4). National crime data can be used for some purposes within a society, but comparisons among countries must be made with great caution.

In recent years, crime rates have increased dramatically in most industrialized and developing nations. With economic development, rates of property crime have usually increased faster than rates of violent crime have. However, social change is not inextricably linked to rising crime rates, as we can see from Japan's experience.

Japan

Japan is one nation that has apparently avoided a long-term increase in crime rates as it has industrialized and urbanized. In 1948, 1.6 million penal code offenses were recorded in Japan, but by 1973 that figure had dropped to 1.2 million, a decline of 25 per cent. From 1962 to 1972, Japan experienced a drop of 20 per cent in all crimes and a 40 per cent drop in serious crimes. Between 1963 and 1972, Tokyo had a 13 per cent decline in crime and Osaka a 37 per cent decline. During the same period, the crime rate in New York City nearly tripled, the rate in West Berlin more than doubled, and the rates in London and Los Angeles increased by about 60 per cent (Clifford, 1976: 1–4). From 1960 to 1974, Japan contained its rate of juvenile delinquency, while the problem increased significantly in magnitude in the United States (Martin and Conger, 1980).

In 1983, the Japanese police were talking of a "crime wave," but statistics indicated that crime was still an insignificant problem compared to other industrial societies, particularly the United States. For instance, in Japan there were nearly twice as many "wanton murders"—or senseless street killings by strangers—in 1982 as there were in 1981, but the total number for 1982 was only thirteen. This is about the same number in Japan—a nation of 118 million people—as New York City with its population of 7.5 million sometimes has on a holiday weekend. From 1981 to 1982, the number of homicides in Japan increased by ten, but the total of 1,764 murders recorded in 1982 was still about 100 less than the number that occurred in 1978. Japan's rate of 1.5 murders per 100,000 people in 1982 was dwarfed by the rate of 9.1 for the United States in that year. Japan has recently experienced some increase in narcotics use, juvenile offenses, computer crime, credit card fraud, and the counterfeiting of designer products, but these crimes are not yet occurring at the same rate that they do in other industrial societies (Haberman, 1983).

Japan's experience since the end of World War II shows that social change is not always accompanied by rising crime rates. Why social change produces higher crime rates in some nations, but not in others, is explored later when we look at theories of crime causation. What is important here is that cross-national differences exist and need to be explained.

China

We do not have reliable crime statistics for China, but observers of that society believe that crime rates have been relatively low since the Communist Revolution of 1949. For instance, it was only in 1980 that China had its first reported armed bank robbery since 1949 (Butterfield, 1980).

In spite of China's apparently low crime rate, the minister of public security reported in 1979 that juvenile delinquency was ten times as common as it

As part of a crackdown on crime in China, offenders are driven through towns wearing signs that give their names and the crimes of which they were found guilty. The banner reads, "To preserve the people's lives and properties."

Reprinted by permission of UPI/Bettmann Newsphotos.

had been in the early 1960s, even though the 1979 rate seemed to be well below that of Western industrial societies. The rise in delinquency was attributed to the continuation of theft, assault, and vandalism that had been regarded as political acts during the Cultural Revolution, but which were socially redefined as delinquency in the 1970s. Other causes of increasing violation of the law in China include a decline in respect for authority, a lack of adequate housing, and the frustration of dealing with the bureaucratization of everyday life (Butterfield, 1980).

Canada

Canada has a significantly lower crime rate than the United States. For instance, metropolitan Toronto has only one-eighth as much murder and one-fifth as much forcible rape as metropolitan Dallas-Fort Worth, even though both cities are of similar size. Canada's crime rates have increased somewhat in the last few years, but they still remain below rates in the United States.

Explanations for this difference vary from one criminologist to another.

One theory is that Canada has a law-abiding tradition that dates back to the settlement of the country in the eighteenth century by people from the thirteen colonies who were loyal to the King of England and unwilling to rebel against authority. The Canadian West was not as lawless as the West in the United States, for the Royal Canadian Mounted Police established order on the frontier. Some criminologists discount the importance of these historical factors and look instead at differences between the countries today. For instance, Canada does not have as large a population of minority groups that are frustrated by blocked opportunities to enter the middle class. Canada's gun-control laws are much stricter than those in most states, and this might also account in part for the lower level of violence (Meisler, 1981).

Cross-National Comparisons of Murder Rates

One offense for which some cross-national data exist is murder. Even for this crime, however, there are some significant variations from one society to another in the definition of the offense. For instance, laws differ in the role assigned to premeditation and responsibility (e.g., see Seidman, 1965). In addition, whether acts of war, civil insurrection, and political terrorism that result in death are recorded as murder or are treated as political acts differs from society to society and depends in part on who has the power to define criminal behavior. These and other problems make even murder difficult to examine cross-nationally.

Until 1975, the United Nations gathered world-wide data on murder under the general category of "all other external causes of death," a broad classification that also included wartime deaths and deaths from internal political violence. In 1975, the United Nations revised its list of causes of death to include one that more accurately measures murder: "homicide and injury purposely inflicted by other persons." It is this category that we use in Table 5.1, where the rates per 100,000 people are given for nations reporting to the United Nations in 1979, 1980, or 1981. The Latin American nations that reported their homicide rates have some of the highest rates in the world, but deaths from political violence may have been counted as homicides and there have been serious problems with the validity of the information reported by those countries (Salas and Wilbanks, 1981). Table 5.1 does not include data from the Soviet Union, from African nations, or from most Asian countries. What seems clear, though, is that the homicide rate in the United States is quite high compared to other industrial societies.

REGIONAL VARIATIONS IN CRIME RATES WITHIN THE UNITED STATES

The comparatively high murder rate of the United States leads us to ask what causes the differences between this country and other industrial societies. We can begin to zero in on an answer to this question by looking at variations in crime rates within the United States. One such variation is by region of the country.

We can see from Table 5.2 that in 1983 the murder rate in the United States was 8.3 per 100,000, and that there were significant variations in this rate for different regions. The rate for the Northeast was 6.8, the rate for

Table 5.1: Homicide and Injury Purposely Inflicted by Others as a Cause of Death, Rates per 100,000*

COUNTRY	RATE PER 100,000	YEAR	COUNTRY	RATE PER 100,000	YEAR
El Salvador	129.4	1980	Singapore	1.8	1981
Guatemala	63.0	1980	Scotland	1.6	1981
Puerto Rico	15.1	1980	New Zealand	1.3	1980
United States**	9.8	1981	West Germany	1.3	1981
Costa Rica	4.7	1981	Austria	1.3	1981
Bulgaria	3.4	1981	Czechoslovakia	1.1	1979
Chile	2.6	1980	Japan	1.0	1980
Hungary	2.6	1980	France	1.0	1980
Panama	2.2	1979	Poland	0.9	1980
Luxembourg	2.0	1980	Netherlands	0.8	1981
Hong Kong	2.0	1981	Greece	0.8	1981
Australia	1.9	1980	England/Wales	0.4	1981
Israel	1.8	1980			

* These figures are provided by the United Nations for "homicides and injury purposely inflicted by other persons" as a cause of death, category AM54 of the 1975 revised classification of causes of death.

** This is the FBI Uniform Crime Reports rate for murder and nonnegligent manslaughter, and is not reported in the United Nations statistics. It is provided here for comparative purposes.

SOURCES: United Nations, *Demographic Yearbook 1981.* New York: United Nations, 1983, pp. 405–411; United Nations, *Demographic Yearbook 1982.* New York: United Nations, 1984, pp. 427–436.

the North Central region was 6.4, the rate for the West was 8.5, and the rate for the South was 10.4. The homicide rate for the South had been about twice the rate for the rest of the nation until recently, when murder rates have become more similar for the different regions. Still, the murder rate in the South is nearly 50 per cent higher than the rate for the rest of the country.

Several explanations have been offered for the South's high murder rate. Because both poverty and minority-group status are linked to murder, some have suggested that the South's high murder rate is a product of the relatively

Table 5.2: Rates of Crime per 100,000 People, by Region of the United States, FBI Data, 1983

CRIME	NORTHEAST	NORTH CENTRAL	SOUTH	WEST	TOTAL UNITED STATES
Murder	6.8	6.4	10.4	8.5	8.3
Forcible rape	26.0	31.0	34.4	44.4	33.7
Robbery	313.9	166.2	171.2	240.5	213.8
Aggravated assault	250.5	212.6	303.7	323.3	273.3
Burglary	1,187.3	1,174.4	1,344.9	1,676.7	1,333.8
Larceny	2,479.8	2,784.8	2,757.5	3,576.4	2,866.5
Motor vehicle theft	577.4	392.1	330.8	487.7	429.3
Crime index total	4,841.7	4,767.6	4,952.9	6,357.5	5,158.6

SOURCE: William H. Webster, *Crime in the United States, 1983: Uniform Crime Reports.* Washington, D.C.: U.S. Government Printing Office, 1984, pp. 44–51. No rates for arson are available for different regions.

large amount of poverty and the relatively large proportion of blacks in that region. Regional differences have also been explained by a "subculture of violence," a set of norms that allows violence to be an appropriate response to certain situations (Wolfgang and Ferracuti, 1967, 1982). Some claim that these norms are more widespread in the South than elsewhere. Attempts to explain regional variations in murder rates by this subculture-of-violence theory are explored later in the book, but what is important here is the existence of differences that a theory of crime causation must explain.

Table 5.2 shows regional variations in rates of the index crimes, with the exception of arson for which no data are available. The South has a higher rate of murder, but its rates of forcible rape and aggravated assault are only slightly higher than the national rates, and its robbery rate is lower than the national rate. Thus any theoretical explanation of the South's high murder rate will have to be specific to lethal violence rather than be a general theory of all violent crime (Gastil, 1971).

Looking at regional variations in rates of property crime, the most notable differences are in the extraordinarily high rates of burglary and larceny in the western states. These differences are difficult to explain. Regional variations in the professionalization of the police might exist, with the police in western states perhaps being more likely to record burglaries and larcenies efficiently than are the police in other regions. The more recent settlement of the West might mean that informal community control of crime is weaker there than it is in more settled areas of the country, but we would then expect the rates for all index crimes to be higher in the West. Another possible explanation is that the relatively casual life style in the West and Southwest might be conducive to theft. Warmer weather there might mean that people are away from their homes more often and leave their property unguarded, and this could inflate property crime rates by creating more opportunities for theft. The weather is also warm in the South, but the lower per capita income there may provide potential thieves with fewer opportunities for theft. We can speculate about the reasons for these regional variations in crime rates, but theories of crime causation should make sense of those variations. This assumes, of course, that the data that show such variations are valid measures of the actual distribution of crime.

VARIATIONS IN CRIME RATES BY SIZE OF COMMUNITY

One aspect of a community that may be conducive to crime is size, and another is the population density of a community. Before looking at the complex relationship between crime rates and population density, we turn to statistical variations in crime rates by size of the community.

Official Crime Statistics

We can see from Table 5.3 that in 1983 crime rates per 100,000 people increased with the size of the community, with few exceptions. For some reason, larceny rates are higher in cities with populations between 100,000 and 250,000 than they are in even larger cities. In addition, rates of murder are higher in rural areas than they are in small towns and cities. With these exceptions,

Table 5.3: Crime Rates per 100,000, by Size of Community, FBI Data, 1983*

CRIME	Total U.S.**	Over 250,000	100,000–249,999	CITIES AND TOWNS 50,000–99,999	25,000–49,999	10,000–24,999	Under 10,000	Rural Counties
Murder	8.6	20.2	10.1	6.3	4.9	3.9	3.6	5.8
Forcible rape	35.1	70.6	49.4	35.4	26.5	18.4	16.2	15.3
Robbery	228.8	713.3	294.5	184.0	126.4	71.6	42.2	16.9
Aggravated assault	282.6	489.9	382.4	285.4	245.5	203.1	197.6	127.0
Burglary	1,382.9	2,190.4	1,989.5	1,518.6	1,326.8	1,043.4	912.0	693.7
Larceny	2,964.2	4,112.4	4,436.9	3,501.1	3,440.0	2,908.9	2,807.6	1,027.6
Motor vehicle theft	443.5	1,042.6	531.2	468.6	364.4	260.9	201.0	103.6
Crime index total	5,345.7	8,639.4	7,693.9	5,999.4	5,534.4	4,510.3	4,180.1	1,989.8

* Data for arson are unavailable.

** These figures differ slightly from those in Table 5.2 because they are based on a smaller proportion of the population and a smaller proportion of all reporting agencies.

SOURCE: William H. Webster, Crime in the United States, 1983: Uniform Crime Reports. Washington, D.C.: U.S. Government Printing Office, 1984, pp. 152–153.

there is a decrease in FBI rates as we read across the row for each index offense. This decrease is most dramatic for robbery, with the official crime rate for this offense being forty-two times as high in large cities as in rural areas.

The growth in the size of cities does not always lead to higher crime rates, even though certain social processes associated with large communities—such as the anonymity of the individual and the disruption of traditional social ties—may be associated with more crime. Since the end of World War II, Japan has become more heavily urbanized, but its crime rate has not increased (Clifford, 1976). Switzerland was also able to keep its crime rate low while urbanizing. Apparently its slow rate of urban growth made it possible to maintain social stability and avoid the disruption of traditional social ties that often accompanies urbanization (Clinard, 1978). Thus the association between size of community and crime rates in the United States should direct our attention to social processes that have occurred with urban growth in this country, rather than lead us to assume that urbanization inevitably and by itself generates crime.

Victimization Surveys

Victimization surveys can produce results about variations in crime rates by size of the community that are somewhat different from those revealed by the FBI's UCR data. This is because the police record where a crime occurs, and the NCS records where the victim lives or where the household is located. Thus, a person living in the suburbs may be robbed or raped in the city. The FBI would record the robbery or rape for the city, but the NCS would record the crime for the victim's suburban place of residence. Likewise, a suburban resident whose car is stolen in the city would have the crime reported in different ways by the FBI and by the NCS.

NCS data for 1981 show that all crimes of violence and all crimes of theft from the person occur at the highest rates in central cities rather than outside central cities. For robberies and assaults, victimization rates are higher in larger metropolitan areas than they are in smaller ones. The pattern for larceny from the person is less clear, but tends to show a higher rate of victimization in larger communities. Rape shows no strong differences in victimization rates by size of the community, but this may be because relatively few rapes are uncovered by the survey (Bureau of Justice Statistics, November 1983a).

For household victimization, rates for 1981 are considerably higher in central cities than they are elsewhere for burglary, larceny from the household, and motor vehicle theft. However, neither burglary nor larceny from the household shows a steady increase with size of the metropolitan area. Motor vehicle theft does show a rising rate with increasing size of the metropolitan area (Bureau of Justice Statistics, November 1983a).

NCS data for 1983 confirm the general pattern revealed by both the 1981 victimization surveys and the 1983 FBI data. In 1983, the NCS study found that victimization rates increased with size of the community for robbery, assault, larceny from the person, burglary, household larceny, and motor vehicle theft. Rape did not show a clear pattern of variation by size of the community. These comparisons are based on the victim's place of residence: rural, suburban, or urban (Bureau of Justice Statistics, May 1984).

In general, both official crime statistics and victimization surveys point in the same direction: Conventional crime occurs more frequently in larger communities, at least within the United States.

Crime within Metropolitan Areas

The first systematic examination of the distribution of crime within metropolitan areas was carried out in the 1920s in Chicago by Clifford R. Shaw and Henry D. McKay (1942, 1969). They followed Ernest W. Burgess in describing the metropolitan area as a series of identifiable concentric rings, depicted in Figure 5.1. In this *concentric-zone model* of the urban community, industry develops near the center of the city to be at the crossroads of transportation and communication. This may not be true of cities that developed after the mass ownership of cars and telephones, and there is evidence that in the future cities may be located at the crossroads of electronic communications rather than at the crossroads of transportation. In Shaw and McKay's model, the central business district is at the center of the metropolis, and is immediately surrounded by an area that is changing from a run-down residential area to one occupied by expanding business and industry. Beyond this are residential areas of increasing desirability and respectability.

This model of the metropolis fits some American cities quite well, but does not describe others very accurately. In some cities, industry has developed on the outskirts, and in others there are multiple centers of business and

Figure 5.1: Shaw and McKay's Concentric-Zone Model of the City

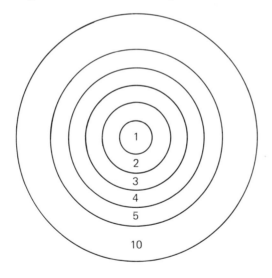

District

1. Central business district
2. Wholesale light manufacturing
3. Low–class residential
4. Medium–class residential
5. High–class residential
10. Commuter's zone

SOURCE: Chauncy D. Harris and Edward L. Ullman, "The Nature of Cities," *The Annals of the American Academy of Political and Social Science* 242 (November 1945), 13. Reprinted by permission.

commerce rather than the single one described by Shaw and McKay. In some nations, government-planned urban development has upset this concentric-zone pattern; one example is Great Britain (Baldwin, 1979). As long ago as the Victorian period, the government built roads through "rookeries," or urban areas inhabited by criminals, in order to disperse offenders throughout the metropolitan region (McIntosh, 1975: 22–23).

Shaw and McKay found that rates of arrest for delinquency—as well as rates of adult crime, truancy, tuberculosis, infant mortality, and mental disor-der—were highest in the center of the city and declined with increasing dis-tance. Since Shaw and McKay completed their research, others have done work that supports their conclusion about the distribution of crime and delin-quency in metropolitan areas (see, e.g., Short, 1969: xxv–liv). Rates of crime and delinquency are usually highest in areas characterized by low incomes, dilapidated and overcrowded housing, transiency, unemployment, broken fam-ilies, and minority groups. These areas are most commonly in the center of large cities (Chilton, 1964; Turner, 1969; Miller, 1974).

Evidence that the highest rates of crime and delinquency occur in the center of cities also comes from research carried out in Canada, Great Britain, Venezuela, Puerto Rico, Uganda, and other countries (Wallis and Maliphant, 1967; Grillo, 1970; Edwards, 1973; Clinard and Abbott, 1973; Jarvis and Mes-singer, 1974; Ferracuti, Dinitz, and Acosta, 1975; Shelley, 1981a). In the Soviet Union, for example, the crime rate of urban areas is about 40 per cent higher than the crime rate of rural areas, even though the rates of the very largest cities are lower than we might expect, for reasons that we will examine in the Cross-Cultural Perspective later in this chapter (Shelley, 1981b).

Looking at data from Chicago from 1900 to 1966, Shaw and McKay found that the delinquency rate for the members of any given racial or ethnic group was higher for members of the group who lived near the center of the city and lower for members who lived in neighborhoods more distant. For instance, people of German ancestry who lived in the inner city had higher rates of arrest for delinquency than did German-Americans who lived in the suburbs. This suggests that it is certain values and norms that are transmitted from generation to generation in an urban neighborhood, rather than the values and norms of any particular racial or ethnic group, that are conducive to violation of the law.

This conclusion is supported by Shaw and McKay's finding that the same urban neighborhoods generally had the highest rates of delinquency over the years, even when there was considerable change in the racial and ethnic com-position of those communities. Areas with high delinquency rates were usually marked by rapid population turnover, socialization into patterns of crime and delinquency, and a lack of good jobs. However, a more recent study of the distribution of delinquency in Chicago found that the conclusion that rates remained the same despite racial and ethnic turnover only fit the data for 1940 and 1950. From 1950 to 1970, changes in the racial and ethnic composi-tion of a neighborhood were often accompanied by changes in delinquency rates. Rates of delinquency remained about the same when a neighborhood was able to maintain its stability in the face of a changing racial and ethnic composition, but in many neighborhoods racial and ethnic succession destabi-lized the community and led to an increased rate of delinquency (Bursik and Webb, 1982).

The major value of Shaw and McKay's work is their systematic documenta-tion of the distribution of crime and delinquency in urban areas, rather than their attempt to develop a theory to explain that distribution. They provide evidence that a theory of crime causation must explain: variations in rates of crime and delinquency within metropolitan areas.

THE GEOGRAPHY OF CRIME

Geographers have provided a picture of crime in metropolitan areas by mapping the location of crimes, the residences of those who commit crimes, and the residences of victims (Georges-Abeyie and Harries, 1980; Brantingham and Brantingham, 1984). Often they use computer graphics to show the distribution of these elements in a metropolitan area.

Crimes of violence are often depicted as a triad of elements: the residences of the offender and the victim, and the place where the crime occurs. However, many crimes of violence—especially homicide and aggravated assault—occur within the home where much interaction takes place. As a result, sometimes the triad is a single point, with the residence of the victim and the offender also being the location of the crime.

Crimes against property are usually depicted as a dyad of elements: the residence of the offender and the place where the property is stolen (although larceny from a person may add the third element of the victim's residence). Most property offenses, as well as most crimes of violence, occur fairly close to the offender's home, with the number of crimes decreasing with greater distance from the criminal's place of residence. People are familiar with their own neighborhoods and so can find targets there; they also know what risks they must avoid near home, even though they may run a greater risk of identification near home. Consequently, criminals' "journeys" or "trips" to the place where they commit their crimes are often short (P. Phillips, 1980; Brantingham and Brantingham, 1984). However, the dyads and triads of crime vary with the kind of offense committed and with the age and sex of the criminal.

Geographers have not mapped dyads and triads for white-collar crime. If they did, they would probably discover that the distance from the home of the offender to the location of the crime, which is usually the place of work, is considerably greater than is the case for most index crimes. Moreover, the places of residence of the victims of white-collar crimes are probably widely dispersed throughout the metropolitan area, and often throughout the nation or the world.

Migration, Population Density, and Crime

Migration may contribute to higher crime rates because of the disruption to the lives of people who move from small towns and rural areas to large cities, or from one country to another. There is also some reason to think that in the cities where many of those migrants live, crowded living conditions may be conducive to high crime rates.

MIGRATION AND CRIME

Research on the relationship between migration and crime has produced mixed results. Studies carried out in Uganda, Kuwait, and several African and South American countries have found that migration is associated with high crime rates (Clinard and Abbott, 1973; Al-Thakeb, 1978; Shelley, 1981b). Migrants to Soviet cities have been found to have higher crime rates than do long-term residents of the same cities (Shelley, 1981b). Immigrants to England from Ireland have been found to have a higher crime rate than the native-born English, a difference attributed to the disruption of traditional controls by family and church, a high unemployment rate, and residence in high crime areas (Radzinowicz and King, 1977: 26). Data from Japan have revealed that the high crime rate of young immigrants to Tokyo from the surrounding countryside is about one and a half times as high as the rate for Tokyo residents who grew up there (Clifford, 1976: 114–115).

Research done in several European countries has yielded somewhat different conclusions. In some of those studies, the crime rates of natives and immigrants are similar, and in others the immigrants have somewhat lower rates than the natives. A study in West Germany concluded that aliens between fourteen and twenty-one had higher crime rates than did their native-born counterparts, but the crime rate for all adult migrants was actually lower than the rate for native-born German adults (Albrecht, Pfeiffer, and Zapka, 1978). Other research from Europe, Australia, Canada, and the United States suggests that recent immigrants—whether permanent residents or "guest workers"—sometimes have crime rates lower than those of the native-born population (Savitz, 1960; Clinard, 1978; Shelley, 1981a). However, studies in these industrial societies do not always support this conclusion; for instance, migration to the United Kingdom and some African migration to France seem to be associated with relatively high crime rates by the immigrants (Ferracuti, 1968).

During the first few decades of the twentieth century, there was a widespread feeling among native-born Americans that high crime rates were due to recent immigrants. In *Culture Conflict and Crime,* one of the first studies of the relationship between migration and crime, Thorsten Sellin (1938) showed that immigrants did not have crime rates higher than native-born Americans. In fact, for many crimes and for many nationalities, the immigrants' crime rates were lower. However, the rates for the offspring of the immigrants often approached the native-born rate. In other words, the crime rates of successive generations of the children of immigrants became more like the crime rate of the native-born. This indicates that crime is a learned behavior, and that socialization into the dominant American culture is likely to be associated with rising crime rates for immigrant groups that had lower rates when they came to the country.

In 1980, about 125,000 refugees entered the United States from Cuba. Because some of these "Marielitos" had served time in Cuban prisons, the American press has given much attention to criminal behavior committed by these refugees in the United States. Law-enforcement officials in many of the cities in which these refugees live have reported that they commit disproportionately large amounts of crime (*The New York Times,* March 31, 1985). However, a study of homicide in Dade County, Florida, found that the murder rate of these Cuban immigrants was no higher than the rate for blacks who were native to the county (Wilbanks, 1984: 26).

The fact that immigrants sometimes have crime rates no higher than the rate for the native-born population is surprising, for there are several reasons to think that the immigrants would have higher rates. Migrants are most often young males, a group particularly prone to crime in most societies. Moving often disrupts ties to family, friends, and community, and this may weaken traditional controls over deviant behavior (Crutchfield, Geerken, and Gove, 1982). The hostility and discrimination sometimes encountered by immigrants might also push them into crime. In addition, there is usually more affluence in the place to which a migrant moves than in the place from which that person came, and this both provides more opportunities for crime and creates a sense of material deprivation conducive to crime. The relationship between migration and crime seems to depend on several factors, including the crime rate of the migrants prior to moving, the crime rate of the native-born population, and the problems of adjustment encountered by the immigrants in their new home.

A study of modernization and crime found that in both industrialized and developing capitalist societies, migration is usually uncontrolled. However, in some socialist societies, migration is controlled. For instance, both China and the Soviet Union have developed policies to minimize the disruption that can occur with internal migration from rural areas and small towns to large cities. In the Cross-Cultural Perspective, we see how this policy has worked in the Soviet Union.

POPULATION DENSITY AND CRIME

One reason that cities may have especially high crime rates is that living conditions there are crowded. In other words, there may be a link between crime rates and *population density*. Overcrowding might lead to aggression among people, and thus population density might be associated with crimes of violence. Dense living conditions could also provide more access to opportunities for crime, whether it be people as targets of violence or property to be stolen.

Research on the relationship between population density and crime does not point to any simple conclusion. Some studies have found little or no relationship between population density and juvenile delinquency when the effects

A Cross-Cultural Perspective: Migration and Crime in the Soviet Union

Urban growth and the movement of people are controlled in the Soviet Union by population policies, an internal passport system, and registration regulations. Because the major cities—such as Moscow, Leningrad, and Kiev—are considered by Soviet planners to be large enough already, people are not permitted to move from rural areas, small towns, and the suburbs into those cities. Only marriage to a resident or a job offer in the city will give a person the right to move there.

Population movement within the Soviet Union is controlled by a passport system that states a person's permanent residence and limits his or her travel within the country. This system was introduced in 1932 and applies to all citizens after their sixteenth birthday. The internal passport system makes it difficult for criminals wanted by the police to escape, for they must show their passports regularly.

One consequence of Soviet migration policies is that the major cities have not grown much in recent years, but small and medium-sized cities have grown because it is relatively easy to secure a permit to live

there. Many people have moved from collective farms to these smaller cities, where they have frequently experienced problems of adjustment to urban life that have led to higher crime rates in those cities.

In addition to curbing the crime rate by restricting migration from rural areas and small towns, the largest Soviet cities have also avoided a crime problem by applying a policy that has been used since the 1920s: Offenders who have been in prison for at least five years, and sometimes less, lose the right to return to their homes in large cities or in surrounding areas after they are released from prison. Consequently, there are fewer offenders in major cities than there would be without state restrictions on migration and place of residence. Many offenders thus move to small and medium-sized cities, causing the crime rates there to increase.

SOURCE: Based on Louise I. Shelley, "Urbanization and Crime: The Soviet Case in Cross-Cultural Perspective," in Louise I. Shelley, ed., *Readings in Comparative Criminology.* Carbondale, Ill.: Southern Illinois University Press, 1981, pp. 141–152.

of income and ethnicity are taken into account (Freedman, 1975: 55–69, 138–142; Booth, Welch, and Johnson, 1976). However, research done in Honolulu, Houston, and Chicago has found that population density and overcrowding are positively associated with rates of crime and delinquency (Schmitt, 1957, 1966; Galle, Gove, and McPherson, 1972; Beasley and Antunes, 1974; Mladenka and Hill, 1976). These studies discovered that a relationship between density and crime exists even when the effects of income, racial and ethnic composition, and education are separated from the effects of population density. In other words, the relationship between density and crime found in these studies is not attributable to the fact that poor people, minorities, and people with little education are the most likely to live in crowded conditions and also the most likely to commit the index crimes that these studies examined.

Density and overcrowding can be defined in several ways, and the definition that is used can influence the results of the research. For instance, one study found no relationship between juvenile delinquency and population density measured by number of people per acre. That same study did find a moderate relationship between delinquency and a measure of density based on number of persons per room in a housing unit, number of housing units per structure, number of rooms per housing unit, and number of residential structures per acre (Galle, Gove, and McPherson, 1972). However, other studies have found no significant relationship between crime and density measured by number of persons per room (Freedman, 1975; Booth, Welch, and Johnson, 1976).

Recently, some researchers have examined the relationship between population density and crime rates by using NCS victimization data rather than official police statistics. These studies have reached somewhat different, and often complex, conclusions. One study found that for property crimes with contact, including robbery from the person, rates were highest where population per square mile was the greatest; however, rates for this kind of crime were not strongly associated with population density within housing units (1.01 or more people per room). Rates of property crime without contact, such as burglary and larceny, and rates of nonproperty assaultive crimes, such as rape and assault, were negatively associated with both measures of density, meaning that these kinds of crime were most common in those areas that had the fewest people per square mile and the least overcrowding within housing units. Motor vehicle theft was not significantly associated with either measure of population density (Shichor, Decker, and O'Brien, 1979; Decker, Shichor, and O'Brien, 1982). In contrast to these results, another study found that population density was positively associated with victimization rates for robbery and assault (Sampson, 1983).

Thus, some research finds that greater population density is associated with higher crime rates for certain offenses, some research shows that population density and rates of certain offenses are not associated with each other, and yet other studies indicate that greater population density is associated with lower rates for certain offenses. More studies that employ both official crime statistics and victimization survey data are needed to disentangle the complex relationship between population density and crime rates.

TEMPORAL VARIATIONS IN CRIME RATES

So far we have seen that crime rates vary by country, by region within a country, and by size of the community. In this section, we will see that crime rates also vary by time of the day, day of the week, month of the year, and over the years. These temporal variations in crime rates seem to reflect differences in patterns of behavior over time.

Crime and Day of the Week and Hour of the Day

Police statistics indicate that murder and forcible rape are most likely to occur during the night-time hours, and least likely to occur in the morning and early afternoon (Wolfgang, 1958; Amir, 1971). The most common time of occurrence for burglaries reported to the police in one suburb was between 6:30 and 10:30 P.M., although for many burglaries it was not possible to estimate the time of occurrence accurately (Conklin and Bittner, 1973). Burglary, murder, and forcible rape are all more likely to occur on weekends than during the week.

NCS victimization data show that the crimes most likely to occur in the evening or at night are car theft and serious crimes of violence such as aggravated assault and robbery from the person. Simple assault, personal larceny without contact, purse snatching, and pickpocketing are least likely to occur in the evening or at night (Bureau of Justice Statistics, October 1983b: 10). These data suggest that variations in the pace of life throughout the day affect opportunities to commit different kinds of crime.

Crime and Seasons of the Year

Police statistics show no strong relationship between month of the year and the frequency of murder, but forcible rape is somewhat more common during the warmer months and somewhat less common in the colder months (Wolfgang, 1958; Amir, 1971). Burglaries are slightly more common in warm months than in cold ones, but the difference is small (Conklin and Bittner, 1973).

Victimization data show that some crimes fluctuate with the seasons. A study that used NCS data for 1973 to 1977 found that household larceny and unlawful-entry burglary peaked in the summer months and reached a low point in the winter. Similar but relatively weak seasonal fluctuations were uncovered for personal larceny of more than $50, forcible-entry burglary, assault, and motor vehicle theft. Rates of robbery from the person did not differ by season. Personal larceny under $50 showed an unusual pattern: Rates peaked in October and reached a low point during the summer. This is apparently because petty theft from the person is a common offense in school. As a result, rates are highest during the months that schools are open, and are especially high early in the school year when there are more new things to steal (Bureau of Justice Statistics, May 1980). More recent NCS data show that "almost all types of personal and household crimes are more likely to occur during the warmer months of the year," with the exception of robbery from the person (Bureau of Justice Statistics, October 1983b: 11).

These temporal variations in murder, rape, burglary, and other offenses are relatively small, but they must be explained. Thus, high rates of rape during the warmest months might be explained by the increased frequency of interaction in June, July, and August, with that interaction sometimes erupting into violent sexual assaults. The slightly higher burglary rates in the warmer months might be accounted for by the fact that many people take their vacations then and leave their homes empty and vulnerable to theft; even if people are not on vacation, they are more likely to leave doors and windows open when the weather is warm.

Annual Trends in Crime Rates

A theory of crime causation should be able to tell us why crime rates rise and fall over the years. However, few theories have tried to explain long-term trends in crime rates.

OFFICIAL CRIME STATISTICS

In Figures 5.2 and 5.3 we can see that the FBI's UCR data show fluctuations in index crime rates since 1933, and a particularly dramatic increase beginning in the 1960s. Between 1933 and 1960, rates were relatively stable, but they began to increase significantly around 1963. Since the mid-1970s, rates have declined in some years and seem to be showing signs of stabilizing or even declining. Between 1973 and 1983, rates per 100,000 people for the FBI's index crimes changed in the following ways:

Murder	− 10.8%
Forcible rape	+ 38.7%
Robbery	+ 17.2%
Aggravated assault	+ 37.8%
Burglary	+ 10.2%

Figure 5.2: Trends in Crimes against the Person, Rates per 100,000 People, FBI Data, 1933–1983

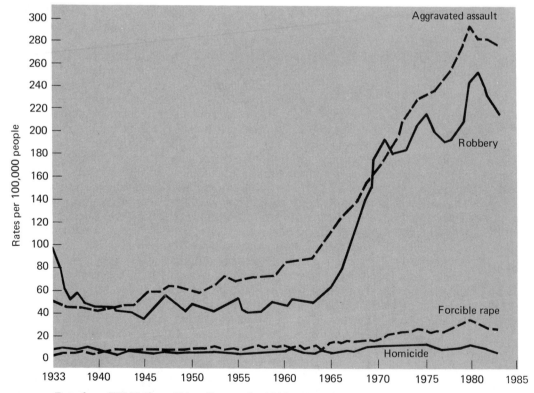

SOURCE: Data from FBI Uniform Crime Reports for 1966–1983 to bring up to date the figure presented in the President's Commission on Law Enforcement and Administration of Justice, *The Challenge of Crime in a Free Society.* Washington, D.C.: U.S. Government Printing Office, 1967, p. 23.

Larceny	+ 39.7%
Motor vehicle theft	− 2.5%
Arson	no data available
Total crime index	+ 25.3%

These data indicate that during the decade the official rate increased for five of the index crimes, the rate declined slightly for motor vehicle theft, and the rate dropped for murder, the least frequent but most serious of the index crimes. These FBI data must be interpreted cautiously, for better crime reporting and recording could have accounted for these changes in rates over the decade. Thus, one self-report study found no significant change in the number or seriousness of acts of juvenile delinquency between 1967 and 1972, even though FBI data showed a substantial increase in arrests of juveniles over that time (cited in Doleschal, 1979: 2).

VICTIMIZATION SURVEYS

Even though the FBI data generally show an upward trend, with some large fluctuations, from 1973 to 1983, NCS victimization data show stability, and

Figure 5.3: Trends in Crimes against Property, Rates per 100,000 People, FBI Data, 1933–1983

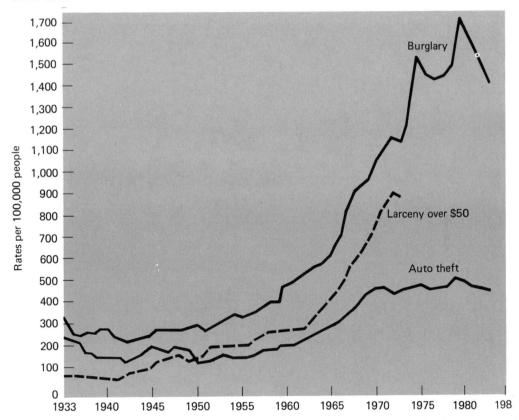

SOURCE: Data from FBI Uniform Crime Reports for 1966–1983 to bring up to date the figure presented in the President's Commission on Law Enforcement and Administration of Justice, *The Challenge of Crime in a Free Society*. Washington, D.C.: U.S. Government Printing Office, 1967, p. 23.

even some decline, in crime rates over that decade. Figures 5.4 and 5.5 show that victimization rates did not change much in the first part of the decade, but declined during the last few years of the decade. Comparing 1973 victimization rates with those for 1983, we find the following changes:

Forcible rape	−10.5%
Robbery from the person	−15.0%
Assault	− 2.0%
Personal larceny with contact	−12.1%
Personal larceny without contact	−16.9%
Household burglary	−22.3%
Household larceny	− 0.4%
Motor vehicle theft	−26.2%

Thus, in per capita rates, the NCS data show consistent declines during the same period that the FBI data show some significant increases (Bureau of Justice Statistics, June 1984; Webster, 1984).

One possible explanation of this discrepancy is that an increasing proportion

Figure 5.4: Trends in Victimization Rates for Violent Crimes, NCS Data, 1973–1983

Rate per 1,000 persons age 12 and older

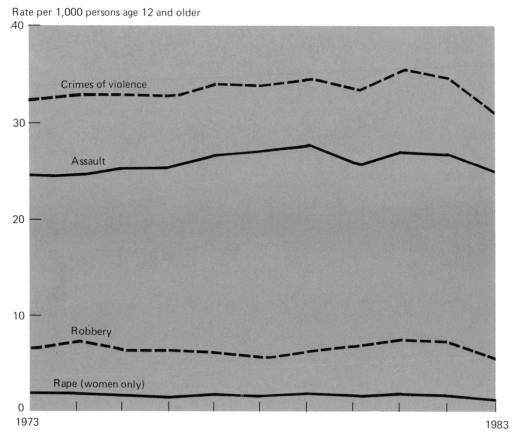

SOURCE: Bureau of Justice Statistics, *Criminal Victimization 1983.* Washington, D.C.: U.S. Department of Justice, June 1984, p. 1.

of the crime that actually occurred during the 1973–1983 period was reported to and recorded by the police. In other words, official statistics could show an increase even if actual victimization remained the same or declined, if a higher proportion of all crimes made their way into the FBI's reports. However, Figure 5.6 indicates that at least for the 1973–1983 period, better reporting of crime to the police cannot account for the differences in trends revealed by FBI and NCS data. In Figure 5.6 we can see that there was little change in the percentage of all victimizations reported to the police, even though slightly higher proportions of victimizations were reported in 1983 than in 1973.

Factors other than better reporting and recording thus seem to account for most of the difference between FBI and NCS crime trends. The offense categories used by the two data collection programs differ, and so do the ways that crime is measured (see Table 3.4, p. 55). For instance, FBI rates are calculated per 100,000 people, and NCS victimization rates are calculated per 1,000 people aged twelve and over. The fact that the FBI bases its rates on the entire population and that the NCS bases its rates only on those aged

Figure 5.5: Trends in Victimization Rates for Selected Crimes, NCS Data, 1973–1983

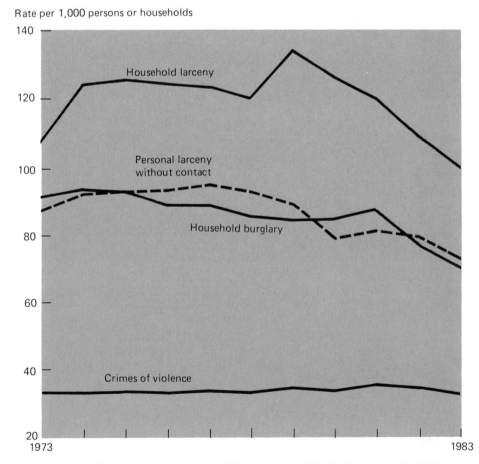

Rate per 1,000 persons or households

SOURCE: Bureau of Justice Statistics, *Criminal Victimization 1983.* Washington, D.C.: U.S. Department of Justice, June 1984, p. 2.

Figure 5.6: Trends in Police Reporting Rates for Selected Crimes, NCS Data, 1973–1983

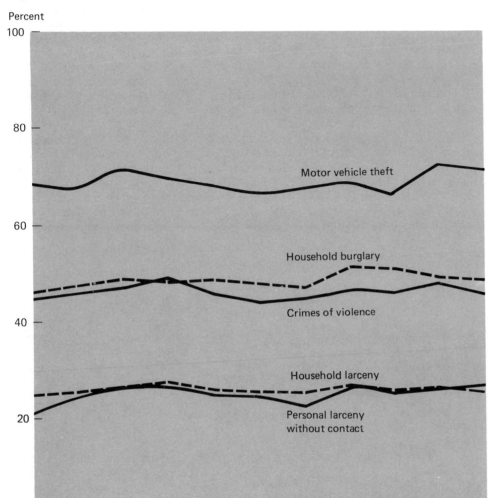

SOURCE: Bureau of Justice Statistics, *Criminal Victimization 1983*. Washington, D.C.: U.S. Department of Justice, June 1984, p. 3.

twelve and over means that changes in the age distribution of the population over time might affect comparisons of trends based on FBI and NCS data. These and other differences in the way that data are collected and presented probably account for some of the difference in the year-to-year trends revealed by FBI and NCS statistics.

SUMMARY

Rates of crime vary from one country to another, by region within a country, by size of a community, and from one time to another. Theories of crime causation should help us to make sense of these variations.

Cross-national comparisons of crime rates are difficult because of differences among countries in their laws and their crime statistics. Three countries that seem to have crime rates lower than the United States are Japan, China, and Canada. In fact, Japan's rates of crime and delinquency have actually declined since the end of World War II. The United States has an extraordinarily high homicide rate compared to other nations that report crime data to the United Nations.

Within the United States, one regional variation in crime rates that has received attention is the South's high homicide rate. This has often been explained by a subculture of violence, but such a theory can explain only the high murder rate because rates of other violent crimes are not especially high in the South. The West has the highest rates of burglary and larceny, but the reasons are not clear.

The FBI's UCR data show that rates of index crimes are highest in larger communities, with few exceptions. NCS victimization data are gathered in a different way from the FBI's data, but NCS data also indicate that for most crimes the victimization rates are highest in the largest metropolitan areas and in the central cities within those metropolitan areas. Shaw and McKay found that crime and delinquency are most common in neighborhoods closest to the center of the city, but their conclusion that rates remain constant in spite of racial and ethnic turnover in a community has been questioned by recent research. Geographers have mapped the residences of offenders and victims and the places where crimes occur. They have found that most offenders commit crimes close to home; violent offenders often commit their crimes within the home. Immigrants frequently have crime rates no higher than, and sometimes lower than, the native-born population, in spite of perceptions by the native-born that the new arrivals are especially prone to crime. The relationship between population density and crime rates is complex and still not clear.

Crime rates vary with time of the day, day of the week, season of the year, and over the years. Crimes of violence, car theft, and burglary seem to be especially likely to occur after dark. Murder, rape, and burglary are more likely to happen on weekends than during the week. Both FBI and NCS data show that when there are seasonal fluctuations in crime, it tends to be committed most often during the summer months, except for petty larceny that commonly occurs during the school year. FBI data show a large increase in crime rates beginning in the 1960s, with some rates declining in recent years. However, NCS data show either stability or a decline in victimization rates from 1973 to 1983, during which time FBI data show an increase in most crime rates. The discrepancy seems attributable primarily to differences between the FBI and the NCS in the collection and interpretation of data, and only slightly due to improved reporting and recording of crime over time.

IMPORTANT TERMS

concentric-zone model   population density

SUGGESTED READINGS

DANE ARCHER AND ROSEMARY GARTNER. *Violence and Crime in Cross-National Perspective.* New Haven, Conn.: Yale University Press, 1984. A series of studies that use data from 110 nations, including a cross-national comparison of homicide rates.

WILLIAM CLIFFORD. *Crime Control in Japan.* Lexington, Mass.: D. C. Heath, 1976. A detailed examination of why rates of crime and delinquency in Japan have remained low and even declined since World War II.

DAVID T. HERBERT. *The Geography of Urban Crime.* New York: Longman, 1982. A brief introduction to the ecology of crime and the work of geographers who have mapped patterns of crime.

CLIFFORD R. SHAW AND HENRY D. MCKAY. *Juvenile Delinquency and Urban Areas,* rev. ed. Chicago: University of Chicago Press, 1942, 1969. An updated version of the classic study of patterns of delinquency in metropolitan areas.

Social Dimensions of Crime

Not everyone is equally likely to commit a crime, or to be the victim of one. Offense rates and victimization rates vary with social characteristics such as sex, age, race, and class. In this chapter we continue our examination of variations in crime rates by looking at the association between these four variables and the rates at which people commit or are victimized by crime.

VARIATIONS IN CRIME RATES BY SEX

Perhaps the best predictor of whether an individual will violate the law is sex: Men commit much more crime than women in every society for which we have data. Even though male-female differences in crime rates vary from one society to another, over time, and from one offense to another, sex is a primary factor differentiating criminals from noncriminals. This could be partly a result of biological differences that make men more aggressive than women, but it is more likely the result of differences in the socialization of males and females. Boys and girls, and men and women, are taught to behave differently and play different roles. This socialization process, in combination with a social structure that assigns statuses to people on the basis of sex, leads to differences in personality and behavior that are linked to the large difference in crime rates between males and females.

Sex and Juvenile Delinquency

To examine male-female differences most fruitfully, we must look at juvenile delinquency and adult crime separately. Delinquency includes acts that are crimes when committed by adults, but it also includes juvenile status offenses (such as disobeying a parent or running away from home) that are prohibited only for those below a certain age, usually sixteen, seventeen, or eighteen. Because delinquency is defined so broadly, differences in expected behavior for boys and girls influence the way that each sex is treated by the juvenile justice system.

Table 6.1 shows the major offenses for which boys and girls under eighteen were arrested in 1983. For all offenses except running away, more boys than girls were arrested. The ratio of male to female arrests varies with the offense. Boys were arrested nearly three times as often as girls for larceny, but boys

Table 6.1: Ten Major Causes of Arrest, Boys and Girls under 18, 1983

| BOYS | | GIRLS | |
Offense	Number of Arrests	Offense	Number of Arrests
Larceny*	277,383	Larceny*	100,052
Burglary*	148,519	Runaways	65,122
Vandalism	85,379	Liquor laws	28,919
Liquor laws	85,240	Disorderly conduct	17,052
Disorderly conduct	81,030	Other assaults (simple)	17,030
Other assaults (simple)	61,457	Curfew and loitering law	
Drug abuse violations	60,908	violations	16,049
Curfew and loitering law		Drug abuse violations	11,779
violations	52,099	Burglary*	10,673
Runaways	47,354	Vandalism	7,778
Robbery*	32,914	Aggravated assault*	5,469

* One of the FBI index crimes

SOURCE: William H. Webster, *Crime in the United States, 1983: Uniform Crime Reports.* Washington, D.C.: U.S. Government Printing Office, 1984, pp. 181, 183.

were arrested fourteen times as often for burglary. For all Part I and Part II offenses, there were 3.7 times as many boys as girls arrested.

In recent years, the delinquency rate for girls has increased faster than the rate for boys, but boys still greatly outnumber girls in arrests for delinquent acts (Office of Youth Development, 1974; Canter, 1982; Webster, 1984). Females do not seem to be catching up with their male counterparts in serious violent crimes or in gang-related delinquency, but they have become more like males in the rate at which they commit larceny, run away from home, and violate liquor laws. The failure to catch up in the more serious crimes may be attributable to the absence among girls of a youth subculture, which acts as a source of recruitment into serious crime (Steffensmeier and Steffensmeier, 1980). A longitudinal study of self-reported female delinquency from 1976 to 1980 found that black girls and lower-class girls were the most likely to admit to violent crimes in three of the five years. Girls between fifteen and seventeen were significantly less involved in delinquency in 1980 than were girls of the same age in 1976. Overall, the frequency of most kinds of delinquent behavior among the girls remained the same or declined over the five years; there was an especially large decline in serious violent crimes, again suggesting that girls are not catching up with boys in these kinds of offenses (Ageton, 1983).

Self-report studies indicate that when a girl commits an act that would be a crime if committed by an adult, she is less likely than a boy to be reported to the police or to be dealt with in court (Clark and Haurek, 1966; Gold, 1970; Chesney-Lind, 1973). Boys who engage in conventional crimes are more likely to be arrested by the police and brought before a juvenile court, partly because of the widely held opinion that girls are not as "bad" as boys or that girls who violate the law are led into crime by "bad" male accomplices. In sum, self-report studies indicate that male-female differences in rates of conventional crime by juveniles are less than indicated by arrest statistics.

Some research reveals that for certain juvenile status offenses, girls are as likely—or even more likely—than boys to be arrested by the police and brought into court (Clark and Haurek, 1966; Wise, 1967; Gold, 1970; Chesney-Lind,

1973). A girl who runs away from home, drinks alcoholic beverages, or has sexual relations is more likely to become involved with the legal system than is a boy who does the same things, even though self-report studies indicate that female involvement in these acts is often no greater than male involvement (Canter, 1982). This difference in treatment by the juvenile justice system is probably related to norms about appropriate gender-role behavior: Boys are expected to "raise hell" but girls are expected to be "well behaved." These expectations lead to more surveillance and control of adolescent girls than of adolescent boys, and result in more arrests and court appearances for girls than would be expected on the basis of sex differences in self-reported delinquency.

Sex differences in delinquency often vary by age group, by racial and ethnic group, and by class. For instance, a study of middle-class delinquency found that there were few differences between boys and girls in self-reported property crimes, even the most serious ones. Larger sex differences in property crimes might exist for the lower class than for the middle class (Richards, 1981).

Sex and Adult Crime

In addition to the male-female differential in juvenile arrests, there is a significant difference between the sexes in arrests of adults. In 1983, for instance, there were 5.4 men eighteen and over arrested for every woman that age who was arrested. This is a higher ratio than for juveniles; in other words, adult crime is even more of a male phenomenon than is juvenile delinquency.

Table 6.2 shows the sex of suspects, both adult and juvenile, who were

Table 6.2: Male and Female Arrests for Index Crimes, 1963 and 1983

| | ALL ARRESTS | | | |
| | PERCENTAGE MALE | | PERCENTAGE FEMALE | |
CRIME	1963	1983	1963	1983
Murder	81.9	86.7	18.1	13.3
Forcible rape	100.0	99.0	0.0	1.0*
Robbery	95.1	92.6	4.9	7.4
Aggravated assault	86.0	86.5	14.0	13.5
Burglary	96.7	93.2	3.3	6.8
Larceny	81.0	70.5	19.0	29.5
Motor vehicle theft	96.3	91.1	3.7	8.9
Arson**	—	87.8	—	12.2
Total index offenses	88.3	79.9	11.7	20.1

* A woman may be arrested for forcible rape is she acts as an accomplice to the man who perpetrates the actual rape.

** No arrest data on arson are available for 1963.

SOURCE: J. Edgar Hoover, *Crime in the United States, 1963: Uniform Crime Reports.* Washington, D.C.: U.S. Government Printing Office, 1964, p. 109; William H. Webster, *Crime in the United States, 1983: Uniform Crime Reports.* Washington, D.C.: U.S. Government Printing Office, 1984, p. 186.

arrested for each of the index crimes in 1963 and 1983. For each offense, significantly more men than women were arrested. The only crime for which more than 14 per cent of the suspects were female in 1983 was larceny.

TRENDS IN FEMALE CRIME

Crime by women has recently received much attention, mainly because of the feminist movement. Some of this attention has exaggerated female involvement in crime. For example, in 1975 *Newsweek* magazine reported that arrests of females for robbery increased by 287 per cent from 1960 to 1973, while arrests for men only increased by 160 per cent over that period. These figures were accurate, but they obscured the fact that in 1960 only 5 per cent of all arrests for robbery were of women, and in 1973 the percentage had only grown to 7 per cent. In other words, nearly all arrested robbery suspects were male in both years. The comparison offered by *Newsweek* of a 287 per cent increase in the number of female arrests contrasted to a 160 per cent increase in male arrests exaggerates the sex difference because the figure for females is based on a small number of arrests in 1960.

The one offense for which there seems to have been a significant change in female involvement between 1963 and 1983 is larceny. For other index offenses, the percentages of all arrested suspects who were women fluctuated by only a few percentage points. In 1963, only 19.0 per cent of all arrests for larceny were of females, but in 1983 that figure had increased to 29.5 per cent. This increase accounted for much of the increase in the total number of arrests of women for index crimes over this period, because larceny is by far the most common index crime for which arrests are made. Without self-report data for women for 1963 and 1983, we cannot determine if there was an actual increase in theft by women over that time. Perhaps the arrest practices of store detectives and the police changed during that period. One response to the large increase in FBI crime rates over this time may have been a decision to arrest people in 1983 who might have been warned and released in 1963. A study of shoplifting in Chicago department stores that was done in the early 1960s found that most suspects were released with a warning rather than formally charged and prosecuted (Cameron, 1964). Whether that study was representative of store policies throughout the country at that time, and whether store policies have changed since the 1960s to bring formal charges against more suspects are questions that cannot be answered with available research.

A systematic review of official statistics, victimization survey data, and self-report studies concludes about the relationship of sex and crime that

> this relation is strong and . . . is likely to remain so into the near future, at least in an absolute sense. On the other hand, in a relative sense, there is evidence that women are becoming more like men in their levels of involvement in crime, with this being particularly true of younger women and in the area of property crime. The areas of female criminality that are changing fastest are those that have been traditionally female, including petty forms of theft and fraud (Nagel and Hagan, 1983: 108).

FEMINISM, WORK, AND CRIME

Some observers have suggested that crime by women has increased in recent years as a result of the feminist movement (*Newsweek*, 1975). One problem with this argument is that arrest data do not show a clear increase in all crimes by women. Another problem is that some of the increase in female crime that has occurred actually preceded the emergence of the feminist movement. Some of the increase in crime by women did come after the development of the feminist movement, but this does not prove that the movement itself was the cause of the increase.

We need to ask how the feminist movement might have led to an increase in crime by women, an increase that is not large except for larceny arrests. It does not seem that women who are most active in the feminist movement are arrested very often for index crimes. Some research on female delinquency finds that violation of the law is not associated with feminist attitudes (Giordano, 1978), and some of that research has even shown that feminist attitudes can inhibit property offenses and violent crimes (James and Thornton, 1980).

Since the end of World War II there has been a large increase in the proportion of women holding jobs outside the home. Some, but probably not most, of this increased involvement by women in the labor force is attributable to the feminist movement and the changes in gender roles that it has produced. Other social forces that have led more women to take jobs include rising rates of divorce and illegitimacy, a delay in the age at first marriage, and the perception that inflation has so eroded the family's buying power that two incomes are needed. Whatever the reasons for increased labor-force participation by women, those women who do hold jobs outside the home may have more opportunities to commit crimes such as larceny and embezzlement. Indeed, as women are promoted to top positions in companies, we might expect that their involvement in white-collar crime would increase too. However, FBI data indicate that most female arrests are not occupationally related. Arrests of women are more common for passing bad checks, credit card or welfare fraud, and shoplifting, rather than for employee theft or embezzlement. One analysis of female crime concludes that increased theft by women is due less to the feminist movement or increased labor-force participation than it is due to changes in merchandising—such as more self-service stores or more buying on credit—that make theft or fraud easier for shoppers, a traditional female role (Steffensmeier and Cobb, 1981).

In one study of employee theft in a large retail organization, data gathered from personnel records, from files kept by the company's security force, and from interviews conducted with the firm's officials revealed that male employees committed more thefts and took more when they did steal than was true of female employees. Of 447 known dishonest workers, 56 per cent were men and 44 per cent women, even though only 40 per cent of the company's workforce was male and 60 per cent was female (Franklin, 1979). This study suggests that given similar on-the-job opportunities for theft, men may commit crime more often than women, even though we would expect female crime to increase somewhat as women gain more opportunities to steal on the job (Figueira-McDonough and Selo, 1980).

The higher rate of labor-force participation by women may have had a more subtle effect on the female crime rate. It may have increased a sense of relative deprivation or entitlement among women who are not working outside the home, or among those who are being paid less than their male colleagues for the same work. If there is a widespread perception—accurate or not—among some women that other women are doing well financially and being fulfilled by their jobs, then women who are not working may feel that they deserve more than they have. This same sense of deprivation can develop if women, whether in the labor force or not, compare their own position unfavorably to that of men. Feminism may have raised expectations faster than reality has changed, and this might have produced frustration that has led to crime by some women. This explanation is consistent with the evidence in Table 6.2 that arrests of women for crimes involving the theft of property increased from 1963 to 1983, but that arrests for murder and aggravated assault declined over that time.

PROSTITUTION AND SEX ROLES

Prostitution is an offense that is closely linked to social inequality between men and women. There are many male prostitutes who cater to men interested in homosexual acts, but most arrests for prostitution are of women offering sex to male clients or of the pimps of those prostitutes. In 1983, 35,485 men were arrested for prostitution and commercialized vice, compared to 83,777 women arrested for the same offenses. This was the only offense for which more women than men were arrested, except for the juvenile status offense of running away (Webster, 1984).

Social inequality between the sexes can make prostitution attractive to some women. Uneducated and untrained women often have no work skills that will get them jobs that pay as well as prostitution, nor are there jobs available to them that offer the same sense of adventure and independence (James, 1976). However, prostitutes in reality probably encounter more male dominance in their jobs than they encounter in the general society. They are expected to serve male clients and dress to fulfill male fantasies. Their male pimps control their incomes and sometimes beat them. Others with whom prostitutes interact are also usually men: the police officers who arrest them, the bail bondsmen who help them to gain their release from jail, the judges who sentence them to jail or prison. Others who are often men and who profit from the prostitute's work include landlords, owners of massage parlors, lawyers, and politicians who gain votes by promising to "clean up vice" just before an election (Heyl, 1979).

SEX AND CRIME IN OTHER SOCIETIES

When women took over some traditionally male roles in Germany during World War II, female crime rates rose to nearly the same levels as male rates. When women returned to traditionally female roles after the war, their crime rates dropped to prewar levels (Radzinowicz and King, 1977: 14–15). This suggests that increasing equality of gender roles might cause male and female crime rates to become more similar. For example, since the end of World War II, the contribution of Japanese women to their nation's crime rate has increased as they have entered the labor market, married later, and become more like men in the roles they play (Clifford, 1976: 125–132).

In a survey of sixty-four countries, the United Nations calculated arrest rates for males and females for 1970–1975. For nations that were still developing economically, there were 12.9 adult males arrested for every adult female arrested, and for juveniles there were 8.3 boys arrested for every girl arrested. In economically developed countries, on the other hand, the ratio for adult arrests was 8.2 males for every female, and for juveniles the ratio was 4.8 boys for every girl arrested. In the United States in 1983, the male-to-female ratio for adult arrests was 5.4, and for juveniles it was 3.7. These figures indicate that females become relatively more involved in both adult crime and juvenile delinquency as a nation industrializes ("United Nations Crime Survey (1977)," 1981). This may be because industrial societies have greater flexibility in gender roles and greater equality between men and women in access to opportunities than do less economically advanced societies.

Sex and Victimization

Men are much more likely than women to be victims of robbery and assault, as we can see in Table 6.3. Women are most apt to be the victims of forcible rape, a crime that is usually defined to include only female victims. The NCS program collects no data on homicide, but the FBI's UCR data show that men are the victims of homicide about three times as often as women (Webster, 1984).

Table 6.3: NCS Rates of Victimization, 1981, Male and Female, Rate per 1,000 Population Age 12 and Over

CRIME	MALE	FEMALE
Crimes of violence	46.2	25.4
Rape	0.1*	1.8
Robbery	9.8	5.2
Assault	36.2	18.5
Crimes of theft	90.7	80.0
Personal larceny with contact	2.7	3.7
Personal larceny without contact	88.0	76.3

* Estimate is statistically unreliable because it is based on a small number of cases.

SOURCE: Bureau of Justice Statistics, *Criminal Victimization in the United States, 1981*. Washington, D.C.: U.S. Department of Justice, November 1983, p. 23.

Table 6.3 also shows that men are more likely than women to be the victims of personal larceny without contact, and that women are slightly more likely to be the victims of personal larceny with contact. Overall, nonviolent crimes of theft victimize males somewhat more often than they do females.

Because the NCS program counts burglaries, household larcenies, and motor vehicle theft as offenses against households rather than against individuals, no victimization rates can be calculated for men and women for these crimes.

VARIATIONS IN CRIME RATES BY AGE

Most crimes are committed by people younger than the general population. In 1983, FBI data showed that 30.4 per cent of people arrested for index crimes were under the age of eighteen and 62.9 per cent were under the age of twenty-five (Webster, 1984). The median age of the population of the country in that year was 30.9.

Age-Specific Arrest Rates

The rate at which people commit crime varies with age. Arrest data do not provide a perfect picture of how involvement in crime varies with age, because young offenders may be more or less likely than older offenders to be arrested for any given crime. However, we can reach some tentative conclusions from Table 6.4, which gives the *age-specific arrest rates*—or number of arrests per 100,000 people in each age category—for the crime of robbery in 1970 and 1980, two census years. We can see that in each year there is considerable variation in arrest rates among age groups. In 1970, the arrest rates rose to a peak at age eighteen and then declined with age. In 1980, a similar pattern occurred, except that the peak age for arrests was seventeen. In both years, there was a precipitous decline in age-specific arrest rates after the mid-twenties.

Another important aspect of Table 6.4 is that the age-specific arrest rate for each group was considerably higher in 1980 than it was in 1970. This suggests more involvement in robbery by people of every age. The increase cannot be attributed to increasing rates of arrest by the police, for their clearance rate for robbery declined from 29.1 per cent in 1970 to only 23.8 per cent in 1980. In other words, by 1980 a smaller proportion of all people who committed robbery were being arrested, but still the age-specific arrest rate increased for every age group.

Peak ages and age-specific arrest rates vary considerably from one offense to another. We can see this by looking at the percentage of all arrests for different offenses that are accounted for by suspects under the age of eighteen. The percentage of suspects arrested in 1983 who were under eighteen and the median age of arrested suspects are shown in Table 6.5 for each of the eight index crimes. We can see that 30.4 per cent of suspects arrested for index crimes were under eighteen, and that their median age was twenty-one. For the four violent crimes—including robbery—only 16.8 per cent of arrested suspects were under eighteen, but 33.9 per cent of all suspects arrested for property crimes were under eighteen. Another way of looking at these figures is to compare the 30.1 per cent of suspects arrested for index crimes

Table 6.4: Robbery Arrests per 100,000 People for Age Groups, 1970 and 1980

AGE GROUP	NUMBER OF ROBBERY ARRESTS PER 100,000 PEOPLE		AGE GROUP	NUMBER OF ROBBERY ARRESTS PER 100,000 PEOPLE	
	1970	*1980*		*1970*	*1980*
Under 15	16.7	19.4	24	122.0	140.2
15	139.4	211.9	25–29	75.8	99.0
16	172.9	265.5	30–34	40.4	55.5
17	189.7	292.5	35–39	21.9	30.0
18	197.5	281.2	40–44	11.6	17.1
19	194.9	242.7	45–49	6.2	9.7
20	172.2	210.6	50 and over	1.5	2.2
21	165.1	196.0			
22	142.1	166.2	Total	43.1	61.6
23	121.8	155.3			

SOURCES: Rates calculated from data in United States Department of Commerce, Bureau of the Census, *General Population Characteristics: United States Summary, 1970.* Washington, D.C.: U.S. Government Printing Office, 1972; J. Edgar Hoover, *Crime in the United States, 1970: Uniform Crime Reports.* Washington, D.C.: U.S. Government Printing Office, 1971; U.S. Department of Commerce, Bureau of the Census, *General Population Characteristics: United States Summary, 1980.* Washington, D.C.: U.S. Government Printing Office, 1983; and William H. Webster, *Crime in the United States, 1980: Uniform Crime Reports.* Washington, D.C.: U.S. Government Printing Office, 1981.

Table 6.5: Arrested Suspects under 18 and Median Age of Arrested Suspects, 1983

CRIME	PERCENTAGE UNDER 18	MEDIAN AGE (ESTIMATED)
Murder	7.4	27
Forcible rape	14.5	25
Robbery	26.3	20
Aggravated assault	12.9	26
Burglary	38.3	19
Larceny	32.3	21
Motor vehicle theft	34.6	20
Arson	37.5	21
Total index crimes	30.4	21

SOURCE: William H. Webster, *Crime in the United States, 1983: Uniform Crime Reports.* Washington, D.C.: U.S. Government Printing Office, 1984, pp. 179–180, 185.

who were between fifteen and nineteen with the 8.2 per cent of the country's population that fell into that age group.

Table 6.5 shows significant variation by offense in the age of arrested suspects. Thus, the median age for those arrested for murder was twenty-seven and only 7.4 per cent of those suspects were under eighteen, but for burglary the median age was nineteen and 38.3 per cent of the suspects were under eighteen. Generally, crimes of violence are committed by people in their early to mid-twenties, and crimes against property are committed most often by people in their late teens or early twenties.

An important problem arises in using the FBI's UCR data on the age of arrested suspects. Most delinquency, especially by males, is group activity, and using individual arrest data can obscure the group nature of law-violating behavior. For instance, young people commit robbery in groups more often than older robbers do (Conklin, 1972; Zimring, 1981). Because much crime by young people is committed in groups, data on the proportion of all arrested suspects who are under eighteen may suggest that the proportion of all crimes committed by people under eighteen is higher than it really is.

Age Distribution and Crime Rates

Because arrest rates differ by age group, and because this seems to reflect a difference among age groups in actual involvement in criminal activity, a society can experience an increase or a decrease in its crime rate if the age distribution of its population changes. In other words, if the young have an especially high crime rate, a society with a large proportion of young people in its population at one time will have a higher overall crime rate than it would at a different time when a smaller proportion of its population is young. The post-World War II "baby boom" produced a significant increase in the proportion of the American population in the high crime rate years from fifteen to twenty-four in the 1960s; between 1960 and 1975, the size of that age group increased about six times as fast as the rest of the population. The dramatic increase in official crime rates during the 1960s seems to have been due in part to the increased proportion of the population in this high crime rate age group (The President's Commission on Law Enforcement and Administration of Justice, 1967a: 27–28).

Table 6.6:   Changing Age Distribution and Crime Rates in a Hypothetical Society

TIME PERIOD	AGE GROUP	POPULATION OF SOCIETY	NUMBER OF CRIMES	CRIME RATES
Time 1	Under 25	100 (25%)	10	10 per 100
	Over 25	300 (75%)	15	5 per 100
	Total society	400 (100%)	25	6.25 per 100
Time 2	Under 25	200 (50%)	20	10 per 100
	Over 25	200 (50%)	10	5 per 100
	Total society	400 (100%)	30	7.5 per 100

SOURCE: John E. Conklin, *Robbery and the Criminal Justice System.* Philadelphia: J. B. Lippincott Company, 1972, p. 23.

The way that a change in the age distribution of a population can produce an overall increase in crime rates can be seen in Table 6.6, where we look at a hypothetical society at two different times. At time 1, one-fourth of this society's population is under twenty-five, and that group commits crime at the rate of 10 offenses per 100 people. The group over the age of twenty-five constitutes three-fourths of the population at time 1 and has a crime rate of 5 offenses per 100 people. The entire population thus has a rate of 6.25 crimes per 100 people at time 1. By time 2 this society has changed so that half of the population is in the high crime rate group under twenty-five. Even though the age-specific crime rates are the same at time 2—10 per 100 for those under twenty-five and 5 per 100 for those over twenty-five—the society's overall crime rate has increased from 6.25 per 100 to 7.5 per 100 simply because of the change in the proportion of the population in the high crime rate age group under twenty-five. Thus, a change in the age distribution of the population, much like the one that resulted from the postwar baby boom in the United States, increased the crime rate in our hypothetical society by 20 per cent.

According to real data for the United States, 17 per cent of the increase in arrests for auto theft between 1960 and 1970 was due to a change in the age distribution of the population (Conklin, 1973). Because auto theft is committed by youthful offenders most of the time, probably less than 17 per cent of the change in the rates of other index offenses can be attributed to changes in the age composition of the population over that decade. For instance, only 9 per cent of the increase in robbery arrests from 1960 to 1970 was due to a change in the age distribution of the population (Conklin, 1973). Another study found that about 13 per cent of the increase in robbery rates from 1950 to 1965 was a result of changes in the size of the fifteen-to-twenty-four-year-old group (Ferdinand, 1969).

Changing age distribution explains some of the increase in index crime rates in the United States during the 1960s and the 1970s, but it does not explain most of it. Instead, there was an increase in the rate at which people of every age committed crime, as we can see in Table 6.4 for the crime of robbery. Looking at changes in the rate of violent index crimes from 1960 to 1970, for instance, we find that changes in the age distribution would have led us to expect a 40 to 50 per cent increase in the rate of those offenses, but instead there was a 200 per cent increase (Silberman, 1978: 31). The important theoretical question thus becomes what social changes, other than the change in the age distribution of the population, produced the increase in the rate at which people of all ages were committing crime.

If age-specific crime rates were to remain stable throughout the 1980s, the overall crime rate in the United States would decline, because the population is growing older and the proportion of people in the high crime rate age groups is declining relative to the rest of the population. In fact, victimization surveys show a decline in crime rates in the early 1980s, and the FBI's UCR data show declines during some of the years in the late 1970s and early 1980s. Even though the changing age distribution might lead us to predict declining crime rates in the 1980s, other forces such as rising unemployment rates or disintegrating families could lead to higher crime rates. In sum, age is but one factor that influences a country's crime rate at any given time.

Age and Victimization

Young people generally have higher rates of victimization than older people. In 1983, FBI data showed that 64.2 per cent of all murder victims were between fifteen and thirty-nine (Webster, 1984). NCS victimization data in Table 6.7 show that rates of other violent crimes are also highest among the young. Excluding the rates for the very youngest victims, we find that rates of rape, robbery, and assault generally decline with increasing age. Crimes of theft also show lower victimization rates for older people; this trend is more pronounced for personal larceny without contact than it is for personal larceny with contact.

A NCS report on crime against the elderly in twenty-six cities found that people over sixty-five had the lowest rates of victimization for rape, robbery, and assault, but the highest rates for pocketpicking and purse snatching (larceny with contact). The elderly were the least likely of all of the age groups to be attacked or injured, and serious injury among them was rare. In part, this was because the elderly were unlikely to resist or to try to protect themselves from criminals (Hochstedler, 1981). However, as we saw in Chapter 4, there may be a sense in which the elderly have a high rate of victimization. They may be at risk less often than younger people because generally they do not go to work, they often live in age-segregated housing (including nursing homes), and they frequently stay indoors out of fear or infirmity. If victimization rates are calculated in terms of time at risk, the elderly's victimization rate may actually be as high as or even higher than that of younger people (Lundquist and Duke, 1982; Stafford and Galle, 1984).

VARIATIONS IN CRIME RATES BY RACE

Variations in crime rates by racial and ethnic group reflect social, cultural, and economic differences among groups. In the past, some have suggested that such variations in crime rates are due to biological differences among racial and ethnic groups, but it is now well established that any biological differences among racial and ethnic groups are unimportant in explaining differences in crime rates. For instance, the crime rates of black Africans are considerably lower than the crime rates of black Americans, even though black Americans have racially intermixed with whites over the centuries, and whites have crime rates lower than black Americans (Bohannan, 1960). Such variations in crime rates need to be explained by sociological theories of crime causation.

Table 6.7: NCS Rates of Victimization, 1981, by Age, Rate per 1,000 Population Age 12 and Over

CRIME	12–15	16–19	20–24	25–34	35–49	50–64	65 and Over
Crimes of violence	58.9	67.8	68.3	43.7	23.3	13.2	7.8
Rape	1.4	2.4	2.0	1.4	0.4*	0.2*	0.1*
Robbery	11.8	12.3	12.3	7.6	5.5	4.6	4.0
Assault	45.7	53.0	54.0	34.7	17.5	8.4	3.7
Crimes of theft							
Personal larceny with contact	128.1	131.9	132.8	100.8	77.8	51.0	22.3
	2.5	3.7	4.4	3.8	2.7	2.9	2.9
Personal larceny without contact	125.5	128.3	128.4	97.0	75.1	48.1	19.4

* Estimate is statistically unreliable because it is based on a small number of cases.

SOURCE: Bureau of Justice Statistics, *Criminal Victimization in the United States, 1981*. Washington, D.C.: U.S. Department of Justice, November 1983, p. 24.

Race, Arrest Statistics, and Self-Report Studies

The FBI presents arrest data for whites, blacks, American Indian or Alaskan Natives, and Asian or Pacific Islanders; it also provides data for Hispanic and non-Hispanic suspects. FBI data do not allow us to analyze differences in arrest rates for white ethnic groups such as Irish-Americans, Italian-Americans, Eastern Europeans, or Jews. However, sociological research has found that the crime rates for Jews, Japanese-Americans, and Chinese-Americans are lower than rates for the total population, and that crime rates for blacks and Mexican-Americans are higher than rates for the total population (Voss, 1963; Wolfgang, Figlio, and Sellin, 1972). Here we will examine differences in arrest rates of blacks and whites, because these two groups account for almost all of the arrests for FBI index crimes; in 1983, for instance, 98.3 per cent of all arrests for index crimes were of blacks or whites.

In 1983 blacks constituted 12 per cent of the population of the United States, but they accounted for 35.7 per cent of arrests for index crimes. Blacks comprised 47.5 percent of arrests for crimes of violence, and 32.7 per cent of arrests for property crimes. For each index crime, blacks are arrested out of proportion to their numbers in the population. According to one estimate, the chance of ever being arrested for an index crime for blacks living in cities of more than 250,000 people is 51 out of 100, compared to a rate of only 14 out of 100 for whites (Blumstein and Graddy, 1981–82). In Table 6.8 the rates of arrest per 100,000 people of the same race are given for whites and for blacks; the third column shows the ratios of blacks' arrest rates to whites' arrest rates. We can see that the likelihood of a black being arrested for an index crime is much greater than the chance that a white will be arrested. Blacks are arrested between 4.7 and 12.2 times as often as whites for violent crimes, and between 2.2 and 3.6 times as often as whites for property crimes. Overall, blacks have an arrest rate for index crimes that is 4.1 times as great as the arrest rate for whites.

Although the rates of involvement are higher for blacks than for whites for all index crimes, crime rates for offenses such as fraud, price fixing, and

Table 6.8:   Rates of Arrest per 100,000 People, by Race, 1983

CRIME	WHITE RATE OF ARREST PER 100,000 PEOPLE	BLACK RATE OF ARREST PER 100,000 PEOPLE	RATIO OF BLACK RATE TO WHITE RATE
Murder	4.4	31.8	7.2
Forcible rape	7.5	52.4	7.0
Robbery	24.4	297.9	12.2
Aggravated assault	77.3	365.6	4.7
Burglary	139.9	463.9	3.3
Larceny	378.6	1,380.9	3.6
Motor vehicle theft	34.8	121.1	3.5
Arson	6.5	14.2	2.2
Total index crimes	673.4	2,727.9	4.1

SOURCES: Arrest rates are calculated using Bureau of the Census data for 1983 on the number of whites (199,520,000) and blacks (28,092,000), and arrest data from William H. Webster, *Crime in the United States, 1983: Uniform Crime Reports.* Washington, D.C.: U.S. Government Printing Office, 1984, p. 187.

embezzlement are higher for whites. It is these white-collar crimes that have the greatest financial costs for American society, even though the criminal justice system focuses its resources "not on the guy who makes millions from powerless people but on the guy who throws a brick through a window" (cited in *The New York Times*, October 18, 1980, p. 26).

We must be wary of using FBI arrest data, for they may distort actual involvement in index crimes by blacks and whites if the police are more likely to arrest black suspects than they are to arrest white suspects. However, most criminologists agree that arrest statistics for blacks and whites reflect a real difference between the groups in their rates of committing crimes, and that the difference in arrests between the racial groups is not primarily a result of racial discrimination by the police. Later in the book, we examine racial discrimination by the police, the courts, and the prisons.

Self-report studies show that blacks report more serious delinquent acts than whites do (Williams and Gold, 1972; Hindelang, Hirschi, and Weis, 1979; Elliott and Ageton, 1980). Some self-report research finds a higher frequency of all delinquent acts by blacks (Elliott and Ageton, 1980), but other studies find that blacks and whites report a similar frequency of involvement in delinquent acts (Williams and Gold, 1972). There is evidence that blacks and whites are more similar in their rates of self-reported involvement in relatively trivial acts of delinquency, but that blacks report serious offenses more often (Hindelang, Hirschi, and Weis, 1979).

Race, Crime, and Background Variables

Differences in crime rates among racial and ethnic groups are a function of group differences in income, occupation, education, family background, and other social characteristics, as well as a function of differences in opportunities to commit crime. This would suggest that if blacks and whites of similar social backgrounds are compared, differences in crime rates between the groups will be reduced or eliminated. However, to suggest that people of different races but similar backgrounds will have the same crime rate is tantamount to suggesting that there are no cultural differences between the groups that result in different crime rates. More specifically, to argue that blacks and whites of similar backgrounds will have the same crime rate is to argue that centuries of discrimination have had no long-term effects on blacks that are conducive to criminal behavior.

Evidence suggests that blacks have higher crime rates than whites, even when individuals of similar backgrounds are compared, but that differences between the groups are reduced in comparisons of people of similar backgrounds. A study of murder in Philadelphia found that when blacks and whites with similar occupations were compared, blacks still committed homicide more often than whites did (Wolfgang, 1958: 39). A study of rape in the same city found that blacks committed rape about four times as often as did whites when people with similar occupations were compared (Amir, 1971: 69–72). Wolfgang, Figlio, and Sellin's (1972) cohort study revealed that 29 per cent of the whites had had police contacts as juveniles, compared to 50 per cent of the blacks. Even when blacks and whites of similar class backgrounds were compared, blacks were more likely to have had police contacts. Table 6.9 shows that blacks of the higher class were actually as likely as whites of the lower class to have had contact with the police. Blacks thus seem to have higher rates of crime and delinquency than whites of similar background,

Table 6.9: Percentage of Each Racial Group with Police
Contacts as Juveniles, 1955 to 1963,
Philadelphia

RACE	SOCIOECONOMIC STATUS	
	Low	*High*
White	36	26
Black	53	36

SOURCE: Adapted from Marvin E. Wolfgang, Robert M. Figlio, and Thorsten Sellin, *Delinquency in a Birth Cohort.* Chicago: University of Chicago Press, 1972, p. 55. Reprinted by permission of the University of Chicago Press. Copyright University of Chicago Press © 1972.

although some research indicates that black-white differences are reduced when people of similar backgrounds are compared (Green, 1970).

Race and Victimization

Blacks are disproportionately likely to be the victims of crime. In 1983, 42.5 per cent of all homicide victims were black, while only 12 per cent of the population was black. Black males who live in cities have about a 5 per cent chance of being murdered, and black males between fifteen and twenty-four are murdered at a rate seven times as high as the rate for the rest of the population. In fact, murder is the primary cause of death for young black males. Some health officials have argued recently that murder among young black males should be considered a public health issue in much the same way that diseases are (Minsky, 1984a).

Table 6.10 shows that blacks have higher victimization rates than whites

Table 6.10: NCS Rates of Victimization, 1981, by Race,
Rate per 1,000 Population Age 12 and Over

CRIME	WHITE	BLACK
Crimes of violence	33.4	49.7
Rape	0.9	1.6
Robbery	6.2	16.9
Assault	26.4	31.2
Crimes of theft	85.3	84.8
Personal larceny with contact	2.9	5.4
Personal larceny without contact	82.3	79.4
Household crimes*		
Burglary	82.7	133.6
Household larceny	118.5	141.6
Motor vehicle theft	16.3	24.0

* For household crimes, households were classified by race of the head of household.

SOURCE: Bureau of Justice Statistics, *Criminal Victimization in the United States, 1981.* Washington, D.C.: U.S. Department of Justice, November 1983, pp. 25, 36.

for rape, robbery, and assault. These NCS data also show that even though blacks, as a group, have a lower average income than whites, they are more likely than whites to be the victims of property crimes. Blacks have higher victimization rates than whites for personal larceny with contact, household burglary, household larceny, and motor vehicle theft. Whites have slightly higher victimization rates for personal larceny without contact.

VARIATIONS IN CRIME RATES BY CLASS

When criminologists examine the relationship between *class*—which is defined as social standing based on economic resources, occupational prestige, political power, or life style—and crime, they usually look at conventional crimes such as murder, rape, robbery, and larceny. However, the most expensive crimes are white-collar crimes, and because these offenses are committed by middle- and upper-class people, we can conclude that the cost of crime is attributable primarily to violations of the law by the middle and upper classes, even though "the crime problem" defined by the FBI, the mass media, and the public usually refers to violations of the law most often committed by the lower and working classes.

Popular wisdom is that the lower and working classes engage in more crime, or at least more of the most serious street crime, than does the middle class. This view has existed for centuries and characterizes societies other than the United States (see, e.g., Chevalier, 1973). People act on their assumption that there is a relationship between crime and class; they avoid slums after dark, leave the doors of their suburban homes unlocked, and expect to be safer when they move from the city to the suburbs.

FBI statistics include no information on the class of arrested suspects, nor do victimization surveys provide us with that information, because victims could not be expected to judge in a reliable way the class of the offender. There is, however, much research that has examined the relationship of class to crime and delinquency. Unfortunately, that research does not lead to a simple conclusion.

Class and Adult Crime

When we look at official measures of crime produced by the police, the courts, or the prisons, we find "a small but consistent inverse correlation of social class with street crime" for adults (Hindelang, 1983: 180). A review of forty-six studies that used arrest data found consistently higher crime rates for lower-class adults (Braithwaite, 1979, 1981). A recent study found a strong relationship between class and adult criminality; crime was associated with an individual's social status, especially as measured by job stability and educational attainment, but not as measured by occupation or current income. Moreover, this study found that adult criminal behavior was not associated with the socioeconomic status of the adult's family of origin. The correlation between class and adult crime in this study was strongest for official arrest data, but was also present in self-report data. In addition, the class-crime link in this study was stronger for blacks than for whites (Thornberry and Farnworth, 1982).

In the few studies that have been done of adult criminality using self-report questionnaires, researchers have found that the class-crime link is less strong in self-report data than in official data. These self-report studies either conclude that the lower class has a higher crime rate than other classes, or that there are no significant differences by class; none of these self-report studies of adults finds that the middle class has a higher crime rate than the lower class (Braithwaite, 1979). Another recent review questions whether self-report data on adults demonstrate that a class-crime link exists: "Among adults, survey-generated criteria of crime are available from too few American studies, and they yield findings too diverse to warrant any confident conclusions" (Hindelang, 1983: 180).

Some have attributed the difference between the relatively strong association between class and adult crime found in official statistics and the weak or nonexistent association found in self-report studies to class bias by the police and the courts. In other words, if the police arrest lower-class suspects more often than they arrest middle-class suspects, arrest data would show that the lower class is more involved in crime, even though self-report studies might show little or no difference among the classes in criminal activity. A review of studies of adults that have used arrest data or self-report questionnaires concluded that class bias by the criminal justice system could not explain away the strong relationship between class and crime found in studies using official statistics. The author suggests that the lower class may be more likely than the middle class to underreport crime in self-report studies, and this might make it seem that lower-class involvement in crime is less than it really is (Braithwaite, 1979, 1981). The author concludes that "[l]ower-class adults commit those types of crime which are handled by the police at a higher rate than middle-class adults" (Braithwaite, 1979: 62).

This same review of the literature concludes that "[a]dults living in lower-class areas commit those types of crime which are handled by the police at a higher rate than adults who live in middle-class areas" (Braithwaite, 1979: 62). The same conclusion applies to juvenile involvement in crime. In other words, people who live in lower-class communities, whatever the class of the individual, are more likely to be involved in crime and delinquency than are people who live in middle-class communities (Gordon, 1967; Clelland and Carter, 1980; Braithwaite, 1981).

One study found that communities that provide higher levels of public assistance (welfare) have lower rates of homicide, rape, and aggravated assault, but that there is no association between levels of public assistance and rates of robbery, larceny, and motor vehicle theft (DeFronzo, 1983). This suggests that reductions in aid to the poor could cause rates of violent crime to rise, but would not affect property crimes to as great a degree, if at all. Other research indicates that homicide rates in metropolitan areas are not significantly related to measures of family income inequality, and that urban areas outside the South have higher homicide rates if they have higher proportions of their populations living in poverty (Messner, 1982, 1983a, 1983b).

Class and Juvenile Delinquency

One review of studies that have examined the link between class and juvenile delinquency found that in forty-four of fifty-three studies that used official statistics, lower-class juveniles had higher rates of delinquency than did middle-class juveniles (Braithwaite, 1979). Another review of the research found a "small but consistent inverse correlation of social class with street crime" by juveniles when official data were used (Hindelang, 1983: 180).

When self-report studies rather than official data are used to look at the link between class and juvenile delinquency, the results are not clear. One review of the research found that these self-report studies provide less support for a class-delinquency link than do arrest data, but that many self-report studies show higher delinquency rates for the lower class and that none finds higher rates for the middle class (Braithwaite, 1979). Another review of self-report studies of delinquency concluded as follows: "About half of the American studies support the hypothesis of an even smaller inverse relationship between various social-class indicators and reported illegal behavior [than is found in studies using official data], and half provide no support for the hypothesis" (Hindelang, 1983: 180).

Table 6.9 provides some data from a cohort study that used police statistics. This table shows a link between class and being stopped by the police for delinquency, with both whites and blacks in the higher class being less likely to be stopped than whites and blacks in the lower class (Wolfgang, Figlio, and Sellin, 1972: 55). However, if the police are more likely to stop lower-class adolescents than they are to stop middle-class adolescents in the same circumstances, these data would not give us a true picture of actual differences between the classes in involvement in delinquency. This is likely to be a greater problem for juvenile delinquency than for adult crime, because delinquency includes a broad range of offenses, from the most serious to the most trivial, and the police may exercise their discretion—and perhaps discriminate by class—most when the offense is relatively trivial.

Self-report studies seem to indicate that class differences in delinquency are most pronounced for the most serious crimes, and smallest for the most trivial offenses. Serious and repetitive violations of the law seem to be most common among the lower classes (Short and Nye, 1958; Reiss and Rhodes, 1961; McDonald, 1969; Gold, 1970; Belson, 1975; Elliott and Ageton, 1980; Clelland and Carter, 1980; Braithwaite, 1981; Elliott and Huizinga, 1983).

Self-report studies that have looked at a broader range of delinquent acts, rather than only the most serious ones, have sometimes concluded that there is little or no association between class and delinquency. One review of the research found that there was a weak-to-moderate relationship between class and official data on violations of the law, but that there was almost no relationship between class and self-reported violations of the law. This study also concluded that any relationship that might have existed between class and self-reported delinquency in the past had declined in strength over time to the point that essentially no relationship between class and delinquency exists anymore (Tittle, Villemez, and Smith, 1978). Other self-report studies have also found no relationship between class and delinquency (Short and Nye, 1958; Nye, Short, and Olson, 1958; Dentler and Monroe, 1961; Akers, 1964; Hirschi, 1969; Krohn et al., 1980). In fact, several self-report studies of juvenile delinquency have even concluded that there is no relationship between class and serious and repetitive violations of the law (Karacki and Toby, 1962; Empey and Erickson, 1966; Shanley, 1967; Williams and Gold, 1972; Cernkovich, 1978a; Johnson, 1980; Krohn et al., 1980).

Contradictory evidence on the association between class and self-reported delinquency also comes from the few studies that have compared the delinquency of people from the lowest class with that of all people of higher social standing. One self-report study that found no overall relationship between class and delinquency did find that boys from the lowest class were the most prone to delinquency. Of those boys whose fathers had been without a job and had received welfare assistance, 62 per cent reported at least one delinquent act, compared to only 40 per cent of the boys whose fathers had not been unemployed or on welfare (Hirschi, 1969: 72). However, another study found no significant relationship between self-reported delinquency—measured only by acts that would be crimes if committed by adults—and the underclass—a class that is below the poverty level, uneducated, often on welfare, and unemployed or working at low-prestige jobs (Johnson, 1980).

One researcher has suggested that there might be stronger evidence for a link between class and juvenile delinquency in economically developing societies where people are categorized at birth into social groups with different perspectives on the world, where access to education is limited, and where social mobility is minimal. This view was supported by the author's research in South Korea. Using both official statistics and self-report data, he found that criminal behavior was confined largely to the lower class, and that the relationship between class and delinquency was strongest for the most serious offenses. The researcher concluded that in developing societies, "class remains an important factor in the explanation of crime and delinquency when educational opportunity is lacking" (Axenroth, 1983: 176).

Methodological Problems

The disagreement between studies based on official statistics and some of the research that has used self-report data to measure juvenile delinquency, as well as the inconsistency among the conclusions of different self-report studies of juvenile delinquency, directs our attention to methodological difficulties that might explain these confusing results. We have already seen that arrest data have problems, particularly that the police may be more likely to arrest some suspects than others, and so we will look here at the problems encountered in self-report studies of juvenile delinquency. Some of these problems also arise in self-report studies of adult crime, but there have been fewer of those studies done and there seems to be more agreement between those few self-report studies and research on adult crime that has relied on official statistics.

One problem encountered by researchers who have studied the class-delinquency association is how to categorize adolescents by class. We have seen that crime by adults does not seem to be strongly associated with the class of the adults' parents, and so it is possible that youths' own job and educational aspirations may be better measures of their class standing than are the occupational prestige or income of their parents. In other words, a class-delinquency association might be more likely to be revealed if class were defined by how well the adolescent does in school, whether the adolescent expects to hold a white-collar or a blue-collar job, whether the individual wants more out of life than he or she feels will realistically be gained, and whether the adolescent expects to be a member of the lower class or the middle class in ten or twenty years (Stark, 1979; Thornberry and Farnsworth, 1982). The class of adolescents has been measured in these ways less often than it has been measured by simply asking them about the occupational prestige of their parents (or usually just their father) or about their family's annual income. Several studies that have measured class only by the occupational prestige of the juvenile's father have found no association between delinquency and class (Hirschi, 1969; Thornberry and Farnsworth, 1982). Perhaps a better measure of the adolescent's class standing would reveal such an association.

Another problem is that many self-report studies of delinquency have gathered data from high school students who are in school on the day that the study is done. These studies miss students who are truant or who have dropped out of school altogether, and these groups may be especially prone to delinquency. In a similar way, studies of adult crime often take a sample of the general population, but in doing so frequently fail to include prisoners, the homeless, and inmates of mental hospitals; certainly the prisoners would report a higher-than-average rate of involvement in crime.

Self-report studies of delinquency often ask about many relatively trivial acts—such as stealing inexpensive items or getting into fights—and then classify an individual as a delinquent if he or she admits to one or more delinquent act. Obviously, the more acts the respondent is questioned about, the more likely that person is to admit to at least one of the acts on the list. In addition, the more delinquent acts there are on the self-report questionnaire, the more likely it is that many of the items will be relatively trivial violations (Reiss, 1975; Hindelang, Hirschi, and Weis, 1979).

In spite of these methodological problems, many self-report studies find higher rates of serious and repetitive delinquency among the lower classes, and none of those studies finds higher rates of serious and repetitive delinquency among the middle class. Official arrest data show even more consistent evidence for a class-delinquency link. Moreover, for adults, arrests show a strong class-crime association, and data from the few existing self-report studies of adults reveal an association between class and crime, although a somewhat weaker one than is found in studies using official data. We must remember that these conclusions about the relationship between class and crime pertain only to offenses that regularly come to the attention of the police. These studies do not define crime in terms of white-collar offenses; if those crimes were included, self-report studies would probably reach different conclusions about the relationship.

We will see later that many sociological theories of crime and delinquency are based on class, even though the relationship between class and violation of the law is still somewhat unclear. These theories rarely consider that involvement in crime and delinquency can affect an individual's class standing by reducing job opportunities or making upward social mobility difficult; unlike sex, age, and race, the variable of class may be both a cause and an effect of crime and delinquency (Thornberry and Christenson, 1984). A recent review of eight theories of crime and delinquency concludes that none of them provides an adequate rationale for predicting an inverse or negative relationship between class and crime without bringing in untested or unsupported assumptions about what the lower class is like (Tittle, 1983). Perhaps sociologists would be on firmer ground in looking for general social processes—such as ways of neutralizing the constraints of the law—that are sometimes correlated with class, rather than treating class itself as a cause of crime and delinquency.

Class and Victimization

The National Crime Survey does not use a single measure of class, but it does gather data on indicators of class such as annual family income, education, employment status, and employment sector. Here we will use annual family income as a measure of the class of both individual victims and households.

Table 6.11 shows that rates of victimization in crimes of violence decline with increasing annual family income. The victimization rates for all three crimes of violence—rape, robbery, and assault—fall with rising income levels; this pattern is least pronounced for assault.

Crimes of theft from individuals show no clear variation by income. Personal

Table 6.11: NCS Rates of Victimization, 1981, by Income, Rate per 1,000 Population Age 12 and Over

CRIME	Less than $3,000	$3,000– $7,499	$7,500– $9,999	$10,000– $14,999	$15,000– $24,999	$25,000 or More
			ANNUAL FAMILY INCOME			
Crimes of violence	66.8	44.7	42.7	40.0	31.1	28.4
Rape	3.6	1.9	1.4	1.0	0.7	0.4
Robbery	15.9	12.1	9.4	7.8	5.7	4.7
Assault	47.3	30.7	32.0	31.1	24.7	23.2
Crimes of theft	106.0	66.2	71.4	81.7	83.6	104.3
Personal larceny with contact	5.5	4.8	3.4	3.3	2.6	2.5
Personal larceny without contact	100.6	61.5	68.0	78.4	81.0	101.8
Household crimes						
Burglary	132.4	98.6	89.4	87.0	79.6	83.2
Household larceny	118.2	119.6	120.8	123.3	129.4	123.0
Motor vehicle theft	11.9	12.4	13.6	20.1	18.9	17.6

SOURCE: Bureau of Justice Statistics, *Criminal Victimization in the United States, 1981.* Washington, D.C.: U.S. Department of Justice, November 1983, pp. 29, 38.

larceny with contact declines with increasing income, but rates of personal larceny without contact—the most frequent theft crime from individuals— show a curvilinear relationship with income: The rate is highest for the lowest and the highest income categories. Except for the very poor, rates of personal larceny without contact increase with rising income levels.

Burglary most often victimizes the poorest people, and victimization rates for this offense decline with increasing income, except for the highest income category. Rates of household larceny are about the same for all income levels, but rise very modestly except for the highest income level. Rates of motor vehicle theft rise with income and reach a peak for families with incomes between $10,000 and $14,999, and then decline somewhat at higher income levels.

In sum, patterns of theft from individuals and from households do not reveal a strong and consistent tendency to rise or fall with income, but crimes of violence do decline consistently with rising levels of annual family income.

SUMMARY

In this chapter, we have examined the relationship of crime and delinquency to each of four social characteristics: sex, age, race, and class.

In recent years, some kinds of juvenile delinquency have become more common among girls, but boys still outnumber girls in arrests. There is differential treatment of the sexes in the juvenile justice system, with girls less likely than boys to be processed formally if they commit acts that would be crimes when committed by adults, and girls more likely than boys to be processed formally if they commit status offenses such as running away from home.

Over the last two decades, there have been some small changes in the relative proportion of males and females arrested for index crimes, but only for larceny has the proportion of female suspects increased significantly. This may be because store detectives and the police have become more likely to treat female thieves formally rather than releasing them with a warning, or because merchandising changes have made theft easier for women who shop, or because women have actually become more likely to steal. Feminism has not had a demonstrable impact on crime by women, and increased participation in the labor force by women seems to have had less of an effect on crime rates than we might expect. Cross-cultural data indicate that males and females are more alike in their involvement in crime in economically advanced societies than they are in developing societies, but even in advanced societies males commit much more crime than females. Males are victimized more than females by violent crime, except for rape, and by personal larceny without contact.

In the United States, most people who commit index offenses are relatively young. Age-specific arrest rates show the age at which the greatest number of suspects are arrested, and also show changes over time in the arrest rates of people of the same age. Changes in the age distribution of a population over time can increase a society's overall crime rate, even if age-specific crime rates do not change. In general, victimization rates are higher for younger people than they are for older people, but the elderly may have a high victimization rate if we take into account their limited exposure to the risk of victimization.

Black Americans are arrested in numbers disproportionate to their numbers in the population, and this is more true for violent crimes than for property crimes. Arrest data seem to reflect a real difference between blacks and whites in their perpetration of index offenses, rather than police bias in the arrest of suspects of different racial groups. Self-report data also indicate that blacks are more likely than whites to commit serious offenses, but some self-report studies find that blacks and whites differ less in the rates at which they commit less serious crimes. Comparing blacks and whites of similar social backgrounds often reduces the difference in their crime rates, but several studies have found that blacks have higher rates of involvement in crime even when people of the same backgrounds are compared. Blacks are more likely than whites to be the victims of violent crimes; blacks are also more likely to be the victims of most property crimes, even though they have a lower average income than whites.

The relationship between class and violation of the law is complex. In general, official arrest statistics show that lower-class adults commit more crimes than do middle-class adults; the few self-report studies of adults find a similar but weaker association between class and crime. Most studies of juvenile delinquency find an inverse relationship between official measures of delinquency and class, but in some studies the relationship is not strong. Self-report studies of delinquency are mixed in their conclusions: Some show an inverse relationship between class and delinquency, and others find no relationship. Methodological problems with self-report studies make it difficult to unravel the exact relationship between class and violation of the law, especially among adolescents. There are mixed relationships between family income and victimization rates for property crimes, but crimes of violence are least common among people with higher incomes.

IMPORTANT TERMS

age-specific arrest rate   class

SUGGESTED READINGS

JOHN BRAITHWAITE. *Inequality, Crime, and Public Policy*. London: Routledge and Kegan Paul, 1979. An examination of the relationship among crime, class, and slums that considers the possible impact of policies to redistribute wealth and power and policies to reduce the residential segregation of classes.

ROLAND CHILTON AND JIM GALVIN, EDS. "Special Issue: Race, Crime, and Criminal Justice," *Crime and Delinquency* 31 (January 1985). A collection that includes several papers on race and violent crime.

JOANN GENNARO GORA, *The New Female Criminal: Empirical Reality or Social Myth?* New York: Praeger, 1982. A study of changing female crime rates and the impact of the women's movement on them, with a consideration of the implications of the findings for criminological theories.

EILEEN B. LEONARD. *Women, Crime, and Society: A Critique of Criminology Theory.* New York: Longman, 1982. A critical assessment of theories of crime that concludes that they fail to explain female crime.

THREE

THE CAUSES OF CRIMINAL BEHAVIOR

Chapter 7 examines biological and psychological explanations of criminal behavior. We look at recent biological research on twins, adopted children, chromosomal abnormalities, and brain functioning that suggests that inherited factors may interact with psychological and social factors to cause crime. We also investigate research by psychologists on the link between intelligence and crime, the personality traits associated with criminal behavior, the psychoanalytic perspective, and conditioning theory. Rules determining criminal responsibility, including the recent debate over revision of the insanity defense, are also discussed.

Chapter 8 focuses on the socioeconomic causes of crime. Aspects of the economy and characteristics of corporations that are conducive to white-collar crime are investigated. Sources of income for organized crime are examined. In looking at conventional crime, we consider the impact of modernization, the relationship between unemployment and crime, and the way that a sense of being deprived can motivate people to violate the law. We look at several theories of delinquency: anomie, differential opportunity, reaction-formation, and lower-class culture as a generating milieu of delinquency. We also consider the subculture-of-violence theory.

The ways that offenders neutralize the law and are free to violate it because of their weak attachments to conventional institutions are considered in Chapter 9. Techniques that people use to neutralize the hold that the law has over them are considered for embezzlement, crime by blacks, murder, and juvenile delinquency. Control theory is discussed, and evidence for this theory is assessed by looking at research on the family, the school, the peer group, religion, and migration.

Chapter 10 focuses on sources of learning to commit crime: the community, delinquent gangs and peer groups, the general culture, the mass media, pornography, and correctional institutions. This chapter presents differential association theory, and considers evidence for that theory from studies of white-collar crime, juvenile delinquency, and professional theft. This chapter also considers the labeling perspective, which proposes that crime and delinquency are the result of the effects of labeling on self-concepts, social opportunities and relationships, and membership in subcultures. Operant conditioning theory and the economist's model of criminal behavior are also examined, with attention given to the way that offenders consider the risks and rewards of crime.

In Chapter 11 we explore opportunities to commit crime and the way that criminal activity is organized. We look at the way that crime is linked to the routine activities in which people engage, and at the way that offenders choose their targets. We examine relationships between offenders and victims, one aspect of the opportunity for crimes of violence. We look at the relationship between crime and facilitating factors such as alcohol, drugs, and firearms. Finally, we explore the way that offenders plan their crimes, and the way that their activities are organized.

The cumulation of acts of crime into criminal careers is the subject of Chapter 12. Here we consider delinquent careers and the career patterns of adult offenders. We also look at the way that career criminals eventually leave a life of crime for a conventional life.

7

Biological and Psychological Causes of Crime

Modern criminology began with the positivist approach of an Italian physician, Cesare Lombroso. His theories of crime causation have since been found deficient, but his emphasis on the collection of data to test hypotheses about criminals became the basis of modern criminology. Much criminological research is now conducted by sociologists, but biological and psychological approaches to the study of crime causation have been important in the past and continue to be so today.

BIOLOGICAL EXPLANATIONS OF CRIME

Biological explanations of crime propose that offenders differ from nonoffenders in some physiological or anatomical way. The idea of a biologically unique criminal minimizes the role in crime causation of social conditions such as poverty and unemployment, and instead attributes crime to individual differences. One example of a biological explanation of criminal behavior can be seen in the movie *Frankenstein*, in which the monster apparently becomes destructive because Dr. Frankenstein's assistant stole an "abnormal" brain rather than a "normal" one to transplant into a corpse.

Over the past two centuries, deviance in general and crime in particular have been seen increasingly in medical terms, being redefined over time as "sick" rather than "bad" behavior (Conrad and Schneider, 1980). This "medicalization" of deviance has given rise to an emphasis on rehabilitation, and has led to a search for individual traits rather than social factors that will explain rule-breaking behavior. Some deviance—for instance, hyperactivity in children—has been explained in terms of biological factors, but the influence of the medical establishment has operated primarily through psychiatry, a branch of medicine that more often emphasizes psychological process than biological factors. The medicalization of deviance in modern society means that we must look carefully at biological and psychological theories of crime, for those theories have played an important part in determining how the criminal justice system responds to criminals.

History of the Biological Perspective on Crime

The biological perspective can be traced to about 1750, but this perspective was most dominant at the end of the nineteenth century and the beginning of the twentieth. With the rise of modern psychology and psychiatry in the early twentieth century, the biological perspective lost influence in criminology, but important work continues to be done by biological researchers.

PHYSIOGNOMISTS AND PHRENOLOGISTS

Between 1750 and 1850, physiognomists and phrenologists tried to show links between criminal behavior and biological factors (Vold, 1979). Physiognomists studied facial features and tried to show a correlation between criminal behavior and characteristics such as the shape of the ears or the eyes. Phrenologists stressed the relationship between the external shape of the skull and an individual's propensity to engage in crime. They thought that studying the shape of the skull would allow them to tell which areas of a person's brain would dominate behavior and possibly lead to crime. Modern research indicates that certain areas of the brain do control particular types of behavior, and that stimulating certain parts of the brain can incite violence, which in turn may be socially defined as crime. However, phrenologists failed to understand the complexity of the brain, and did not demonstrate any relationship between skull shape, behavioral control centers in the brain, and criminal behavior. Both phrenologists and physiognomists failed to test their theories in a methodologically sound way, but they did draw attention to the possibility that offenders and nonoffenders might differ in measurable ways.

LOMBROSO'S THEORY OF THE ATAVISM

Cesare Lombroso explored what he thought were the physically distinct features of criminals. After examining the skull of a notorious Italian criminal, he observed:

> At the sight of that skull, I seemed to see all of a sudden, lighted up as a vast plain under a flaming sky, the problem of the nature of the criminal—an atavistic being who reproduces in his person the ferocious instincts of primitive humanity and the inferior animals. Thus were explained anatomically the enormous jaws, high cheek bones, prominent superciliary arches, solitary lines in the palms, extreme size of the orbits, handle-shaped or sensile ears found in criminals, savages and apes, insensibility to pain, extremely acute sight, tattooing, excessive idleness, love of orgies, and the irresistible craving of evil for its own sake, the desire not only to extinguish life in the victim, but to mutilate the corpse, tear its flesh and drink its blood (cited in Taylor, Walton, and Young, 1973: 41).

Lombroso theorized that criminals were *atavisms,* people "born out of time" who were similar to primitive people or lower animals in their biological makeup (Ferrero, 1911). This theory owed much to the influence of Darwinism at the end of the nineteenth century, but the idea that people reverted to an earlier stage of evolutionary development was not widely accepted even then.

Lombroso also erred in his ideas about what features could be inherited. For example, the tattoos that he said were characteristic of criminals were obviously not inherited. Some of the features that he thought were typical of offenders may have been the product of both inheritance and diet, with the latter being a function of income, education, and other social factors.

Lombroso made several important mistakes in testing his theory. He failed to select in a careful way a control group from the general population with which to compare criminals. In addition, many of the differences between criminals and noncriminals that he documented were small enough to have occurred by chance.

Lombroso's most important contribution to modern criminology was his application of measurement and the testing of hypotheses. As a result of this positivist method, his ideas on crime causation underwent revision, and he increasingly took social and environmental factors into account. In the final edition of his textbook on the criminal offender, Lombroso suggested that born criminals might account for as few as one-third of all offenders. Other types were insane criminals and occasional offenders who were the products of a poor social environment. Nevertheless, the born offender remained at the center of Lombroso's work, and he never did systematic research on the social causes of criminal behavior.

POST-LOMBROSIAN RESEARCHERS: GORING AND HOOTON

Several researchers built on Lombroso's ideas. The Englishman Charles Goring (1870–1919) sought to test Lombroso's theory that offenders had certain physical defects or anomalies. Goring found no significant differences between offenders and groups from the general population in skull shape, eye color, hair color, or various other physical traits. He did find what he thought was a real difference in height and weight, with offenders being shorter and lighter than nonoffenders. Still, Goring (1913: 173) concluded that "there is no such thing as a physical criminal type."

Ernest Hooton, an American anthropologist who worked on crime causation during the 1930s, criticized Goring's research. Hooton (1939) contended that criminals were the products of environmental influences on organically inferior people. However, he failed to provide a clear meaning for the idea of physical inferiority or the way that it might lead to criminal behavior. He offered no satisfactory evidence that "physical inferiority" was inherited rather than acquired. Moreover, Hooton's research contained important methodological problems; for instance, he did not compare offenders with a carefully chosen and random sample of nonoffenders.

SHELDON'S THEORY OF SOMATOTYPES

One biological theory that relies on psychological traits is William Sheldon's theory of *somatotypes* or body types. This theory focuses on differences among individuals in embryonic development, and claims that people with different body types have different temperaments that affect their propensity to engage in crime and delinquency.

Sheldon, an American psychologist and physician, developed a rating scheme to classify bodies as one of three basic types. One study found that endomorphs, who are slow, "soft," and comfort-loving, exhibited no particular tendency to be delinquent, nor did ectomorphs, who are described as lean and fragile. However, mesomorphs, described as muscular, active, and aggressive, were twice as common among delinquents as they were among the general population (Glueck and Glueck, 1950, 1956). Nevertheless, a recent review of biological theories of crime concluded that "empirical research has revealed little evidence for the unique temperamental traits that Sheldon ascribed to the three somatotypes" (Pollock, Mednick, and Gabrielli, 1983: 309). There is no strong support for Sheldon's contention that specific combinations of body types and temperaments determine whether people will violate the law.

Modern Biological Research on Crime

Since the end of World War II, biologists have used various strategies to test for the possible impact on crime and delinquency of physical traits and inherited characteristics. Some of this research points to explanations of crime and delinquency that might fit with learning theories developed by psychologists and sociologists.

TWIN STUDIES

One potentially rewarding approach to the study of biological influences on criminal behavior is the study of twins. Identical twins develop from a single female egg and have no hereditary differences. Fraternal twins develop from two eggs and do have hereditary differences. Researchers can thus look at the relative impact on crime of heredity and environment by comparing the criminality of identical twins with the criminality of fraternal twins of the same sex. Evidence for genetic factors would take the form of a higher *concordance rate*, or similarity of criminal behavior, between identical twins than between fraternal twins.

The results of studies done in the United States, Japan, and Europe between 1929 and 1962 are consistent with the idea that inherited factors influence criminal behavior. The concordance rates for identical twins were between 60 and 70 per cent in these studies, but the concordance rates for fraternal twins were only 15 to 20 per cent. However, because of methodological problems with these studies, they exaggerated the importance of genetics (Pollock, Mednick, and Gabrielli, 1983).

In what is perhaps the best twin study to date, Karl O. Christiansen (1974, 1977) examined all 3,586 twin pairs born in one area of Denmark between 1881 and 1910. He found that if one identical twin had a criminal conviction, the other twin also had a conviction in 35 per cent of the cases. The rate of concordance was only 12 per cent for fraternal twins. Similar results were produced from a study of twins in Norway (Dalgaard and Kringlen, 1976). Both studies yielded smaller differences in rates of concordance between identical twins and fraternal twins than early researchers had found; this was probably due to the poor methodology of the older studies. Still, the recent research provides some evidence that is consistent with the role of inherited traits in the causation of crime.

Even this recent research does not prove beyond any doubt that genetic factors play an important role in the causation of crime. Identical twins are more alike biologically than fraternal twins, and recent researchers acknowledge that because identical twins look more like each other, they are probably more likely than fraternal twins to have similar environments when young and to receive similar treatment by parents, relatives, peers, and teachers. As a result, we would expect identical twins to be socialized in ways that are more alike than is true of fraternal twins.

ADOPTION STUDIES

An ideal method to test the relative importance of biological and environmental influences on crime would be to study identical and fraternal twins who are separated at birth and who never have contact again, and then compare their crime rates as adults. Because this situation is too rare to provide sizeable samples for study, researchers have turned to other approaches. One that is promising is the study of adopted children, who are usually separated from their biological parents at a young age and often never see them again. Researchers have compared the criminality of adoptees with that of their biological parents and their adoptive parents.

A study of all 14,427 adoptions that occurred in Denmark from 1924 to 1947 found that children who had biological parents with criminal convictions had a greater chance of themselves being involved in repetitive property crimes, but they had no greater propensity to engage in violent crimes. Among sons raised by adoptive parents, only 13.5 per cent had a criminal conviction if neither their biological parents nor their adoptive parents had a criminal conviction. If their adoptive parents had been convicted of a crime but their biological parents had not, the proportion of the sons convicted of crime rose slightly to 14.7 per cent. However, if at least one of the biological parents had been convicted of a crime and the adoptive parents had not been, 20 per cent of the sons had a conviction. If both the biological and the adoptive parents had criminal convictions, then 24.5 per cent of the sons also had criminal convictions. Similar results were found for female adoptees. These data are consistent with the idea of a biological influence on criminal behavior, but the researchers did not claim that the data proved that inherited traits cause crime. Instead, they cautiously concluded that inherited traits might lead some people who are raised in certain ways and who live in certain circumstances to become criminal more often than people in the same situation who lack the inherited traits (Mednick and Volavka, 1980; Mednick et al., 1982; Ellis, 1982; Reinhold, 1982b; Pollock, Mednick, and Gabrielli, 1983).

According to one review of adoption studies, the evidence on genetic involvement in crime causation is even stronger than these researchers assert. This review states that the evidence provided by adoption studies approaches the limits of certainty in demonstrating a genetic influence on crime causation, with an adopted person's chance of being convicted of a serious crime more accurately predicted from knowledge of the criminal record of that person's biological parents than from knowledge of the criminal record of that person's adoptive parents. According to this observer,

> to the degree that causal statements can ever be made with finality in science, the adoption studies carried out in the decade just past seem to be making the following, cautiously worded pronouncement about the involvement of genetics in criminal behavior possible: Significant amounts of the observed variation in human tendencies to behave criminally appear to be the result of some genetic factors, presumably operating on the functioning of the nervous system (at least for the variations observed in criminal behavior other than describable as victimless and status offenses) (Ellis, 1982: 57).

THE XYY CHROMOSOME

The possibility that abnormalities in the sex-determining chromosome could account for crime received much attention during the 1960s. There are twenty-three pairs of chromosomes in humans, one of which is the sex chromosome pair. The female usually has an XX pair, and the male normally has an XY pair. Beginning with the discovery of an *XYY chromosome* complement in some men in 1961, several unusual combinations have been found. During the 1960s there was speculation in the press and by some criminologists that men with the XYY pair might be especially prone to aggressive and violent crime. This idea apparently reflected the assumption that if the Y chromosome in the sex-determining pair makes a person a male, an extra Y should make that person a "supermale," hence a more violent person than the average male.

A cohort study in Denmark tested 4,139 tall men from a cohort of 31,436 men born in Copenhagen from 1944 to 1947 (Witkin et al., 1976). The reason that only tall men were studied is that earlier research had shown that XYY men are taller than average. This study found only twelve men with an XYY combination. The infrequency of this unusual chromosome complement suggests that even if it is associated with criminal behavior, it could only account for relatively little of the crime that is committed. This Danish study found that 42 per cent of the twelve XYY men had been convicted of at least one crime, compared to only 9 per cent of the XY group. In spite of the small number of men with the XYY combination, this difference was statistically significant; that is, the difference was very unlikely to have occurred by chance. However, the crimes for which the XYY men were convicted were not violent ones; there was no meaningful difference between the XYYs and the XYs in convictions for violent offenses.

The XYY men showed significantly lower levels of intelligence than did the XY men, but both groups had attained similar educational levels. Comparing XYY men with XY men of similar intelligence, educational attainment, height, and social status, the researchers found that the XYY group was still more likely to have a criminal record. The researchers concluded that the XYY chromosomal combination does not seem to predispose men to violent crime, but may be tied to a higher-than-average likelihood of being detected for other kinds of crime (Witkin et al., 1976).

A follow-up to this study that used the same data found that differences in intelligence could not fully explain the excess criminality of the XYYs over the XYs. The XYYs were found to have different electroencephalogram (EEG) readings of brain activity, and lower galvanic skin resistance (GSR) readings that measured arousability by noxious stimuli and rate of recovery after arousal (Volavka et al., 1977). In other words, the XYY combination may be linked to nonviolent crime through factors that are associated with brain functioning and the autonomic nervous system.

SEX DIFFERENCES

Earlier we examined differences in crime rates between males and females. The fact that male and female crime rates differ to varying degrees from one society to another suggests that much of the sex difference in crime rates is due to social and cultural factors. However, some of the difference could be the result of biological differences between the sexes.

One review of sex differences in aggressiveness cites developmental studies that show that children under six do not seem to imitate the behavior of same-sexed adults (Maccoby and Jacklin, 1980; Mednick et al., 1982). However, most studies of children under six reveal that boys are significantly more aggressive than girls; none of those studies shows more aggressiveness among girls. The data thus "suggest strongly that greater male aggressiveness is present in children before social learning can explain it. It is a likely hypothesis that greater aggressiveness in males is related to their higher levels of male sex hormones" (Mednick et al., 1982: 30). There is, however, little direct proof that male-female differences in aggressiveness are caused primarily by differences in sex hormones. Moreover, an association between sex hormones and aggressiveness would not constitute proof that sex hormones cause crime and delinquency, for aggressiveness can take many forms other than violation of the law.

There is some evidence that levels of the male sex hormone testosterone may be associated with differences in aggressiveness, and even assaultive crime, among men. Some data indicate that plasma testosterone levels are correlated with self-reported physical and verbal aggression. Some research on samples of prisoners shows that plasma testosterone levels are higher among offenders who have committed violent crimes than among those incarcerated for nonviolent crimes; one study found that rapists who are more violent have higher plasma testosterone levels than less violent rapists. Experiments that have administered psychological tests, which supposedly measure aggressivity or hostility, to prisoners and to nonprisoner control subjects have reached contradictory conclusions about whether testosterone levels are associated with aggressiveness or hostility (Mednick and Volavka, 1980: 134–135; Mednick et al., 1982: 30–31).

There are a few studies that suggest that crime committed by women is more likely to occur in the four premenstrual days and the four days of menstruation than it is to occur at other times during the menstrual cycle (Shah and Roth, 1974). In recent years, attention has been paid to *premenstrual syndrome* (*PMS*), a set of symptoms that includes tension, nervousness, irritability, fatigue, headaches, cramps, and depressed moods. PMS does not manifest itself in the same way in all women who suffer from it, and some doubt that it is a single condition. Even though PMS has been introduced in British courts as a factor to mitigate the sentences of some female offenders, as we see in the Cross-Cultural Perspective, the evidence for its association with crime is still

---

A Cross-Cultural Perspective: Premenstrual Syndrome and Criminal Behavior in England

In 1981, Sandie Smith, a twenty-nine-year-old English barmaid, was sentenced to three years on probation for threatening to murder a police officer with a knife. Previously, she had been convicted of almost thirty other offenses, including arson and assault, and she was already on probation for killing a woman when she threatened the police officer.

Also in 1981, Christine English, a thirty-seven-year-old English woman, was conditionally discharged for one year after pleading guilty to "manslaughter by reason of diminished responsibility." Originally, she had been charged with murder for killing her lover with her car after an argument.

In each of these cases, the defendant's punishment was reduced because she successfully claimed that premenstrual syndrome (PMS) had caused her to commit the crime. According to Ms. Smith's defense attorney, all of her crimes coincided with her premenstrual phases, which caused her to become "a raging animal" every month unless she receive hormone treatments. Ms. English's lawyer claimed that at the time she ran her lover down with her car, she was experiencing "an extremely aggravated form of premenstrual physical condition" that she had suffered from for years.

British judges have thus used PMS as a mitigating factor in sentencing women, and some observers believe that PMS may even become grounds for acquittal in the future. However, there has been much debate in England about the use of PMS as a legal defense. The syndrome is difficult to define precisely. There is doubt about how accurately the hormonal changes that accompany the menstrual cycle have been measured in cases that have come before the courts. Moreover, it is often difficult or impossible to separate the effects of hormonal change from the effects of individual personality or social circumstances. One doctor who has studied the association between premenstrual symptoms and mental health in more than five hundred women doubts that PMS is a cause of aggressive behavior. Another physician who has treated women for PMS for years has claimed in court that some women become seriously mentally disturbed prior to menstruation, and that this problem can be treated with hormones.

SOURCE: Based on "British Legal Debate: Premenstrual Tension and Criminal Behavior," *The New York Times*, December 29, 1981, p. C3.

unclear. Women experiencing PMS may simply be more likely to be arrested for crimes they commit during their premenstrual and menstrual days, perhaps because their reaction time is slower then or because they are more fatigued. Moreover, the changes associated with menstruation do not cause most women to commit crime, and women who do violate the law commit crimes at other times during their menstrual cycles (Shah and Roth, 1974).

BRAIN DYSFUNCTIONS AND LEARNING DISABILITIES

There is some evidence that brain disorders may cause violent outbursts that violate the law. Epileptic seizures may lead to crime through the lack of control over behavior. Most epileptics never commit crime, but there is evidence that the rate of epilepsy is higher among delinquents than among nondelinquents. Many violent offenders seem to have defects in the frontal and temporal lobes of the brain that are associated with impaired self-control. Overall, the evidence on the link between epilepsy and crime is contradictory, and a conclusion that epilepsy is associated with crime is unwarranted at this time (Pollock, Mednick, and Gabrielli, 1983).

Delinquents seem to be more likely than nondelinquents to have minor neurological problems. There is also some evidence that the parents of violent delinquents have more neurological problems than do those of nonviolent delinquents, suggesting the possibility of a genetic factor associated with adolescent violence. Violent delinquency is not inherited behavior, but children may inherit a susceptibility to stress that could lead them to engage in violence in certain situations (Adams, 1979).

Some research also shows that some delinquents and criminals produce abnormal electroencephalogram (EEG) readings of brain activity (Strasburg, 1978; Mednick and Volovka, 1980; Mednick et al., 1981, 1982; Pollock, Mednick, and Gabrielli, 1983). One review of the research literature suggests that the EEGs of criminals may be similar to those of normal people at younger ages, suggesting that antisocial behavior may be associated with, though not necessarily caused by, "brain immaturity" (Mednick et al., 1981, 1982).

There is good evidence that delinquency is associated with *learning disabilities,* which are "impairments in sensory and motor functioning which lead to deviant classroom performance, and are the product of some abnormal physical condition" (Holzman, 1979: 78). The causes of learning disabilities are not well understood, but they seem at least partly rooted in biology. One learning disability is dyslexia, the failure to attain language skills commensurate with intellectual abilities. Another is aphasia, a problem of communicating verbally or understanding others' speech. A third learning disability is hyperactivity, or excessive inattentiveness and restlessness. One study found that hyperactive children were twenty times more likely to become seriously delinquent during adolescence than were children without that disorder, and that upper-class children who were hyperactive were as likely to be arrested as lower-class children who were hyperactive (James H. Satterfield, cited in *The Boston Globe,* November 26, 1982).

Some people may be more biologically predisposed than others to crime and delinquency, although many people who are predisposed that way still learn to conform to the law. Brain disorders and learning disabilities can predispose individuals to violence, but these problems can also lead to rejection and stigmatization of people who seem unintelligent or unable to function socially. This rejection by itself may be conducive to violation of the law. Brain disorders and learning disabilities may be reflected in poor academic performance and rejection by teachers, both of which may be conducive to delinquency. Thus brain disorders and learning disabilities may directly lead to delinquency and crime, or they may increase the likelihood of delinquency and crime indirectly by leading to social rejection or academic failure.

Biology and Modern Criminology

There are several reasons that modern criminologists have paid little attention to biological explanations of crime and delinquency. One is that relatively little research on crime and delinquency has been done by biologists and medical researchers. Another reason is that the poor quality of much early research and the political abuse of the biological approach in Nazi Germany have made biological perspectives on crime suspect in the eyes of many criminologists. As a result, many criminologists have prematurely dismissed biological theories of crime, and have reacted negatively to theories that attribute criminal behavior to inherited traits.

Many criminologists seem to react hostilely to the biological perspective on crime because that perspective is viewed as a threat to the ideology of welfare liberalism and social change to which they adhere. Heredity appears unchangeable, and thus a theory that stresses biological causes of crime seems to imply that efforts to reduce crime through social change are misguided.

Another reason that criminologists have paid little attention to biological research in recent years is that this work does not seem to explain geographic, temporal, and social variations in crime rates. Biological explanations do not help us to understand why crime rates vary from one nation to another, from one region to another, or among communities of different sizes. Likewise, biological theories do not seem to explain changes in crime rates over time, for there is no evidence that increases and decreases in crime rates are associated with changes in biological factors. Biological explanations are also not of much help in making sense of variations in crime rates by sex, age, race, or class. Biological factors might account for some of the difference between the sexes in crimes of violence, but they do not seem to explain differences in property crimes. Biological research has not yet offered a good explanation of why crime rates peak in the late teens and earlier twenties, and then decline with age. There is also no evidence that biological differences among racial groups explain differences in crime rates among those groups; racial groups are socially defined categories rather than biologically distinguishable groupings. Finally, there seems to be no way for biological explanations to account for class differences in crime rates, for the factors on which biological researchers have focused are not associated with class standing in any obvious way.

Modern biological researchers do not dismiss nonbiological explanations of crime and delinquency, nor do they claim that all criminals and delinquents have physiological or anatomical disorders that cause them to violate the law. Indeed, biological criminologists often go only so far as to say that some physical factors are associated with a propensity to crime and delinquency, not that such factors cause people to violate the law. Thus, genetic factors are usually seen as interacting with the familial and social environment to increase the probability that a person will violate the law, rather than seen as operating alone to cause crime and delinquency (Adams, 1979; Mednick and Volavka, 1980; Rowe and Osgood, 1984).

One criticism of biological work on crime is that inherited traits are specific in nature, but crime is a very broad concept. Thus, for biological researchers to make progress in their search for the causes of crime, they must focus on links between specific inheritable traits and specific kinds of criminal behavior. In a sense, there cannot be an inherited predisposition to violate a socially created law, but it is possible that certain inherited predispositions may be linked to behavior such as violence that is likely to be defined as crime.

Inherited traits can create a "range of potential" for behavior, even if they do not determine behavior; in other words, biological factors may limit the kind of behavior a person will engage in, even if the constraints are very broad. Often biological factors interact with social and environmental influences to make certain behavior more likely, as we can see from the following example from research on monkeys:

> It has been demonstrated that aggressive behavior can be evoked in free-ranging monkeys by stimulation of implanted intracerebral electrodes. However, such stimulation produces differing results depending upon the hierarchical structure of the monkey colony. Monkeys exhibit aggressive behavior with this stimulation when a submissive monkey is present as a target, but such responses are inhibited (despite the brain stimulation) in the presence of a dominant animal (Shah and Roth, 1974: 106).

Research on humans suggests that the hierarchical structure of social relationships may influence an individual's propensity to homicide, but this research did not look at biological predispositions that might interact with the social context to produce violent behavior (Henry and Short, 1954).

A few criminologists have worked to develop an interdisciplinary approach to the study of crime and delinquency (Jeffery, 1979; Mednick and Volovka, 1980; Ellis, 1982), but more work on the interaction of biological, psychological, and social factors is needed. One effort to link genetic and environmental factors in the study of crime causation proposes the model in Figure 7.1. This approach suggests that only neurochemical factors control behavior directly, and that they are influenced both by genetics and by environment. Behavior then affects the environment in which the individual lives, and this in turn influences behavior in a feedback loop, within certain genetic constraints (Ellis, 1982).

PSYCHOLOGICAL EXPLANATIONS OF CRIME

The once popular view that the criminal is biologically different has been replaced during the twentieth century with the idea that the criminal is somehow psychologically abnormal. This view that offenders are "crazy" or "unbalanced" underlies the philosophy of rehabilitation that leads to the counseling of offenders by psychiatrists, psychologists, and social workers. The logic of this approach is that because only certain individuals commit crimes, something must distinguish them from those who do not break the law.

Mental Deficiency Theory

The mental deficiency theory of crime maintains that the offender either lacks the intelligence to appreciate the reasons for the existence of the law and thus violates it, or is unable to control his or her actions even if aware of the law. Nonoffenders are seen as intelligent enough to understand the law and control their actions.

Figure 7.1: A Model of Crime Causation

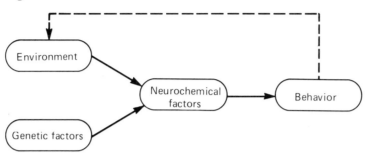

SOURCE: Lee Ellis, "Genetics and Criminal Behavior: Evidence through the End of the 1970s," *Criminology* 20 (May 1982), 44. Reprinted by permission.

IQ AND CRIME

Intelligence, which is usually measured by IQ (intelligence quotient) tests, has been linked to crime and delinquency by many researchers. Sometimes they claim that intelligence is inherited, but most modern researchers do not claim that intelligence is solely biological in origin. IQ tests have repeatedly been shown to contain cultural biases, in spite of efforts to develop unbiased tests. For instance, whites may average somewhat higher scores on IQ tests than do blacks because those tests reflect the cultural biases of the whites who design the tests. As a result of such problems, critics claim that IQ tests measure social learning rather than native intelligence (Gartner, Greer, and Reissman, 1973). The inadequacy of IQ tests is one reason to look at research on the link between intelligence and criminality with some skepticism.

Another reason for some skepticism is the inadequate research design that some of these studies employ. For example, some researchers have administered IQ tests to prisoners and then compared the prisoners' IQs with those of a group from the general population. Thus, a survey conducted in 1982 found that mentally retarded people—those with very low intelligence levels—constituted between 9 and 30 per cent of the prison inmates in different states, with an overall percentage closer to 9 per cent. If 9 per cent of inmates were retarded, this would be about three times the rate at which retarded people are found in the general population (*The New York Times*, June 14, 1982). Research that compares inmates' IQs with those of the general population encounters several methodological problems. First, prisoners are not necessarily representative of all people who violate the law; for instance, prisoners may be the least competent of all offenders. Thus, researchers are often comparing *prisoners* with the general population, not *criminals* with the general population. Second, the "general population" to which the prisoners are compared probably includes many people who have violated the law but who were not in prison at the time of the study. As a result, researchers often end up comparing those offenders who are imprisoned with a sample of the general population that is not in prison but includes some offenders. Such a research design does not allow us to say much about what distinguishes criminals from noncriminals. A better approach would be to administer IQ tests to a randomly chosen cross section of the nation's population (including prisoners), gather evidence on that sample's involvement in crime from official arrest records and self-report questionnaires, and then examine the relationship between IQ and both officially recorded and self-reported crime.

Evidence on IQ and crime   One study that employed a good research design to study the relationship between intelligence and delinquency concluded that if boys of the same class are compared, delinquents generally have lower IQs than nondelinquents. In other words, a lower-class delinquent usually has a lower IQ than a lower-class nondelinquent, and a middle-class delinquent generally has a lower IQ than a middle-class nondelinquent (Reiss and Rhodes, 1961). This study also found that lower-class boys are more likely to be delinquent than middle-class boys of the same level of intelligence. Thus, class affects delinquency (whether measured by self-reports or court records), and intelligence as measured by standardized IQ tests is also related to delinquency.

Wolfgang, Figlio, and Sellin's (1972) cohort study also looked at IQ, class, and delinquency. The researchers found that the average IQ of boys who had been stopped by the police was 101, compared to an average of 108 for boys who had not been stopped. Table 7.1 shows the average IQ scores of black and white delinquents and nondelinquents from different classes. This table indicates that the largest IQ differences are between white and black boys of the same class and delinquency status; differences by race range from eight to eleven points. IQ differences by class range from three to five points. IQ differences are three to five points lower for delinquents than for nondelinquents of the same race and class. There is thus a small but consistent tendency for IQ and delinquency to be associated with each other.

Table 7.1:   IQ, Class, and Race of a Cohort of Boys

	AVERAGE IQ SCORE	
	Lower Class	*Higher Class*
White nondelinquents	107	111
Black nondelinquents	97	100
White delinquents	102	107
Black delinquents	94	97

SOURCE: Marvin E. Wolfgang, Robert M. Figlio, and Thorsten Sellin, *Delinquency in a Birth Cohort*. Chicago: University of Chicago Press, 1972, p. 62. Reprinted by permission of the University of Chicago Press. Copyright University of Chicago Press © 1972.

An English cohort study confirmed Wolfgang, Figlio, and Sellin's results. In the English study, boys who were to become delinquent as teen-agers scored an average of 95 on IQ tests at ages eight and ten, and boys who did not become delinquent during their teen years scored an average of 101 at ages eight and ten. This difference of six points, combined with the finding that there was a higher proportion of the future delinquents among those who scored the lowest on the IQ test, showed that performance on IQ tests at a young age is a strong predictor of future delinquency (West, 1982).

Hirschi and Hindelang (1977) reach similar conclusions about the relationship between IQ and delinquency from their systematic review of the research literature. They claim that sociologists regularly deny individual differences between criminals and noncriminals because "kinds of people" theories are seen as nonsociological. They show that criminology textbooks either ignore or argue against the role of intelligence in the genesis of crime and delinquency. They go on to document a small but consistent and reliable difference of about nine points between the IQs of delinquents and the IQs of nondelinquents. Evidence for this difference comes from studies carried out in diverse settings using different IQ tests and controlling for race and class. Hirschi and Hindelang conclude that IQ is an important correlate of delinquency that seems to be as closely linked to delinquency as race and class. Wolfgang, Figlio, and Sellin's cohort study, on the other hand, found race to be a more important correlate of delinquency than intelligence.

Intelligence is related to delinquency, whether delinquency is measured by self-reports or official statistics. However, the relationship of intelligence and delinquency is weaker in self-report studies than it is in studies that use police or court records, possibly because offenders with lower IQs are arrested more often than offenders with higher intelligence levels. Hirschi and Hindelang report that they know of no recent research that refutes this relationship of IQ test scores and delinquency, a relationship that they claim is not the result of class or cultural biases in IQ tests, the methodological inadequacy of those tests, or the instability of IQ scores over time.

Hirschi and Hindelang state that differences in IQ between delinquents and nondelinquents are consistent with some sociological theories of crime causation. For instance, if intelligence affects school performance and attitudes toward the school and its teachers, lower intelligence may be associated with a lower "stake in conformity," which can increase the chance that an adolescent will engage in delinquent behavior.

Interpreting research on IQ and crime One criticism of the conclusion that delinquency and crime are related to intelligence is that IQ test scores, which supposedly measure native intelligence, are significantly influenced by the social environment. By changing social conditions, IQ test scores can be raised by even more than the nine-point difference that Hirschi and Hindelang found between delinquents and nondelinquents.

Another criticism of the conclusion that intelligence is linked to delinquency and crime is that instead of low intelligence producing trouble in school and thus generating delinquency, it may be that lower-class status is associated with both delinquency and trouble in school, and trouble in school may lead to a failure to learn. This failure to learn might then be reflected in lower IQ scores, which would produce a correlation between class, IQ scores, and delinquency. Lack of motivation to do well in school might also show up in the results of IQ tests, which can be seen as a measure of academic performance rather than of basic intelligence.

A structuralist critique of the evidence linking IQ and delinquency is that this association exists only because of specific responses by institutions such as the school to low levels of intelligence, low IQ test scores, and poor academic performance. Thus,

> the absence of access to desirable social roles plus premature and/or inappropriate negative labeling mutually reinforce one another and lead to alienation, a rejection of the rejectors. Alienation, in turn, leads to delinquent behavior. The behavior generated by institutional structures through opportunity and labeling may then feed back into the institutional structure, generating responses which reinforce that behavior (Menard and Morse, 1984: 1349).

An empirical test of this theory with self-report data revealed that structural variables—access to desirable social roles, negative labeling, alienation, and delinquent peer-group association—explained significant amounts of both serious and nonserious delinquency, and that IQ, academic aptitude, and school performance added very little to the explanation of delinquency. The researchers concluded that IQ is not causally linked to delinquency, but is instead an individual characteristic that institutions may or may not reward. Consequently, it is "the institutional pattern of behavior that (a) is causally related to delinquent behavior and (b) must be altered if the frequency or type of aggregate delinquent behavior is to be reduced or changed" (Menard and Morse, 1984: 1374).

Another problem with determining the relationship between intelligence and violation of the law is that intelligence probably varies considerably among different types of offenders. Embezzlers may well have higher IQ levels than the general population, because they can embezzle funds only if they have attained a position of trust in the business world, and intelligence may play a role in achieving such a position. On the other hand, sex offenders such as child molesters seem to have lower than average IQ levels. Intelligence may influence an individual's social position and thus affect the opportunities that are available for crime. For instance, a retarded person is unlikely to gain access to the economic power necessary to engage in price fixing or false advertising.

Personality Characteristics

Many studies have tried to determine if any personality traits are more common among criminals than among the general population. A 1953 survey of 113 studies concluded that no personality traits were consistently and systematically linked to criminality (Schuessler and Cressey, 1953). Forty-two per cent of the studies that were reviewed showed that the personality traits of offenders differed from those of the general population, but the differences were usually small, of questionable validity, and inconsistent with the results of other research. Studies of this sort might be more likely to reveal personality trait differences if specific types of offenders were compared with the general population. Thus a comparison of embezzlers with the general population might show embezzlers to have certain personality traits, and a comparison of bank robbers with the general population might show that bank robbers differ from the general population in personality traits, and probably differ from embezzlers as well.

Another review of studies of personality traits and criminality found that 81 per cent of the ninety-four studies examined showed a statistically significant difference in personality traits between offenders and control groups (Waldo and Dinitz, 1967). However, the differences were small, even though they were greater than would have occurred by chance fluctuations in sampling. This review concluded that the role of personality in the genesis of criminal behavior remains unclear.

THE CRIMINAL MIND

Researchers have not yet found a "criminal personality," but some psychologists and psychiatrists persist in the search for personalities or personality traits that distinguish criminals from noncriminals. This was the thrust of a study by Samuel Yochelson and Stanton E. Samenow (1976; 1977; Samenow, 1984). In a recent book, Samenow (1984: 5; emphasis added here) declares current thinking about the causes of crime "dead wrong" and makes the following claim:

I shall expose the myths about why criminals commit crimes, and I shall draw a picture for you of *the personality of the criminal* just as the police artist draws a picture of his face from a description. I shall describe how criminals think, how they defend their crimes to others, and how they exploit programs that are developed to help them.

It seems unlikely that all criminals—from the corporate price fixer to the sadistic rapist, from the professional burglar to the desperate addict, and from the organized crime leader to the juvenile shoplifter—would have the same personality, but that is the basis of Yochelson and Samenow's work.

In *The Criminal Personality*, Yochelson and Samenow (1976, 1977) report that in working with criminals they initially found that traditional psychiatric concepts and techniques were ineffective, and so they began a search for evidence on the psychology of the criminal in order to develop a workable treatment program. Their evidence comes from interviews with 255 offenders, many institutionalized in St. Elizabeths Hospital in Washington, D.C., and the rest from referrals by the police or the correctional system. They did not use a control group with which to compare these criminals, and the criminals were not in any sense a representative sample of all offenders, so Yochelson and Samenow's conclusions are based on a methodologically flawed research design.

Yochelson and Samenow claim to have identified "thought patterns" that exist among all offenders, whether blacks from the ghetto or whites from the suburbs, whether grade-school dropouts or college graduates. As a result, they argue that the criminal personality is not the product of socioeconomic or other environmental factors. They identify fifty-two "errors of criminal thinking" that form the criminal personality. Some of the errors of criminal thinking that lead offenders to violate the law include:

• chronic lying,
• a view that other people's property is their own,
• unrelenting optimism,
• great energy,
• fear of injury or being insulted,
• intense anger,
• manipulativeness, and
• an inflexibly high self-image.

Without a control group, however, there is no way to show that these personality traits are more common among criminals than among the general population.

Yochelson and Samenow then sought a way to treat people with this criminal personality. Traditional therapy seemed ineffective because the offenders were manipulative, mimicked psychiatric jargon, and faked insight into their problems. Job training did not work either, according to Samenow, who has said, "I'm all for job training, but if that's all you do, you'll simply have a criminal with job skills. And he'll use those skills to gain entry into new avenues of crime" (cited in Krost, 1982: 8). Yochelson and Samenow developed a technique of confronting offenders with their flaws, subjecting their thoughts and actions to detailed examination, and forcing them to accept responsibility for their behavior. Much like the technique used by Alcoholics Anonymous, their approach was rigid in demanding full conformity to the rules and in being most effective for offenders who had hit "rock bottom" and saw their only options as prison, suicide, or change. By eliminating "criminal thinking" through this "exercise in self-disgust," Yochelson and Samenow hoped to create a morally responsible person.

Did their approach work? Samenow reports that of the 255 interviewed offenders, only thirty completed the 500 hours of therapy that the program required. Of the thirty, twenty showed improvement, although precise measures of their improvement are not provided. The kind of evidence offered by Yochelson and Samenow cannot tell us whether their method works. The twenty offenders who completed treatment may have changed even without the program. They are only a small part of the initial group of offenders, and may not even be representative of that group, much less of all criminals in society. Even a success rate of 67 per cent (twenty out of thirty) may be no better than would have been produced by an untreated control group over the same period.

THE PERSONALITIES OF RAPISTS

One problem with studying the personality of the criminal is that different kinds of crime may be committed by people with very different personalities. Moreover, the same crime may be committed by people with several types of personalities. For instance, a clinical study of rapists concluded that there were three psychodynamic patterns among rapists. The most common were "power rapists," who wanted to possess the victim sexually rather than harm her, and who used sexuality to express mastery and control. Next most common were "anger rapists," who discharged their contempt and hostility toward all women through the act of rape; these men often harmed and degraded their victims. The third and least common type was the "sadistic rapist," who eroticized aggression toward the victim and took gratification in her anguish and suffering (Groth, 1979).

Knowing that the perpetrators of a single crime such as rape have very different personalities can be important in developing policies to treat criminals and counsel victims. Different kinds of rapists pose different threats to society, and they may respond to different kinds of treatment. Victims who are raped by different kinds of offenders may have quite different experiences, and counseling them may thus have to take different forms. In addition, advice to women about how to react to a rapist at the time of the crime—for instance, "resist at all costs" or "comply with the offender's demands"—often assumes a single kind of rapist, and knowledge of the different personalities of rapists might make advice-givers more cautious. For instance, resisting a sadistic rapist could lead to murder, but resisting a power rapist might prevent the crime.

AGGRESSIVENESS AND CRIME

One personality trait sometimes associated with crime and delinquency is the inability to tolerate frustrating situations without resorting to aggression and violence. Frustration that arises from not being able to achieve a goal may lead to aggression that sometimes takes the form of crime, either against the frustrating object or against another object (displaced aggression). There is some evidence that children who are the most assertive, daring, prone to fight, quick to anger, and resistant to discipline are also the most likely to violate the law later in life (Radzinowicz and King, 1977: 89). One study that found a link between childhood aggressiveness and adult crime discovered that eight-year-old boys who were rated highly aggressive by their parents and friends had committed much more crime than their peers by the age of thirty. Aggressive girls did not develop into criminals as adults any more often than nonaggressive girls did (Leonard Eron, cited in *The Boston Globe*, August 28, 1983).

Few psychologists today believe that aggression follows directly and simply from frustration, and even when frustrated people become aggressive they may channel their aggression into acceptable activities such as athletic or academic competition rather than engage in crime. Most psychologists consider a host of variables that are conducive to aggressive acts. They focus primarily on "nonbiological intraindividual determinants" of aggression while acknowledging other influences (Megargee, 1982: 82). One psychologist (Megargee, 1982) identifies the following determinants of whether an individual will respond aggressively to a situation:

1. Instigation to aggression: the total of all internal factors motivating the person to commit an aggressive or violent act;
2. Habit strength: learned preferences for the use of aggressive behavior in a particular situation;
3. Inhibitions against aggression: learned preferences to avoid aggression against a certain target;
4. Stimulus factors: environmental influences facilitating or impeding aggressive behavior; and
5. Competition: making a choice among several responses to the situation so that the individual's needs are met in the best way.

Even a model as complex as this does not incorporate influences on aggressive behavior such as genetic predisposition, endochrinological balance, the availability of weapons, differences in political power and economic resources, and many situational factors. Psychologists, biologists, and social scientists who have studied aggression in recent years have recognized that the causes of aggression and violence are very complex, even though they generally focus their attention on one set of variables.

THE PSYCHOPATHIC PERSONALITY

The psychopathic personality is a hypothesized cluster of personality traits thought to lead to criminal behavior. A *psychopath* (or sociopath) is an asocial, aggressive, and highly impulsive person who feels little or no guilt for antisocial activity and who cannot form lasting bonds of affection with others. Psychopaths are asocial in the same way as infants: They have not learned to control their desires and impulses. Psychopaths show poor judgment, do not learn easily from experience, are uncooperative, and are not easily influenced by social demands. They are narcissistic and interested only in the gratification of their immediate impulses. They seek pleasure, variety, and excitement rather than security and stability. Because of their impulsiveness, psychopaths' crimes seem purposeless to others. Because they are present-oriented, they rarely plan their crimes in much detail. When frustrated, they become furious and aggressive, and are unable to sublimate or rechannel their impulses. They feel little anxiety or remorse after hurting other people. Psychoanalysts have described psychopaths as loners with a warped capacity for love, and as cold and compassionless people who treat others as a means to their goal of personal pleasure (McCord and McCord, 1964; Cleckley, 1964; McCord, 1983).

One estimate is that 2 to 5 per cent of the noncriminal population can be described as psychopaths, and that about 10 per cent of known offenders fit this category. However, the term "psychopath" has been given many definitions, and studies often disagree on the incidence of this personality type (McCord, 1983).

There is some evidence that psychopaths and normal people respond similarly in learning tasks that are positively rewarded, but that normal people learn well and psychopaths learn poorly those tasks that are negatively reinforced. Psychopaths

> show signs of slower autonomic nervous system responses to punishment, and they differ significantly in pulse and heart rates. In general, research indicates that psychopaths are less fearful of punishment, are less anxious, respond more efficiently to stress, are less mature neurologically (that is, less able to learn from punishment), are more eager for excitement, and have a greater propensity for violence than nonpsychopaths (McCord, 1983: 1315).

Some research indicates that psychopaths are physiologically insensitive, compared to nonpsychopaths. Psychopaths seem less able to learn from physical punishment, and they are less responsive to skin-conductivity stimuli. This may be a result of inherited traits, such as an adrenal gland deficiency in producing or releasing the hormone epinephrine. However, this relative insensitivity to pain could also result from socialization experiences while young or from being abused as a child (Glaser, 1979; McCord, 1983). There is also evidence that psychopaths are especially likely to have brain dysfunctions and neurophysiological dysfunctions, but whether these problems are caused by heredity, accidents, physical abuse, childhood diseases, or environmental factors is unclear (McCord, 1983).

Most psychopaths have a childhood history of rejection, often severe rejection, by at least one parent. Many were institutionalized while young, and their parents frequently had a criminal record or a history of alcoholism, desertion, or neglect. One review of studies on the origins of the psychopathic personality concludes that

> (1) rejection, in combination with damage to such areas of the brain as the hypothalmus, results in psychopathy; and that (2) rejection, in the absence of neural disorder, can result in psychopathy if other influences in the environment (such as a criminal role model, differential association with criminals, or complete neglect) help direct the person in a criminal direction (McCord, 1983: 1316).

A critique of the concept of the psychopath   Some social scientists have criticized the use of the concept of the psychopathic personality to explain criminal behavior. One critic states that the psychopath is "in fact, *par excellence,* and without shame or qualification, the model of the circular process by which mental abnormality is inferred from anti-social behavior while anti-social behavior is explained by mental abnormality" (Wootton, 1959: 250). For instance, let us take an individual who commits a "senseless" mass murder. Because the press and psychologists quoted in the press often have a difficult time explaining the murder, they may say that the killer has a psychopathic personality. They assume this because the murder makes little sense. In other words, they assume that anyone who would do such a thing must be asocial, impulsive, aggressive, and compassionless—characteristics of the psychopathic personality. The murderer might well be a psychopath, but the problem is that this term may be used even if there is no information available about the offender's actual personality. Information about the killer's personality that is independent of the act of murder is needed to assess his or her personality; personality cannot be assumed from the act itself. This does not mean that the concept of the psychopath is useless, but only that the term is sometimes used without direct evidence to label an offender.

Another problem with the concept of the psychopathic personality is that different psychiatrists and psychologists often give quite different meanings to the term. This may be one reason that anywhere from 7 to 26 per cent of different samples of inmates have been classified as psychopaths (McCord, 1983). This variation might be a result of differences in the characteristics of the inmates, but it could also reflect differences among psychiatrists and psychologists in the meaning that they give to the term psychopath. The label might tell us more about the psychiatrist or psychologist classifying the inmate than it does about the inmate who is being classified.

THE VIOLENT CHILD

Recent research has explored the origins of violence in children fifteen and under, focusing particularly on children who kill (Collins, 1982; Nelson, 1983a). One study of homicidal behavior by children between three and twelve included a three-year-old who held a knife to his mother's neck as she slept and a ten-year-old who twice tried to kill his mother. The psychiatrist who did this study found that compared to nonhomicidal children who were also psychiatric patients, the homicidal children were more likely to

- have a history of psychomotor seizures,
- have attempted suicide,
- have fathers who had been violent to their mothers,
- have fathers who had been homicidal, and
- have mothers who had been hospitalized for psychiatric reasons (Collins, 1982).

Other research has found that violent children between thirteen and nineteen typically have psychiatric symptoms and neurological problems; many have been physically abused by their parents, and that is often a cause of their neurological problems.

One study found two kinds of murderers under the age of sixteen. One was the "nonempathic murderer" who did not have the ability to put himself or herself in another person's place. These children had histories of assaultive behavior, did not cope well with stress, and had spent their first year of life with little affection, either in an institution or with a mother who was not nurturing. One fifteen-year-old boy who killed a six-year-old girl said, "I don't know the girl so why should I have any feelings about what happened to her?" (cited in Nelson, 1983a: C8). The second type of child killer was the "sexual-identity conflict murderer." These were boys who carried weapons because they lacked physical confidence, often as a result of being taunted as effeminate. Their mothers were dominant, and their fathers absent or passive. Sometimes their parents actually encouraged them to commit crime. One thirteen-year-old boy who had his face rubbed in the mud by another boy was told by his parents to do whatever was necessary to defend himself. The boy got a large knife and stabbed his tormentor in the heart as his father watched (Nelson, 1983a).

Many, perhaps most, of these children who commit murder can be classified as psychopaths. They have experienced severe rejection by one or both parents while young, and often they have no role model in the home from whom they can learn empathic behavior. The physical abuse that many of these child murderers have suffered can produce brain dysfunctions and neurological problems that are associated with psychopathy.

The Psychoanalytic Perspective

Another psychological approach to crime causation is the *psychoanalytic perspective* developed by Sigmund Freud (1930, 1962; 1933) and August Aichhorn (1935, 1951). Freud proposed three aspects to the personality. The "id" is composed of instincts and drives that need immediate gratification; it characterizes unsocialized and unrestrained individuals. The "superego" is social authority or conscience; it represents parental authority expressed in the individual as a continuing acceptance of cultural norms and values. The "ego" is the mediating force that tries to adjust the id drives with the demands of the superego by rechanneling and sublimating those drives. A state of "balanced conflict" exists among the three elements in healthy and integrated personalities.

The psychoanalytic approach sees people as antisocial by nature. Thus, a newborn baby needs to be socialized to avoid becoming a criminal (Aichhorn, 1935, 1951). All people are thought antisocial by nature, in contrast to Lombroso's view that some people are born criminals and others are born noncriminals. Lombroso, especially in his early work, focused on heredity as a cause of crime in some people, implying that external circumstances had a limited impact on behavior. By contrast, the psychoanalytic position is that external circumstances lead to the socialization of most people, and that those who become criminals do so because of inadequate socialization.

The id-ego-superego framework allows for the possibility of a "socialized criminal" (Aichhorn, 1935, 1951). If the social environment tolerates, supports, or even requires criminal behavior, a person may be socialized into a life of crime (Jenkins, 1955; Russell and Harper, 1973). Psychoanalysts imply that the superego is society's conscience, but in fact various social demands are placed on people. Individuals who are isolated from law-abiding influences and exposed to crime-generating ones may learn to conform to social demands that are contrary to the law.

Part of the socialization process involves the repression of instinctual drives by pushing them back into the unconscious. When these repressed instincts break through, crime may result. In these cases, offenders may not know why they have committed a crime. Some psychoanalysts claim that certain people commit crimes because of guilt developed in childhood. Crime then becomes a way to get the punishment they feel that they deserve in order to atone for forbidden desires. This might be true of offenders who commit crimes carelessly and are easily arrested, but if this theory were generally true, we would expect offenders to be arrested far more often than they now are. Most offenders try to avoid arrest, and some who seem to be careless are probably incompetent or distracted rather than trying to atone for forbidden desires.

NEUROSES AND CRIME

A neurosis is a functional disorder in which a person has some difficulty in coping with everyday life. Neurotics usually seem nervous, inhibited, and over-conforming rather than aggressive, and so their disorders are probably not closely linked to crime (Radzinowicz and King, 1977: 86). Neurosis has also been seen as an alternative to juvenile delinquency rather than a cause of it.

One neurosis that some people have associated with crime is the obsessive-compulsive neurosis, which can lead to certain nonaggressive crimes and to sexual perversions such an exhibitionism and fetishism. This neurosis has also been linked to kleptomania, a compulsive form of stealing sometimes thought to be caused by a desire for sexual excitement rather than financial gain. However, kleptomania seems to be a label that is applied to middle- and upper-class thieves who can afford a psychiatrist. The same behavior by a poor person would probably be labeled larceny. There is little evidence that kleptomania exists as a functional disease that can explain theft. For instance, one study of fifty-six shoplifters found almost no relationship between law-violating behavior and any neurosis or psychosis (Cameron, 1964). Shoplifters were understandably upset about being arrested, but there was no evidence of an obsessive-compulsive neurosis that led to theft. The fact that most shoplifters do not repeat the behavior and the fact that shoplifting increases just before Christmas suggest that this form of theft is usually a way to stretch a budget and provide for material needs, rather than a form of behavior not under the shoplifter's conscious control (Robin, 1963).

PSYCHOSES AND CRIME

A psychosis is a disorder characterized by a lack of contact with reality. Sometimes psychoses involve hallucinations that lead to irrational violence, but not all psychotics are dangerous. Definitions of psychoses are sometimes vague, but probably no more than 5 per cent of all prison and jail inmates are psychotic (Strasburg, 1978: 68). It is not clear what proportion of the general population is psychotic, but if it does not differ much from the proportion of inmates who are psychotic, then psychosis is not associated with crime. Moreover, many prisoners may be psychotic without their particular problem having caused them to violate the law. It is also possible that some prisoners become psychotic as a result of their prison experiences, and so their problem might not have existed prior to their violation of the law.

The psychosis that has most often been linked to criminal behavior is *schizophrenia*, which involves disordered thought patterns characterized by fantasy, delusion, and incoherence. Paranoid schizophrenics have delusions of persecution; they are nervous and sensitive to interpersonal cues, they act and speak primarily with reference to themselves, demand much of loved ones but criticize them for their lack of appreciation, and feel unfairly rejected by others. Schizophrenia is sometimes associated with acts of violence, including homicide, particularly against people who are thought to be threatening to the schizophrenic. One study of ninety-seven boys in a correctional school found that 81.8 per cent of those who had engaged in serious violence such as murder or rape exhibited symptoms of paranoia, and only 16.7 per cent of the less violent boys (who had engaged in fist fights, set fires, or threatened others) showed symptoms of paranoia. The violent boys also exhibited more neurological disorders and were more likely to have been physically abused by their parents (Adams, 1979).

PSYCHOANALYTIC EXPLANATIONS OF ASSASSINATIONS

Psychoanalytic explanations have been offered for political assassinations in the United States. Unlike political murders elsewhere, American assassinations have rarely been motivated by a political goal or been associated with a political group. The one exception among presidential assassinations was the 1950 attempt on the life of President Harry Truman by two Puerto Rican nationalists.

Otherwise, American assassins have been motivated primarily by personal needs, and this has led to psychological explanations for their actions.

One psychiatrist observes that most assassins in the United States have been younger children in their families, and usually they have had older brothers. This situation can lead to rebellion and resentment because of low status in the family. Hatred of a powerful father can become murderous, leading to an attack on the president as an authority figure who symbolizes the father. American assassins thus seem to be striking more at a symbol of authority than at a particular individual who holds certain political views. One psychiatrist sees assassins as paranoics who have lost touch with reality, developed delusions of grandeur and persecution, and hated authority (Donald Hastings, cited in Brody, 1981). Other psychiatrists believe that assassins are characterized by depression and despair over their self-worth; these assassins try to counteract those feelings by creating a new self-image that is worthy of respect and attention through the dramatic act of political murder (Brody, 1981; Freedman, 1981).

A CRITIQUE OF THE PSYCHOANALYTIC PERSPECTIVE

Psychiatrists sometimes disagree about how to classify specific offenders in psychoanalytic terms, in part because those terms are not always precisely defined. Because many of the concepts of the psychoanalytic perspective are difficult to measure, hypotheses about the causes of crime are not easily tested. As a result, there is little systematic research that shows that neuroses and psychoses lead to specific kinds of crime.

Psychoanalytic work on crime often takes the form of case studies of offenders. In these studies, psychiatrists are usually aware that a crime has been committed before they begin to study the patient. Through a process of "biographic reconstruction," psychiatrists "demonstrate" that certain traits and aspects of the patient's background led to the crime. These case studies do not constitute evidence for the psychoanalytic explanation of crime, because psychiatrists might well find a "dormant capacity for delinquency in any normal individual" (Rettig, Torres, and Garrett, 1977: 234).

A study of 257 indicted male defendants found that psychiatrists classified 154 of them as dangerous. There was little difference between the defendants classified as dangerous and those classified as nondangerous in class, past criminal behavior, or past hospitalization in a mental institution. The most important characteristic distinguishing the two groups was the current charge against the defendant, which was known to the psychiatrist before the defendant was questioned. Defendants charged with the most serious crimes were the most likely to be found dangerous by the psychiatrists, although few of the examining psychiatrists gave the current charge against the defendant as the reason for classifying the individual as dangerous. In other words, the psychiatrists seemed to take the crime with which the defendant was charged, classify the defendant as dangerous if it was a serious crime, and then construct an explanation of why that defendant was dangerous (Cocozza and Steadman, 1978).

Until we have evidence on the psychological characteristics of the general population, we cannot know whether criminals differ psychologically from other people. Proponents of the psychoanalytic perspective rarely gather evidence on the psychological state of the general population, because they are usually concerned with doing therapy rather than with testing theories. As a result, many of the ideas of the psychoanalytic perspective on crime remain untested.

Conditioning Theory

According to the British psychologist, Hans Eysenck (1977), people acquire behavior in two ways. One way is through rational learning that involves the central nervous system. People learn to engage in behavior that is pleasurable and rewarding, and they try to avoid behavior that is painful and unrewarding. The sooner the pain or pleasure results from their actions, the more effect that pain or pleasure will have on their future behavior. Thus, if much time elapses between a crime and its punishment, the sanction will have relatively little effect on the offender's future behavior, because the rewards of the crime (such as stolen property) are gained when the crime is committed.

The second way that behavior is acquired is through conditioning, which works by the contiguity of stimuli rather than by reinforcement (the mechanism by which the first kind of learning occurs). This second type, often called *classical conditioning,* is exemplified by Pavlov's famous experiment with dogs that salivated at the sound of a bell; the bell elicited that behavior because it was associated with other stimuli. Eysenck argues that it is this classical conditioning that forms the basis of what we call conscience, the internalized force that leads us to conform to norms and laws. Criminals are thus people whose consciences do not restrain them from violating the law. Their inadequate conditioning may stem from their "low conditionability," something that may be linked to a deficient autonomic nervous system that makes it more difficult to acquire law-abiding behavior.

The effectiveness of conditioning depends on the sensitivity of the autonomic nervous system that a person has inherited (a biological influence) and on the quality of conditioning that a person receives during childhood (a social environmental influence). Some people seem to have physical makeups that allow them to ignore pain and punishment with relative ease (Shah and Roth, 1974; Glaser, 1979; Mednick and Volavka, 1980; McCord, 1983). These individuals seem to recover more slowly when aroused by noxious stimuli and seem to be aroused less easily by such stimulation. Minimal brain dysfunction can also reduce a person's ability to learn from experience (Shah and Roth, 1974). These physiological characteristics affect conditionability; they also seem to be linked to psychopathy. Biological and psychological predispositions can affect the ability to learn from experience, and the inability to be conditioned can lead to crime and delinquency.

A CRITIQUE OF CONDITIONING THEORY

Conditioning theory does not tell us who decides what will be positively or negatively rewarded in a society, or why values vary from one society to another. The theory pays little attention to the way that culture and social structure influence individual choices and elicit certain behavior by giving or withholding rewards. The theory seems to minimize people's ability to make rational choices on their own. Conditioning theory also seems to work better for property crimes, which involve immediate tangible rewards, than it does for crimes of violence, which do not as obviously involve direct rewards.

Psychology and Variations in Crime Rates

Psychologists have rarely tried to make sense of geographic, temporal, and social variations in crime rates. Thus we have no reason to believe that variations in crime rates from one society to another, from one region to another, or among communities of different sizes can be explained by differences among the residents of those places in intelligence, personality traits, neuroses or psychoses, or conditioning. Similarly, we have no evidence that variations in crime rates over time are the result of changes in any of these psychological variables. For instance, it seems unlikely that the dramatic increase in the rate of index crimes in the United States during the late 1960s was caused by short-run changes in intelligence, personality, neuroses or psychoses, or conditioning.

Whether psychological factors can explain variations in crime rates by sex, age, race, or class is less clear. Males and females are socialized differently, and differences in personality traits that result from socialization might be linked to male-female differences in rates of crime and delinquency. Males and females also differ in the rate at which they suffer certain mental disorders; this might explain some of the sex difference in crime rates, except that there is no strong evidence that mental disorders cause criminal behavior. If men and women are conditioned differently to seek rewards and avoid pain, this could account for differences in crime rates between the sexes. Intelligence does not seem to be a source of male-female differences in rates of crime and delinquency.

Differences in crime rates by age also do not seem to be explained very well by psychological theories. Neither IQ test scores nor personality traits seem to change dramatically over the course of a lifetime for most people, but involvement in crime does vary significantly over the life cycle. There is little reason to think that the psychoanalytic perspective or conditioning theory can help us to make sense of the relationship between age and crime.

Differences in crime rates among racial groups do not seem to be easily explained by psychological theories either. Blacks score lower than whites on IQ tests, but those tests are widely regarded as biased against blacks because they are designed by whites. Moreover, the IQ scores of blacks can be raised significantly by education and by changing the social environment, suggesting that IQ scores are best seen as the product of the socially structured opportunities available to members of different racial groups. Other psychological theories of crime also do not seem to do a very good job of explaining racial differences in crime rates.

Class differences in crime rates are not explained well by psychological theories. IQ scores are lower for the lower classes, but this is probably due mainly to the poor quality of the schools that the lower classes attend. There may be class differences in personality traits, the frequency of neuroses and psychoses, and conditioning, but these differences have not been shown to explain class differences in rates of crime and delinquency.

Psychology and the Criminal Law

Psychological perspectives on crime have long been important in determining the legal responsibility of people who violate the law. Modern psychology questions the ability of some people to form criminal intent, a necessary element of most crimes, and the legal system may relieve people of responsibility for their actions that violate the law if they cannot form criminal intent. The legal system's emphasis on the individual offender focuses attention on the psychology of the law breaker, rather than on the social environment in which the offender lives. This serves to uphold the existing social system, because individuals rather than social conditions are blamed for crime.

RULES DETERMINING CRIMINAL RESPONSIBILITY

One legal rule on criminal responsibility that is used in some states today is the *M'Naghten rule,* which was originally spelled out in a case in Great Britain in 1843, well before the advent of modern psychology and psychiatry. The M'Naghten rule establishes a "right and wrong test": For defendants to prove a lack of criminal responsibility because of insanity, they have to demonstrate either 1) that at the time of the crime they were under a defect of reason so as to be unable to know the nature and the quality of the act, or 2) that if they were aware of the nature of the act, they did not know that the act was wrong. The M'Naghten rule raises difficult issues. It is concerned with the rational and cognitive elements of human thought, or what a defendant knows, rather than with human emotions and desires and with mental disorders. The law speaks of the "rational man," but it rarely consults modern behavioral science to determine what would be "rational" behavior for a particular person in a given situation. "Reasonable" often means what a judge thinks is reasonable in a situation, and what is reasonable for a judge earning $50,000 may not be reasonable for an unemployed parent of five living in a slum.

One attempt to improve the criteria for determining criminal responsibility was made in a 1954 case in which the Court of Appeals for the District of Columbia held that defendants were not guilty if they could show that their actions were products of a "mental disease or mental defect." This Durham rule is now used only in a few jurisdictions in the United States, for it is too general to provide jurors with much guidance for their deliberations.

The Model Penal Code drawn up by the American Law Institute (ALI) in 1955 is the basis of a rule of criminal responsibility that is widely used today. This *Brawner rule* states that a person should be found not guilty "if at the time of such conduct as a result of mental disease or mental defect, he lacks substantial capacity either to appreciate the criminality of his conduct or to conform his conduct to the requirements of the law." This rule focuses on a defendant's understanding of his or her conduct, as well as on the defendant's ability to control that conduct. This rule is now used in most states and in the federal circuit courts (Kaufman, 1982).

Research indicates that the likelihood that a jury will find a defendant not guilty by reason of insanity does not vary much with the type of insanity rule that is used (Simon, 1967; Caplan, 1984). This is probably because only ambiguous cases raise the issue of insanity and because juries find it difficult to determine if mental disturbance is permanent or temporary. Nevertheless, the rules used to determine criminal responsibility have continued to receive much attention from lawmakers and lawyers. The assassination attempt on President Reagan in 1981 generated much public debate on these issues.

THE HINCKLEY CASE AND THE INSANITY DEFENSE

On March 30, 1981, John W. Hinckley fired four shots at President Reagan in an assassination attempt that he hoped would win him public attention and the love of actress Jodie Foster. Reagan and three others were wounded. Hinckley later pleaded not guilty by reason of insanity. Under federal law, the prosecutor had to prove beyond a reasonable doubt that Hinckley was sane; the defense attorney did not have to prove beyond a reasonable doubt that Hinckley was insane. More than a year after the shooting, Hinckley was found not guilty by reason of insanity and sentenced to an indefinite term in St. Elizabeths Hospital in Washington, D.C. The verdict caused a public outcry and much criticism by lawmakers, and led to a reevaluation of the insanity defense.

There was strong public reaction to the 1982 jury verdict that John Hinckley, who had attempted to assassinate President Reagan, was not guilty by reason of insanity.

Reprinted by permission of UPI/Bettmann Newsphotos.

Some public officials reacted to the Hinckley verdict by demanding the abolition of the insanity defense; Idaho, Montana, and Utah essentially did abolish it, but the constitutionality of their reforms is questionable. Critics of the jury's verdict pointed out that Hinckley had purchased a gun, stalked the president, knew what he was doing when he fired the shots, and that those things indicated that Hinckley had committed the crime intentionally. Some critics of the insanity defense would not allow it to be used if a crime is committed intentionally, even if the defendant's psychological condition meant that he or she was unable to control his or her behavior. Opponents of this view claim that it would reverse the development of the criminal law since the 1843 M'Naghten decision (Taylor, 1981).

The abolition of the insanity defense probably would not have a major impact on the crime rate, for it is rarely used. One study found that only one in every 4,000 defendants in Massachusetts is acquitted as a result of an insanity plea (Dietz, 1984). The most recent national data on the insanity defense are for 1978, a year in which about ten million suspects were arrested and about three-fifths of that number were formally charged with a crime.

Of those defendants, about two-thirds pleaded guilty. There were only 1,625 successful pleas of insanity in 1978, about one-tenth of 1 per cent of the number of defendants who were tried (Caplan, 1984). There is some evidence that the use of the insanity defense may have increased in recent years; for instance, in New York state the annual average number of successful insanity pleas increased from eight in the late 1960s to about one hundred in the early 1980s (Caplan, 1984).

One reason that the insanity defense may have become more widely used in recent years is that there has been growing pressure to release mental patients after shorter periods in custody. The courts have expanded the civil rights of mental patients; for instance, John Hinckley must have a hearing for possible release every six months that he is hospitalized. In addition, psychiatrists today prefer to return patients to the community rather than institutionalize them, and the law requires that patients be released unless they are still mentally ill and dangerous. However, psychiatrists are not able to predict future dangerousness very well, and so vesting power in them to determine a release date seems to be asking too much of them. For example, a study of mental patients who had committed felonies found that 14 per cent of those classified as dangerous by psychiatrists were rearrested for violent crimes within three years of their release, but 16 per cent of those classified by psychiatrists as nondangerous were rearrested for violent crimes within three years. This suggests that psychiatrists cannot predict future behavior well enough to determine when mental patients who have committed felonies should be released (Henry J. Steadman, cited in Pines, 1982).

Another possible reason for the increased use of the insanity defense in recent years is the renewed use of the death penalty since 1977. If the alternative to an insanity plea is the risk of execution, then defendants charged with capital crimes will have a strong incentive to plead not guilty by reason of insanity. The link between the insanity plea and capital punishment can be seen in the experience of Great Britain, where the proportion of defendants found not guilty by reason of insanity declined noticeably after that country abolished capital punishment in 1965 (Wilson, 1983: 185).

Those who argue for abolition of the insanity defense sometimes claim that such a change would make it possible to imprison dangerous offenders for longer periods. Defendants found not guilty by reason of insanity are usually hospitalized from two to three years, although in some jurisdictions they are hospitalized longer (Caplan, 1984). Critics of the insanity defense point to cases in which people who have committed murder and been found insane have been released after a few months or a few years of hospitalization (*The Boston Globe*, July 1, 1982). However, others claim that defendants who are found not guilty by reason of insanity are usually confined in hospitals for as long as they would be imprisoned had they been found guilty of the same offense.

REFORMING THE INSANITY DEFENSE RULES

The Hinckley assassination attempt has led to proposals to change the rules of criminal responsibility. One suggested change would place the burden of proof to show insanity on the defense, rather than require the prosecution to prove sanity. Still, the defense could require the prosecution to prove all elements of the crime that is charged; one element is intent, which in turn is closely related to the concept of sanity (Kaufman, 1982). Another suggested reform is to introduce more widely a verdict used in eight states in 1983:

"guilty but mentally ill." If a defendant is found guilty but mentally ill, then the jury, the judge, or a board of mental health professionals would determine whether the defendant should be sent to prison or to a mental hospital (Wicker, 1982; Nesson, 1982). Critics claim that use of the "guilty but mentally ill" verdict avoids the hard question of whether a defendant is criminally responsible for violating the law, and that it is impractical, and possibly unconstitutional (Rubenstein, 1982; Kaufman, 1982).

In 1983, several professional associations took positions on the insanity defense, mainly in response to the furor caused by the Hinckley verdict. The American Psychiatric Association (APA) took a stand in favor of continued use of some form of the insanity defense in cases that involved serious mental illness, which meant psychoses rather than "personality disorders" and antisocial personalities. However, as we have seen, research has not yet established a close association between psychoses and criminal behavior. The APA also suggested that standards and procedures be tightened to protect the public against the premature release of individuals who might still be dangerous. The APA expressed skepticism about periodic reassessments of patients to determine their dangerousness to society, acknowledging that psychiatrists had much difficulty in predicting dangerousness. The association opposed the "guilty but mentally ill" verdict, seeing it as a disguised form of abolition of the insanity defense and as a way for juries to avoid important issues of criminal responsibility. No stand was taken on whether the defense or the prosecution should be required to demonstrate sanity or insanity (Boffey, 1983b).

Also in 1983, the American Bar Association (ABA) supported changes in the insanity defense to narrow its scope and to require the defense to assume the burden of proof in demonstrating insanity (Margolick, 1983). The ABA suggested that defendants who were aware of the wrongfulness of their conduct should be held criminally responsible, even if they later claimed that they had been unable to control their actions or had acted under an "irresistible impulse." The ABA rejected the part of the Brawner rule that deals with volition and self-control, because it is not possible in practice to distinguish undeterrable acts from undeterred acts. The ABA retained the other part of the Brawner rule, the need to appreciate the criminality of the behavior. In addition, the ABA opposed the "guilty but mentally ill" alternative. Under the revisions suggested by the ABA, Hinckley probably would have been found guilty as charged.

Finally, in 1983 the American Medical Association (AMA) voted to abolish the insanity defense, a position opposed by both the APA and the ABA. The APA called the AMA's action "an emotional overreaction to the Hinckley verdict" (cited in *The New York Times*, December 7, 1983, p. B8).

The insanity defense will continue to be a source of controversy in the future. Changes in the rules of criminal responsibility may be important in redefining the conditions under which people who violate the law can be punished. However, the insanity defense will probably continue to be raised in a very small proportion of all criminal cases, and so reforms in the rules of criminal responsibility are unlikely to have much effect on the crime rate.

SUMMARY

Much criminological research today is done by sociologists, but biologists and psychologists have contributed in important ways to our understanding of criminal behavior.

Early biological theories of crime—such as the theories of the physiognomists and phrenologists, Lombroso's theory of the atavism, and Sheldon's somatotype theory—have little empirical support and receive little attention today, but they were significant in the development of criminology.

Modern biological research has produced important findings that may ultimately fit into a general theory of crime causation. Twin studies find that identical twins, who are genetically alike, are more similar in their criminal behavior than are fraternal twins, who share fewer inherited traits. These findings have been explained by environmental influences as well as by inheritance. Adoption studies seem to provide evidence for an inherited propensity to crime; this propensity is also influenced by the social environment. Criminality can better be predicted from the criminality of an adopted person's biological parents than from the criminality of his or her adoptive parents. Research on the XYY chromosome suggests that this rare condition may be associated with a tendency to engage in nonviolent crimes; men with an XYY chromosome may be more likely to get caught for their crimes because they are less intelligent, or they may be less easily conditioned by punishment than are normal men. There is mixed evidence about the effects of sex hormones on behavior, but they might account in part for men's higher rates of violent crime. In Great Britain, symptoms associated with the onset of menstruation have been used to mitigate the punishment of a few female defendants. Brain dysfunctions and learning disabilities, particularly hyperactivity, seem to be correlated with involvement in crime and delinquency. Most biologists who study criminal behavior today are cautious in their conclusions, treating inherited predispositions to certain behavior as factors that interact with environmental influences. However, because biological explanations do not seem to make sense of geographic, temporal, and social variations in crime rates, many criminologists have not paid much attention to biologists' research on crime and delinquency.

One psychological approach to the study of crime and delinquency proposes that law violators have lower levels of intelligence than people who abide by the law. Research shows a small but consistent difference in IQ levels between delinquents and nondelinquents, even when class and race are taken into account. This research has been criticized because IQ scores can be changed by environmental factors, because IQ tests are culturally biased, and because structural factors determine what is made of IQ socially.

Researchers have not found a single criminal personality type, but efforts continue to identify such a cluster of traits. It is more likely that different kinds of offenders will have different personalities; in fact, research on rape finds that there are at least three personality types among men who commit that offense. Today psychologists usually regard aggressiveness, which seems to be linked to some crimes, as the product of many complex and interacting factors. The psychopathic personality, which has origins in both physiology and the environment, and especially in rejection by parents, seems to be linked to criminal behavior.

The psychoanalytic perspective sees crime as the result of inadequate socialization, although an individual may also become a criminal if socialized to conform to the demands of a group whose norms conflict with the law. Neuroses are not closely associated with criminal behavior, but some psychoses, particularly schizophrenia, might be linked to crimes of violence. The psychoanalytic perspective has been used to explain assassinations in the United States, where political murders are motivated more often by personal needs than by political goals. The case study approach used by psychoanalysts makes it difficult to test their theory of crime causation in a way that meets the requirements of scientific research.

Conditioning theory proposes that criminal behavior is the product of rational learning and classical conditioning, both of which are influenced by inherited characteristics and the social environment.

There is little reason to think that psychological explanations can help us to understand geographic or temporal variations in crime rates. Psychological factors might help to explain variations in crime rates by sex, age, race, and class, but there have been few systematic attempts to use psychological variables to make sense of differences in crime rates among people with those social characteristics.

Psychological perspectives on crime causation are used by the criminal justice system to determine if a defendant is criminally responsible. Several rules, most of them quite vague in their wording, are now used in the United States to determine if a defendant is not guilty by reason of insanity. The Hinckley verdict of not guilty by reason of insanity has led to a reevaluation of these insanity rules. Acquittals because of insanity are rare, and, as a result, changes in the insanity defense are unlikely to have much effect on crime rates.

IMPORTANT TERMS

atavism
Brawner rule
classical conditioning
concordance rate
learning disabilities

M'Naghten rule
premenstrual syndrome
  (PMS)
psychoanalytic perspective

psychopath
schizophrenia
somatotype
XYY chromosome

SUGGESTED READINGS

LINCOLN CAPLAN. "Annals of Law: The Insanity Defense," *The New Yorker*, July 2, 1984, pp. 45–78. A fascinating account of the Hinckley case and the recent controversy over the insanity defense.

HANS EYSENCK. *Crime and Personality.* London: Routledge and Kegan Paul, 1977. A detailed statement of the conditioning theory of criminal behavior.

SARNOFF A. MEDNICK ET AL., "Biology and Violence," in Marvin E. Wolfgang and Neil Alan Weiner, eds., *Criminal Violence.* Beverly Hills, Calif.: Sage Publications, 1982, pp. 21–80. A useful essay that reviews recent biological research on criminal behavior.

NORVAL MORRIS. *Madness and the Criminal Law.* Chicago: University of Chicago Press, 1982. An important examination of issues raised by the rules of criminal responsibility and the insanity defense.

GEORGE B. VOLD. *Theoretical Criminology*, 2nd ed., prepared by Thomas J. Bernard. New York: Oxford University Press, 1979. A textbook that examines the development of biological and psychological theories of criminal behavior.

8

Socioeconomic Causes of Crime

Until recently, a common way of dealing with arson was to focus on the individual who sets fires. Seeing the arsonist as a deviant—perhaps a "pyromaniac" with severe psychological problems—led nowhere in the prevention of arson, a crime that has destroyed major parts of our cities. A much better approach, and one already bearing some fruit, focuses on the social-structural causes of arson. There is an important link between legitimate institutions—particularly banks, real-estate developers, and insurance companies—and arson-for-profit schemes by gangsters, professional arsonists, landlords, and corrupt political officials (Brady, 1983a). This approach suggests that arson can be stopped only by reforming the social structure. Better regulation of banks, real-estate developers, and insurance companies might reduce the incidence of this crime. Studies of the relationship between arson and the deterioration of neighborhoods suggest that arson might also be reduced by citizen-action groups, arson-prediction methods, better communication between the community and the police, housing revitalization, and changes in environmental design (Brady, 1982; Cook and Roehl, 1983). In sum, the crime is most effectively understood and best controlled by paying attention to the socioeconomic context within which it occurs, not by focusing on the psychology of the individual offender.

In this chapter, we look at the social, economic, and cultural causes of white-collar crime, organized crime, and conventional crime (especially juvenile delinquency). In the following chapter, we examine the social and psychological processes by which people neutralize or weaken their commitment to the law. Then, in Chapter 10, we explore the ways that such individuals actually learn to commit crime.

SOCIOECONOMIC CAUSES OF WHITE-COLLAR CRIME

Several aspects of the social and economic system of the United States are conducive to white-collar crime. The American economy is based as much on the stimulation of new demands as on the fulfillment of existing demands. Competition in the business world creates pressure to increase consumer demand for products and pressure to capture existing markets. This results in advertising, which sometimes goes beyond "puffing one's wares" to fraud, a crime characterized by the intent to deceive. Some advertising is thus actually criminal. Advertising can also stimulate demand that leads to theft if that demand is not fulfilled. Advertising fuels consumption in the American economy, but by urging people to consume and maintain an expensive life style, it can also lead to larceny, robbery, and embezzlement.

Free Enterprise: Profits and Competition

The American ideology of free enterprise stresses two goals: the pursuit of profits and open competition among sellers. Each goal can be conducive to violation of the law by business people.

THE PURSUIT OF PROFITS

The emphasis on consumption and the use of advertising help to create profits for firms. Some economists have suggested that companies seek a "satisfactory profit" rather than the maximum profit, and that corporations have goals other than making a profit. However, profits are basic to the corporation, even if other considerations play some role in corporate decision making.

In a study of sixty-four retired middle managers of large corporations, the largest number of them cited the pressure to show profits and keep costs in line as the major pressure on middle management. About nine-tenths of the retired executives said that the various pressures on middle managers sometimes lead to unethical behavior; 78.2 per cent of these executives said that such pressures can lead to criminal acts. Pressure on executives is more likely to lead to unethical behavior than to crime, but the drive for profits is a source of pressure that sometimes leads managers to violate the law (Clinard, 1983).

Firms seem most likely to violate the law to increase profits when the economy is unstable and profits are declining. The drive for profits can lead to antitrust violations such as price fixing, which is the illegal setting of prices by firms acting in collusion rather than depending on the free market to determine prices; this is an offense that the federal government explicitly states will be prosecuted. Profit seeking can also push business people into the arms of gangsters to secure capital for investment and expansion; this sometimes leads to the takeover of legitimate businesses by organized crime (Grutzner, 1972; Lubasch, 1983). Economically weak firms may try to recoup their losses by "selling out to the insurance company"; that is, they may hire a "torch" to burn down the plant in order to collect the fire insurance. Arson increases during recessions when firms are in financial difficulty.

One of the largest losses in any crime in history involved an attempt to create a profitable enterprise. The conspirators sought to make the Equity Funding Corporation of America "the largest, fastest growing, most successful financial institution in the world and in the process thereby to gain fame and fortune for themselves" (Parker, 1976: 122). Their fraud involved the writing of fake life insurance policies that were sold to other insurance companies at a discount, a practice known as reinsurance. What was peculiar about this massive fraud was not the extraordinarily large losses involved, but that the conspirators created a situation in which their firm would actually have lost more money every year the fraud continued. Their crime created the illusion of making money while it was in fact losing money. The crime was apparently too complex for even its perpetrators to understand.

COMPETITION

The second element of free-enterprise ideology is open competition among firms, which is theoretically beneficial to the consuming public because it reduces profits to a "fair" level. However, competition can also lead firms to try to capture a larger share of the market through illegal acts such as false advertising or bribery. Individual firms do not seek to maximize competition for themselves and reduce their own profits to a "fair" level. Instead, they seek to reduce the strength of their competitors and maximize their own profits. To do this, they may turn to price fixing to drive competitors out of business, or to efforts to get banks to charge competing firms higher rates of interest. Competition has also led to the theft of new ideas through industrial espionage.

Competition in foreign markets has involved businesses in the bribery of officials to secure contracts and establish plants. In recent years, the increased internationalization of trade, the rise of multinational corporations, and the growing interdependence of nations have generated concern about white-collar crime in the international arena. Competition among the corporations of the world sometimes leads to clearly illegal behavior such as assassinations, and sometimes into "gray" areas that involve unethical behavior that may not violate existing laws. Only since the passage of the Foreign Corrupt Practices Act of 1977 have firms based in the United States that pay bribes to foreign officials been in violation of American law. Even now, another unethical practice—the shipping to foreign buyers of products banned in the United States, such as carcinogenic TRIS-treated infant clothing—is not prosecuted as a crime in the United States. Competition and the search for new and profitable markets encourage this behavior, especially when the law does not cover the situation adequately or when the criminal justice system does not punish such actions.

Market Structure and Crime

Some white-collar crimes are more likely to occur in certain market structures or economic circumstances (Leonard and Weber, 1970; Kramer, 1982). For example, seller concentration—a large share of the market being controlled by a few leading producers—is conducive to price fixing. A small number of buyers or a great deal of wealth in the hands of a few buyers—called buyer concentration—can give buyers the power to demand bribes and kickbacks from sellers. When goods and services are in short supply, consumers may bribe those who control scarce resources in order to meet their needs; we see an example of this in the Soviet Union in the Cross-Cultural Perspective.

Another aspect of market structure conducive to business crime is the price elasticity of demand. When demand is price-inelastic—that is, when there will be little reduction in the demand for a product if its price increases—firms may engage in price fixing to increase profits. A slow growth rate of demand in a given market is another condition that can lead to business crimes such as false advertising.

Product differentiation, which is the ability to distinguish one's product from a competitor's product, can lead to false or deceptive advertising. Sometimes the opposite situation, trying to make one's product seem as much like another product as possible, leads to crimes such as copyright or patent infringement. Consumer demand for designer clothing or designer cosmetics is conducive to the counterfeiting of those products.

A Cross-Cultural Perspective: Bribery in the Soviet Union

Market conditions determine how well the demands of consumers will be met. When goods and services are scarce, consumers may bribe those who control economic resources. One Soviet dissident notes that "the prevalence of bribery in Russia is accentuated by the fact that many goods are in short supply and are distributed in accordance with an elaborate network of privileges. Since people cannot buy wanted items in the usual way, they have to bribe those who control the privilege system" (Chalidze, p. 156).

Another Soviet dissident, who is an attorney, describes the process of bribery in more detail:

Entering into relations with representatives of the government, dealing with industry, commerce, and services, the Soviet citizen, readily and without thinking about it, uses corruption to get what is

necessary for him—most often what is vitally necessary. In the same automatic way, the average Soviet citizen gives a ruble to a salesman in a store to get a piece of meat, 300 rubles to an official of the Ministry of Communication to have a telephone installed in his apartment, or 3000 rubles to an official of the District Executive Committee to get a government apartment. If he does not pay these bribes his family will not have meat; he will be forced to wait five or six years before a telephone is installed; he will remain for years with his large family in a single room in a communal apartment (Simis, p. 298).

SOURCES: Valery Chalidze, *Criminal Russia: Crime in the Soviet Union.* New York: Random House, 1977; Konstantin M. Simis, *USSR: The Corrupt Society.* New York: Simon and Schuster, 1982.

MARKET CONDITIONS AND THE ELECTRICAL PRICE-FIXING CONSPIRACY

During the 1950s, executives from companies that manufactured heavy electrical equipment conspired to fix the prices that contractors, including the federal government, would pay for their products. This was done by determining a "reasonable" division of the market among the companies, based on past sales, and by allowing the company that was supposed to win a contract to submit the lowest bid, while the other companies submitted higher bids (Geis, 1967).

Several of the market conditions conducive to white-collar crime were present in the electrical equipment industry during the time of this price-fixing conspiracy. A relatively small number of companies controlled most of the market in electrical products. Large short-term fluctuations in profits led to efforts by these companies to stabilize prices. They thought that demand was price-inelastic, and that their customers would tolerate small price increases for electrical products without complaining or reducing their purchases. These conditions led to the elaborate price-fixing conspiracy that culminated in the 1961 convictions of twenty-nine firms and several of their executives, seven of whom actually served time in jail (Geis, 1967).

This price-fixing case received little attention in the press, and a 1976 antitrust case against manufacturers of folding cartons did not receive much notice in the mass media either. Antitrust cases of this sort are usually not reported in a prominent way for the following reasons:

- They involve diffuse harm;
- There is a lack of awareness that corporations are "juristic persons" capable of crime;
- Newspapers are large organizations that are not inclined to link other large organizations to crime; and
- Newspapers depend on large corporations for advertising revenue (Evans and Lundman, 1983).

Trust and Credit

Some business crimes stem from the economic system's reliance on trust and credit. Business people have faith that others will fulfill their obligations honestly; when that trust is violated, crimes may occur. Robert Vesco exploited his business colleagues in Investors Overseas Services by looting about half a billion dollars from that international corporation (Hutchison, 1974). Employers sometimes violate the trust of employees and union leaders by engaging in illegal labor practices. Merchants abuse the trust of their customers when they misrepresent prices, engage in deceptive credit practices, or substitute inferior goods upon delivery. Corporate directors violate stockholders' trust when they fail to disclose information about illegal contributions to political candidates and bribes to foreign officials. The Trustee's Bankruptcy Report on the Equity Funding Corporation of America fraud concluded that EFCA had violated the trust of other members of the insurance industry, saying that

> only someone with an exceedingly skeptical bent of mind would have . . . inferred fraud. Such an inference would have been hostile to the presumption of good faith and honest-dealing which customarily prevails in American business practice. To the Trustee, that presumption, though sometimes grievously abused, is probably indispensable to a vigorous and productive economy (cited in Parker, 1976: 166).

One trust relationship that is conducive to certain crimes is credit, which is given on the creditor's faith that the borrower will repay the money. Many of the crimes that involve the abuse of credit involve business people who defraud other large businesses. Business credit fraud is sometimes planned in advance, with a new company established to defraud suppliers, or a legitimate business converted into a firm that abuses its creditors. Banks and corporations sometimes continue to extend credit to a firm, even though that firm's shaky financial condition makes it unlikely that it will be able to repay its debts (Levi, 1981). One businessman who aspired to wealth through fraudulent credit practices was Tony DeAngelis, who borrowed millions of dollars by using as collateral for his loans salad oil that he said was stored in large tanks. His creditors trusted him, but failed to check on the existence of the salad oil. When the tanks were found to be empty, DeAngelis defaulted on the loans and his creditors lost millions of dollars (Miller, 1965).

The widespread use of credit cards in the United States is also conducive to crime, including the counterfeiting of cards, the fraudulent use of them to place telephone orders, and the use of stolen, lost, and altered cards.

Corporations and Crime

Much American business is conducted by large corporations. Various aspects of these organizations—such as their bureaucratic structure, their large size, their impersonality, their specialization and delegation of responsibility, and their use of rationality in decision making—are conducive to crime (Conklin, 1977; Clinard and Yeager, 1980).

SIZE AND BUREAUCRATIC STRUCTURE
Large size and bureaucratic structure are often associated with the fragmentation of responsibility and the difficulty of pinpointing who made a particular decision. Supervisors often blame underlings for the company's violation of the law, and underlings claim that supervisors encouraged them to break the law to meet corporate goals.

The division of tasks in a large corporation may enhance bureaucratic efficiency but make it difficult to exercise control over business activities. The Equity Funding Corporation of America fraud resulted in part from a fragmented corporate structure, which allowed conspirators to act in relative secrecy (Dirks and Gross, 1974: 240). The decentralization of General Electric in 1950 broke that large corporation into several relatively autonomous divisions, each of which was under pressure to show a profit. The need to stabilize profits at a high level led to price fixing, an offense that was made easier by the fragmentation of the company.

Corporate crimes can result from organizational defects such as poor information flow, lack of coordination in the bureaucracy, inaccurate promotional material, failure to deal adequately with complaints after an inaccurate advertisement, or failure to tell sales representatives all of the relevant facts about a product (Hopkins, 1980; Ermann and Lundman, 1982). A study in Australia of fifteen companies that had committed white-collar crimes involving an organizational defect found that official sanctions caused at least 60 per cent of the companies to make significant organizational changes to reduce the chance that the problem would recur (Hopkins, 1980).

IMPERSONALITY

Large size and bureaucratic structure are correlated with impersonality. Employees of large corporations may find it easy to steal from the company if they have little loyalty to the firm. Crime against the employing firm is less common in Japan, where workers traditionally remain with one company for their entire working lives, than it is in the United States, where job mobility is great and there is little tradition of loyalty to one firm (Clifford, 1976). In addition, when union-management conflict is necessary to increase wages and benefits, workers may believe that management is not concerned with their welfare and will make concessions only grudgingly. This attitude may be used to justify employees' crimes against the firm.

Dissatisfied workers who feel exploited or underpaid and executives who are frustrated by not being promoted or by an unsatisfactory salary may justify theft or embezzlement as the only way to gain deserved compensation for low pay or poor working conditions (Hollinger and Clark, 1983b). Some observers believe that workers steal to increase their spendable incomes; the policy implication is that theft can be reduced by paying workers more (Jaspan, 1974). Another view is that because many jobs are dull, repetitive, lacking in prestige, or unchallenging, workers steal for job enrichment or to increase their self-esteem (Zeitlin, 1971; Altheide et al., 1978). For instance, a wealthy lawyer allegedly stole $607,000 in bonds because he was "fascinated by the challenge of constructing elaborate schemes to steal money" (Carmody, 1974). Theft for challenge is also a common motive in many computer crimes (Parker, 1976). The impersonality of the work environment in large corporations and on plant assembly lines can give rise to the need to create a challenge that workers can meet, and this may take the form of crime against the company. Giving workers a vested interest in the company's success and integrating them into the firm might help to reduce employee theft (Hollinger and Clark, 1983b).

RATIONAL DECISION MAKING

The rational decision making of large corporations can also be conducive to business crime. Given a low risk of apprehension, a small likelihood of being convicted in court, and a negligible chance of a meaningful criminal sanction, corporate executives may knowingly violate the law or enter "gray areas" where they know they may be violating the law. It may seem rational, if not moral or legal, for executives to violate the law if their gains are great and their risks are small. Even if the company is convicted of a crime, it will probably gain more in profits than it loses in fines, and individual executives may gain more in promotion and salary than they lose from criminal sanctions (Stone, 1974: 45–46).

Development of New Technology

Technology develops in a cumulative fashion, and new opportunities to violate the law often accompany breakthroughs in technology. The high-tech and computer industry has provided both new opportunities for crime and new techniques to commit traditional crimes such as embezzlement.

Computer crime, which can broadly be defined as any violation of the law in which a computer is the target or the means, often involves large losses. Computer crime includes many kinds of offenses:

- introduction of unauthorized data into a system,
- manipulation of authorized data,
- creation of unauthorized files,
- unauthorized use of passwords or accounting codes, often called "hacking,"
- theft of hardware, software, or computer time, and
- use of the computer as a weapon (Parker, 1976; McLellan, 1983; Green, 1984).

One example of the computer being used as a weapon occurred in 1979, when someone purposely tampered with a computerized flight plan guiding a plane's automatic pilot, causing a crash in which 257 people were killed (McLellan, 1983). Another computer crime is "shaving," in which someone programs a computer to round off each employee's pay check down to the nearest ten cents and then deposit the extra few pennies in the offender's account. One programmer made $300 a week with this scheme, an amount that was two and a half times his regular salary. Another computer crime involved tapping into an oil company's computer to get information that allowed the offending company to underbid the victimized company for leasing rights (Green, 1984).

Various social and economic factors have led to an increase in computer crimes. The tremendous reduction in the cost of computers in recent years means that individuals and small businesses can afford them. This has two effects. First, individual "hackers" have an instrument with which to tap into computerized files, an act that has recently become the focus of federal law enforcement. Second, the inexpensive computers owned by small businesses usually do not have good built-in security measures, and so they are vulnerable to violation (Green, 1984).

Several aspects of computer technology are conducive to crime. It is relatively easy for a knowledgeable computer programmer to hide a program or a modification within a larger program, or to destroy records and leave no "trail" of the crime. Computer software or programs are relatively easily copied. The courts have treated this act as copyright infringement (Sanger, 1983). In 1983, one company with sales of $26 million claimed to have lost between $20 million and $40 million because of illegal reproduction or piracy of its software (*The New York Times*, January 5, 1983). The chips used in computer hardware are small but expensive, and have been a target of thieves, who then sell them to companies that cannot purchase enough chips in the legitimate market (Reinhold, 1984). Another aspect of computer technology is that computers emit radio waves or "compromising emanations" that can be decoded with the proper equipment. The federal government calls this the "Tempest" problem and worries about electronic espionage that might reveal secret information in computerized files (Broad, 1983).

One aspect of computer technology that is of growing importance is electronic fund transfers (EFT), which include all payment systems that permit transactions or exchanges in which value is represented by electronic messages, rather than by paper such as currency or checks. *EFT crime* is thus any violation of the law that would not have occurred except for the presence of an EFT system. This includes crimes that involve automated teller machines and wire transfers from bank to bank by a company's computer. There is no good source of data on the extent of EFT crime, but so far it seems to be a very small proportion of all crimes involving financial institutions. However, EFT crime will probably become a more important problem as the number of financial transactions conducted electronically grows. For instance, automated teller machines create several possibilities for crime, including the following:

- use of a stolen card and personal identification number to steal funds from an account,
- intentional withdrawal of more money than one has in an account,
- use of a counterfeit card,
- physical attack on the machine itself, and
- robbery of a customer who has just withdrawn money from a machine.

Corporate EFT crime includes an employee's misuse of a company's bank account number and code number to order a transfer of funds into a personal account. Internal EFT crime by bank employees who "shave" accounts for personal gain or who use confidential information for blackmail may also increase in the future (Colton et al., 1982; Bureau of Justice Statistics, February 1984).

SOCIOECONOMIC CAUSES OF ORGANIZED CRIME

The tendency in American society to pass legislation that prohibits the consumption of widely demanded goods and services has produced a situation conducive to vast profits for people who are willing to supply those illegal goods and services. One example is Prohibition.

Prohibition and Organized Crime

Prior to the passage of the Eighteenth Amendment, which prohibited the manufacture, sale, and transportation of alcoholic beverages, there were gangsters in many American cities, but they were not well organized. The efforts of religious, white, native-born Americans in small towns and rural areas to protect the dominance of their cultural values led to Prohibition in 1920.

The Prohibition Amendment made a widely demanded product illegal. The consequence was that those willing to supply illegal alcoholic beverages could charge higher prices than consumers had paid when those beverages were legal and in more plentiful supply. The relatively price-inelastic demand for alcohol created a situation somewhat like that which leads to price fixing in the business world. In each case, sellers sought monopoly control in a given market in order to establish higher prices than would exist under a system of open competition among sellers.

The Eighteenth Amendment was repealed during the Great Depression, partly for economic reasons. People needed the jobs that the liquor industry could provide, and the government hoped to raise more tax revenue from the legal sale of alcoholic beverages (Gusfield, 1963). Repeal was also a result of the unenforceability of the law and the public's reactions to the tactics used by the Prohibition Bureau. National prohibition became a thing of the past in 1933, but gangsters had become well organized as a result of this unsuccessful experiment in the legislation of morality.

Organized Crime after Prohibition

When Prohibition ended, gangs turned to other illegal enterprises for revenue. They became involved in prostitution, though they are not much involved in it today. The major sources of revenue for organized crime today seem to be narcotics and loan sharking, and perhaps gambling. However, gangsters have shown ingenuity in making a profit from many different illegal activities, including bankruptcy fraud and the disposal of toxic wastes.

GAMBLING

According to some scholars and most law-enforcement officers, many bookies work for or are members of organized crime "families." One sociologist who has had access to evidence gathered by law-enforcement agencies suggests that 95 per cent of illegal gambling in the United States is controlled by organized crime (Cressey, 1969). However, research in New York City, where the largest number of organized crime families in the country are located, indicates that organized crime does not seem to have a firm control over gambling and that bookies operate in a competitive market rather than as agents of organized crime. Because the gambling business is unpredictable, bookies often turn to loan sharks, who do have ties to organized crime, in order to borrow money to keep their gambling operations afloat (Reuter and Rubinstein, 1978; Reuter, 1983). Bookies thus provide a source of income for organized crime not because their profits are channeled directly to gangsters, but because they pay high interest rates to loan sharks who are members of organized crime.

LOAN SHARKING

Loan sharks are a major source of income for organized crime. They meet a demand for money that is not met by legitimate institutions such as banks and finance companies. The interest rates on their loans are illegally high and well in excess of what borrowers pay to legitimate institutions. Loan sharks frequently charge an interest rate of 20 per cent per week. This "six for five" formula means that a loan of $500 on Monday must be repaid with $600 the following Monday. Rates this high involve loan sharks in the crime of usury.

Loan sharks thrive on the difficulties that some people encounter in getting loans from legitimate institutions. Many borrowers from loan sharks are poor credit risks who are turned down by banks and finance companies; other borrowers need money for purposes of which legitimate institutions would disapprove, such as the repayment of gambling debts or the financing of a drug deal. Loan sharks are willing to lend money to such people with less financial information or collateral than legitimate institutions require. This means that many who borrow from loan sharks have difficulty repaying their loans on time. When this happens, a loan shark may threaten violence against the borrower or the borrower's family. However, a study of loan sharking in New York City found violence and intimidation to be less common than some accounts suggest, as borrowers and lenders often have close ties. Borrowers usually repay their loans because they hope to be able to secure loans from the loan shark again (Reuter, 1983).

In the United States, loan sharking is a major activity of established organized crime gangs, but nonracketeers also engage in this illegal activity, according to a study in New York City (Reuter, 1983). Loan sharks are also common in Japan, where about 14,000 of these *sakarin* make loans at illegally high rates and assault or kill those who do not repay their loans (Chapman, 1983a).

NARCOTICS

The money lent by loan sharks who are linked to organized crime often comes from the profits made from the importation of illegal narcotics, especially heroin. Laws against the sale and possession of narcotics lead to high profits for those who are willing to take the risk of importing and distributing drugs. As a result, heroin and other drugs are far more costly to users in the United States than would be the case if those substances were legal.

The illegality of heroin generates crime in two ways. First, it creates drug crimes such as importation, sale, and possession. Then indirectly, the illegality of heroin creates secondary or drug-related crimes such as larceny, robbery, and prostitution, which addicts commit to get the money to pay for their expensive narcotics. The supply-demand balance for heroin is similar to that for illegal alcoholic beverages during Prohibition, except that there is less choice involved in an addict's use of heroin. There is a relatively constant demand for heroin among addicts, and this makes it possible for gangsters to raise prices without losing much business.

Government programs to reduce drug use and drug-related crimes by curtailing the importation of narcotics can backfire. Reducing the supply of heroin entering the country may have little immediate effect on addicts' demand for the drug, but prices may rise as demand remains steady and supply declines. When this happens, addicts may commit more crime in order to get the money to pay for the more expensive drug. Thus, a government program that succeeds in reducing the amount of an addictive drug that is imported can increase street crime by addicts without reducing drug use in any significant way.

A contrary argument is made by James Q. Wilson (1983: 212–213), who claims that law enforcement can and has reduced, or at least has stabilized, the addict population by curtailing the supply of heroin. One study of addicts found that the confiscation of drugs may drive prices up, but that quality falls as a result. Addicts seem to be less sensitive to the cost of heroin than to the quality of the drugs they are using. Consequently, government seizures of heroin might push some addicts into treatment; if this happens, it will more likely be the result of lowered drug quality than the result of higher prices (Baridon, 1976).

BANKRUPTCY FRAUD

Organized crime has sometimes taken advantage of the trust inherent in credit transactions in the business world to engage in a type of bankruptcy fraud known as the "scam" (DeFranco, 1973). In a scam, racketeers purchase a business that has a good credit rating or establish a "front business" with a name much like one of a respected firm. They stock up on merchandise bought on credit. They demand quick delivery, pay for initial orders with cash so as to establish and maintain good credit, and buy to the limit on credit, excusing nonpayment by the rapid expansion of their business or by the busy season of the year, the Christmas season being a favorite time for this crime. The goods they buy are appealing to consumers, can be purchased in volume, and are easy to transport and hard to trace. Office equipment, television sets, and toys are examples. The racketeers sell these goods as quickly as they can through discount houses and by mail orders, and then disappear and leave their creditors with unpaid bills. The widespread use of credit in the world of commerce makes it possible for gangsters to commit this kind of crime.

DISPOSAL OF TOXIC WASTE

Organized crime has been adaptable in moving into newly profitable areas of illegal activity. For instance, the disposal of toxic waste material produced by industry has become difficult and expensive because of strict environmental protection laws. Garbage companies owned by organized crime have developed highly profitable, but dangerous and illegal, methods of waste disposal. One method involves mixing toxic materials with recycled fuel oil (Blumenthal, 1983; Oreskes, 1984; Block and Scarpitti, 1985).

Organized Crime and the Economic System

The activities of organized crime are closely interwoven with the economic system. Illegal goods and services are supplied by gangsters at a high cost to consumers and at great profit to organized crime. Gangsters act as brokers who meet an unfulfilled public demand for illegal goods and services. Because of the illegal nature of their enterprise, gangsters seek monopoly control of a market, sometimes using violence to drive out competitors who threaten their profits. Organized crime serves economic functions for some people; for example, loan sharks make money available to people who cannot borrow elsewhere. Gangsters in the United States, Japan, and elsewhere often adopt the economic strategies and managerial skills of legitimate business to carry out their illegal profit-making ventures, and they frequently invest their illegal profits in legitimate enterprises.

SOCIOECONOMIC CAUSES OF CONVENTIONAL CRIME

Conventional crime is influenced by the economic system in many ways. Modernization affects crime rates in significant ways. Changes in the value of goods can create new opportunities for crime. Unemployment and crime are related to each other in complex ways. If a culture encourages people to strive for material success, dissatisfaction that is conducive to the committing of crime may develop among the unsuccessful. Sociologists have sought to explain the impact of these and other socioeconomic factors on crime and delinquency.

Modernization and Crime

The process of economic development has affected the amount and characteristics of crime in both capitalist and socialist societies. In general, high proportions of all of the crimes committed in economically developed societies are property crimes, because with prosperity there are more opportunities to steal. In less developed societies, property crimes usually make up a smaller proportion of all crimes, and violent crimes are relatively more common (Clinard and Abbott, 1973; Shelley, 1981a). The overall crime rate tends to rise with economic modernization, but some of that increase seems to be due to the development of a professional police force that keeps better records. With economic development also comes an increase in the relative amount of crime by juveniles and by women. One review of the research concludes that in developing societies, women rarely commit more than one-tenth of all crimes, but in economically advanced societies they are responsible for as much as one-sixth of all crimes (Shelley, 1981a: 141).

Some societies have avoided high and rising crime rates as they have modernized. High overall crime rates have been avoided where traditional group ties and cultural values have been maintained; Japan and some Middle Eastern nations are examples. Control over urbanization and migration has also reduced the rate at which crime has increased (see the Cross-Cultural Perspective in Chapter 5). Harsh treatment of criminals—including long prison sentences or capital punishment—seemed to contain the crime problem in societies such as Stalin's Soviet Union and Franco's Spain. Eastern European nations have checked the growth of crime by redistributing income and guaranteeing jobs. By contrast, crime seems to have increased in advanced economic systems such as the United States where there is great income inequality and where everyone is urged to strive for material success (Shelley, 1981a: 142).

Opportunity and the Economy

Property crime rates increase especially dramatically with economic development because of growing opportunities for theft. Within developed economies, fluctuations in the value of certain goods can also create new opportunities for crime. For instance, the enormous increase in the market value of gold and silver during the 1970s changed the theft patterns of burglars, who began to leave behind televisions and stereos in favor of jewelry and silverware. Street criminals began to grab gold necklaces from women's necks, injuring and in a few cases even killing their victims. This increase in the theft of precious metals had several consequences: longer waiting lists for bank safe-deposit boxes; the updating of insurance policies; the establishment of refineries in the United States to melt down stolen jewelry, coins, and silverware; and advertisements by metal dealers to buy gold and silver with "no questions asked" (Peterson, 1980).

Other unusual crimes have developed as the value of goods has increased. "Bee rustling"—the theft of bee hives—became a problem as the cost of a bee colony climbed from $25 to $65 between 1975 and 1982. A truckload of one hundred hives could net the thieves $6,500 for one night of work, and the placement of hives far from their owners' homes meant that there was little risk of detection (*The New York Times*, August 22, 1982). Timber theft from national forests increased from 1,050 incidents in 1971 to 6,800 cases in 1980. This change seemed due to the increased use of wood-burning stoves as natural gas and oil became more expensive. To meet the great demand for firewood, thieves operating in bands of ten to fifteen stole tens of millions of dollars of wood from national forests, causing environmental damage in the process (Twomey, 1982).

Unemployment and Crime

Unemployment is related to crime and delinquency in complex ways (see, e.g., Thompson et al., 1981). Some crimes cannot occur unless a person is working; embezzlement and price fixing are examples. In such cases, higher unemployment rates might reduce crime. Other offenders mix employment and crime by "moonlighting" in crime, by using a job as a front (as with a professional fence), or by using legitimate income as a stake for a crime (as in drug deals). For moonlighters, more unemployment might increase criminal activity, but for those who use a job as a front or use their income for a stake, unemployment might reduce crime. Some people, especially youths, alternate between employment and crime, and in these cases more unemployment might increase crime and delinquency. Finally, some offenders are committed to crime as a source of income. They would not work even if jobs were available, and so a higher unemployment rate would not affect their criminal activity (Sviridoff and Thompson, 1983).

There may be an important difference between people who are working or are temporarily unemployed, and people who have been out of work for a long time or who have stopped looking for jobs. The difference between having a job or not having a job at any given moment may be less significant (Votey and Phillips, 1974). Even more important than finding a job is keeping a job over time, for having a job binds people to legitimate institutions and gives them a "stake in conformity" that they do not want to jeopardize by involvement in crime (Jeffery, 1977: 167–171). Criminals tend to have poorer work records and higher rates of unemployment than do nonoffenders, but some research indicates that more and better job opportunities might lead some offenders to select legitimate sources of income over illegal ones (Freedman, 1983: 106). People who hold unattractive jobs that pay poorly, are boring, and offer little room to advance may not think that they stand to lose much if they are arrested (Cook, 1975; Orsagh and Witte, 1981). As a result, finding a good job to which a person can feel committed over time seems to be more important than simply holding some job.

A study of released inmates concluded that employment in the postrelease period and the steadiness of that employment were strongly associated with lower arrest rates. However, experiments to help ex-convicts to find work through job counseling and job placement have not been very successful, nor have subsidized or government-created jobs been shown to be very effective in reducing crime (Rossi, Berk, and Lenihan, 1980).

One explanation of delinquency focuses on youth's lack of access to jobs that provide the income they need to participate in peer-group activities and buy the clothes, records, and other things that will win them the esteem of their friends. The exclusion of young people from adult work roles, and the increased competition that youths have recently encountered from greater numbers of female workers, deprive young people of income and make them financially dependent on their parents longer (Phillips and Votey, 1981). Juvenile delinquency has thus been attributed to the "structural position of juveniles in an advanced capitalist economy" that excludes the young from well-paying jobs by child labor laws, compulsory education, and minimum wage laws (Greenberg, 1977b: 220).

Overall, aggregate data for the nation show that fluctuations in the unemployment rate are no more than weakly related to the rate of index crimes. A review of ten studies done before 1975 found that seven revealed no significant relationship between unemployment and crime (Gillespie, 1975). Research since 1975 also provides "no strong support for the proposition that 'unemployment causes crime'" (Orsagh and Witte, 1981: 1059). A recent review of the evidence concludes as follows: "There is a cyclical pattern to the crime rate, with crime rising over the cycle with unemployment—but only weakly, so that changes in crime rates are dominated by other factors" (Freedman, 1983: 106).

Relative Deprivation and Crime

Even more important than poverty or unemployment as a cause of crime may be the way that poor or unemployed people perceive their situation. Most poor and unemployed people are law-abiding, and the crime rates of the poor in many developing nations are lower than the crime rates of Americans who have higher absolute standards of living. For instance, blacks in the United States have higher incomes, on the average, than do black Africans, but black Americans also have higher crime rates than black Africans.

What seems important, then, is people's relative standard of living. Resentment of poverty is probably more common among the poor in a wealthy nation than it is among people who have an absolutely lower standard of living in a poor nation (Toby, 1967). Quetelet observed in the nineteenth century that the rural poor in Europe were generally honest, but that the urban poor who were nearer to great wealth and temptation were more prone to crime. Relative rather than absolute poverty was given as the reason for this difference (Radzinowicz and King, 1977: 77). Evidence from the contemporary United States shows that crime rates are highest in cities where the difference between the income of the poor and the income of the rich is the greatest (Eberts and Schwirian, 1968).

The discrepancy between people's expectations and their capabilities can motivate them to violate the law. Expectations are the goods and conditions of life to which people think they are rightfully entitled, and capabilities are the goods and conditions of life they believe they can attain and maintain under the current social system (Gurr, 1970). The discrepancy between the two is called *relative deprivation*. Crime is probably more likely to occur when there is much relative deprivation with regard to deeply held goals such as material success. Crime may also occur when people think they have exhausted all constructive means to reach their goals and believe that legitimate opportunities to reduce their relative deprivation are closed to them. Crime is not, however, the only reaction to a sense of relative deprivation, for relative deprivation can also lead to political action, a social movement, suicide, or alcoholism. However, those who control political power often define the actions of the relatively deprived as crime, whether those actions are larceny, political protest, or terrorism.

Relative deprivation becomes greater when expectations increase or when capabilities decrease. A sudden drop in prosperity might reduce perceived capabilities, but relative deprivation more often increases because of a growth in expectations. In developing nations, the "demonstration effect" leads to a desire for a better standard of living among people who move to large cities where a wealthy life style can be observed firsthand. Capabilities usually do not rise as fast as expectations, and thus relative deprivation increases and crime rates rise (Clinard and Abbott, 1973).

IDEOLOGY AND EXPECTATIONS

The ideology of a society influences people's expectations, and thus affects the extent of relative deprivation and the amount of crime in the society. For instance, the United States and Great Britain have significantly different rates of homicide and robbery, in spite of similarities between the two societies. One reason for the different crime rates may be a difference in national ideologies. Great Britain's ideology does not emphasize social mobility to the same extent that the ideology of the United States does. The actual amount of movement from one class to another is not much different in the two societies, but Americans are more likely to think that their society is open to advancement, and this creates high expectations. When this perception of an open system is coupled with a strong emphasis on individualism—the belief that people succeed or fail on the basis of their own merits, rather than because of the way that society is organized—the scene is set for frustration if one fails to become wealthy or powerful. This is especially true if barriers to success, such as racial discrimination, are endemic to the society.

Data from the United States, where values promote the idea of equal opportunity for everyone, indicate that inequality is associated with higher rates of property crime (Danziger and Wheeler, 1975). However, a comparative study of sixty-two nations found that in other societies, inequality apparently does not lead to higher rates of property crimes as it does in the United States. In these other countries, inequality seems more closely associated with other forms of behavior, such as political action and social protest (Stack, 1984).

Anomie and Crime

An important effort to link crime to American cultural values was Robert K. Merton's 1938 paper on social structure and anomie. Merton (1968) sought to relate particular types of behavior to the social position of the people engaging in the behavior. Whereas Freud tried to explain deviance by the failure of the social structure to socialize people to control their natural impulses, Merton looked instead at social pressures that caused deviant or criminal behavior. He saw crime as rooted in the social system rather than as intrinsic to the makeup of humans. He was not interested in explaining the behavior of each and every individual, but in explaining differences in rates of behavior for different groups and categories of people.

GOALS AND MEANS

Merton's explanatory approach is based on a distinction between culturally defined goals and the norms that regulate the means to achieve those goals.

Goals are the valued purposes and interests that the culture holds out as legitimate objectives for all members of society. American culture emphasizes equal opportunity for all to attain the goals of wealth and power. Indeed, these goals are highly valued in most cultures (Gurr, 1970: 25–26). American culture encourages everyone to have the same high ambition, and treats the failure to achieve cultural goals as an individual failing rather than as a flaw in the social system. This belief protects the social system from criticism. The culture's emphasis on the measurement of individual worth by material success produces a society with a built-in incentive to achieve. This has helped the nation attain a high overall standard of living, but has also generated relative deprivation and crime among those who do not achieve the goals of wealth and power.

The second factor in Merton's theory can be described as the institutionalized means to reach the cultural goals. Norms, which define acceptable ways to reach cultural goals, are derived from the values or preferences of the society, rather than from the pure technical efficiency of the means in reaching goals. Thus, performing a successful bank robbery might be the most technically efficient way for an uneducated and unskilled person to attain material well-being, but social and legal norms define this as an unacceptable way to achieve wealth. Instead, norms emphasize hard work at a socially approved occupation over a lifetime, coupled with deferred gratification of the rewards of material success, as the appropriate way to achieve financial well-being.

ANOMIE

Social equilibrium exists when satisfactions accrue to people who use the institutionalized means to reach the culturally approved goals. When there is a disjunction between means and goals, *anomie* or normlessness results. A disjunction may result from the socially structured incapacity of people to use the approved means to reach cultural goals. Thus, racial discrimination in education, employment, and housing makes access to the institutionalized means of achieving success difficult for blacks and other minorities. Discrimination by class is another socially structured incapacity. Success may require a good education, which is less available to the poor, and "good manners," which are defined by the preferences of those who hold wealth and power. These socially structured incapacities are experienced as low capabilities, and can lead to relative deprivation that causes crime.

Socially structured incapacities might not produce anomie in a society in which success goals are not held out to everyone. The relative significance of material well-being in comparison to other goals may be the same in the United States and other nations, but the absolute strength of the drive to attain material success is probably greater in the United States than elsewhere. This has been called the American "fetishism of money" (Taylor, Walton, and Young, 1973: 94). This fetishism is spurred by the mass media, including television and magazines such as *Time, Newsweek,* and *People.* Television commercials urge consumers to spend money on goods and services that will bring them happiness. Sometimes the message to consume is more subtle. For instance, the large kitchens that are shown in television commercials for dish soap, scouring pads, and floor wax can be found only in homes that a small proportion of Americans can afford. Television viewers may vaguely sense being disadvantaged because the kitchens they see in television commercials are so much better than their own; they may even begin to hope that they will someday have enough money to afford a home with such a kitchen, which seems to them to be "just an average American kitchen."

MODES OF ADAPTATION

Merton develops a paradigm of five *modes of adaptation* to the social structure. He looks at the ways that individuals who occupy different social positions adapt to cultural goals and the institutionalized means to reach those goals. Table 8.1 indicates acceptance of a goal or means by a plus sign (+), rejection of a goal or means by a minus sign (−), and rejection of a goal or means and the substitution of a new goal or means by a plus-minus (±) sign.

Table 8.1:   Merton's Five Modes of Adaptation

MODES OF ADAPTATION	GOALS	MEANS
I. Conformity	+	+
II. Innovation	+	−
III. Ritualism	−	+
IV. Retreatism	−	−
V. Rebellion	±	±

+ = acceptance

− = rejection

± = rejection of goals or means, and substitution of new goals or means

SOURCE: *Social Theory and Social Structure*, 1968 Enlarged Edition, by Robert K. Merton (Copyright © 1968, 1967 by Robert K. Merton. Published by The Free Press, a Division of Macmillan, Inc.).

Conformity   The first mode of adaptation, *conformity*, is by far the most common adaptation to goals and means in a stable society. This pattern involves acceptance of cultural goals (such as material wealth), and the acceptance of the institutionalized means to reach those goals (such as a legitimate occupation).

Innovation   *Innovation* is the mode of adaptation most relevant to the analysis of criminal behavior. Here the goal is accepted, but means are used that society regards as unacceptable. Innovation is especially common when the goal that is sought is charged with great emotion. Thus the strong emphasis on material wealth as a sign of individual worth in the United States produces a powerful emotional investment in that goal, leading to a readiness to resort to illegal means to attain it when acceptable means are unavailable. The author of a study of shoplifting in department stores concluded that such theft is closely related to the acquisitiveness of American society and the emphasis placed on material symbols of success. She claims that theft is encouraged because department store goods are "dazzlingly arrayed before people who have been exhorted to desire them" (Cameron, 1964: 171).

Innovation occurs when business people resort to price fixing or embezzlement to attain material wealth for themselves or profits for their firms. Innovation also describes crimes such as tax fraud and larceny, which occur when the desire for more money or goods leads to violation of the law. The pressure to violate the law may be greatest among the lowest classes, because they are most distant from the goal of financial security and because their access to institutionalized means to attain material success is the most limited. However, as we have seen, the relationship between class and crime is not clear-cut, even though serious and repetitive index crimes seem to be most likely to be committed by people at the bottom of the stratification system. Merton's anomie theory emphasizes the disjunction between goals and means, and this approach is general enough to apply to property crimes committed by members of all classes.

The rise of many big-city political machines in the nineteenth-century grew out of efforts by Irish immigrants, who found industry and wealth controlled by native-born Americans, to gain power and status for themselves. When Italians arrived in the country some time after the Irish, they not only found that wealth was controlled by the native-born and that political power was controlled by Irish-Americans, but also that society's need for unskilled labor was less than it had been in earlier years. With the stimulus of Prohibition, some Italian immigrants innovated by using criminal means to achieve material wealth and political influence (Bell, 1962). Another view attributes the rise of Italians in organized crime not to blocked opportunities to achieve wealth and power, but rather to a rational choice of crime as an easy and exciting way to get rich (Lupsha, 1981). Just as not all Irish-Americans became politicians, so not all Italian-Americans became gangsters, but in each case some of the members of an ethnic group innovated by using new means to reach societal goals. Irish-American politicians used acceptable and legal means, and Italian-American gangsters employed unacceptable and illegal means.

Some observers claim that blacks and Puerto Ricans have recently taken over certain organized crime activities from Italian-Americans (Ianni, 1976). However, others argue that there has been little ethnic succession of Italian-Americans by blacks and Hispanics, except that some Italian-American gangsters have "licensed" members of those ethnic groups to help with low-profit, risky crimes at the street level (Lupsha, 1981). There is also some evidence of a recent growth in organized crime activities in the United States by crime cartels run by Chinese, Japanese, and Vietnamese immigrants (Raab, 1984a, 1984b).

Ritualism   Merton's third mode of adaptation, *ritualism*, holds little significance for the study of crime. Ritualists accept society's norms about appropriate means to reach cultural goals; for example, they hold regular jobs that produce steady incomes. However, ritualists scale down or give up cultural goals. They may keep working but realize that they will never achieve material success.

Retreatism   In *retreatism*, cultural goals are abandoned and institutionalized means are also rejected. Retreatists, such as skid-row alcoholics and drug addicts, are seen as alienated dropouts from society. Their rejection of cultural goals and their unwillingness to use accepted means to reach those goals are often interpreted as a challenge to the goals that most people hold. Their behavior may be regarded as immoral and criminal, even if there is no easily identified victim of their actions.

Rebellion   The final mode of adaptation is *rebellion*. Here, a person seeks to create a new social structure that will more effectively allow people to meet what the rebel considers appropriate goals. Rebels attack the value system of the ruling class and seek to replace it with an "ideal universal concept of justice" (Schafer, 1974: 30). The goals of rebels include the humanitarian treatment of all members of society; they oppose what they see as the exploitation of some groups to further the narrow interests of those who control power and wealth. Rebels have an "altruistic-communal motivation" for crime, rather than an egoistic motivation, and their offenses are directed toward nonpersonal goals. They seek to set an example for their followers and want publicity for their crimes. They pose a threat to lawmakers because they not only reject society's goals, but also propose to replace those goals with their own. Some acts of rebellion involve conventional crimes such as vandalism, burglary, arson, and murder. Other rebellious acts, such as treason and conspiracy to overthrow the government, are defined as crimes by those who control power in order to punish people who challenge the status quo (Schafer, 1974; Blumberg, 1974).

Conflict theorists see rebellion or political criminality as a struggle for authority or control over scarce resources. This struggle involves a dialectic, with the powerful trying to maintain the status quo and the powerless trying to gain power through dissent, evasion, disobedience, or violence. Those who control power often use the law to define behavior by political resisters as crime, especially if that behavior involves violence. The powerful justify such laws as necessary to defend the government, arguing that the special interests of resisters must be subordinated to the interests of the collectivity. Often the laws that are used to prosecute political resisters are vague and applied without the usual legal constraints of due process (Turk, 1982).

CRITIQUE OF ANOMIE THEORY

Merton's anomie theory is quite general, but it has stimulated important theoretical work on the values of different groups and the availability of legitimate and illegitimate means to reach cultural goals. The theory's assumption that everyone accepts the same cultural goals and that everyone is encouraged to achieve those goals does not describe many societies very well. Even in the United States, anomie theory seems to apply primarily to the goal of financial success and to crimes against property; it does not explain crimes of violence very well. Critics also suggest that in the United States anomie theory may apply better to men than to women, because men are socialized to pursue material success as a measure of self-worth more than women are (Leonard, 1982). If this is true, then anomie theory may help us to explain why men have higher crime rates than women do.

Differential Opportunity and Delinquency

During the 1950s, many cities in the United States experienced juvenile gang warfare, which involved assaults and sometimes murders. Not only did gang "rumbles" provide the basis for many newspaper, radio, and television reports, but they seeped into the popular culture in plays and movies such as *West Side Story.* During this era, criminologists focused their attention on juvenile delinquency, especially gang delinquency.

The great attention to gangs during the 1950s and 1960s, and the subsequent decline in interest in gangs, seem attributable to social and political influences on what criminologists study, rather than to an increase in gang delinquency during the earlier period and a decline in more recent years. According to one perspective, gangs were of interest in the 1950s and 1960s because the dominant political ideology then was centrist and because sociological theories were interactionist and subcultural. When ideological polarization occurred during the late 1960s, criminologists began to focus either on the larger social and economic structure or on individuals, and started to pay less attention to groups such as gangs. Gangs were largely ignored during the 1970s because of the popularity of labeling theory, which focused on status offenses and on the way that the juvenile justice system operates (Bookin-Weiner and Horowitz, 1983).

OPPORTUNITY AND GANG DELINQUENCY

One influential work on juvenile gangs is Richard A. Cloward and Lloyd E. Ohlin's *Delinquency and Opportunity: A Theory of Delinquent Gangs* (1960). Their *differential opportunity theory* combines Merton's anomie theory and

Sutherland's differential association theory, a learning theory that we examine later.

Cloward and Ohlin follow Merton in their emphasis on cultural goals and the means that people use to reach those goals. Merton claims that deviance in the form of innovation occurs when people lack access to the legitimate means to reach culturally approved goals. Cloward and Ohlin add to this theory by suggesting that people's access to both legitimate and illegitimate means is socially structured. In other words, there is "differential opportunity" to reach cultural goals by legitimate means, and there is also "differential opportunity" to use illegitimate means to reach those goals.

Differential opportunity theory focuses on the discrepancy between what lower-class juveniles want and what is available to them. It assumes that the "discrepancies between aspirations and legitimate chances of achievement increase as one descends in the class structure" (Cloward and Ohlin, 1960: 86). Lower-class youths learn their goals from the larger culture and are "unable to revise their aspirations downward" (Cloward and Ohlin, 1960: 86). As a result, their lack of access to legitimate means to reach cultural goals produces intense frustrations, and they search for illegitimate means to reach cultural goals. This theory is much like Merton's, except that Cloward and Ohlin go on to show how even these illegitimate means are differentially distributed in the society.

Cloward and Ohlin's theory suggests that two kinds of opportunities are differentially distributed. First, there are differences in access to "learning structures," which are the "appropriate environments for the acquisition of the values and skills associated with the performance of a particular role" (Cloward and Ohlin, 1960: 148). Sutherland's differential association theory focuses on the process by which these values and skills are learned through interaction with others; Cloward and Ohlin draw on this theory in their differential opportunity theory. Second, there are differences in access to what Cloward and Ohlin call "performance structures," the opportunity to join with others who share a similar problem of adjustment and the opportunity to gain peer approval for one's behavior. In other words, delinquents must not only learn certain values and skills, but they must also have support for the performance of delinquent behavior once they have learned those values and skills. According to differential opportunity theory, the social structure of a community determines the access that lower-class youths will have to both learning and performance structures. In other words, the social structure of the community affects the kind of subculture, and the kind of juvenile gang, that will develop in an area.

Criminal gangs *Criminal gangs* seek material gain, power, and prestige through illegitimate means such as theft. Gangs of this sort develop in communities where there are close ties between juvenile delinquents and adult criminals. Adult criminals, such as gangsters and professional thieves, transmit to young people in the neighborhood the values and skills that are important to the perpetration of crime. This is most likely to occur in stable lower-class communities where adult offenders are closely integrated with adults who hold conventional values.

Conflict gangs *Conflict gangs* provide a way for adolescents to achieve prestige in the eyes of their peers. When their relationships with adults in the community are weak, and when they lack access to both legitimate and illegitimate means to achieve success, juveniles may establish their own success goals (such as having a reputation for being tough) and develop their own means (such as gang fights) to achieve those goals.

Retreatist gangs *Retreatist gangs* are formed by juveniles who have failed to use both legitimate and illegitimate means to achieve success. They lack access to the illegitimate means used by criminal gangs, because they do not have close relationships with the adults in their community. They also lack the ability to attain prestige in a conflict gang. As a result, these juveniles abandon success goals and retreat into the use of drugs or alcohol. The drug user and the alcoholic establish life styles in which the routine of a job, commitment to convention, and self-restraint are missing. However, critics of this idea note that the daily search for heroin and the money with which to buy it involves addicts in a way of life that requires much planning, energy, and commitment (Finestone, 1964; Preble and Casey, 1972).

CRITIQUE OF DIFFERENTIAL OPPORTUNITY THEORY

Cloward and Ohlin see gang delinquency as related to the goals and means of the larger society and to the organization of the local community. They suggest that the integration of people of various ages in a community influences the kind of gang delinquency in an area, but they do not explain why a single community often has several types of gangs at the same time. Critics have also questioned whether the retreatist gang really exists, for addicts and alcoholics seem to be solitary more often than they are members of organized gangs.

Like Merton, Cloward and Ohlin assume that people are socialized with the desire for cultural goals, but confront obstacles to reaching those goals. Cloward and Ohlin offer no evidence that lower-class gang boys are socialized to want to reach those cultural goals, and no evidence that the discrepancy between goals and legitimate means is greater for lower-class gang members than for other lower-class youths. Like Merton, Cloward and Ohlin focus on social-structural factors such as institutionalized access to opportunities, rather than on individual decisions about how to act. A better approach might be to look at the way that people actually use available opportunities or seek out opportunities, as well as focus on differences in the socially structured opportunities available to different groups.

In spite of its shortcomings, Cloward and Ohlin's differential opportunity theory has been an important contribution to the study of delinquency. It has also influenced social policies, such as those of the Great Society programs of the 1960s, that have tried to reduce crime and delinquency by increasing the legitimate opportunities available to the lower classes.

Class, Values, and Delinquency

Very closely related to Merton's and to Cloward and Ohlin's social-structural theories of delinquency are social-psychological theories that emphasize class differences in values and responses to blocked opportunities. Two important theories of this sort are Albert K. Cohen's (1955) reaction-formation theory and Walter B. Miller's (1958) theory of lower-class culture.

WORKING-CLASS DELINQUENCY AND REACTION-FORMATION THEORY

In *Delinquent Boys*, Albert K. Cohen (1955: 25) develops a theory to explain why a juvenile delinquent subculture that he characterizes as "nonutilitarian, malicious, and negativistic" is found among working-class male adolescents. Cohen sees delinquency as a collective solution to a shared problem: blocked opportunities to achieve cultural goals. However, he is concerned only with certain kinds of delinquency: gang wars and vandalism, rather than profit-oriented theft.

Cohen describes the dominant American values in much the same way that Merton does: striving for success through hard work and discipline, deferring gratification, being ambitious, maintaining hope for the future, relying on oneself rather than on others, using individual skills to get ahead, respecting property, and controlling violence and aggression. Cohen claims that working-class adolescent males pick up these values from their parents, who share middle-class values even though they are members of the working class. Adolescents also learn middle-class values from the mass media and from former members of the working class who have entered the middle class. In addition, schools are important sources of middle-class values. Teachers communicate middle-class values and often come from the middle class themselves, and schools are organized around middle-class values such as discipline and self-reliance. According to Cohen, working-class adolescents are at a disadvantage in school, for their background does not equip them for academic success in this middle-class setting. Because they are too young to form a family or to hold a job that pays well, working-class adolescents lack legitimate opportunities to achieve culturally approved goals.

Working-class male adolescents share a problem of adjustment because of the double burden of class and youth. This shared condition is conducive to the development of a group solution to their common problem. They define their predicament in similar terms and have ample opportunity to interact. Often they band together in groups that define goals that they can achieve.

Because they are emotionally attached to middle-class goals that they cannot attain, these working-class boys must repudiate those goals. This produces a *reaction-formation*, a reversal of middle-class values. For instance, if the middle class favors the control of aggression, the working-class male adolescent subculture will award prestige for the use of violence. If the middle class reveres property, the working-class gang will value the senseless destruction of property. This reaction-formation is a psychological defense against the failure to achieve strongly held desires. Seeking the exact opposite of what is valued by the middle class is a way to repudiate those goals and validate the goals that replace them. The new goals also increase solidarity among the working-class boys by making the middle class a common enemy.

Cohen thus links a particular class (the working class) to specific values (aggressiveness and destructiveness) that, in turn, cause certain kinds of law-violating behavior (gang fights and vandalism). The type of delinquency that Cohen is interested in thus originates from a repudiation of middle-class values, rather than from conformity to working-class values.

Critique of reaction-formation theory   Cohen's theory, like Merton's, requires a culture that encourages everyone to strive for the same goals, especially material success. We can see in the following Cross-Cultural Perspective that Argentina is one society in which Cohen's theory does not work very well; little "nonutilitarian, malicious, and negativistic" working-class delinquency occurs there, apparently because the lowest classes are not socialized to seek middle-class goals.

Cohen's reaction-formation theory does not explain middle-class delinquency very well. Neither does it explain why some delinquents turn away from violations of the law and leave gangs as they grow older, while other delinquents move on to adult crime. Cohen's emphasis on age explains why

A Cross-Cultural Perspective: Delinquency in Argentina

To test the usefulness of Albert K. Cohen's reaction-formation theory of delinquency, Lois B. DeFleur studied boys who had violated the law and appeared in court in Córdoba, Argentina, a city of 600,000 people.

Contrary to Cohen's theory that much theft by working-class adolescent males would be nonutilitarian, DeFleur found that Córdoban boys who appeared in court sold the stolen goods or personally used them in about 80 per cent of their thefts. For these boys, stealing was a means to get money and goods, rather than a nonutilitarian activity as in Cohen's theory. DeFleur found little evidence that delinquency in Argentina was malicious, the second element in Cohen's theory. "Malicious jokes or tricks, senseless vandalism, and unprovoked assaults on others" were relatively uncommon among the Argentine boys. DeFleur also found little evidence for the third element of Cohen's reaction-formation subculture, negativism. There was no clear evidence that the Argentine boys were expressing hostility toward people who had more property. They did envy them, wanted to have their possessions, and expressed scorn for people who worked hard, but they did not show "open animosity" toward the middle or upper classes, nor did they deliberately flout authority. In sum, DeFleur found little evidence of a reaction-formation subculture in Córdoba. At most, there were scattered indicators of such a subculture, and even these occurred infrequently.

DeFleur did find juvenile street gangs in Córdoba. Most of them engaged in the theft of property, which was usually sold to adults. There were traditional neighborhood rivalries and gang fights, but fighting was not the gang's primary reason for existence. There was little drug use by gang members, for drugs were too expensive for these poor boys. The gangs in Córdoba represented an instrumental-theft subculture; theft was a way to pursue pleasure, not an end in itself, as it was in Cohen's reaction-formation theory.

Cohen's theory did not fit the experience of the Argentine boys very well because their culture does not emphasize success and status-striving for everyone. Latin countries are more often characterized by a rigid class structure that encourages people to keep to their inherited station in life. Cohen's theory, on the other hand, requires a strong commitment to achievement and upward mobility. In Argentina, status-striving is a recent development, and one that has not yet filtered down to the lower classes. In other words, there is no cultural theme of equal opportunity shared by all of the classes in Argentina, and this is an essential ingredient of Cohen's theory of gang delinquency.

SOURCE: Lois B. DeFleur, *Delinquency in Argentina: A Study of Córdoba's Youth.* Pullman, Wash.: Washington State University Press, 1970.

some males move out of delinquency as they gain access to other sources of prestige such as jobs and families, but his emphasis on class does not tell us why most delinquents give up illegal behavior even though they remain members of the working class.

LOWER-CLASS CULTURE AND DELINQUENCY

Contrary to Cohen's theory that nonutilitarian, working-class male delinquency has its roots in the rejection of traditional middle-class values is the position of Walter B. Miller (1958). Miller proposes that gang delinquency in lower-class communities is a result of positive efforts by adolescents to achieve goals that are spelled out in the *focal concerns,* or values, of a lower-class culture. The lower-class culture that Miller suggests is the "generating milieu" of delinquency exists among the 15 per cent of the population that he calls the "hard-core lower class" and to some extent among another 25 to 45 per cent of the population that is directly influenced by lower-class values. Miller made these estimates in the 1950s; the proportions are probably considerably lower today because of a reduction in the proportion of Americans living in poverty and because of the assimilation of many Americans into the middle class.

Focal concerns Miller examines six lower-class focal concerns, or areas of interest that elicit widespread, persistent attention and emotional involvement. The focal concern of "trouble" refers to situations that bring unwelcome or complicating involvement with official authority. Issues of staying out of trouble and getting into trouble are of daily concern to the lower class, according to Miller. The lower class avoids illegal behavior, he says, in order to keep out of trouble, rather than because it is committed to a law-abiding way of life. The lower class seeks to avoid violating the law, but at the same time may admire those who violate the law.

A second focal concern is "toughness," a concern with masculinity, physical prowess, bravery, and daring. A third is "smartness," the capacity to outwit or "con" others and avoid being duped oneself. Through clever verbal exchanges, lower-class youths can achieve prestige by demonstrating maximum use of their mental abilities and minimum use of their physical strength. There is an apparent contradiction here, for toughness can inhibit the display of smartness, and smartness can inhibit the display of toughness; both, however, are of concern to the lower class, according to Miller.

Another focal concern of lower-class culture is "excitement," the concern with thrills, risks, and the avoidance of boredom. The life of the poor may be unstimulating because of the lack of money with which to pay for leisure goods and activities, and this may be a source of the lower class's interest in exciting activities. Indeed, a study of teen-age gangs earlier in this century found that avoidance of boredom was a major reason for gang delinquency (Thrasher, 1927, 1963). The search for excitement can also lead to gambling and to the use of alcohol and narcotics.

Another focal concern of the lower class is "fate," an interest in luck, fortune, and jinxes. The poor often feel, and with some justification, that their lives are governed by external forces over which they have little or no control. Related to this concern with external control is a sixth focal concern, "autonomy." This refers to a desire to be one's own master, which is often expressed as "no one's going to push me around."

Critique of lower-class culture theory Miller sees the gang as a social setting within which juveniles can gain prestige by acting in accordance with the focal concerns of their class. This theory might lead us to believe that all members of the lower-class, even adults, will violate the law regularly, for the theory does not distinguish between offenders and nonoffenders from the lower class in terms of their focal concerns. In addition, Miller does not explain the origins of these focal concerns. In contrast to Miller, Cohen is concerned with the values and norms of working-class male adolescents. He treats their delinquency as deviance from middle-class values, rather than as conformity to lower-class values. Cohen and Miller diverge in their explanations of delinquency, but both examine the role of values that are linked to class.

Opportunity, Values, and Class:
An Evaluation of Delinquency Theories

James F. Short, Jr., and Fred L. Strodtbeck (1965) have tested the theories of Cloward and Ohlin, Cohen, and Miller. They gathered data from boys between sixteen and eighteen who belonged to gangs ("gang boys"), lower-class boys of the same age who did not belong to gangs ("lower-class boys"), and middle-class boys who did not belong to gangs ("middle-class boys").

To test Cohen's reaction-formation theory, Short and Strodtbeck looked for indications of bitterness and contempt toward middle-class values among the gang boys. Cohen's theory also led Short and Strodtbeck to expect that the gang boys would evaluate deviant values more highly than middle-class values.

Miller's theory of lower-class culture as a generating milieu of gang delinquency states that the lower class has a distinctive value system; this suggests that both gang boys and lower-class boys should evaluate middle-class values less favorably than middle-class boys do. According to Short and Strodtbeck, Miller's theory also implies that gang boys and lower-class boys should evaluate lower-class values more highly than they do middle-class values. In addition, Miller's theory suggests that gang boys and lower-class boys should evaluate deviant values more highly than middle-class boys do.

According to Short and Strodtbeck, Cloward and Ohlin's differential opportunity theory indicates that gang boys should be indifferent toward membership in the middle class, even if they are eager to improve their own economic well-being. As a result, lower-class boys should be "cool" toward middle-class values, and gang boys should evaluate deviant values more highly than middle-class boys do. Differential opportunity theory also implies that middle-class values will not be as highly endorsed by gang boys as by middle-class boys.

Short and Strodtbeck found little empirical support for any of these theories. The three groups of boys all evaluated middle-class values equally highly, and all three groups evaluated middle-class values more highly than "nearly all other subcultural images, especially those that are unquestionably illegitimate" (Short and Strodtbeck, 1965: 59). None of the theories would have predicted these results. Short and Strodtbeck (1965: 65) concluded that "there is evidence of neither differential nor low legitimation of the behaviors represented by the middle-class images by any population." They also found that neither the gang boys nor the lower-class boys evaluated lower-class values significantly more highly than they did middle-class values; this suggests that the three theories of delinquency are inaccurate or incomplete.

PRESCRIBED AND PROSCRIBED NORMS

Short and Strodtbeck found that gang boys evaluated behavior in much the same way as nondelinquents of the lower class did and in much the same way as middle-class boys did. All three groups accepted what middle-class norms prescribed or recommended. There were, however, differences in their evaluation of things that middle-class values proscribed or disapproved. Goals approved by middle-class values were meaningful to all three groups of boys, but the gang boys were more tolerant of theft and violence, which were proscribed by middle-class standards. The values of the gang boys thus allowed rather than required delinquent behavior. Boys became delinquent because they lacked commitment to conformity, rather than because they accepted norms that forced them to violate the law (Short and Strodtbeck, 1965: 72–76; also, see Briar and Piliavin, 1965).

A study in Uganda uncovered data consistent with Short and Strodtbeck's interpretation of their data. The research in Uganda found little difference between offenders and nonoffenders in their perceived need for greater material well-being. However, the offenders were more likely to believe that success was possible only if they violated the law and that it would be difficult for them to earn much money without breaking the law. These offenders believed in hard work to achieve success, but thought that opportunities to follow that legitimate path to success were restricted and that crime was therefore justified (Clinard and Abbott, 1973: 182–186).

One way to interpret Short and Strodtbeck's conclusion that there was no difference between delinquents and nondelinquents in prescribed norms, but that there was a difference in proscribed norms, is to assume that the gang boys did not condemn theft and violence because they had been improperly socialized. However, the fact that they shared many values with middle-class boys is evidence that they had been socialized in a way similar to middle-class boys. The gang boys' acceptance of behavior disapproved by middle-class values may better be seen as a difference in values rather than as a lack of values.

CLASS, VALUES, AND DELINQUENCY

Class by itself does not cause crime and delinquency. Instead, violation of the law is a result of factors associated with class, such as values, goals, and socially structured opportunities. We would thus expect delinquents from all classes to have certain values, goals, and opportunities in common, and also to differ from nondelinquents of all classes in those factors.

One study that looked at lower-class, middle-class, and upper-class delinquency tried to explain youthful misbehavior in terms other than class. The researcher found that commitment to values such as short-run pleasure-seeking, thrills, excitement, trouble, toughness, conning, and the search for a "fast buck" was associated with self-reported involvement in delinquency, and this was true for all classes. This study also revealed less commitment to conventional value orientations such as hard work, delayed gratification, formal education, and various themes of the Protestant ethic among boys of all classes who engaged in delinquency (Cernkovich, 1978c). This research suggests that class is a less important predictor of delinquency than values, and that values are imperfectly correlated with class.

There is reason to believe that some people are able to violate the law because they can "stretch values" (Hyman, 1966). These individuals may share values with the middle class and the law-abiding, but because of weak attachments to family, school, and work, they believe that they have little to lose from violating the law. They may thus be more flexible in interpreting social constraints on their behavior. For instance, one middle-class value is respect for property; the related norm is that property should not be stolen, damaged, or used without the owner's permission. This norm is adhered to by most people, but some people are able to stretch the norm by reinterpreting it to define a purse on an office desk as property that can be stolen because the owner was careless enough to leave it unattended. The stretching of norms to permit violation of the law probably occurs among members of all classes, including poor people who shoplift and wealthy executives who engage in price-fixing conspiracies.

Short and Strodtbeck (1965: 248–264) suggest a similar interpretation of their finding that all three groups of boys in their study supported prescribed middle-class values, but that gang boys held different attitudes toward acts proscribed by these values. They propose that some lower-class males may find it more practical to be deviant in certain situations. These boys may react to situational pressures in ways that allow them to neutralize norms prohibiting certain behavior. Because American society lacks rites of passage, or formal processes, by which adolescents enter adulthood, some adolescents experiment with various forms of "adult" behavior. In these circumstances, it may be rational for boys to break the law if that behavior allows them to gain prestige among their friends. Short and Strodtbeck argue that if there is a small chance of serious consequences such as arrest, and a great chance to gain prestige from fighting or theft, it makes sense for gang boys to violate the law. The payoff in social approval is immediate, but punishment is uncertain and remote in time.

JUVENILE GANGS TODAY

Since the mid-1960s, there has been relatively little theoretical or empirical work on delinquent gangs, compared to the efforts expended on gangs during the decade from 1955 to 1965. There is evidence, however, that gangs continue to thrive in many American cities, and have even developed in many smaller communities. For instance, Walter B. Miller has identified 2,200 gangs with about 96,000 members in 300 communities (cited in *The Boston Globe,* July 10, 1981).

One city that has experienced major problems with gang delinquency is Los Angeles, which in 1984 had 420 gangs with a total of 40,000 members. In 1983, Los Angeles had 214 gang-related homicides, compared to 351 in 1980, 267 in 1981, and 205 in 1982 (Cummings, 1984). Gangs have existed in Los Angeles since the 1920s, but increased significantly in number and membership in the late 1970s and early 1980s. One explanation is that Hispanic and Southeast Asian immigrants have banded together for self-defense and to provide the social ties that families have traditionally provided. Some black and Hispanic groups in Los Angeles are involved in drug dealing; they act as entrepreneurs interested in profit rather than as retreatists. Vietnamese gangs in Los Angeles specialize in the extortion of "protection money" from merchants (King, 1982; Oppenheim, 1983; Cummings, 1984).

Since the 1950s, gangs have focused on protection of their "turf," an area of the city they define as theirs. Gangs often organize along militaristic lines to protect their neighborhood from "invaders"; people have been killed just for venturing into "enemy territory." In communities where arson has razed entire blocks in recent years, turf has become a less important basis for gang solidarity. One police officer has said, "There is no land to fight over. In many of the poor neighborhoods of the city, turf consists of a block full of abandoned buildings" (cited in Chambers, 1983). Another officer says that the emphasis today has shifted from turf to the sale of drugs, but that gangs continue to define strictly who controls the sale and distribution of drugs in each community (Chambers, 1983).

The Subculture of Violence

One theory of the origin of violent crime that uses norms and values as explanatory variables is the *subculture-of-violence theory* developed by Marvin E. Wolfgang and Franco Ferracuti (1967, 1982). They state that the norms shared by a group of people may define violence as an appropriate response to certain circumstances. They claim that these norms have a reality of their own and that they influence behavior, sometimes leading people to engage in violent crime in order to conform to others' expectations (Della Fave, 1974). Wolfgang and Ferracuti do not explore the historical and social-structural origins of these norms in detail, but they imply that the norms originate in the social conditions of certain countries, classes, and racial and ethnic groups. Because the theory is presented as a cultural explanation of violent crime, rather than as a social-structural explanation, Wolfgang and Ferracuti emphasize norms, values, and beliefs rather than the specific social conditions that give rise to a subculture of violence.

Wolfgang and Ferracuti claim that there are identifiable subcultures in which violence and aggression are regarded as a proper response to threats, insults, or the display of a weapon. A *subculture* is a patterned way of life similar in some ways but different in others from the dominant culture of a society. It includes specific standards of behavior that are learned and transmitted from generation to generation. In a subculture of violence, these norms differ from those of the dominant culture in expectations about the use of interpersonal aggression. As a result, the more integrated into a subculture of violence an individual or a group is, the greater the likelihood that the individual or group will engage in violent crime. Violence in such a subculture is rarely accompanied by guilt, because violence is not considered wrong or deviant. Violent individuals in a subcultural setting such as this are not pathological, but instead are conformists to the values of their group.

EVIDENCE ON THE SUBCULTURE OF VIOLENCE

Wolfgang's study of homicide in Philadelphia found evidence consistent with the subculture-of-violence theory. Forty-three per cent of the homicide offenders had been arrested previously for crimes against the person, and about one-fourth of the homicide victims had been arrested for crimes against the person (Wolfgang, 1958: 178). Whites had a murder rate of 1.8 per 100,000, and white males between twenty and twenty-four had a rate of 8.2 per 100,000. Blacks, on the other hand, had a murder rate of 24.6 per 100,000, and black males between twenty and twenty-four had a homicide rate of 92.5 per 100,000 (Wolfgang, 1958: 33, 66). The homicide rate for young black males was thus much higher than the rate for any other group. Wolfgang and Ferracuti later interpreted these and other data as support for their theory that among certain groups, such as young black males in large American cities, and in certain nations, such as Colombia with its pattern of violence known as *violencia*, there exist norms that support the use of interpersonal violence.

There is other evidence that a subculture of violence may exist among black Americans. One study of fifty black offenders found that about 70 per cent of them carried firearms because they anticipated attacks by others; this defensive posture could lead to crimes of violence (Schultz, 1962). There is also some evidence that blacks are more likely than whites to engage in angry fistfights, even though blacks do not report that they feel group support for this activity. The value that blacks place on "staying cool" leads to more talk about fighting than actual fighting (Erlanger, 1974). Evidence contradictory to the idea that there is a subculture of violence among black Americans comes from a study that found that although whites commit less homicide than blacks, whites are more likely to report that they own firearms, are more likely to have been assaulted, and are more tolerant of assaultive behavior (Doerner, 1978).

A study of forcible rape found no subculture of rape, but concluded that a general subculture of violence was an important source of rape. According to the researcher, a sociocultural framework preceded and determined the formation of personalities conducive to rape. In addition, this sociologist found a high rate of rape among lower-class black male youths in peer groups, a

The subculture-of-violence theory attempts to explain the high rates of violent crime among certain groups. Here two gangs of adolescent boys are engaged in a knife fight.

Copyright by J. P. Laffont-Sygma. Reprinted by permission of Sygma.

category of people that Wolfgang and Ferracuti claim shares a subculture of violence (Amir, 1971: 320–324).

The evidence is still inconclusive, but there do seem to be violence-prone groups that may share the norms and attitudes of a subculture of violence. For a subculture of violence to exist, three elements must be present:

1. A group that shows norms and attitudes that differ from those of the culture of the larger society;
2. A means to transmit the norms and attitudes to the next generation; and
3. Contact among the members of the group to keep the norms and attitudes alive.

In the United States, firearm ownership does not fit these criteria. There is no regular interaction among gun owners. Ownership of firearms for defense and protection is a function of the amount of violent crime in a community, rather than a function of the perceptions, attitudes, or social background of gun owners. In sum, the three conditions necessary to a subculture of violence do not fit the data on gun ownership in the United States (Lizotte and Bordua, 1980).

HOMICIDE IN THE SOUTH: TESTING FOR A SUBCULTURE OF VIOLENCE

Several criminologists have tried to explain differences between the homicide rates of southern states and the homicide rate of the rest of the country in terms of a subculture of violence (Hackney, 1969; Gastil, 1971; Loftin and Hill, 1974; Erlanger, 1975; O'Connor and Lizotte, 1978; Messner, 1982, 1983a, 1983b). Earlier in the book we saw that southern states have homicide rates higher than other regions, even though homicide rates in different parts of the country have become more similar in recent years. However, the South does not have especially high rates of other violent crimes.

The methodology usually employed to test the effect of cultural values on the homicide rates of different regions is to isolate the effects of economic and social factors on homicide rates, and then attribute the remaining variation in regional homicide rates to cultural differences, such as the norms of the subculture of violence. The problem with this approach is that it includes no direct measure of regional variations in norms and values. As a result, if the measurement of economic and social factors is inadequate or incomplete, the residual effect of cultural factors may be exaggerated. One study concluded that the economic, educational, and racial composition of the states was relatively unimportant in explaining regional variations in homicide rates, and suggested that a subculture of violence explained such variations (Hackney, 1969). However, a later study that employed a more sophisticated measure of poverty found that poverty explained much of the state-by-state variation in homicide rates (Loftin and Hill, 1974). Thus an index that better measured poverty left a smaller residual variation in homicide rates that could be attributed to the subculture of violence.

A recent study found that the homicide rates of 204 metropolitan areas in the United States were influenced by the region in which the city was located and by its racial composition, even when factors such as poverty were controlled (Messner, 1983a). In other words, the higher homicide rates in the southern cities and in the cities with larger black populations could not be accounted for by low income alone. However, this study, like most previous ones, provided no direct measure of subcultural values and perspectives.

Another study concluded that poverty does have a significant effect on a metropolitan area's homicide rate, but that the impact of poverty on the homicide rate varies from one region to another. This study also found that greater income inequality between races is associated with higher levels of criminal violence, and that the relative size of a metropolitan area's black population is associated with its homicide rate, even after economic factors are accounted for (Williams, 1984).

The precise role of the subculture of violence in explaining regional variations in homicide rates is still unclear. The high rate of firearm ownership and the widespread opposition to gun-control laws in the South, along with that area's military tradition, history of lynching, and aggressive defense of womanhood all suggest to some sociologists that attitudes in southern states toward the use of violence might differ from attitudes in other regions. However, the South differs little from other regions in the ownership of handguns, the weapon most often used in crime. Instead, the South's higher rate of firearm ownership is due to regional differences in the ownership of rifles and shotguns, which are rarely used to kill people (Wright, Rossi, and Daly, 1983).

Another indirect kind of evidence cited as an indication of the greater tolerance of violence in the South is the fact that all southern states now have capital punishment, and that most of the people on Death Row and most of the people who have been executed in recent years are in southern states. One sociologist has commented that "both murder and the death penalty reflect mostly the extent to which there exists a subculture in which killing is considered a morally obligatory response to a large range of rebuff or disagreement, outweighing the moral tenet that all life is sacred" (Glaser, 1971: 57).

One reason for the high homicide rate of blacks throughout the country might be that many of them, or their parents, were brought up in the South, where they learned norms and values conducive to violence. With migration from the South, those norms and values might have become diffused throughout the country (Pettigrew and Spier, 1962). There are obviously many causes of violent crime in the United States, but the diffusion of a subculture of violence that has a southern origin might be one such cause.

CRITIQUE OF THE SUBCULTURE-OF-VIOLENCE THEORY
Some groups, regions, and countries do have high rates of criminal violence, but there is as yet no strong evidence supporting a role for the subculture of violence in the genesis of violent crime. This may be because the appropriate research design to test for this relationship has not been developed or implemented. Some researchers have inferred norms and attitudes supporting the use of violence from the high rates of violent crime among certain groups, and then explained those high rates of violent crime by the inferred norms and attitudes. This tautological approach provides no independent evidence that norms and attitudes supporting violence exist among groups that have high rates of violent crime.

We also have no direct evidence that southerners hold the values of a subculture of violence (Reed, 1971; Ball-Rokeach, 1973; Curtis, 1975). More research on cultural differences among regions of the country might be done by carrying out surveys or by examining regional variations in preferences for art, literature, music, or sports (Messner, 1983a). Even if such regional variations were found, they might not explain differences in violent crime rates, for one study concluded that violence is more an outcome of the nature of social interaction in certain groups than a result of different norms and values about when violence is appropriate (Ball-Rokeach, 1973).

SOCIOECONOMIC FACTORS AND VARIATIONS IN CRIME RATES

The social, economic, and cultural factors examined in this chapter help us to make sense of the variations in crime rates that we looked at in earlier chapters.

Cross-national variations in crime rates seem to be due to differences among countries in social structure, economy, and culture. For instance, some white-collar crimes are more likely to occur in certain kinds of economies; thus, price fixing occurs in the American economy as business people try to enhance profits, and bribery by consumers is more common in the Soviet Union where goods and services are in short supply. The degree to which a society relies on laws to make widely desired goods and services illegal influences the development and strength of organized crime in the society. Variations in rates of conventional crime from one society to another are attributable in part to the level of economic development, the extent of relative deprivation, the degree to which everyone feels entitled to material success, and the opportunities that are available to achieve culturally approved goals.

Just as cross-national variations in crime can be explained by differences in the social structure, economy, and culture of a country, so regional variations can also be explained by similar differences among areas within a country. The subculture-of-violence theory proposes that variations in violent crime can be explained by regional differences in norms and attitudes toward violence, but we lack strong supporting evidence for this theory.

Variations in crime rates by size of the community may also be related to the factors examined in this chapter. For example, the economic conditions characteristic of urban communities differ from the economic conditions in small towns and rural areas, and these differences may explain in part the higher crime rates of larger communities. In addition, the close proximity of people from different classes in large communities may increase relative deprivation among the poor and lead to more conventional crime than occurs in the relatively more homogeneous small towns and rural areas.

Temporal variations in crime rates can be accounted for by changes in the social structure, the economy, and the culture. Changes in market conditions can lead to an increase or a decrease in white-collar crime. Technological breakthroughs and a growing reliance on trust and credit create new opportunities for white-collar crime. The passage of laws that prohibit the consumption of widely desired goods and services results in more opportunities for organized crime; this happened during Prohibition, and again more recently with the development of strict controls on the disposal of toxic wastes. The modernization process leads to changes in rates of conventional crime, especially rates of property crime. Conventional crimes also increase or decrease as groups experience relative deprivation, anomie, and blocked opportunities.

Variations in crime rates by sex, age, race, and class are also related to the social structure, the economy, and the culture. For example, most white-collar crimes are committed by middle-aged or older white men of the middle or upper classes. The time needed to advance to the positions in which white-collar crime is committed means that white-collar offenders are usually middle-aged or older. White-collar offenders are usually white men, because discrimination by sex and race has closed many higher-level positions in corporations to women and minorities. As such discrimination is reduced, we would expect more white-collar crimes to be committed by women and minorities.

Anomie theory, differential opportunity theory, reaction-formation theory, and the theory that lower-class culture is a generating milieu of gang delinquency all account for the higher rates of serious and repetitive conventional crime among the lower and working classes. These theories help to account for the high rate of crime by young people, for these people are the most remote from the cultural goal of material success and are probably the most likely to encounter blocked opportunities. These social-structural theories also account for the high crime rates of blacks, who have had opportunities to achieve material success blocked by racial discrimination. The subculture-of-violence theory proposes that blacks' high rate of violent crime is due to a difference between their norms and attitudes toward violence and whites' norms and attitudes toward violence, but there is no strong and consistent evidence that this is so. Social-structural theories of crime and delinquency do not seem to do a good job of explaining low crime rates for females; in some cases, these theories were specifically designed to explain violations by males. We might expect that the blocked opportunities encountered by women would lead them to commit crime at a higher rate than men, but this is not the case. This may be because men more than women are socialized to pursue the cultural goal of material success, and are thus more likely to turn to crime when they do not reach that goal.

We have not looked at all of the ways in which the social, economic, and cultural factors examined in this chapter can explain geographic, temporal, and social variations in rates of white-collar, organized, and conventional crime. From this brief discussion, however, we can see that social, economic, and cultural theories are useful in explaining variations in crime rates.

SUMMARY

In this chapter, we have examined the social and economic causes of white-collar crime, organized crime, and conventional crime (with an emphasis on juvenile delinquency).

American free-enterprise ideology emphasizes profit-seeking and competition. The pressure to make profits sometimes leads executives and corporations to violate the law, and efforts to outperform competitors can lead to offenses such as price fixing. Certain market conditions are conducive to white-collar crime. Trust and credit may be abused, as was the case in the Equity Funding Corporation of America fraud. Large corporations have characteristics such as large size, bureaucratic structure, impersonality, and rational decision making that are conducive to white-collar crime and employee theft. As new technology develops, opportunities are created for crime; computer crime and EFT crime are examples of costly offenses that have become problems in recent years.

Prohibition provided an opportunity for gangsters to become highly organized in their pursuit of profits. Since Prohibition ended in 1933, organized crime has turned to other sources of income, including gambling (according to some accounts), loan sharking, narcotics, bankruptcy fraud, and the illegal disposal of toxic wastes. Gangsters use the techniques of legitimate business to make a profit, and this is true in Japan and other countries as well as in the United States.

Conventional crimes, especially property crimes, increase with economic development. Modernization also brings increased participation in crime by juveniles and by women. New opportunities for crime develop as an economy modernizes, and changes in the value of certain goods (such as precious metals) may alter patterns of crime. Unemployment rates are not closely associated with crime rates, although a few studies have found a weak relationship. Employment may be more important for the social ties it provides than for the income it produces. One source of criminal behavior is relative deprivation, a situation that exists when people believe they are entitled to more than they can achieve by the legitimate means available to them. A culture that emphasizes the possibility of upward mobility for everyone can create relative deprivation among people who do not achieve financial success.

Anomie theory proposes that a disjunction between cultural goals and access to legitimate means to attain those goals can lead to certain kinds of crime.

Innovation occurs among those who strongly pursue cultural goals with means that are not socially approved; examples include petty theft by the poor and price fixing by corporate executives. Retreatists and rebels are often defined as criminals by those who control power.

Differential opportunity theory emphasizes access to both legitimate and illegitimate means to reach cultural goals. The social structure of a community affects access by lower-class youth to both learning and performance structures. As a result, the kind of gang that delinquents form—criminal, conflict, or retreatist—depends on the relationship of young people to adult criminals and the relationship of adult criminals to conventional adults in a community.

Reaction-formation theory proposes that working-class male adolescents learn middle-class values, but because they are not equipped to succeed in school and at work, they reject these values and create values opposite to them. They support violence and the theft and destruction of property, and this leads to "nonutilitarian, malicious, and negativistic" behavior. This theory does not explain delinquency in Córdoba, Argentina, because poor boys there are not socialized with the hope that they will join the middle class, and thus they do not have to react against middle-class values.

The theory that delinquents react against middle-class values differs from the theory that the lower class is a generating milieu for gang delinquency. In this theory, delinquency is seen as a kind of conformity to the values or focal concerns of the lower class: trouble, toughness, smartness, excitement, fate, and autonomy.

An empirical study that evaluated differential opportunity theory, reaction-formation theory, and lower-class culture theory found little support for any of them. Instead, gang boys seemed to favor the goals of the middle class, but did not feel bound to avoid deviance from middle-class norms. Delinquents seemed to be able to "stretch" values, and they often had more to gain in peer prestige from violating the law than they had to lose from such behavior. Today, juvenile gangs are still an important problem in the United States, but less theoretical and empirical work is being done on gang delinquency than was done from 1955 to 1965.

The subculture-of-violence theory proposes that among certain groups and in certain areas there is a set of norms that support violent responses to certain situations. Some groups, such as urban blacks in the United States, and some regions, such as the South, do have high rates of criminal violence. However, there is no strong evidence that these groups and regions have distinctive norms and attitudes that support violence, or that such norms and attitudes lead to violent crime.

The social, economic, and cultural factors that we have looked at in this chapter are helpful in explaining geographic, temporal, and social variations in different kinds of crime.

IMPORTANT TERMS

anomie
computer crime
conflict gang
conformity
criminal gang
differential opportunity
  theory

EFT crime
focal concern
innovation
mode of adaptation
reaction-formation
rebellion
relative deprivation

retreatism
retreatist gang
ritualism
subculture
subculture-of-violence
  theory

SUGGESTED READINGS

MARSHALL B. CLINARD AND PETER C. YEAGER. *Corporate Crime*. New York: Free Press, 1980. An analysis of antitrust offenses, false advertising, bribery, tax evasion, and the production of unsafe products by American corporations.

RICHARD A. CLOWARD AND LLOYD E. OHLIN. *Delinquency and Opportunity: A Theory of Delinquent Gangs*. New York: Free Press, 1960. An important theoretical statement of differential opportunity theory.

JOHN E. CONKLIN. *"Illegal but Not Criminal": Business Crime in America*. Englewood Cliffs, N.J.: Prentice-Hall, 1977. A brief synthesis of sociological work on the costs, causes, and punishment of white-collar crime.

PETER REUTER. *Disorganized Crime: The Economics of the Visible Hand*. Cambridge, Mass.: MIT Press, 1983. A study that calls into question some of the conventional wisdom on the activities and power of organized crime in the United States.

MARVIN E. WOLFGANG AND FRANCO FERRACUTI. *The Subculture of Violence: Towards an Integrated Theory in Criminology*. Beverly Hills, Calif.: Sage Publications, 1967, 1982. An important theoretical statement of the subculture-of-violence theory.

9

Social Control and Commitment to the Law

Because most people learn to abide by the law, or are at least aware that the law commands widespread respect, they can engage in crime or delinquency only after they have minimized their commitment to the law. People neutralize the power of the law by justifying their offenses to themselves and to others. Some people are weakly attached to conventional institutions, and this leaves them relatively free to violate the law. In this chapter, we explore the ways that neutralization of the law and the absence of social control lead to behavior that violates the law.

NEUTRALIZING THE LAW

The theories of anomie, differential opportunity, reaction-formation, and lower-class culture that we have examined all suggest that social forces push some juveniles into delinquency. A contrasting perspective is that delinquents exercise some free will, choosing to violate the law rather than being forced to do so by the social structure. According to this view, delinquents do not hold values that are diametrically opposed to dominant values, as reaction-formation theory suggests, nor are they members of delinquent subcultures that require them to violate the law, as differential opportunity theory and reaction-formation theory imply (Matza and Sykes, 1961; Matza, 1964).

Drift

David Matza (1964) proposes that some adolescents are in a state of *drift*, a condition of limbo between a conventional life style and a criminal life style with no strong attachment to either. Juveniles drift into delinquency in an almost accidental and unpredictable way through their exercise of personal choice. Becoming delinquent involves neither a compulsion to deviate nor the complete freedom to choose how to behave. Matza does not say why juveniles continue to engage in delinquency over time, nor does he indicate why they are drawn to delinquency in the first place. In other words, he does not specify the rewards of delinquent behavior.

In describing everyday delinquency rather than explaining its causes, Matza returns to the ideas of the classical school of criminology, particularly free will. He suggests that one motive for delinquency is existential in nature: Adolescents need to "make things happen" to assure themselves of their existence and their mastery over the world. For some adolescents, delinquency involves less risk of failure, and more potential gains, than schoolwork or athletics.

Delinquent, Dominant, and Subterranean Values

Part of the attractiveness of delinquency for juveniles may be that it has much in common with the leisure activities of the dominant classes. Rather than see society as split into various strata with different norms and values—as do Cloward and Ohlin, Cohen, and Miller—Matza and Sykes (1961) examine contradictions within the dominant value system. Thus, the dominant or middle-class value system exhorts people to work hard and defer gratification, but it also encourages them to seek excitement and go on occasional sprees. The search for adventure is best regarded not as a deviant value but as a *subterranean value* in the dominant value system. In other words, the value is subordinate or below the surface in the dominant value system, and is sought by most people only occasionally and in appropriate circumstances. Delinquents can then be seen as people who act in accordance with subterranean values in inappropriate circumstances. For instance, vandalism is tolerated, within limits, on Halloween, but people who destroy property at other times may be labeled delinquent. Matza and Sykes (1961: 717) see the delinquent not as alien to society, but as "a disturbing reflection or a caricature" of society's values. The delinquent's "vocabulary is different, to be sure, but kicks, big-time spending, and rep have immediate counterparts in the value system of the law-abiding" (Matza and Sykes, 1961: 717). The motivational thrust behind delinquent behavior is thus normal and derived directly from conventional morality.

Evidence that delinquents have a strong bond to dominant values is the fact that they often express respect for law-abiding citizens. If delinquents held values opposed to dominant ones, they probably would regard law-abiding behavior as incorrect or immoral. Their recognition of the moral validity of dominant values suggests an attachment to the larger culture, even if that bond is broken at times.

The fact that delinquents are often selective in choosing targets for their offenses is additional evidence that they recognize the dominant morality. Theft and violence by delinquents are often directed against people who are held in low social regard, such as prostitutes, alcoholics, homosexuals, or other delinquents. This suggests that delinquents can distinguish victims of whom the larger society approves from victims who would elicit negative reactions.

Techniques of Neutralization

Social norms that define expected or appropriate behavior for particular situations often lack specificity as to how and when they apply. In other words, norms have flexibility and act only as "qualified guides for action" (Sykes and Matza, 1957: 666). Thus, a norm that theft is wrong may be qualified so that theft is tolerated—or even actually encouraged—if one is hungry or needs to feed one's hungry children, if theft is from another criminal, or if theft is from a large and impersonal corporation (Jones, 1941, 1964; Smigel, 1956).

Individuals can avoid moral blame and maintain self-esteem while violating the law if they tell themselves and others that they had no criminal intent or that their behavior was justified. People who have accepted the law as legitimate find it difficult to launch frontal assaults on dominant norms, and so they remove the constraints of the law by justifying their behavior in some way. These justifications, which Sykes and Matza call *techniques of neutralization*, are tangential blows against dominant norms and help to render inoperative the social controls that would otherwise check law-violating behavior, enabling but not requiring people to break the law (Minor, 1981). These justifications make it possible for people to commit crime and delinquency without serious damage to their self-image. Deviance such as this has been described as apologetic rather than oppositional deviance (Sykes and Matza, 1957: 667).

Techniques of neutralization are sometimes extensions of patterns of thought prevalent in society, and are thus learned from the general culture. Techniques may also be subcultural in origin; that is, they exist among certain groups whose norms and values differ from dominant norms and values. Techniques of neutralization are then learned in association with members of these subcultures through the process of differential association that we examine in the next chapter.

The five techniques of neutralization that Sykes and Matza look at are used prior to violation of the law to allow an offender who otherwise accepts the moral validity of the law to break it. Rationalizations may also occur after the crime, but there is less need to justify a crime that has already been committed than to neutralize the law that would have blocked the individual from committing the crime in the first place.

DENIAL OF RESPONSIBILITY

One technique of neutralization is the *denial of responsibility*, a denial by an individual of personal responsibility for his or her own actions. People may claim that a criminal or delinquent act was an accident or assert that it was caused by factors beyond their control, such as negligent parents, wayward friends, a broken home, or poverty. Those who use this technique often feel acted upon by others and by the social environment, rather than in control of their own lives. Other people may avoid crime and delinquency because they accept personal responsibility for their own behavior. When asked why he had not become a criminal, one nonoffender said: "I was given a certain amount of responsibility and learned to become responsible, and accept the fact that I was accountable for my actions" (cited in Rogers, 1977: 91).

Crime is also justified by this technique in other societies. For instance, in the Soviet Union, where the theft of socialist (state-owned) property is legally regarded as a more serious crime than the theft of private property, the public nevertheless sees the theft of socialist property as "innocent and normal behavior" (Chalidze, 1977: 190). Soviet citizens sometimes justify their theft of state property by denying responsibility, pointing to the way that the failures of the state economy have forced them to steal: "If I could get it in the stores, I wouldn't steal it at work"; or "There are lots of things the State fails to provide, so we have to take them for ourselves" (Chalidze, 1977: 190).

To the extent that the positivist approach to the explanation of criminal behavior has seeped into the popular culture, it may be used to deny responsibility. Sociological research that shows a link between violation of the law and factors such as poverty or minority status can be used by delinquents and criminals to argue that those factors forced them to violate the law, thereby absolving them of personal responsibility for their actions. For instance, one theory of heroin addiction is that it is a sickness in which addicts use heroin to prevent the physical pain of the withdrawal symptoms that would occur

"In extenuation, Your Honor, I would like to suggest to the court that my client was inadequately parented."

if they stopped using the drug. This theory has been used by addicts to justify their continued use of heroin and their involvement in crimes to support their habit (Lindesmith, 1968; McAuliffe and Gordon, 1974).

Walter B. Miller (1974) has said that the civil rights movement of the 1950s added a "justificatory vocabulary" to traditional explanations for gang activity and other kinds of juvenile delinquency. Gang behavior was not much different in the 1960s than it was in the 1950s before the civil rights movement, but in the 1960s gang members were more likely to attribute their behavior to "exploitation by the power structure, restitution for past injustices, and brutalization by the system" (Miller, 1974: 233). One example of this kind of justification for crime was black activist Eldridge Cleaver's "political" defense of his rape of white women:

> Rape was an insurrectionary act. It delighted me that I was defying and trampling upon the white man's law, upon his system of values, and that I was defiling his women—and this point, I believe, was the most satisfying to me because I was very resentful over the historical fact of how the white man had used the black woman. I felt I was getting revenge (Cleaver, 1968: 14).

Professional fences also deny responsibility for their crime of receiving stolen goods. They deny responsibility by saying that they do not steal anything, claiming that it is thieves who steal and the public that buys "hot" goods from fences. Fences claim that if they did not act as middlemen, others would do so. They say that because they do not commit theft or cause theft, the popular image of the thief does not fit them (Klockars, 1974: 139–150).

Denial of responsibility has also been used to justify white-collar crime and political corruption. In his final months in office, President Nixon blamed subordinates such as tax lawyers and advisors for his problems. In his resignation speech, he blamed the press that had reported the Watergate incident and Congress that had forced him to leave office. Few juvenile delinquents can maintain a noncriminal self-concept in the face of as much contrary evidence as confronted Nixon.

Rationalizations similar to Nixon's are also used by white-collar criminals. Executives say that their corporation violated the law because their subordinates misunderstood orders or took the law into their owns hands; subordinates may say that their supervisors told them to violate the law for the good of the company. What little information we have on the denial of responsibility by white-collar criminals is usually in the form of rationalizations for offenses that have already been committed. We lack good evidence that these justifications are used prior to violation of the law to make it possible for business people to reduce their commitment to the law and commit a crime.

DENIAL OF INJURY

A second technique of neutralization is the *denial of injury*, the claim by offenders that no one will be hurt by their crime, even if it technically violates the law. Nonoffenders sometimes say that they do not violate the law because of their ability to perceive injury to others and because they are concerned about inflicting harm on others. In other words, sensitivity to others may keep some people away from crime and delinquency (Rogers, 1977). Those who violate the law may be less sensitive to the effect that their behavior has on victims, or may regard their victims as objects or means to their own ends rather than as individuals who suffer when victimized.

An offender may say that victims who lose money or have property damaged can afford the loss, or that they can recover their losses from their insurance company. Offenders often see the losses incurred by insurance companies as unreal, even though policyholders pay higher premiums to offset the costs of claims paid by the insurance company.

One instance of thieves regarding their crimes as causing no real loss to anyone comes from a study of eighty-eight workers in a midwestern electronics assembly plant (Horning, 1970). Workers rationalized their theft as causing no injury by making a distinction among three kinds of property in the plant: property that belonged to the company, property that belonged to employees, and property of uncertain ownership. Property classified as being of uncertain ownership was small, plentiful, inexpensive, and expendable, and the company did not regulate its flow within the plant. The property did belong to someone or to the company, but if workers could categorize it as being of uncertain ownership, they thought they were doing no injury if they stole it. Almost all workers reported pilfering goods from the plant, but few expressed any guilt at doing so, because work-group norms supported theft when it was confined to property of uncertain ownership and limited to what was needed for personal use. The conditions under which theft was tolerated were communicated to workers through "folktales" about thefts that had occurred in the past.

Delinquents use the denial of injury technique to justify their violation of the law. Car thieves justify their offenses by saying that they are only "temporarily borrowing" cars, rather than permanently depriving owners of their cars. Gang fights are defined as private quarrels that are no one else's business. Sometimes delinquents and adult offenders actually claim that their crimes are socially useful. They may claim to be "Robin Hoods" who steal from the rich and give to the poor. In India, the crime of dacoity, a violent form of theft by gangs, has been justified in this way (Clinard and Abbott, 1973: 40–41). In a similar fashion, professional fences sometimes justify their crimes as a way to redistribute property from wealthier neighborhoods to poorer ones (Klockars, 1974).

Criminals sometimes claim that it is appropriate to victimize certain targets, but that other targets should be avoided. The general public seems to think that theft from a large corporation is preferable to theft from the government, which in turn is better than theft from a small business (Smigel, 1956). People seem to believe that large corporations can afford the loss because they are insured, are highly profitable, can raise prices to compensate for their losses, and cheat customers anyway. Large corporations are also unpopular because they are seen as impersonal, inefficient, and unresponsive to the best interests of their customers and clients (Smigel and Ross, 1970: 4). This "rip-off mentality," which seems to have been especially widespread in the 1960s, has been used to justify theft from large corporations. Shoplifters often rationalize their crimes to the extent that they may speak of "getting property" rather than "stealing" (Weiner, 1970: 216). Computer thieves offer similar justifications when they distinguish harm to individuals (which is immoral) from harm to organizations (which is not always immoral) (Parker, 1976, 1983). One safe-cracker justifies his thefts in a similar way:

> We [professional thieves] would never beat the average working man or anything like that. . . . When I was a young kid learning, I stole anything. But later on I became a professional and started hanging around with professionals and learned from them that you didn't steal from a home or small place of business; you only stole from a big place that could afford the loss (King and Chambliss, 1984: 13).

Crimes without victims—such as homosexual acts (which are still illegal in many states), gambling, and drug addiction—are often justified as involving no injury. These consensual offenses are usually uncovered by proactive police work rather than in response to citizen complaints. The lack of complainants in these offenses has been used to argue that no one is injured. Statutory rape has also been justified as involving no injury to an underage female who consents to sex.

Denial of injury has been used to justify white-collar crime and political corruption. In rationalizing the Watergate burglary and its cover-up as necessary for national security, President Nixon not only claimed that no injury had been done, but that he had actually intended to do good. In a similar vein, a Westinghouse executive responded as follows to a question from a congressional committee about whether he knew that his meetings with other executives to fix the prices of electrical equipment were illegal: "Illegal? Yes, but not criminal. I didn't find that out until I read the indictment. . . . I assumed that criminal action meant damaging someone, and we did not do that" (cited in Geis, 1967: 144). The executive was wrong; not only did the criminal convictions and the jail sentences served by some executives show quite clearly that harm had been done, but the fact that plaintiffs recovered millions of dollars in civil damages from the offending companies also indicated that financial harm had been done.

DENIAL OF THE VICTIM

A third technique of neutralization is the *denial of the victim,* the claim that a crime is justified as rightful retaliation against the victim. Offenders see the victim as a wrongdoer, rather than seeing themselves as wrongdoers, and use that attitude toward the victim to justify the offense.

Certain targets of crime are more likely than others to be socially approved or tolerated, including prostitutes, alcoholics, homosexuals, and unscrupulous shopkeepers who sell shoddy merchandise or adulterated food. Offenders may appeal to widely held ideas about valued and disvalued people to justify their acts. People who are able to recognize that victims suffer, in spite of what those victims may have done to "deserve" victimization, are probably more likely to avoid criminal behavior. One nonoffender says: "If there is something I want, I work for it because I don't want to hurt anyone else by trying to obtain it by other means. I always try to remember that other people have feelings too" (cited in Rogers, 1977: 92). Offenders do not seem to share this view, but instead think it is acceptable to victimize certain people. For instance, con artists who engage in fraud and trickery justify their behavior by the complicity of their victims, who are seen as having "larceny in their hearts" (Maurer, 1974). Similarly, a rapist may justify his crime by saying that the victim "deserves" to be raped because she is sexually experienced, promiscuous, or has a bad reputation, and that such a woman is "public property" and does not have the right to reject him as a sex partner (Hills, 1980: 67).

CONDEMNATION OF THE CONDEMNERS

Another technique of neutralization is the *condemnation of the condemners*, the assertion that it is the motives and behavior of the people who are condemning the offender, rather than the motives and behavior of the offender, that should be condemned. Actions of the condemners, including police brutality and political corruption, are used to justify an offender's violation of the law. People who remain nonoffenders often can concede the imperfection of the condemners without using it to justify their own violation of the law (Rogers, 1977: 96).

Many kinds of offenders justify their actions by condemning the condemners. Murderers and bank robbers compare the harsh punishments they receive with the lack of punishment for politicians who send young men to their deaths in pointless wars. Political criminals or rebels use the corrupt and self-serving nature of the political system to justify crimes aimed at changing the system (Schafer, 1974). Professional criminals claim that their behavior does not differ much from that of politicians, business offenders, and the police. Fences point out that some of their best customers are judges and police officers (Klockars, 1974: 139–150). Corrupt political leaders point to the crimes of other politicians in the past to justify their own behavior. Thus, President Nixon sometimes referred to acts that allegedly occurred during the Kennedy and Johnson administrations, and Nixon's autobiography includes several references to Senator Edward Kennedy and the Chappaquiddick incident (Nixon, 1978).

APPEAL TO HIGHER LOYALTIES

The fifth technique of neutralization is the *appeal to higher loyalties*, an attempt to justify violation of the law by the demands of a group—such as a juvenile gang or a corporation—that is smaller than the whole society but that requires its members to conform to standards that may be incompatible with the law. Those who place loyalty to the larger social system and its laws above loyalty to individuals or a group are more likely to stay away from crime. One noncriminal expressed this as follows: "I am not a criminal . . .

because I trust the system. I am willing to sacrifice for it. I believe in it" (cited in Rogers, 1977: 94).

Different types of offenders justify their violations of the law by appealing to higher loyalties. Juvenile delinquents rationalize their acts by peer pressure and the need not to let their friends down. Police officers justify graft and corruption by the need to remain loyal to fellow officers (*Knapp Commission Report on Police Corruption*, 1972). Nixon's appeal to national security was an effort to justify violations of the law by demands higher than the law. In a 1977 interview, he strongly implied that whatever the president did was not a crime because the president was above the law. Another use of loyalty to demands higher than the law was by an electrical company executive involved in the price-fixing conspiracy; he said, "I thought that we were more or less working on a survival basis in order to try to make enough to keep our plant and our employees" (cited in Geis, 1967: 144).

OTHER TECHNIQUES OF NEUTRALIZATION

Other techniques of neutralization can also be used to justify crime and delinquency. A person who uses a "defense of necessity" may justify an act by saying that it is required by the circumstances; this differs from the denial of responsibility in that the offender accepts responsibility for the act while claiming that it was necessary. Stealing food to feed one's starving children might be justified as a necessary act for which an offender accepts full responsibility. Another technique is the "defense of the ledger," which is used by offenders who claim that the good and evil they have done balance out favorably over time (Klockars, 1974; Minor, 1981).

EVIDENCE ON TECHNIQUES OF NEUTRALIZATION

Several researchers have found that techniques of neutralization play an important role in the genesis of crime and delinquency, but others believe that it is too early to assess the validity of neutralization theory as an explanation for violation of the law (Minor, 1981).

Embezzlement and the Techniques of Neutralization

Earlier in the book, we examined Donald R. Cressey's (1953, 1971) study of imprisoned trust violators or embezzlers. Cressey concluded that people violate an employer's trust and embezzle funds when they face a nonshareable financial problem, become aware that they can solve that problem by turning the skills and opportunities of their job in a criminal direction, and can "apply to their own conduct in that situation verbalizations which enable them to adjust their conceptions of themselves as trusted persons with their conceptions of themselves as users of the entrusted funds or property" (Cressey, 1953, 1971: 30). These "verbalizations" are what Sykes and Matza call techniques of neutralization. They permit people to define the relationship between a nonshareable financial problem and an illegal solution to that problem in a way that makes embezzlement seem justifiable.

Cressey found that justifications were used either before or at the time of the crime; after the offense, there was no need for the verbalization. Verbalizations were often applications of general cultural values to an offender's specific situation. For instance, embezzlers said the following:

- "Some of our most respectable citizens got their start in life by using other people's money temporarily."
- "In the real estate business there is nothing wrong about using deposits before the deal is closed."
- "All people steal when they get in a tight spot" (Cressey, 1953, 1971: 96).

The vagueness of some business practices made it possible for embezzlers to say they were only using the money "temporarily" and to claim that they were "only borrowing," even though they took the money without the owner's knowledge and rarely repaid it. For example, deposits with real-estate agents are in the possession of the agents, but the agents do not own the money. They may convert such funds to personal use, claiming that the money was not being used and that they planned to replace it. However, embezzlers usually find that they take more than they can replace, and accounting procedures can make the replacement of the money even more difficult than the theft of the funds.

Justifications for Crime by Blacks

Another study that uncovered techniques of neutralization asked 150 black men between the ages of fifteen and thirty the following: "It is said that black men violate the criminal law more frequently than others. If this statement is true, are there any reasons you feel why such a higher violation rate exists?" (Davis, 1974: 74).

The men, who were approached on the street, said that the legal system lacked legitimacy for blacks, and gave various reasons for a general "justification for no obligation" to the law by black men. More than four-fifths of the men thought that laws had been created by whites to control blacks, that blacks lacked equal access to participation in social institutions, and that unequal access to opportunities is unjust and indicative of hypocrisy about democratic ideals. At least two-thirds of the men said that racial discrimination had a long history and that whites had supported it over the centuries, that blacks were not obligated to obey the law because they had been forcibly brought to the country and had no choice in citizenship, and that blacks were not protected by the law in the same way that whites were. More than half of the men said that blacks are a conquered people who had lost the first battle between the races, and that it was not logical to expect whites to grant them any rights.

For black men who find themselves in a state of drift and without a strong commitment to a conventional life style, these justifications may support involvement in crime. Crime by blacks may result from grievances about unjust conditions and a subsequent lowering of respect for the law and its enforcers. Illegal activity may then be accepted as a solution to those grievances. This study did not test directly for the presence of Sykes and Matza's techniques of neutralization among black criminals, but it shows that one group of streetwise black men think that crime by blacks is a result of the ease with which blacks can neutralize the constraints of the law.

Justifying Murder

In a study of sex-related and robbery-related murders and execution-style homicides, several justifications for these acts of lethal violence were uncovered (Dietz, 1983). Street violence was justified by the need to protect oneself or one's property, the need to control others and keep them from using violence, the need to protect a reputation from personal affronts, and the need to ward off unprovoked attacks. In sex-related and robbery-related murders, offenders sometimes forced themselves to think of the victim as an object rather than as a person with feelings. Sometimes these murderers killed to prevent the victim from reporting the crime to the police and testifying in court. In execution-style homicides, "hit men" sometimes justified their crimes by saying that the victim "deserved to die" or by claiming that the murder was a "public service."

Delinquency and Techniques of Neutralization

More direct evidence on the techniques of neutralization comes from a study of delinquency by Travis Hirschi (1969). Data were gathered in 1964 from interviews with California junior and senior high school students, and from school and police records. Self-reports were used to measure personal involvement in six delinquent acts: theft of property worth less than $2, theft of property worth $2 to $50, theft of property worth more than $50, auto theft, vandalism, and battery (beating someone up). The number of acts that a student admitted to formed the index of delinquency. Because few students had engaged in many delinquent acts, those who admitted to no acts were compared with those who admitted to one or more. It is questionable whether someone who has stolen only a pencil from a store should be classified as delinquent, or would be likely to be so classified by a judge, but this way of measuring delinquency was required by the data in order to explore relationships between self-reported delinquency and the acceptance of statements used to justify violation of the law.

DENIAL OF RESPONSIBILITY
Hirschi measured support for the denial-of-responsibility technique by asking students if they thought that criminals were to blame for their actions. Because few respondents—only 12 per cent of the sample—said that criminals should not be held responsible for their actions, Hirschi could not use this question to measure support for this technique of neutralization.

Another indicator of support for the denial-of-responsibility technique was the following: "I can't seem to stay out of trouble no matter how hard I try." Students who agreed with this statement might be able to deny personal responsibility for their behavior and justify violation of the law. Thus, we might expect that those who agreed most strongly with this statement would be the most likely to report involvement in delinquent acts, and those who most strongly disagreed would be the least involved in delinquency. Hirschi's data show that this was the case. Sixty-three per cent of the boys who strongly agreed with the statement admitted at least one delinquent act, but only 25 per cent of those who strongly disagreed with the statement admitted at least one delinquent act. Those who expressed intermediate levels of agreement with the statement showed intermediate levels of self-reported delinquency (Hirschi, 1969: 207). These findings provide tentative support for a link between denial of responsibility and juvenile delinquency.

Hirschi's study was replicated by Michael J. Hindelang (1973), who gathered data from boys and girls in rural New York state in 1971. This study provided similar support for an association between this denial-of-responsibility item and self-reported delinquency.

DENIAL OF INJURY

Hirschi tested for the technique of neutralization called denial of injury with the following statement: "Most things that people call 'delinquency' don't really hurt anyone." Agreement with this statement would suggest greater ease in denying harm to potential victims of delinquent acts and should thus be associated with more involvement in delinquency. This was the case: 72 per cent of those who strongly agreed with this statement reported at least one delinquent act, but only 31 per cent of those who strongly disagreed with the statement reported a delinquent act (Hirschi, 1969: 208). Hindelang's (1973) replication of Hirschi's study found similar support for a link between this statement and self-reported delinquency.

DENIAL OF THE VICTIM

The item that Hirschi used to measure denial of the victim was the following: "The man who leaves the keys in his car is as much to blame for its theft as the man who steals it." This particular item was not related to self-reported delinquency; the percentages who admitted at least one delinquent act were similar for those who agreed and those who disagreed with the statement (Hirschi, 1969: 210). Hindelang (1973) did not find support for this technique of neutralization either. Hirschi suggests that had he phrased the question as "The *sucker* who leaves the keys in his car . . .," he might have found an association between responses to this statement and self-reported delinquency. The item that Hirschi did use might have said too little about the respondent's attitude toward the victim by referring to him simply as a man.

CONDEMNATION OF THE CONDEMNERS

Condemnation of the condemners was measured by asking for responses to the following: "Policemen try to give all kids an even break." Agreement should be associated with low involvement in delinquency, because those who think that the police are fair should be less able to justify violating the law. The evidence supports this: 35 per cent of the boys who strongly agreed with the statement admitted a delinquent act, but 58 per cent who strongly disagreed with the statement reported a delinquent act (Hirschi, 1969: 211). Hindelang (1973) also found an association between this statement and self-reported delinquency.

APPEAL TO HIGHER LOYALTIES

Hirschi could not test the technique of appealing to higher loyalties with the data he collected, nor did Hindelang ask about this technique.

CONCLUSION

Hirschi's and Hindelang's studies tentatively support a positive association between three of the five techniques of neutralization and self-reported involvement in delinquent acts. Their work lends some support to Sykes and Matza's theoretical ideas, but does not provide a definitive test of those ideas. For instance, Hirschi's and Hindelang's data do not allow them to conclude that the techniques of neutralization were used prior to committing the delinquent acts to make it possible for the boys to neutralize the constraints of the law.

CRITIQUE OF NEUTRALIZATION THEORY

Neutralization theory implies that people who are committed to a conventional life or who have not yet engaged in deviance will be the most likely to need to use techniques of neutralization. However, one study found that these techniques are used both by youths who disapprove of deviance and therefore need to neutralize norms, and by youths who already approve of the deviance and should therefore not need to use neutralization techniques. Moreover, the relationship between the acceptance of neutralizing excuses and subsequent deviant behavior existed only for people who had already committed that deviant act in the past, not for people who had never violated the norm before. This suggests that techniques of neutralization may only develop and be used after people commit an initial act of delinquency or crime, and that the techniques may not precede violation of the law as Sykes and Matza suggest. Overall, however, this study concluded that "the acceptance of neutralizing verbalizations does have some empirical consequences for subsequent behavior" (Minor, 1981: 314).

The process of neutralizing the law is a social-psychological one by which potential offenders justify crime or delinquency by employing general arguments about when such violations are acceptable. Neutralization theory might be criticized for ignoring aspects of the social structure that make it easy or difficult to justify violations of the law. These social-structural aspects have been explored in control theory, which proposes that people who are the most weakly attached to social institutions are the most free to violate the law.

CONTROL THEORY

The *control theory* of delinquency developed by Travis Hirschi (1969) proposes that people who engage in delinquency are free of intimate attachments, aspirations, and moral beliefs that bind them to a conventional and law-abiding way of life. Delinquents are not forced into delinquency so much as they are free to commit delinquent acts because they lack ties to the conventional social order. Delinquency violates other people's expectations about appropriate behavior. If people do not care about the opinion of others, they are free to deviate from norms. Most people have deviant impulses from time to time, but whether they act on those impulses depends on their attachments to others.

Delinquents believe in the conventional order even as they violate its norms; the critical factor is the extent to which they believe that they should obey norms. Hirschi (1969: 198) says that "delinquency is not caused by beliefs that require delinquency but is rather made possible by the absence of (effective) beliefs that forbid delinquency." This position is similar to Matza's notion of drift: The delinquent is midway between crime and convention, between deviance and conformity. It is also consistent with Short and Strodtbeck's (1965) finding that gang boys support middle-class prescriptive norms but do not support some middle-class proscriptive norms. In sum, delinquents do not hold norms that require delinquency, but rather lack norms that strongly oppose such behavior. The absence of proscriptive norms is related to the lack of attachment to social institutions, and both leave some adolescents free to violate the law.

Control theory does not make clear the motivations that give rise to violation of the law, but rather looks at the institutions that create barriers to the expression of deviant motivations (Eve, 1978). The desire to acquire material goods, the need for social approval, and association with other law violators can all push a person to violate the law. However, if a person experiencing those pressures to violate the law is also subject to social control that results from attachment to family, school, job, and friends, that control may counteract the pressure to violate the law.

The Family

One institution that is basic to all societies is the family. It socializes the young and provides surveillance over their behavior. It also controls the behavior of both adults and young people who value the good opinion of other family members.

Hirschi's research shows that delinquents are much less closely attached to their parents than nondelinquents are. The critical factor is not whether the parents are always physically present to supervise the behavior of the child, but whether the parents are "psychologically present" when the child faces a temptation to violate the law. If the parents are not present in the child's mind, he or she is free to commit a delinquent act without giving any thought to how the parents might react. Nonoffenders sometimes say that they abide by the law because they take their parents' feelings into account when deciding how to act (Rogers, 1977: 37–42). Nondelinquents are also more likely to say that their parents know where they are most of the time, and this acts as a check on their behavior; by contrast, delinquents are more likely to say that their parents are often unaware of their whereabouts.

The closer a child's relationship with his or her parents, and the more intimate the communication with them, the less likely that child is to be delinquent. Relationships with mothers and fathers are of equal importance in controlling delinquency (Hirschi, 1969: 102). Through attachment to a parent, children learn to care about parental expectations. Attachment to parents seems to be important for children of all classes and all racial and ethnic groups. Even adolescents in high crime rate groups are less likely to be delinquent if they have close relationships with their parents.

The School

A second important institution in controlling delinquency is the school. The most academically successful students are the least likely to be delinquent, for they are most attached to the school and its teachers. Adolescents are more likely to be delinquent if they do not care what their teachers think of them; again the expectations of "significant others" are important in controlling delinquency. As Hirschi (1969: 127) says, "Positive feelings toward controlling institutions and persons in authority are the first line of social control. Withdrawal of favorable sentiments toward such institutions and persons at the same time neutralizes their moral force."

Hirschi's research shows that students who are not much concerned with their teachers' opinions and who dislike school also have the weakest relationships with their parents. These adolescents are the most likely to report that they have committed delinquent acts.

The Peer Group

The third type of attachment that is important in control theory is relationships with the peer group. Hirschi finds that delinquents are more likely to have delinquent friends than nondelinquents are. However, the relationship between friendships and delinquency is less clear-cut than the commonly assumed pattern of poor family relationships leading to attachment to peers, which then leads to delinquency. Instead, adolescents who have weak relationships with their parents tend to have weak relationships with their peers, and those closest to their parents have the greatest number of close friends. Attachment to peers does not necessarily produce attitudes conducive to delinquency, for the more adolescents respect the opinions of their friends, the less likely they are to be delinquent. Those who are more delinquent and more likely to have delinquent friends are also less likely to say that their friends are worthy of respect. Contrary to the picture of the juvenile gang as a warm and supportive group similar to a family, Hirschi finds that delinquents do not have warm and intimate relationships with each other, or with anyone else for that matter.

Conventional Lines of Action and Adult Activities

Thus far, the picture that control theory offers of the delinquent is of someone who lacks strong attachments to parents, teachers, or peers. Delinquents are in a state of drift and are free to deviate from social norms. Another link in the chain of circumstances leading to delinquency is an individual's aspirations to conventional lines of action, such as education and work. Adolescents who have such aspirations do not want to jeopardize their chances of success, for they risk losing their "stake in conformity" by getting into trouble with the law.

Young people who do not aspire to conventional lines of action are more involved in adult activities during adolescence. Adult privileges without adult responsibilities may help to compensate for a bleak outlook on the future. Delinquents are more likely than nondelinquents to see their high school years and the years immediately after as the time in their lives when they will be the happiest. They are especially likely to engage in delinquency because their lack of orientation toward the future frees them from conventional pursuits such as education and a career.

As a measure of involvement in adult activities, Hirschi uses the age at which an individual began to smoke cigarettes and the number of "adult activities"—smoking, drinking, and dating—in which the person is involved. Each indicator shows a significant relationship to self-reported delinquency. Thus, adolescents who began smoking before they were thirteen were the most likely to admit a delinquent act; those who began to smoke between thirteen and fifteen were less likely to admit a delinquent act; those who started after fifteen were even less likely to report a delinquent act; and those who did not smoke at all were the least likely to report a delinquent act (Hirschi, 1969: 167). Involvement in the three adult activities was directly associated with a higher rate of self-reported delinquency. Boys who smoked, drank, and dated reported delinquent acts three times as often as boys who engaged in none of those activities (Hirschi, 1969: 168).

In conclusion, adolescents who have fewer attachments to family, school, peers, and conventional lines of action are more likely to engage in delinquency because they do not feel that society's rules are binding on them and do not fear the disapproval of others. This perception can be seen as a "master technique of neutralization" supported by the specific techniques of neutralization that we have examined.

EVIDENCE ON CONTROL THEORY

There is much evidence to support control theory. Hirschi's survey provides evidence that delinquency is associated with weak attachments to conventional institutions and lines of action. Other studies, too, support control theory.

Comparing Delinquents and Nondelinquents

A study of juvenile delinquency by Empey and Lubeck (1971) found some support for control theory. They used a group of boys who had been labeled delinquent in juvenile court and another group of boys who had not been so labeled. They then combined the two groups and looked at those factors that distinguished delinquents from nondelinquents.

Empey and Lubeck's research design was not ideal. It would have been better to sample a cross section of a given age group and measure delinquency both by official arrests and by self-report questionnaires. In addition, Empey and Lubeck did not take into account factors that might make the police and the courts more likely to find a boy delinquent. Thus, we cannot know for certain whether coming from a broken home is a cause of delinquent behavior or a cause of the delinquent label being imposed by the police and the courts.

Empey and Lubeck began their research with the theory that lower-class status reduces school achievement, which produces strain that leads to identification with peers, and this in turn draws boys into delinquency. Their analysis of the data led them to formulate a more complex explanation for delinquency. They found that lack of integration into institutions, particularly the family and the school, predicted delinquent behavior. Specifically, measures of strain—such as disharmony in the family and dropping out of school—were directly associated with peer identification, and peer identification was tied to delinquency.

The interrelationships of the critical variables related to delinquency in Empey and Lubeck's research are portrayed in Figure 9.1; a one-headed arrow means one-way causation, and a two-headed arrow means that variables have effects on each other. Hirschi's theory is diagrammed in simple terms in Figure 9.2; here four variables have direct effects on delinquency, but the four variables have no clearly specified causal relationships with each other. For instance, lack of family ties is correlated with weak ties to the school, but Hirschi does

Figure 9.1: Empey and Lubeck's Model of Delinquency

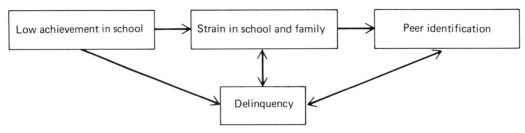

SOURCE: Reprinted by permission of the publisher, from *Explaining Delinquency: Construction, Test, and Reformulation of a Sociological Theory* by LaMar T. Empey and Steven G. Lubeck. Lexington, Mass.: Lexington Books, D. C. Heath and Company, Copyright 1971, D. C. Heath and Company. (Adapted)

Figure 9.2: Hirschi's Model of Delinquency

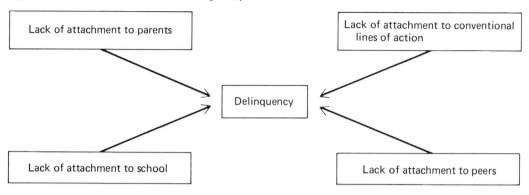

SOURCE: Based on Travis Hirschi, *Causes of Delinquency*. Berkeley, Calif.: University of California Press, 1969.

not claim that one directly causes the other. Hirschi's model can be described as follows: Lack of attachment to parents, to the school, to peers, and to conventional lines of action each increases the likelihood of delinquency.

Empey and Lubeck's model is more complicated. Low achievement in school leads directly to delinquency, but it also has an indirect effect on delinquency by producing strain in school and in the family, which in turn leads to delinquency, and by increasing peer identification, which is associated with delinquency. Strain in school and in the family leads directly to delinquency, and also leads indirectly to delinquency by increasing peer identification. In addition, strain is affected by a juvenile's involvement in delinquency; in other words, being arrested and taken to court produce problems for boys with their parents and teachers. Peer identification leads to delinquency, and involvement in delinquency affects identification with peers, both directly and indirectly, by producing strain in school and in the family. This model is a less satisfying one than Hirschi's model of direct, one-to-one relationships between causes and delinquency, but it is a more accurate reflection of the complex processes that lead to delinquency.

Delinquency and the Family

Much research on crime and delinquency points to the crucial role of the family. This is not surprising, for the family is the primary institution in the socialization and supervision of children.

SOCIALIZATION

The way that children are socialized by their parents is a major factor in the causation or prevention of crime and delinquency. A study that asked students why they had not become criminals found that many said that their parents had taught them right from wrong and had been models of hard work and honesty. The students said that their parents had taught them important values about how to behave, and that they abided by the law because they believed in·those values rather than because they feared punishment (Rogers, 1977: 36–45). In comparison with nonoffenders, delinquents are more likely to say that their childhood experiences with their parents were unpleas-

217

ant and that they rejected their parents as models while they were young (Medinnus, 1965). In general, crime seems to be more common in societies where young people have less contact and less identification with their parents during childhood (Bacon, Child, and Barry, 1963).

Socialization by parents is most likely to reduce the chance that children will violate the law if

- parents clearly define their expectations,
- there is a close relationship between parents and their children,
- parents control their reactions toward their children's rebellious behavior, and
- parents reward the learning of expected behavior and withhold rewards for the failure to learn that behavior (Toby, 1974).

People can also be socialized to break the law. They may learn values, norms, and skills from the members of a criminal or delinquent subculture. Few parents intentionally socialize their children to violate the law, but the failure to recognize their children's crime and delinquency as deviant and the use of ineffective methods of punishment can socialize children to break the law (Hirschi, 1983). In addition, the learning of contradictory values and norms, sometimes called ambivalent socialization, can lead to compulsive behavior that violates the law (Toby, 1974).

In a longitudinal study in which records describing the family environments of boys were compared with their criminal convictions three decades later, the researcher found that six variables were predictive of adult criminality. One variable that was not associated with later criminal convictions was the absence of the father from the home. Adult criminality was more common among men whose childhood had been characterized by parental conflict, lack of supervision, and an absence of maternal affection. Boys were also more likely to become criminals as adults if their parents were aggressive, if their father had engaged in deviance, and if their mother had lacked self-confidence. Thus, the behavior and psychology of the parents, and the way that they treated the boys while young, were highly predictive of whether those boys would be convicted of crimes as adults (McCord, 1979).

SIZE OF THE FAMILY

Delinquents are more likely to come from larger families than nondelinquents, even when children of the same class are compared. Hirschi (1969: 240) found that only children reported at least one delinquent act 33 per cent of the time, children with one sibling reported delinquent acts 39 per cent of the time, those with two siblings reported delinquency 44 per cent of the time, those with three siblings reported delinquency in 46 per cent of the cases, and those with four or more siblings reported a delinquent act 49 per cent of the time.

The reason for the relationship between delinquency and family size is unclear, but it may be because there is more disharmony in larger families. In addition, parents in larger families might retreat more from interaction with their children, leading to neglect and a weakening of family bonds. At the very least, a child will receive fewer hours of parental attention in a large family than in a small one, because parents' attention must be divided among more children in a large family. The monitoring and punishment of deviant behavior are probably least effective in large families (Hirschi, 1983).

Brothers and sisters can be important in the socialization of children. Younger children may imitate older siblings who are delinquent, or react against that delinquency by conforming to the law. Older siblings may become more conforming to the law if they take on some of the responsibility of raising younger brothers and sisters. The sex of younger and older siblings may be an important variable in explaining delinquency, and so may be birth order (Wilkinson, Stitt, and Erickson, 1982).

A cohort study done in England casts some light on the association between family size and delinquency. In this study, the impact of family size on delinquency was much greater among families with a low social standing than it was among families that were better off. The researcher concluded as follows: "Presumably higher-status families, who have better education, housing and income can manage a larger number of children without their becoming delinquent" (West, 1982: 37).

DISCIPLINE

Parental discipline is another important factor in the genesis of delinquency. "Defective discipline" is much more common among delinquents than among nondelinquents (Glueck and Glueck, 1962). Defective discipline includes excessively strict parental control over children (leading to hostility among children), excessively lenient control (leading to isolation of children and their subsequent resentment of others), and virtually nonexistent discipline (leading to a lack of conscientiousness among children). There is also some evidence that if parents punish their young children severely, those children will have a higher likelihood of engaging in aggressive delinquent behavior later in life (Welsh, 1978).

Consistency of discipline seems more important than whether the discipline involves a punitive approach or a love-oriented method (McCord and McCord, 1959). Consistency is needed in dealing similarly with each member of the family so that children feel they have been treated fairly in comparison to their brothers and sisters, and consistency is also needed in dealing with one child over time.

Recent research at the Oregon Social Learning Center finds that parental discipline is necessary to teach children to avoid the use of force and fraud. Parents must monitor their children's actions, recognize deviant or criminal behavior when it occurs, and punish that behavior. If parents care too little about their children to pay attention to their actions, if parents fail to supervise their children, if they do not regard their children's deviant behavior negatively, or if they do not punish their children for breaking the rules, then their children will be more likely to violate social conventions and the law (Patterson, 1980; West, 1982; Hirschi, 1983; Wilson, 1983). This explanation seems to fit some of the correlates of delinquency, such as the greater tendency for the children of criminals to become delinquent and the high rate of delinquency among children with large numbers of siblings.

"EMPTY SHELL" FAMILIES

Some children live in an *"empty shell" family,* one in which both parents are physically present in the home, but one that involves limited or conflict-ridden interaction between parents and between parents and children. This situation creates confusion and instability in children and weakens their attachment to their parents. In Empey and Lubeck's (1971) study, disharmony between parents and children was correlated with delinquency and with peer identification that led to delinquency; disharmony between the parents themselves had similar effects.

BROKEN HOMES

There has been much speculation and research on the broken home as a cause of delinquency and crime. Broken homes include those that are not structurally intact for various reasons: the death of a parent, divorce, desertion, separation, and illegitimacy (in which case the family was never completed).

Studies of the role of the broken family in delinquency causation are not clear in their conclusions, partly because many studies have employed inadequate research designs. Because broken families are more common among the lower classes and among minority groups, and because those groups have higher rates of officially recorded crime and delinquency, researchers need to separate the effects of class and minority-group status on crime and delinquency from the effects of family structure on crime and delinquency. For instance, some research shows that among the middle class, neither officially recorded nor self-reported delinquency is associated with coming from a broken home (Grinnell and Chambers, 1979; Richards, Berk, and Foster, 1979). Researchers need to use self-report measures to determine if there are real differences in delinquency and crime between adolescents from broken homes and those from intact homes, because adolescents from broken homes may be more likely to be arrested and found delinquent in court than are adolescents who come from intact homes (Nye, 1958; Hirschi, 1969).

The most carefully designed studies seem to find a relationship between delinquency and broken homes. That relationship is relatively weak, but delinquents are slightly more likely than nondelinquents to come from broken homes (Nye, 1958; Dentler and Monroe, 1961; Hirschi, 1969; Hennessy, Richards, and Berk, 1978). Children in families in which remarriage has occurred seem to be slightly less likely to report delinquent acts than are children in families that have only one parent, but the difference is not statistically significant (Perry and Pfuhl, 1963).

One study of broken homes and delinquency found that different family contexts influence various kinds of delinquency in different ways. Running away, truancy, and motor vehicle theft were strongly related to a specific kind of broken home, one in which both biological parents were absent. Vandalism and theft were more highly associated with school and peer contexts than with the structure of the family. In sum, certain kinds of broken families may produce particular kinds of delinquent acts (Rankin, 1983).

There is some evidence that broken homes may have greater effects on girls and preadolescent boys than on adolescent boys (Toby, 1957; Austin, 1978). Compared to girls and preadolescent boys, adolescent boys are not especially well supervised by their parents, whether they live in an intact home or in a broken one. Thus, there is little difference between the delinquency rate of adolescent boys from broken families and the delinquency rate of adolescent boys from intact homes. However, the relative lack of supervision of adolescent boys is probably a cause of their high rate of involvement in delinquency, compared to girls and preadolescent boys. The difference between coming from a broken home or an intact family is more likely to be important for girls and preadolescent boys, because these two groups are usually better supervised in intact families than in broken ones. Consequently, delinquency among girls and preadolescent boys is more common among those who come from broken homes than among those from intact homes, at least according to some research. Other research does not support this conclusion; for instance, a national survey of adolescents failed to confirm this relationship between family structure and delinquency among girls. Broken homes did increase the rate of self-reported delinquency in this study, but in comparable ways for both boys and girls (Canter, 1982). Earlier research may have found a sex differential in the impact of broken homes on delinquency because those studies used official data, which may reflect sex discrimination in the processing of adolescents by the police.

Contradictory findings about the relationship between broken families and delinquency may be due in part to the use of different kinds of samples of adolescents. One researcher tentatively concluded that the relationship between delinquency and father-absence may be strongest for those groups that are the least tolerant of divorce, and that broken homes may make less difference for groups that are more accepting of divorce. If this were true, then researchers who study groups that are relatively tolerant of divorce—for instance, urban Protestants—would be likely to find less of an association between broken homes and delinquency than would researchers who use samples that are less tolerant of divorce. Future research should try to "specify the social characteristics of the children for whom the broken home has significant behavioral consequences" (Wilkinson, 1980: 39).

Broken homes and delinquency in other societies   There is some evidence that broken families are associated with delinquency in other societies. Delinquents in the Soviet Union apparently are likely to come from broken homes, though carefully designed research is lacking (Connor, 1970). In Japan, adolescents who are living with their parents are arrested about half as often as adolescents who are not living with their parents (Clifford, 1976: 114–115). This may be because of a lower level of parental supervision among adolescents who are not living with their parents, but it could also be due to a higher likelihood that the police will arrest adolescents who are not living with their parents. Research on the relationship between broken families and delinquency in other societies is inconclusive for the same reasons that such research is inconclusive in the United States: reliance on official records rather than on self-report data, and failure to compare delinquents and nondelinquents of the same class and minority group.

SEPARATION OF CHILDREN FROM THEIR PARENTS
One factor that might be related to delinquency is the early separation of children from their parents. Regular or prolonged separation from parents during the early years could make it harder for children to develop feelings for others later, and lack of empathy could be linked to delinquency and crime.

There is some evidence that delinquency is more common among the children of parents who both work outside the home (Austin, 1982). Hirschi (1969: 237–239) found that 37 per cent of the boys whose mothers were housewives reported a delinquent act, 44 per cent of the boys whose mothers worked part time outside the home reported a delinquent act, and 50 per cent of those whose mothers were employed full time outside the home reported delinquency. An earlier study (Nye, 1958: 53–59) also found more delinquency among adolescents whose mothers worked outside the home. Whether this relationship still exists today, when a much higher proportion of mothers hold jobs, is unclear.

Any negative effects on children of having both parents work outside the home might be attributable to a loss of supervision. However, conflict between a husband and a wife might also result from the wife's working outside the home, or the wife might take an outside job to escape from a problematic family situation, such as an alcoholic and unemployed husband. In these cases, intrafamily conflict related to working outside the home, rather than lack of supervision, might be the cause of delinquency.

FAMILY COHESIVENESS

What seems most important in determining whether a child will become delinquent is the cohesiveness of the family, the quality of interpersonal relationships in the family, communication between parents and children, and emotional support of the children by their parents (Hirschi, 1969; Hindelang, 1973; Ferracuti, Dinitz, and Acosta, 1975; Poole and Regoli, 1979; Wiatrowski, Griswold, and Roberts, 1981). Attachment of a child to caring parents and parental supervision of that child seem to be more important factors in preventing delinquency than is the simple presence of two parents in the home. For instance, there seems to be less delinquency in broken homes than there is in unhappy intact families (Nye, 1958; Belson, 1975). One study of delinquency in three cultures found less family cohesiveness, less confiding in parents, and less stable home situations among delinquents than among nondelinquents (Rosenquist and Megargee, 1969). Higher levels of hostility within the family have also been found to be associated with more deviant behavior in a study done in Mexico (Meadow et al., 1981).

The quality of family relationships may be associated in different ways with various kinds of crime. For instance, one study found that adult males who had been most exposed as boys to conflict and aggression between their parents were especially likely to commit crimes against people (such as murder, rape, and kidnapping); men who had lacked maternal affection as boys and men whose fathers had engaged in deviance were the most likely to be arrested for crimes against property (such as larceny, car theft, and burglary) (McCord, 1979).

Control theory's assumption that attachment to parents inhibits delinquency receives mixed support from research on drug users. Heroin users are more likely than nonusers to have been deprived of the experience of living in a cohesive family while young (Chein et al., 1964). Adolescents seem to be most likely to turn to drugs if they disagree with their parents or have weak or cold relationships with them (Anderson, Chiricos, and Waldo, 1977). However, one study finds that even though attachment to non drug-using parents inhibits adolescent drug use, close attachment to parents who are perceived by their children to be drug users does not seem to inhibit drug use by adolescents. In fact, there were hints in this study that attachment to drug-using parents might even increase drug use by children in some circumstances, apparently through the social learning of that behavior (Jensen and Brownfield, 1983).

In explaining why Switzerland has relatively low rates of juvenile delinquency, Marshall B. Clinard (1978) focuses on the close ties and good communication between young people and adults. He suggests that Swiss adolescents often prefer interaction in heterogeneous age groups to interaction in peer groups, and that people of various ages often participate together in outdoor activities. Interaction of various age groups also occurs in the large Swiss army. In addition, many Swiss continue to live with their parents after they become young adults. Clinard attributes Switzerland's relatively small problem with youth crime to the culture's emphasis on harmony and compromise, which sustain close ties between people of different ages, both within and outside the family.

The family is an especially important institution in the genesis or the prevention of delinquency and crime. The size and structure of the family are important, but what seems most critical is the quality of relationships among family members. Harmonious relationships between parents, and between parents and children, help to prevent delinquency and crime. Indeed, the relationship between violation of the law and factors such as family size and structure might be due to differences in the quality of relationships in families of different sizes and structures.

Delinquency and the School

Crime and delinquency are more common among people who have lower levels of academic achievement and who are most weakly attached to their schools and teachers. School is an "apprenticeship to maturity" that eases the passage from adolescence to adulthood (Hirschi, 1969; Wiatrowski, Griswold, and Roberts, 1981). However, if academic pressure is coupled with a high likelihood of failure, adolescents may feel that school is irrelevant to their future, ungratifying, and unrewarding. They will then see their grades as unimportant and spend less time on homework; these factors lead to lower academic achievement. Their ties to the school will then weaken, and they may drift into delinquency (Hirschi, 1969: 170–183; Hindelang, 1973; Rettig, Torres, and Garrett, 1977: 248). Poor academic performance in high school is also strongly predictive of being arrested for crime as an adult (Polk, 1980).

Nondelinquents often mention their commitment to education and their respect for their teachers' good opinions as reasons for not turning to crime. They also say that education is important to their future and that they do not want to risk their stake in conformity by violating the law (Rogers, 1977: 52–53).

Students with lower IQ levels may be more delinquent because they are less attached to the school and its teachers and less likely to experience academic success (Hirschi and Hindelang, 1977). Delinquency is correlated with poor grades, dislike of school, hostility toward teachers, and little effort at doing schoolwork (Hirschi, 1969; Empey and Lubeck, 1971).

Evidence that weakened attachment to the school is linked to delinquency was uncovered in Wolfgang, Figlio, and Sellin's (1972) cohort study. Table 9.1 shows that boys with more contacts with the police were more likely than boys with fewer police contacts to

- have changed schools frequently;
- have lower IQs,
- have completed fewer grades, and
- have a lower overall level of achievement.

Wolfgang, Figlio, and Sellin attributed the relationship between school achievement and number of police contacts to the effects of race on both school achievement and delinquency, but a reanalysis of their data concluded that school achievement had an independent and important effect on the likelihood that an individual would be stopped by the police for delinquent behavior (G. Jensen, 1976).

Table 9.1: School Experiences by Number of Contacts with the Police, Averages

	NO POLICE CONTACTS	ONE POLICE CONTACT	MORE THAN ONE POLICE CONTACT
Number of school changes	3.5	3.6	4.6
IQ	108	104	98
Highest grade completed	11.2	10.8	9.2
Modal achievement level	High	Average	Very low

SOURCE: Marvin E. Wolfgang, Robert M. Figlio, and Thorsten Sellin, *Delinquency in a Birth Cohort.* Chicago: University of Chicago Press, 1972, p. 66. Reprinted by permission of the University of Chicago Press. Copyright University of Chicago Press © 1972. (Adapted)

DELINQUENCY AND DROPOUT

A study of delinquency and dropping out of school concluded that bonds to school could, in some circumstances, actually be conducive to delinquency (Elliott and Voss, 1974). By forcing unsuccessful students to attend school until sixteen, compulsory education laws create a frustrating situation that stigmatizes those students as failures and reduces their self-esteem. Some students rebel by engaging in delinquency, which leads to more rejection and alienation, and thus to more delinquency. Some frustrated students drop out of school, and when they do their involvement in delinquency declines. Dropouts thus become less delinquent when they sever their bonds to the school, and delinquency is common among those who are forced to stay in school but feel alienated from it. In this sense, school is "the critical generating milieu for delinquency" (Elliott and Voss, 1974: 203).

This study directs attention to the quality of a student's ties to the school. Staying in school by itself is not an indicator that a student is concerned with the good opinion of teachers and administrators, nor that a student is afraid to jeopardize his or her future by doing poorly in school. What is important is the student's attachment to the school, the schoolwork, and the teachers. Some students who are enrolled in school do not feel that attachment, and so are not inhibited from engaging in delinquent behavior.

SCHOOLS AND DELINQUENCY IN OTHER SOCIETIES

There is some evidence from the Soviet Union that weak school ties may be associated with delinquency. The delinquency rate of school dropouts in the Soviet Union is much higher than the rate of adolescents who remain in school. Dropouts are thought to be especially prone to delinquency because they are outside "the system of semi-formalized primary-group relationships which should influence . . . behavior in officially approved directions" (Connor, 1970: 291). This is consistent with control theory, which predicts that higher rates of delinquency will exist among people who lack attachment to such institutions.

Similar evidence comes from a comparison of delinquents and nondelinquents in poor communities in San Juan, Puerto Rico. This study found that the delinquents did much worse than the nondelinquents did on every measure of school performance and attitudes toward school (Ferracuti, Dinitz, and Acosta, 1975).

Delinquency and the Peer Group

Hirschi's conclusion that weaker peer-group ties are associated with higher rates of delinquency is challenged by other research, perhaps because Hirschi did not adequately distinguish ties to conventional peers from ties to delinquent ones. One national study found no relationship between attachment to peers and self-reported delinquency (Wiatrowski, Griswold, and Roberts, 1981), but other research has found that greater identification with peers is linked to higher rates of delinquency (Empey and Lubeck, 1971; Hindelang, 1973; Elliott and Voss, 1974). This may be because the adolescent subculture is "oppositional" to the dominant, middle-class culture, and so closer ties to the peer group may be associated with more delinquency (Elliott and Voss, 1974).

One study looked carefully at the effects of both parents and delinquent friends on self-reported delinquency, and concluded that both had independent effects on delinquency. However, the delinquent peer group had a greater effect on delinquent behavior for adolescents who had the weaker family ties than it did on the behavior of adolescents who had more family support. Adolescents who had little support from their parents were more open to the influence of their delinquent peers, and adolescents who were wary of harming their good relationships with their parents were more likely to stay away from delinquent peers (Poole and Regoli, 1979).

A study of adolescent gangs among Chinese-Canadians found that those gangs emerged as a consequence of poor family supervision and guidance. Traditionally, the Chinese family in North America has been strong and able to insulate young people from trouble with the law, but in Canada in recent years this cohesive family unit has not been as strong as it once was, and so young Chinese-Canadians have turned to gangs. In part, this may be an escape from family pressure to succeed in school, which creates problems for recent immigrants who lack the necessary language skills (Joe and Robinson, 1980).

The peer group is an important predictor of marijuana use among adolescents in both the United States and France. There is less marijuana use in France, but in both countries users are more oriented to their peer group than nonusers. Moreover, users in each country are less committed than nonusers to conventional institutions such as the school and the family (Kandel and Adler, 1982).

A study of juvenile theft in Great Britain found that the desire to be accepted by peers was a major source of the motivation to steal. Boys imitated other juvenile thieves with whom they interacted, and their peers often encouraged or dared them to take property. The peer group can also reduce theft, because juveniles are sometimes deterred from stealing when a member of their peer group is arrested (Belson, 1975).

Delinquency and Religion

One bond that may prevent delinquency, but was not incorporated in control theory, is membership in organized religion or a belief in religious precepts. Studies in Great Britain and Puerto Rico have found less delinquency among boys who attend church more often and among boys who express stronger religious interests (Belson, 1975; Ferracuti, Dinitz, and Acosta, 1975). However, research done in the United States provides somewhat contradictory results on the relationship between religion and delinquency, even though much of that research finds a weak to moderate inverse relationship—that is, there is less delinquency among the more religious (Jensen and Erickson, 1979; Elifson, Petersen, and Halaway, 1983).

In a study of metropolitan areas in the United States, a significant association was found between official crime rates and church membership, measured by number of members per 1,000 people in the metropolitan area. Communities with a higher proportion of church members tended to have lower crime rates. This relationship was strongest for property crimes, and somewhat weaker though still statistically significant for violent crimes (Stark, Doyle, and Kent, 1980).

In a national survey of sixteen-year-old males from eighty-seven high schools, the impact of religious commitment on delinquency was revealed to vary significantly with the degree of religious commitment in the social environment. In schools in which religious students were a majority, the more religious an individual student was, the less likely it was that he engaged in delinquency. In these schools, the personal convictions of students were reinforced by the social environment. However, in schools that were highly secularized, there was no relationship between religious commitment and delinquency. In these schools, the more religious students were no less likely to be delinquent than were the less religious students. These results suggest that earlier researchers may have come to contradictory conclusions about the relationship of religious commitment and delinquency because studies done on the West Coast, where schools are more secularized, often found no relationship between religion and delinquency, but studies done elsewhere in the United States, where religious commitment is likely to be greater, more often found that religion inhibits delinquent behavior (Stark, Kent, and Doyle, 1982).

Religion is but one of a large set of influences on delinquent behavior, and one that interacts with the influence of the family, the school, and the peer group to inhibit or cause delinquency. One study that used religious salience—the strength of a belief in the power of prayer—and religious orthodoxy as measures of religiosity found a weak to moderate relationship between religion and delinquency, and concluded that religion was not a significant predictor of delinquency when compared to other factors such as the family and the peer group (Elifson, Petersen, and Halaway, 1983). A study of Mormon teen-agers found that measures of religion—especially church participation—were moderately strong predictors of deviant behavior, particularly alcohol and drug use. The researchers concluded that self-reported deviance could be predicted best by combining measures of religious involvement with measures of peer expectations and measures of relationships with parents; this conclusion is consistent with control theory (Albrecht, Chadwick, and Alcorn, 1977). Another study found that the social-control effects of religion were greatest when secular controls were absent or weak; individual religiosity seemed to inhibit deviance only in environments that did not contain other social-control mechanisms to induce conformity (Tittle and Welch, 1981).

Migration and the Disruption of Social Bonds

Earlier in the book we saw that migration is sometimes associated with an increase in crime rates of the people who move. This increase in criminality seems most likely to occur when migration from one nation to another or migration within a nation disrupts social bonds and weakens the informal control of behavior by family, school, peer group, religion, and community. The social integration of groups is sometimes undercut by population turnover and the arrival of newcomers and transients; this seems to have a greater impact on intentional crimes than on impulsive offenses (Stark et al., 1983). However, in some cases a group maintains its social bonds while moving, or recreates those bonds in its new home, and this may keep crime rates from increasing.

UGANDA

In Uganda and other developing nations, crime rates have often increased as people have become detached from traditional institutions through "detribalization" (Clinard and Abbott, 1973: 108–131). One study found that Ugandans who left their villages and moved to the large city of Kampala, especially to its slum shantytowns, were likely to have high rates of crime unless they established new social bonds in the city. Migration thus caused crime rates to increase by weakening attachments to the groups that had traditionally controlled deviant behavior. This process has been described as follows:

> The decline of intimate communication in an urban setting means that the breaking of rules results in almost none of the informal censure common in the villages; often the police are the only means of control. The broader experiences offered, coupled with increased education, weaken parental authority and other traditional controls not only of the youth but of all persons (Clinard and Abbott, 1973: 89).

Migration may not be disruptive if the "receiving community" contains groups into which immigrants can be integrated or if individuals move from one place to another in groups. However, people who move alone and lack social ties in their new community are more likely to become involved in crime because there is little to control their behavior. In the study of Uganda, it seemed to be relatively unimportant for migrants to the city to maintain direct ties to their village; what was important was that they form attachments to relatives and other immigrants from their village in the city to which they had moved (Clinard and Abbott, 1973: 127).

JAPAN

In three of five major regions of economic development in Japan, there were increases in crime rates during the period of development. The largest increase, in the city of Kishima, was largely due to the fact that the workers involved in the development of the city moved into the area temporarily and without families or friends. Apparently, these migrants accounted for much of the increase in this city's crime rate, something that might not have occurred had they brought with them a network of family and friends (Clifford, 1976: 151–159).

Social Bonds in Other Societies

One way to examine the usefulness of control theory is to see whether it helps us to understand cross-national differences in rates of crime and delinquency. If control theory is valid, we would expect the lowest rates to exist in societies characterized by close attachments to institutions. One effort to use control theory in this way suggests that it can account for the relatively low rate of delinquency in India (see the Cross-Cultural Perspective). A study of ten nations in which there is less fear of crime than in the United States found that a common characteristic of those societies was an ability to create or maintain effective social-control agencies, especially the family (Adler, 1983). Let us look briefly at the role of social bonds in several societies.

CHINA

China is a society apparently characterized by a low rate of conventional crime, although statistics are not made publicly available. The country is also characterized by the presence of strongly integrated groups. Chinese citizens

A Cross-Cultural Perspective: Delinquency in India

Compared to other societies, in India juvenile delinquency is relatively uncommon and not especially serious when it does occur. This conclusion is based on both official records and self-report studies. Why is delinquency relatively rare in India?

Part of the answer is that India's economy is a peasant or agrarian one, and in such an economy young people are not superfluous as they are in advanced industrial economies. In postindustrial societies such as the United States, the absence of much need for unskilled labor means that young people must postpone their entry into the labor force. This often leads to an adolescent subculture that is sometimes supportive of delinquency. In contrast, a peasant economy makes use of unskilled labor, and children and adolescents are thus integrated into the social network of their community. In India, where many businesses are run by families, children are introduced into the economic system by their families at a young age.

Young Indians are integrated into their society to an even greater degree than their participation in the labor force would suggest. Indian society is organized in terms of role relationships that create for everyone a set of obligations to the family, the subcaste, and the community. People are expected to care for others, even distant relatives and employees. Social bonds create much interdependence. Thus, agricultural workers and landowners have mutual obligations and patterns of respect that extend beyond their relationship as worker and employer. As a result, an "employer becomes almost a surrogate parent to the worker and is obliged to look after the employee's (and the employee's family's) welfare. The worker, in turn, has obligations to the employer (or provider) that are not due simply to economic dependence, but are defined by the work role itself" (p. 78).

Because all Indians are enmeshed in a complex network of social relationships, their deviance is of concern to many other people. Informal control induces conformity. Indians learn at a young age what others expect of them and learn to conform to the expectations of those with whom they have close relationships. There is a "psychological presence" not only of the child's parents, but also of an extended family network, a subcaste, and a community. Young people thus develop a stake in the status quo, and even a degree of power to say how they will be treated.

Indian culture defines young people as a part of the social structure, not as outsiders to it. Social activities are rarely segregated by age, "hangouts" for adolescents are practically nonexistent, and there is no adolescent subculture conducive to juvenile delinquency.

SOURCE: Based on Clayton A. Hartjen and S. Priyadarsini, *Delinquency in India: A Comparative Analysis.* New Brunswick, N.J.: Rutgers University Press, 1984.

learn an ideology of attachment to the country and to a version of communist ideology; they are thus subordinated to supraindividual concerns. Moreover, the Chinese family is a primary institution that exerts control over individual tendencies to deviate from the law. Young Chinese are also tied to society through state-run recreational facilities that occupy much of their free time.

The regimentation and lack of privacy in China have been compared to life in an army barracks (Butterfield, 1982). Two institutions that maintain social control by public scrutiny of behavior are the *danwei* (or workplace) and the street committee. All Chinese belong to a *danwei* through the school they attend or the office or factory in which they work. The *danwei* often provides housing, schooling, and medical care. It must give permission to marry and to divorce. Ties to the *danwei* are so strong that the Chinese are more likely to be asked their *danwei* than their name if they travel to another community. The urban street committee also controls behavior, searching people's homes, recommending job assignments and housing changes, and even deciding who may have children (Butterfield, 1982). These and other institutions make the Chinese very sensitive to the expectations of other people and help to curb delinquency and crime.

JAPAN

The Japanese have traditionally had strong ties to their family, to the company for which they work, and to the community in which they live. Bonds to such tightly knit groups offer security and success to individuals, and ensure conformity by requiring the fulfillment of social responsibilities. The group nature of Japanese society is so strong that crime rates are low even in densely populated urban areas, where we might expect social bonds to break down and crime rates to be high (Clifford, 1976).

In Japan, individual behavior is guided by obligations to family, employer, neighborhood, and society, rather than by self-interest. The Japanese know that they will benefit socially and economically by conforming to the expectations of others. Americans usually speak of their rights, but the Japanese more often think of the debts they owe to others. The social structure of Japan is similar in its group orientation to some communist nations such as China that also seem to have low crime rates, but Japan provides striking evidence that crime is more a result of the social structure of a society than a product of the society's political and economic ideology. In other words, the capitalist society of Japan and the communist society of China seem to have low crime rates because both have created or maintained social bonds that tie people to groups and institutions.

In recent years, Japan has experienced a rising rate of juvenile delinquency, even though its current rate is well below that of the United States. Much of this delinquency occurs in the schools; some has taken the form of assaults against teachers. Close to 90 per cent of Japanese delinquents are middle or upper class, and they are now a younger group than they were even a few years ago. One explanation for this increase in delinquency is the breakdown of a traditional educational system that once inculcated respect for authority. Japanese leftists claim that the rising delinquency rates of the 1980s are a result of educational policies that favor the brightest students, neglect others, and create for all students "an examination-hell atmosphere from which violence is bound to erupt" (Chapman, 1983b: 3). Competition for academic success has led some students to feel ignored or discriminated against by teachers, weakening their bonds to teachers and the school and freeing them to engage in delinquent behavior.

THE SOVIET UNION

The Soviet Union has also apparently experienced an increase in juvenile delinquency in recent years (Shipler, 1978a, 1978b). This increase has been attributed to rapid urbanization, the breakdown of family and social ties, and the fact that more parents are working outside the home. Migration to cities is thought to disorient people and break up families; this is one reason that population movement has been controlled by the state. These explanations of delinquency are untested, but they are consistent with control theory.

ISRAEL

One nation that has undergone rapid social change and experienced more crime and delinquency as a result is Israel. Until recently, Israel had a very low crime rate, but between 1975 and 1980 there was a tripling in the rate at which new criminal files were opened by the police. This has been attributed to the disruption of the social order by war and the ever-present threat of war, and to the sweeping away of traditional values by increased materialism (Radzinowicz and King, 1977; *The New York Times*, November 22, 1980).

SPAIN

Spain had a relatively low crime rate under Franco's dictatorship, but with his death in 1975 and the introduction of democracy, social control loosened and urban crime—especially by violent juvenile gangs—increased. There was a 44 per cent increase in burglary and robbery in Spain in the first year after Franco's death, but the homicide rate remained low and stable over that time (Markham, 1977). It is not clear that we can attribute the growth in Spain's crime rate to political liberalization alone, but this change was accompanied by loosened social control that might have increased burglary and robbery rates. Another possibility is that crime was simply recorded more completely after Franco's death, creating the illusion of an increase in the crime rate.

Critique of Control Theory

One shortcoming of control theory is that it does not identify the social-structural sources of motivations to break the law. Attachment to the family, the school, and the peer group can keep people from violating the law even when other social forces—such as poverty—might impel them to engage in crime and delinquency. However, a complete theory of crime and delinquency needs to explain the way that social, economic, and cultural forces produce the motivation to break the law.

Attachments to different institutions probably take on varying degrees of importance at different stages of the life cycle, and control theory needs to identify the relative significance of bonds to different institutions for people of various ages. For instance, good relationships with parents may be more important than close attachments to peers for five-year-olds, but less important than close attachments to peers for fifteen-year-olds. In its present form, control theory does not tell us whether this is so.

The way that bonds to different institutions interact with each other also needs to be more fully delineated. Empey and Lubeck looked at this interaction, but we need more information on problems such as how relationships with parents affect attitudes toward school and work, how bonds to teachers during adolescence influence adult work history, and how attachment to family and to job among adults is related to involvement in criminal behavior. For instance, a young father with strong bonds to a wife and children and a strong attachment to his career might experience conflict between his loyalties to family and to job; in some cases, this might cause frustration that leads to violence in the home or theft at work. In sum, control theory needs elaboration, and researchers must study the complex relationships among attachments to different institutions.

TECHNIQUES OF NEUTRALIZATION, CONTROL THEORY, AND VARIATIONS IN CRIME RATES

We do not now have enough evidence on the distribution of the techniques of neutralization to know whether they can account for variations in crime rates. One country might have more crime than another because its culture includes beliefs that make it easier to neutralize the law and engage in crime and delinquency. Differences in access to techniques of neutralization might also help to explain variations in crime rates by region, by size of the community, or over time; however, we have no evidence that this is so. Similarly, socialization experiences and access to criminal subcultures might account for some of the variations in crime rates by sex, age, race, and class; again we lack supporting evidence. More research on the way that techniques of neutralization vary from one society to another and vary within a society by region, community, and social group might help us to explain differences in crime rates.

Control theory does make sense of cross-national variations in crime rates, for nations that have lower crime rates seem to be characterized by stronger and more extensive bonds to family, peer group, school, community, and nation. We have little evidence that regional variations in crime rates in the United States can be explained by differences in the strength of attachments to institutions, but the West's high rate of property crime might be due in part to the relatively weak attachments to community of the many people who have moved there from other parts of the country. Variations in crime rates by size of the community might also be accounted for by control theory; attachment to community seems weaker in larger cities than in small towns and rural areas, and interpersonal relationships in large communities have often been described as weak and segmented. We lack good evidence that fluctuations in crime rates over time parallel changes in social bonds to institutions such as the family, the school, the peer group, the community, and organized religion; however, some scholars have attributed increased crime rates to a reduced emphasis on obligations and responsibilities to others (Wilson, 1983; Davies, 1983).

Control theory helps us to explain variations in crime rates by sex, age, race, and class. Adolescent boys probably have high rates of delinquency because they are usually supervised less carefully than girls and preadolescent boys, two groups that have relatively low delinquency rates. Age variations in crime rates can also be explained by control theory. Adolescents are concerned with breaking away from their parents, and this creates pressure on parents to exert less control. Adults marry, have children, take jobs, and settle down in a community; these social bonds help to account for the decline in crime rates with age. Blacks' high crime rates may be due in part to their weaker attachment to jobs, with the lack of promising jobs to which they can form strong attachments being a product of racial discrimination and the poor quality of the education available in many public schools. The higher rates of family dissolution and illegitimacy among blacks also suggest that differences in the quality of family relationships between blacks and whites might account for some of the difference in crime rates between the groups. Finally, class differences in crime rates might exist because poorer families tend to be larger, are more likely to be broken, and are more likely to experience financial strain; these factors may be associated with reduced control over deviant behavior. In addition, lower-class students may feel that they cannot win the good opinion of their middle-class teachers, or may believe that education will gain them little in improved job prospects even if they did form close attachments to their teachers.

We have little research that demonstrates that variations in crime rates among different groups, regions, and countries are directly due to variations in attachments to institutions. Control theory is, however, compatible with some of these variations in crime rates, and more research might show that this theory can account for those variations.

SUMMARY

Most people must neutralize the hold that the law has over them before they can violate the law. People who are in a state of drift and lack strong bonds to the conventional order are free to engage in delinquency and crime, but they are not forced to do so, according to some sociologists. The values of law violators have some things in common with the dominant value system, but delinquents and criminals act on subterranean themes in the dominant value system in inappropriate situations. Techniques of neutralization, which are used to justify delinquency and crime prior to the deviant act, include the following: denial of responsibility, denial of injury, denial of the victim, condemnation of the condemners, and the appeal to higher loyalties. These techniques are used by many kinds of offenders—juvenile delinquents, professional criminals, and white-collar offenders.

Evidence that these techniques of neutralization are associated with violation of the law comes from a study of embezzlers, a survey of black men interviewed on the street, a study of sex-related and robbery-related murders and contract killings, and several studies of juvenile delinquency. However, we lack good evidence that offenders use these techniques prior to violating the law, and we do not know what aspects of the social structure make it easy or difficult to justify violations of the law.

Control theory proposes that people engage in delinquency or crime when they are free of intimate attachments to the family, the school, and the peer group, and when the aspirations and moral beliefs that bind them to a conventional way of life are weak. The absence of a "psychological presence" of parents leaves adolescents free to violate the law without being afraid of how their parents will react. Close ties between adolescents and their parents inhibit delinquent behavior, as do strong ties to the school and its teachers. Some research also finds that delinquents have relatively weak ties to their peers. Adolescents who do not aspire to conventional lines of action such as school and work, but who want to engage in adult activities before assuming adult responsibilities, are also especially likely to engage in delinquency.

Comparisons of delinquents and nondelinquents generally support control theory, but the interrelationship of variables is more complex than Hirschi's initial formulation of the theory suggested. The way that parents socialize their children, particularly the way they discipline them, is related to delinquency and crime. Children raised in large families also seem more prone to delinquency. If relationships between parents and their children, and between the parents themselves, are characterized by conflict or poor communication, children are more likely to become delinquents. The relationship between broken homes and delinquency is only weak to moderate, but is stronger for some groups than for others. There is also some evidence that having both parents work outside the home is associated with higher rates of delinquency. In general, more cohesive families seem to help to insulate their children against trouble with the law.

Delinquents have weaker ties to schools and teachers than nondelinquents do, and delinquents do less well in their academic work. Delinquency is especially common among academically poor students, but poor students who drop out of school seem to become less delinquent because they reduce the frustration that they encountered as students.

The relationship between the peer group and delinquency is not entirely clear, but many studies find that delinquents usually have delinquent friends. Whether those friends led them into delinquency, or whether they chose those friends after violating the law, is unclear.

Some research indicates that there is less delinquency among adolescents who are more religious. Studies also suggest that religion may interact with the family, the peer group, and the school to curb delinquency.

Under some conditions, migration disrupts social bonds and increases criminality. This occurs when traditional social bonds are broken by moving and are not replaced by other attachments that inhibit criminality.

Control theory has several shortcomings. It does not identify the social-structural sources of motivations to violate the law. It has not yet specified the relative importance of different kinds of attachments for people of various ages. Control theory has also failed to spell out the way that attachments to different institutions interact with each other to prevent or cause crime and delinquency.

We do not yet have enough evidence on the distribution of the techniques of neutralization to account for geographic, temporal, and social variations in crime rates. Control theory does seem capable of explaining those variations, with attachments to institutions being the weakest in those countries and among those groups that have the highest crime rates.

IMPORTANT TERMS

appeal to higher loyalties	denial of injury	"empty shell" family
condemnation of the	denial of responsibility	subterranean value
condemners	denial of the victim	technique of neutralization
control theory	drift	

SUGGESTED READINGS

WILLIAM CLIFFORD. *Crime Control in Japan.* Lexington, Mass.: D. C. Heath, 1976. A fascinating exploration of a society that seems to have kept crime rates low by maintaining traditional group ties.

DONALD R. CRESSEY. *Other People's Money: A Study in the Social Psychology of Embezzlement.* Belmont, Calif.: Wadsworth, 1953, 1971. A study that shows how embezzlers neutralize the law before stealing from their employers.

TRAVIS HIRSCHI. *Causes of Delinquency.* Berkeley, Calif.: University of California Press, 1969. An important statement and test of control theory.

GRESHAM M. SYKES AND DAVID MATZA. "Techniques of Neutralization: A Theory of Delinquency," *American Sociological Review* 22 (December 1957), 664–670. An important paper that presents the five techniques of neutralization and shows how delinquents use them to neutralize the law.

10

Learning to Commit Crime

Crime arises from needs that can be met by violating the law. Because most people are attached to the legal order, or at least know that the law commands widespread respect, they must justify their criminal acts and be relatively free of bonds to the legitimate social order before they can break the law. Criminals must learn techniques for neutralizing the law, and they must also learn the skills and motives that are needed to violate the law. For instance, they learn how to recognize opportunities for crime, how to break into safes, how to reduce victim resistance, and how to find outlets for the property they steal. The degree to which such skills must be learned varies from crime to crime. Thus, no particular skill is needed to steal an unattended bicycle, but finding a safe that contains a large amount of money, breaking into the building, and cracking the safe require considerable skill.

SOURCES OF LEARNING TO COMMIT CRIME

Offenders can learn motives and techniques for violating the law from a multitude of sources. Some of the sources that we will look at here include the community, the peer group, the general culture, the mass media, pornographic material, and correctional institutions.

The Community

Opportunities to learn to commit crime are linked to the social organization of a community. Learning about crime seems to be more possible when there are close ties and frequent interaction among people of different ages within a community (Kobrin, 1951; Cloward and Ohlin, 1960: 162–165). Interaction between teen-agers and adult criminals, as well as between teen-agers in gangs and preteens, provides an opportunity to engage in criminal activity under the supervision of more experienced offenders. An unusual instance of this was reported in 1980 in Washington, D.C., where two adults were arrested for training teen-agers to rob banks. The two men recruited the teens on the street, wrote a robbery note, drove them to a bank, and instructed them to give the note to a female teller. If the youths left the bank before getting the money, they were given a "pep talk" and driven to another bank. When successful, the youths were paid $50 to $135 for the robbery (*The New York Times*, November 2, 1980).

Local criminals sometimes act as role models for young people to emulate, as we can see from the following childhood memory of one of the robbers in the 1950 Brinks holdup:

> "When I was a kid, we all knew what a big-time crook was, and most of us looked up to them. I was always working to make money from the time I could walk. You wanted money because the parents were so poor. And I had all kinds of legitimate jobs, but they didn't pay nothing. But these racket guys would drive up in those big touring cars filled with pretty girls and all the money they wanted. I remember one of them giving us kids five bucks each just to stand and watch his car while he and the girl went to eat at a restaurant. Jesus, five bucks was almost as much as my father made in a week" (cited in Behn, 1977: 60).

Delinquent Gangs and Peer Groups

One example of how the integration of different age groups can give rise to crime comes from a study of a New York City gang. This group of young adults provided a setting where even younger delinquents gathered. The younger boys were on trial by the older boys, who occasionally took them along to "case a job." Many of the gang's exploits were planned by an adult criminal who collected information on places to burglarize, planned the crimes, and made contacts with fences for the disposal of the stolen goods. In such a highly integrated set of age groups, learning criminal motives and techniques is made easy for the gang members and for the young delinquents or "predelinquents" who interact with them (Bloch and Niederhoffer, 1958: 198–201).

Learning to commit crime often occurs within delinquent gangs, but many adolescents also learn not to be delinquent from their peers. Those who are concerned with their reputation and believe that they have an investment in abiding by the law cite the influence of their peers as a major reason for not violating the law (Rogers, 1977: 45–49). Adolescents who do not have a stake in conformity may join gangs and learn criminal motives and skills from peers who encourage and reward violation of the law.

In the gang, adolescents come to respect older criminals, develop specific skills such as car theft, learn how to cooperate with other offenders, and become aware of fences, shady lawyers, bondsmen, and corrupt politicians and police officers (Rettig, Torres, and Garrett, 1977). One professional robber reports that he first got involved in an adult gang of robbers because as an adolescent he had a reputation as a skilled car thief. Members of the gang approached him to steal a getaway car for a robbery, and he was gradually accepted into the gang on a permanent basis (Conklin, 1972).

The General Culture

People sometimes learn criminal motives from the general culture. For instance, the increase in violent crimes after the end of wars is particularly dramatic in nations that were actively involved in the war, were victorious, and suffered large combat losses. The best explanation of this seems to be that violence is legitimized by war. People apparently believe that if their leaders can solve problems with violence, it is also a suitable means for them to resolve interpersonal differences (Archer and Gartner, 1976, 1984).

The techniques of neutralization that we examined earlier are part of the general culture and are used to justify violations of the law. For instance, embezzlers sometimes learn motives for their crimes from the general culture, justifying their offenses by the ambiguity that surrounds the ownership of money and property, and saying that they are only "borrowing the money temporarily" (Cressey, 1953, 1971).

Forcible rape is another crime that is closely linked to the values of the culture. Cultures that emphasize *machismo*—the demonstration of masculinity through the manipulation and exploitation of women—are likely to have more rape and other violence against women than are cultures that deemphasize differences between the sexes and provide men and women with the same opportunities (Brownmiller, 1975; Hills, 1980; Schwendinger and Schwendinger, 1983). We can see an example of this in Brazil in the Cross-Cultural Perspective. One sociologist believes that rape and violence against women would be less common if "our culture considered it masculine to be gentle and sensitive, to be responsive to the needs of others, to abhor violence, domination, and exploitation, to want sex only within a meaningful relationship, to be attracted by personality and character rather than by physical appearance, to value lasting rather than casual relationships . . ." (Russell, 1975: 264–265). Conflict theorists claim that sexist values, and the economic inequality that often accompanies them, are the product of capitalism (Schwendinger and Schwendinger, 1983). However, until we have better data on the incidence of rape in noncapitalist industrial societies and until variations in rates of rape among different capitalist societies are explained, this hypothesis is unproven.

The Mass Media

In 1983, the average daily television viewing time per household in the United States was seven hours and two minutes (Rothenberg, 1984). Social scientists have done much research on the consequences of such heavy television viewing, focusing especially on the large amount of violence that viewers see. Students who watch more television have poorer grades, whatever their parents' income or however much homework they do, and we have seen that low academic achievement is associated with a higher probability of delinquency (*The New York Times*, November 9, 1980).

Violence in the media might have a cathartic effect and actually reduce violence by releasing tensions that might lead to violence, but most research does not support this hypothesis (Goranson, 1969). There is evidence, however, that exposure to television violence elevates short-term aggressiveness among children, and this could lead to delinquency and crime (Bandura, Ross, and Ross, 1961; Liebert and Baron, 1972; Cater and Strickland, 1975; Muson, 1978; Garofalo, 1981). A review of about 2,500 studies and reports published since 1970 concludes that there is "overwhelming" scientific evidence that watching large amounts of violence on television leads to aggressive and violent behavior in children. This report, by the National Institute of Mental Health, calls television "a formidable educator whose effects are both pervasive and cumulative" (cited in Reinhold, 1982a: C27).

Longitudinal research suggests that exposure to televised violence while young even affects behavior in later years. A study that measured the viewing habits of eight-year-olds, and then studied them again ten years later, concluded that for boys "the best single predictor we had on how aggressive these people were at eighteen was the violence in the programs they viewed at age eight" (Leonard Eron, cited in Bennetts, 1981: 25). There was no relationship between the viewing of television violence when young and aggressive

A Cross-Cultural Perspective: Machismo and Murder in Brazil

Brazilian culture has traditionally supported the use of violence by men against women who insult their dignity. This has sometimes led husbands to kill their unfaithful wives, even when those husbands expect to have an unchallenged right to engage in extramarital sex themselves.

A 1979 murder trial and its aftereffects have produced a change in Brazilian culture's support for this kind of violence. In this trial, Raul "Doca" Street, a forty-five-year-old man, shot and killed Angela Diniz, his thirty-two-year-old lover, after she ordered him to move out of her expensive villa so that she could replace him with someone else. She also hit him in the face with a handbag. At Street's trial, his attorney justified the killing by calling the victim "a luxurious Babylonian prostitute" and "a lascivious woman." The attorney said that his client had suffered "a violent moral aggression" and had murdered the victim out of "legitimate defense of his honor." Women who were present inside and outside the courtroom applauded the defendant and carried signs of support for him. A jury of five men and two women convicted him of involuntary homicide, and he was given a two-year suspended sentence and allowed to go free.

According to some observers, this case caused an increase in the number of murders of women by "affronted" men, who were typically acquitted or given light sentences. One feminist describes the months following Street's trial as "a hunting season on women." Brazilian women, led by a small group of militant feminists, became increasingly angry over the murder of women in defense of "masculine honor." They de-

manded a retrial of Street to show that women could not be killed merely for insulting a man's honor. Eventually, an appellate court, acting on an appeal from a member of the victim's family, declared that the verdict of involuntary homicide was invalid, and ordered a new trial.

In the retrial, which ended in December 1981, Street was convicted and sentenced to fifteen years in prison. At the new trial, military police had to force an opening through five hundred angry feminist protesters. The atmosphere at the new trial was one of condemnation of machismo killings, rather than the supportive atmosphere of the first trial only two years earlier. Some Brazilians believe that the second verdict, and the protest over killing in defense of "masculine honor" that followed the first verdict, have weakened this justification for murder. In three cases tried during the two weeks after the second verdict, three men were found guilty of murdering their wives to defend their honor.

The increased education of Brazilian women, their greater participation in the labor force, and the leadership of a small group of militant feminists all helped to produce this change in Brazilian culture. Machismo as a legally acceptable excuse for the murder of women who insult men's honor is becoming a thing of the past. In the future, Brazilian men may no longer be able to learn this justification for violence against women from the general culture.

SOURCE: Based on Jim Brooke, "Feminism in Foreign Lands: Two Perspectives: Macho Killing in Brazil Spurs Protesters," *The Boston Globe*, January 3, 1982, pp. A23, A24.

behavior by teen-age girls. Perhaps only the boys were encouraged or reinforced in their expressions of violence, which they modeled after what they saw on television. In addition, what the boys watched on television when they were eighteen was not related to their aggressiveness at that age, possibly because television violence was no longer realistic to them or perhaps because the modeling effect only occurs earlier in life (Lefkowitz et al., 1977). In response to commonly heard methodological criticisms of this and similar studies, one of the researchers in this study states the following:

Now, it could have been said that aggressive youngsters like violent programs to begin with. But because of the methodology we used to control the experiment, we were fairly certain this was a cause and effect relationship, with television viewing preceding the aggressive behavior. The highly aggressive youngsters who were watching nonviolent programs were significantly less aggressive by age eighteen than the youngsters who were not aggressive at eight but who had watched violent programs; they turned out to be more aggressive in the end. We later repeated the study, and found the same thing. Furthermore, the more violent the program, the more aggressive the children became (Leonard Eron, cited in Bennetts, 1981: 25).

Media attention to real acts of violence may also trigger additional violence in the general population. Thus, after the assassination of President John F. Kennedy in 1963, there was an increase in aggravated assaults and robberies throughout the country. Similar increases occurred in 1966 after two widely reported crimes: the murder of eight nurses by Richard Speck and the killing of fourteen people by Charles Whitman from a tower at the University of Texas (Berkowitz and Macaulay, 1971). One study even found a noticeable increase in the homicide rate after heavyweight championship boxing matches, and an especially great increase after those matches that were most heavily publicized (Phillips, 1983). News stories about violence that is rewarded, such as a championship fight, seem to be followed by a short-term increase in the nation's homicide rate, but news accounts of violence that is punished, such as a murder for which the perpetrator is executed or imprisoned for life, seem to be followed by a short-term drop in the country's homicide rate; apparently, the homicide rate is not affected by reports of violence that is neither punished nor rewarded (Phillips and Hensley, 1984).

For some people under certain circumstances, exposure to media violence can increase aggressiveness. Why this aggressiveness sometimes takes the form of crime and delinquency, and other times takes legitimate forms such as athletic or academic competition, is unclear. Thus, one recent study concluded that television did not have a significant effect on the later aggressive behavior of young boys and girls or on teen-age boys, contrary to many other studies (Milavsky et al., 1983). A study conducted at Harvard University to explore children's reactions to televised violence concluded that children were usually able to distinguish fantasy—such as cartoon violence—from real life, and were probably unlikely to imitate fantasy violence (cited in Chira, 1983). Television networks often point to the methodological flaws of the many studies that show a link between media violence and aggressiveness, and cite the smaller number of studies that fail to find such an association. However, these networks solicit billions of dollars in advertising from companies on the assumption that what people see on television does influence their behavior.

The general thrust of the research done to date is that the mass media, and their portrayal of violence, probably contribute to crime and delinquency in the larger society, but that factors other than exposure to media violence are also important in the explanation of crime and delinquency. The age of the viewer is important, with young viewers probably being the most vulnerable to the effects of media violence. More realistic violence, and violence that forms the central theme of a show, probably have the greatest impact on viewers (Seymour Feshbach, cited in Bennetts, 1981). A useful position is that of psychologist Leonard Berkowitz (cited in Bennetts, 1981: 25): "There is no one factor at work, but one of the things that happens is that people get ideas as well as inclinations, and if their inhibitions happen to be weak at the time, these ideas or inclinations can be translated into open behavior." This position can, with little modification, be fitted into control theory: People exposed to media violence may engage in violent behavior if they lack attachments to conventional institutions and lines of action, or if they have techniques available for neutralizing the constraints of the law.

Pornography

There is a widely held view that people who view or read pornography are more likely to commit sex offenses, because they learn to see such behavior as rewarding or because they are stimulated to act on their sexual fantasies. *Pornography* is material that is intended to arouse people sexually by portraying sexual matters in visual or verbal terms. *Obscene material* is material, often pornographic in nature, that has been declared illegal because it poses a threat to the state or to organized religion, violates common morality, has no redeeming social value, or appeals to the prurient or lascivious interest.

Pornographic material does arouse people sexually, although not everyone responds to it in the same way. Those who are most likely to be aroused sexually by pornography are the young, the college educated, the religiously inactive, and the sexually experienced. Most men are sexually aroused when they view pornography; women are more likely to experience sexual arousal mixed with guilt and disgust.

Exposure to pornography rarely causes any major changes in the viewer's sexual behavior, except for short-term increases in masturbation or sexual intercourse with regular partners. No effects on sexual morality have been found, nor is there evidence that pornography causes sex crimes (The President's Commission on Obscenity and Pornography, 1970; Goldstein and Kant, 1973). In fact, the legalization of pornography in Denmark in 1966 preceded a decline in arrests for sex crimes. From 1959 to 1969, arrests for exhibitionism dropped by 58 per cent (primarily as a result of fewer reports from victims), arrests for voyeurism dropped by 80 per cent, arrests for child molesting declined by 69 per cent, and arrests for physical indecency with adult women fell by 56 per cent (a decline apparently unrelated to the legalization of pornography). Rates of rape and other serious offenses against adult women seemed unaffected. Falling numbers of arrests do not necessarily prove a decline in criminal behavior; they could simply indicate more police or public tolerance of the behavior. However, the data are consistent with the hypothesis that the legalization of pornography reduced sex crimes in Denmark. At the very least, the data suggest that the legalization of pornography did not increase sex crimes (The President's Commission on Obscenity and Pornography, 1970; Gagnon, 1974: 253).

One study that looked at exposure to pornography among several groups—including the general population, regular users of pornography, child molesters, homosexuals, transsexuals, and rapists—found that most people had been exposed to erotic material of some sort during adolescence. Rapists were the most likely to have been exposed to sexually explicit material before the age of thirteen; this was the only indication in the study that people exhibiting deviant sexual behavior were more likely to have been exposed to explicit pornography during their preadolescent years. During adolescence, rapists and child molesters actually saw less pornography than people from the general population. The researchers suggested that a reasonable exposure to pornography, especially during adolescence, reflects sexual interest and curiosity that coincide with normal adult patterns of acceptable heterosexual interest and practice. Less-than-average exposure during adolescence may reflect either active avoidance of heterosexual stimuli or an environment in which such material is absent (Goldstein and Kant, 1973).

Among the sex offenders in this study, there was no clear-cut pattern of antisocial sexual activity following arousal by pornography. Erotic material was a factor in a few offenses, but sex crimes are more likely to be associated with lowered inhibitions due to alcohol consumption, rejection by wives or lovers, and interaction with peers who suggest sex crimes. Sex offenders rarely mentioned pornography as stimulating, but some did mention being aroused by material depicting violence. There was little overt imitation of the behavior displayed in pornographic material, although that material sometimes produced sexual fantasies. For sex offenders, these fantasies typically led to masturbation, even in adulthood, rather than to sex crimes. Among the general population, such fantasies led to masturbation during adolescence but usually to sexual activity with established partners during adulthood.

Two experiments have found that pornography that combines sex with explicit violence against women increases aggressiveness toward females. Nonviolent erotic material does not have the same effect (Sullivan, 1980). However, these experiments used college students as subjects, and measured aggressiveness by the subjects' administration of electric shocks and by subjects' responses to questionnaires. We cannot generalize from these studies and say that violent pornography increases actual sex offenses among the population at large. There is some evidence that men who are already angry may have their level of aggressiveness increased by exposure to hard-core pornography, but this is not the same as showing that exposure to hard-core pornography causes sex crimes among the male population at large, or even among men who are already angry (Gray, 1982).

Exposure to pornography can weaken condemnation of rape by both men and women. One experiment found that students who were exposed to more pornographic films recommended more lenient prison sentences for convicted rapists than did people who were exposed to less pornography (*The Boston Globe*, November 21, 1982). Another study found that viewers of films showing extreme violence against women, even films that were not very sexually explicit, became "more callous in the face of the films' portrayals of violence toward women and more likely to believe that a woman who was raped wanted to be" (Goleman, 1984: C1).

Correctional Institutions

Another commonly mentioned source of learning to commit crime is the correctional institution. Prisons, jails, and juvenile detention centers have been described as "schools of crime" where relatively inexperienced offenders are thrown into daily contact with skilled criminals. Conversations in these settings often focus on crime, spreading criminal motives and techniques from more experienced offenders to less knowledgeable inmates, and possibly increasing involvement in crime by those inmates after they are released.

There are no reliable data on the extent to which this kind of learning actually takes place. Many offenders are quite skilled in crime before they are incarcerated. There seems to be no clear relationship between the length of time that inmates are imprisoned and the likelihood that they will return to crime when released (Von Hirsch, 1976: 113). Indeed, the longer that inmates spend in prison, the less efficient and more out-of-practice they may become in the commission of crimes that require skill (Irwin, 1970: 147). Thus, any learning of criminal motives and skills by an inmate may be counterbalanced by the loss of efficiency that occurs with the passage of time.

To the extent that criminal motives and skills are learned in an institution, this seems to occur during an inmate's middle stage of confinement. Inmates are less likely to pick up skills when they are first incarcerated or when they are about to be released (Radzinowicz and King, 1977: 271–272). In addition, whether inmates learn criminal motives and skills is probably related to personal characteristics. For instance, inmates who have families and plan to "go straight" when released are probably less likely to learn criminal motives and skills than are inmates who have no family ties and are committed to a life of crime.

Incarceration can lead to crime in indirect ways. The prison experience may be conducive to the formation of motives to engage in crime. The deprivations of prison life, including lack of freedom and demeaning treatment, can cause resentment that is later used to justify crime (Sykes, 1958). Material deprivations and crowded living conditions lead to the exploitation and manipulation of inmates by each other, and sometimes to homosexual rape, assault, and even homicide (Silberman, 1978: 379–381). Because prisoners lack opportunities to make their own decisions and take responsibility for their own lives, they do not acquire the everyday skills needed to lead law-abiding lives once they are released, and this can push them back into crime after they leave prison (Kassebaum, Ward, and Wilner, 1971; Cordilia, 1983).

In addition to learning the motives and skills to commit crime from their prison experiences, and sometimes from other inmates, offenders also learn motives and skills from adults in the community, from peers in gangs, from the general culture, and from the mass media. One theory of crime causation that looks at the process by which people learn to commit crime is differential association theory.

DIFFERENTIAL ASSOCIATION THEORY

Edwin H. Sutherland introduced *differential association theory* in the 1939 edition of his criminology textbook. He modified the theory in 1947, but it has remained the same since then (Sutherland and Cressey, 1978). This theory seeks to explain why crime rates are distributed as they are among various groups and why any given individual does or does not become a criminal or a delinquent. Because the theory purports to be a theory of all crime and delinquency, it is very general in nature.

Principles of Differential Association Theory

The first principle of differential association theory is that criminal behavior is *learned*. This assertion denies the possibility that individual pathology or biological factors cause crime. It also claims that criminal behavior is not unique to or invented anew by individuals, but is instead learned from others. This is questionable, for some crimes—such as the Equity Funding Corporation of America fraud or one kidnapper's attempt to have ransom money delivered through a computerized bank terminal—seem to be unique to the offender (Parker, 1976). Many aspects of an offender's behavior may be learned from others—for example, the motives and justifications for the crime—but the criminal's specific actions may result from a combination of skills, ideas, and opportunities that are available only to that individual.

The second major statement of differential association theory is that most learning of criminal behavior takes place *in face-to-face interaction* with other people. This means that differential association theory regards the mass media as relatively unimportant in the causation of criminal behavior, even though there is some evidence that criminal motives and skills may be learned from the mass media. Differential association theory was developed before mass ownership of television; today 98 per cent of all American households have television sets. This major change in the role of the mass media requires a modification of differential association theory to incorporate learning directly from the mass media.

The third principle of the theory is that people learn from others both the *techniques of crime and the direction (legal or illegal) of motives, drives, and attitudes.* However, some crimes require little or no skill. For instance, the murder of a spouse requires little skill, especially if a handgun or a knife is available, and many forms of theft require little skill. Embezzlers have to learn "verbalizations" that allow them to use their accounting skills for illegal ends, but they do not need to learn specific techniques of embezzlement (Cressey, 1953, 1971: 147–151).

Differential association theory then proposes that *the direction of motives and drives is learned from definition of the law as favorable or unfavorable.* This assumes that people orient their actions toward the law; in other words, the law is not irrelevant to any individual in deciding how to behave. Some situations are defined as favorable to violation of the law; thus, an unattended bicycle may be seen as a chance to steal. However, the same situation may also be defined as unfavorable to violation of the law, with the unattended bicycle being viewed as a chance to alert the owner to the risk of theft or as a chance to watch the bicycle until the owner returns. Some people define the situation in one way, and others define it differently. The way that the situation is defined depends on the favorable or unfavorable definitions of the law that have been learned in the past.

The primary proposition of differential association theory is that a person becomes delinquent or criminal because of *an* EXCESS *of definitions favorable to violation of the law* OVER *definitions unfavorable to violation of the law.* This principle stresses association with criminal or noncriminal definitions, but does not require contact with criminal or noncriminal individuals. One can learn definitions favorable to violation of the law from law-abiding people, and one can learn definitions unfavorable to violation of the law from criminals. Parents may not violate the law but verbally approve of theft for certain purposes (such as feeding a family) or in certain situations (such as in a large store). Parental approval of this sort may convey to children a definition favorable to violation of the law. On the other hand, a professional thief may convey to youngsters the need to avoid violence against victims of theft. Some offenders even warn others away from behavior that they themselves engage in. For instance, heroin addicts often tell nonusers to stay away not only from heroin but also from marijuana, the drug with which many of them began.

Critical to differential association theory is the *ratio* of definitions favorable to violation of the law to definitions unfavorable. Any one individual holds both types of definitions. It is only when the definitions favorable to violation of the law exceed the definitions unfavorable that a person turns to crime or delinquency. There is an obvious difficulty in measuring these definitions of the law so that an exact ratio can be calculated for any given person.

Definitions of the law are a result of associations with criminal and noncriminal patterns that vary in *frequency, duration, priority, and intensity.* It is the nature of associations with criminal and noncriminal patterns, rather than the mere fact of those associations, that is important. Associations that are more frequent play a larger role in the balance between definitions favorable to violation of the law and definitions unfavorable to violation of the law. Associations that endure over the longest time are the most significant in determining criminal behavior. Associations that occur earlier in life—in childhood or in adolescence—are the most important in forming definitions of the law; this is called priority. Finally, the intensity of associations is important. This means that the prestige of the source of the definition of the law and the individual's emotional reactions to the source are significant in learning definitions of the law. Thus, a young child who learns a definition favorable to violation of the law from a parent who presents that definition frequently and over long stretches of time will be more influenced in the direction of violating the law than an adult who is exposed to a definition favorable to violation of the law by a passing acquaintance whom the adult sees infrequently and for short periods.

Critique of Differential Association Theory

The theory of differential association stresses the ratio of definitions favorable to violation of the law over definitions unfavorable to violation of the law. It may be mistaken in looking at definitions of the law in general, for individuals violate specific laws. Thus, a person might not need to hold an overall unfavorable view of the law before committing a crime; holding an unfavorable definition of one specific law may be enough.

Differential association theory examines the learning process by which people become criminals, but it does not explain why people have the associations they do. Because the theory does not tell us how the associations that expose people to different definitions of the law are distributed throughout the social structure, it does not fulfill its goal of explaining why crime rates are distributed as they are among various groups.

Because differential association theory looks at the individual's perception of the situation, rather than at the actual situation itself, the theory is a social-psychological rather than a social-structural one. It is not, however, a purely psychological theory, because it does not consider personality traits and psychological variables to be important factors in crime causation. In answer to critics of differential association theory who say that it does not account for an individual's receptivity to certain definitions of the law, Sutherland and Cressey (1978) claim that the way that people react to the patterns to which they are exposed is a result of their past associations. In other words, a person's current response pattern is learned in the same way that criminal behavior is learned. Likewise, the search for opportunities to commit crime is seen as a product of past learning experiences.

One criticism of differential association theory is that it may better describe how some people initially become involved in crime and delinquency than why people continue in a criminal career. Thus, the direct rewards of crime— such as money, euphoria from illegal narcotics, or prestige among peers— may be a sufficient cause of continued violation of the law.

Because differential association theory is so general and imprecise, it is not easily tested. Even if the concepts of the theory could be defined in measurable terms, an enormous amount of data would be needed to test the theory. Consider, for example, the difficulty of measuring not only all associations with criminal definitions, but also all associations with noncriminal definitions, from the time a person is conscious of the social environment. To test the theory, it would be necessary to measure how frequent all of those associations are, how long they last, how they vary in significance because of the person's age, and how the person reacts emotionally to the various sources of definitions. Because this measurement process cannot realistically be accomplished, some sociologists have tried to test the theory by examining hypotheses derived from it. For instance, differential association theory has been reconceptualized as follows:

> Overt criminal behavior has as its necessary and sufficient conditions a set of criminal motivations, attitudes, and techniques, the learning of which takes place when there is exposure to criminal norms in excess of exposure to corresponding anticriminal norms during symbolic interaction in primary groups (DeFleur and Quinney, 1966: 7).

This reformulated version of the theory seems to be internally consistent, and it yields testable hypotheses. However, full verification of differential association theory would require extensive research that examines many specific hypotheses generated by the theory, and this has not yet been done.

Modifications of Differential Association Theory

Because of the shortcomings of differential association theory, several modifications of the theory have been proposed. Two important ones are differential identification theory and differential association-reinforcement theory.

DIFFERENTIAL IDENTIFICATION THEORY

Differential identification theory stresses the way that people choose models for their behavior. The choice of models does not necessarily involve interaction with others in intimate personal groups, as required by differential association theory. Instead, according to differential identification theory, "a person pursues criminal behavior to the extent that he identifies himself with real or imaginary persons from whose perspective his criminal behavior seems acceptable" (Glaser, 1956: 440). This approach has been described as follows:

> Differential identification allows for human choice, and stresses the importance of vocabularies of motives existing in the wider culture independently of direct intimate association. That is, direct, social and symbolic support for deviance need not necessarily coexist before deviant action is undertaken. . . . Once this step has been taken, differential association becomes important only to the extent that personal interaction is a considerable factor in criminality and the "excess of definitions favorable over those unfavorable" is now seen to be involved with the relative weightings purposively given to these factors by the actor (Taylor, Walton, and Young, 1973: 129–130).

Testing differential identification theory would require the application of role theory to people who do and do not violate the law, and this might be somewhat easier than testing differential association theory.

DIFFERENTIAL ASSOCIATION-REINFORCEMENT THEORY

Another important modification of differential association theory is Burgess and Akers's (1966; Akers, 1985; Akers et al., 1979) *differential association-reinforcement theory.* This social learning theory is broader than differential association theory. It states that learning occurs through operant conditioning in both nonsocial and social situations, even though most learning results from interaction with others. People learn attitudes and techniques conducive to crime from positive reinforcement (rewards) and negative reinforcement (punishments) that result from their own behavior, whether it is criminal or law-abiding. Thus, an absence of rewards from attending school or holding a menial job would make criminal behavior seem more attractive.

Evidence on Differential Association Theory

There is some research that is consistent with differential association theory. Much of this research focuses on the relationship between delinquent behavior and patterns of interaction among adolescents, demonstrating that the associates of delinquents are other delinquents and that delinquency is often a group phenomenon. Even though this evidence is consistent with differential association theory, the absence of a time dimension in the research makes it impossible to conclude that the learning of delinquent behavior from others precedes and causes violation of the law.

EVIDENCE AGAINST DIFFERENTIAL ASSOCIATION THEORY

Differential association theory does not explain all crimes. For instance, it is not consistent with some evidence on rural offenders or with research on landlords who violate rent-control regulations (Clinard, 1942; 1944; 1952, 1969). In addition, some check forgers operate alone and apparently lack the associations with criminal patterns required by differential association theory (Lemert, 1953). Some crimes are evidently invented anew by offenders who do not experience the learning process proposed in differential association theory; unique situations can generate or facilitate crimes without the offender learning criminal motives or techniques from others.

Offenders who are not part of a criminal subculture or who have no ties to criminals may lack exposure to the patterns and associations needed to learn criminal motives and skills. One study of shoplifters found that often they had no contact with a criminal subculture or with other criminal patterns. Few of those who were apprehended had prior convictions, most were "respectable" people who were employed or were housewives, many did not live in poor neighborhoods, most took inexpensive merchandise with little resale value, and many were ignorant of the arrest process (Cameron, 1964: 146–148). These characteristics suggest a lack of contact with a subculture that could have provided the shoplifters with criminal motives and techniques.

WHITE-COLLAR CRIME AND DIFFERENTIAL ASSOCIATION THEORY

Differential association theory is useful in explaining crime in the business world. White-collar crime arises in part from learning cultural goals, such as material success, and then pursuing those goals through illegal means. Because there is no enforceable code of business ethics to limit the pursuit of those goals to legal means, definitions unfavorable to violation of the law may not readily be learned in the world of business. For instance, after the conviction of the electrical equipment manufacturing companies and their executives for price fixing in 1961, neither the National Association of Manufacturers nor the Chamber of Commerce of the United States publicly condemned the violators.

Some business crime results from what C. Wright Mills (1956) calls "structured immorality," a characteristic of the corporate milieu that leads to a lack of personal responsibility among some people in the business world. Individuals who are most assimilated into the organization are probably the most likely to violate the law, and those new to the world of business are less likely to do so because they are more apt to be guided by the definitions unfavorable to violation of the law that they bring with them from the outside world. A study of attitudes toward bribes and payoffs made by business people to foreign officials found that experienced executives who were enrolled in business school programs were more tolerant of such bribes and payoffs than were undergraduate business students who lacked experience in the world of business (M. Jensen, 1976). This suggests that experience in business is conducive to the learning of definitions supportive of bribes and payoffs. Whether these definitions lead to actual violation of the law depends on factors such as exposure to definitions unfavorable to violation of the law and the presence of opportunities to break the law.

Learning from superiors and from peers in the company is probably a more important determinant of business crime than is the personality of the individual. A former head of the Securities and Exchange Commission's Division of Enforcement states this bluntly: "Our largest corporations have trained some of our brightest young people to be dishonest" (Stanley Sporkin, cited in Kohlmeier, 1976: 53). Social pressure to violate the law has been described as follows for the Equity Funding Corporation of America fraud:

> Corporations can and do create a moral tone that powerfully influences the thinking, conduct, values, and even the personalities of the people who work for them. The tone is set by the men who run the company, and their corruption can quickly corrupt all else. A startling thing about Equity Funding is how rarely one finds, in a cast of characters big enough to make a war movie, a man who said, "No, I won't do that. It's wrong." As for the majority who were sucked in and drowned, their motives were many and mixed. The important thing is that the fraud unerringly pressed upon their weaknesses, some of which they were unaware of at the time, and quickly overthrew them almost before they realized what had happened (Blundell, 1976: 46).

Executives convicted in the 1961 electrical equipment price-fixing case said that when they came to their jobs, they found price fixing to be an established way of life (Geis, 1967). They felt pressure to violate the law in order to achieve corporate goals, even though company presidents later said that these executives were self-aggrandizing people who had violated company rules to advance their own careers. The executives did admit later that if they had refused to violate the law, they would have been transferred within the company rather than dismissed, but they also said that loyalty to the company was what led them to violate the law.

Differential association theory fits much of what we know about white-collar crime. Business people learn definitions favorable to violation of the law, such as loyalty to the corporation over loyalty to the law. This learning process includes techniques of neutralization that are conducive to violation of the law. It also involves the segregation of business people from the law-abiding public, thus making them relatively immune to public criticism and limiting their exposure to definitions unfavorable to violation of the law. This isolation is more common in small towns than in large cities, where there is a more diverse social life and a more cosmopolitan atmosphere. One study found that executives in larger cities were more tolerant of government regulation of business than were executives in smaller towns (Lane, 1954: 102–103). This study also found fewer violations of the law by firms located in larger cities than by those in smaller towns. The researcher attributed this to negative attitudes toward government regulation in small towns and to the isolation of business people in smaller communities from attitudes favorable to regulation.

From his study of the black market that developed when prices were regulated by the Office of Price Administration (OPA) from 1942 to 1947, Marshall B. Clinard (1952, 1969) concludes that most black market violators learned their crimes from other people. He avoids the question of who invented those crimes in the first place, an issue that differential association theory also ignores. Clinard claims that definitions of the situation and justifications for black market violations were transmitted from one business person to another in conversations and were described in the general press and in business trade papers. He suggests that differential association theory is consistent with aspects of the black market such as the similarity of offenses, the shared attitudes of business people toward government regulation, and the failure to condemn people who violated the regulations. However, this evidence does not prove that business people learned to commit their crimes in face-to-face interaction with people who held criminal definitions of the law. The similarity of their violations may have been due to a common response to OPA regulations, the market structure of certain industries, and available opportunities to violate the law.

Donald R. Cressey (1953, 1971) assesses the usefulness of differential association theory in his study of embezzlement. He finds that offenders did not learn specific techniques and skills for embezzlement through interaction with others, but rather employed regular job skills to commit their crimes. They learned rationalizations for their offenses from the general culture, but most of them could not give specific sources of their justifications for theft. Cressey concludes that the general emphasis of differential association theory is correct, in spite of his finding that the associations of embezzlers did not change prior to their thefts in a way that would have produced an excess of definitions favorable to violation of the law.

Even though research on embezzlement and black market violations indicates that differential association has its limitations, the theory seems to be consistent with two conclusions about white-collar crime. First, it is often learned from the general culture, from the ideology of business, and from peers and superiors in the firm. Second, it is frequently associated with the isolation of business offenders from norms and values that support the law. In spite of its consistency with some of what we know about white-collar crime, differential association theory needs to be tested further to show that it is the best possible explanation for such offenses.

JUVENILE DELINQUENCY AND DIFFERENTIAL ASSOCIATION THEORY

Juvenile gangs reinforce and stimulate delinquency by supporting law-violating behavior and by offering protection from outsiders to gang members who break the law. A study of juvenile theft in Great Britain found that association with other adolescents who had already stolen property was very important in leading to theft by boys, especially if that association began when a boy was quite young, continued over a long time, and involved boys who stole frequently (Belson, 1975).

Research in the United States reveals that much delinquency takes place in groups, although the extent to which this is true varies with the specific offense and the sex of the offender (Erickson and Jensen, 1977; Giordano, 1978). One study concludes that juvenile shoplifters often learn attitudes and techniques from other juveniles. Because older juveniles are more likely to steal by themselves, and younger thieves are more likely to steal in groups, the researcher suggests that younger thieves learn motives and skills from others but are eventually able to steal by themselves (Cameron, 1964: 148–149). Other research is consistent with the idea that delinquent behavior is learned from other juveniles (Matsueda, 1982).

Several studies focus on the ability of differential association theory to explain adolescent use of drugs and alcohol. One study finds that differential association theory must be modified, even though it is generally supported by the data. Peer groups seem to have a direct effect on drug and alcohol use among teens, independent of the internalized definitions of the law held by adolescents. Differential association theory in its original form suggests that peer groups affect behavior by their impact on these definitions, and the data do not support that idea. Moreover, definitions held by adults who are important in the adolescents' lives do not seem to play a role in marijuana use; peer groups or a drug subculture, rather than adults, seem to affect the use of marijuana by teens. However, adolescents' use of alcohol is influenced by adult definitions, and this finding is compatible with differential association theory. In conclusion, this study suggests that peer groups' definitions help to generate some kinds of delinquent behavior, but that their impact varies with the kind of behavior in question (Jaquith, 1981).

Support for differential association theory also comes from a study of drug use by adults in Texas. This research, which found a close relationship between drug use by close friends and self-reported drug use, assumed that intensity of association was more important than frequency of association. This study has its limitations, however. Drug users in Texas may differ from drug users in other parts of the country. Frequency of association could be more important than intensity of interaction, and so the drug-using behavior of close friends might not be the most important factor leading to drug use. Even more importantly, people may rationalize their own drug use by saying that their best friends also use drugs, rather than start to use drugs after learning certain definitions from their close friends. This study thus provides only tentative support for differential association theory (Dull, 1983).

PROFESSIONAL THEFT AND DIFFERENTIAL ASSOCIATION THEORY

Evidence consistent with differential association theory also comes from studies of professional thieves. Members of the subculture of professional thieves teach new recruits the skills that make expert theft possible, and immersion in the subculture isolates the thieves from noncriminal patterns (Sutherland, 1937; Maurer, 1955, 1964; 1974; Letkemann, 1973). The process of *tutelage* or instruction provides new thieves with knowledge of how to spot opportunities for theft, how to plan thefts, and how to carry out thefts. Thus, burglars learn specific skills such as how to enter a building or how to blow open a safe. Robbers learn how to interpret the body language of potential victims, how to control victims, and how to show self-confidence and mastery during the crime. Con artists learn how to lie convincingly, how to size up and manipulate victims, how to display a winning personality, and how to look respectable.

Pickpockets learn to look unobtrusive in public, be cautious, and use the opportunities with which they are presented. Manual dexterity is a source of professional pride for pickpockets. Good pickpockets are expected to have the skill to take money from a victim if they can figure out where the victim is carrying his or her money. Pickpockets learn timing, speed, misdirection, concealment, rhythmic movement, and dexterity. They learn to blend these skills into a "single, almost instantaneous, and practically invisible act of theft"

(Maurer, 1955, 1964: 41). Pickpockets also learn about garments and their pockets, and how to take wallets from different pockets. These skills are learned through direct interaction with skilled pickpockets: "One thief turns out another. That is, he teaches him" (Maurer, 1955, 1964: 157). Pickpockets first learn that it is possible to steal from other people. Then they learn specific skills, practice them, and are evaluated by other thieves, so that they refine their skills and eventually become accepted as professionals by other pickpockets. If thieves are arrested and imprisoned, as most eventually are, their pickpocketing skills may grow rusty because they cannot practice them in prison.

Most thieves "have a line"—or a personal work preference and related skills—even though they usually avoid strict specialization. Their skills can be adapted to various crimes, but they prefer to stay close to their "line" to ensure their safety. A study of burglars in the United States found that most of the successful ones had engaged in a wide variety of crimes (Shover, 1973: 41–44). Research on professional theft in the United States in the mid-1960s also found considerable versatility among professional thieves (The President's Commission on Law Enforcement and Administration of Justice, 1967b: 96–101). This contradicts the conclusion of Sutherland's (1937) study of a professional thief, which found much specialization among thieves. Either the nature of professional theft changed over those three decades, or Sutherland's single informant provided a distorted picture of professional theft in the 1930s.

A study of professional thieves in a Canadian prison concluded that early involvement in juvenile delinquency seems to be a prerequisite for an adult career as a professional criminal (Letkemann, 1973). As juveniles, these thieves learned such things as how to avoid attention when stealing and what a typical police reaction to a certain crime might be. Their usual pattern was a gradual progression from awkward juvenile theft, to some learning from other thieves while incarcerated, to trial and error with new forms of theft, and then to learning from skilled thieves and from personal experience. These professional thieves learned mechanical skills, social skills such as the management of victims, and organizational skills such as planning and executing a crime. They learned these things from other prisoners, from members of their gang, and from thieves they met in bars. In this way, safecrackers learned about different styles of safes and how to break into them; this information had to be continually updated. Thieves paid close attention to common knowledge on which their livelihood and freedom depended; one example is the fact that people are more likely to be away from their homes at some times than at others. Other information that the thieves learned was less readily available to the general public, such as how to blow open a safe or how to plan a bank robbery.

Again we find evidence consistent with differential association theory, but no firm support for the theory as it is formally stated. In other words, there is no concrete evidence from these studies of professional thieves that they initially became thieves because of an excess of definitions favorable to violation of the law over definitions unfavorable to violation of the law. To demonstrate this would involve a measurement task that might be impossible; it would also require a comparison of professional thieves with a sample from the general population who did not become professional thieves.

THE LABELING PERSPECTIVE

Since Edwin Lemert's (1951) pioneering work on the labeling of deviant behavior, much attention has been directed to the effects on individuals of being treated as deviants. Labeling is a general perspective on deviance that has been applied to mental illness, homosexuality, and even stuttering. Because crime and delinquency are forms of deviant behavior, this perspective should help us to understand some of the causes of law-violating behavior. Here we will focus on the effects that labeling has on individual criminals and delinquents, rather than on the way that certain kinds of behavior are initially defined as deviant by the larger society or by specific interest groups.

The labeling perspective assumes that people first violate a norm by chance or for unexplained reasons. This initial act of deviance, called *primary deviation,* sometimes elicits reactions from others. These reactions often take the form of stereotyping and rejecting the deviant. Thus, one study suggests that offenders are treated more harshly by the courts if they fit the stereotype of a "normal primitive," an image of lower-class blacks and other minorities whose limited education, lack of job skills, orientation to the present, possession of weapons, and immaturity are thought to predispose them to violence (Swigert and Farrell, 1976, 1977). Another stereotype is of lower-class delinquents, who are thought to violate the law because of blocked opportunities, poor education, or other defects of the social structure; this contrasts with the stereotype of middle-class delinquents, who are said to violate the law because of a temporary lack of commitment to adult roles and values, a view that relies on social-psychological factors and control theory (Cernkovich, 1978b). Ideas about why different types of people break the law can influence the way that those people are treated by the criminal justice system.

Differences in norms about parental supervision of the sexual activity of sons and daughters can lead to the labeling of one sex but not the other as delinquent, even though the behavior of both sexes is the same. Many girls who are brought into juvenile court are there for reasons related to their "adult" sexual activity, even though the formal proceedings may be based on running away from home or "incorrigibility." By contrast, the males with whom they were sexually involved are rarely labeled delinquent for the same behavior.

People who engage in socially disapproved behavior are labeled as disvalued individuals. Their status as a deviant sometimes becomes a *master status;* that is, other aspects of their behavior are submerged in a social identity as a deviant. The labeling perspective directs attention away from the causes of primary deviation, or rule breaking, and focuses instead on the people and institutions that have the power to label behavior deviant (Schur, 1971, 1979). The processing of rule breakers by institutions, such as prisons and mental hospitals, keeps deviants at a distance from the rest of society. Deviant acts would occur even if there were no such institutions, but "their nature, distribution, social meaning, and implications and ramifications are significantly influenced by patterns of social reaction" (Schur, 1969: 115). The assumption of the labeling perspective is that a major cause of continued deviant behavior is the way that people who initially violate norms are treated by lawmakers, police officers, judges, psychiatrists, and others who have the power to affix the label "deviant." Deviant behavior that is a product of this labeling process is called *secondary deviation.*

Labeling and Self-Concepts

One way that the labeling of deviant behavior leads to secondary deviance is through the effects of the label on the self-concept of the person who has

People who are arrested may have their self-concepts changed and begin to see themselves as criminals or delinquents.

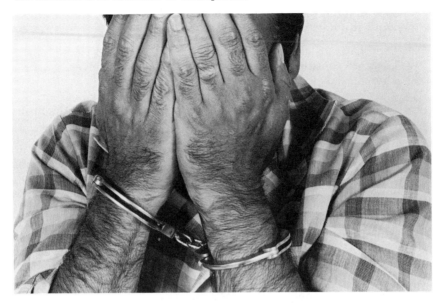

Photo by Phyllis Graber Jensen. Reprinted by permission of Stock, Boston. © by Stock, Boston, Inc., 1980.

been labeled. People who violate the law and are arrested by the police and tried in court may have their conceptions of themselves altered and come to think of themselves as criminals or delinquents. Court appearances have been called "status degradation ceremonies" in which people accused of violating the law are recast as unworthy persons (Garfinkel, 1956). These people may then reject other people and become hostile to society in order to maintain their self-esteem (Schrag, 1974). Being labeled criminal or delinquent in court can thus produce a self-fulfilling prophecy, so that people behave in ways consistent with their altered self-concepts. In other words, once they are labeled criminal by the police, the courts, and the prisons, people may continue to behave as criminals.

The labeling perspective would suggest that the first time that youngsters engage in minor vandalism or petty theft, they might think little of it. If they are arrested, brought to court, and treated as delinquents, they may come to think that they have done something drastically wrong and that perhaps they are unworthy people. As a result, they may begin to associate with others who have also been labeled as troublemakers, and this could lead them into additional and more serious delinquency. A study of adolescent shoplifters found that those who had been exposed to the police by store officials were more likely to engage in subsequent shoplifting than were adolescent shoplifters who had not been subjected to the police (Klemke, 1978). This is consistent with the labeling perspective's assumption that processing a deviant can amplify or increase deviance, rather than deter violation of the rules.

Rather than engage in more deviance because of being labeled, some people who are labeled deviant react by trying to change their behavior to conform to social expectations. The fact that many juveniles who are arrested are appre-

251

hended only once can be interpreted to mean that the status degradation ceremony that occurs in juvenile court persuades some of them to avoid delinquency in the future. This is probably most likely to occur for first-time offenders with the following characteristics:

- They have a stake in conformity.
- They are sensitive to others' evaluations of themselves.
- They are labeled in private rather than in public.
- They are not committed to a delinquent or criminal career.
- They are able to remove the label with good behavior in the future. (Thorsell and Klemke, 1972).

Some labeled offenders try to disavow the label, saying that they are innocent or that their behavior caused no harm. Techniques of neutralization that are used prior to violating the law may be used by offenders later to help themselves to disavow the label and avoid self-rejection (Covington, 1984). In other cases, a label can reinforce deviance. For instance, a changed self-concept and a stake in nonconformity can push some labeled offenders further into a criminal career. The conditions that produce these different results are unclear. We need more research on the factors that determine the consequences of labeling for people who violate the law.

SELF-CONCEPTS AND CONTAINMENT THEORY

Self-concept plays an important role in the *containment theory* of crime and delinquency (Reckless, 1973, 1978). This theory proposes that people are insulated to various degrees against pressures to commit deviant acts by "external" and "internal" factors. External containment results from attachments to family, community, and other parts of the social structure. Internal containment is composed of the following "self" components:

1. A favorable image of self in relation to other persons, groups, and institutions.
2. An awareness of being an inner directed, goal oriented person.
3. A high level of frustration tolerance.
4. Strongly internalized morals and ethics.
5. Well developed ego and superego (Reckless, 1978: 189).

Greater strength of either internal or external containments will reduce vulnerability to crime and delinquency, but "the inner containment is the more important in the mobile, industrialized settings of modern society" (Reckless, 1978: 189).

There is some evidence that juvenile delinquents have poorer self-concepts than nondelinquents do, and that delinquents are more likely to believe that they will break the law, not finish school, and be unsuccessful (Dinitz, Scarpitti, and Reckless, 1962; Jensen, 1973). Delinquency has been seen as a defense against low self-esteem caused by doing poorly in school (Mann, 1981). Delinquents seem to be less likely than nondelinquents to be committed to long-range goals, and they are more likely to strive beyond their means, be impulsive, have a short time perspective, and feel unable to control themselves (Dinitz, Scarpitti, and Reckless, 1962; Reckless, 1973; Jensen, 1973).

In contrast to delinquents and criminals, those who abide by the law tend to see themselves as accountable for their actions. They feel good about themselves and behave accordingly, taking into account the "hypothesized reactions" of others before they act. This is much like what Hirschi calls the "psychological presence" of parents and authority figures. Noncriminals see themselves as vulnerable if they deviate from the law, and they fear the loss of material rewards and the good opinion of others (Rogers, 1977: 64–68).

There is some evidence that negative self-concepts are associated with crime and delinquency, but some research suggests that the relationship between self-concept and violation of the law is not a strong one (Farrell and Nelson, 1978). One study concludes that self-esteem has a negligible impact on subsequent delinquency, but that involvement in delinquent behavior does lower subsequent self-esteem somewhat (McCarthy and Hoge, 1984).

REJECTING THE LABEL

An individual's self-concept is a product of many influences. It is influenced by the reactions of others, but it is also the product of choice and reflection by the individual. The label attached by the criminal justice system can affect a person's self-concept, but the individual can also reject or fight the label. Self-concepts are constructed in an active way. The opinions of others are considered and sometimes incorporated into the self-concept, but those opinions may also be rejected as inconsistent with a person's idea of himself or herself (Scimecca, 1977).

White-collar criminals   Not all people who are labeled criminal undergo a change in self-concept. For instance, white-collar criminals violate the law, but few of them are arrested and convicted. White-collar offenders often believe that because they are so rarely treated as "real criminals," they must not be criminals. This view is even shared by some law enforcers. The head of the Antitrust Division of the Department of Justice expressed this nicely in 1940:

> While civil penalties may be as severe in their financial effects as criminal penalties, yet they do not involve the stigma that attends indictment and conviction. Most of the defendants in antitrust cases are not criminals *in the usual sense*. There is no inherent reason why antitrust enforcement requires branding them as such (cited in Sutherland, 1949, 1983: 54; emphasis added here).

White-collar offenders may be seen as "respectable," meaning that they are generally law-abiding, but it is interesting to keep in mind a question Ralph Nader once asked a congressional committee, "Do you give credit to a burglar because he doesn't burglarize 99 per cent of the time?" (cited in Geis, 1974: 276). White-collar criminals see their offenses as "technical violations of governmental regulations" and are thus able to maintain a noncriminal self-concept, even when labeled criminal in court. A General Electric vice-president, who was on his way to jail after a conviction for price fixing, said to the press: "All of you know that next Monday, in Philadelphia, I will start serving a thirty-day jail term, along with six other *businessmen* for conduct which has been *interpreted* as being in conflict with the *complex* antitrust laws" (cited in Geis, 1974: 273; emphasis added here). Here we see a convicted criminal disavowing the label of criminal. This is easier for offenders who do not fit the stereotype of the typical criminal, who are treated with leniency by the courts, and who enjoy the support of their families, friends, and colleagues.

Juvenile delinquents   The official label "delinquent" is sometimes rejected by adolescents who are processed by the juvenile justice system. For instance, teen-agers who steal cars to "joy ride" often fail to see themselves as "real criminals," claiming that they merely "borrowed" the car for a time.

Conventional criminals   Adult offenders are also able to disavow the label "criminal." Professional fences see themselves as decent people who perform a socially useful function (Klockars, 1974: 151–161). Professional thieves compare their behavior to the dishonest actions of politicians and corporate executives. Robbers claim that they are "not too dishonest" because they steal from their victims in a direct way, rather than sneaking around in a house at night to commit a burglary (Inciardi, 1975: 71–72). Apprehended shoplifters often disavow the label of criminal when first caught, but the threat of prosecution usually forces them to redefine themselves as offenders; this happens because they fear exposure and lack support for a noncriminal definition of self (Cameron, 1964: 159–170).

THE EFFECTS OF LABELING ON SELF-CONCEPTS
Some research suggests that the effects of official labeling on the self-concepts of delinquents and criminals may not be as great as the labeling perspective proposes. One study found that labeling by law enforcers had no major effect on self-satisfaction, identification with other delinquents, or future commitment to delinquency (Hepburn, 1977). A longitudinal cohort study found that a single delinquent experience often had a limited effect, and that being labeled once as a delinquent did not necessarily transform a person (Polk, 1980). Delinquents often express concern with the outcome of their cases, but their appearances in court may not be obviously stigmatizing and may not have major effects on their self-esteem (Mahoney, 1974).

The effects of labeling seem to vary with the individual who is labeled. One study found that the self-concepts of lower-class white delinquents appear to be more influenced by an appearance in juvenile court than are the self-concepts of other delinquents (Ageton and Elliott, 1973). Self-concepts of delinquents may be less influenced by official sanctions than by the frequency and seriousness of the delinquent's illegal acts. Thus, a self-concept may be grounded more in actual behavior than in official reactions to that behavior, with the police and the courts validating or rubber-stamping an individual's self-concept rather than applying a totally new label.

Even if official labeling affects a person's self-concept, it does not necessarily increase delinquent or criminal behavior, for there is no strong evidence that changes in self-concepts cause changes in law-violating behavior (Mahoney, 1974). Moreover, any effects that the labeling has may fade with time.

There is thus some evidence that official labeling by the criminal justice system may not have the dramatic effects suggested by the labeling perspective. However, the effects of labeling might be subtle and complex, and occur only over long periods. In addition, research on labeling, self-concepts, and violation of the law may simply not yet have uncovered all of the effects of stigmatizing people as criminals or delinquents.

Labeling and Opportunities

A second effect of labeling—in addition to its possible effects on self-concepts—is the reduction of opportunities and the harm to the social relationships of people who are labeled by the criminal or juvenile justice system. Even if self-concept does not change, a person may experience difficulty in relationships with parents, friends, teachers, or potential employers if those people react negatively to the label of delinquent or criminal.

A study of 196 adolescent boys sought to determine if juvenile court intervention had reinforced their deviance by producing "spoiled" identities or by harming their relationships with people who viewed them with mistrust and suspicion because of their official status as delinquents (Foster, Dinitz, and Reckless, 1972). In general, the boys did not believe that their contact with the law had created any major problems for them in their social relationships. They perceived no negative effects on their friends' attitudes toward them. Few of the boys thought that being in trouble with the law would cause them any special problems at school, because they would be protected by the secrecy of juvenile court records and by their ability to separate their out-of-school life from their role as student. The boys believed that their court experiences would not influence their parents' attitudes toward them, other than simply confirming attitudes that their parents already held. This conclusion is consistent with other research that finds that parent-child relationships are well established before court appearances and are not substantially influenced by those appearances (Mahoney, 1974).

The boys in this study did think that their contact with the courts might have some negative effects in two areas: their relationships with the police and their relationships with future employers. About half of the boys said that the police would be more likely to keep an eye on them because they had been to court, but they thought this problem could be solved by convincing the police that they had given up delinquency. Nearly half of the boys believed that future employers might hold their court appearances against them, but many thought that this liability would be unimportant if they avoided encounters with the law in the future. The boys also counted on the passage of time and the secrecy of juvenile court records to minimize their problems with future employers.

This study concluded that the labeling perspective overemphasizes the effects on the individual of stigmatization by the juvenile courts. Such labeling may actually close legitimate opportunities or harm social relationships, but the boys in this study did not generally perceive this to be the case. However, nearly half of the boys had been involved with the juvenile justice system before, and a study of the impact of their first court appearance might have found more dramatic effects on their social relationships.

Even though somewhat more than half of the boys in this study thought that their appearance in juvenile court would not hurt them with future employers, there is some evidence that job opportunities may be closed if potential employers learn about a person's problems with the law (Erickson and Goodstadt, 1979). In fact, even the knowledge that a job applicant has been acquitted of charges seems to make some employers less willing to offer that person a job (Schwartz and Skolnick, 1962). As a result, the law in the United States now prohibits employers from asking about arrests, limiting them to questions about actual criminal convictions. The law also "seals" or keeps secret juvenile court records so that job opportunities are not denied to those who get into trouble with the law at a young age.

Labeling and Subcultures

In addition to the effects of labeling on self-concepts and social relationships, labeling can push people into subcultures in which they learn criminal motives and skills. Thus, contact with other offenders can result directly from the imposition of the label of delinquent or criminal, regardless of any change in self-concept. Once contact has been made with the members of a subculture, the learning process described by differential association theory may increase law-violating behavior. This learning process can then affect the offender's self-concept, even if labeling by the police or the courts did not have that effect. Thus, a woman convicted of prostitution may be approached by a pimp, by drug dealers, or by gangsters who see her "spoiled identity" as making her vulnerable to exploitation. By pushing an offender into a subculture, labeling can make reintegration into society difficult and increase the probability that people will repeat their crimes.

Critique of the Labeling Perspective

Figure 10.1 shows the labeling perspective in schematic form. The perspective proposes that primary deviation, or rule breaking, sometimes leads to the labeling of the rule breaker. This can affect an individual's self-concept and opportunities and drive the person into a subculture. In the subculture, the individual may undergo a change in self-concept through differential association with other deviants. In these ways, the labeling process can amplify or increase deviant behavior, leading to secondary deviation.

The labeling perspective has some shortcomings. It does not tell us why some people engage in primary deviation, and why other people do not break rules or do so infrequently. The labeling perspective helps us to understand what society makes of primary deviation, but it tells us little about rule breaking that is not socially labeled. The perspective fails to make clear the conditions under which labeling will alter self-concepts, restrict opportunities, hurt social relationships, and drive deviants into subcultures. It has also not made clear when a label will be accepted by a rule breaker, and when a deviant will reject or disavow a label. There is little empirical evidence that demonstrates that labeling by the criminal justice system actually increases crime or delinquency. Experiences with the criminal justice system sometimes deter potential offenders, and some offenders who are labeled and then commit more crime might have gone on to commit more crime even if they had not been labeled. The labeling perspective is useful in directing our attention to social processes that may, under some circumstances, reinforce tendencies to violate

Figure 10.1: The Labeling Perspective

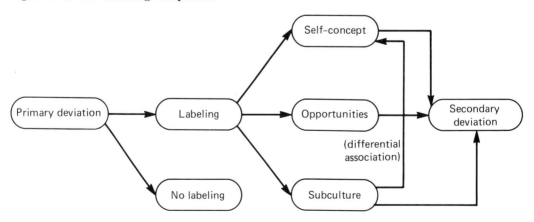

the law, but it is not yet a fully developed and empirically tested theory of crime and delinquency.

REWARDS AND RISKS OF CRIME

Differential association theory suggests that people turn to crime when their attitudes become supportive of crime—that is, when their definitions favorable to violation of the law outweigh their definitions unfavorable to violation of the law. The labeling perspective suggests that being processed by the criminal justice system changes self-concepts and social relationships and pushes people into criminal subcultures. Another approach sees criminal behavior as learned and reinforced through the intrinsic rewards and risks that it offers to offenders. This perspective is derived from operant conditioning theory and from economists' work on crime.

Operant Conditioning and Crime

Operant conditioning theory emphasizes the interaction of the person and the environment; people's behavior affects the world around them in ways that in turn influence their future behavior. The reasons for an initial criminal act may be accidental, experimental (curiosity), or instrumental (goal seeking), but an individual is more likely to continue that behavior over time if it is found to be intrinsically rewarding. Thus, a boy who steals property—or even forgets to pay for something that he picks up in a store—will find the act rewarding if he is not caught, for he has the item and still has his money. Over time, this boy's thefts may become more frequent and more consciously planned, and may involve increasingly expensive goods. Positive reinforcement of this sort is probably most common for property crimes, but aggression against others can also escalate if it is reinforced (Berkowitz, 1974).

The Economist's Model of Criminal Behavior

The *economist's model* of criminal behavior focuses on instrumental rather than expressive offenses. An *instrumental crime* is one in which an offender gets some satisfaction from the product of the crime, and an *expressive crime* is one in which the act itself fulfills an emotional need for the offender. Instrumental crimes are commonly planned in advance, but expressive crimes are more often impulsive. Economists look at crimes purposefully chosen by offenders to achieve certain ends; they see offenders as acting in a conscious manner, making reasoned and informed choices in much the same way that intelligent consumers do. Economists admit that the criminal's rationality is "bounded," or limited, in certain ways, but they do not specify what the limitations on rationality are.

Like operant conditioning theory, the economist's model regards crime as caused by its consequences. If the rewards of crime are great and its risks small, and if the rewards from a noncriminal way of life are comparatively small and its risks relatively great, people may rationally choose to violate the law. Potential offenders thus consider the rewards (or benefits) and the risks (or costs) of criminal and noncriminal behavior before breaking the law. Table 10.1 shows some of the many risks and rewards of criminal activity. Money is one of the rewards from property crimes, but many of the rewards

Table 10.1: Risks and Rewards of Theft

RISKS (OR COSTS)	REWARDS (OR BENEFITS)
Being caught and punished (lost freedom if imprisoned; lost money if fined)	Money earned from crime
Loss of benefits from legal work (paid vacation, social security, medical insurance)	Freedom from taxation
	Excitement of criminal activity
	Satisfaction in a crime successfully carried out
Time to learn criminal skills	Much leisure time
Costs of equipment to do the crime	Reputation as a successful criminal
Risk of injury while stealing (by police or by victim)	Free room and board if caught and imprisoned
Work involved in casing a target and carrying out the crime	
Anxiety about punishment	
Stigma of being labeled a criminal	

SOURCE: Adapted from Gwynn Nettler, *Lying, Cheating, Stealing.* Cincinnati, Ohio: Anderson Publishing Company, 1982, p. 97. Reprinted with permission.

from crime are noneconomic, including excitement and challenge, satisfaction in carrying out a difficult crime, prestige in the eyes of other offenders, and the chance to be one's own boss.

RISKS
Before looking in more detail at some of the rewards of crime, we will consider some of its risks or costs. The primary risk is the threat of arrest, conviction, and imprisonment. Offenders sometimes plan their crimes to minimize these risks.

Most people who continue in crime for any significant amount of time are eventually arrested. Sometimes they are turned in by informants, sometimes they are caught because the police happen to be near the scene of the crime, and sometimes they are arrested because of efficient police investigative work. The probability of arrest for any single crime is relatively low, with the overall clearance rate for index crimes in 1983 being only 20.6 per cent, but the chance of being arrested for at least one crime if a large number of crimes are committed is quite high. Even if an offender has an 80 per cent chance of escaping arrest for a given offense, the chance of escaping any arrest if two such crimes are committed is only 64 per cent, the chance of not being arrested if three offenses are perpetrated is 51 per cent, the chance of not being arrested if ten offenses are committed is only 11 per cent, and the chance of escaping any arrest if the offender commits twenty crimes is only 1 per cent (Glaser, 1978: 86–90). In other words, the chance of not being arrested for a single crime may be quite high, but the chance of never being arrested over the course of a criminal career is quite small. Consequently, most criminal careers are eventually interrupted by arrest.

Continued criminal activity may make offenders more expert, thus minimizing their chance of being arrested, but with continued success many offenders become overconfident and careless. Moreover, chance factors play an important role, and in a real sense an offender's luck will eventually run out if he or she continues to violate the law.

REWARDS
In spite of the high probability of being arrested, convicted, and imprisoned sometime during a criminal career, many offenders find that the rewards, or

perceived rewards, of crime justify continued violation of the law. Some offenders believe that the income they derive from crime is more certain and more substantial than the income they could earn from the legitimate jobs that are available to them (Holzman, 1982). However, even if all offenders were paid the amount that they realize from their criminal activities, many of them would probably continue to violate the law because of the noneconomic rewards of crime.

One noneconomic reward of criminal behavior is the challenge of violating the law and getting away with it. This element of challenge is important in many computer crimes:

> A general characteristic of computer programmers is their fascination with challenges and desire to accept them. In fact, they face the great challenge of making computer systems do their bidding day in and day out. Telling a programmer that a computer system is safe from penetration is like waving a red flag in front of a bull. The challenge of an unauthorized act often overshadows the question of morality (Parker, 1976: 47–48).

Another important noneconomic reward from crime is excitement. A study of "the criminal mind" concludes that "thinking about the crime is exciting. Committing the crime is exciting. Even getting caught is exciting. Trying to figure out a way to beat the rap is exciting" (Stanton E. Samenow, cited in Serrill, 1978: 90). For juvenile delinquents, excitement and relief from boredom are often motives to violate the law (Thrasher, 1927, 1963; Mayo, 1969; Belson, 1975; Csikszentmihalyi and Larson, 1978). A study of adolescent shoplifting found that equal numbers stole for instrumental reasons and for expressive reasons such as excitement (Klemke, 1978). One study treats middle-class delinquency as a form of play, claiming that much middle-class delinquency serves needs similar to those served by other forms of leisure: adding interest to the daily routine, providing entertainment, learning new techniques and skills, and learning social rules (Richards, Berk, and Foster, 1979).

We need to ask why violating the law is fun for some people. It may be that breaking rules set by others is satisfying, perhaps because it gives the rule breaker a feeling of autonomy. Sometimes the physical activity involved in a criminal or delinquent act is pleasing, or the consequences of the act are gratifying in some way. For instance, there may be an aesthetic element involved in vandalism, with vandals enjoying the visual, auditory, and tactile sensations resulting from their "creative conversion" of material things (Allen and Greenberger, 1978). The fun or "kicks" derived from crime may be short-lived, and this might lead to continued criminal activity. Some thieves claim that stealing is hard work with little thrill about it, and some say they are very tense while committing their crimes, but many offenders seem to be motivated by the challenge, excitement, and relief from boredom that they derive from criminal activity.

Some crime is motivated by a desire to preserve individual or collective honor or to preserve an organization. Trying to maintain one's self-image when insulted by another person can lead to homicide (Luckenbill, 1977). A study of Chicano gang violence found that preservation of the gang's collective honor and the self-esteem of its members often led to gang violence (Horowitz and Schwartz, 1974). The execution of informants in the ranks of organized crime gangs is motivated partly by revenge and partly by a need to maintain the organization in the face of external threats. Some white-collar crime, such as price fixing, is the result of efforts to preserve the profitability of a firm and the continued employment of its workers.

The Risks and Rewards of Crime

Different crimes offer different kinds of rewards and risks, and so an offender's choice of criminal activity may be influenced by the perceived benefits and costs of a particular crime. For instance, some thieves commit robberies to gain quick access to cash, even though they risk identification. Other thieves commit burglaries to avoid identification and confrontation with the victim, but they must then convert the stolen goods into cash.

WHITE-COLLAR CRIME

For white-collar offenders, the risks are relatively small. Few are convicted of a crime, and those who are usually are punished leniently. The instrumental nature of white-collar crime lends itself to a careful calculation of the costs and benefits of violating the law. For instance, in designing the Pinto, Ford Motor Company calculated the number of expected severe burn injuries and deaths that were likely to result from the car's defective fuel tank, considered the profits from the sale of the Pinto without modifications to the fuel tank, and went ahead with production. This strategy led to criticism of Ford as negligent, and produced indictments and a trial for reckless homicide in Indiana (Swigert and Farrell, 1980–81; Kramer, 1982; Cullen, Maakestad, and Cavender, 1984).

PROFESSIONAL THEFT

Professional thieves gain many rewards from their crimes in addition to money and excitement. They mention satisfaction in a job well done, the leisure time between jobs, being their own boss, the nonroutine nature of theft, and the intrinsic fascination of stealing (Sutherland, 1937). Especially for those who lack the education and skill to get a good job, the choice of theft as a source of income may be rational. One professional robber says that he began working at a legitimate job, earning between $70 and $100 a week. He started committing a few crimes to supplement that income, soon got used to spending $200 a week, and then became more involved in crime. He says that "as you advance, your mode of living, your clothes change in accordance. Your apartment changes. You can't go back" (cited in Jackson, 1969: 22). A safecracker says that he uses his money to party, travel, and generally enjoy himself. He sets an amount to steal and when he reaches that goal, he stops stealing and spends his money (Jackson, 1969: 113). These motives for theft are not limited to the United States. Criminals in Kampala, Uganda, gave the following as reasons for stealing: the need to buy clothes and luxury items for girlfriends and prostitutes, their desire for weekly visits to nightclubs, and their need for better housing and more spending money (Clinard and Abbott, 1973: 89).

ROBBERY

A study of "casual robbers" in the United States found that they stole to buy drugs and clothing, to maintain or enhance their standing among peers, and to create a more exciting life. Their "adventurous deviance" was more pleasurable because it was risky, but they tried to keep their risks to a "manageable level" (Lejeune, 1977: 125).

Other robbers are more systematic in their crimes. For instance, one study found that two robbers who committed nearly two hundred crimes in an eighteen-month period had decided to engage in robbery in a very calculating way. They had some money but lacked good job prospects and disliked the manual labor available to them. They wanted to make money quickly and decided on crime, which they saw as a business with risks and rewards like any other job. They spent four days in a public library doing research to find the best way to get money quickly and safely. They examined crime statistics, including the number of crimes committed, the amounts stolen, and the chances of arrest and conviction. They decided on armed robbery. They understood the risks they were taking, and picked robbery because it was direct and did not require them to convert property into cash. To reduce the risk of being injured by victims or the police, they carried firearms (Jackson, 1969: 20–21). Few offenders select their crimes this carefully, but these two robbers considered the rewards and risks of crime in a way that is consistent with the economist's model of the rational offender.

BURGLARY
A study of burglars found that excitement and solidarity with peers were considerations in the decision to commit crime, but that money was the primary motivating factor. Only 10 per cent of the offenders said that they would continue to commit burglary if all of their financial needs were met. Seventy-three per cent said that they would abandon burglary if their financial needs were satisfied, and 17 per cent were uncertain what effect financial security would have on their criminal activity (Reppetto, 1974: 21–23). These burglars did not steal for survival; they usually spent their money on clothes, drugs, or alcohol. Few people ever think that all of their financial needs are met, and so it is unlikely that many burglars would give up crime because they thought that they had enough money.

ARSON
Motives for crime vary with the offense. Knowing that a crime has been committed does not tell the criminologist, the police, or the public why that crime was committed. For instance, some fires are set deliberately. Some of these crimes of arson may be motivated by "pyromania"—a supposed psychological abnormality in which the arsonist or "firebug" derives pleasure from seeing things burn. Other motives for arson include revenge against the inhabitants or owners of a building, and desire for profit. People who seek a profit from arson have diverse motives. Landlords may burn buildings they cannot rent, maintain, or pay taxes on. Manufacturers suffering economic hardship "sell out to the insurance company" by burning a plant and collecting the insurance. Welfare recipients may burn themselves out of buildings so that they will be given preference for public housing and extra welfare grants. Arsonists may burn buildings if others pay them to, or they may burn a building so that they can steal and sell copper tubing or plumbing from the building (Nettler, 1978: 25–26).

CAR THEFT
Another offense with multiple motives is car theft. Some thieves steal cars for "joy riding"—to have a good time and enjoy prestige in the eyes of their peers. Others steal cars for short-term transportation; this results from situational pressures for rapid mobility and from the lack of other ways to get around. Some car thefts are for transportation over longer periods; these thieves keep stolen cars for personal use for some time. Cars may be stolen to commit other crimes, such as burglaries and robberies, because stolen cars cannot be traced to the offenders. Amateur thieves sometimes strip cars of

their tires or batteries, and well-organized professionals steal cars, repaint them, and ship them out of state or out of the country for sale (McCaghy, Giordano, and Henson, 1977). The declining rate of recovery of stolen cars and the increasing age of arrested car thieves suggest that professionals have become more involved in car theft in recent years (*The New York Times*, November 26, 1984, p. A13).

DRUG USE

Drugs such as marijuana, cocaine, and heroin can be seen as rewarding for their physiological effects on users, and also for the profits they yield for those who import and sell drugs. Organized crime has long been involved in the highly profitable heroin trade, and increasing numbers of middle- and upper-class Americans have recently been lured into the lucrative cocaine trade (Lindsey, 1982).

The effects of drugs One study of marijuana use found that people who first try the drug by themselves often experience no pleasurable effects (Becker, 1973). Those who use marijuana for the first time in the presence of experienced users get feedback from them about the proper way to smoke, how to perceive the drug's effects, and how to enjoy those effects. People who continue to use marijuana do so because they find it personally rewarding.

Various addictive drugs are used by physicians, especially anesthesiologists, who seek relief from the tension and exhaustion caused by their jobs. Drugs offer an escape, a way to relax, and a euphoria that allows some medical personnel to maintain a sense of competence at their jobs. Doctors and nurses have easy access to drugs and are generally aware of the positive effects of the drugs, while minimizing the potential dangers of prolonged use (Winick, 1964; Altman, 1983a, 1983b).

Many heroin users are given the drug free by friends and acquaintances the first time they use it; few first-time users have been looking for heroin on their own (Chein et al., 1964). Peer influence is a major force in initiating youths into heroin use. The idea that it is usually schoolyard pushers who lure youths into heroin use is incorrect (Hunt and Chambers, 1976). The effects of the first use of heroin are sufficiently strong for some people that they do not need to learn from others how to enjoy the effects of the drug; one book on heroin is entitled, *"It's So Good, Don't Even Try It Once"* (Smith and Gay, 1972). For many users, however, it is necessary to learn to experience the effects of heroin as pleasurable. This is especially true for long-term use in a society in which the drug is illegal and therefore expensive, as it is the United States (Goode, 1974).

Causes of heroin addiction There is disagreement about the causes of heroin addiction. One long-standing theory developed by Alfred Lindesmith (1938, 1947, 1965, 1968, 1975) holds that heroin addicts become hooked when they make a connection in their minds between the administration of the drug and the alleviation of withdrawal symptoms—such as sweating, nausea, trembling, and hallucinations—that occur when the amount of heroin in the body gets too low. Addicts crave heroin. Whether this craving is psychological or physiological, or some combination of the two, is not clear, but craving does occur in people who have been addicted but are no longer using heroin.

Research by McAuliffe and Gordon (1974, 1975) with street addicts in Baltimore concludes that addicts need a drug that staves off withdrawal pain, but want a drug that produces euphoria. Whereas Lindesmith discounts the importance of the desire for euphoria, McAuliffe and Gordon present strong evidence that pleasurable sensations are the primary reason that addicts use heroin. They find that almost all addicts would like to get high every day, even though commitment to a conventional life style—including a family and a legitimate job—and lack of money keep some addicts from getting high more than two or three times a week.

McAuliffe and Gordon asked addicts how much heroin they actually used and how much heroin they would need to prevent withdrawal. They called the ratio between the two figures *"the deluxe ratio,"* the amount of heroin used in excess of the amount needed to prevent withdrawal. If Lindesmith is correct, the amount used would be about the same as the amount needed to prevent withdrawal; possibly a bit more would be used to insure against withdrawal. However, the deluxe ratio was 2.4 to 1; in other words, addicts used nearly two and a half times as much heroin as they needed to prevent withdrawal. This large ratio was clearly a result of a desire for euphoria. Addicts thus seem to use heroin because they enjoy the reward of getting high, even though they do need some heroin to prevent the pain of withdrawal.

Heroin use and crime   The rewards of heroin use can lead to addiction. In the United States, this inevitably leads addicts to violate the law, because the sale, possession, and use of heroin are illegal. In Great Britain, the use and possession of heroin are legal for addicts who are registered with the government and who are prescribed heroin or other addictive drugs by licensed physicians.

The use of heroin in the United States leads to crime in other ways as well. There are state and federal laws against the possession of "works," the hypodermic syringes that are used to administer the drug intravenously. Some addicts have adapted to such laws by gathering in "shooting galleries" where syringes are passed from one user to another (Howard and Borges, 1972). This allows fewer addicts to possess needles, and some addicts can thus avoid violating the law against the possession of works. Shooting heroin in the presence of others also provides group support for drug use and psychological protection against outsiders, and gives users a chance to observe addicts who are "on the skids" and thus get a realistic but depressing view of their own future. Because heroin users know that there is a good chance of contracting hepatitis from shared needles, those who share needles are acting self-destructively. However, the rewards of needle-sharing—not having to buy and carry works and the camaraderie of using heroin in a group—make this activity a favored one by some users.

Heroin addicts also engage in crimes that are secondary to their addiction. Where heroin is illegal, the cost of the drug is far above what it would be in an unrestricted market. One sociologist estimates that a heroin habit now costing between $25 and $100 per day would cost no more than $1 a day if heroin were legally available (Glaser, 1978: 297). The cost of illegal heroin is so great that few addicts can support a habit on the income derived from legitimate work. McAuliffe and Gordon (1974) found that the average daily cost of a heroin habit was $40. If such a habit were supported with income from a legitimate job, the habit alone would require a net annual income of about $15,000. To have this much money left after taxes, social security payments, and other deductions would require a gross income of nearly $20,000. Fewer than half of the families in the United States earned this much money in the year that McAuliffe and Gordon did their research. Because heroin addicts tend to come from less educated groups and from disadvantaged minorities, it is clear that few of them can rely on legally earned income to support their habits. As a result, most addicts turn to crime. Table 10.2 shows the sources of income for male and female street addicts in a study carried out in Miami. We can see that criminal activities were mentioned by the largest number of addicts as a source of income; only about half as many mentioned legitimate jobs as a source of income with which to buy drugs. Smaller numbers mentioned public assistance and family and friends as sources of income to support their habits. In McAuliffe and Gordon's study, 96 per cent of the addicts who got high every day committed crime to support their habits. Addicts' criminal activities included drug sales, pickpocketing, shoplifting, burglary, robbery, con games, gambling, and prostitution (McAuliffe and Gordon, 1974; Inciardi, 1979; Wilson, 1983). One study found that female addicts in Miami engaged in many different crimes to support their habits (Inciardi, 1980c); a study of female addicts in San Francisco revealed that 62 per cent of them had engaged in prostitution (Rosenbaum, 1981, 1982).

Table 10.2: Sources of Support for Drug Use and General Economic Needs among Active Street Addicts in Miami, Florida*

SOURCE OF INCOME	MALES	FEMALES
Criminal activity	97.4%	94.9%
Legitimate employment	49.4%	43.6%
Public assistance	20.0%	18.8%
Family and friends	12.5%	31.6%

* Columns add to more than 100% because addicts mentioned several sources of income.

SOURCE: James A. Inciardi, "Heroin Use and Street Crime," *Crime and Delinquency*, Vol. 25, No. 3 (July 1979), p. 341. Copyright © 1979 by the National Council on Crime and Delinquency. Reprinted by permission of Sage Publications, Inc.

Most heroin addicts engaged in some crime even before they became addicted, suggesting that people who become addicts often experienced the rewards of crime before they started to spend the proceeds of their crimes on heroin (Greenberg and Adler, 1974; McGlothlin, Anglin, and Wilson, 1978; Inciardi, 1979). Studies have found that 50 to 80 per cent of all addicts were arrested for crime before becoming addicted to heroin, but that they generally increased their criminal activities greatly after becoming addicted (Baridon, 1976; McBride and McCoy, 1981; Gropper, 1984). For instance, one study found that a sample of 237 addicts committed an estimated total of 500,000 crimes during an eleven-year period (*The New York Times*, March 22, 1981). Robberies of drug dealers and disputes over the control of drug trafficking account for many murders as well; in 1981, nearly one-fourth of New York City's 1,832 homicides were drug-related (Buder, 1983a).

Criminal activity seems to decline when addicts enter treatment or kick their habits. One study found that addicts' crime rates were 84 per cent lower when they were not dependent on heroin than when they were using the drug on a regular basis (*The New York Times*, March 22, 1981). However, other research indicates that addicts' involvement in crime remains greater after addiction than it was before addiction (Vorenberg and Lukoff, 1973; Cushman, 1974; Stephens and Ellis, 1975; Silberman, 1978). This suggests that the rewards of crime may still be sought when crime is no longer necessary to support a drug habit. Money previously spent on heroin may be used for a car or a better apartment. At best, treatment programs seem to moderate rather than eliminate addicts' involvement in crime.

Critique of the Rewards-Risks Model

The idea that crime can be explained by its intrinsic rewards and risks directs our attention to motives for violating the law. One problem with this model is that it suggests that people choose to commit crime in a rational way. Some offenses, such as white-collar crime, seem to involve more careful calculation than do other crimes, such as forcible rape, and the rewards-risks model thus seems to explain some crimes better than others.

The rewards-risks model fails to tell us exactly how potential offenders weigh the various benefits and costs of criminal and noncriminal behavior. For instance, how does an offender calculate the probability of arrest, or balance a small chance of a prison sentence against a high probability of making a small financial gain from a property crime? The rewards-risks model also does not examine the sources of people's methods of evaluating rewards and risks. Thus, for people who have little stake in conformity, a small financial gain may be worth risking arrest for; others who have a greater stake in conformity may think that even the possibility of a large financial gain is not worth a small risk of arrest. The rewards-risks model thus fails to spell out in detail the actual process of balancing rewards against risks, the reasons that people balance rewards and risks differently, and the way that the social structure influences the balancing of rewards and risks.

LEARNING THEORIES AND VARIATIONS IN CRIME RATES

The learning theories examined in this chapter suggest some ways that geographic variations in crime rates might be explained. If there are geographic differences in the definitions favorable and unfavorable to violation of the law to which people are exposed, differential association theory might help to explain variations in crime rates by nation, region, and size of the community. Geographic variations might also be due to cross-national, regional, or community differences in the groups that control power and label behavior criminal. For instance, the difference between the United States and Great Britain in rates of drug addiction and secondary crimes associated with addiction has been attributed to the definition of drug addiction as a crime in the United States and as a medical problem in Great Britain (Schur, 1962, 1965; Judson, 1974). Another possible explanation of geographic variations in crime rates is that people in different places may balance rewards against risks differently. For instance, if people living in one country have a low stake in conformity, they may be willing to take more risks to gain the rewards of crime than are people in another country who have a greater stake in conformity. To date, however, we have little direct evidence that such cross-national, regional, or size-of-community variations in crime rates can be explained by the learning theories explored in this chapter.

Learning theories do not seem to provide very good explanations for temporal variations in crime rates. For differential association theory to explain changes in crime rates, it would have to tell us why an increasing or decreasing number of people have an excess of definitions favorable to violation of the law over definitions unfavorable to violation of the law. The theory does not make clear why that might happen, and thus does not do a very good job of explaining changes in crime rates. Labeling theory would suggest that the kind of behavior defined or treated as criminal fluctuates over time as certain groups gain power or change their views about the kind of behavior that is threatening to them. However, there have been few efforts to use the labeling perspective to explain temporal variations in crime rates. Similarly, there have been few attempts to use the rewards-risks model to explain changes in crime rates, although the way that people evaluate and balance rewards and risks might change over time in ways that would help us to explain increases or decreases in crime rates.

Learning theories might help us to make sense of variations in crime rates by sex, age, race, and class. Differential association theory suggests that exposure to criminal and noncriminal definitions of the law varies by social group, with males, young people, minority groups, and the lower classes being the most likely to commit crime because they are the most likely to be exposed to an excess of definitions favorable to violation of the law over definitions unfavorable to violation of the law. This explanation does not, however, tell us why differences in definitions of the law are distributed in society in this way, nor does it provide direct evidence that these groups actually differ in their exposure to definitions favorable and unfavorable to violation of the law. The labeling perspective suggests that one reason that official crime rates may be higher among certain groups is that those groups lack the power to define what kind of behavior will be defined as criminal. Young people, minorities, and the lower classes may thus be especially likely to have the kind of behavior in which they engage defined and treated as crime by older people, dominant racial and ethnic groups, and the middle and upper classes. This approach would not explain the higher crime rate of males, because for the most part it has been men who have written and enforced criminal laws. The rewards-risks model might suggest that people with different social characteristics evaluate the rewards and risks of criminal and noncriminal behavior differently, but there is little direct evidence that this is so.

In sum, the learning theories examined in this chapter might help us to explain some of the geographic, temporal, and social variations in crime rates that we have looked at, but there have been few explicit attempts to use those theories to make sense of such variations.

SUMMARY

People learn skills and motives to commit crime from various sources. The social structure of some communities is conducive to learning criminal and delinquent behavior. Many delinquents become involved in violation of the law by learning from older adolescents in gangs. People also learn criminal motives and techniques from the general culture. The mass media, especially television, are another source of learning to commit crime. Exposure to porno-graphic material does not seem to cause sex offenses, but violent pornography may have this effect on people who are otherwise predisposed to commit such crimes. There is little solid evidence that correctional institutions act as "schools of crime," but some sociologists believe that interaction among in-mates in prisons and jails is an important source of criminal motives and skills.

Differential association theory proposes that crime and delinquency are learned through face-to-face interaction. Techniques and motives are learned from definitions of the law in favorable or unfavorable terms. People violate the law when definitions favorable to violation of the law exceed definitions unfavorable to violation of the law. These definitions result from associations with criminal and noncriminal patterns that differ in frequency, duration, priority, and intensity. This theory is not easily tested, but some research is consistent with it. The theory has been modified in two forms: differential identification theory, which emphasizes the emulation of role models, and differential association-reinforcement theory, which stresses social learning.

Differential association theory fits much of what we know about white-collar crime, although the theory has not been subjected to rigorous testing. Business offenders seem to be exposed to definitions favorable to violation of the law within the company, and they seem to be somewhat isolated from definitions unfavorable to violation of the law. Research on juvenile delinquency is also consistent with differential association theory. Much delinquency occurs in groups, and delinquents seem to interact frequently with other delinquents. Professional thieves are often introduced to crime through tutelage by experi-enced thieves.

The labeling perspective proposes that some people who engage in primary deviance, or rule breaking, are labeled delinquent or criminal by institutions such as the police and the courts. This can change an individual's self-concept, close off opportunities, alter social relationships, and push people into subcul-tures. This leads to secondary deviance, or repeated rule breaking by those who see themselves as criminals or delinquents. There is mixed evidence about the actual effects of labeling on self-concepts, and it is not certain that changes in self-concepts necessarily lead to more violation of the law. However, delin-quents seem to have poorer self-concepts than nondelinquents do. Some devi-ants are able to reject the label of criminal or delinquent. This is especially common among white-collar offenders, who have much support for a noncrimi-nal self-concept. It is not clear that labeling closes off opportunities for all labeled deviants, but some adult offenders seem to have their job opportunities reduced. For juveniles, the secrecy of court records means that others will probably not learn of their violations of the law, and so opportunities may not be affected in significant ways. In some cases, labeling pushes delinquents and criminals into a subculture, leading to a changed self-concept and more crime as a result of differential association with other offenders.

Crime offers offenders various rewards or benefits, and produces certain risks or costs for them. Operant conditioning theory focuses on the reinforce-ment of criminal activity. Economists look at the rational choice of behavior in terms of its rewards and risks. The major risk that most crime poses is the possibility of arrest and punishment. Rewards vary from crime to crime. Monetary gain is a primary reward, but challenge, excitement, and autonomy are other benefits derived from criminal activity. Some offenses, such as arson and car theft, provide different kinds of rewards to different offenders, and so we cannot specify the rewards of a particular crime without knowing what motivated the offender. Heroin addicts seem to be motivated by a desire for euphoria, although they need a certain amount of the drug to prevent the pain of withdrawal. The rewards-risks model focuses our attention on the factors that motivate offenders, but it may exaggerate the rationality of some criminal activity. This model needs to provide more details on the exact way that offenders consider the rewards and risks of crime, and it needs to look at the influence of the social structure on the way that people balance rewards and risks.

Differential association theory, the labeling perspective, and the rewards-risks model may help us to make sense of the geographic, temporal, and social variations in crime rates, but so far there have been few explicit attempts by researchers to show how these learning theories explain those variations.

IMPORTANT TERMS

containment theory
"the deluxe ratio"
differential association-
  reinforcement theory
differential association
  theory

differential identification
  theory
economist's model
expressive crime
instrumental crime
the labeling perspective
machismo

master status
obscene material
operant conditioning theory
pornography
primary deviation
secondary deviation
tutelage

SUGGESTED READINGS

DARYL A. HELLMAN. *The Economics of Crime.* New York: St. Martin's Press, 1980. An introduction to the economist's model of criminal behavior.

BRUCE JACKSON. *A Thief's Primer.* New York: Macmillan, 1969. An examination of the rewards and risks of criminal activity, as reported by one thief.

PETER LETKEMANN. *Crime as Work.* Englewood Cliffs, N.J.: Prentice-Hall, 1973. A study of professional theft in Canada, focusing on the learning of criminal motives and techniques.

EDWIN M. SCHUR. *Interpreting Deviance: A Sociological Introduction.* New York: Harper & Row, 1979. A textbook that provides a useful introduction to the labeling perspective.

EDWIN H. SUTHERLAND AND DONALD R. CRESSEY. *Criminology,* 10th ed. Philadelphia: Lippincott, 1978. A textbook that presents and uses differential association theory.

11

Opportunity and Organization to Commit Crime

Even if the social structure is conducive to crime, and commitment to the law is weakened by techniques of neutralization or detachment from institutions, and criminal motives and skills are learned, crime cannot occur unless there are opportunities, situations, facilitating factors, and organization that allow people to break the law. The "routine activities approach" looks at the way that crime develops from everyday patterns of behavior. Before an offender can violate the law, targets of crime must be identified; the value of property and the vulnerability of victims are often considered by offenders in choosing their targets. Certain relationships among people seem to be especially conducive to crime; for instance, violent crime is frequently a result of arguments among intimates. Alcohol, drugs, and firearms are factors that may facilitate crime under some conditions. In this chapter, we also look at the way that offenders plan their crimes and organize gangs to perpetrate offenses.

THE ROUTINE ACTIVITIES APPROACH

The *routine activities approach* sees crime as a function of people's everyday behavior. This approach includes three elements: motivated offenders, target suitability, and guardianship. In earlier chapters, we have examined the factors motivating offenders to commit crime. The second element is target suitability, which refers to the form and value of property, the visibility and accessibility of targets, and the vulnerability of property and people to victimization. The third element is guardianship, the presence of people who can protect targets from victimization. The routine activities approach proposes that crime occurs when motivated offenders are present near suitable targets that are not adequately protected. This approach can help us to explain crime rates, forecast trends in crime rates, and plan future needs for criminal justice services and personnel (Cohen and Felson, 1979; Cohen and Cantor, 1980, 1981; Cohen, 1981; Cohen, Kluegel, and Land, 1981).

The routine activities approach suggests that the presence of an abundance of goods that can be stolen will be associated with a high rate of property crime. In fact, economically developing societies do encounter rapidly rising rates of theft (Clinard and Abbott, 1973). A study of Sweden's crime rates from 1950 to 1979 found that theft increased as more goods became available; this increase in theft seemed to be better explained by changes in opportunities for theft than by changes in income inequality (Stack, 1982).

Guardianship can be measured in several ways, all of which try to gauge the extent to which people in the course of their daily behavior do, or do not, protect property and individuals from crime. Some recent changes in patterns of behavior may have reduced guardianship, and thus increased crime rates. These changes include the following:

- a large increase in the proportion of women holding jobs outside the home,
- an increase in the proportion of all households that have only one person,
- more recreational activity outside the home, and
- more frequent and longer vacations.

We would expect crimes such as burglary to decrease if recreational activities became more home-centered, even though this might create more opportunities for interaction among intimates that could lead to violent crime.

We can use the routine activities approach to help us to explain why there is a low rate of property crime in Switzerland (Clinard, 1978). Swiss cities have low rates of robbery, even though opportunities are plentiful. The Swiss carry much cash and rarely use checks. This makes them vulnerable to robbery, and increases the potential gain from robberies of stores, where cash is available because customers typically do not pay with checks or credit cards. Moreover, the Swiss leave property in public places with little fear of theft; in other words, they lack a tradition of guardianship. The lack of guardianship and the presence of available targets for theft suggest that Switzerland should have a high rate of property crime, but it does not. The routine activities approach would lead us to expect that this is because there are relatively few motivated offenders in Switzerland. To understand why a country has the crime rate that it does, we must examine all three elements of the routine activities approach.

A Critique of the Routine Activities Approach

Researchers who have used the routine activities approach have so far focused on property crimes rather than violent crimes. They have typically used demographic variables such as age, sex, race, and class as indicators of people's daily behavior (Cohen and Cantor, 1981). What is needed is to test the routine activities approach more fully with direct evidence about people's life styles and patterns of behavior, rather than to assume how people with different social background characteristics behave (Cohen, 1981). Some research finds that the relationship among the variables specified in the routine activities approach is more complex than statements of the theory indicate (Carroll and Jackson, 1983).

TARGETS OF CRIME

There is a nearly unlimited number of targets for crime. What is important is the way that these targets are perceived by potential offenders. An offender may see a bank with both a front and rear entrance, a nearby expressway, and weak security as an excellent opportunity for a bank holdup; law-abiding citizens will view the same bank simply as a place to deposit and withdraw funds. The crime-generating process examined in previous chapters—the social-structural pressure to commit crime, the neutralization of the law, and the acquisition of criminal motives and skills—is necessary but not sufficient for crimes such as bank holdups; without an opportunity, there will be no crime.

The victim selected by an offender depends in part on the specific skills the offender possesses. Some criminals specialize in one kind of offense, but many are quite versatile. Even experienced professional thieves usually "hustle" for opportunities for crime, rather than seek specific targets. They read newspapers, swap information with other thieves and fences, and keep their eyes open for targets for crime. Specialization would force them to pass up lucrative opportunities. Many thieves prefer certain crimes but do not limit themselves to those offenses (Gould et al., 1966; Letkemann, 1973).

Property Crimes

Thieves consider several factors in choosing targets for their crimes. The form of the property to be stolen is important, as is the value of that property. Target vulnerability and the likelihood of victim resistance are also considered by thieves.

FORM OF THE PROPERTY

The form of the property to be stolen is important. If assets are in the form of computerized data, most thieves will have to avoid computers as targets for crime because they lack the necessary skills. However, assets in this form are vulnerable to theft by computer operators who have the necessary skills (Parker, 1976, 1983). Some have suggested reducing theft by eliminating cash and replacing it with computerized assets, thereby making property inaccessible to many thieves, at least until they develop computer skills (Lederman, 1981).

Most thieves steal cash or property. Stolen property is either for personal use or is converted into cash. Conversion of stolen property into cash requires access to a fence, a receiver in stolen goods who usually pays the thief one-tenth to one-third of the retail value of the stolen merchandise. Young burglars often steal goods that they dispose of among their acquaintances, but older and more experienced burglars are more likely to steal goods that they convert into cash or drugs with fences (Reppetto, 1974: 20–21). Amateur shoplifters ("snitches") often take small, easily concealed goods for personal use. Professional shoplifters ("boosters") usually steal more expensive items and sell them to professional fences or to jewelry stores and clothing shops that are primarily legitimate retail outlets (Cameron, 1964).

The conversion of property into cash is time-consuming, and this is an important consideration for offenders who require cash immediately, as do thieves who are heroin addicts looking for a fix. Selling stolen goods to a fence can be risky as well as inconvenient, because the police may trace stolen property back to the thief through a fence. For these reasons, some offenders prefer the direct theft of cash from victims and turn to robbery. Robbery has the important advantage over other forms of theft of providing offenders with immediately usable assets that cannot be traced back to them. Robbery also requires relatively little preparation in most cases, and there is an abundance of potential targets. Robbers often claim that burglary is more trouble than robbery because it involves entry into a house or building, a search for valuable goods, the physical labor of carrying the goods from the building, and the need to convert those goods into cash. Robbery is faster, more direct, and provides readily usable assets, but it also involves the risk of a violent confrontation and the risk of identification by the victim.

VALUE OF THE PROPERTY

Thieves who commit robbery, burglary, and other types of theft consider from which victims they can get the most money with the least risk. Pickpockets usually select their "marks" or victims by criteria such as sex (men being thought to carry more money), age (older people being thought to carry more money), and race and ethnicity (whites being thought to carry more money) (Maurer, 1955, 1964). For robbers, the holdup of a commercial establishment such as a supermarket or bank will typically net more money than the robbery of an individual on the street (Conklin, 1972). Burglars have to locate the money or valuable property once they enter a building, even if they have chosen a potentially lucrative target.

Offenders usually choose victims on the basis of general expectations about how much money or property they will get. Sometimes they are systematic in calculating their profits in advance, especially if the crime involves elaborate planning and substantial risk. One gang of jewelry store robbers regularly sent its "straightest-looking" member into a store a few days before a planned crime in order to examine the jewelry and decide whether the robbery was worth the trouble and risk it would involve. The gang would then steal only the most valuable jewelry and fence it with a receiver of stolen goods in a different state. The members of the gang had a very good idea of how much they would gain in a particular holdup. Another robber secured information about the number of employees working for a firm and the approximate amount earned by each worker; his robbery of the company on payday netted him an amount that was very close to his estimate (Conklin, 1972).

The amount of money that a given target will yield is often calculated in detail by professional thieves, who seek as large a "score" as possible while keeping risks to a minimum. By contrast, opportunistic thieves look for smaller gains and are less methodical in assessing what they will get from a theft. Still, even opportunists consider what they are likely to get from potential victims. They observe how expensively potential victims are dressed and watch to see who "flashes a large wad of bills." Sometimes they try to improve their odds of a large score by stealing on paydays and on days when welfare checks are delivered.

Vulnerability of Victims

A major factor that criminals consider in choosing a target is the vulnerability of their victims. Check forgers believe that some stores are more willing to accept checks from strangers, and are therefore easier to victimize. For instance, supermarkets are seen as easy "marks," but men's clothing stores are thought to be relatively invulnerable to check passing (Jackson, 1969). Shoplifting is also easier in certain stores. For instance, stores that emphasize self-service seem to accept shoplifting as a cost of doing business. Managers may even think that if shoplifting is infrequent, their merchandise is not attractive enough or accessible enough to customers (Cameron, 1964: 17–19).

Opportunistic robbers—typically young, male members of minority groups who often operate in gangs—tend to choose victims who are elderly, female, and alone. In other words, they seek victims who are vulnerable because of their age, sex, or lack of company, even though these victims usually carry less money than other potential victims (Conklin, 1972: 89–91). Because these opportunists often lack experience and skill in committing crime, they place greater emphasis on victim vulnerability and the minimization of risk than they do on the size of the score. In contrast, professional robbers have a broader conception of vulnerability; for them, a vulnerable target is one from which they can steal after considerable planning. For example, the 1950 Brinks robbery was directed against a target that would be seen as invulnerable by most robbers, but careful observation and planning showed the thieves that the Brinks office lacked adequate security and was vulnerable to theft (Behn, 1977).

Certain obstacles to theft may turn offenders away from particular targets. Exact-fare requirements on buses may reduce robberies of bus drivers, but lead thieves to steal from the stores or newspaper stands that make change for bus riders. Since 1940, there has been an increase in bank security, including the installation of electronically controlled doors and cages, alarm systems, and closed circuit television. These measures have eliminated sneak theft from banks, a crime in which thieves go behind a counter, grab money from a till, and run from the bank (Inciardi, 1975: 15–19).

In a study of residential burglary, nearly one hundred convicted burglars were shown slides of buildings and asked to pick the type of target from which they usually stole (Reppetto, 1974). They were then asked why they chose the particular building. Older offenders usually selected single-family houses because of easy access and affluence, and younger offenders picked housing projects and multiple-family houses for their easy access. Overall, the burglars cited the following as reasons for their selection of particular targets:

- ease of access (44 per cent of all burglars),
- appearance of affluence (41 per cent),
- an inconspicuous setting (21 per cent),
- isolation of the neighborhood (19 per cent),
- the absence of police patrols (19 per cent), and
- lack of surveillance by neighbors (12 per cent).

The type of information that the burglars said they wanted about a target before committing a burglary included

- whether occupants were present (70 per cent),
- whether there was a burglar alarm (36 per cent),
- what valuables were available (34 per cent),
- where escape routes were located (20 per cent),
- the location of entrances to the building (15 per cent), and
- the presence of police or security patrols (14 per cent).

The importance of occupancy is shown by the fact that the more hours of the day a dwelling was unoccupied, the greater the chance it would be burglarized. Offenders learned whether anyone was home primarily by observing the dwelling, but sometimes they made telephone calls, questioned neighbors, or looked for signs of nonoccupancy such as piles of newspapers or mail. They learned if there were valuables to be stolen by peeping in windows and by tips from friends and fences.

One study suggested that vulnerability to burglary might be minimized by symbolic barriers to theft, rather than by creating actual physical obstacles (Barbara B. Brown, cited in *The New York Times*, November 17, 1983). Neatly trimmed hedges, for instance, can easily be passed through or around by a burglar, but, by showing that the residents feel a sense of protectiveness or territoriality about their homes, these hedges can indicate that potential intruders should keep out. Shrubs and trees can make a house seem well cared for and less exposed, and thereby minimize the chance of burglary. The way that houses are situated on a street, or the fact that a street is a cul-de-sac, can also create a sense of territoriality that potential burglars will be reluctant to violate.

Thieves try to minimize their risk by selecting targets that are not likely to be under police or neighborhood surveillance. They prefer targets that are isolated from the view of passersby, whether the police or private citizens. Even those who rob commercial establishments try to conceal themselves from public view during the crime, picking establishments that are set back from the street or positioning themselves inside the store so as to be invisible from the street. "Lookouts" are often stationed outside the building to report any threat of intrusion.

Robbers often use nonverbal cues to assess the vulnerability of potential victims. A study that asked inmates who had been convicted of violent attacks on strangers to rate people who had been videotaped while walking on the street found that the people who were rated "easy to mug" by the inmates showed distinctive body movements that signaled that they would be good targets:

> Specifically, the most muggable people tended to take strides that were of unusual length, either too short or too long. Instead of walking heel to toe, they walked flatfooted. Instead of swinging their left arm while striding with their right foot, they moved their left arm and left foot, then right arm and right foot together. Instead of the usual figure 8-like sway of upper body and lower body, the most muggable people seemed to move their torsos at cross purposes to the bottom half of their bodies.
>
> And instead of moving "posturally" (letting the movement start from within the body core), potential victims seemed to move "gesturally" (moving one part of the body, an arm for instance, as though the movement started outside the body). Indeed, the most muggable people seemed to walk as though they were less in touch with their bodies (study by Betty Grayson, described in Foreman, 1981: 21–22).

These movements were more important to offenders in choosing a victim than were age and sex. Body movement seemed to indicate something about the way that people presented themselves to the world. Muggers read movement as an indicator of vulnerability, but this seemed to occur without their conscious awareness of the factors discovered by the researcher.

VICTIM PRONENESS

One measure of vulnerability is the frequency with which people are victimized repeatedly. There may be *victim proneness* among certain people because of their personal characteristics, social situation, physical location, or relationship to offenders (Wolfgang and Singer, 1978; Nelson, 1980; Sparks, 1981a). In a study of robbery in Boston, twenty-three of ninety victims who were held up in 1968 were robbed again during the next two and a half years, even though the city's robbery rate suggested that only one or two of them would have been robbed again in that time if robberies were randomly distributed across the city's population (Conklin, 1972: 96–97). Whatever made these victims vulnerable to robbery in the first place continued to make them vulnerable, and whatever measures they took to reduce their vulnerability seemed to have little effect.

Multiple victimization, or victim proneness, seems to be due to several factors, including:

1. Precipitation or provocation: The victim does or says something that causes an offender to violate the law;
2. Instigation or perpetration: The victim actively encourages a crime or takes criminal action against another person;
3. Facilitation: The victim places himself or herself at risk by deliberation, recklessness, or negligence;
4. Vulnerability or invitation: Some people are unusually susceptible because of personal attributes, social status, or entry into a risk-filled situation;
5. Cooperation: The victim is a party to a consensual crime such as gambling or prostitution;
6. Attractiveness: Affluence will often attract offenders; and
7. Impunity: Offenders can expect that the victim will not report the crime to the police or testify in court, perhaps because the victim is also breaking the law (Sparks, 1981a, 1982).

VICTIM-OFFENDER RELATIONSHIPS

The selection of targets for violent crimes such as murder, aggravated assault, and rape is often associated with the relationship between the offender and the victim. To understand what "opportunity" means for crimes of violence, we must look at the interaction and relationship between participants in the crime. These relationships were first explored systematically by Hans von Hentig (1948, 1967) in *The Criminal and His Victim,* and have been studied more recently with data from police records and victimization surveys (see, e.g., Wolfgang, 1958; Hindelang, 1976).

Social Characteristics of Victims and Offenders

Many studies that have examined the relationship between victims and offenders have focused on demographic or social characteristics such as age, sex, and race. Here we will focus on the race of victims and offenders.

MURDER

Studies of homicide that have relied on police statistics have found that a disproportionately high number of all murders involve black offenders and black victims. Homicides involving white offenders and white victims are also common. Fewer than 10 per cent of all murders cross racial lines, as we can see from Table 11.1. The three studies shown in this table all indicate that when murderers cross racial lines, blacks are more likely to kill whites than whites are to kill blacks.

FORCIBLE RAPE

Forcible rape is patterned by race in much the same way that murder is, with most rapes being intraracial and black offender-black victim rape being disproportionately common. Table 11.2 shows that both a study done in Philadelphia and a study done in seventeen large American cities found that the majority of all reported forcible rapes involved black rapists and black women as victims. (The FBI provides no data on the race of rape offenders and victims.)

Table 11.1: Racial Characteristics of Homicide Offenders and Victims in Three Studies

RACE OF OFFENDER/RACE OF VICTIM	WOLFGANG (PHILADELPHIA)	CURTIS (17 CITIES)	FBI UCR DATA* (NATIONAL)
black/black	72%	66%	45%
white/white	22%	24%	47%
black/white	4%	6%	5%
white/black	2%	4%	2%
Total	100%	100%	99%

* Data are for 10,919 offenses with a single offender and a single victim.

SOURCES: Adapted from Marvin E. Wolfgang, *Patterns in Criminal Homicide.* Philadelphia: University of Pennsylvania Press, 1958, p. 379; Lynn A. Curtis, *Criminal Violence: National Patterns and Behavior.* Lexington, Mass.: D. C. Heath, 1974, p. 21; William H. Webster, *Crime in the United States, 1983: Uniform Crime Reports.* Washington, D.C.: U.S. Government Printing Office, 1984, p. 9.

The Philadelphia study found that when rapists crossed racial lines, it was slightly more common for whites to rape blacks than vice versa, but the seventeen-city study found that virtually all cross-racial rape was by blacks against whites.

AGGRAVATED ASSAULT

Aggravated assault is another offense that typically involves victims and offenders of the same race. The seventeen-city study found that 66 per cent of reported aggravated assaults involved black offenders and black victims, 24 per cent involved white offenders and white victims, 8 per cent involved black offenders and white victims, and only 2 per cent involved white offenders and black victims (Curtis, 1974: 21). Because spouse beating and child abuse are forms of assault that are greatly underreported, and because these kinds of assault typically involve people of the same race, police data such as those used in the seventeen-city study probably underestimate the intraracial nature of aggravated assault.

ROBBERY

Robbery involves theft, violence or threat of violence, and a confrontation between an offender and a victim. This crime occurs between people of the

Table 11.2: Racial Characteristics of Rape Offenders and Victims

RACE OF OFFENDER/RACE OF VICTIM	AMIR (PHILADELPHIA)	CURTIS (17 CITIES)
black/black	77%	60%
white/white	16%	30%
black/white	3%	10%
white/black	4%	*
Total	100%	100%

* less than ½ of a per cent.

SOURCES: Adapted from Menachem Amir, *Patterns in Forcible Rape.* Chicago: University of Chicago Press, 1971, p. 44; Lynn A. Curtis, *Criminal Violence: National Patterns and Behavior.* Lexington, Mass.: D. C. Heath, 1974, p. 21.

same social background less often than other violent crimes. For instance, many robberies involve offenders and victims of different races. The seventeen-city study found that 47 per cent of armed robberies were by blacks against whites, 38 per cent by blacks against blacks, 13 per cent by whites against whites, and 2 per cent by whites against blacks. Proportions were similar for unarmed robberies (Curtis, 1974: 21). A victimization survey carried out in eight major cities found that robbery most commonly involved a black offender and black victim, next most often a black offender and white victim, next most commonly a white offender and white victim, and rarely a white offender and black victim (Hindelang, 1976: 190).

Relationships between Victims and Offenders

Police statistics on the race of victims and offenders suggest that the opportunity for crimes of violence is socially structured. Most intimate interaction takes place among people of the same race, and so it makes sense that crimes of violence arising from disagreements and confrontations would also involve members of the same race. We now look directly at the personal relationships between victims and offenders.

MURDER

The most recent available data on victim-offender relationships in murders comes from the FBI's Uniform Crime Report. In 1983, 28.2 per cent of all murders involved relationships between the offender and the victim that were not known to the police. Of all homicides, 18.7 per cent involved an offender and a victim in the same family, 36.9 per cent involved boyfriends, girlfriends, friends, or other acquaintances, and 15.0 per cent involved strangers (Webster, 1984: 11).

In 100 cases of marital homicide in Philadelphia from 1948 through 1952, wives killed their husbands almost as often (47 times) as husbands killed their wives (53 times) (Wolfgang, 1958). A study in Houston in 1969 found that thirteen husbands and common-law husbands killed their wives, and that twenty-four wives and common-law wives murdered their husbands (Lundsgaarde, 1977: 54). Women who commit murder seem to be more likely than male murderers to kill someone with whom they have an intimate relationship. This is probably especially true when traditional gender roles limit women's interaction to the home; it may be less often the case when women work outside the home and interact more with people outside the family.

The study of murder in Houston found that the criminal justice system treats murderers who are strangers to their victims more severely than it treats other murderers. We can see this in Table 11.3. Strangers who committed

Table 11.3: Criminal Justice Response to Different Kinds of Murders, Houston, 1969

RELATIONSHIP BETWEEN OFFENDER AND VICTIM	NUMBER	PERCENTAGE ESCAPING ANY LEGAL PENALTY	MEAN PRISON TERM OF THOSE CONVICTED
Strangers	55	36%	27.9 years
Friends or associates	68	53%	10.1 years
Relatives	77	61%	7.6 years

SOURCE: Adapted from Henry P. Lundsgaarde, *Murder in Space City: A Cultural Analysis of Houston Homicide Patterns.* New York: Oxford University Press, 1977, p. 232. Reprinted with permission.

murder were the least likely to escape any punishment, and received the longest prison sentences when convicted. Murderers who were friends or associates of their victims were more likely to escape punishment, and received shorter prison sentences than strangers who committed murder. Finally, relatives who committed murder were the most likely to escape punishment, and received the shortest sentences if convicted.

According to law-enforcement experts, one kind of murder by strangers has become epidemic in recent years, accounting for as many as 4,000 of the 21,012 murders in 1982, according to one estimate. This kind of murder involves "serial murderers," killers who slay strangers and then move on to other areas of the country in search of more victims. These murderers are distinguished from "mass murderers," who kill several victims at the same time. There seem to be more serial murderers today than even a decade ago, although this conclusion is tentative. In 1984, the Department of Justice reported more than thirty instances in which a killer had murdered at least six victims over a stretch of time. Many serial murderers prey on runaways or on men and women involved in prostitution. Several male serial murderers have been homosexuals who apparently killed their victims after sex. Others seem to have chosen their victims randomly. Serial murderers seem to be particularly intelligent, commonly have knowledge of police methods, and are often personally charming, a quality they use to lure unsuspecting victims into lethal situations that often involve sex (Lindsey, 1984a; also, see Levin and Fox, 1985).

FORCIBLE RAPE

In study of rape in Philadelphia, 42 per cent of the cases involved victims and offenders who were complete strangers to each other, and in 10 per cent of the rapes the victim had only a very general knowledge of the offender. Even though 48 per cent of the victim-offender relationships were primary ones (acquaintances, close neighbors, close friends or boyfriends, family members, or relatives), only 14 per cent of all relationships were classified as intimate: 6 per cent of the rapists were close friends or boyfriends, 5 per cent were family members, and 3 per cent were relatives (Amir, 1971: 234).

The seventeen-city survey found that 10 per cent of rapes involved an intimate social relationship between victim and offender prior to the crime (family member, close friend, or lover), 29 per cent involved acquaintances, 53 per cent involved strangers, 4 per cent involved nonprimary contacts, and information was missing for 14 per cent of the rapes (Curtis, 1974: 59–60).

NCS victimization data show a relatively constant rate of rape victimization from 1973 to 1979, but also reveal an increase in the number of rapes per capita by nonstrangers over that period. During that time, NCS data show that an average of 65 per cent of all rapes were committed by strangers (Bureau of Justice Statistics, April 1982).

One relationship between the rapist and the victim that has received considerable attention in recent years is the rape of women by their husbands or ex-husbands. According to one study, 14 per cent of women who have ever been married have been the victim of a rape, or an attempted rape, by their husbands or ex-husbands (Russell, 1982). As of December 1984, twenty-seven states did not permit the prosecution for rape of a husband who was living with his wife. Other states have changed their laws to define sexual violence as rape if it occurs between husbands and wives, whether they are living together or are separated (Margolick, 1984). Rape in marriage is an underreported offense, and when it is reported the police usually treat it as an assault rather than a rape, if they even deal with it as a crime. Not until 1984 was a husband convicted of raping a wife with whom he was living.

ASSAULT

In the seventeen-city survey of violent crime, 13.9 per cent of officially recorded aggravated assaults occurred between members of the same family; 31 per cent involved lovers, friends, and acquaintances; 20.6 per cent were attacks by strangers; and 10.1 per cent were assaults involving a felon or a police officer. In the remaining 24.3 per cent of the aggravated assaults, the relationship between the victim and the offender was unknown (Curtis, 1974: 46–47, 58).

NCS victimization data show that rates of aggravated assault by strangers were stable from 1973 to 1979, as were rates of aggravated assault by non-strangers. Victimization rates for simple assaults by both strangers and non-strangers rose during the same period. From 1973 to 1979, an average of 56 per cent of aggravated assaults were by strangers, and an average of 53 per cent of simple assaults were by strangers (Bureau of Justice Statistics, April 1982).

The relationship between victim and offender in assaults is difficult to determine, because many assaults occur within the family and are not reported to the police, and perhaps not even to interviewers in victimization surveys. Fear of retaliation, embarrassment, and the desire to protect even abusive family members all contribute to the underreporting of family violence. As a result, assaults between spouses and parental violence against children are more common than is suggested by official crime statistics, and probably more common than is indicated by victimization surveys (Steinmetz and Straus, 1980; Gelles, 1982).

ROBBERY

Robbery, or the theft of property by the use or threat of force, rarely involves people who are closely associated with each other. Because thieves have access to the property of people they know well, they do not need to use force to steal from them; they can simply take the property by stealth in a larceny. In addition, a potential robber's need for cash can be explained to those with whom he or she is close, and so the would-be robber may be given or loaned the necessary money rather than have to steal it. Concern for people whom they know well may lead robbers to think that if they must use force to steal, they might as well use that force against strangers, rather than against relatives or friends. Moreover, strangers are less likely to be able to identify them to the police. Thus, it is not surprising that 76 to 86 per cent of all robbers are strangers to their victims (Curtis, 1974; Hindelang, 1976).

Two kinds of prior relationships do seem to give rise to robbery with some frequency: relationships between prostitutes and their clients, and relationships between homosexual partners. A study in New York City found that one in five muggings—a colloquial term for strong-armed street robberies—involved a prostitute's client, a homosexual, or a chronic drunk (Burnham, 1968). A study of robbery in London revealed that one robbery in eight involved a "preliminary association of short duration between victim and offender (mainly for heterosexual or homosexual purposes)" (McClintock and Gibson, 1961: 16).

CRIMES AGAINST PROPERTY

Interaction between people with prior social ties is sometimes conducive to criminal behavior. These prior ties are especially important as a factor leading to murder and aggravated assault, somewhat less important in the crime of forcible rape, and even less significant for robbery. The role of prior social relationships between victims and offenders is unclear for property crimes such as larceny, burglary, and auto theft. There is no particular reason to expect a prior relationship between thieves and the victims of these offenses. Some larcenies may involve offenders and victims who are related to each other, because this gives the offender easy access to the victim's property, but one victimization survey found that 90 per cent of the victims of personal theft were complete strangers to the perpetrators of the crime (Hindelang, 1976: 162).

Victim Precipitation

Victim precipitation means that the person who suffers eventual harm from a crime plays a direct role in causing the crime to be perpetrated. For instance, a homicide victim may be the first to use force. In one case encountered in this author's robbery study (Conklin, 1972), an incarcerated offender reported that he had regularly used a knife to hold up drugstores because "a knife was quieter than a gun." A few months after the interview, this offender attacked another inmate with a homemade knife. The other inmate took the knife away and stabbed the attacker to death. This is a clear case of a victim-precipitated murder.

Victims who act in particular ways with regard to potential offenders may create opportunities for crimes where none existed before. Thus, a man who enters a bar, picks an argument with another customer, and draws a knife has in a sense contributed to his own murder if the other person responds by killing him with a handgun. This may not absolve the murderer of legal responsibility, but it could mitigate the punishment.

One definition of victim precipitation suggests that we need much information to assess the role of the victim in the causation of a crime:

> Victim precipitation occurs when the offender's action in committing or beginning to commit a crime is initiated after and directly related to an action (be it physical or verbal, conscious or unconscious) on the part of the victim. The offender perceives the victim's behavior as a facilitating action (including temptation, invitation) to the commission of the crime. The action of the victim might be said to have triggered the offender's behavior (R. A. Silverman, cited in Curtis, 1974: 96).

There is a continuum from deliberate provocation by the victim, to some involvement by the victim, to little or no victim contribution. The intent of the offender must be considered on a continuum from deliberate premeditation, to some intent, to none at all. Victim precipitation exists when offenders have little or no intent to commit a crime and victims clearly provoke them to commit a crime. Real-life situations are usually less clear-cut. Information on the interaction between the offender and the victim, and the state of mind of each, is difficult to get after a crime has been committed, especially if one participant is murdered. Witnesses may describe how the crime developed, but it is difficult to gather data on the perceptions and expectations of the participants.

MURDER

About one murder in four is victim-precipitated (Wolfgang, 1958: 254; Curtis, 1974: 82–84), although one study found that 38 per cent of a sample of homicides were caused in part by the victim (Voss and Hepburn, 1968). Victims of victim-precipitated murders are especially likely to be male and black and to have prior criminal records. Female murderers are more likely than male murderers to be involved in victim-precipitated murders, because female murderers have often been provoked by their male victims.

In a study of interaction between offenders and victims prior to murder, about half of the seventy cases were found to involve prior hostility or physical violence between the offender and the victim (Luckenbill, 1977). Homicides were not usually one-sided events in which a passive victim was attacked by the murderer. In nearly two-thirds of the murders, the victim initiated the interchange, the offender stated an intent to harm the victim, and the offender then killed the victim. The interaction among the offender, the victim, and the audience to the murder can be analyzed in the following stages:

1. The offender first feels personally injured by the victim's behavior, which can be intentional or unwitting; this may include physical or verbal insults, gestures, or refusal to comply with the offender's wishes;
2. The offender then seeks to restore "face" by retaliating, expressing anger or contempt, or casting the victim as an unworthy person;
3. The victim next reacts to the offender's behavior by defining violence as the appropriate solution to the disagreement;
4. The offender interprets the victim's behavior as intentional noncompliance with his or her wishes;
5. Commitment to violence develops and actual violence is made more likely by the presence of weapons; and
6. The offender "drops" the victim and then flees, voluntarily stays at the scene, or is involuntarily held at the scene by witnesses to the murder (Luckenbill, 1977).

Another study looked at the interaction leading to 159 incidents of homicide and assault and found similar patterns of behavior. Physical violence typically followed an "identity attack," a failure to influence the antagonist, threats, and sometimes efforts at evasive action or mediation. Offenders retaliated in an effort to reestablish a favorable identity, and the situation escalated into assault or murder. Each individual responded to the other's actions and the implications of those actions for his or her well-being and honor. Consequently, it is difficult to classify violent crime as offender-precipitated or victim-precipitated. Victims often acted aggressively, but they attacked less often and were more likely to take evasive action than were the offenders. Efforts at mediation and evasion suggest that offenders and victims may not share norms that support violence as the appropriate response to an identity attack (Felson and Steadman, 1983).

FORCIBLE RAPE

There is a cultural stereotype, which has been eroded somewhat by feminists, that rape victims often contribute to their own victimization (Weis and Borges, 1973). This belief reflects the mistaken idea that rape is primarily a sexual act rather than a violent crime, even though victims experience rape as violence rather than sex. The widely held view that some victims provoke rapists, and even enjoy the act, is used to defend rapists' actions as justifiable, excusable, or understandable.

The idea that rape is often a victim-precipitated crime overlooks an important difference between rape and homicide. In the events leading to a homicide, the lives of both the eventual victim and the eventual murderer are usually at risk. However, in a confrontation between a rapist and a woman, only the woman is at risk. Thus, most murders are symmetrical in terms of the risk of being killed, but rapes are asymmetrical in terms of risk.

Nevertheless, the view that rape victims precipitate their own victimization persists in the minds of the public and the jurors who decide rape cases. Many people regard situations in which a woman places herself at risk—for instance, by hitchhiking or by telling dirty jokes in a bar—as a form of victim precipitation. The idea of a "dating bar rape"—in which a male and a female meet in a bar, leave together, and later have sexual intercourse that the women claims to have occurred without her consent—is sometimes used by jurors to justify their acquittal of a defendant.

One researcher concluded from his study of rape in Philadelphia that 19 per cent of the cases were victim-precipitated, in that the victim had actually agreed to have sexual relations with the offender—or had been thought to have agreed to this by the offender—but had retracted before the act, or had not reacted "strongly enough" when the suggestion of sex was first made by the offender. This researcher also categorized rapes as victim-precipitated if they were preceded by "risky situations marred with sexuality," such as a woman using "indecent" language or gestures or behaving in a way that could be taken as an invitation to sexual relations (Amir, 1971). Application of this extremely broad definition of victim precipitation led the researcher to conclude that nearly one rape victim in five contributes to her own victimization, even though "contribution" here seems to encompass anything outside a very restricted range of puritanical behavior.

Using a different definition of victim precipitation of rape, the seventeen-city survey of violent crime found that only 4 per cent of rapes were victim-precipitated, 83 per cent were not, and 13 per cent could not be classified easily or accurately (Curtis, 1974: 87–90). In this study, rape was defined as victim-precipitated if a female agreed to sexual relations and clearly invited them verbally or by gestures but then retracted before the act.

CRIMES AGAINST PROPERTY

Theft can be precipitated by property owners. Individuals who leave their homes vacant while on vacation, allow mail and newspapers to collect on the porch, and leave windows and doors open while away provide potential burglars with obvious signals that the dwelling is an easy target. People who leave car keys in the ignition facilitate car theft, because a thief does not even have to possess the skill to start the car without a key. Similarly, leaving property where it can easily be stolen encourages theft. A study of crime in Uganda found that immigrants to a large city from small villages brought with them a tradition of leaving property unguarded, thus encouraging theft. In the village, thieves could be observed and recognized, so the tradition of leaving property unguarded did not lead to theft there. In the city, similar informal controls were absent and the tradition frequently led to theft (Clinard and Abbott, 1973).

Offenders who lack a strong commitment to crime as a way of life may break the law when they happen upon easy opportunities to gain something with little risk. Sometimes they are drawn into crime because of victim precipitation. Thus, marginally committed offenders may steal unattended property, enter an empty house through an open window, or attack someone who insults them.

FACILITATING FACTORS: ALCOHOL, DRUGS, AND FIREARMS

Three factors that are often present when crimes are committed, but do not actually cause crime, are alcohol, drugs, and firearms. The high frequency with which alcohol, drugs, and firearms are present during crimes suggests that they are facilitating factors that increase the chance that an interaction or a situation will lead to criminal violence or theft.

Alcohol and Crime

There is substantial evidence that alcohol use and crime are correlated with each other (Pittman, 1974; Petersilia, Greenwood, and Lavin, 1977; Collins, 1981a, 1981b). A 1979 survey of the inmates of state prisons found that nearly 30 per cent of them said that "they had drunk heavily just before they committed the offense for which they were convicted," and another 20 per cent said that they had been drinking but not heavily (Bureau of Justice Statistics, January 1983: 1). Such self-reports may be questioned as to their validity, because inmates may try to diminish their personal responsibility for violating the law by blaming it on the effects of alcohol.

This survey of inmates also found that alcohol use varies from one kind of offender to another. Slightly higher proportions of property offenders than of violent offenders had been drinking just prior to their offense; the same pattern held for heavy drinking in the year prior to the crime (Bureau of Justice Statistics, January 1983). Offenders incarcerated for burglary, rape, and assault were especially likely to be heavy drinkers, both just before the crime and during the year before the offense. Drug offenders were the least likely to be very heavy drinkers, but we can see from Table 11.4 that even they were frequently heavy users of alcohol.

Table 11.4: Alcohol Use by Type of Offense, 1979, Percentages

CURRENT OFFENSE	VERY HEAVY DRINKING IN THE YEAR PRIOR TO THE OFFENSE	VERY HEAVY DRINKING JUST PRIOR TO THE OFFENSE
Violent	35	60
Homicide	33	56
Assault	45	62
Rape	41	65
Robbery	34	60
Other violent	36	63
Property	40	68
Burglary	43	71
Forgery or fraud	32	59
Larceny	31	61
Other property	44	68
Drugs	28	46
Public order	37	55
Total	36	62

SOURCE: Bureau of Justice Statistics, *Prisoners and Alcohol.* Washington, D.C.: Bureau of Justice Statistics, U.S. Department of Justice, January 1983.

Alcohol is present in a significant proportion of homicides and assaults, and a smaller proportion of rapes, according to studies that have used official crime statistics. The Philadelphia homicide study found that alcohol was present in 63.6 per cent of all cases. In 10.9 per cent, the offender had been drinking; in 9.2 per cent, the victim had been drinking; and in 43.5 per cent, both the offender and the victim had been drinking. Inebriated victims sometimes precipitated their own murders by being the first to use violence.

Alcohol also seems to play a role in various sex offenses. The Philadelphia study of forcible rape found that alcohol was present only in the victim in 10 per cent of the cases, only in the offender in 3 per cent of the cases, and in both the offender and the victim in 21 per cent of the reported rapes (Amir, 1971: 98). Alcohol can also facilitate offenses such as incest, child molestation, and child abuse. A common pattern for incest is an unemployed man with an absent wife and an available daughter (or, less commonly, a stepdaughter), coupled with a pattern of heavy drinking by the man (Gebhard et al., 1965). Physical and social isolation of the family and tension within the marriage are also conducive to incest. These conditions are especially likely to lead to incestuous behavior if the strong norms against it are neutralized by the heavy consumption of alcohol. Other sex offenses, such as child molestation, are also associated with alcohol use (McCaghy, 1967, 1968).

Several explanations have been offered for the relationship between alcohol use and crime. One explanation is that alcohol may reduce inhibitions and trigger law-violating behavior in some people. The reduction of inhibitions from alcohol consumption is suggested by the results of the Philadelphia homicide study, which found that murders in which alcohol was present involved more violence and brutality than did murders in which neither the offender nor the victim had been drinking (Wolfgang, 1958). Another piece of evidence that is consistent with this disinhibition explanation comes from a study of robbery, which found that alcohol was present in 71 per cent of the crimes that were committed on the spur of the moment, but only in 44 per cent of the crimes that were planned (G. D. Wolcott, cited in Petersilia, Greenwood, and Lavin, 1977: 81).

A second explanation of why alcohol use is linked to crime is that people who are actively involved in a life of crime may rely on alcohol to reduce their anxiety or to build up their courage for crimes they have planned (Collins, 1981a; 1981b). However, the inmate survey found that heavy alcohol consumption was typical daily behavior for one inmate in five; it was not something they did just before committing a crime. Thus, many offenders seem to be heavy drinkers even when not engaging in crimes, and so they probably do not drink just to build up their courage. It is more likely that they are problem drinkers who occasionally commit crimes when their inhibitions are reduced by alcohol.

A third explanation of the association of alcohol use and crime is that groups have norms about how people who are under the influence of alcohol should behave. Among some groups, drunkenness is seen as a "time out" from conventional demands; in this situation of relaxed behavioral standards, aggressive or even criminal behavior may be tolerated or expected. There is little research on differences among groups in their norms about "drunken comportment," but if such differences exist they would help us to explain why alcohol use and crime are associated with each other in different ways for various groups (MacAndrew and Edgerton, 1969).

We do not yet have enough research to tell us why alcohol use is associated with crime. More studies are needed to make clear "(1) the role of alcohol in the criminal situation, (2) the prevalence of alcoholism among criminals, and (3) the criminal history of alcoholics" (S. Greenberg, 1981: 106–107; also, see Wilbanks, 1981).

Drugs and Crime

Earlier in the book, we saw that many kinds of drug use are defined as crime, and that the need to support a drug habit can lead to secondary crimes. Drugs can also facilitate crime by reducing inhibitions or clouding a user's judgment, much as alcohol may facilitate crime. The extent of drug use among offenders can be seen in a 1976 survey of 624 male felons in California prisons, which revealed that 42 per cent of them had used or been addicted to drugs—usually heroin—during the three years before their current incarceration. Inmates who had used drugs reported more property crimes than did nonusers (Peterson and Braiker, 1981).

In the 1979 survey of state prison inmates, nearly a third of them reported that they had been under the influence of an illegal drug at the time of the crime for which they were incarcerated (Bureau of Justice Statistics, March 1983). Seventeen per cent were under the influence of marijuana, 9 per cent had been using heroin, and 5 per cent had been using cocaine. Table 11.5 shows the percentage of inmates under the influence of any illegal drug when they committed the offense for which they were incarcerated at the time of the survey. Burglars, robbers, and drug offenders were the most likely to have been under the influence of a drug at the time of their crime. Homicide, rape, and public-order (often drunkenness) offenders were the least likely to have been using an illegal drug.

Table 11.5 also shows that 56 per cent of all prisoners had used illegal

Table 11.5: Illegal Drug Use by Type of Offense, 1979, Percentage

CURRENT OFFENSE	ILLEGAL DRUG USE		
	Ever	*Month Prior to Offense*	*Under Influence at Time of Offense*
Violent	75	53	30
Homicide	64	41	21
Assault	73	47	27
Rape	64	39	22
Robbery	86	66	38
Other violent	79	59	34
Property	80	58	35
Burglary	85	64	40
Forgery or fraud	69	45	25
Larceny	78	53	30
Other property	75	51	30
Drugs	92	74	47
Public order	69	42	19
Total	78	56	32

SOURCE: Bureau of Justice Statistics, *Prisoners and Drugs.* Washington, D.C.: Bureau of Justice Statistics, U.S. Department of Justice, March 1983, pp. 3–4.

drugs in the month prior to their offense, and that 78 per cent had used illegal drugs some time in the past. Again, burglars, robbers, and drug offenders reported the most illegal drug use. Homicide, rape, and public-order offenders reported illegal drug use least often (Bureau of Justice Statistics, March 1983).

The inmate survey did not compare inmates' alcohol use with that of the general population, but it did compare inmates' drug use with use by the general population. For each illegal drug, a higher proportion of inmates than of the general population reported that they had ever used the drug. The difference was especially great for heroin; only 2 per cent of the general population reported ever having used this drug, but 30 per cent of the inmates had used this drug at some time. Inmates were also more likely to have used an illegal drug recently than were people in the general population.

The greater amount of drug use by inmates does not, however, tell us the reason for the association between drug use and crime. Inmates may have had their crimes facilitated by the effects of drugs, but they may also have been more likely to be arrested because they were known by the police to be drug users, or because the drugs affected their behavior in ways that drew the attention of the police.

Firearms and Crime

Firearms are often used in crime in the United States. In 1983, 44 per cent of all reported murders were committed by handguns, 7 per cent by shotguns, 4 per cent by rifles, and 3 per cent by other or unknown kinds of firearms (Webster, 1984: 8). Thus, more than half of all murders involve firearms. Firearms are also used to facilitate crimes such as robbery and rape. In 1983, 37 per cent of all reported robberies were committed with a firearm (Webster, 1984: 18). The FBI does not report the use of firearms in rapes and burglaries, but one study found that 21 per cent of all rapists intimidated their victims with some weapon (although not necessarily a firearm), and another study found that 8 per cent of burglars carried a firearm and 16 per cent carried some other weapon (Amir, 1971: 150; Reppetto, 1974: 107).

The relationship between firearms and crime is complex. Firearms might, under some circumstances, deter potential offenders from crime. Thus, a robber might think twice about holding up a store in which the owner had shot another thief the week before. Ownership of firearms for protection against criminals might make people feel more secure and affect their behavior in ways that help to keep crime rates low, for instance, by encouraging a storekeeper who feels safer to stay open at night, thereby providing informal control over nearby sidewalks and streets. On the other hand, firearms that people keep for self-protection are often stolen by burglars, who may then use them for illegal purposes (Wright, Rossi, and Daly, 1983; Kates, 1984).

Crime and firearms may also be related in another way: Fear of crime might cause people to arm themselves. Most firearms in private hands in the United States are not for self-defense against criminals, but for other purposes such as hunting, target shooting, or collecting. One survey found that only about one gun owner in three gives self-defense as a reason for owning a firearm (DuBow, McCabe, and Kaplan, 1979: 133–134), and a recent review of research suggests that only 10 to 20 per cent of all firearms are for self-defense against other people (Wright, Rossi, and Daly, 1983). Most evidence indicates that the victims of crime are no more likely to arm themselves than are people who have not been victimized, and that people who are afraid of crime are no more likely to buy weapons than people who are not afraid of crime (Wright, Rossi, and Daly, 1983).

Firearms may also facilitate the commission of crime. The presence of a weapon during an argument can lead to an escalation of violence, producing a murder when an assault would have occurred if no firearm had been present. Firearms may also give some robbers and rapists the courage to commit crimes that they would otherwise have avoided. Guns can act as catalysts, pushing people over the borderline between the wish to act violently and the actual commission of a violent crime. However, a recent assessment of research concludes that there is "little or no conclusive evidence to show that gun ownership among the larger population is, per se, an important cause of criminal violence" (Wright, Rossi, and Daly, 1983: 137). Switzerland, for instance, has widespread private ownership of firearms but no tradition of using guns to settle interpersonal disputes, and so it has a low rate of criminal violence with firearms (Clinard, 1978). The mere presence of weapons does not cause crime, and so restricting firearm ownership by the general population might not be an effective way to prevent criminals from getting firearms illegally. On the other hand, such restrictions might make access to firearms by potential offenders

A Cross-Cultural Perspective: Firearms in Israel

Israel is a nation "pervaded by guns, but . . . not excited by them." This attitude is largely due to the fact that all men and women serve in the army and are taught to use firearms carefully. An Israeli political scientist contrasts American attitudes toward firearms with attitudes in his country as follows:

America and Israel are both immigrant societies, but immigrants to America come as individuals, whereas in Israel people immigrate as part of a people, and therefore the conceptions of security are different. The holding of a gun in Israel is interpreted as more of a commitment to collective security than as a sign of unyielding commitment to self-defense in an individual sense. In America it is much more connected to a fear of crime, and here [in Israel] much more connected with national defense, an external threat, the idea of a people's army. When we see individuals carrying guns, we see them almost as organs of the community.

Both automatic weapons and handguns are common in Israel, but firearm ownership is strictly regulated outside the military and the system of national security. Possession of a firearm without a license can lead to a seven-year prison term; ammunition is also strictly controlled. Licensing clerks determine who will get a firearm license, and they may reject applicants because they have no need for a weapon, have been institutionalized in a mental hospital, have a police record, are under twenty years old, or are on active military duty. About one applicant in five is rejected.

Firearms are not used by criminals in Israel very often, although there has recently been some concern with the theft of firearms by criminals from licensed owners and from the military. The police estimate that there are three to four times as many unlicensed and illegal firearms in the country as there are licensed weapons, but many of the unlicensed weapons are in the hands of private collectors rather than criminals.

Overall, Israel, much like Switzerland, has a relatively low crime rate with little use of firearms by murderers, robbers, and rapists. This is true in spite of the pervasive ownership of weapons in the country, a situation tied to military and security measures for the nation as a whole rather than associated with individuals' efforts to protect themselves from criminals.

SOURCE: Based on David K. Shipler, "To Pistol-Packing Israelis, a Gun Is a Patriotic Badge," *The New York Times*, April 13, 1981, p. A2.

more difficult and reduce crime to some degree. Tight restrictions on firearm ownership in Japan, for example, have often been cited as a reason for that society's low crime rate. In the Cross-Cultural Perspective we see that Israel is a nation that has both widespread ownership of firearms and strict controls on those weapons.

In 1982, the total number of index crimes involving firearms and Part II offenses involving the carrying and possessing of weapons, many of which were firearms, was more than 500,000. In contrast, a report from Great Britain, which has about one-fourth of the population of the United States, showed that in 1982 the English police recorded only 1,935 crimes in which firearms were used or threatened, an increase from 1,401 such offenses in 1976. England thus has a much lower rate of firearm-related crime than the United States, even though England's rate of such offenses has increased in recent years (Thomas, 1984).

FIREARMS AND MURDER
With about 120 million firearms, including 50 million handguns, in private hands in the United States, and with about half of all households having at least one firearm, there is a good chance that one will be present at the scene

Firearm ownership is widespread in Israel. Here a picnicker is carrying a pistol in a park in Jerusalem.

SOURCE: Copyright © 1981 Micha Bar-Am. Reprinted by permission of the New York Times.

of a bitter argument or a fight (DuBow, McCabe, and Kaplan, 1979; Wright, Rossi, and Daly, 1983). If a firearm is used during an altercation, murder is a likely result. Thus, one study found that the increased number of handguns in Detroit between 1963 and 1971 accounted for most of the substantial increase in murders in that city over that period (Fisher, 1976). Other studies have also found a relationship between gun ownership and homicide rates (Seitz, 1972; Cook, 1983).

Firearms can change what might have been an assault into a murder. Firearm assaults lead to death about four to seven times as often as attacks with other weapons, so if a firearm is present during an assault there is a much greater chance that someone will be killed. Firearm assaults are fatal about 13 per cent of the time, knife attacks are fatal about 3 per cent of the time, and attacks with hands, fists, and feet are fatal only 1.7 per cent of the time (Morris and Hawkins, 1970: 66). These data suggest that because guns are the most deadly weapons, their easy availability might be associated with a higher homicide rate (Cook, 1983). However, we cannot infer from these statistics that substituting knives for guns in the hands of assailants would reduce fatalities, because assailants who decide to use firearms might be more single-minded in their desire to kill victims, and they might be more intent on doing so even if they had to use a knife (Wright, Rossi, and Daly, 1983).

FIREARMS AND ROBBERY

Relatively few studies have asked offenders what role the firearm plays for them in the commission of a crime. One study of robbery did conclude that the idea that firearms serve mainly expressive purposes is probably incorrect. Rather than using weapons as psychological props to create a sense of omnipotence or masculinity, as some psychologists and psychiatrists suggest, robbers usually employ weapons primarily for instrumental purposes—to acquire money more easily and with less resistance and to ensure a safe escape from the scene of the crime (Conklin, 1972: 108–112).

Paradoxically, the use of firearms by robbers may prevent violence, because victims are less likely to resist offenders who carry guns (Conklin, 1972; Block, 1977). When victims do resist, offenders may increase the level of intimidation by cocking the pistol, holding it to the victim's head, or using it as a blunt instrument to hit the victim. Sometimes, of course, firearms are used to shoot victims, and then robberies may lead to serious injury or death. Victims who resist armed robbers are about three times as likely to be injured seriously as are victims who do not resist (Block, 1977, 1981; Nelson, 1983b).

We cannot say exactly how much robbery would be prevented if no firearms were available, but at least some marginally committed and opportunistic robbers would probably give up that form of theft if they could not get a gun. Some of them might turn to nonviolent crimes such as burglary, shoplifting, and larceny. Even if they continued to commit robberies without firearms, that might be preferable to robberies committed with guns.

GUN CONTROL AND CRIME RATES

There is mixed evidence as to whether crime can be reduced by controlling access to firearms. One study that compared five states with strong gun-control laws to five states with weak laws found that the states with the strong laws had lower homicide rates. In these states, a smaller proportion of the homicides that did occur were perpetrated with firearms (Criminal Division, U.S. Department of Justice, 1968). Although this study suggests that strong gun-control laws might reduce the homicide rate, the results can also be interpreted to mean that the states that were able to pass strong gun-control legislation were the states in which people were more opposed to the use of firearms to begin with or were the states in which firearms were relatively unimportant to residents. Thus, both the low murder rate and the gun-control law may have been products of a nonviolent, antiweapon attitude on the part of the state's residents. This attitude, rather than the law itself, might account for a low homicide rate.

In recent years, several states have passed laws that have attempted to reduce crime by controlling firearms. One approach is to control the possession and use of firearms by the general public. Thus, in 1975 the Bartley-Fox law was implemented in Massachusetts to require a one-year jail sentence for anyone caught carrying an unlicensed firearm. One evaluation of the impact of this law found that it seemed to have reduced the incidence of gun assaults, but that it also produced a more than offsetting increase in assaults with weapons other than guns, apparently because people who avoided carrying firearms turned to other weapons to commit assaults. Gun robberies were reduced by the law, but armed robberies without firearms increased; however, the increase in robberies without firearms did not offset the decline in gun robberies. The law reduced homicides with firearms without any increase in nongun homicides. Thus, the Bartley-Fox law had some effect in reducing homicides and robberies with firearms. However, the researchers concluded that it was the publicity about the intent of the law, rather than the severity or certainty of the sanctions that were actually imposed, that produced this reduction in firearm crime; the researchers were unwilling to attribute the changes to the impact of the mandatory jail term (Pierce and Bowers, 1981). A more recent evaluation of this law concluded that

> although there is some evidence that the Massachusetts Bartley-Fox Amendment achieved at least an initial impact on gun-related crime, there is substantial reason to believe that long-range effects are not to be expected or will be considerably reduced in magnitude. In other words, there is some evidence that under some conditions gun-related crimes can be reduced through gun control legislation, but this outcome will be neither very common nor especially pronounced (Wright, Rossi, and Daly, 1983: 308).

In 1980, New York state implemented a law similar to Bartley-Fox, except that in New York the mandatory sentence of one year was applied only to people who had been convicted of a crime in the previous five years. There is no evidence that this law has reduced street crime with firearms, and many who have been convicted under the law have not served the "mandatory" one year in jail (Basler, 1982; Barbanel, 1984).

A strategy tried by other states, including Michigan and Florida, requires judges to impose an additional prison term on offenders convicted of a serious crime in which they used a firearm. A study in Detroit found that crime rates declined after the implementation of a two-year mandatory additional penalty for the use of a firearm in a serious crime, but it concluded that the decline did not seem to be attributable to the new law. The decline began before the law was implemented, and unarmed violent crime as well as crime with firearms showed a decrease. The law's lack of impact was attributed to the fact that "offenders were not responsive to a mandatory two-year increment in sanctions for offenses which already carry maximum sentences much greater than two years" (Loftin, Heumann, and McDowall, 1983: 310). Thus, the law did not increase the perceived certainty or perceived severity of punishment in a significant way. The law would have affected rates of murder, robbery, and assault only if offenders who used weapons in those crimes placed relatively little value on the use of weapons, and this apparently was not the case. The fact that Detroit's population was heavily armed when the law was passed probably meant that offenders placed great value on being armed because of the high probability that they would encounter armed resistance from their victims (Loftin and McDowall, 1981; Loftin, Heumann, and McDowall, 1983; also, see Loftin and McDowall, 1984).

Research has not demonstrated that gun-control laws that require mandatory jail sentences for anyone carrying an unlicensed weapon or for anyone using a firearm in a serious crime can have a long-run effect on the use of firearms in crime. Sometimes "mandatory" penalties are not imposed. Either the police do not arrest everyone who carries an illegal firearm, or prosecutors and judges fail to impose the required sentence. Even if the criminal justice system imposed the mandatory penalty, it is not clear that felons would give up their firearms.

THE CONTINUING DEBATE OVER GUN CONTROL

In spite of the uncertain effects of gun-control laws, most Americans support stronger laws than we now have. A 1983 poll found that 59 per cent of Americans favored stricter legal controls on the sale of pistols, and polls since 1975 have found a majority supporting this proposal. In 1983, 44 per cent favored and 48 per cent opposed a law that would ban the sale and possession of pistols (*The New York Times*, June 20, 1983). The town of Morton Grove, Illinois, banned pistols in 1981, and a few other communities have enacted similar ordinances, but local laws of this sort are not likely to have much effect on the nation's crime rate. People can easily find firearms in nearby communities and carry them to the town where they are banned.

One reason that federal gun-control laws are relatively weak is not for lack of public support for stronger laws, but rather because of the power of the National Rifle Association (NRA). This well-financed organization of about two million members can mobilize its supporters to write to members of Congress and oppose any gun-control legislation that is being considered. In 1980, the NRA contributed more than $2 million to political campaigns, and in 1982 it spent $3.5 million on lobbying activities. The NRA uses magazine advertisements to argue against stricter gun-control laws. Many NRA members are "single-issue" voters who will vote against candidates who favor tougher gun-control laws. Because most voters who support tougher gun-control laws will not vote for or against candidates solely because of their stand on gun control, NRA members pose a more significant risk of lost votes to candidates, and thus many politicians vote against gun control out of fear of alienating the opponents of stronger gun-control laws.

In recent years, several lobbyist groups—such as People against Handguns, the National Coalition to Ban Handguns, and Handgun Control, Inc.—have fought for stronger gun-control laws. These organizations have been hampered by a lack of funds, by little support from "single-issue" voters, and by well-organized opposition from the NRA and the firearms industry.

The debate over gun control continues. Opponents claim a constitutional right to bear arms, even though the Constitution specifies that this right is not to be abridged because of the need to raise a national militia. The handguns involved in murders and robberies are not designed for military use, nor do their owners buy them for that purpose. Another argument against stronger gun-control laws is that criminals will find guns even if stronger laws are passed. Proponents of stronger gun-control laws claim that the laws might reduce crime, but we lack solid research data to support that argument. Further research may clarify the effects that different kinds of gun-control laws can have on various forms of crime.

PLANNING CRIME

Most criminals plan their crimes to some degree. Sometimes this planning is elaborate and takes place over weeks or months, but often offenders plan their crimes only a few hours before committing them or even at the scene when an opportunity arises. One study found that 18 per cent of one sample of offenders had not planned their crimes at all, 61 per cent had planned their crimes less than a hour ahead of time, 7 per cent had planned them at least an hour before or earlier the same day, and 14 per cent had planned them the day before or earlier. Thus, only one-fifth of these offenders had planned their crimes more than an hour before committing them (Erez, 1980).

Planning includes consideration of what might go wrong during the crime, and the way that obstacles might be surmounted. Criminals sometimes have to secure items with which to carry out their crimes, such as nitroglycerin to blow open a safe, a firearm to intimidate a bank teller, or bogus certificates to use in a stock fraud. Planning may also require offenders to allocate duties to various gang members or to different conspirators if collusion is required.

The degree to which offenders plan their crimes is important, because measures to reduce crime by "target hardening"—that is, adding locks, bars, or other devices to secure property—may deter offenders who act impulsively but not offenders who plan their crimes carefully well in advance. On the other hand, those who plan their crimes might be deflected to other targets if they weigh the possible obstacles to a crime in advance (Erez, 1980). The deterrent effect of punishment, which we examine later, is also closely related to the extent to which offenders plan their crimes.

Forcible Rape

Some crimes are planned in detail, but many seem to occur spontaneously. One study found that 71 per cent of forcible rapes were planned, with offenders deliberately trying to force the victim into sex. Another 11 per cent of the rapes were partially planned, with vague plans being hastily made after an encounter with a potential victim. About one-sixth of the rapes were "explosive," with the offender having no earlier intention of committing a rape but impulsively perpetrating one when an opportunity presented itself (Amir, 1971: 141).

Shoplifting

Shoplifting is carefully planned by professional "boosters," and even amateur "snitches" who steal for personal use may plan their thefts before entering a store (Cameron, 1964). Shoplifting often involves the intention to pick up certain merchandise, a plan to leave the store, and a way to dispose of the stolen goods.

Burglary

Other thieves also plan their crimes. Thus, three-fourths of one sample of burglars did some planning prior to entering the building (Reppetto, 1974: 17–18). Many burglars "case a job" in order to minimize their risks; for instance, they may carefully examine the architecture of a building for ease of entry and escape. Burglars often first try to enter through an unlocked door, and only if that fails do they climb in through a window. If burglars cannot make a quick entry, they may seek a different target. Casing also involves looking for alarm systems, occupants of the building, and nearby witnesses. Learning about police and security patrols in the area may also be part of this planning phase (Letkemann, 1973).

Robbery

Some robberies are planned only a few minutes before they occur, with offenders piecing together the elements of a crime by improvisation (Lejeune, 1977). One study found that more than 40 per cent of juvenile robbers and 25 per cent of adult robbers had not even intended to commit the robbery before it occurred (Feeney and Weir, 1973). In another study of robbery, an inmate reported that he and a friend were riding in a taxi and his friend pulled a knife, grabbed the driver around the neck, and demanded his money; the inmate said that he had not even known that his friend was going to commit a robbery until it was under way. In another case, a professional robber who usually planned his offenses with a partner well in advance went into a liquor store to buy some beer. When the clerk refused to sell to him because he was drunk, he pulled a gun and demanded money. His partner outside in the car was taken by surprise because they had not planned the robbery, but he ran into the store to help. After the robbery, they drove away, but their license number was traced and they were arrested. When they engaged in planned robberies, they always stole a car to avoid being traced (Conklin, 1972: 97).

Robbers often case their targets. They may look at the architecture of a bank as well as its location; a bank on a street corner near a superhighway makes a fast getaway possible. Risk, which is often a function of the number of victims and witnesses likely to be at the scene, is also assessed. In trying to neutralize obstacles, offenders often look at the crime from the victim's perspective, asking how victims would be likely to react to the crime and how important the money is to the victim.

Planning a crime sometimes involves a careful assessment of the best time to commit the offense. A time is picked that will maximize the score and minimize the obstacles. Businesses that pay employees in cash are most likely to have large sums of money on hand on paydays. One robber prefers to do holdups on rainy days, because he can then wear a coat to conceal a weapon and because he will not seem suspicious as he runs from the scene of the crime (Letkemann, 1973: 140). Robbers sometimes choose a time when the streets are empty of people and cars, because this makes their escape easier. They may also watch the flow of people in an establishment, counting the number of people in a store or a bank on the same day at the same time for weeks or months ahead of a planned robbery. They may also try to figure out when messengers carry money to night depositories or when store managers are away from the premises. One of the best known of all bank robbers, Willie Sutton, developed a technique described as follows:

First, he would study a bank carefully until he learned how many employees worked there, when they arrived for duty and what their duties were.

He invariably entered the bank after the arrival of the first employee, usually a porter or guard, then welcomed the other employees at gunpoint. When the manager arrived, he would warn him that his employees would be the first to be shot if there was trouble. The robber and his helper or helpers were always gone before the bank opened for public business (Krebs, 1980: A31).

White-Collar Crime

White-collar crime usually involves elaborate planning. The electrical equipment price-fixing conspiracy that culminated in the conviction of companies and executives in 1961 involved detailed planning. One conspirator describes the techniques used by the offenders as follows: "It was considered discreet to not be too obvious and to minimize telephone calls, to use plain envelopes if mailing material to each other, not to be seen together on traveling, and so forth . . . not to leave wastepaper, of which there was a lot, strewn around a room when leaving" (cited in Geis, 1967: 143). The conspirators "hid behind a camouflage of fictitious names and conspiratorial codes," called their meeting roster the "Christmas card list," and referred to their gatherings as "choir practice" (Geis, 1967: 143). They also used public telephones and met at trade association meetings and at remote sites to ensure their anonymity.

THE ORGANIZATION OF CRIMINAL BEHAVIOR

Criminologists, the public, and the criminal justice system often treat crime as the act of an individual. For instance, statistics on crime incidents and arrests emphasize the individual nature of crime (Short, 1974). However, much crime is carried out by organized groups. Criminologists need to learn how criminal organizations influence behavior, and how and why individuals organize into these collectivities (McIntosh, 1975).

Professional Theft

Professional thieves often organize for specific offenses, but many of them are loners who only work with others sporadically. Often there is no permanent organization of the thieves, even though social ties among them provide access to accomplices when they are needed (Jackson, 1969). Groups of professional thieves are frequently in a state of flux. There may be some stability of membership in these gangs, but usually there are changes as thieves drop out, move, are imprisoned, or are replaced.

For any given offense, professional thieves allocate specific tasks to members of the gang. Individuals may have specialties, but most are quite versatile. The different roles and specialties of the gang members must be coordinated so that the group functions smoothly to carry out the crime. Gangs seek the most efficient organization to deal with the problems they must solve to carry out the crime. For instance, the 1950 Brinks robbery involved eleven thieves with various skills, although the robbery probably could have been perpetrated, perhaps even more efficiently, with fewer gang members.

The picture of professional thieves painted by "Chic Conwell," a professional thief interviewed by Edwin H. Sutherland (1937) in the 1930s, seems in need of modification today. Conwell described thieves as having very narrow specialties; recent information suggests much greater versatility. Conwell described thieving gangs as having an esprit de corps, a "we-feeling" that provided the thieves with group support. There was also a code of behavior that required mutual aid, payment of debts to other thieves, and honest dealing with other thieves. Current information suggests that loyalty of this sort is now no more than an elusive ideal. Most thieves will do anything to stay out of prison, including making a deal with the police or a district attorney to turn in an accomplice. One thief reported that there "is no loyalty among thieves today. There's no such thing at all. They have absolutely no loyalty. They'll beat one another to the money, you know, anything they can, they'll beat one another for their girls, or anything" (King and Chambliss, 1984: 78).

ARGOT

Gangs of criminals are often characterized by *argot* or cant, a specialized language that differentiates offenders from others and creates solidarity among them (Maurer, 1955, 1964; Lerman, 1967). This language is used when criminals are with other members of the underworld, but usually not when dealing with noncriminals, because their argot would identify them as deviants. The argot of criminals is closely linked to the kinds of crime they commit. For instance, pickpockets employ an elaborate argot in which different pockets and different means of taking wallets are given slang terms. The "stall" in the "whiz mob" picks out a "mark" and "steers" that potential victim into position so that the "tool" can take the wallet (Maurer, 1955, 1964).

ROLES IN THE GANG

Gangs of thieves assign roles to their members to ensure the efficient completion of all aspects of the crime. Safecrackers often work with partners; one acts as a lookout and another enters the building, opens the safe, and steals the money (Letkemann, 1973: 79). Most robberies involve multiple offenders, so different tasks must be assigned to participants in the crime. Most roles in robbery gangs are relatively easy to perform and are thus interchangeable among offenders, but role allocation ensures that all tasks will be performed. One such role is the "wheel man," who steals a car, maps an escape route, and drives to and from the robbery site. This role is critical in a robbery, because there is great risk in getting away from the scene of the crime in a car that cannot be identified. The wheel man may also act as a "lookout" or "peek man" for the gang, or may leave the car and take an active part in the holdup. Occasionally the driver is hired for a fixed percentage of the profits, usually 10 per cent. Some robbers who begin as "10 per centers" later join robbery gangs as full-fledged members (Conklin, 1972: 99–100).

OUTSIDERS TO THE GANG

Gangs of professional thieves sometimes require the assistance of people who do not take part directly in the crime. They may use a tipster to locate a particularly large score, paying that person 10 to 25 per cent of the profits if the crime is successful. One robber preyed on drug pushers who were vulnerable because they could not report the crime to the police; he paid the tipster who guided him to local drug dealers (Conklin, 1972: 89). Tipsters are probably used more often by burglars than by robbers. Robbers usually know where to find money, but burglars often need information about which buildings contain money or valuable property and exactly where in the building that money or property is located.

Thieves often use a fence as an outlet for stolen goods, but the fence is not a member of the gang. One study found that with the exception of addict-thieves, most thieves are part of a network that links them to each other and to fences who purchase stolen merchandise and may even direct the thieves in their criminal activities to some extent (Walsh, 1977). Because thieves are often ignorant of the actual value of the property they steal and because they frequently need cash quickly, fences may try to drive down the prices they pay to the lowest levels acceptable to the thieves. Fences may say that an item is incomplete, useless, out of season, of poor quality, or otherwise undesirable; they also use deception in figuring the value of the stolen goods (Klockars, 1974).

Another role of some importance to professional thieves is the fixer, a lawyer or other person who is not a member of the gang but who contacts the police, judges, or victims to have charges dismissed (Sutherland, 1937; Letkemann, 1973; King and Chambliss, 1984). Amateur thieves try to avoid detection, but professionals assume that they will be arrested occasionally and therefore seek to avoid conviction when this happens. Toward this end, professionals may use fixers to act as brokers who offer to return stolen property to victims if they will drop their complaints against the thieves. Fixers may also bribe police officers, judges, and jurors so that their client will be acquitted or given a light sentence.

Professional thieves sometimes rely on loan sharks to provide them with money that they need to pay for disguises, trucks, or other equipment. Loan sharks can also be a source of money with which to pay a bail bondsman or a fixer if the thief is arrested, or to pay a defense lawyer if the case goes to trial. Thieves who are released on bail or acquitted may then commit more crimes to get the money with which to repay the loan shark (Gould et al., 1966).

Organized Crime

Organized crime has the characteristics of a formal organization: a division of labor, coordination of activities through rules and codes, and an allocation of tasks to various roles in order to achieve certain goals (Cressey, 1969, 1972). The organization seeks profit from crime, and tries to preserve itself in the face of external and internal threats.

The hierarchy of an organized crime "family" shown in Figure 11.1 includes a boss with absolute authority over the members, an underboss who acts as chief deputy and assistant, a staff of counselors or advisors, a series of lieutenants who act as buffers between the higher echelons and the lower-level workers, and soldiers who operate illegal or legitimate activities for the family (The President's Commission on Law Enforcement and Administration of Justice, 1967c: 7–10).

Three major roles are necessary to the functioning of an organized crime family: the corrupter, the corruptee, and the enforcer. The corrupter "bribes, buys, intimidates, threatens, negotiates, and sweet-talks himself into a relationship with police, public officials, and anyone else who might help 'family' members secure and maintain immunity from arrest, prosecution, and punishment" (Cressey, 1972: 36). Corruptees are usually public officials who are not members of the family; they are necessary to the functioning of organized crime. The third critical role is the enforcer, who "makes arrangements for killing and injuring (physically, financially, or psychologically) members, and occasionally nonmembers" (Cressey, 1972: 38).

Figure 11.1: An Organized Crime Family

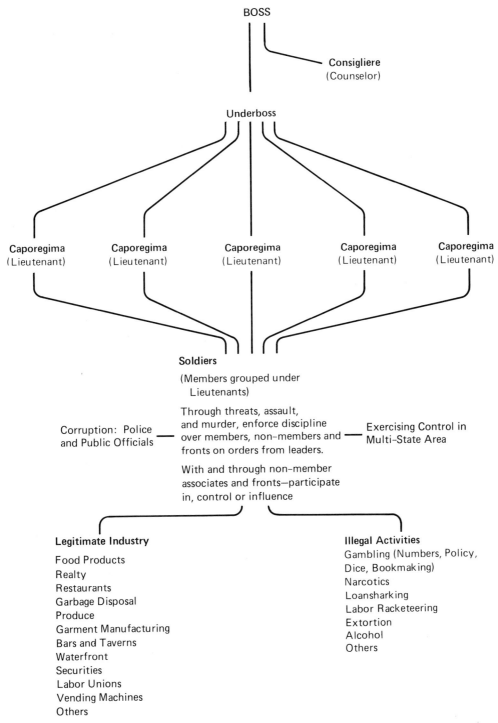

SOURCE: The President's Commission on Law Enforcement and Administration of Justice. *Organized Crime.* Washington, D.C.: U.S. Government Printing Office, 1967, p. 9.

One innovative piece of research on organized crime shows that the roles in organized crime "families" are often linked by kinship rather than by the formal bureaucratic hierarchy described by others (Ianni, 1972). Certain relatives work together in various criminal activities, and other members of the kinship group are involved in legitimate activities. Kinship ties and intermarriage may also loosely bind together organized crime gangs in different cities. In Japan, organized crime gangs are tightly knit groups that demand loyalty and the fulfillment of obligations, but kinship ties are not the basis of Japanese gangs (Clifford, 1976: 119–120).

A NATIONAL CONFEDERATION?

One question about the structure of organized crime in the United States is whether it is organized at the national level or only at the local level. This issue has been hotly debated for years and is not a trivial one, for the answer to the question of how organized crime is structured determines how law enforcement can best combat it.

It is clear that some American cities have gangs or "families" of organized criminals variously called the Mafia, La Cosa Nostra, or the Mob. According to one estimate, La Cosa Nostra families include about 1,700 active members, with about ten times that number involved as associates (Werner, 1983). Law-enforcement officials and even members of organized crime do not agree on how many families exist or which cities have them, although one often-heard figure is twenty-five "families" in the country (Albanese, 1983).

Many law-enforcement officials and some criminologists believe that these gangs are knit together in a highly organized national confederation led by a commission of powerful bosses. This conclusion is based mainly on transcripts of bugged conversations among gangsters; unfortunately, these transcripts are not readily available for analysis and verification. Moreover, these conversations do not necessarily provide accurate information about the structure of organized crime. Gangsters may boast of their numbers and their organization without actually having that strength and structure, much as juvenile delinquent gangs in the 1950s claimed "reserve forces" and "allies" of thousands of members who proved nonexistent when a gang war occurred.

Some criminologists have made a strong case that organized crime is not highly organized at the national level by examining the testimony of gangsters and finding many internal inconsistencies in this "evidence" for a nationally organized La Cosa Nostra (Hawkins, 1969). Observation of a New York City crime family found no evidence that it was linked to a national organization, although no evidence was found that such ties did not exist (Ianni, 1972: 89). Another study of the Mafia in New York City, where it is probably stronger than anywhere else in the country, concluded that it "may be a paper tiger, reaping the returns from its reputation while no longer maintaining the forces that generated the reputation" (Reuter, 1983: xi). The press and the police may contribute to the popular impression that the Mafia controls crime through a centrally coordinated organization, even though its actual control over criminal activities seems to be quite limited. A study of organized crime in Seattle found that organized crime was "a coalition of politicians, law-enforcement people, businessmen, union leaders, and (in some ways least important of all) racketeers. Who dominates the coalition varies from city to city and from time to time" (Chambliss, 1978: 9). This study concluded that organized crime was not run by a national commission, and that its activities were not primarily even under the control of private citizens.

Organizations of criminals called "families" do exist at the local level in some cities, even though it may be difficult to determine who is a member of the family and who is merely hired to perform specific tasks for the gang. Some loose ties exist among families throughout the country, but there is little solid evidence of a highly structured bureaucracy led by a commission of bosses that "serves as a combination board of business directors, legislature, supreme court, and arbitration board" (Cressey, 1969: 111). When families come into conflict with each other in competition for a new market or for control of a new criminal activity, well-respected and powerful family bosses may be asked to step in and resolve the conflict. Instead of a single national organization, informal patron-client relationships and kinship ties at the local level, and to a lesser extent at the national level, seem to make possible some coordination among gangsters when it is needed (Albini, 1971; Ianni, 1972; Conklin, 1973).

SUMMARY

In this chapter we have looked at the way that offenders seek suitable targets that are not protected by owners or bystanders. Opportunities for crime are a function of people's everyday behavior, according to this routine activities approach.

Criminals consider various aspects of potential targets for crime: the form and value of property, and the vulnerability of victims. Some victims are more prone to victimization than others because they have characteristics or occupy roles that make them especially vulnerable.

One aspect of the opportunity for crime is the relationship between offenders and victims. Murder, forcible rape, and aggravated assault usually arise out of interaction between people of the same race, but robbery is more often cross-racial. Murderers and their victims frequently have close social relationships prior to the crime; the same seems true of assaults. Rapists and their victims are often complete strangers, or have nonintimate social relationships with each other before the crime. Robbers and their victims are usually strangers, as are most thieves and their victims.

Sometimes a victim precipitates an offense, contributing to his or her own victimization. Homicide victims are often the first to use abusive language or force in an interaction that culminates in murder. Rape victims sometimes enter risky situations, although this does not absolve rapists of legal responsibility for their crimes. Owners of property precipitate crimes by leaving their property unguarded and vulnerable to theft.

Alcohol and drugs sometimes facilitate crime. There is an association between alcohol use and crime, with many offenders being drunk or under the influence of alcohol when they violate the law. Similarly, many offenders are under the influence of illegal drugs when they engage in crime. More research is needed to determine the precise manner in which drugs and alcohol are associated with the commission of crime.

In the United States, many offenses are committed with firearms. Guns seem to facilitate crimes such as murder and robbery. Assaults with firearms are more likely to produce death than are attacks with other weapons, and so the presence of a firearm seems to make murder a more likely outcome of an altercation. However, countries such as Switzerland and Israel have relatively low crime rates even though they have widespread ownership of firearms. The effects of gun-control laws on crime rates are unclear. Mandatory penalties are often not applied, and additional penalties for the use of a firearm in a serious crime do not seem to deter most offenders. The debate over the impact of gun-control laws continues. A majority of Americans favor stronger laws, but such restrictions are opposed by the well-financed and powerful National Rifle Association.

Many offenders do not plan their crimes far in advance, or even at all, but some engage in efforts to neutralize obstacles, maximize gain, and minimize risk. Most white-collar crimes involve elaborate planning, but conventional crimes can be either well planned or relatively spontaneous.

Professional thieves sometimes organize into gangs that allocate roles before committing crimes. These gangs often rely on outsiders such as tipsters, fences, fixers, and loan sharks. Organized crime families are highly structured at the local level, but seem to be only loosely organized at the national level. Some criminal activities are thus highly organized, but many offenses are carried out with little forethought by one or two offenders who do not plan their crimes much in advance.

IMPORTANT TERMS

argot	victim precipitation
routine activities approach	victim proneness

SUGGESTED READINGS

JAMES J. COLLINS, JR., ED. *Drinking and Crime: Perspectives on the Relationships between Alcohol Consumption and Criminal Behavior.* New York: Guilford, 1981. A collection of eight papers that review research on the link between alcohol use and crime.

JOHN E. CONKLIN. *Robbery and the Criminal Justice System.* Philadelphia: Lippincott, 1972. A study of robbery in Boston that examines the extent to which different kinds of robbers plan their crimes.

DENNIE F. PACE AND JIMMIE C. STYLES. *Organized Crime: Concepts and Controls,* 2nd ed. Englewood Cliffs, N.J.: Prentice-Hall, 1983. An up-to-date textbook on organized crime in the United States, including law-enforcement activity in response to it.

EDWIN H. SUTHERLAND. *The Professional Thief.* Chicago: University of Chicago Press, 1937. A classic examination of professional theft through the eyes of "Chic Conwell," a thief active in the earlier part of this century.

JAMES D. WRIGHT, PETER H. ROSSI, AND KATHLEEN DALY. *Under the Gun: Weapons, Crime, and Violence in America.* New York: Aldine, 1983. An authoritative examination of the relationship between firearms and crime, including an assessment of the pros and cons of gun-control laws.

12

Criminal Careers

A person who commits crimes repeatedly has a *criminal career.* A career has been defined as a "sequence of movements from one position to another in an occupational system made by an individual who works in the system" (Becker, 1973: 24). Criminal careers are not "occupations" as we commonly understand that term, but a sequence of crimes over time can be analyzed much like a career in a legitimate occupation, for both involve skills, tasks, and commitment over time (Letkemann, 1973; Gibbs and Shelly, 1982). As long ago as 1893 it was recognized that "correct statistics of offenders can be developed only by a study of the total life histories of individuals" (Otto Kobner, cited in Petersilia, Greenwood, and Lavin, 1977: 2–3). Another student of crime noted in 1917 that the proper study of crime requires an examination of "the manner in which criminality develops in the course of a human lifetime" (Georg Von Mayr, cited in Petersilia, Greenwood, and Lavin, 1977: 3).

Even though criminal careers are similar to legitimate careers in some ways, we must be alert to differences between them. Legitimate careers develop in stable contexts, such as within a corporation or a law firm. Criminal careers usually develop in less formal contexts; for instance, robbers' and burglars' careers develop outside a stable organizational context, even though gangsters have careers within the relatively stable setting of an organized crime "family." In addition, criminal careers often lack the well-defined sequence of stages and the pattern of upward mobility that are frequently characteristic of legitimate careers. Although some legitimate workers do not experience these changes during their career, and some offenders do gain in status over their lifetime, there is probably less upward mobility in deviant careers than in legitimate ones. Careers in crime are also less structured and perhaps more dependent on individual initiative in seeking out rewards than are legitimate careers. Moreover, criminal careers develop in secrecy from established authorities, whereas legitimate occupations often have the support of social institutions (Luckenbill and Best, 1981).

We can study criminal careers by examining the autobiographies of individual offenders. These accounts reveal much about the subjective states and actual experiences of offenders, although they may not be representative of all criminals. Another approach is to develop conceptual typologies, or categorizations, of criminal careers. Arrest statistics have also been used to study the careers of offenders, but because relatively few crimes lead to arrest, these data seem to tell us more about contacts with the criminal justice system

Charles Manson, convicted of the Tate-LaBianca murders in California, claimed to have killed thirty-five people. His long criminal record includes convictions for car theft, forgery, pimping, and many juvenile offenses.

than about actual involvement in criminal behavior (Petersilia, Greenwood, and Lavin, 1977).

Knowledge of criminal careers has practical value. If we know why offenders get involved in a life of crime, we may be able to implement policies that prevent criminal careers from developing. If we know why some career offenders "retire" from crime, we may be able to create programs that hasten their departure from crime. There is evidence that relatively few career criminals account for a large proportion of all of the crime that occurs. This suggests that the punishment and treatment of career offenders might have a significant impact on the crime rate. As we will see later, career criminal programs have been developed to concentrate the criminal justice system's resources on offenders who repeatedly commit serious crimes.

ANALYZING CRIMINAL CAREERS

The analysis of criminal careers requires attention to the social conditions that influence the development of patterns of crime. Labeling by the criminal justice system can affect an individual's life chances, and thus make criminal activity more or less likely. Criminal careers can be analyzed by looking at an individual's alternation between legitimate work and criminal activities. We also need to examine the way that people are recruited into criminal careers, and especially the way that involvement in juvenile delinquency is linked to adult criminal careers.

Career Contingencies

Criminal careers depend on various *contingencies,* or factors that determine movement from one criminal role to another, or from one crime to another (Becker, 1973). For instance, organized crime and lucrative offenses primarily involve males, even though sex-segregation in the underworld—and in the upperworld as well with white-collar crime—varies from one crime group to another. Women are at a disadvantage in being recruited into crime groups, in the criminal career paths that are available to them, and in their access to opportunities for learning criminal skills and gaining the rewards of crime. Gender-role socialization, differences in expectations for men and women, and patterns of parental surveillance of boys and girls also limit females' access to certain criminal careers (Hoffman-Bustamante, 1973; Steffensmeier, 1983).

Career contingencies include apprehension for violating the law. People who break the law, are arrested by the police, and are convicted in court may later engage in crime because of the social contacts they make while incarcerated. Experience with the criminal justice system may contribute to a criminal career by causing bitterness or by closing off job opportunities. However, offenders may also commit more crime if they are not arrested and convicted, because successful crimes can reinforce their law-violating behavior by providing them with rewards. Short-run rewards of peer prestige and money can create a "mobility trap" for juvenile delinquents, who gain immediate prestige and property at the cost of long-term upward mobility if they are expelled from school, are socially stigmatized, or become known to the police as offenders. The absence of legitimate opportunities for upward mobility can make a criminal career more appealing (Wiley, 1967).

The Labeling Perspective

The labeling perspective focuses on the development of deviant careers, including careers in crime. People who break rules repeatedly and are labeled deviant by others may organize their lives around deviant behavior. What begins as casual experimentation with rule breaking can become a deviant career, or "a whole sequential process in identity formation" (Rettig, Torres, and Garrett, 1977: 192).

Most people who break the law repeatedly are eventually arrested and convicted. As criminals say, "If you want to play, you have to pay," or "If you can't do the time, don't do the crime" (Silberman, 1978: 75–76). As we saw earlier in the book, the chance of avoiding arrest for any given crime is good, but the chance of never being arrested if one commits many crimes is small. Offenders who are more skilled may go longer without an arrest, but eventually they "take a fall."

The response by the criminal justice system to people who break the law creates a set of contingencies that can push some individuals into criminal careers. The criminal justice system seems to deal more harshly with some people than with others. For instance, the police react to suspects on the basis of the seriousness of the offense, the individual's demeanor, the complainant's preferences, and the requirements of the police department (Piliavin and Briar, 1964; Black, 1980). The arrest, conviction, and imprisonment of an individual may be more likely if he or she is seen as a member of a criminal subculture who is likely to continue to commit serious crimes, rather than perceived as someone who violated the law because of poor judgment or situational pressures (Cloward and Ohlin, 1960: 12). Reactions to defendants by the criminal justice system may be based on valid assumptions about the likelihood that different kinds of people will continue in a life of crime, but these reactions can also elicit patterned and persistent behavior. In other words, the label "criminal" can structure other people's responses to the offender; some people, for example, will refuse to hire an ex-convict. Responses of this sort can then act as contingencies that influence the development of a criminal career.

The "Zigzag Path": Criminal Careers and Legitimate Pursuits

Criminal careers vary considerably. One study of thieves found that most followed a "zigzag path" back and forth between criminal and noncriminal pursuits (Glaser, 1974). Offenders would commit crimes, go to prison, try to get a job when released, and often return to crime later. Contacts with other criminals and the difficulty of finding a good job often made a return to crime the "path of least resistance" (Rettig, Torres, and Garrett, 1977: 4). The effects of situational factors such as peer influence and financial need were mediated in part by the ex-convict's commitment to a criminal career or commitment to a legitimate career, but tempting situations sometimes drew even those who were committed to a conventional way of life back into crime. However, people who are committed to a conventional way of life apparently engage in less crime than people who are committed to a criminal career, even if they do not stay away from crime altogether (McAuliffe and Gordon, 1974).

Success at crime can lead to continued criminal activities, and success in legitimate pursuits can lead to a continuation of those activities. Once people have engaged in crime and escaped arrest, they may think that the risk of negative consequences from crime is small and that the rewards are great. Even if they are caught the first time, they may receive only a "slap on the wrist" in court and believe that the chance of a harsh sanction is small. Serious failure in either criminal activities or legitimate pursuits can lead people to shift to the other form of behavior. Thus, losing a job might push a person into crime, and being arrested might lead someone else to look for a legitimate job (Glaser, 1974).

Recruitment into a Criminal Career

Recruitment into a criminal career often begins during adolescence, with early delinquency often being a prerequisite for an adult career in theft and violence. While still in their teens, future career criminals learn skills and motives, what a criminal way of life involves, and how the police react to different crimes (Letkemann, 1973). Access to criminal careers seems to be greater in communities where there are close ties between adolescents and adult criminals who can act as role models and communicate to the adolescents the values and skills necessary to crime. Access to criminal careers is also greater where there are stable relationships between people with conventional values and people with criminal values (Cloward and Ohlin, 1960). In such communities, a delinquent subculture is more likely to develop, and involvement in this subculture increases the likelihood of entry into adult criminal careers.

Adult offenders must also learn criminal skills and motives. For instance, to move from various forms of hustling into a specialty as a professional fence, one career criminal had to acquire considerable knowledge about merchandise, including what he should pay for it and how much he could sell it for. This fence also needed "ability, energy, ingenuity, and certain persuasive skills," as well as a willingness to deceive both the buying public and the thieves who sold to him (Klockars, 1974: 177). To become a buyer of stolen goods required a modest amount of capital, skills about how to purchase goods, opportunities to buy goods for less than their retail price, a regular source of supply, a predictable demand for goods, and the ability to avoid arrest and imprisonment. The fence also needed a convincing front that would keep the police away but still attract customers looking for low prices.

Career criminals are recruited from various settings. Sutherland (1937) found that professional thieves had rarely been amateur thieves in slum areas, but instead came from legitimate occupations and severed their ties to the legitimate world after a period of unemployment. They spent time in bars and hotels where professional thieves gathered. Bartenders, taxi drivers, bellhops, waiters, and prostitutes who worked in "proximity to the social universe of the professional" sometimes entered a life of crime by taking tangential roles in the commission of crime (Inciardi, 1975: 60). Often they began by playing a small part in one crime, and were called on later for more important roles in other offenses, gradually acquiring the skills and status of professional thief. Others became career criminals by applying specific job skills to crime; for example, a printer might become a counterfeiter, or a locksmith might become a safecracker.

Typologies of Criminal Careers

One way to analyze criminal careers is to construct a typology of offenders and their patterns of criminal activity. A typology is developed from criteria that a criminologist thinks are important in distinguishing one criminal career from another. Such a typology assumes that there is some specialization among offenders in the kinds of crime they commit.

GIBBONS'S TYPOLOGY OF CRIMINAL ROLE CAREERS

Don C. Gibbons (1982) has developed an influential typology of "criminal role careers," which are patterns or sequences of criminal behavior and related social situations. He suggests that a good typology will describe real offenders accurately and will be comprehensive. With such a typology, criminologists can develop specific theories that explain each criminal role career. A typology can also be used to develop treatment methods for various kinds of offenders.

Gibbons's typology is not a logically exhaustive set of criminal career types. Instead, he selects several dimensions that he thinks are important aspects of criminal careers and then describes a set of criminal role careers in terms of those characteristics. The dimensions that he examines are the offense itself, the interactional setting of the behavior (alone or with others), the offender's self-concept and attitudes, and the pattern of crime over the offender's lifetime. Gibbons also looks at the offender's class background, family background, peer-group associations, and contacts with law-enforcement agencies. From these dimensions, he derives the following types of criminal role careers:

1. Professional thieves
2. Professional "heavy" criminals
3. Semiprofessional property offenders
4. Naive check forgers
5. Automobile thieves—"joyriders"
6. Property offenders, "one-time losers"
7. Embezzlers
8. White-collar criminals
9. Professional "fringe violators"
10. Personal offenders, "one-time losers"
11. Psychopathic assaultists
12. Statutory rapists
13. Aggressive rapists
14. Violent sex offenders
15. Nonviolent sex offenders
16. Incest offenders
17. Male homosexuals
18. Opiate addicts
19. Skid Row alcoholics
20. Amateur shoplifters (Gibbons, 1982: 225).

Critique of Gibbons's typology This typology has several problems. Gibbons does not indicate why he selected these career types and not others. For instance, there is empirical evidence for distinguishing between two types of opiate addicts: "hard-core addicts" who get high on heroin nearly every day and usually commit crime to support their habits, and "weekenders" who get high on heroin only a few times a week (although they use heroin daily) and are less often involved in crime (other than the offenses of purchasing and possessing heroin) (McAuliffe and Gordon, 1974). Gibbons's typology would be more accurate if he replaced his "opiate addict" career criminal with these two kinds of addicts.

Gibbons's decisions about what constitutes a criminal role career sometimes seem to be based more on intuition than on empirical evidence. For example, research indicates that some offenders consciously choose between robbery and burglary as specialties, but that other thieves switch back and forth between these offenses (Conklin, 1972: 87–88). Gibbons includes robbers and burglars in the professional heavy criminal category and also in the semiprofessional property criminal group; it might be more accurate to create six distinct types: professional and semiprofessional robbers, professional and semiprofessional burglars, and professional and semiprofessional thieves who engage in various property offenses. Any typology will include certain assumptions about what factors are critical in distinguishing one criminal career from another, but those assumptions should be as consistent with the empirical evidence as possible.

Gibbons's typology is not really a typology of criminal careers, if the term "career" means the development of criminal behavior over time in a patterned way. He does not stress the cumulative nature of criminal behavior, offenders' deepening involvement in crime, or the way that experiences at one time lead to later career developments. In other words, his typology has a static quality, whereas criminal careers by definition evolve dynamically over time.

Another problem with Gibbons's typology is that some of the criminal role careers that he identifies are careers in only the most limited sense of the term. There is a problem in speaking of an embezzler role career, because few embezzlers are involved in crime over time. Likewise, statutory rape—sexual intercourse with a female under the legal age of consent—is probably not the basis of a criminal role career very often; few men seem to have a long-term commitment to engaging in intercourse with young women. Incest is probably not the basis of a criminal career very often either; it may be a repeated offense, but it is usually with the same partner and is likely to cease after the offender is caught.

Gibbons states that comprehensiveness is a criterion of a good typology, but he also acknowledges that many offenders cannot be categorized easily. A study by Hartjen and Gibbons (1969) assessed the usefulness of an earlier version of Gibbons's typology by trying to classify 655 offenders who were on probation. Using three probation officers to classify the offenders, Hartjen and Gibbons concluded that only 48 per cent of the probationers could be fitted into one of the twenty-six career types they used. In only 22 per cent of the cases did all three probation officers agree on how to classify offenders. Of the 312 offenders who were assigned to a career type by either two or three of the probation officers, 60.8 per cent of them fell into four categories and all of them fell into seventeen of the career types. Hartjen and Gibbons concluded that the typology they used included some dramatic but relatively rare criminal career types. They suggested a revision of the typology to include more mundane offenses, such as nonsupport of dependents and traffic violations, but Gibbons's (1982) most recent typology does not include these career types.

Typologies of criminal careers can be useful, but they must be based on empirical evidence on patterns or sequences of crimes. There is evidence that many offenders are versatile in their selection of crimes, and typologies usually emphasize specialization. The proportion of all crimes that can be accounted for by career criminals who specialize in one kind of offense is thus smaller than is implied by typologies such as Gibbons's.

CHAIKEN AND CHAIKEN'S TYPOLOGY OF OFFENDER TYPES

Another potentially fruitful approach to the development of typologies is to categorize people by the specific combinations of offenses that they commit over time. A survey of nearly 2,200 adult male inmates in three states identified ten types of offenders by the combination of offenses they had committed. Chaiken and Chaiken (1982a, 1982b, 1983, 1984) found that these ten types differed in their rates of committing crime, their persistence in crime, and their personal characteristics. Table 12.1 shows these ten offender types and the kinds of crimes they committed.

Chaiken and Chaiken gave the most attention to the first type of offender, the violent predatory offender. This offender engages in robbery, assault, and drug dealing, and sometimes in burglary and other kinds of theft. The violent predatory offender commits a disproportionate amount of all of the crime committed by inmates, is usually quite young, has been arrested frequently, began to commit crime at an early age, rarely has any family obligations, and has an irregular employment record. Violent predatory offenders are difficult to identify from official records, because they are young and the juvenile

Table 12.1: Ten Offender Types by Combinations of Offenses Committed

GROUP	ROBBERY	ASSAULT[a]	BURGLARY	THEFT,[b] FRAUD, FORGERY, CREDIT CARD CRIMES	DRUG DEALS	PERCENT OF STUDY SAMPLE[c]
Violent predators (robber-assaulter-dealers)	+	+	?	?	+	15
Robber-assaulters	+	+	?	?	0	8
Robber-dealers	+	0	?	?	+	9
Low-level robbers	+	0	?	?	0	12
Mere assaulters	0	+	0	0	0	5
Burglar-dealers	0	??	+	?	+	10
Low-level burglars	0	0	+	?	0	8
Property and drug offenders	0	??	0	+	+	6
Low-level property offenders	0	0	0	+	0	8
Drug dealers	0	0	0	0	+	6

Note: + = Group member commits this crime, by definition.
0 = Group member does not commit this crime, by definition.
? = Group member may or may not commit this crime. Analysis shows that nearly all members of the group do.
?? = Group member may or may not commit this crime. Most don't.

[a] Assault includes homicide arising out of assault or robbery.
[b] Theft includes auto theft.
[c] Percentages add to 87%. The remaining 13% did not report committing any of the crimes studied. Some serious crimes (e.g., rape, kidnap) were not included in the self-report survey. Respondents with missing data (150 out of 2190) were excluded in calculation of percentages.

SOURCE: Marcia R. Chaiken and Jan M. Chaiken, "Offender Types and Public Policy," *Crime and Delinquency,* Vol. 30, No. 2 (April 1984), p. 198. Copyright © 1984 by Sage Publications, Inc. Reprinted by permission of Sage Publications, Inc.

records that would indicate their heavy involvement in criminal activity are unavailable for use by researchers, probation officers, prosecutors, and judges.

DELINQUENT CAREERS

One way to examine criminal careers is to look at lifetime patterns of delinquency and crime for a sample of individuals born in the same year. A cohort study of this sort was conducted by Wolfgang, Figlio, and Sellin (1972) in a project described in Chapter 2. They used school records, police and court records, and draft board records to study 9,945 males who were born in 1945 and lived in Philadelphia from their tenth through their eighteenth birthdays. The design of this study made it possible to examine past contacts with the juvenile justice system, but did not allow the researchers to question individuals and administer self-report questionnaires to learn about offenses that never came to the attention of the police and the courts.

Chronic Offenders

Wolfgang, Figlio, and Sellin found that a relatively small proportion of the boys in the cohort accounted for a large proportion of all of the cohort's contacts with the police that resulted in written reports. Table 12.2 shows the proportion of the cohort that had no contact with the police (nondelinquents), the proportion that had one contact (one-time offenders), the proportion with two to four contacts (nonchronic offenders), and the proportion with five or more contacts (chronic offenders). Only 6.3 per cent of the 9,945 boys were chronic offenders, but this group accounted for 51.9 per cent of all of the cohort's contacts with the police. The nonchronic group accounted for 12.4 per cent of the cohort, but 32.3 per cent of all police contacts. If the nonchronic and chronic groups are combined into a category of "career delinquents"—that is, those with more than one police contact as a juvenile—we find that the 18.7 per cent of the cohort classified as career delinquents accounted for 84.2 per cent of all police contacts for the cohort. There is thus a high concentration of police contacts among a relatively small proportion of the cohort.

A more recent cohort study in Racine, Wisconsin, looked at the police contacts of both juveniles and young adults and found a similar concentration of police contacts among a small percentage of three different cohorts. Between 5 and 7 per cent of the people in each cohort accounted for more than half of all nontraffic contacts with the police, and about 20 per cent of each cohort accounted for 80 per cent of all nontraffic police contacts in the cohort. Moreover, 8 to 14 per cent of each cohort accounted for all of the felony arrests in the cohort (Shannon, 1982: 3).

Patterns of Delinquent Careers

Wolfgang, Figlio, and Sellin examined several issues related to delinquent careers. They discovered that boys who had one contact with the police and then had no more contacts usually had engaged in relatively trivial offenses the first time. However, boys with at least two police contacts were more likely to have been stopped the first time for a relatively serious offense that involved injury, theft, or damage.

Table 12.2:   Police Contacts among Members of a Cohort

TYPE OF OFFENDER	PERCENTAGE OF COHORT	PERCENTAGE OF ALL OF COHORT'S POLICE CONTACTS
Nondelinquents	65.1	0
One-time offenders	16.2	15.8
Nonchronic offenders	12.4	32.3
Chronic offenders	6.3	51.9

SOURCE: Marvin E. Wolfgang, Robert M. Figlio, and Thorsten Sellin, *Delinquency in Birth Cohort.* Chicago: University of Chicago Press, 1972, p. 89. Reprinted by permission of the University of Chicago Press. Copyright University of Chicago Press © 1972. (Adapted)

Of the boys with at least one police contact, 53.6 per cent were stopped a second time. Of those stopped a second time, 65.1 per cent went on to a third contact with the police, and of those with three or more contacts, the chances of being stopped an additional time ranged from 70 to 80 per cent. In other words, the likelihood of never again being stopped by the police for delinquency is greatest after the first contact with the police; after a second contact, the chance of continuing in a delinquent career is greater. Another study found even higher "transition probabilities" among a sample of 1,591 adults arrested for violent crimes; the chance of being arrested again after any given arrest was about 80 per cent, whatever the individual's prior arrest history (Miller, Dinitz, and Conrad, 1982).

In the Philadelphia cohort study, juveniles who were first stopped by the police at a very young age were more likely to have another police contact than were juveniles whose first contact with the police came at a later age. Early age at first contact also seems to be associated with a long career in crime and delinquency, a rapid development of that career, and involvement in serious offenses (Peterson and Braiker, 1981; Miller, Dinitz, and Conrad, 1982). Early contact with the police may indicate a serious behavioral problem that is conducive to a criminal career, or early contact with the police may subject individuals to a labeling experience in juvenile court that closes off legitimate opportunities, breaks conventional bonds, and pushes people into lives of crime.

There was no apparent relationship between the type of offense for which a juvenile was stopped by the police and the number of contacts the juvenile had with the police, contrary to an expectation that offenders would specialize over their delinquent careers. There was a slight tendency for boys to be stopped for the same type of offense, but except for theft crimes this tendency was weak. If police contacts reflect actual behavior, it seems that delinquents begin anew each time they commit a delinquent act. A more recent study also found no clear offense patterns among delinquent youths (Lab, 1984).

The Philadelphia cohort study found that the time between police contacts became compressed over the course of an individual's delinquent career. The average time from first contact to second contact was sixteen to eighteen months. However, the average time from second contact to third contact was only ten months, and the average time from the third to the fourth contact was only eight months. The interval continued to decrease with additional police contacts, so that the average time between contacts after the twelfth one was only about three months. A similar compression of arrests as the criminal record lengthens has been found for adult offenders (Miller, Dinitz, and Conrad, 1982). It is unclear whether this compression results from increased criminal or delinquent activity once a career begins, or whether it occurs because the police are more likely to arrest people they consider to be troublemakers because of their past contacts with the police.

Juvenile Delinquency and Adult Criminal Careers

Wolfgang and his colleagues (1974) have recorded police contacts up to the age of twenty-six for a sample of 567 members of the original Philadelphia cohort of boys. The probability of being stopped by the police before eighteen was .35; that is, thirty-five of every 100 males in the original cohort had contact with the police as a juvenile. The probability of any police contact from age ten to age twenty-six was .43, and 23 per cent of the adults in the sample of 567 had a police contact between eighteen and twenty-six.

The likelihood of police contact as an adult for a person who had been stopped by the police as a juvenile was .44, but the probability of contact as an adult if a person had not been stopped as a juvenile was only .12. Thus, a male with a juvenile record was nearly four times as likely as a male without a juvenile record to have a police contact as an adult. Even though males who had been stopped by the police as juveniles were much more likely to have trouble with the police as adults than were males who had not been stopped as juveniles, it is also true that many people who had had contact with the police as juveniles did not go on to have trouble with the police as adults.

It is not too surprising that many juvenile offenders do not go on to commit crimes as adults, because often their delinquent acts would not be crimes if committed by adults. There is no reason to expect that a fifteen-year-old boy apprehended for underage drinking or skipping school will commit robbery or burglary as an adult, or even as an adolescent. Researchers have found weak or nonexistent relationships between such status offenses and serious acts of delinquency (LeBlanc and Biron, 1980; Rojek and Erickson, 1981–82, 1982; Kelley, 1983). Because juvenile delinquency includes status offenses as well as acts that would be crimes if committed by adults, juvenile delinquents cannot simply be seen as criminals who happen to be under the age at which people are legally treated as adults.

Even juvenile delinquents who do commit serious crimes often realize that when they become adults, the chance of a harsh punishment increases greatly. They may be aware that their juvenile record is secret and that they start

A Cross-Cultural Perspective: Juvenile Delinquency and Adult Crime in England

An English cohort study that examined delinquent and criminal careers began with 411 boys who were eight and nine years old in 1961. Sixty-one per cent of the boys who were later convicted of delinquent acts were eventually convicted of crimes as adults, but only 13 per cent of the boys who were not found delinquent went on to be convicted as adults. Some adult criminals had avoided any contact with the law as adolescents; in fact, nearly one-fourth of the adults who had two or more convictions had never been found delinquent. Boys who were convicted of delinquent acts at the earliest ages were the most likely to become persistent adult offenders.

There was little specialization by type of offense by the age of twenty-one, although there was some continuity in aggressive behavior over time. Each of the following factors enhanced the likelihood that a boy would be arrested and convicted: low family income, large family size, criminal parents, poor child-rearing, and low IQ level. Parents who had been convicted of crimes tended to have children who were also convicted of criminal and delinquent acts, but there was no evidence that the parents taught their children to violate the law or encouraged them to do so. Instead, criminal parents seemed to be poor at supervising their children, sometimes because of their own imprisonment, and therefore they were less likely to be "psychologically present" when their children found themselves in situations in which they were tempted to violate the law. There may also have been some police bias against children whose parents were known criminals, with the police being more likely to arrest rather than to warn those children if they were caught violating the law.

SOURCE: Based on David P. Farrington, "Longitudinal Research on Crime and Delinquency," in Norval Morris and Michael Tonry, eds., *Crime and Justice: An Annual Review of Research*, Vol. 1. Chicago: University of Chicago Press, 1979, pp. 289–348.

with a clean slate when they reach adulthood. These considerations lead some juvenile offenders to avoid breaking the law when they become adults. Other juvenile offenders settle down when they become adults, taking full-time jobs, getting married, and having children. These changes take them away from the street life and gangs that are conducive to criminal activities and reduce their motivation to engage in crime.

There is, nevertheless, a relationship between juvenile delinquency and adult criminal careers, both in the United States and in England (see the Cross-Cultural Perspective). Some attribute this relationship less to the continuity of behavior over time than to the effects of the juvenile and criminal justice systems on young people (Wolfgang, Figlio, and Sellin, 1972; Shannon, 1982). This view focuses on the labeling of juveniles as an important factor in the development of adult criminal careers, and often leads to support for a strategy of *radical nonintervention* (Schur, 1973; Shannon, 1982). A radical nonintervention policy would minimize official reaction to delinquency in an effort to prevent the labeling of adolescents that could drive them into criminal careers. Another view is that adolescent offenders who represent the most serious threats to society are the most likely to be labeled delinquent, and it is they who are also the most likely to go on to engage in crime as adults. In other words, some delinquents will become adult offenders even without official intervention when they are young. To date, researchers have not provided persuasive evidence of whether the relationship between juvenile delinquency and adult criminal careers is a result of labeling, a result of continuity of behavior over time, or some combination of the two.

ADULT CRIMINAL CAREERS

One way to look at criminal careers is to examine the lifetime criminal and noncriminal experiences of one kind of offender. Petersilia, Greenwood, and Lavin (1977) used this approach to study forty-nine men who were serving sentences in a California prison for armed robbery and who had been in prison at least once before. They used self-reports of criminal activity as well as official data on arrests and convictions to trace the careers of these habitual offenders.

Career Patterns

The armed robbers had been incarcerated an average of half of their criminal careers, and they averaged about twenty years from first self-reported offense until current incarceration. Collectively, the forty-nine robbers reported 10,505 offenses over their careers, an average of 214 per offender. They had moved from crimes such as auto theft and burglary when they were juveniles to more serious offenses such as robbery when they became adults. The average age at first arrest was fifteen, but 29 per cent had begun significant criminal activity by twelve, 75 per cent had started by fifteen, and 90 per cent had started by eighteen. Over their careers, the average amount stolen in a crime was about $250, but their average annual income from crime was only a few thousand dollars.

There was no strong tendency toward crime specialization among these offenders; they often switched from one offense to another. They would continue one kind of crime as long as it proved successful and as long as they could find opportunities. Other studies support this finding of little specialization by type of crime (Gould et al., 1966; Blumstein and Cohen, 1980; Petersilia, 1980; Peterson and Braiker, 1981; Rojek and Erickson, 1982). One study of thieves involved in commercial burglary and truck hijacking found considerable versatility in the choice of crimes (Gibbs and Shelly, 1982). A study of 1,591 offenders chosen because they had been arrested for a serious violent crime found that 93 per cent of them showed "no discernible pattern of violence" in their arrest histories; few habitually violent offenders were found in the sample (Miller, Dinitz, and Conrad, 1982: 59).

The armed robbers were more likely to be arrested for any given crime as adults than they were as juveniles; arrest rates were calculated in terms of number of arrests per self-reported crime. Why they became less successful in avoiding arrest as their criminal careers progressed is not clear. Few of them believed that they were watched more carefully by the police because of their prior record. They may have become more careless over time, perhaps because their long experience in crime had made them overly confident.

These armed robbers continued to commit crimes after their earlier releases from prison because they had difficulty getting good jobs, lacked financial resources, and continued to interact with other offenders. A criminal record can be an impediment to securing a good job, but even more important may be an offender's lack of job skills and experience. The jobs that these career criminals found were often low-paying, menial jobs with little or no opportunity for advancement. Those ex-convicts who managed to get good jobs did have lower offense rates than the ex-convicts who found poor-paying jobs or no jobs at all.

Planning Crimes

Relatively few of the armed robbers did much planning of their crimes. One-fourth did no planning or preparation at all, about half did very little planning, and one-fourth planned their crimes to some extent. Planning was more common when the offenders were young adults or adults than when they were juveniles, but even planning of crimes by adults was quite limited. Offenders typically included in what plans they did make the location of the crime, the presence of police patrols, when money would be present, whether there was an alarm on the premises, where a getaway car would be stolen, what disguise (if any) to wear, and how to escape from the scene of the crime. Many offenders said that they made few detailed plans, and some said that they did not think about their crimes in advance. Offenders seemed to distinguish between planning and premeditation, the latter including mental preparation for the crime and thinking about how they would overcome any obstacles they encountered.

As the habitual armed robbers got older, they increasingly operated by themselves. This allowed them to keep the profits of their crimes for themselves and reduced the risk that a partner would be arrested and cooperate with the police. Some offenders used fences or drug dealers to meet certain needs, but in general there was a decline in reliance on others over time.

Use of the Stolen Money

While the armed robbers were juveniles, their crimes tended to fulfill expressive needs, such as peer approval, revenge, hostility, excitement, and a sense of being grown up. Over the course of their criminal careers, financial needs

Table 12.3: Use of Money Gained from Crimes

USE	JUVENILE PERIOD	YOUNG ADULT PERIOD	ADULT PERIOD
High living	58.8%	37.2%	33.3%
Drugs and drinking	11.8%	30.2%	23.8%
Self-support	11.8%	16.3%	21.4%
Family support	2.9%	9.3%	16.7%
Debts	2.9%	2.3%	2.4%
Other	11.8%	4.6%	2.4%
Number of offenders	34	43	42

SOURCE: Adapted from Joan Petersilia, Peter W. Greenwood, and Marvin Lavin, *Criminal Careers of Habitual Felons.* Santa Monica, Calif.: Rand, 1977, p. 77. Reprinted with permission.

became relatively more important. The increased importance of financial needs suggests that economic assistance or a job that pays well might draw some older criminals away from crime and into a conventional way of life. We can see from Table 12.3 that the armed robbers increasingly used their money to support themselves and their families as they grew older, and that they used the proceeds of their crimes less for "high living." However, Table 12.3 also indicates that adult offenders were more likely than they were as juveniles to spend the fruits of their crimes on drugs and alcohol. In general, the careers of the armed robbers interviewed in this study began early in life, often between the ages of fourteen and seventeen, and for expressive reasons, with instrumental reasons becoming more important over time (Petersilia, 1980).

In a survey of 624 male California inmates who were serving time for felonies, the researchers discovered that 47 per cent reported that economic distress was an important reason for their crimes; offenders who cited this reason reported fewer violent offenses than did inmates who said that they had other motivations for their crimes (Peterson and Braiker, 1981). Thirty-five per cent of the felons reported that their desire for high living and high times motivated them to commit crime; these offenders reported the most frequent commission of offenses. Finally, 14 per cent of the inmates reported that temper was an important reason for their crimes, which were frequently violent. These three motivations for crime—economic distress, a desire for high living and high times, and temper—were found to be statistically unrelated to each other. Table 12.4 shows the specific reasons that the 624 felons cited for committing their crimes.

Intensive and Intermittent Career Criminals

Petersilia, Greenwood, and Lavin's research on armed robbers led them to distinguish between two kinds of career criminals: intensives and intermittents. *Intensive offenders* engage in criminal activity that begins at an early age and is sustained over time, consciously planned, persistent, skilled, and frequent. In contrast, *intermittent offenders* engage in irregular and opportunistic crimes with low payoffs and great risks, and do not think of themselves as professional criminals. Intensive criminals see themselves as career criminals, have a specific goal for their crimes (such as supporting high living or a drug habit), and try to avoid arrest but do little planning of their crimes. Compared to the intermittent offender, the intensive criminal steals more money in each

Table 12.4:   Self-Reported Reasons for Committing Crimes, Percentages

REASON	IMPORTANT	UNIMPORTANT
To get money for rent, food, self-support	65	35
To get money for good times and high living	52	48
Good opportunity	51	50
Because of drugs or alcohol	47	53
Couldn't get a job	47	54
Losing a job	46	54
To get money for drugs	41	58
Trouble with wife or girlfriend	35	65
Heavy debts	30	69
Excitement and kicks	25	75
Blew up or lost his cool	24	75
Friends' ideas	23	77
Revenge or anger	21	78
Just felt nervous and tense	19	81
Gang involvement	8	92

Note: Some rows do not add to 100 per cent because of rounding.

SOURCE: Adapted from Mark A. Peterson and Harriet B. Braiker, with Suzanne M. Polich, *Who Commits Crimes: A Survey of Prison Inmates.* Boston: Oelgeschlager, Gunn & Hain, 1981, p. 94. Reprinted with permission.

crime and is more likely to injure the victim. Intensives commit relatively serious crimes and engage in crime often, admitting to an average of fifty-one crimes per year, compared to an average of only five self-reported offenses per year for intermittent offenders (Petersilia, Greenwood, and Lavin, 1977).

A survey of 624 male felons in California prisons estimated that the average incoming prisoner had committed about fourteen serious crimes per year during the three years prior to his incarceration. However, this average conceals the fact that most inmates had committed few offenses, and a small number had committed many. More than half of the inmates had committed fewer than three offenses per year while on the street, but the most criminally active of the inmates accounted for more than sixty serious offenses per year (Peterson and Braiker, 1981). Another study that showed the disproportionately large number of crimes accounted for by intensive offenders found that 6 per cent of all suspects arrested in Manhattan for robbery, assault, burglary, and rape in 1979 were responsible for nearly one-third of all crimes of that sort reported in that year. These intensive offenders averaged thirteen prior arrests and committed an average of thirty-four crimes per year (*The New York Times,* April 9, 1981). In Chapter 15, we will see that this high rate of crime by intensive offenders has been the basis of programs that focus the criminal justice system's resources on the apprehension, conviction, and imprisonment of career criminals.

LEAVING A LIFE OF CRIME

In Chapter 6, we saw that the rate of arrest for index offenses declines with age; for instance, in 1983, only 9.3 per cent of all suspects arrested for index crimes were over the age of forty. We will see later that there is considerable evidence that programs to rehabilitate offenders have been, for the most part, ineffective. If rehabilitation programs cannot account for the small number of arrests of older people, what does? One possibility is that criminals "exit" or "retire" from criminal careers as they get older for reasons that have little to do with treatment programs.

The idea that criminals "burn out" or "mature out" of crime comes from studies of narcotics addicts. Heroin addicts are often young, and samples of addicts rarely include many older addicts. The absence of older heroin addicts cannot be accounted for solely by overdose deaths. Some addicts apparently stop using opiates, either on their own or as a result of an effective drug treatment program. Addicts who join such programs may already be "burned out" physically and mentally by the burdens of maintaining a habit and may thus be ready to stop using addictive drugs.

Exiting can be defined as a successful disengagement from a previous pattern of criminal behavior. If a criminal career is seen as a "zigzag path" or alternation between criminal and noncriminal activities, we then need to ask what conditions or contingencies promote the change from criminal activities to noncriminal pursuits (Meisenhelder, 1977; Shover, 1983). Offenders may grow tired of the "hassles" of continued involvement with the criminal justice system. Habitual offender laws, which provide longer sentences for people convicted of a third or a fourth felony, may lead some career criminals to reconsider their commitment to a life of crime; the application of these laws sometimes takes offenders out of circulation and thus interrupts or ends a criminal career. Inmates sometimes compare their likely future with the older inmates they observe, and develop a fear of dying in prison. Offenders may undergo a change in identity, and come to see themselves as different from what they were when young. The realization that a life of crime is a "dead end," and that crime nets them little in the long run, may accompany this changed view of self. Offenders sometimes scale down their material aspirations and develop a stronger interest in a settled and conventional way of life. Changes such as these may cause offenders to try less risky crimes, lead them to reduce the frequency with which they commit offenses, or push them out of a life of crime altogether (Meisenhelder, 1977; Shover, 1983).

Reasons for Leaving a Career as a Professional Thief

Evidence from biographical and autobiographical accounts of professional thieves suggests various motives for leaving a life of crime. Thieves may give up crime they violate the code of the criminal subculture and are ostracized by other thieves; if they become inefficient as a result of increasing age, fear, narcotics, or alcohol; if they can no longer find other thieves to work with them; if they cannot guarantee themselves immunity from conviction and incarceration because they have lost the trust of a fixer or the police; or in rare cases if they make a "big score" (Sutherland, 1937: 24–25). Thieves may also leave a criminal career if a long prison term shocks them into reforming, if they take a legitimate job, or if they marry into the legitimate world (Inciardi, 1975: 73–74; Shover, 1983). Over time, thieves may see that the financial rewards of a legitimate job actually outweigh the financial rewards of crime, for few thieves ever make much money from crime (Krohm, 1973; Petersilia, Greenwood, and Lavin, 1977: 71; Silberman, 1978: 68).

Whatever their reasons for retiring from crime, professional thieves who do so of their own volition and who still retain their skills at theft may be seen as "retired" professional thieves rather than as new members of the conventional world (Sutherland, 1937). Thieves who leave criminal careers may not regret their past behavior, and may reflect with nostalgia on the excitement and the scores of the past. They may retain a "latent criminal identity," an affinity for others who are involved in crime (Irwin, 1970: 202). They may never fully break their bonds with criminals and may never become fully integrated into the conventional world. In a sense, exiting or retiring from crime can be seen as a change in criminal identity from a manifest to a latent form.

Reasons for Leaving a Career as a Drug Dealer or Smuggler

An in-depth study of upper-level drug dealers and smugglers, most of whom trafficked in marijuana and cocaine, found that about 90 per cent of those who were observed and interviewed had decided to get out of the business (Adler and Adler, 1983). Early in their criminal careers, they had seen their drug dealing as temporary. As they grew aware of the restrictions and sacrifices imposed by a deviant career, and as they tired of life as a fugitive, they decided to abandon this career. What had once been a novel form of activity had become routine, exhausting, dangerous, and isolating. However, they were bound to their careers as dealers and smugglers by the rewards of money, drugs, and sex; by their commitment to a deviant career; and by the difficulty of finding another way to earn a good income. As a consequence, dealers and smugglers oscillated between a deviant career and a legitimate way of life, often for years after they had decided to leave the deviant career. They moved out of dealing and smuggling temporarily, and then back into the drug business, a process described as "phaseout and re-entries" (Adler and Adler, 1983: 201). They found it hard to stay out of the drug underworld because they were unable or unwilling to reduce their drug use and change their extravagant life style, and so their "exits" were usually temporary rather than permanent.

Exiting and Theories of Crime Causation

The theories of crime causation we examined in earlier chapters suggest why some offenders may leave a life of crime. A complete theory of criminal behavior should be able to explain why some people break the law and others do not, and also why some people who engage in crime eventually disengage from a criminal career (Frazier, 1976). Here we will look at some of the implications of different criminological theories for the process of exiting.

DIFFERENTIAL ASSOCIATION THEORY

Differential association theory would explain exiting by a change in a career criminal's ratio of definitions favorable to violation of the law over definitions unfavorable to violation of the law. In other words, just before leaving a criminal career, an offender should interact more with others who provide definitions that are not favorable to continued criminal activity, or should interact less with people who are sources of definitions favorable to violation of the law.

There is no research that directly supports or refutes this explanation of exiting. However, this explanation is questionable, because many offenders probably decide to leave a criminal career while in prison, where their exposure to definitions favorable to violation of the law is great and where they are isolated from definitions unfavorable to violation of the law. Some inmates might decide to exit because they are exposed to law-abiding values held by a correctional officer, a social worker, a visiting family member, or even another inmate who decides to go straight.

Another problem with using differential association theory to explain exiting is that Sutherland proposed that associations are more important if they occur early in life (the priority factor); this would suggest that an older career criminal would require very intense and frequent exposure to definitions unfavorable to violation of the law to change the ratio of definitions in a way that would lead to exiting. In a few cases, this might occur through religious conversion.

THE LABELING PERSPECTIVE

The labeling perspective offers a better explanation of why career criminals continue to commit crime than of why some of them abandon a life of crime. As criminal careers develop, the label "criminal" or "ex-convict" is more firmly affixed by the criminal justice system and the public. A criminal record, sometimes even an acquittal, signifies to the rest of the world a continuing intention to do social harm (Schwartz and Skolnick, 1962; Stebbins, 1971). There is little reason to change that label as long as an individual is involved in crime, and thus we would not expect a change in the label to precede the abandonment of a criminal career. Even an offender who decides to terminate a life of crime faces continued labeling as an ex-convict and closed-off job opportunities and social contacts. More positive support from the criminal justice system and from people with whom the ex-convict interacts would make exiting easier.

Exiting sometimes involves deviance-disavowal by an offender or the relabeling of an offender by others (Frazier, 1976; Meisenhelder, 1977). Relabeling may take the form of *certification,* the social verification by the criminal justice system or by conventional people that an offender is rehabilitated. Certification can ease the transition from a criminal career to membership in the conventional social world (Meisenhelder, 1977).

The labeling perspective also bears on exiting to the extent that it helps us to understand why offenders do not leave criminal careers. Offenders can avoid certain costs or penalties associated with the abandonment of a criminal career by maintaining a deviant identity. Leaving a career in crime often means awkward interaction with others about aspects of an earlier life in crime; this may include direct insults and embarrassment. Fear of these social consequences can make exiting unpleasant and anxiety-provoking, and keep some offenders in a criminal career (Stebbins, 1971).

ANOMIE AND DIFFERENTIAL OPPORTUNITY THEORY

Theories that focus on anomie and differential opportunity would suggest that exiting is caused either by increased access to legitimate means to reach socially approved goals, or by reduced aspirations. There is some evidence that changes in aspirations are associated with the decision to abandon a criminal career (Shover, 1983). Research indicates that securing a job that holds promise for career advancement may be important to exiting, but this evidence fits as well or better with control theory as it does with anomie or differential opportunity theory, because it seems that the bond to the conventional order offered by a job is more important than the income produced by the job (Meisenhelder, 1977; Shover, 1983).

CONTROL THEORY

Control theory would propose that a career criminal "retires" when he or she forms bonds or attachments to conventional people, institutions, and ways of behavior. Just as adolescents who lack ties to family, school, peers, or a job are the most likely to become delinquents, so older offenders may be more likely to move out of crime when they form such attachments.

Control theory probably offers the most convincing explanation of the process of exiting. Exiting usually seems to require the acquisition of meaningful bonds to the conventional social order, the opposite process to the one that control theory describes as giving rise to delinquency. Thieves leave a life of crime as they form attachments to a life of conformity and develop a reluctance to give up those new bonds by risking further imprisonment. One important tie to the conventional order is a job that seems to have the potential for advancement and that is seen as meaningful and economically rewarding. A good job shifts a criminal's attention from the present to the future, and provides a solid basis for the construction of a noncriminal identity. It also alters an individual's daily routine in ways that make crime less likely (Meisenhelder, 1977; Shover, 1983).

Good personal relationships with conventional people such as a spouse, a lover, children, or peers create bonds to the social order that an individual wants to protect. These people may then be "psychologically present" if the individual faces situations that offer a temptation to violate the law. Family members and lovers also provide a place of residence, food, and help in the development of everyday skills such as paying bills and scheduling time (Irwin, 1970). Other bonds that may lead people away from crime include involvement in organized religion and in extravocational and extradomestic activities, such as sports and hobbies (Irwin, 1970: 203). However, attachments of this sort are usually less important in the exiting process than are ties to jobs and to other people (Meisenhelder, 1977; Shover, 1983).

Exiting and the Correctional System

Correctional treatment programs are designed to rehabilitate offenders. In other words, administrators see prisons as places where inmates should learn to "go straight." However, some researchers suggest that the conditions necessary for exiting are largely outside the control of the correctional system (Meisenhelder, 1977; Petersilia, 1980). Some critics of the correctional system even claim that it impedes the process of exiting. In prison, inmates often learn a way of life directly opposed to what they need to leave a criminal career. They depend on the prison administration for their material needs, but after release they must rely on themselves to meet those needs. In prison their time is structured for them, and much of the time they are idle; after release, they must learn how to structure their time to keep themselves from drifting back into crime. Prison life is easier for inmates who do not spend much time thinking about their future, but outside prison they must construct goals for themselves. In sum, changes produced by prison often hinder offenders who might otherwise leave a life of crime (Cordilia, 1983).

In order to leave a life of crime, the released inmate must "keep out of the old bag," a way of life that involves the commission of felonies and a high likelihood of arrest and conviction (Irwin, 1970). The "old bag" offers excitement and glamor, but also physical danger and the risk of a return to prison. Some observers believe that the only way to leave a criminal career is to stay away from all criminal behavior; this opinion is similar to the claim of Alcoholics Anonymous that alcoholics cannot drink at all without risking a relapse.

An ex-convict's first few weeks on the street after release are especially critical. During that time, the individual must become reaccustomed to the outside world, which has a faster pace and less routinization than life in prison. Often a released offender feels like a foreign traveler during the first few weeks on the street (Irwin, 1970).

As the ex-convict develops bonds and as time passes, the motivation to stay away from crime increases. The longer the individual stays away from crime, the less the chance that he or she will return to crime. Conversely, the greater a person's past involvement in crime and the longer a person's criminal career, the less the chance of abandoning a life of crime (Kitchener, Schmidt, and Glaser, 1977; Glaser, 1979).

The successful termination of a criminal career seems to require detachment from other offenders and from a criminal subculture, and attachment to a conventional way of life that usually involves a family, law-abiding friends, and a job that holds promise for the future. The process by which offenders detach themselves from one way of life and become attached to another is not yet fully understood, but more research on this process may reveal as much about the causes of crime as do studies that focus on the way that people become involved in crime in the first place.

SUMMARY

Individual acts of law breaking may cumulate over time into a criminal career, which is similar in some ways to a legitimate career but which also differs in important ways.

Certain contingencies influence the development of a criminal career. An individual's sex can close off access to illegitimate occupations. Another important contingency is contact with the criminal justice system, which can influence the course of a criminal career through the labeling process. Offenders often alternate in a "zigzag path" between criminal activities and legitimate pursuits. They are often recruited into criminal careers through a delinquent subculture or from occupations close to the underworld.

Typologies can be useful in developing theories to explain different kinds of criminal behavior and in establishing effective treatment methods. Typologies must be tested for their empirical validity; that is, researchers must determine if typologies accurately and completely describe patterns of criminal behavior. One potentially fruitful approach is to develop typologies that categorize offenders by specific combinations of crimes that they commit over time.

Studies of delinquent careers find that a small number of offenders account for a very large proportion of all contacts with the police in any cohort. The chance of being stopped again by the police increases as the number of police contacts increases. People who have contact with the police while very young are especially likely to have further contacts and to go on to commit crimes as adults. Delinquents show little inclination to specialize in one type of crime; this is true of adult career criminals as well. The time between police contacts becomes compressed as a delinquent career lengthens, indicating either increased delinquent activity or more attention to known offenders by the police. People who have police contacts as juveniles have a much greater chance of being stopped by the police as adults than do people who have no police contacts as juveniles. This may be because of the labeling effects on young offenders, or it may be because of a continuity of law-violating behavior over time.

Most adult offenders do not plan their crimes in much detail. As they grow older, they increasingly spend the money from their crimes for instrumental rather than expressive purposes. Intensive career criminals commit many more crimes than intermittent offenders do. These intensive offenders also engage in more planning and are more skilled and persistent in their criminal activity. As a result, they account for a disproportionately high percentage of all serious crimes.

Career criminals exit or retire from a life of crime for many reasons, but the exiting process usually involves a growing detachment from offenders and a criminal subculture, and a growing attachment to a conventional way of life that includes a family and a job. Different theories of crime causation would explain exiting in different ways, but control theory seems to make the most sense of the data we now have on the exiting process; meaningful social bonds are usually acquired before an offender leaves a criminal career. The correctional system seems to play a relatively minor role in the process of exiting.

IMPORTANT TERMS

certification	exiting	intermittent offender
contingency	intensive offender	radical nonintervention
criminal career		

SUGGESTED READINGS

JAN M. CHAIKEN AND MARCIA R. CHAIKEN, WITH JOYCE E. PETERSON. *Varieties of Criminal Behavior: Summary and Policy Implications.* Santa Monica, Calif.: Rand, 1982. A summary of a research project that produced a typology based on the combinations of crimes that offenders commit over time.

CARL B. KLOCKARS. *The Professional Fence.* New York: Free Press, 1974. A fascinating autobiographical account of the development of one kind of criminal career.

JOAN PETERSILIA, PETER W. GREENWOOD, AND MARVIN LAVIN. *Criminal Careers of Habitual Felons.* Santa Monica, Calif.: Rand, 1977. A detailed examination of the criminal careers of forty-nine armed robbers.

RICHARD P. RETTIG, MANUAL J. TORRES, AND GERALD R. GARRETT. *Manny: A Criminal-Addict's Story.* Boston: Houghton Mifflin, 1977. An interesting account of one offender's life, illustrating the various contingencies that lead to different kinds of criminal behavior.

NEAL SHOVER. "The Later Stages of Ordinary Property Offender Careers," *Social Problems* 31 (December 1983), 208–218. An important paper on the exiting process that is based on interviews with retired offenders.

FOUR

REACTIONS TO CRIME

Chapter 13 deals with community reactions to crime. We look at the informal social control of criminal behavior, including the way that architectural design may foster control and thereby curb crime. Bystander responses to crime, and collective reactions such as urban patrol groups, are explored. The community's isolation of offenders and recent efforts at community-based corrections are also examined.

Chapter 14 provides an overview of the criminal justice system. We look at the history and organization of the police and the way that officers do their job. We examine aspects of the courts, including bail, preventive detention, and plea bargaining. We look at prosecutors, defense attorneys, judges, and juries. Disparities in sentences by race and by sex are investigated. Prison conditions and parole are also examined. Finally, we explore the changing role of the victim in the criminal justice system.

Deterrence and incapacitation are the topics of Chapter 15. We consider the idea that the threat of punishment can keep people from violating the law, and look at research that has tested this idea. We explore aspects of the criminal act and the sanctioning process that influence the deterrent effect of penalties. We also examine the way that the deterrence perspective affects the operation of the criminal justice system. Finally, we look at incapacitation, the idea that crime can be prevented simply by locking up offenders.

In Chapter 16 we look at retribution or "just deserts," the idea that punishment should inflict suffering on offenders commensurate with the harm they have inflicted on others. We examine the way that this idea has influenced the operation of the police, the courts, the prisons, and the use of capital punishment.

Rehabilitation is explored in Chapter 17. We explore the effect on the criminal justice system of the idea that offenders should be treated in ways that will reform them and keep them away from crime in the future. We also examine evaluations of treatment programs to see whether they are effective in changing offenders.

Chapter 18 looks at the conservative, liberal, and radical approaches to the crime problem. It investigates crime and politics in the United States since the 1960s, and then explores three major strategies of reducing crime: reforming the criminal justice system, situational crime prevention, and dealing with the causes of crime.

13

Community Reactions to Crime

Toward the end of the last century, the French sociologist Emile Durkheim (1895, 1933: 73) defined crime as behavior that shocks the sentiments found in all "healthy" consciences. According to Durkheim, these sentiments are intensely held and specific to particular situations, and commonly form the basis of criminal codes. Crime is thus behavior that offends a shared sense of what is valued and worth pursuing, and punishment is a reaction to that behavior.

Societal reactions to crime often lead to *social control*, a process that brings about conformity to society's norms and laws. One kind of reaction to crime is *formal social control*, the effort to bring about conformity to the law by agents of the criminal justice system such as the police, the courts, and correctional institutions. We examine these agents of formal social control later in Chapter 14.

Informal social control, or the reactions of individuals and groups that bring about conformity to norms and laws, includes peer and community pressure, bystander intervention in a crime, and collective responses such as citizen patrol groups. There is some reason to believe that the amount of formal social control varies inversely with the amount of informal social control; that is, the agents of the criminal justice system will exercise more control when informal social control is weaker (Black, 1976: 107–111).

One sociologist has even treated some criminal behavior as a kind of informal social control, arguing that violent and property crimes are sometimes the results of efforts to engage in self-help, correct injustice, and pursue justice against perceived wrongdoers (Black, 1983). Murders in which people kill because they feel insulted by their victims, vandalism in which youths destroy school property because of hostility toward teachers who have hurt their self-esteem, and theft from stores that overcharge customers can be seen as efforts to correct serious wrongs perpetrated by others—that is, as efforts to exercise informal social control over unjust actions. Sometimes informal efforts to control crime actually violate the law; for instance, vigilante groups that lynch suspected offenders violate due process rights and may break federal laws by denying others their civil rights.

INFORMAL CONTROL OF CRIME

Because only 1 or 2 per cent of all serious crimes are reported to the police and lead to arrest, conviction, and imprisonment, the formal sanctions of the criminal justice system may be less important in controlling criminal behavior than are informal sanctions such as group censure and bystander intervention. Loss of esteem in the eyes of relatives and peers may be a more significant cost for an offender than a court's judgment that a crime has been committed (see, e.g., Chambers and Inciardi, 1971: 300). For instance, white-collar offenders seem to be affected more by accusation and indictment than by a criminal conviction. Concern for the good opinion of friends, relatives, and neighbors is a strong force controlling deviant behavior in Japan, where an internal "social policeman" seems to induce conformity out of fear of losing face (Clifford, 1976).

Community and Informal Social Control

By creating fear, mistrust, and suspicion, crime can reduce interaction among the residents of a community (Conklin, 1975). As social solidarity in a community weakens, informal control over behavior dissipates. This can increase crime rates because interpersonal pressures on potential offenders to abide by the law are attenuated. One indicator of the effectiveness of a community's standards in controlling deviance is the proportion of all crimes in the community that are committed by local residents. In a study of crime in Honolulu, Andrew Lind (1930: 218) concluded: "An area capable of maintaining the strength of its prohibitions is likely also to discourage its wayward residents from attempting the violation of taboos within the boundaries of the district, although it may not succeed in entirely repressing the behavior." Similarly, another study found that riot activity during the 1960s was more common where there was no "extensive informal social interaction," and thus little informal control over potential rioters (Warren, 1969).

MECHANICAL AND ORGANIC SOLIDARITY

Simple preindustrial societies, such as tribal groups, are characterized by more intimate relationships and more social integration than are modern industrial societies. In simple societies, primary groups such as the family and the peer group are relatively stronger than they are in complex societies. These simple societies are held together by what Durkheim (1895, 1933) called *mechanical solidarity*, a unity based on shared values and norms and on the similarity of functions performed by all members of the society. Children in these simple societies learn shared values and norms through face-to-face interaction, and this socialization process perpetuates the collective conscience over the generations.

In larger and more complex societies, primary groups diminish in relative strength, and secondary groups such as corporations, labor unions, and schools become more important. Interpersonal relationships become less intimate, and people carry out very different tasks in their daily lives. Complex societies are integrated by *organic solidarity*, a unity based on an interdependence of functions, much as in a complex biological organism. In modern industrial societies, the collective conscience is less strong than it is in simple societies, and so legal institutions develop to control behavior. Sanctions are designed to restore disrupted social situations. The overall severity of formal sanctions seems to decrease in complex societies, as normative diversity increases and some acts that are violations of the collective conscience in simpler societies are redefined as private matters (Durkheim, 1895, 1933; Green and Allen, 1981–82). However, legal sanctions are still invoked against people who violate intensely held values and norms.

SMALL TOWNS AND LARGE CITIES

Related to the idea that informal social control is stronger in simpler societies is the notion that informal control is greater in small towns than in larger cities. If informal social control is indeed stronger in small towns than in large cities, this would help to explain a fact that we examined earlier in the book: Crime rates, in general, decline with decreasing size of the community.

Evidence on the real nature of informal social control in small towns is mixed. A study of the Massachusetts Bay Colony in the seventeenth century found that the small size and cultural homogeneity of the community helped to control deviant behavior by pressuring potential deviants to conform (Erikson, 1966: 169–170). Informal controls operate most effectively where people know each other well and interact on a regular basis, and small and homogeneous communities may be best suited to this kind of interaction. Outsiders who try to commit crime in small communities may be more easily recognized as strangers and thus be treated with suspicion. As James Q. Wilson (1968: 115) notes, in small towns "teachers, parents, and little old ladies keeping watch on flower gardens are apt to notice any strange or objectionable behavior and they will want to 'do something' about perceived threats to property."

In general, there is probably less informal social control in large cities than in small towns. The large size of the city means that residents may have a difficult time distinguishing strangers from residents, and the heterogeneity of the city means that many neighborhoods will include a variety of values and norms. Nevertheless, many cities are characterized by informal social control. Thus, Swiss cities grew slowly and were able to maintain strong community ties that provided informal social control and thus kept crime rates relatively low (Clinard, 1978: 103–107). In addition, well integrated and homogeneous urban neighborhoods, such as Boston's North End, are often able to exercise informal control over both residents and outsiders.

One piece of evidence that community integration is generally greater in small towns than in large cities comes from a study of people's willingness to admit strangers to their homes to use the telephone (Milgram, 1970: 1463). Residents of small towns were more willing to allow strangers to use their phones than were residents of urban middle-class housing projects. Small-town residents were also more likely to open their doors to speak with strangers, and urban residents were more likely to find out what strangers wanted by talking to them through the door.

Urban residents encounter more people on a day-to-day basis and have to screen out some of the input they receive in order to prevent "informational overload" (Milgram, 1970: 1462). A multitude of demands on city dwellers may generate "norms of noninvolvement" that lead to mistrust of strangers, a desire for privacy, and withdrawal from social interaction (Milgram, 1970: 1463). Urban residents are more likely than the residents of small towns to deal with others in terms of the roles they occupy rather than on a personal basis. Thus, urban residents will probably be concerned only with paying for their groceries at a supermarket checkout counter, but small-town residents may ask the local grocer how his sick wife is feeling or how his children are doing in school.

A study of reactions to crime in cities, suburbs, small towns, and rural areas in Missouri found that large-city residents were the most likely to think that crime would occur in their community. These people were also the most likely to say that their neighbors would not call the police about a burglary that they observed. A majority of the residents of all communities believed that their own community was safe, but city dwellers were the least likely to feel that way. When asked what made their own community safe, more residents of rural areas and small towns than residents of suburban and urban areas mentioned informal controls, such as a social network in the community that would lead bystanders to intervene in a crime. In comparison to the residents of small towns and rural areas, people in the suburbs and cities were more likely to say that crime in their community was kept in check by formal agents of control such as the police. Urban residents were thus the most likely to expect crime, and they relied more on formal than on informal means to control crime in their community (Boggs, 1971).

One study examined formal and informal social control in two Israeli communities (Schwartz, 1954, 1976). One community was a collective in which there was no formal mechanism to resolve legal disputes. The other community was a semiprivate settlement that had a judicial committee to handle legal disputes. According to the researcher, the collective did not require a legal committee because behavior was informally controlled through intense and frequent face-to-face interaction. On the other hand, the semiprivate settlement had considerably less interaction and less consensus; much everyday behavior was not visible to the members of the community. Consequently, informal control was less effective, and formal control was needed. This evidence suggests that the structure of interpersonal relations may be more important than size alone in determining the degree of informal control in a community. Intense and regular interaction, normative consensus, and surveillance of behavior all seem to be conducive to the informal control of behavior.

DIFFERENCES AMONG URBAN COMMUNITIES
In developing nations, the process of migration from tribal villages to large cities sometimes reduces informal control over deviant behavior. For instance, in Liberia

> the effectiveness of tribe and family as agents of social control has always depended upon the cohesiveness of the particular unit. In the urban areas, this cohesiveness increasingly gives way to individualism and the vacuum created by the decline in family and tribal authority has only been filled by the impersonal sanctions of the law (Zarr, 1969: 194).

A comparison of two communities in the city of Kampala, Uganda, found that the area with less crime had greater social solidarity, more interaction among neighbors, more participation in local organizations, less geographic mobility, and more stable family relationships (Clinard and Abbott, 1973: 149). There was also greater cultural homogeneity and more emphasis on tribal and kinship ties in the community with the lower crime rate; these conditions seemed to alleviate the anonymity that recent migrants to the city might otherwise have felt. Crime in the community with the lower rate was prevented in part by strong primary group ties among residents, which made strangers to the area conspicuous.

A study of two neighborhoods in Cambridge, Massachusetts, supports these conclusions. Although residents of the two communities were similar in several ways, the community with the higher delinquency rate was less socially integrated. Residents of the community that had the higher delinquency rate were more heterogeneous in religion and ethnicity, knew fewer neighbors by name, thought they had less in common with their neighbors, and liked the community less. They were no more tolerant of deviance than were adults in the community that had less delinquency, but the residents of the high rate area were less likely to do something about delinquency if they observed it. More adults in the area with the high delinquency rate said that people ought to mind their own business and not interfere when the children of their neighbors committed delinquent acts. This unwillingness to do something about observed violations of the law creates "an atmosphere in which delinquency can grow more easily. . . . [T]he lack of social integration appears to have certain direct effects in a lowered level of social control of delinquent and pre-delinquent activities" (Maccoby, Johnson, and Church, 1958: 49, 51). Here we see that the informal control of crime and delinquency is greater in some urban neighborhoods than in others. The degree of informal control seems to be related to the social structure and the nature of social relationships in a community, rather than to the absolute size of the community.

Feeling unsafe in an urban neighborhood usually means not having a sense of security when in public places such as streets, sidewalks, and parks (Jacobs, 1961). Fear of venturing out-of-doors at night means that the streets may become deserted; informal controls that would check crime if people were there are absent. The presence of people on the street creates surveillance of public places and attracts the attention of others to the streets, thereby reducing opportunities for crime. Better lighting may increase surveillance, because activities will be more easily observed and people will be more likely to venture onto brightly lit streets and sidewalks. A study of slum neighborhoods in Chicago found "impersonal domains" that were deserted and seen as dangerous at night, even though informal control over deviance was maintained in those areas during the day by business persons and their customers (Suttles, 1968: 36–37).

In Figure 13.1, we diagram a "crime cycle" in which responses to crime can change behavior in ways that actually increase the crime rate. Less interaction in public places may decrease informal social control, leading to an increase in both the actual and the perceived crime rate, which can then decrease interaction in public and begin the cycle anew.

Architecture and Informal Social Control

Informal control of criminal behavior can be enhanced through architectural design. Oscar Newman (1972, 1973) is an architect who claims that citizen involvement in crime prevention is needed and that it is possible to construct

Figure 13.1: The Crime Cycle

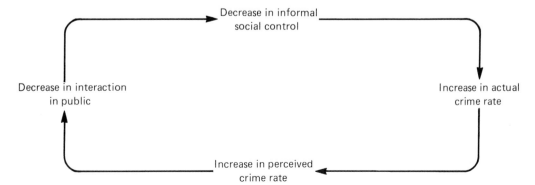

residential complexes that deter crime by creating *defensible space.* Defensible space involves the subdivision and design of housing to allow residents to distinguish stranger from neighbor. The design of housing can reinforce or create opportunities for surveillance of a building and its surrounding grounds by eliciting from residents a feeling of territoriality and a sense of proprietary interest in the protection of the community.

A survey of residents of New York City housing projects found that more than half felt unsafe. Newman (1973: 92) claimed that this sense of insecurity had important consequences: "Fear, in itself, can increase the risk of victimization through isolating neighbor from neighbor, witness from victim, making remote the possibility of mutual help and assuring the criminal a ready opportunity to operate unhampered and unimpeded." Project residents were less threatened by crime if they knew more of their neighbors, and they were more likely to know their neighbors in housing projects where architectural design facilitated interaction.

Housing design can enhance interaction and foster interest in nearby areas, thereby creating informal control over behavior. Crime may be reduced by making the interior spaces of large buildings visible to people outside the building. Design can define private and semiprivate space near and within buildings. For instance, the area enclosed by an L-shaped building often becomes the focus of surveillance and informal control by residents of the apartments that face the enclosed area, especially if the building is only a few stories high. Apartment clusters also create zones of influence by residents if shared areas are defined as private and are carefully watched. When children play in hallways or on playgrounds near a building, parents often watch those areas to protect their children from strangers. Filling the space around housing projects with play equipment, benches, or athletic facilities can attract people and attention, and keep children near home where they will be under surveillance by parents and neighbors.

Newman (1973: 59) states that residents of housing projects will feel safer if they can "see and be seen, hear and be heard, by day and night." Surveillance deters crime, and it also reduces anxiety by creating an image of a safe environment. People who feel less anxious will spend more time in public places, thereby increasing surveillance and the informal control of behavior. Surveillance must be backed up with a willingness to intervene in a crime, either personally or by alerting the police, or mere observation will have little effect. If potential offenders believe that they will be seen committing a crime, but will not be interfered with or reported to the police by the witness, they will not be affected much by surveillance; only a real risk of apprehension can deter offenders (Merry, 1981; Murray, 1983).

EVIDENCE ON DEFENSIBLE SPACE AND CRIME

There is some evidence on the impact of architectural design on crime rates. Because much of the research on defensible space has been done in public housing projects, we do not know if this concept can be applied to other kinds of living environments (Taylor, Gottfredson, and Brower, 1980). One researcher concludes that the defensible space concept can be used to prevent vandalism and burglary in the indoor public areas of apartment buildings, but that it may not apply to other crimes and to other areas. Even for indoor areas and for vandalism and burglary, the impact of defensible space design on crime seems to be small, although consistent (Booth, 1981). A review of research on defensible space and crime carried out in Great Britain finds that the concept may have some "limited relevance to levels of delinquency (particularly vandalism) in English housing areas" (Baldwin, 1979: 55).

Overall, the idea that defensible space design can dramatically reduce crime lacks strong empirical support. Some of Newman's ideas on defensible space are difficult to test, either because they are unclear or because they are difficult to define in operational terms (Baldwin, 1979). Researchers testing the idea of defensible space often fail to account for the possible displacement of crime from well-designed housing projects to nearby targets; thus, crime may be shifted to other locations rather than prevented when the defensible space concept is implemented.

CRITIQUE OF THE DEFENSIBLE SPACE MODEL

A major flaw in Newman's defensible space model is that it pays attention to physical design features but slights or ignores social variables. For instance, the model ignores the demographic characteristics of the people who live in a housing area. Thus, a project that includes many teen-agers and many elderly people will probably have a higher crime rate than a project limited to the elderly, whatever the defensible space design of each project. The model also pays little or no attention to other social aspects of the area, such as neighborhood stability, residential mobility, employment rate, and racial integration. According to some critics, then, defensible space is a concept that lacks social reality (Taylor, Gottfredson, and Brower, 1980; Booth, 1981).

Another problem with the model is that the built environment can affect the crime rate either by encouraging residents to take action against potential offenders who violate the defensible space, or by reducing opportunities for crime through controlled access or "target hardening" (for example, locks and bars on doors and windows). To test the idea of defensible space, it is necessary to separate these two processes. The defensible space model claims that crime is controlled by environmental influences on residents' behavior, but so far there is more evidence that the built environment reduces crime by limiting opportunities to break the law (Heinzelman, 1981). Moreover, we have little evidence that potential offenders perceive defensible space measures as a threat and adjust their behavior accordingly (Taylor, Gottfredson, and Brower, 1980).

Sometimes the design of the built environment impedes informal social control, as in areas with high-density housing. However, those areas may attract more police officers, which might enhance formal control of crime there (Gillis and Hagan, 1982). In other words, the characteristics of the physical environment may be associated with both formal and informal social control, rather than just with informal control as the defensible space model implies.

One critique concludes that we need a revised defensible space model that takes into account recent advances in the study of human territoriality. This revised model would pay more attention to barriers that deter access by unwanted outsiders, territorial markers that show that an area is cared for, and signs of incivility that indicate the disintegration of civil order in an area. This revised model would look at the way that sociocultural characteristics affect territorial behavior; for instance, culturally homogeneous neighborhoods probably exert more territorial control than do heterogeneous neighborhoods. A revised model would look not only at physical design, but also at the traits of people who might exercise territorial control and the ways that social networks are formed and affect territorial control (Taylor, Gottfredson, and Brower, 1980, 1984).

INDIVIDUAL RESPONSE TO CRIME

Informal control of crime depends not only on the surveillance of public places by the residents of a community, but also on the willingness of those people to take action if they see a crime in progress. The combination of cooperative surveillance and willingness to intervene has been called *protective neighboring* (Schneider and Schneider, 1978). Protective neighboring seems to be more common among people with higher incomes, among long-term residents of a community, and among homeowners. Just as crime and delinquency are less common among people who have a stake in conformity, so it seems that efforts to control crime and delinquency are also more common among people who have a stake in conformity.

The most common action that people take in response to a crime is to call the police to report it. Occasionally, people intervene in a crime. This is probably least likely where fear of crime leads people to withdraw from social contacts, stay home at night, and avoid strangers. These reactions minimize the likelihood that anyone will be around to observe a crime, and they cause those people who are on the street to adopt a self-protective stance and avoid intervening personally in a crime.

Bystander Responses to Crime

The issue of bystander response to emergencies such as crimes has been called the *Good Samaritan problem* (Ratcliffe, 1966). The crime that most dramatically brought this problem to public attention was the 1964 murder of Kitty Genovese in Queens, New York. This crime occurred in a middle-class neighborhood that had a relatively low crime rate. A man attacked Kitty Genovese at about three o'clock in the morning when she was returning from work. She screamed, and lights went on in nearby apartments. People looked out and one witness shouted at the assailant to leave the woman alone. The assailant left but soon returned. Again lights went on and again the assailant left. When he returned a third time, he killed Miss Genovese. The three attacks took place over a period of about thirty-five minutes, and at least thirty-eight witnesses knew of the violence. When the witnesses were later asked about their failure to take action, some said they had been too tired to do anything and others said they had not wanted to get involved.

At first, social scientists were unable to provide a convincing explanation of the bystanders' failure to help the victim. Letters to the newspapers suggested printing the names of the nonresponsive witnesses. Others blamed the police, saying that New Yorkers were afraid of the police and were therefore unwilling to call them in an emergency. What was puzzling was that no help was forthcoming from a group as large as thirty-eight; had only one or two people observed the crime, it might have been possible to point the finger at a few heartless individuals. Many commentators concluded that something must be wrong with society as a whole; several gave apathy as the cause of the problem, concluding that people just no longer cared about their fellow citizens.

THE LAW AND THE GOOD SAMARITAN PROBLEM

Anglo-American law does not generally require witnesses to emergencies such as crimes to help victims, unless the witness caused the victim's plight. Thus, in 1984 only three states had laws that required intervention in emergencies

(Dowd, 1984). In contrast, most European countries have laws that punish "Bad Samaritans" with criminal sanctions. For instance, a few dozen citizens of France are punished each year for failure to help the victims of emergencies (Geis, 1981).

There is some question as to whether laws that require bystander assistance have much effect on the behavior of people who witness emergencies. There is limited evidence suggesting that if such laws exist, people will know about them and will be more likely to condemn nonresponsive bystanders. However, there is no evidence that knowledge of such laws increases the chance that people will actually intervene in an emergency (Zeisel, 1966). One reason is that bystanders may fear legal action by the victim or by the victim's surviving dependents if the rescue attempt fails. Bystanders may also fear being attacked by the offender if the crime is in progress, or being the target of reprisals later if the crime has been completed. As one observer points out,

> the original Good Samaritan extolled by St. Luke was fortunate in not arriving on the scene until after the thieves had set upon the traveler, robbed him, and beaten him half to death. The Samaritan cared for him and showed him great kindness, but he did not put himself in any peril by doing so. Perhaps this is about as much as can be reasonably asked of the ordinary mortal man (Barth, 1966: 163).

REACTIONS TO EMERGENCIES

How then do people respond when faced with a crime or other emergency that requires action? Lawrence Zelic Freedman (1966) suggests that the initial response is fear of being hurt and fear of reprisals. Often witnesses cannot fit the unusual event into any familiar category of past experience. Thus, the failure of the witnesses to the Genovese murder may be attributed in part to the crime seeming "totally incongruous in a respectable neighborhood"; this "created a sense of unreality which inhibited rational action" (Milgram and Hollander, 1970: 208). Before witnesses take action, they must clearly define the situation as an emergency that requires personal intervention. Emergency situations are often ambiguous to witnesses; for example, several witnesses to the Genovese murder interpreted it as a "lovers' quarrel." Witnesses often fail to respond appropriately; they deny to themselves that anything so unusual could be happening in their presence. What appears to be apathy may in fact be massive inhibition or paralysis of consciousness resulting from internal conflict. Freedman (1966: 175) claims that in response to emergencies,

> apathy and indifference are the least likely primary psychic vectors. . . . The sequence as I see it is, first, the intense emotional shock—characterized predominantly, but not exclusively, by anxiety; second, the cognitive perception and awareness of what has happened; third, an inertial paralysis of reaction, which as a non-act becomes in fact an act; and fourth, the self-awareness of one's own shock anxiety, non-involvement which is followed by a sense of guilt and intra-psychic and social self-justification.
>
> I do not assume that these things happen in such neat sequence. For all practical purposes they seem to occur simultaneously.

Witnesses may justify their inaction by claiming that the victim and the offender must know each other, which may be the case. Research indicates that bystanders are much more likely to intervene in assaults between strangers than to offer help when it seems that the assault involves a married couple (Dowd, 1984). Witnesses are probably more likely to intervene if they believe that the victim is totally innocent and if they can identify in some way with the victim. Similarly, witnesses probably find it easier to tolerate the victimization of people who occupy disvalued social statuses, such as prostitutes, homosexuals, or members of minority groups. If a witness's identification with a victim is slight, the chance that the witness will assist the victim is probably also low (Sorokin, 1930; Shils, 1967; Blumenthal et al., 1972).

Experimental studies of bystander response Social-psychological experiments have cast light on the reasons that witnesses to emergencies help under some conditions but not others. Bibb Latané and John M. Darley (1970), who conducted several of these studies, claim that neither public apathy nor the absence of norms that require emergency assistance can explain bystander nonresponse. In a series of experiments, they clarify the characteristics of situations that are conducive to bystander intervention. Personality traits that might plausibly influence helping behavior did not bear any relationship to such action. Situational determinants of bystander assistance are so strong that differences among the personalities of witnesses pale in significance as determinants of their behavior.

Before bystanders will intervene, they must make a series of decisions. A negative decision at any point means that they will not help the victim. They must notice the situation, and define it as an emergency. Then they must determine that they have a personal responsibility to do something; if they think that the situation is none of their business, they will not help. Bystanders must also decide what kind of aid to offer—personal intervention, or calling the police or an ambulance. Finally, bystanders must decide how to implement the course of action upon which they have decided (Latané and Darley, 1970: 34–35). The social context within which this decision-making process occurs will influence the outcome.

One reason for the public's condemnation of the nonresponsive bystanders in the Genovese murder was the failure of a large number of witnesses to help. The commonsense assumption is that if there are more people around, the chance that at least one will help should be greater. However, social-psychological research demonstrates that the presence of others at the scene of a crime or an emergency actually inhibits helping behavior. People might be embarrassed to help for fear that their assistance will turn out to be unwanted or unneeded. When no witness in a group of bystanders immediately offers help, others may assume that their interpretation of the situation as one requiring aid is wrong; if help were needed, would not someone already have offered it? People in groups take cues from others, and if no one helps they may reinterpret the event. This has been referred to as *pluralistic ignorance:* Witnesses in a group fail to help because they interpret the failure of other witnesses to help as a sign that no help is needed (Latané and Darley, 1970: 38–42).

Witnesses who are alone when they observe a crime or an accident are more likely to help than are witnesses who are in groups of two or more. Lone witnesses are more likely to seek information about the situation, to help the victim by their own efforts, and to report the situation to someone else who can provide assistance. A witness who is with another person is more likely to help the victim if that witness is personally acquainted with the other witness than if the other witness is a stranger; this is probably because personal knowledge breaks down pluralistic ignorance by making communication between witnesses more likely. However, pairs of witnesses who know each other are less likely to help victims than are witnesses who are alone. One reason for this is that there is no *diffusion of responsibility* when there is only one witness present (Latané and Darley, 1970: 90–91, 106–112). Diffusion of responsibility occurs in groups of witnesses because people can say to themselves that someone should act but that it need not be themselves, because other potential helpers are present. Especially when a victim's cries for help are not directed toward a specific bystander, people who witness an emergency can soothe their consciences by claiming that someone else should help or that others are equally responsible if no one helps. Indeed, the larger the group of bystanders, the more responsibility is diffused and the less likely it is that help will be offered (Latané and Darley, 1970: 97–98).

One experiment that suggests that bystander intervention is more likely when responsibility is focused on a particular bystander was conducted on Jones Beach, Long Island. A "victim" placed a blanket near another bather, turned on a radio, and a short time later said to the bystander, "Excuse me, I'm going up to the boardwalk for a few minutes. Would you watch my things?" This committed the bystander to watch the radio. Other bystanders were only asked for a match and were thus not committed to watching the radio. In a few minutes, a "thief"—who was actually part of the experiment—picked up the radio, which was playing loudly, and walked away with it. Another participant in the experiment observed the reactions of bystanders. Of twenty uncommitted witnesses who later said that they had noticed the theft, only four tried to stop the thief. However, of twenty committed bystanders, nineteen made some effort to stop the thief. Prior contact between the victim and the bystander had focused responsibility on the committed bystanders to take some action when the theft occurred (Thomas Moriarity, cited in Horn, 1973).

Other aspects of the situation also affect the likelihood of bystander assistance to the victim. Familiarity with the location is important; help is probably more likely to be given if witnesses are in their own neighborhood than if they are in a strange neighborhood. Bystanders also consider the risks of providing help; they may be less willing to help if a weapon is present or if there are several offenders rather than one. Offering help may be a function of other activities in which the witness is engaged at the time; for instance, help is probably more likely to be given if a witness is standing on the street doing nothing than if a witness is rushing to a doctor's appointment or a job interview (Darley and Batson, 1973).

Bystanders who are self-assured, feel good about themselves, or have specialized training in first aid, life saving, or medical and police techniques seem to be especially likely to help others (Geis, 1981; J. Greenberg, 1981; Dowd, 1984). People who seek training in such skills may be more inclined to help to begin with, or they may learn an ethic of helping behavior as they learn those skills (Geis, 1981).

A study of thirty-two people who had intervened in actual crimes of violence or theft found that all but one were men, and that these men tended to be above average in height and weight and were usually larger than the offenders they confronted (Geis, 1981). Perhaps size and sense of competence led more men than women to risk taking action when faced with a crime in progress. However, an experimental study at the University of Virginia staged a theft and found that 73.9 per cent of the women but only 47.2 per cent of the men tried to stop the theft (Austin, 1979). This experiment, which elicited a promise from the bystander to watch the "victim's" goods, led the researcher to conclude that women might be more unwilling than men to break a promise, or that women perhaps feel more empathy for victims than men do. These explanations would not, however, tell us why nearly all of the bystanders who intervened in actual crimes in the first study were men.

Help seems to be more likely to be given by people raised in small towns than by people raised in large cities (Latané and Darley, 1970: 117). Solid supporting evidence is lacking, but help may also be more common in a small town than in a large city. If this were true, it might be because diffusion of responsibility and pluralistic ignorance are less common in small towns where people are more likely to know each other. Witnesses are more willing to help victims whom they know or with whom they have interacted prior to the crime (Latané and Darley, 1970: 105–111). Interaction creates empathy with the victim, but even more importantly, it seems to negate the diffusion of responsibility by creating a sense of duty to help in the witness who had been in contact with the victim.

Bystanders who witness crimes and fail to help are not apathetic; they are aroused even when they do not act. Failure to act immediately can lead bystanders to rationalize their inaction. The presence of other witnesses, especially strangers, leads bystanders to think that if help were required, someone would have offered it and that they are not solely responsible for seeing that the victim is rescued.

COLLECTIVE RESPONSE TO CRIME

People sometimes band together in a collective response to crime. They may work for a political candidate who promises "law and order," meet to plan a crime-prevention program, or even unite in a civilian patrol group to perform tasks that they think that the police are not doing adequately. Group action of this sort has been both condemned as a mob taking the law into its own hands and praised as citizen involvement in crime prevention.

A Historical and Comparative Perspective

Collective response to crime has a long history. Ancient Roman plebeians engaged in community self-help when they threw alleged offenders from the Tarpeian rock. Early Germans raised a hue and cry, took up arms, blew horns, chased suspects, and occasionally lynched them (Pound, 1921). More recently, "people's police" have sometimes had to be restrained from attacking innocent people in the Soviet Union. In China, people informally police their communities, and Africans in tribal villages sometimes impose harsh punishment on suspected criminals (Radzinowicz and King, 1977: 181). In the Cross-Cultural Perspective, we see an example of citizen self-help in dealing with the crime problem in urban Brazil.

The history of vigilante activity in the United States covers more than two centuries. The first recorded movement was in the 1760s in South Carolina, where a group called the Regulators sought to bring order to communities in the Back Country (Brown, 1963). The Regulators apparently reduced crime, but they violated the due process rights of suspects. They elicited much hostility and were eventually disbanded when they began to mete out severe punishment, select victims rashly, and even supervise the morals and family life of law-abiding citizens.

Vigilante groups on the American frontier developed in response to a per-

A Cross-Cultural Perspective: Lynchings in Brazil

Rising crime rates in the Brazilian cities of Rio de Janeiro and São Paulo have elicited a variety of public responses. A majority of the public favors restoration of the death penalty. People have moved from houses to apartment complexes that are protected by armed guards. Residents of some neighborhoods have hired guards to stand watch on street corners. More Brazilians are carrying weapons. In some communities, crime is controlled by "death squads" of off-duty police officers who beat and kill "known offenders."

Perhaps the most dramatic response to Brazil's crime problem is citizen involvement in the lynching of suspected offenders. A public opinion poll in December 1983 found that 26 per cent of a sample of the residents of Brazil's two largest cities approved of lynchings, and an additional 33.1 per cent favored such action "depending on the crime." These lynchings seem to be a response to the perception that the criminal justice system has been ineffective in controlling crime. One lynching is described as follows:

> Osvaldo Otávio Pires was brought handcuffed into Elio's Bar in the Jardim Guanhambu slum on the outskirts of São Paulo at about 8 A.M. on April 2. Over 100 men, women and children had gathered in the small wooden building to await his arrival.
>
> Mr. Pires, 33 years old, was thrust onto a bench facing the crowd and the handcuffs were removed. He was allowed to smoke a cigarette and drink a glass of rough liquor, but no one moved when he asked to see his two small children. Witnesses recalled that his hands were trembling.
>
> Mr. Pires, long feared in Jardim Guanhambu, then heard an array of charges of armed assault brought by people filling the bar. After 20 minutes, participants in the meeting later told reporters, a voice was heard to say, "All those in favor of death raise their hands." Dozens of arms were lifted; apparently no one objected.
>
> Mr. Pires was pushed out of Elio's Bar and the crowd fell on him with sticks, poles and stones. Once he lay dead in the dusty street, the police were called. When they arrived, they took the names and addresses of 43 people who said they had joined in the lynching. No arrests were made.

SOURCE: Based on Alan Riding, "Brazilians Turn to Lynchings to Fight Soaring Crime Rate," *The New York Times*, April 15, 1984, pp. 1, 12.

ceived lack of social order, rather than in response to specific crimes. Because the new frontier communities often lacked the resources to hire law-enforcement officials, because they were usually far from towns that could provide those officials, and because they were near to open spaces to which suspects could flee, frontier vigilante groups sometimes developed as a way to establish social control over crime and bring stability to the community.

The leaders of many vigilante movements in the West were young men from the East who sought power and prestige and wanted to establish an orderly community in which they could pursue their ambitions. The rank-and-file members of these vigilante movements were often drawn from the middle classes, and the lower classes provided most of the targets of these movements.

Vigilante organizations in the West ranged in size from a dozen to as many as 8,000 participants; usually they had a few hundred members. Most groups lasted only a few weeks, but some endured for over a year. In nearly half of the recorded vigilante movements, there was at least one execution of an alleged offender, usually after a brief and formal—but extralegal—"trial."

Vigilantes traditionally espoused popular sovereignty, the right of the people to wield power in their own best interests (Brown, 1969: 141–142). They also supported the idea that people had the right to revolt against established authority if it failed to maintain order. Vigilante groups sought to preserve and protect the life, liberty, and property of their members and the other residents of the community, and in this sense their extralegal efforts to preserve civil order were conservative (Little and Sheffield, 1983).

Some vigilante movements were socially constructive, dealing with specific problems of disorder and then disbanding; these movements usually represented the consensus of the community. By contrast, socially destructive vigilante movements encountered stiff opposition and produced community strife. Movements became socially destructive when they failed to exercise control over violent or sadistic members. The possibility that vigilante movements, including civilian patrol groups in today's cities, may become battlegrounds for personal and group conflicts rather than represent genuine community consensus is one reason to distrust such movements. Such consensus is difficult to establish in large and heterogeneous cities.

Urban Patrol Groups

Vigilante groups on the American frontier developed to provide social control of deviant behavior. Just as the Western frontier was in transition from wilderness to settled territory, so can the transition from a small preindustrial city to a heavily industrialized urban center be understood as a kind of frontier. In Great Britain in the eighteenth and nineteenth centuries, urbanization and industrialization created a kind of frontier, a transition between social forms, that left growing cities without effective law enforcement. Just as vigilante groups emerged in the American West, so did private "prosecution societies" develop in these English cities. These prosecution societies sought to make the criminal justice system more accessible and more effective. They supported the rule of law and rarely meted out sentences on their own (Little and Sheffield, 1983).

One of the earliest recorded cases of urban vigilante action followed the Jack the Ripper murders in London in 1888. Vigilante groups, composed of college students and laborers, patrolled the streets of East London to prevent further crimes and capture the killer. Surveillance was so complete that "some of the plainclothes men who were strange to the neighborhood were watched by members of the Whitechapel Vigilante Committee, while they in turn came under the scrutiny of detectives" (Cullen, 1965: 89–90).

In the United States today, about five million citizens belong to crime-stopping groups such as Neighborhood Watches, which are sponsored by sheriffs in about 2,500 communities. These groups usually communicate directly with the local police, patrolling the streets in radio-equipped cars or on foot with walkie-talkies (Robbins, 1982). They do not punish suspected criminals, but instead seek to deter crime and rowdiness with their presence, turning over apprehended suspects to the police. Their patrol activity is usually routine, even dull, and they have few contacts with offenders. In general, these groups seek to supplement the police rather than to replace them. They differ from frontier vigilantes because they operate in a context in which there is already a fully developed system of law enforcement.

When law enforcement seems to be ineffective, people may mete out punishment on their own, as we saw in the Cross-Cultural Perspective. A similar case occurred a few years ago in Skidmore, Missouri, where a group of enraged citizens watched as a habitual offender who seemed to have been treated very leniently by the criminal justice system was shot to death. Although the killing occurred in broad daylight in front of about thirty people, no one was willing to help the police find the killer. Apparently, the citizens felt that "justice" had been done (Rose, 1981).

A study of twenty-eight civilian patrol groups in American cities found that seventeen of them could be classified as supplemental groups that sought to assist the police rather than to oppose them. Seven groups were adversarial, in that they thought people had to defend themselves against the police as well as against criminals. The other four groups were mixed in their attitudes toward the police (Marx and Archer, 1971, 1972, 1973). The police usually regard adversarial patrol groups as spies on their activities or as challengers to their authority. Patrol groups that are adversarial to the police and opposed by the police are the kind of group most likely to engage in violence, as well as the type most likely to be the target of police violence. In general, there is more community support for supplemental patrol groups than for adversarial ones; the latter are less likely to represent community consensus and may create or exacerbate intergroup conflict in the community.

One patrol group that has received much attention is the Guardian Angels. This organization, which now has branches in many large cities, is comprised primarily of young Hispanics and blacks who patrol subway stations and subway cars in groups, wearing red berets and Angel T-shirts in order to deter robbery and assault. Guardian Angels are trained in karate, resuscitation methods, and the legal requirements for citizen arrests (Robbins, 1981). In some cities, this group is supported by the police, but in other cities officials have been silent or critical of the Angels. The effectiveness of the Angels in preventing crime is unclear; they may simply displace crime to other locations or to a time when they are not around. However, many subway riders say that they feel safer when they see a group of Guardian Angels nearby; this greater sense of security may make people more willing to ride the subways, thereby creating more informal social control because of the presence of a greater number of people in public places (Michaels, 1981).

Since 1960, there has been a rapid growth of private security forces in American communities. Suburban areas and well-to-do urban neighborhoods have hired private guards to patrol the streets as a deterrent to crime (Stein, 1981; *The New York Times,* September 18, 1983). These private security guards supplement the local police, stopping offenders and holding them for the police to arrest. The fact that these private guards are paid for by the residents of a neighborhood raises the possibility that middle-to-upper-income people might prefer to hire private security forces for their own community, rather than pay more taxes to hire additional police officers for the city as a whole. This "privatizing of social control" could thus reduce the patrolling of the streets of poor neighborhoods and enhance the security of well-to-do areas that can afford such guards (Shearing and Stenning, 1983: 503; Teltsch, 1984).

OBSTACLES TO URBAN PATROL GROUPS

Patrol groups face several problems (Marx and Archer, 1971, 1972). To sustain the interest of their members and the support of the community, they need to make the crisis to which they are responding continuously felt. Patrol groups need a charismatic leader to inspire confidence in their members and in the residents of the community. Patrol groups need to be formally organized, and they require financial support. They have a better chance of survival if

Here a member of the Guardian Angels patrols a New York City subway car.

Photo by Christopher Brown. Reprinted by permission of Stock, Boston. © by Stock, Boston, Inc., 1983.

they have an ideology that states positive, specific goals; vague targets such as crime and disorder do not seem to sustain patrol groups for long. These groups are also most effective in limited and well-defined settings, such as housing projects and rock concerts, where there are homogeneous populations separated from other people by clear boundaries. Even if all of these conditions are met, patrol groups face difficulties:

> Self-defense groups often lack a clear mandate from the groups they wish to serve and their legal position regarding the use of force and citizen arrests is ambiguous. They may have trouble defining their task. The tendency of the groups to lack the resources for recruiting, screening, and training appropriate manpower and for sustaining motivation beyond that which stems from a deeply felt crisis (along with the degree of autonomy some groups have) may contribute to ineffectiveness and abuses. And even if internal problems are solved, the groups may face harassment from the police (Marx and Archer, 1971: 68).

THE FUNCTIONS OF URBAN PATROL GROUPS

Urban patrol groups serve important symbolic and participatory functions for their members. They enhance the self-esteem and sense of power of those who are involved, leading patrol-group members as well as other community residents to think that they can do something about crime. If people believe that the patrols are effective in making the streets safer, even if they are not, people may be more willing to use the streets at night.

Patrol groups probably provide more structured surveillance of a community than is possible through informal observation by residents. The surveillance provided by patrol groups is likely to be more effective in deterring crime than is unorganized surveillance, because the chance that a member of a patrol group will take direct action is probably greater than the chance that a private citizen will intervene personally or call the police. Patrol groups can thus create surveillance, stimulate interaction in public places, and help to reduce crime by providing support for the formal control agents and by increasing informal control by community residents.

Community Crime-Prevention Strategies

There is evidence that people who participate in patrol groups and other community efforts to fight crime are drawn to those organizations not by their fear of crime, but rather by a general desire to improve neighborhood life. Indeed, most community crime-prevention efforts develop from neighborhood organizations that have a more general orientation toward community revitalization or toward providing services for local youths (Lewis and Salem, 1981). A survey in Chicago found that most people did not participate in any organized program to reduce crime, but that the 10 per cent who did were usually already active in a local voluntary association. Crime had to reach a certain level of salience before these people would turn their efforts to crime prevention, but fear of victimization by itself did not seem to draw many people into such crime-prevention efforts and may even have kept some potential recruits from taking action (Lavrakas and Herz, 1982).

One study of community crime-prevention efforts explicitly avoided an approach that treats collective responses to crime as the product of fear of victimization, pointing out that similar levels of crime elicit very different responses in different communities. Every community studied by the researchers devoted some energy and resources to fighting crime, and people everywhere seemed to believe that collective efforts can reduce the crime rate. In general, people did not see crime as a problem that could be isolated from other social problems, and so their crime-prevention efforts were usually part of a broader effort to improve the neighborhood. Some communities followed a "social problems" approach to deal with the general conditions thought to be the source of the crime problem; other communities used "victimization-prevention" strategies to deal more directly with crime by increasing surveillance or by developing protective measures. Instead of being linked to perceptions of the crime rate, participation in these collective efforts to reduce crime seemed to be associated with the social and cultural context of the community— that is, with the family status, socioeconomic position, and race and ethnicity of the residents. Participation in community-wide efforts is more likely in communities where residents are more integrated into the community and have more permanent ties to the area through home ownership and long-term residence (Podolefsky and DuBow, 1981).

COMMUNITY REACTIONS TO OFFENDERS

People frequently react to crime by assuming that it is the activity of people very different from themselves—either offenders of a different race or class, or criminals who live somewhere else. This "we-they" distinction allows people to condemn offenders more harshly, because they are not then condemning people like themselves or the residents of their community. "We" form a peaceful and homogeneous community, but "they" bring crime and violence to the community and must be excluded or locked up to ensure safety. This negative identification with offenders allows people to see criminals as completely different from themselves, and permits them to think that they could never violate the law. This negative identification also pushes offenders out of conventional society and makes it difficult for them to maintain ties to the society or become reintegrated once they have been ostracized.

One case in which several of these attitudes toward criminals as outsiders came together was in the events leading to the lynching of Leo Frank after the murder of a thirteen-year-old factory worker in Georgia in 1913 (Dinnerstein, 1968). Frank was singled out as the girl's murderer in part because he was Jewish (in a Protestant community), from the North (in a southern community), an industrialist (in a farming community), and an employer of young women (in a community that supported traditional gender roles). There was little or no evidence to link Frank with the murder, but he was taken from prison and hanged by a mob after his death sentence was commuted by the governor. Even when an offender is not actually an outsider as Frank was, he or she may be redefined as an outsider or as different. For instance, in referring to local black criminals, a black political leader once remarked, "We don't consider criminals to be a brother. We consider them to be an enemy and they will be dealt with as such" (cited in Wallace, 1971: 3).

Isolating the Offender

People often place distance between themselves and criminals by establishing social agencies and institutions that take responsibility for law violators. When confronted with a convicted offender, people often prefer that the criminal be sent to a prison some distance from their own community. This attitude reflects a view of the offender as a dangerous outsider, and it reinforces that view by isolating the offender from conventional society. The popular view that crime results from personal shortcomings rather than from social conditions helps to justify the isolation of individual offenders in prisons, instead of leading to the development of social policies that might reduce crime. The isolation of offenders can lead to "prisonization," or immersion in a subculture of inmates that may reinforce criminal behavior. The geographic isolation of prisons also tends to increase demographic differences between inmates, many of whom are young members of minority groups from urban areas, and correctional officers, who tend to be older whites from rural areas and small towns.

The isolation of offenders makes it difficult to reintegrate them when they are released from prison; this pushes them back into a life of crime and perpetuates the crime problem. Prison programs that train inmates for jobs are of little use if no one will hire ex-convicts when they are released. People with criminal records have a harder time finding good jobs than do people without records (Schwartz and Skolnick, 1962; Goodstadt, 1979). Many employment agencies will not even handle clients with criminal records, because they know that many firms will not hire them.

Community-Based Corrections

In recent years there has been an increasing recognition that most criminals who are sent to prison eventually return to society, and that most rehabilitation programs in prison have little or no beneficial effect. The result has been the growth of *community-based corrections,* an approach to punishment that includes a reduced emphasis on the "warehousing" of offenders in large prisons far from their homes and an increased emphasis on keeping offenders within their own community. Some efforts have been made to develop small correctional facilities in the towns and cities where offenders live. These institutions make it easier for relatives and friends to visit inmates, help to maintain offenders' ties to the community, and make it easier to find jobs when offenders are released.

WORK-RELEASE AND EDUCATION-RELEASE
Another aspect of community-based corrections is work-release and education-release programs. These programs place incarcerated offenders in a less secure housing situation outside the main prison. Inmates work or go to school during the day and return to the institution at night. This helps to maintain social ties, gives inmates access to jobs and educational facilities in the outside world, and yet provides security for the community.

HALFWAY HOUSES
Another community-based correctional program is the *halfway house.* This is an institution with little or no security where offenders who have been released from prison live with other ex-convicts. The halfway house eases the offender's transition back into the community; the released ex-convict is not confronted with an abrupt change from prison to freedom that many offenders find difficult to manage.

The commonly held public attitude that ex-convicts are different and dangerous underlies what is often considerable community resistance to the establishment of local halfway houses for ex-convicts, juvenile delinquents, or alcoholics. A national survey found that four of every five people favored the general idea of a halfway house, but only half of those questioned would support one if it were located in their own neighborhood (Joint Commission on Correctional Manpower and Training, 1968: 13–17). Another study of community resistance to halfway houses for juvenile delinquents found that people believed that these institutions would tarnish their community's image, cause local property values to drop, subject the community to victimization by the house's residents, and set a bad example for their children (Coates and Miller, 1973).

Community resistance to halfway houses can be neutralized by having a halfway house represented by house parents rather than by a government agency, by getting residents of the house to renovate it and thus increase its value, by using staff and peer pressure to reduce crime by house residents, and by having house residents be well-groomed and well-dressed so as to increase interaction between them and residents of the community. These measures might be supplemented with a low-profile approach to introducing the house to the community, including discussions with local political leaders and a campaign to neutralize community resistance (Coates and Miller, 1973).

Measures that make offenders seem human to the public and that show that the exclusion and rejection of offenders only perpetuate the crime problem may ease the reintegration of offenders into the community. This would make the lives of ex-convicts more productive and help to reduce crime rates. However, overcoming the community's tendency to isolate offenders is a difficult and challenging task.

SUMMARY

Reactions to crime by the community and the criminal justice system can help to control crime. Formal control by the criminal justice system seems to be less important in keeping crime in check than is informal control. These two forms of social control may be inversely related to each other.

Informal control is most effective when interaction is common and the surveillance of behavior is possible. These conditions are probably more common in small towns than in large cities, but some large cities contain communities in which such conditions exist. In large cities, where crime rates are often quite high, people frequently assign the task of crime prevention to the formal control agents of the criminal justice system. There is, however, much variation among urban communities; people seem especially willing to play an active role in crime prevention in socially integrated and stable neighborhoods. The unwillingness of citizens to help to prevent crime can begin a crime cycle in which their responses to crime influence behavior in ways that actually cause crime rates to rise.

The idea of defensible space maintains that architectural design can increase citizen involvement in the crime-prevention process by encouraging people to exercise control over the territory in which they live. This process may reduce some kinds of crime in certain housing situations, but overall the evidence that defensible space can have a major impact on the crime rate is not strong. A revised defensible space model that takes into account the social characteristics of residents and the way that people form networks might describe more accurately the way that informal control can check crime.

For informal social control to be effective in reducing crime, people must be willing to call the police or intervene in a crime. The Good Samaritan problem arises when witnesses fail to take action of this sort. Nonresponse to observed crimes is a product of the ambiguity of some crime situations, a sense of unreality when watching a crime in progress, pluralistic ignorance that results from thinking that if no one else is helping it must be because no help is needed, and a diffusion of responsibility among witnesses. Other factors that can affect the chance that a bystander will intervene include whether the person feels self-assured, whether the person is trained in offering assistance, and the kind of community in which the person was raised.

Collective action in response to crime has a long history, dating back at least to 1760 in the United States and even earlier in other societies. Vigilante groups in the American West sought to create order in the absence of a criminal justice system, taking upon themselves the responsibility for preserving life, liberty, and property from suspected criminals. Today, urban patrol groups operate in the context of a functioning, but often ineffective, criminal justice system. These groups usually seek to supplement the police by patrolling the streets and calling the police to the scene of a crime or holding suspects until the police arrive. In recent years, there has been a privatization of crime control as well-to-do people have hired their own security guards to reduce the risk of victimization in their neighborhood. In general, however, citizen involvement in crime prevention does not seem to be a direct result of the fear of victimization, but is instead usually a part of ongoing efforts to improve the community and is related to the social characteristics of the community.

Rejection of offenders by the community can contribute to the crime problem by severing offenders' bonds to conventional society. The isolation of criminals in prisons remote from their homes weakens their attachments to family and community and makes it difficult for them to stay away from crime after they are released. In recent years, community-based correctional programs have tried to reduce this isolation through work-release and education-release programs and through the use of halfway houses.

IMPORTANT TERMS

community-based corrections

defensible space

diffusion of responsibility

formal social control

Good Samaritan problem

halfway house

informal social control

mechanical solidarity

organic solidarity

pluralistic ignorance

protective neighboring

social control

SUGGESTED READINGS

JOHN E. CONKLIN. *The Impact of Crime.* New York: Macmillan, 1975. A more detailed exploration of the topics examined in this chapter: informal social control and individual and collective responses to crime.

BIBB LATANÉ AND JOHN M. DARLEY. *The Unresponsive Bystander: Why Doesn't He Help?* New York: Appleton-Century-Crofts, 1970. A series of experiments bearing on the Good Samaritan problem.

DAN A. LEWIS, ED. *Reactions to Crime.* Beverly Hills, Calif.: Sage Publications, 1981. A collection of papers that investigate different aspects of the impact of crime on society.

OSCAR NEWMAN. *Defensible Space: Crime Prevention through Urban Design.* New York: Macmillan, 1972. A detailed presentation of the defensible space model of reducing crime through architectural design.

14

The Criminal Justice System

Every modern society has a criminal justice system that exercises formal social control over its members. We need to understand this system in order to make sense of the careers of criminals, for the criminal justice system shapes offenders' behavior as well as punishes them. Labeling by the criminal justice system can, under some circumstances, contribute to the development of criminal careers, but arrest and conviction can also keep people from violating the law by instilling in them a fear of punishment. A prison sentence may also reduce crime by cutting an offender's ties to accomplices, causing criminal skills to grow rusty, or pushing an offender into treatment. However, a prison sentence may also contribute to crime by creating a desire to strike back at society, reducing ties to conventional people, and exposing an offender to other criminals. Thus, the criminal justice system can prevent crime or contribute to it.

In this chapter, we examine three components of the criminal justice system—the police, the courts, and the prisons. In the following three chapters, we look at the principles on which this system is based. The criminal justice system is sometimes based on the idea of deterrence, the notion that the threat of sanctions can prevent crime by creating a fear of punishment in those who might break the law. A second basis for the system is retribution, the idea that offenders deserve to suffer for the harm they have caused, and that their punishment should be in proportion to that harm. A third perspective is rehabilitation, which proposes that criminal sanctions should aim to reform convicted offenders so that they will stay away from crime in the future.

The effectiveness of the criminal justice system in meeting the goals of deterrence, retribution, and rehabilitation depends on coordination among the various agencies of law enforcement. Critics have claimed that the American criminal justice system is not really a system at all, in the sense of being a set of agencies that are coordinated with each other, seek the same goals, and try to implement a single policy to deal with crime. There are important linkages among the police, the courts, and the prisons, as we can see in Figure 14.1, but these agencies do not form a unified system. Thus, when we speak of the criminal justice system we are talking about these different law-enforcement agencies and the linkages among them, rather than about a single, well-coordinated system.

The criminal justice system has been described as a funnel or sieve that sorts out cases (The President's Commission on Law Enforcement and Administration of Justice, 1967a; Vera Institute of Justice, 1981). Only some of all

Figure 14.1: Case Attrition in the Criminal Justice System

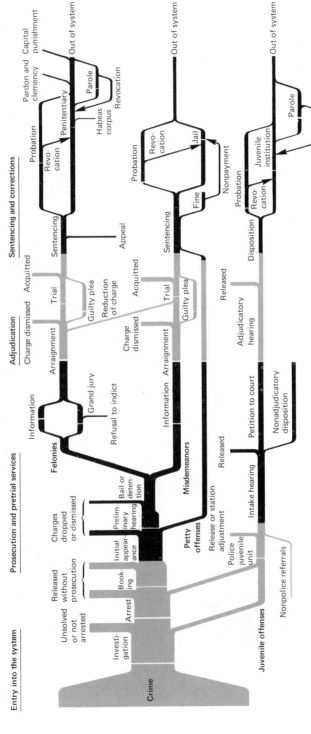

Note: This chart gives a simplified view of caseflow through the criminal justice system. Procedures vary among jurisdictions. The weights of the lines are not intended to show the actual size of caseloads.

SOURCE: Bureau of Justice Statistics. *The American Response to Crime.* Washington, D.C.: U.S. Department of Justice, December 1983, pp. 2–3. Adapted from the President's Commission on Law Enforcement and Administration of Justice, *The Challenge of Crime in a Free Society.* Washington, D.C.: U.S. Government Printing Office, 1967.

347

crimes that are committed are reported to the police, and many of those that are reported do not produce an arrest. Arrested suspects sometimes have the charges against them dropped or are acquitted in court; of those who are convicted and sentenced, many are not sent to prison. This funnel or sieve effect that characterizes the criminal justice system is one of *case attrition,* with cases being sorted out as they proceed through the system and with relatively few crimes that occur ending up with a perpetrator being convicted and imprisoned. This process of case attrition is shown in Figure 14.1.

A detailed study of case attrition for felony cases in New York City estimated that about half of all felonies in 1971 were reported to the police, and that the police made an arrest in about one-fifth of the felonies of which they learned. Overall, the police made 100,739 felony arrests, of which 75,661 proceeded to some disposition by the criminal justice system. Only 42,129 of the felony arrests, or 56 per cent of the arrests disposed of by the criminal justice system, produced a conviction on some charge. Twenty-seven per cent of the arrests, or 20,503 cases, led to a jail or prison sentence. However, only 5 per cent of the arrested suspects, or 3,811 defendants, were sentenced to "felony time," or more than one year in jail or prison (Vera Institute of Justice, 1981). Figure 14.2 shows the attrition of felony cases from arrest until final disposition.

Figure 14.2: Disposition of Felony Arrests in the Criminal Process, New York City, 1971

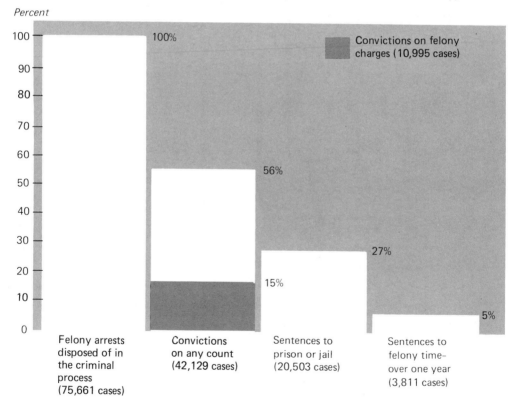

In 1973 the Comprehensive Data Systems program developed a Computerized Criminal Histories/Offender-Based Transaction Statistics (CCH/OBTS) system to gather information on defendants' prior criminal behavior and responses to that behavior by the criminal justice system. The federal Bureau of Justice Statistics did not direct states' attention to that program until 1981, and its initial report in November 1983 provided data for only four states, which asked to remain anonymous because their data had not been fully verified (Bureau of Justice Statistics, November 1983b). If this CCH/OBTS system is refined and implemented by all states, it would provide important information on the operation of the criminal justice system, including case attrition, and on the role that the police, the courts, and the prisons play in the careers of criminals.

THE POLICE

The police are the first formal line of defense against crime, for only if the police arrest suspects will the rest of the criminal justice system come into play in trying, convicting, and punishing offenders.

History of the Police

For centuries, societies have had some kind of a police force, an armed group of specialists who keep order and deal with violations of the law. The first modern police force was organized in London in 1829 by Sir Robert Peel, with officers nicknamed "bobbies" after their founder. This police force differed from earlier law-enforcement units in being full time, paid, uniformed, and organized for the city as a whole. Standards of literacy and character were established, and recruits were trained to perform their duties (Bayley, 1983).

Public police forces have existed in the United States since early in the seventeenth century, but it was only in Boston in 1837 that the first modern police force was organized, along the same lines as London's department. By the 1870s nearly all large American cities had their own police force, which provided all citizens, rather than just wealthy ones, with the services of criminal investigation. Urbanization had weakened the informal social control provided by families and neighbors, and the police were needed as a formal means of controlling deviance. Another important factor in the rise of American police forces was the threat to the social order posed by mob violence in nineteenth-century cities (Bayley, 1983).

Marxist criminologists regard the police in capitalist society as a tool used by the bourgeoisie to maintain a social order that is profitable to themselves and that exploits laborers (Harring, 1981, 1983; Spitzer, 1981). Marxists have shown how capitalists have historically used the police to quell collective action by organized labor. They point to the unequal treatment by the police of suspects from disadvantaged classes and racial and ethnic groups. However, there is evidence that members of all classes agree on the need to punish those crimes to which the police devote most of their attention: murder, rape, assault, and theft. Moreover, these crimes are the subject of police activity in socialist and communist societies, as well as in capitalist ones. In addition, the criminal law is probably not the most important mechanism for maintaining the social order, nor is it a very effective tool for the dominant class to use in controlling all members of society (Sparks, 1980b).

There is, however, good evidence that the criminal justice system responds to threats to the social order. For instance, one study found that a city's expenditures on its police force can be predicted by the racial composition of the city's population and by the level of black mobilization activity in the city. Cities with larger black populations spend more on salaries, operations, and capital expenditures for the police than do cities with proportionally fewer blacks. In addition, cities with more political activity by blacks have higher rates of police capital expenditures. One explanation of this is that police expenditures are increased when minorities are seen as a threat to the dominant racial group (Jackson and Carroll, 1981).

Organization of the Police

The police in the United States are organized at four levels. The first to develop were county sheriff's departments, followed by municipal police departments. Next there were established state police departments, first in Texas and then in Massachusetts. Federal marshalls, established in 1789, were the first federal police agency. Over time, the national government has expanded its policing activities, with the Bureau of Investigation—renamed the Federal Bureau of Investigation in 1935—being established in the Department of Justice in 1908 (Bayley, 1983).

Municipal police departments are organized hierarchically, with a police chief or superintendent at the top. Detectives and specialized investigative units—robbery, vice, and homicide, for instance—focus on solving crimes. One important aspect of police departments, compared to other bureaucracies, is that the individual at the lowest level of the hierarchy—the patrol officer on the street—has the most contact with the public and with criminal suspects, and also has a great deal of autonomy because superiors have difficulty directly supervising the officer's activities. Within police departments, conflict and competition often develop between administrators concerned with efficiency and productivity, and officers on the street who must deal with the public and with suspects (Reuss-Ianni, 1983).

For the police, fighting crime is but a small part of their job. In cities of more than 50,000 people, only forty-five of every 100 officers on duty at any time are actually on patrol. The police spend only about 15 per cent of their time dealing with crime; they spend the rest filing reports, providing ambulance service, or managing traffic (*U.S. News & World Report*, November 1, 1982). Much police effort is also expended in maintaining social order. For instance, to keep peace on skid row—a run-down area of the city frequented by the homeless, the unemployed, the alcoholic, and those without families—the police must cultivate personal relationships to gain knowledge about the people who live there (Bittner, 1967).

In their efforts to maintain order and enforce the law, the police in a democratic society are required to act in accordance with the legal rights of citizens and certain constraints upon official behavior, which have been spelled out in the Constitution, legislative enactments, and judicial decisions. As part of a bureaucracy, however, the police have an ideology that emphasizes order, efficiency, and initiative. These values are sometimes in tension with the value of legality. Thus, " 'law' and 'order' are frequently found to be in opposition, because law implies rational restraint upon the rules and procedures utilized to achieve order. Order under law, therefore, subordinates the ideal of conformity to the ideal of legality" (Skolnick, 1975: 9).

The conflicting demands under which the police operate sometimes lead them to abuse their authority. For instance, departmental pressure on officers to use their initiative and to be efficient in solving cases may lead to violations of due process rights, such as illegal seizure of evidence or coercion of a confession. Laws that define "victimless crimes" such as gambling, possession of drugs, or prostitution require the police to make arrests for consensual crimes in which the participants do not define themselves as victims; in such cases, the police may find it easy to justify taking a bribe not to make an arrest. Stressful work conditions may increase police sensitivity to challenges to their authority and make brutality against citizens more likely. The camaraderie of the police subculture may encourage retaliation against those who assault or kill fellow officers. In sum, police abuses of their authority seem to be structurally induced, rather than the product of personality flaws in individual officers. Sometimes, entire departments engage in systematic violations of the law, as we see in the Cross-Cultural Perspective.

Periodically, police corruption scandals occur, often before elections and frequently with an activist press involved. A commission may be established to document police corruption and bring charges against officers; action against those who pay bribes is less common. For a time, the department may be "cleaned up," as officers become wary of accepting bribes. Eventually, matters usually get back to "normal," with at least small favors for the police becoming common again. An exception to this pattern seems to be the New York City Police Department, which has been able to sustain an effort to control corruption for more than a decade. In 1972, the Knapp Commission was established to investigate charges by officer Frank Serpico that corruption was rampant

---

A Cross-Cultural Perspective: Police Corruption in Mexico

In Mexico, the police "have become symbols of corruption, abuse of power and in some cases outright criminality." A newspaper editorial claims that Mexicans see the police officer as "a hot-tempered individual, capable of extreme cruelty and easily corruptible." One lecturer and author writes: "Society has come to fear the police more than it fears criminals." Indeed, the distinction between police officer and criminal is often unclear, as Mexicans were reminded when a former officer was shot to death while resisting arrest after kidnapping and murdering an eleven-year-old boy.

When it was revealed that an illegal detective corps in Mexico City had run secret jails where people were beaten until ransoms were paid, Mexico's new president dismantled the unit. However, this unit was so feared by Mexicans that some were afraid of the consequences of letting its officers loose on the public. One newspaper remarked: "They are too dangerous to be cast into the ranks of the unemployed."

Widespread corruption from the bottom to the top of the Mexican police force has led to public cynicism toward the government. When the police march in parades, they are heckled. A major source of this hostility is the "mordidas," or bribes, that the police demand from drivers they accuse of violating traffic laws. These bribes are distributed upward throughout the police organization, and are often justified by the poor salaries that officers are paid or by the fact that they had to "buy" their jobs. This corruption pervades not only the police, but also district attorneys' offices and the court system. As one official notes, "With defenders of the law acting outside the law, the citizen doesn't stand a chance."

SOURCE: Alan Riding, "Criminals in Mexico: How Many Are Policemen?" *The New York Times*, February 13, 1983, p. 12.

in the department. The commission found that a majority of officers were engaged in some corrupt practices, and distinguished between "grass eaters" who did not pursue payoffs actively but did accept them, and "meat eaters" who expended much effort in soliciting bribes and payoffs (*The Knapp Commission Report on Police Corruption,* 1972). A 1982 report found that departmental pressure to avoid corrupt practices was still strong, and that officers continued to fear indictment and punishment. Reorganization of the department, intensive supervision, and the internal investigation of corruption—including systematic informing on dishonest officers by others who were assigned to report to the Internal Affairs Division—have kept corrupt practices at a lower level than before the Knapp Commission (Farber, 1982b).

The Working Personality of the Officer

Police officers develop a *working personality,* a distinctive approach to situations and events that they encounter in their jobs (Skolnick, 1975). This working personality develops in response to the danger of the job, the authority vested in the police officer, and the need to appear efficient in the performance of assigned duties. The police learn to respond to "symbolic assailants," who threaten community standards and the police themselves with violence and with disregard for other people's property. Officers learn how to do their jobs from the police subculture, which shares values such as conformity and authority with the larger culture, but includes specific values of its own such as suspiciousness and the need to maintain respect for the police at all costs. New recruits quickly learn the values and norms of this subculture. For instance, one study found that officers soon agreed that they sometimes had to use force to gain citizen compliance and that respect in tough areas depended on their willingness to use force (McNamara, 1967).

SUSPICIOUSNESS

Suspiciousness is a key element of the police officer's working personality. Officers learn to suspect that a crime is being committed or is about to be committed in situations to which other people would not give a second thought.

What is not clear, even after many judicial decisions, is exactly when an officer's suspiciousness is a legal basis for making an arrest. We can see this problem by looking at three cases decided by the Supreme Court in 1968. In one case (*Terry* v. *Ohio*), the Court ruled that an officer had behaved legally when he stopped two men who had been walking back and forth in front of a store and looking in the window. The Court found that the men's behavior was a reasonable basis for the officer's suspicion, even though an average citizen might not consider such behavior suspicious. In the same year, the court decided another case (*Peters* v. *New York*) in which it supported the actions of an officer who had patted down a suspect to find concealed weapons after he stopped the suspect tiptoeing down the hallway in the officer's apartment building. The Court held unanimously that this was a reasonable search because the officer suspected that the man was about to commit a burglary, a suspicion borne out by the burglar's tools found on the suspect. In the third case (*Sibron* v. *New York*), the Court ruled that an officer had not behaved legally in stopping and searching a man whom the officer had watched interacting with "known addicts" over an eight-hour period. From the perspective of the police subculture, someone who associates with known addicts for that long is quite likely to be an addict as well, but the Supreme

Court held that mere association with other addicts was not a reasonable basis for stopping and searching someone.

DISCRETION

Another important aspect of the working personality of the police officer is the exercise of *discretion*, the use of judgment to decide what action to take. Delegated discretion is clearly given to the police, such as the power to decide when to give a traffic ticket; unauthorized discretion is that which the police exercise but for which they may not have authority, such as making decisions on the basis of a suspect's race or sex (Skolnick, 1975). The way that the police exercise discretion helps to define the outer limits of permissible behavior. They may regard some offenses as mere nuisances, and decide to warn an individual rather than make an arrest. In general, the police are most likely to exercise discretion in dealing with minor offenses; in serious crimes, they have less freedom in deciding how to treat suspects and usually make arrests.

One decision that is difficult for the police to make is when to use force against a citizen. The police are legally justified in shooting people under certain circumstances, such as when an officer or another person is attacked by an armed offender or when a fleeing suspect poses a threat of serious harm to an officer or other people. The decision to shoot must be made quickly and under stressful conditions, and it is not always clear what action is called for. As a result, legal constraints on police use of force combine with dangerous situations on the street to make it difficult for officers to decide whether to shoot suspected offenders.

Another situation in which the police must exercise discretion is the "domestic dispute." The police have traditionally dealt with arguments or assaults between people who live together by making a judgment about the possible consequences of either arresting someone or trying to settle a dispute by mediating between the parties, even though few officers have been trained in crisis-intervention techniques (Oppenlander, 1982). An officer may judge that an arrest in a domestic disturbance will heighten conflict in the household over the long run, or believe that the complainant will not press charges in court. In these cases, the officer may decide not to make an arrest. Officers may choose to make an arrest if they think that the conflict will flare up again as soon as they leave. Feminist organizations have protested this use of police discretion, claiming that many wives are abused repeatedly by their husbands because the police are reluctant to make arrests. This is true, but so is the officer's contention that many women refuse to help in prosecuting their husbands, often out of fear, and that arrests can exacerbate tensions in the household. A recent Police Foundation study, which we examine in the following chapter, found that arrest deters future domestic violence more than does an effort to mediate a dispute. This finding lends support to the demand by feminist groups that more arrests be made in domestic disputes.

One study of police discretion found that an officer's decision about how to act in dealing with interpersonal disputes depended largely on the neighborhood in which the disputants lived. The police were more likely to deal formally with disputes in poor communities than in other areas. An officer's compliance with a complainant's request for action also varied with the socioeconomic status of the neighborhood (Smith and Klein, 1984). In this study, the exercise of police discretion seemed to be based not on the offense, but rather on the socioeconomic status of the community in which the fight occurred.

The decision to arrest a suspect is often based on the nature of the interaction between the officer and the suspect. In dealing with juvenile suspects, officers consider the youth's prior record, but also assess the suspect's character by his or her group affiliations, age, race, hair style, dress, and demeanor. Demeanor includes how contrite the suspect is about the offense, how much respect the adolescent shows the officer, and how afraid of possible sanctions the juvenile seems to be (Piliavin and Briar, 1964; Black, 1980). Fitting the image of a dangerous delinquent by being a member of a male delinquent gang can also increase a suspect's chances of being arrested (Morash, 1984).

One study found that an officer's decision to take a suspect into custody was influenced by

- the dispositional preferences of the victim,
- the race and demeanor of the suspect,
- the presence of bystanders, and
- the seriousness of the offense.

Males and females were equally likely to be arrested, and antagonistic behavior by suspects of either sex increased the chance of arrest. Bystanders increased the probability of arrest, because the police thought that they needed to show others that they were in control of the situation. In addition, arrest was less likely if the victim and the suspect knew each other, because this indicated that the victim would be less likely to help in prosecuting the suspect (Smith and Visher, 1981).

Police discretion is, ideally, based on an officer's best judgment about the future course of a suspect's behavior and the likely effects of an arrest or a warning, but this judgment must be made within legal constraints. For instance, if an officer judges that one suspect is more likely than another one to commit more crime if not arrested, and thus arrests the first suspect and only warns the second one, this decision involves illegal discrimination rather than delegated discretion if the only basis for the officer's decision is that the first suspect is black and the second one white.

Discretion and racial discrimination   There is mixed evidence on whether the police discriminate against minority groups. The complexity of this issue can be seen in a study based on data collected in 1965 and 1966 in Boston, Chicago, and Washington, D.C., by observers who rode in police cars and systematically observed police behavior (Black and Reiss, 1970; Black, 1980). The researchers found that the police were much more likely to arrest a black juvenile suspect than a white juvenile suspect. However, two factors other than racial discrimination seemed to explain this difference. One was that more of the black juveniles were stopped for serious crimes, and the police acted on the legal basis of seriousness of the offense in arresting more of the black suspects. Second, most complaints about black juveniles came from black adults, and they were more likely than white adults who complained to the police about white juveniles to demand that the police make an arrest, rather than merely warn the juvenile. In making arrest decisions, the police thus seemed to respond to the seriousness of the crime and the preferences of the complainant, rather than to the race of the suspect.

One study of police discretion found that the race of the suspect had little effect on police arrest decisions in encounters without complainants, except that the police were more likely to arrest black females than white females in such encounters. In encounters with both a complainant and a suspect, police arrest decisions were not affected by the race of the suspect. However, the police were more likely to make arrests in encounters with a white complainant than in encounters with a black complainant. Police discretion thus seemed to involve racial discrimination against black complainants rather than against black suspects (Smith, Visher, and Davidson, 1984).

Much research, especially that done outside the South in recent years, finds that the race of the suspect is a less important influence on the police arrest decision than are factors such as the seriousness of the offense, prior criminal record, demeanor, and the socioeconomic status of the neighborhood in which a police encounter occurs. However, even when these other variables are taken into account, some studies find that race remains as a factor that influences the disposition of a case. For instance, one study found that there was more evidence of racial bias by the police in deciding to send juvenile suspects to court than there was of racial bias in court decisions. This racial bias by the police increased the chance that a youth from a minority group would have a record, which could then contribute to a criminal career by affecting police actions and court decisions in the future (Dannefer and Schutt, 1982).

If the police discriminate by race, we would expect that black offenders would stand a greater chance of being arrested than would white offenders who committed the same offense. We can test this for the crime of robbery, which involves a face-to-face confrontation between offender and victim. If the police "overarrest" black robbers, we would expect the proportion of all arrested suspects who are blacks to be higher than the proportion of all robbers that victims report to be blacks. We can see, however, from Table 14.1 that in a study of robbery in Boston the police actually "underarrested" black robbers in comparison to white robbers. In the first six months of 1964, 55 per cent of all robbers were blacks, according to victims, but only 44 per cent of all suspects arrested for robbery were blacks; this suggests that black robbers had a smaller chance than white ones of being arrested for their crimes. The data for 1968 show a similar pattern. This research does not support the contention that the police are more likely to arrest black suspects than to arrest white suspects (Conklin, 1972). A study of robbery in 1974 in Milwaukee, Wisconsin, found that the percentage of all arrested robbery suspects who were blacks was about the same as the percentage of all robbers identified as blacks by victims (Pruitt and Wilson, 1983). A study that used victimization survey data and FBI arrest data concluded that there was "virtually no criminal justice selection bias for either rape or robbery but there [was] such bias for assault, especially aggravated assault" (Hindelang, 1978: 101).

The observational study of the police carried out in Boston, Chicago, and Washington, D.C., in the mid-1960s uncovered a significant amount of prejudice among the police, with about three-fourths of the officers classified as very prejudiced or considerably prejudiced against blacks on the basis of spon-

Table 14.1: Percentage of All Robbers Who Are Blacks

PERCENTAGE WHO ARE BLACKS	1964*	1968*
By victim identifications	55%	66%
By arrest data	44%	53%

* Data are for the first six months of each year.

SOURCE: Adapted from John E. Conklin, *Robbery and the Criminal Justice System*. Philadelphia: J. B. Lippincott Company, 1972, p. 33.

taneous comments and behavior. Some of this prejudice was learned from the officers' relatives and neighbors when young, but prejudice also developed from on-the-job experiences that led officers to believe that all members of a racial group should be regarded with suspicion because that group had a relatively high rate of involvement in crime. This study found that prejudice, an attitude, was not necessarily associated with discrimination, which is behavior. The observers saw forty-four cases of police assault on citizens during seven weeks of around-the-clock observation; in many of these assaults no arrest was made. They found a higher rate of undue force used against whites than against blacks. Black and white officers used violence with about the same frequency, and usually against members of their own race, something that seemed to reflect the areas to which the officers were assigned. The police may have been less likely to use violence against blacks during this period because of the threat of an urban riot, for riots occurred in many cities from 1965 to 1968. The gains of blacks in the area of civil rights may also have convinced some officers that police abuses would be reported and lead to trouble for them. In addition, officers may have adjusted their behavior in the presence of observers to avoid the appearance of discrimination, although they apparently did not adjust their verbal comments to avoid the impression of racial prejudice (Reiss, 1968, 1971).

One area in which the police may discriminate by race is in the shooting of civilians. A study of police shootings in Chicago between 1974 and 1978 found that if rates of being shot by the police were calculated for blacks, Hispanics, and whites by dividing the number of shooting victims of each group by the number of people of that group arrested for "forcible felonies"—defined as murders, rapes, robberies, assaults, and burglaries—then whites were somewhat more likely to be shot than blacks and Hispanics, although differences among the groups were relatively small. Rates were calculated in this way to account for group differences in involvement in serious crimes, the situations that most often led to police shootings. This study suggests that the police are about equally likely to shoot whites, blacks, and Hispanics; that is, the police do not seem to discriminate by racial or ethnic group (Geller and Karales, 1981). A study of police shootings in Memphis, Tennessee, found that the police were more likely to shoot blacks than whites, even if differences between the groups in involvement in criminal activity were taken into account (Fyfe, 1981). This suggests that police discrimination against minorities in the use of force may exist in some cities but not in others. Differences in the relative power of minorities, the organization of the municipal police department, and the department's administrative directives may help to account for such city-to-city variations in the use of force by the police against minorities (Fyfe, 1981; Waegel, 1984).

Discretion and sex discrimination　There is evidence that the police respond differently to male and female defendants. One study in a midwestern city found that from 1948 to 1976, police disposition of males and females became more similar for juvenile and adult misdemeanors and for adult felonies, but that males and females continued to be treated differently for juvenile status offenses and juvenile felonies. Overall, treatment of the sexes became more alike over time, but sex discrimination had not disappeared by the 1970s. Female status offenders were treated more leniently and paternalistically even in the 1970s (Krohn, Curry, and Nelson-Kilger, 1983).

A study that covered the period from 1934 to 1979 found that sex differentials in arrests had diminished in most offense categories, with the largest changes occurring in the 1960s and 1970s. Women showed the most significant increases in arrests for petty property crimes—such as larceny, fraud, and forgery—and for vagrancy and disorderly conduct, which were often related to prostitution. The researchers concluded that the narrowing of the sex differential has not yet produced a convergence of male and female arrests. This narrowing seemed to be due to changes in law-enforcement practices and changes in FBI statistical coverage of a larger part of the nation, as much or even more than it was due to changes in actual behavior by men and women (Steffensmeier and Cobb, 1981). The following changes seemed to have produced increased arrests of females:

1. A decline in chivalry and sympathy for female defendants;
2. A possible increase in the surveillance of women because of growing attention to crime by women;
3. Increased social and legal pressure to administer the law in a nondiscriminatory way;
4. Professionalization and bureaucratization of the police;
5. Improvements in police recording practices, including a greater likelihood of recording a suspect's sex; and
6. Changes in welfare agencies, which have led to more prosecution of crimes such as fraud and larceny (Steffensmeier and Cobb, 1981).

The Clearance Rate

To measure their effectiveness in dealing with crime, the police use the *clearance rate*, or proportion of offenses that they solve to their satisfaction (Skolnick, 1975). Many cleared cases lead to arrest, prosecution, and conviction, but the police also classify as cleared some cases that do not produce an arrest. Sometimes an offender cannot be arrested because he or she is deceased, out of the country, or in prison in another state. Thus, a man who kills his wife and then commits suicide would leave the police with no one to arrest for the murder, but the police would still call the homicide cleared. In other cases, the police strongly believe that they know who committed a crime, but lack the evidence to make an arrest; often these crimes are classified as cleared.

There are some problems with relying on clearance rates to measure the effectiveness of the police. Because the police themselves decide when a case is cleared, they can classify cases as cleared to make themselves look good. This might mean that the actual offender in a crime that is erroneously marked cleared will no longer be hunted by the police; such "false clearances" could reduce the deterrent effect of the law. Another difficulty with clearance rates is that a crime committed by several offenders may be marked cleared with the arrest of a single suspect; this action exaggerates the police's effectiveness in arresting criminals. Departmental pressure to clear cases can lead the police into illegal actions to draw people into behavior for which they can be arrested. Critics see this as illegal entrapment, but supporters justify it by saying that only people predisposed to crime would be drawn into it.

In the Boston robbery study, close attention was paid to the way that the police cleared cases. The clearance rate for all robberies recorded by the police in the first six months of 1964 was 37.4 per cent; for the first six months of 1968, it was 35.8 per cent. Looking at cleared robberies for the 1968 period,

38 per cent of the clearances resulted from an arrest at or near the scene of the crime, with the police interrupting the robbery or finding a suspect nearby. Another one-fifth (19.7 per cent of the clearances) resulted directly from information supplied by the victim or a witness; this included giving the police the name or address of the robber or identifying a "mugshot." Nearly as many robberies were cleared by victim identification of a suspect in another case; 18.2 per cent of the clearances resulted from victims saying that they were robbed by someone whose photograph was shown to them by the police or by an offender they picked out of a lineup. Another 17.9 per cent of the clearances resulted from what we might call "multiple clearance by confession." This method, which did not use the victim as a check, involved suspects who confessed to similar offenses about which the police asked them. In cases of this sort, suspects know that the police will not charge them with the additional crimes to which they confess, and may even be more lenient on the offense for which they were arrested, if the suspect cooperates and helps the police to clear their books. These multiple clearances by confession are used to make the department look more efficient at solving crimes. The final method by which robbery cases were solved was by a detective's investigation; this method accounted for only 6.2 per cent of all clearances (Conklin, 1972).

THE ROLE OF THE DETECTIVE IN CLEARING CASES

There are several reasons that detectives solve relatively few robberies. One is that if robbers escape from the scene of the crime, there is usually little that detectives can do to find them. There is rarely any physical evidence, such as fingerprints, and victims' descriptions are often vague and unreliable. Those few cases that detectives do solve may well be the most serious robberies, such as bank robberies and grocery store holdups.

A recent study of the role of detectives in solving crimes concludes that their efforts are as important as the investigative work of patrol officers in solving robberies and burglaries. Robbery and burglary cases were divided into three categories within the department:

1. Cases that could not be solved with a reasonable amount of effort;
2. Cases that are solved by circumstances, requiring only the arrest of a suspect and the development of the case for prosecution; and
3. Cases that could be solved with a reasonable amount of effort.

Many robberies and burglaries were not even assigned to detectives for investigation because there were few or no leads or because the case was solved by circumstances, but of those cases that were assigned to detectives, many were solved by investigation. This investigative process included interviews with witnesses and informants, discussions with other police officers, and an examination of the department's files. Interviews with victims led to few arrests (Eck, 1984).

A detective's decision to investigate a victim's complaint about the theft of property is affected by the characteristics of the victim and the crime. Detectives are more likely to spend time in a follow-up investigation if there is some evidence that might help them to solve the crime. In burglary cases, victims living in relatively well-to-do communities seem to receive more attention from police investigators than do victims who live in poor communities. Minority-group members who are burglary victims seem to be only slightly less likely than white victims to receive favorable treatment by police investigators. Police activity in the follow-up investigation of violent crimes is influenced to some degree by the willingness of the victim to aid in the prosecution of the case (Bynum, Cordner, and Greene, 1982; also, see Sanders, 1977).

A study of responses to reported burglaries found that a southern sheriff's department was more likely to use evidence technicians to dust for fingerprints when entry into the building involved force or when the property that had been stolen was "a marker of the self." Jewelry, silver, and firearms were items that recalled the past or had special personal significance for victims, and the sheriff was more likely to make special investigative efforts when such property had been taken. Dusting for fingerprints rarely led to an arrest, but it did help to foster good public relations and to restore the victim's peace of mind after a serious breach of the home "as a private place and as a territory of the self" (Stenross, 1984: 400).

The police are especially likely to investigate complaints about crimes that have certain characteristics: These crimes are serious, provide evidence, occur in relatively well-to-do neighborhoods, have a victim who is willing to prosecute, and involve the loss of property with personal significance. The race of the suspect does not seem to be a major factor in either the arrest decision or the decision to shoot a suspect. However, the police seem to be more responsive to a white complainant who wants an arrest made than they are to a black complainant who makes the same demand. We can see that not every crime is equally likely to produce an arrest. The nature of police work thus introduces several contingencies into an offender's career, with offenders who have certain traits and who commit certain kinds of crime being especially likely to be arrested and processed by the courts.

THE COURTS

In the United States, suspects are presumed to be innocent from the time they are arrested by the police until they are found guilty or innocent in court. As a consequence, they have a right to gain their release pending the disposition of charges against them. Usually after some delay, a prosecutor brings charges against the suspect, a defense attorney helps the defendant to get acquitted or to secure the most lenient sentence possible, and a judge or a jury decides guilt or innocence. Often a defendant pleads guilty in return for an agreed-upon sentence that is less than the one that might result from a trial. When judges sentence the guilty, they sometimes give very different penalties to offenders who have similar criminal records and have been convicted of similar offenses.

Bail and Preventive Detention

The Eighth Amendment states that "excessive bail shall not be required" of criminal defendants, even though the practice has developed of denying bail to defendants in crimes that carry the death penalty. *Bail* is a system designed to ensure that defendants will show up to face charges against them when their trial is scheduled, while allowing them to remain free until the trial takes place. To do this, an amount of money is set that must be deposited with the court before the defendant can be released. Because bail requires suspects to pay money, it discriminates against those with low incomes who cannot afford their release. As a result, jails that hold suspects for trial are usually filled with poor defendants (Shenon, 1983).

A study conducted in Philadelphia concluded that defendants who were detained on bail—either because bail was denied or because they could not afford bail—differed from the average defendant entering the criminal justice system. Those who were detained on bail were more likely to be charged with serious crimes, more likely to have many prior arrests and convictions, more likely not to have shown up for trials in the past, and more likely to have been arrested when out on bail in the past. Thus, defendants held on bail seemed to be especially likely to commit new crimes ("bail crimes") if released, and especially likely to "default," or not show up for trial, if released. However, a significant number of the detained defendants, 13 per cent of the total, were classified as "low risks" who might have been released with little threat of bail crime or default. If these low-risk detainees had been released, jail overcrowding would have been alleviated (Goldkamp, 1983).

Defendants are released in several ways. Some are released on their own recognizance, a promise to appear for trial. Others gain their release by placing with the court an amount of cash equal to the bail set by the judge or by giving the court security equal in value to the amount of bail, such as a savings account pass book or a deed to real estate. Because most defendants have little money or property, a system of bail bondsmen has developed in the United States to help defendants gain their release.

Bail bondsmen write a bail bond, a kind of insurance policy, that guarantees the court that they will pay the full amount of the bail if the defendant fails to appear for trial as scheduled. In return for this guarantee, the bondsman charges the defendant 5 to 10 per cent of the total amount of the bail to write the bond. This fee is like an insurance premium; the defendant does not get it back if he or she appears for trial, because the bondsman assumes a risk for that money.

Bondsmen justify their services by saying that they allow defendants to be free pending trial, that they remind people of trial dates and thus reduce the number of defaults, and that they assume the risk of having to pay the court a large sum of money if the defendant does not appear for trial. In fact, these self-justifications are not supportable, except that bondsmen do make it easier for defendants to gain their release. In addition, bondsmen have often been involved in corrupt practices; one Kentucky official remarked that before that state replaced bondsmen, they "preyed on the poor, bribed judges and bailiffs, and paid jailers to send them customers" (cited in Sheppard, 1979: A22).

Bondsmen's assertion that they reduce the default rate by reminding defendants of trial dates can be tested. Illinois and Kentucky have eliminated the bail bondsman by allowing defendants to place 10 per cent of the amount of the bail with the court as a deposit, which is returned when they appear for trial, even if they are found guilty. Both states have found that defendants appear for trial as often under this percentage-deposit system as they did when released by bail bondsmen; thus, bail bondsmen seem to provide no useful service in reminding defendants to show up for trial. Moreover, both Illinois and Kentucky have found that their system of returnable deposits saves defendants much money that would otherwise have been lost to bondsmen. An experiment in two Massachusetts courts with a similar percentage-deposit system found that the default rate was actually lower than it was with bondsmen, and that defendants in the two courts saved a total of $78,000 in returned deposits over a six-month period (Conklin and Meagher, 1973).

Long delays from arrest until trial provide opportunities for defendants who are released on bail to commit crimes (Sorin, 1984). Concern with such "bail crimes" has led critics of the criminal justice system to call for *preventive detention,* a system that holds some defendants without bail. Washington, D.C., has a little-used preventive detention system that has been in effect since 1971, and preventive detention was authorized for the federal court system in 1984. In about half of the states, judges are allowed to consider whether a defendant is dangerous to others in making a decision to release the defendant prior to trial (Taylor, 1984). Even where preventive detention is not specifically authorized, judges often set very high bails for defendants they believe will endanger the safety of others or commit bail crimes. These defendants are held in jail when they cannot afford to make bail.

Most European nations have preventive detention systems that allow judges to hold defendants in jail without bail. For instance, French law allows judges to deny pretrial release to suspects if a judge believes it is the only way to protect evidence, prevent the coercion of witnesses, or avoid unlawful concertation between the defendant and accomplices. French law also permits judges to hold suspects without bail if they believe that it is required in order to prevent a repetition of the crime, to protect the accused, or to guarantee the appearance of the suspect in court. Informally, French judges also deny bail when they believe that a defendant needs a "taste of prison" to be rehabilitated or think that it would be psychologically harmful to release a suspect who will eventually be imprisoned; these reasons for denying bail are not stipulated in French law (Gerety, 1980).

In the United States, numerous objections to a system of preventive detention have been raised (Ervin, 1971). It may be unconstitutional, because setting no bail seems to violate the Eighth Amendment's requirement of setting a reasonable bail; however, as of 1984, the Supreme Court had not ruled that preventive detention was unconstitutional. Another objection to preventive detention is that it imprisons people for acts they might commit if they were released, and accurately predicting the behavior of pretrial releasees is difficult (Angel et al., 1971; Floud and Young, 1981; *British Journal of Criminology,* July 1982). Even the best predictors of what released suspects will do before they are tried make many errors, especially the error of incarcerating defendants who would not actually have engaged in any crimes if they had been released (Angel et al., 1971).

Preventive detention might contribute to criminal careers, for defendants who are held in jail awaiting trial are less able to consult with their attorneys and contact witnesses to help in their defense, and they may make a worse impression on judges or jurors in court. Preventive detention may thus set in motion a cycle in which suspects thought to be dangerous are denied bail, are then more likely to be convicted as a result of being held in jail, and thus have a worse criminal record that is used to hold them without bail again in the future. In addition, the denial of bail can cause defendants to lose their jobs, force their families to go on welfare, sever their bonds to the conventional order, and even make criminal behavior by their children more likely.

Prosecutors

Prosecutors, or district attorneys, are lawyers who are elected officials. Often they see themselves as independent of public control, while still serving the public, and regard themselves as lawyers whose behavior should reflect the standards of the legal profession (Neubauer, 1974). They work on behalf of the public to bring charges against defendants and to ensure that justice is done. Prosecutors are concerned with all aspects of the criminal case; they interact with police officers, defense attorneys, judges, jurors, witnesses, victims, and defendants.

Prosecutors measure their success by a conviction rate, just as the police measure their effectiveness by a clearance rate. Some prosecutors blame the police when they are unable to get convictions, claiming that the police are more concerned with clearing cases than with presenting cases that can produce convictions. The police, on the other hand, often accuse prosecutors of being too willing to reduce charges from felonies to misdemeanors just to secure convictions, rather than using the resources of the prosecutor's office to convict suspects on more serious charges (Shipp, 1981). Prosecutors do screen cases brought by the police to find the ones that are the most likely to produce convictions. Once defendants are convicted, prosecutors are not necessarily concerned with getting judges to mete out the harshest possible sentences (Neubauer, 1974; Stanko, 1981–82). Prosecutors are concerned with fairness, rather than with getting the longest possible prison sentence or with getting a conviction in a case in which the evidence does not warrant it.

Defense Attorneys

The American criminal justice system is based on an adversary model or "fight theory" that assumes that the correct verdict will emerge if the prosecutor presents the best case against the defendant and the defense attorney presents the strongest case for the defendant. Later we will see that many more criminal cases are settled by guilty pleas by defendants than are settled by trials that use this adversary model. The expertise of defense attorneys is important in helping defendants to get the best possible sentence in exchange for a guilty plea. When cases are tried before a judge or a jury, defense attorneys can help defendants to get acquitted, convicted on the least serious charge, or sentenced as leniently as possible.

Because many defendants are poor or have limited financial resources, defense attorneys often must be appointed and paid for by the court. The cases of *Gideon* v. *Wainwright* (1963) and *Argersinger* v. *Hamlin* (1972) guaranteed free counsel to any indigent defendant facing the threat of incarceration. Within the legal profession, attorneys who specialize in criminal law are often held in low regard, because of the social standing of their clients and because they tend to have relatively low incomes. As a consequence, criminal law usually attracts the less expert lawyers, and so defendants are not very well served in court.

In a study of the criminal justice system in a small Illinois city, the defense attorneys acted as counselors who tried to keep defendants out of court and do the best for them. Defense attorneys interpreted the law for their clients, and tried to get them the "normal" penalty or "going rate" for the offense with which they were charged. At the arraignment, judges informed defendants of the maximum penalty for the crime with which they were charged; the threat of a very long sentence—which few defendants actually received—made them more than willing to seek the advice of defense attorneys (Neubauer, 1974).

Defense attorneys are an integral part of the court system. They interact cordially with prosecutors and judges, rather than behave in an adversary manner, for good relationships with other court personnel make plea bargaining easier and help defense attorneys to get trial dates postponed when necessary. The close relationship of defense attorneys with other court personnel dilutes the adversary nature of the American criminal justice system, a system that seems designed to produce the most expeditious processing of cases (Blumberg, 1979).

Judges

In lower criminal courts, where most criminal cases are first heard, one of the judge's primary functions is to ratify agreements between defense attorneys and prosecutors about the sentences that defendants will receive for pleading guilty. When cases go to trial, judges act as decision makers, or as supervisors of the proceedings when cases are tried before juries. Perhaps the most important function for the judge is the sentencing of convicted offenders.

Judges are supposed to sentence convicted offenders on the basis of legal criteria: the nature of the crimes for which they have been convicted, and perhaps their criminal records. Criminologists have been concerned that judges may sentence offenders on the basis of extralegal criteria such as race, age, or sex. As we will see, most research indicates that sentences are based primarily on legal criteria, although sentences are sometimes influenced by personal characteristics of defendants that are supposed to be irrelevant to punishment.

Juries

The jury has been criticized as a group of amateurs who lack the legal training to make decisions that have major effects on defendants' lives. Others have defended the jury as important to a democracy, because it involves the average citizen in the process of defining and meting out justice. However, no more than 5 per cent of all felony cases that are prosecuted involve jury trials, as guilty pleas account for most convictions (Baldwin and McConville, 1980).

An important study of the American jury asked judges to fill out questionnaires about the jury trials over which they had presided. In about four-fifths of the cases on which data were collected, judges agreed that jurors had reached the same verdict that they themselves would have reached. In the remaining cases, juries were much more likely to acquit defendants when judges said they would have convicted them, rather than convict defendants that the judges would have acquitted. The jurors seemed to require more proof to find guilt beyond a reasonable doubt than did the judges, and so we might say that juries are "defendant-friendly." However, it may also be that defendants guessed correctly that in their particular cases they would fare better with juries than with judges, and chose jury trials as a result. The judges thought that the juries performed quite well, considering the evidence carefully and taking longer to reach verdicts in cases that the judges thought were the most difficult from a legal point of view (Kalven and Zeisel, 1966).

In contrast to this study's conclusion that juries are somewhat more lenient toward defendants than are judges, a more recent study found that juries were significantly more likely than judges who tried cases to convict defendants (Levine, 1983). This study of more than 58,000 felony trials concluded that since the 1950s there has been a growth in public conservatism toward crime that supports harsher treatment of defendants, and this change underlies a shift toward more convictions by juries. This researcher's methods differed from those of the earlier study, and so we must be cautious in attributing differences between the conclusions of the two studies to actual changes in jury behavior over time.

The Constitution requires a jury of the defendant's peers, but the exact meaning of this idea is unclear. During the twentieth century, the Supreme Court has required that black defendants have a jury of their peers, and the exclusion of blacks from juries has been used by the Court to invalidate convictions of black defendants. The courts have been less willing to hear cases from young defendants—say, those under the age of thirty—who claim that the juries deciding their fate are composed almost exclusively of people much older than they are, and that they are therefore not being tried by juries of their peers. Many surveys find that young people differ significantly from older people in attitudes and behavior, and so it would seem that a young defendant might not get a fair trial before a jury of much older people. However, the courts have not agreed, nor have they applied the idea of a jury of one's peers to characteristics such as class or level of education.

Plea Bargaining

Probably 95 per cent of the guilty verdicts in American courts result from *plea bargaining,* an informal but structured process of negotiation in which the prosecutor and the defense attorney agree about a guilty plea and the sentence that the prosecutor will recommend to the judge. In the United States, plea bargaining has long been acknowledged as integral to the processing of criminal defendants. It has also been used in Great Britain for years, but only recently has it been publicly acknowledged to be an important way of obtaining guilty verdicts.

Because defendants can request trials or delays, which are costly and time-consuming for the court, prosecutors are often willing to agree to a reduced charge or a light sentence in exchange for a guilty plea. Because prosecutors have the power to go to trial and ask for a severe sentence, defendants are frequently willing to plead guilty and accept a penalty less than the one they might receive if convicted in a trial (Rosett and Cressey, 1976; Maynard, 1984). One study found that judges sentenced defendants to longer terms if they asked for trials than if they pleaded guilty. Judges seemed to adopt the position that if a defendant took some of the court's time to have a trial, which is of course the defendant's legal right, then the judge would take some of the defendant's time by meting out a longer prison sentence (Uhlman and Walker, 1980). The sentence differential between defendants who have jury trials and those who plead guilty is especially likely to characterize jurisdictions where most defendants are induced to plead guilty (Brereton and Casper, 1981–82).

Plea bargaining has both critics and supporters. Critics claim that it may induce innocent defendants to acquiesce to a guilty plea in order to get a more lenient sentence than they would if they demanded a trial and were found guilty by a judge or a jury. Critics also complain that plea bargaining goes on behind closed doors, and that this keeps the legal process from public view and makes abuses more likely. Including defendants in the plea negotiation conference might help to minimize the routine way that defendants are treated by the courts. In addition, claim some critics, defendants cannot be sure that judges will mete out agreed-upon sentences after the defendants plead guilty in court. Sentences given out as a result of plea bargaining usually fall far short of maximum sentences so as to induce defendants to plead guilty.

Some critics argue that this means that the penalties resulting from plea bargaining are invariably less than justice demands.

Supporters of plea bargaining argue that the criminal courts could not function if every defendant asked for a trial. Resources of the courts would have to be multiplied many times to process all of the cases if plea bargaining were not used to resolve most charges. Supporters claim that plea bargaining provides just sentences—that is, penalties proportional to the harm caused by offenders—even if those penalties fall short of the legal maximum. They point out that the actual penalties meted out are much longer in the United States than they are in other Western democracies, and that plea bargaining keeps punishment from being even more severe than it already is (Rosett and Cressey, 1976).

Probation

One penalty that judges sometimes impose on convicted offenders is *probation*, a form of supervised release. Probation originated in the work of a Boston shoemaker named John Augustus, who began to supervise offenders and report on them to the court in 1841. In 1878 Massachusetts became the first state to pass a probation law; today all states and the federal government provide probation for at least some kinds of offenders (Gottfredson, 1983).

Probation is designed to offer convicted offenders treatment outside prison where they can maintain their ties to conventional society. Judges, with the help of probation officers who present them with presentence reports, try to select for probation those offenders who seem to be the best risks to stay away from crime. In addition to providing probationers with services, this system aims to control behavior through surveillance by probation officers to whom offenders have to report regularly (Gottfredson, 1983). However, many probation officers are so overburdened with cases that they have little time to supervise their clients or provide them with services. Probation is less expensive than incarceration, which is one reason that more than twice as many offenders were on probation as were in the nation's jails and prisons at the end of 1982 (Bureau of Justice Statistics, September 1983, August 1984b).

Sentence Disparity

A major problem with American courts is *sentence disparity*, the difference in the criminal sanctions that are meted out to people who are convicted of similar offenses and who have similar criminal records. For instance, there is significant variation in sentences from one state to another, from one city to another, and from one judge to another in the same city. Later in the book, we will examine sentence disparity in terms of the principle of retribution, but here we consider the influence that a defendant's characteristics—particularly race and sex—have on the kind or length of sentence that a judge metes out.

RACE AND SENTENCING

The fact that blacks constitute a disproportionately high percentage of all inmates in American jails and prisons, perhaps as much as half of all prisoners, while being only 12 per cent of the population, has led some critics of the criminal justice system to blame the imprisonment of so many blacks on racial discrimination by the judges who sentence offenders. Much research has been done on racial discrimination in the sentencing of offenders, particularly for capital offenses, but the results are not conclusive. In noncapital crimes, the research seems to indicate that race plays a less important role in sentencing than do legal factors such as the offense and the defendant's prior criminal record (Kleck, 1981; LaFree, 1981; Pruitt and Wilson, 1983; Hagan and Bumiller, 1983; Peterson and Hagan, 1984). When these and other legally relevant criteria are taken into account, race either disappears as a factor influencing sentencing or more often diminishes significantly in importance. However, some research finds that race does affect sentencing (Thornberry, 1979; Christianson, 1981). One study even concludes that both severity and leniency may exist toward black defendants, with the social context and nature of the crime determining the meaning that is given to race by the criminal justice system (Peterson and Hagan, 1984).

A useful distinction is between "direct" discrimination—in which race or ethnicity plays a part in the sentencing decision, even after taking into account seriousness of the crime and prior criminal record—and "organizational" discrimination—in which economically disadvantaged people are more likely to be convicted or to get a long prison term because they cannot afford to be released on bail or pay for a private attorney. Organizational or economic discrimination may not be based directly on race, but it affects the way that blacks are treated by the criminal justice system, because they have lower incomes, on the average, than whites, and are thus more affected by organizational discrimination (Unnever, 1982). Thus, some of what seems to be racial discrimination may actually be due to disadvantages suffered by blacks, such as poverty, lack of job skills, unemployment, low levels of education, and residence in blighted urban areas (Levey, 1979).

The relationship between direct discrimination and organizational discrimination is complex and has important consequences for social policy. Evidence of direct racial discrimination would require civil rights remedies, but evidence of organizational discrimination would point to the need for policies to alleviate the burden of poverty for people of all races. Most recent research finds that race plays some part in sentencing, but that its role seems to be diminishing and that its effects are compounded by the higher poverty rate of blacks.

A study in a large northeastern city found that sentence severity was not affected by race, once the seriousness of the charge and prior criminal record were taken into account. Blacks did receive harsher sentences than whites, but this was because blacks were charged with more serious crimes and had more prior arrests for serious crimes. There was also a tendency for blacks to be sent to prison more often than whites, and for whites to be put on probation more often; this tendency persisted even when legal and extralegal variables were taken into account. This study also found organizational or economic discrimination, with harsher penalties given to defendants who could not afford pretrial release or a private attorney. This economic discrimination fell most harshly on blacks, who tended to be poorer than whites (Spohn, Gruhl, and Welch, 1981–82).

Research conducted in California, Texas, and Michigan found that blacks and Hispanics received harsher sentences than whites in felony cases, even when they were charged with the same offenses and had similar criminal records. Minorities were more likely than whites to be released after arrest; but whites were more likely to be placed on probation, to be sent to jail rather than to prison, to get shorter sentences, and to serve less time in prison. There were no differences between whites and minorities in being considered for treatment programs in prison. In Michigan, but not in California or Texas, the parole board equalized sentences somewhat by releasing minority inmates earlier to compensate for their longer court-imposed sentences. The researcher did not attribute her findings to deliberate racial discrimination, but rather to the beliefs of many judges that minority offenders had characteristics—such as coming from broken homes or having poor employment records—that made them likely to return to crime if they were given short sentences. However, there was no evidence in this study that minority offenders had higher rates of returning to crime after release. The lighter sentences for whites seemed to be partly due to the fact that they were more likely than blacks and Hispanics to engage in plea bargaining, which led to convictions but also produced relatively lenient sentences. Blacks and Hispanics, on the other hand, were more likely to have jury trials, which could produce an acquittal but led to longer sentences when defendants were convicted (Petersilia, 1983; Rohrlich, 1983).

Discrimination against racial and ethnic minorities sometimes takes subtle forms. For instance, a study of sentencing in California found that being white, black, or Hispanic did not directly affect sentences, but that these groups were treated differently because judges emphasized different factors, such as type of offense and prior record, in determining sentences for members of each group. Thus, judges used the prior records of Hispanic defendants to justify longer sentences for them, but were less likely to use the prior records of white and black defendants to justify longer sentences for them (Zatz, 1984).

Procedures adopted by the courts—such as release prior to trial, the assignment of defense attorneys to indigent defendants, and the use of information about job history and family stability—seem to result in longer sentences for minority-group members than for whites, even when direct racial discrimination does not occur. Changes in court procedures could reduce the impact of race and ethnicity on sentencing. For instance, a study in Milwaukee, Wisconsin, found that between 1967 and 1977 judges became more "race neutral" in their sentencing of convicted robbers and burglars, and came to rely more heavily on legal factors such as offense and prior record. Growth in the caseloads of the courts forced the development of a more bureaucratic system of criminal justice, and this led to more reliance on formal rules that punished offenders on the basis of legal criteria rather than individual characteristics. In addition, the diminishing impact of race on sentencing was a result of an increasingly liberal judiciary and more professionalized prosecutors and defense attorneys (Pruitt and Wilson, 1983).

One review of the research on racial discrimination in sentencing concludes that in noncapital cases, the evidence is largely against general or widespread overt discrimination against blacks, even though there is discrimination in some jurisdictions and for some offenses (Kleck, 1981). However, in cases involving the death penalty, there have been several recent studies that indicate that race plays a role in sentencing.

Race and capital punishment   The major reason that the Supreme Court declared the states' death penalty laws unconstitutional in the 1972 case of *Furman* v. *Georgia* was that the application of those laws had shown an excessive degree of arbitrariness, especially in the more frequent use of capital punishment for black defendants. Since 1972, three-fourths of the states have enacted new death penalty laws to satisfy the criteria required by the Supreme Court, but these new laws have not eliminated racial discrimination in the use of the death penalty (Bowers and Pierce, 1980a; Bowers, 1984). Recent studies have found that race, location within a state (urban versus rural jurisdiction, for example), and other variables affect decision making in capital cases. This is true for different stages of capital cases: indictment, prosecution, reaching a verdict, sentencing, and appealing a verdict (Bowers and Pierce, 1980a; Bowers, 1983, 1984; Paternoster, 1983).

Recent studies have found that the race of the victim is an important predictor of which homicides will result in the death penalty (Bowers and Pierce, 1980a; Zeisel, 1981; Bowers, 1983, 1984; Paternoster, 1983; Samuel R. Gross and Robert Mauro, cited in Joyce, 1984a). For instance, a study of homicide in Florida in 1976 and 1977 found that people charged with killing white strangers were more likely to be indicted for first-degree murder (a capital offense) than were people accused of killing black strangers. Differences by race at the stage of bringing formal charges (indictment) thus accounted for the more frequent imposition of the death penalty on people who killed white strangers (Radelet, 1981). Table 14.2 shows the results of a study of homicides in eight states from 1976 to 1980. Defendants in homicide cases were much more likely to receive the death penalty if their victims were white than if their victims were black. This suggests that the courts place greater value on the lives of whites than on the lives of blacks (Joyce, 1984a). One study found that the importance of the victim's race was limited to felony-murders—homicides committed during the commission of another felony such as a rape, burglary, or robbery. In nonfelony homicides, black offenders who killed whites were by far the most likely of all murderers to be sentenced to death in Florida, Georgia, and Texas (Bowers and Pierce, 1980a).

Until 1977, forcible rape was a capital offense in some states; in that year, the Supreme Court ruled in *Coker* v. *Georgia* that the death penalty could not be imposed for rape. Until that decision, there was much racial discrimination in the administration of the death penalty for rape, particularly in the South for black males convicted of raping white females (Kleck, 1981). One study finds that black men accused of raping white women still receive harsher penalties than do white men who rape white women, or black men who rape black women; rapes of black women by white men seem relatively rare. It

Table 14.2: Race and the Death Sentence in Eight States, 1976–1980

STATE	WHITE VICTIMS			BLACK VICTIMS		
	Homicides	*Death Penalty*	*Per Cent*	*Homicides*	*Death Penalty*	*Per Cent*
Florida	1,803	114	6.3	1,683	14	0.8
Georgia	773	67	8.7	1,345	12	0.9
Illinois	1,214	35	3.0	1,866	10	0.5
Oklahoma	581	40	6.9	252	3	1.2
North Carolina	850	21	2.5	966	4	0.4
Mississippi	208	17	8.2	639	5	0.8
Virginia	646	15	2.3	742	4	0.5
Arkansas	396	13	3.3	398	2	0.5

Note: Homicides are cases in which negligence was not a factor and known suspects at least fifteen years old were identified.

SOURCE: Study by Samuel R. Gross and Robert Mauro; table reprinted from Fay S. Joyce, "Courts Study Link between Victim's Race and Imposition of Death Penalty," *The New York Times*, January 5, 1984, p. A18. Copyright © 1984 by The New York Times Company. Reprinted by permission.

thus appears to be the race of the victim, or a combination of the race of the victim and the race of the offender—rather than the race of the offender by itself—that is most important in determining sentences for convicted rapists (LaFree, 1980).

Much of the research on the death penalty that has found past discrimination in rape cases, and past and current discrimination in homicide cases, relies on data from the South. In part this is because all southern states, but only some nonsouthern states, now have the death penalty; and in part it is because southern states have meted out capital punishment much more often than those nonsouthern states that have death penalty laws. Between 1977, when executions were resumed after a ten-year hiatus, and the end of 1984, twenty-nine of the thirty-two executions that were carried out occurred in southern states. One study has found that outside the South, black homicide defendants seem less likely than white ones to be sentenced to death or actually executed (Kleck, 1981).

SEX AND SENTENCING

A recent review of the research on the differential treatment of men and women in the criminal justice system concluded that women were more likely than men to be released on their own recognizance (without bail), but that when bail was set there seemed to be no difference by sex in the amount at which it was set. Sex did not seem to make a difference in the decision to prosecute a defendant, nor were there differences by sex in the use of plea bargaining or in the likelihood of being convicted. At the sentencing stage, there was a small but consistent differential leniency toward female defendants, even when variables such as prior criminal history and the nature of the offense were taken into account (Nagel and Hagan, 1983). These findings of no differences by sex in prosecution, plea bargaining, or conviction, but a difference by sex in the sentencing of convicted offenders, were confirmed by a study in Dade County, Florida (Curran, 1983).

Although the juvenile courts seem to treat girls more harshly than boys for certain offenses (e.g., see Chesney-Lind, 1973), the criminal courts seem to sentence women more leniently than men. However, women are less likely to have a prior criminal record and more likely to commit less serious crimes, and so we must compare the fate of male and female defendants who have similar histories of criminal activity and who face similar charges. When this is done, somewhat contradictory conclusions are reached. Some studies find that men and women with the same records and facing the same charges are sentenced similarly by the courts, and other studies find that women are treated more leniently (Parisi, 1982).

The differential leniency toward female defendants has sometimes been attributed to "chivalry." Some claim that women who exhibit behavior that is socially defined as appropriate for women are the most likely to be treated leniently. Thus, older white women who are apologetic and submissive are less apt to be treated severely by the criminal justice system than are women who are black, young, and hostile toward authorities. Similarly, women who are more economically dependent on their husbands may be treated more leniently than women who are economically independent, perhaps because judges think that the courts need to exert less formal social control over women who are controlled by the men on whom they are economically dependent (Kruttschnitt, 1982).

Greater leniency by judges toward female defendants is due to factors other than chivalry. Judges may think it impractical to incarcerate women who have young children. They may believe that women are only led into crime by men and are unlikely to violate the law on their own. Women may also seem to be less dangerous or more easily rehabilitated than male offenders (Steffensmeier, 1980).

In spite of continuing leniency toward women, recent years have seen an increase in the number of women in prison. Between 1974 and 1983, the number of women incarcerated in state and federal prisons increased by 133 per cent, compared to an 86 per cent increase in male prisoners. However, in 1983 only 4.4 per cent of all inmates were women, and women's incarceration rate of 14 inmates per 100,000 women in the population was much lower than the male rate of 349 inmates per 100,000 men (Bureau of Justice Statistics, October 1983a: 5).

THE PRISONS

Probably no more than 1 or 2 per cent of all serious crimes lead to the imprisonment of an offender, but most people who commit many crimes eventually end up in jail or prison. Prison sentences probably deter some people from crime, even though the certainty of punishment is relatively low in the United States today.

History of Prisons

For centuries, jails and prisons were places to hold people before they were punished for their crimes, rather than places of punishment for convicted offenders. People were locked up until they could be executed, stoned, or subjected to other forms of suffering. Jails, which are institutions run by cities or counties, serve much the same purpose today, holding defendants until they can be tried in court. Defendants who are found guilty in court are given a criminal sentence such as a fine, time on probation, a sentence to a state prison or local correctional institution, or the death penalty.

In the late eighteenth century, the Quakers in Philadelphia developed a use for prisons different from the earlier practice of holding people until they were punished. The Quakers believed that even the worst offenders could be saved, and they sought to do this by requiring offenders to serve long periods in total silence in prison, hoping that this would lead prisoners to reflect on their mistakes and see the correct way to behave. These institutions were called penitentiaries, because the Quakers thought that inmates would grow penitent about their crimes while reflecting on their lives. However, inmates often died in prison, and those who were released often had become mentally ill while incarcerated (Leland, 1982b).

In the nineteenth century, prison reformers developed an institution at Auburn, New York, that used a different philosophy of punishment: Put prisoners to work and teach them to become law-abiding by instilling in them the work ethic. Since then, inmates have often been put to work, although usually only for part of each day and often at menial and poorly paid tasks.

In contrast to the view that prisons originally had a humanitarian impulse behind them, a more recent view is that they were and continue to be weapons of class conflict, a tool used by the powerful and the wealthy to control the "dangerous classes" (Rothman, 1971; Foucault, 1978; Ignatieff, 1978). This position has been criticized for incorrectly assuming that the state controls the punitive regulation of behavior, that the state's moral authority and power are the major sources of social order, and that all social relationships can be described in terms of power and subordination (Ignatieff, 1981).

Prison Overcrowding

In recent years, American prisons have become overcrowded, and it seems that this will be a problem throughout the 1980s and perhaps beyond. At the end of 1983, state and federal prisons were operating at about 110 per cent of their capacity, on the average. One inmate in Ohio notes that state veterinarian services standards recommend forty-three square feet of space for a calf that is more than five weeks old, and that he only has thirty-two square feet of living space in his cell (Lieber, 1981: 28). Overcrowding creates unpleasant living conditions for inmates: lack of privacy, arguments and fights over the use of limited space, and the threat of sexual assaults. Poor living conditions in prison have increased the chance of prison riots and led to the prisoners' rights movement.

Figure 14.3 shows changes in the number of state and federal prisoners from 1925 to 1983. A significant increase began in 1972 as a result of more Americans entering their twenties, the age group that has the highest imprisonment rate. As this large age cohort has entered its thirties, a time when criminal activity tapers off, the prison population has stopped growing as quickly, even though it continues to increase for other reasons. These other reasons include

Figure 14.3: Number of Sentenced State and Federal Prisoners, Yearend, 1925–1983

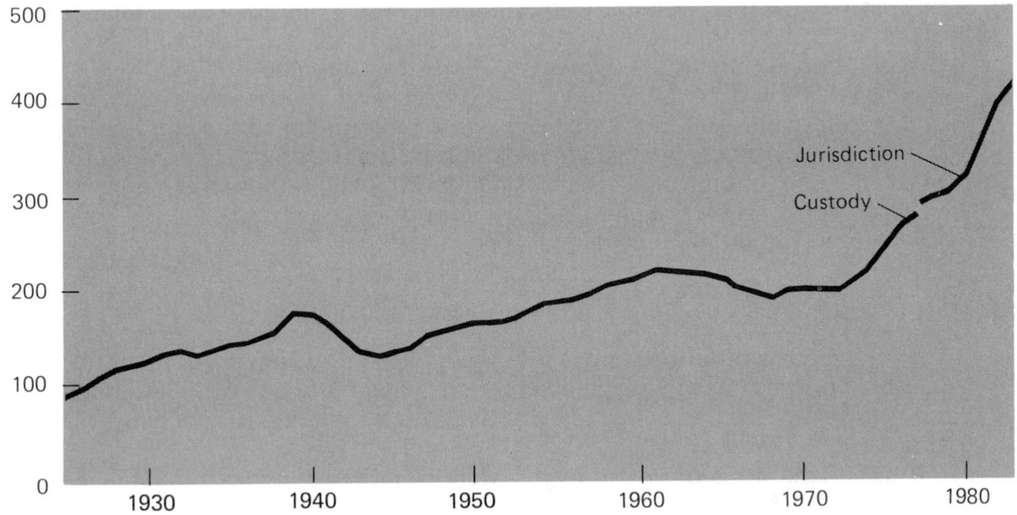

Note: Prior to 1978, National Prisoner Statistics reports were based on the custody population. Beginning in 1978, focus is on the jurisdiction population. Both figures are shown for 1977 to facilitate year-to-year comparison.

SOURCE: Bureau of Justice Statistics, *Prisoners in 1983.* Washington, D.C.: U.S. Department of Justice, April 1984, p. 3.

mandatory minimum sentences, laws that give judges less discretion in sentencing, and tightened parole release (Blumstein, 1983). Even though the rate of increase in prisoners slowed somewhat from 1982 to 1983, the Bureau of Justice Statistics (April 1984) estimates that even at the 1982–1983 rate of increase about five hundred beds must be added to American prisons each week to keep them from becoming even more overcrowded.

The fact that the increase in the prison population was slower from 1982 to 1983 than it was in the preceding two years suggests that the problem of prison overcrowding is being alleviated. Some states have adopted early release programs to reduce overcrowding, even though this practice has been criticized as being excessively lenient. The courts have sometimes stepped in to alleviate overcrowding. Thus, at the end of 1982, the entire prison system in seven states was operating under court order, and twenty-four jurisdictions were running at least one prison under court order. In some states, prison overcrowding has been reduced by housing state prison inmates in county jails, a temporary solution that might give a state time to find other solutions (Bureau of Justice Statistics, April 1984). New cells are also being constructed; nearly 42,000 beds were added to prisons during 1981 and 1982, more were in the process of being added, and still more were planned. The cost of adding each new cell for an inmate is $60,000 to $90,000, and so taxpayers have sometimes turned down proposals to add prison space. However, a national survey reveals that Americans believe that more prisons are needed, and that many people are willing to pay for them with higher taxes (Krajick, 1982).

Some critics of prison overcrowding oppose the construction of new facilities, claiming that the new prisons would be filled to capacity in short order as judges send more people to prison and parole boards keep inmates behind bars longer. These critics call for shorter prison terms, or no prison sentence at all for less serious offenders, as the way to reduce overcrowding. Research is inconclusive on the issue of whether building more prison cells will result in a larger prison population rather than alleviate overcrowding. One study claimed to show that increased prison capacity led to an equal growth in the number of inmates in two years (Abt Associates, Inc., 1980). However, a reanalysis of the data concluded that the relationship between prison capacity and prison population is still unclear. Some judges who do not send offenders to prison because of overcrowded conditions might do so if there were less overcrowding, but during the late 1950s and the 1960s there was empty space in some state prisons, suggesting that empty cells may not always be filled (Blumstein, Cohen, and Gooding, 1983).

Prison Riots

Prison overcrowding sometimes sets the stage for an inmate uprising. Other causes of prison riots include ineffectual prison administrators, real or imagined grievances by inmates, and racial discrimination by administrators and correctional officers (McKay, 1983).

One of the most dramatic prison riots of recent years occurred at Attica (New York) State Prison in 1971. Prisoners took control of part of the prison and held officers hostage. The state acceded to many of the inmates' demands, but refused to grant them amnesty for offenses committed during the uprising. An assault by the state police enabled the state to regain control of the prison, but during the assault the police killed twenty-nine prisoners and ten correctional employees who were being held hostage.

Another major riot occurred in 1980 at the New Mexico State Prison at

An inmate at Walpole (Massachusetts) state prison waits as correctional officers inspect cells after a prison riot.

Photo by Michael Dobo. Reprinted by permission of Stock, Boston. © by Stock, Boston, Inc., 1977.

Santa Fe. Gangs of convicts held control of the prison for a day and a half, taking a dozen guards hostage and torturing and sexually assaulting them. Armed prisoners tortured and mutilated other inmates, and thirty-three inmates were killed by other prisoners before the uprising was subdued (Lieber, 1981). One sociologist has attributed this riot to changes by the prison administration toward a more coercive system of control, rather than to overcrowding, poor food and services, lapses in security, conspiracies by administrators, or a "new breed" of inmate who was more prone to violence. The administration's shift from a policy of accommodating inmate power to a policy of using force and restrictions on inmates to maintain order set the stage for the riot (Colvin, 1982).

The Prisoners' Rights Movement

One response to overcrowding, guard brutality, poor food, lack of access to lawyers, and other deprivations of prison life is the *prisoners' rights movement*, which has been led by ex-convicts and attorneys on behalf of people still in

373

prison. Since the late 1960s, this movement has successfully brought cases to the courts, particularly the federal courts. These cases have led to judicial rulings that treatment must be provided for inmates, that minimum standards of shelter and food must be met, and that inmates' constitutional rights cannot be abridged. One summary of the accomplishments of the prisoners' rights movement of the late 1960s and the 1970s concludes that it established the following principles:

> (1) prisoners retain certain constitutional rights in spite of conviction and incarceration; (2) [pretrial] detainees retain even greater constitutional protections; (3) many existing practices and conditions within prisons and jails abridge those retained rights and protections; (4) correctional officials carry the burden of justifying the restriction of constitutional rights; and (5) the Civil Rights Act is an appropriate tool for protecting and enforcing the constitutional rights of prisoners and detainees (Krantz, 1983: 1192).

Prisons and Race

The fact that as many as half of all federal and state prisoners are blacks has led some people to claim that the criminal justice system discriminates by race. Blacks have about seven times as high a per capita rate of imprisonment as whites, and during the 1970s the imprisonment rate for blacks increased faster than the rate for whites (Levey, 1979; Christianson, 1981; Blumstein, 1982). We have seen that most sentences are meted out according to legally relevant criteria, but race plays some role in sentencing in certain jurisdictions.

Even if all racial discrimination in sentencing were eliminated, the prisons would still include a disproportionately high number of blacks, because blacks, to a much greater degree than whites, commit those crimes defined by the law and regarded by the public as the most serious ones, and those crimes therefore carry the longest sentences. Because more blacks than whites are convicted of serious crimes, in proportion to their numbers in the population, and because the crimes that blacks are most likely to be convicted of when compared to whites are the most heavily punished offenses, more blacks go to prison and stay there a long time. By one estimate, differences in arrest rates, which do not seem to exaggerate blacks' actual involvement in crime, account for about 80 per cent of the difference in incarceration rates between blacks and whites (Blumstein, 1982). However, there is some research that indicates that racial discrimination accounts for some of the higher incarceration rate of blacks (Carroll and Mondrick, 1976; Thornberry, 1979; Christianson, 1981).

Racial discrimination in prison is an important part of inmates' lives. The Attica Prison riot and other uprisings have been attributed, at least in part, to racial antagonisms between guards, who are typically white, and inmates, many of whom are black. A study of a medium-security prison in the South sought to determine if blacks and whites were treated differently by guards. Using self-report questionnaires, the researchers found that black and white inmates engaged in equal amounts of rule-breaking behavior, but that blacks were more likely to be disciplined formally for their violations. Part of this differential treatment was directly due to racial discrimination; some of it was due to the fact that blacks were more likely than whites to have prior criminal records, and guards were likely to see any inmate with a prior record as dangerous and in need of discipline when that inmate violated prison rules. Taking formal disciplinary action against an inmate can cause hostility that may lead to further violation of the rules (Poole and Regoli, 1980).

Parole

Prison overcrowding and the high cost of incarceration can be alleviated by releasing inmates before they complete their full sentences. They can then be supervised on the street and sent back to prison if they violate the conditions of their release. This system is called *parole.*

A state parole board meets regularly to review an inmate's progress toward rehabilitation, and to determine whether the inmate can be safely released if certain conditions are met. Parole board decisions cause anxiety and bitterness in prisoners, who often see these decisions as arbitrary and in violation of their due process rights (Irwin, 1970). One study found that the most annoying thing to inmates about serving time in prison was never knowing when they would be released: 52 per cent mentioned this problem, and only 12 per cent mentioned the next most commonly voiced complaint, being treated like a child by the prison staff (Kassebaum, Ward, and Wilner, 1971: 31).

If the parole board decides to release an inmate, it specifies the conditions of release, which typically include a steady job, staying away from known offenders, and avoiding the use of alcohol and illegal drugs. The parolee is required to meet regularly, perhaps once or twice a month, with a parole officer to discuss problems of adjustment and signs of progress. Parole officers frequently know of violations of parole conditions, but usually do not send inmates back to prison for minor infractions. Instead, parole officers "save" these infractions so that if a major one occurs, such as arrest for a new crime, their decision to revoke parole and send the parolee back to prison can be justified with a list of infractions.

Not all inmates who leave prison are paroled. Some choose to "wrap up" their sentence, that is, to complete the full sentence in prison. The use of parole has been restricted in response to criticisms of the system: The granting of parole seems arbitrary and perhaps in violation of due process rights, and the behavior of parolees is difficult to predict and to monitor (Von Hirsch and Hanrahan, 1978). A few states have abolished parole altogether, and others have limited its use through sentencing reforms. Even where parole is widely employed, inmates usually must serve a minimum part of their sentence before they are eligible.

THE VICTIM IN THE CRIMINAL JUSTICE SYSTEM

The American criminal justice system includes many defendants' procedural rights to protect them against the power of the state. Some people complain that this emphasis on defendants' rights neglects "victims' rights," or what those who are victimized are entitled to. It may seem unfair that fines paid by criminals go into the state's coffers rather than back to the victims. Critics also complain about the slowness of the legal process, which costs victims and witnesses time and money to sit in court hallways awaiting trials.

In recent years, more attention has been paid to victims, as district attorneys have realized that cases cannot be prosecuted successfully without cooperative victims and witnesses. One resulting change is the "shield law," which protects rape victims from being questioned about their previous sexual experiences, and thus enhances the likelihood that rapes will be reported to the police and that victims will testify in court. Another change has been to listen to the victim's wishes before sentencing an offender or paroling an inmate. State systems of compensation and restitution have also been developed to repay victims for their losses.

Compensation

Compensation is a system in which the state repays victims for their financial losses or physical injuries. Under this system, it is not necessary to arrest and convict an offender for a victim to be compensated, nor does a convicted offender have to be financially solvent for the victim to be repaid for his or her losses. In 1983, thirty-six states had laws that provided compensation for victims, even though many of these programs were not well-funded or well-publicized.

Compensation has been justified in several ways. Some say that the state has an obligation to protect the welfare and safety of its citizens, and that when it fails to prevent crime, it should pay victims for their losses. Another rationale for compensation is that it may prevent victims from becoming angry at the criminal justice system and alienated from the political system (Schafer, 1968; Stookey, 1981). Even though compensation programs are sometimes aimed at improving public attitudes toward the criminal justice system and the government, research indicates that many victims who have sought compensation are disenchanted with the criminal justice system. Indeed, administrative obstacles to securing compensation and the inadequate rewards provided to victims seem to engender more discontent toward the legal system among applicants for compensation than exists among people who do not apply for compensation (Elias, 1983, 1984).

A few states have developed compensation programs that are funded by convicted offenders. These programs combine compensation with restitution. In Tennessee, for instance, to fund the compensation system, court clerks are supposed to collect a $21 fee from anyone convicted of a crime against person or property, and the Department of Correction is required to collect a $5 monthly levy from anyone on parole, probation, or work-release. However, neither court clerks nor correctional workers usually collect these fees, and so funds are not available to compensate victims (*The New York Times,* October 28, 1979).

Compensation programs must deal with the problem of the victim's contribution to the crime. Earlier in the book, we saw that victims sometimes precipitate a crime or contribute to their own victimization, and in such cases the state might choose not to compensate the victim. For instance, someone who first uses force against another person and then ends up badly injured in a fight might not be compensated if the state compensation board found that the crime would not have occurred without the victim's initiating actions. In Great Britain, compensation is limited to "deserving cases," and this is determined in part by the degree to which the victim is to blame for his or her own victimization (Schafer, 1968).

Restitution

A system of *restitution* requires offenders to make monetary payments or provide services, either to the victim or to the community at large (Galaway, 1977). Relatively few criminal courts have used restitution extensively, but growing concern for victims' rights has led some judges to require offenders to repay victims for their losses.

Some claim that restitution makes offenders take responsibility for their behavior, and thus helps to rehabilitate them (Deming, 1976). Others claim that offenders who repay their victims may not feel guilty for their crimes if they believe that they have corrected their wrongs, and that this may make it more likely that they will continue to commit crime. Restitution might improve crime reporting if victims thought they would be repaid for their losses. Moreover, by easing public hostility toward offenders, restitution might help to minimize the isolation of offenders from conventional society and make it easier to reintegrate them into society after they are released from prison. Restitution would also reduce the burden on taxpayers if it replaced a system of state compensation (Barnett, 1977; Bridges, Gandy, and Jorgenson, 1979).

The Changing Role of the Victim

Many states have implemented programs to help the victims of crime, including compensating them for their losses and requiring offenders to make restitution. Victims have been given a greater voice in the sentencing of offenders, although defendants are usually allowed to respond to victims' statements. In some jurisdictions, victims must be notified of hearings and trials, and be informed when an inmate is being considered for parole or escapes from prison (McNamara, 1983).

District attorneys have started to pay more attention to the role of the victim in the criminal justice system. They can help to deal with a victim's fear of retaliation by the offender, frustration with delays in court, and intimidation by a defense attorney's cross examination. District attorneys can also impress on victims and witnesses the importance of testifying in court. In some jurisdictions, victims have even been included in plea bargaining conferences with the district attorney, the defense attorney, and the defendant (Heinz and Kerstetter, 1981).

Several states now permit victims to testify at parole board hearings, and to make known their wishes about whether a prisoner should be released. The federal prison system implemented this reform in 1984. The director of the National Prison Project of the American Civil Liberties Union opposed this reform, claiming that it could curb the civil rights of prisoners who are poor and uneducated, because they might end up with longer sentences if they were confronted with an articulate victim at a parole board hearing (Werner, 1984).

One potential tool for improving the victim's experience with the criminal justice system is television. Since 1981, the Supreme Court has allowed television in the courtroom to telecast trials and other proceedings; in 1984, forty states permitted at least some coverage of court events. This coverage might educate the public about the nature of the criminal justice system, including its delays and the way that cross examination is conducted. However, television tends to present only the most sensational cases, ignoring mundane ones and paying little attention to the details of building a case. This could leave television viewers unprepared for their experiences as victims or witnesses in actual cases. Nevertheless, televised courtroom proceedings might have a beneficial effect in letting victims know that punishment is meted out to offenders, as we can see in the following example:

> When a California nursery school operator and six employees were arraigned 10 days ago on charges of sexually abusing 18 pupils, the court proceedings were televised. The broadcast had a beneficial effect on an unexpected group—the victims. "The children saw the defendants in court and in custody," said Lael Rubin, the Los Angeles County deputy district attorney who is prosecuting the case. "It was very reassuring to them" (Friendly, 1984: E22).

SUMMARY

The criminal justice system aims to mete out justice and reduce the crime rate. In doing so, it also influences the development of criminal careers. This system has been described as a funnel or sieve that sorts out cases as they pass from the police through the courts and to the prisons.

The police were first formally organized at the municipal level in the nineteenth century. They are organized so that the most important contacts with the public and with suspects are by patrol officers, who are not easily supervised by administrators. The working personality of a police officer includes a demand for respect, suspiciousness, and the exercise of delegated and unauthorized discretion. The exercise of discretion is influenced by what an officer sees as the likely consequences of an arrest or a warning, by the community in which an offense occurs, by a suspect's demeanor, and sometimes by race and sex. Much research indicates that the police do not discriminate in dealing with black and white suspects, but there is some evidence that they are less likely to arrest females than males for certain offenses.

The police measure their effectiveness with clearance rates, which are indicators of the proportion of offenses they solve to their satisfaction. They sometimes inflate clearance rates by encouraging suspects to confess to multiple offenses. Relatively few robberies and burglaries are solved by police detectives.

Suspects who are arrested by the police have the right to have bail set at a reasonable level. The bail system discriminates against the poor. Percentage-deposit bail systems are as effective as bondsmen in getting defendants to show up on time for trial, and they save defendants money as well. Preventive detention has been proposed as a way to reduce "bail crimes," those offenses that are committed between the time of pretrial release and the trial.

Prosecutors, who bring criminal charges against defendants on behalf of the state, measure their effectiveness by conviction rates. Defense attorneys try to get their clients acquitted, or at least get them the lightest possible sentences. Because many defendants are poor, defense attorneys are often appointed by and paid for by the state. Prosecutors and defense attorneys theoretically engage in a "fight" or adversary process, out of which the truth is supposed to emerge. In practice, they often engage in plea bargaining over guilt and an appropriate sentence in order to save the time and resources of the court. Judges then ratify the negotiated plea and sentence, treating defendants more leniently for helping to speed up the processing of cases. Judges preside over trials, but their most important function is probably the sentencing of convicted offenders. Juries also try cases, but no more than 5 per cent of all felony cases are tried before a jury. In general, juries seem to perform quite well, in spite of their lack of legal expertise. Convicted offenders are sentenced in various ways, one of which is probation, a form of supervised release.

One problem with the courts is sentence disparity. Legal criteria are usually the basis of judges' sentences, but race sometimes plays a role in the sentencing of offenders. This may be due to direct racial discrimination, but often it is a result of organizational or economic discrimination that affects minorities more because of their lower incomes. Criminal justice procedures rather than direct racial discrimination seem to account for most of the disparity in sentences among racial and ethnic groups. However, in capital cases, murderers who kill blacks are punished less severely than murderers who kill whites.

The sex of a defendant makes some difference in the sentencing of convicted offenders, with women being treated somewhat more leniently than men.

Prisons in the United States are overcrowded, but there is some evidence that demographic changes and prison reforms are beginning to alleviate this problem. Not everyone agrees that building more prisons is the best solution to this problem, because judges might simply imprison more offenders if there were more cells. Overcrowding, ineffectual prison administrators, coercive control strategies, inmate grievances, and racial discrimination sometimes lead to prison riots. Another response to these problems has been the prisoners' rights movement, which has achieved important gains through the courts since the late 1960s. Prisoners are sometimes released on parole prior to the expiration of their sentence, and are then supervised on the street to help them to become rehabilitated.

Recently, victims have come to play a more important role in the criminal justice system. Compensation programs and penalties of restitution are designed to repay victims for their financial losses and physical suffering. In some states, victims can testify before a judge about the sentence they believe is appropriate for an offender, and in some places they can appear before a parole board to say whether they think that an offender should be released. The criminal justice system would probably function more efficiently if it counseled victims and witnesses and tried to incorporate them more into the processing of defendants.

IMPORTANT TERMS

bail
case attrition
clearance rate
compensation
discretion

parole
plea bargaining
preventive detention
prisoners' rights movement

probation
restitution
sentence disparity
working personality

SUGGESTED READINGS

BURT GALAWAY AND JOE HUDSON, EDS. *Perspectives on Crime Victims*. St. Louis: C. V. Mosby, 1981. A collection of papers that deal with the role of the victim in the criminal justice system, including papers on compensation and restitution.

JOHN IRWIN. *The Felon*. Englewood Cliffs, N.J.: Prentice-Hall, 1970. An important examination of prison from the inmate's perspective, written by a former prisoner who is now a sociologist.

DAVID W. NEUBAUER. *Criminal Justice in Middle America*. Morristown, N.J.: General Learning Press, 1974. An empirical study of the components of the criminal justice system in a small American city.

ARTHUR ROSETT AND DONALD R. CRESSEY. *Justice by Consent: Plea Bargains in the American Courthouse*. Philadelphia: Lippincott, 1976. An examination of the pros and cons of plea bargaining, including a detailed look at one case from the perspective of the defendant, the prosecutor, the defense attorney, and the judge.

JEROME H. SKOLNICK. *Justice without Trial: Law Enforcement in a Democratic Society*, 2nd ed. New York: John Wiley, 1975. A fine account of how police officers do their job, based on first-hand observations.

15

Deterrence and Incapacitation

One justification for punishment is *deterrence*, the inhibition of criminal activity by state-imposed penalties. This rationale is a utilitarian one—that is, it is based on the idea that punishment should help a society to prevent crime. Deterrence is a philosophy of punishment, but it raises empirical issues that social scientists have explored through research. For instance, research indicates that the deterrent effect of sanctions is related to the nature of the act to be prevented and to the severity, certainty, and promptness with which punishment is applied.

THE DETERRENCE MODEL

Deterrence is based on assumptions about why criminals violate the law and how the law can affect their behavior. Many of these assumptions are centuries old, but recently empirical data have been collected to test their accuracy.

History of the Idea of Deterrence

Philosophers such as Cesare Beccaria (1738–1794) and Jeremy Bentham (1748–1832) argued that the punishment of criminal acts can deter potential offenders by making the negative consequences of crime greater than its rewards. Writing in the eighteenth century, Beccaria (1764, 1963: 42) stated that the goal of crime prevention should be pursued with punishments "which will make the strongest and most lasting impression on the minds of men, and inflict the least torment on the body of the criminal." He believed that punishment should be as certain as possible and as harsh as necessary to deter potential offenders, but that "all beyond this is superfluous and for that reason tyrannical" (Beccaria, 1764, 1963: 43). For Beccaria, punishment should be consistent with the principle of retribution or just deserts, a principle that we examine in the next chapter.

For much of the twentieth century, the notion of deterrence was ignored or held in disrepute by social scientists, because positivists focused attention on individual and social pathologies as causes of crime. The idea of rehabilitation thus dominated the field of corrections. However, beginning with an influential paper published by the Norwegian law professor Johannes Andenaes in 1952, there has been a rebirth of interest in deterrence. Since the mid-1960s, much research has been done on the deterrent effects of punishment (Andenaes, 1952, 1974, 1975; Zimring and Hawkins, 1973; Gibbs, 1975; Blumstein, Cohen, and Nagin, 1978; Cook, 1980; Hagan, 1982).

Assumptions about Behavior

The deterrence model assumes that people engage in an act only after carefully and rationally considering its costs (or risks) and benefits (or rewards). People who comply with the law seek the rewards of conformity and try to avoid the costs of deviance. Punishment supposedly induces compliance, because people fear punishment and do not want to risk their stake in conformity. In the deterrence model, the rationale for punishment is to affect future behavior, rather than to inflict pain that offenders supposedly deserve because of their past actions; the latter is the retribution or just deserts rationale for punishment.

The deterrence model assumes a degree of free will or voluntarism; it suggests that people choose how to behave, even if they are limited in their choice by social, psychological, and biological factors. However, not all behavior is governed by a careful consideration of costs and benefits, for much behavior is unplanned or habitual. Moreover, internalized values and beliefs, sometimes referred to as "conscience," often guide behavior. Other behavior may be avoided because people lack the skill or the opportunity needed to commit an act.

As we have seen in earlier chapters, rational choice is involved in some criminal behavior. Some offenders consider risks carefully and try to minimize them by planning their crimes. They consider possible gains from the crime and pick targets accordingly. However, even these offenders often lack good information on the real risks of arrest and conviction, and on the rewards to be gained from a particular crime. More importantly, many offenders do not consider risks and rewards as rationally as is assumed by the deterrence model. Many act on impulse; murderers who kill "in the heat of passion" are one example.

We know relatively little about how the deterrent effect of punishment operates for different people and for various crimes. Because the motivations of criminals differ, to deter crime it may be necessary to devise penalties that are a function of the type of offender and the kind of crime. This would produce an unwieldy and probably unconstitutional system of law. For example, the law might provide one penalty for an armed robber who stole to support a heroin habit, and a different penalty for an armed robber who stole on the spur of the moment. This might be unconstitutional because it would deny equal protection of the law to people who committed the same crime. It would also probably be unworkable because it would be difficult to prove an offender's motivation in court. Even if these difficulties could be solved, we do not yet have enough information about criminals' motivations and the penalties that would deter different kinds of offenders to construct and implement such a system of punishment.

Deterrence and Other Effects of Penalties

In the deterrence model, a criminal penalty acts as a negative inducement or cost to discourage people from engaging in behavior that violates the law. However, deterrence is not the only effect of punishment. The very existence of a criminal penalty for an act indicates moral condemnation of the behavior and a corresponding support for certain values; people learn these attitudes through socialization and formal education. The law has an "eye-opener effect," in that it directs attention to punished acts and invites reflection on the reasons that those acts are condemned (Andenaes, 1974: 110–128). The actual punishment of offenders makes credible the threat of a sanction and helps to convince people that the government's effort to deter crime is a serious one. Punishment also keeps some people in line by convincing them that those who violate the law gain no advantage over those who abide by the law (Zimring and Hawkins, 1973: 88–89).

One analysis of the factors that inhibit criminal behavior suggests that three forces operate independently and have additive effects on keeping crime in check:

1. Moral commitment, or internalized legal norms;
2. Social disapproval, or fear of informal sanctions by peers; and
3. Threat of legal punishment, or fear of physical and material deprivation from legally imposed sanctions (Grasmick and Green, 1980).

Usually, only the third of these factors is called deterrence. All three inhibiting forces are associated with criminal behavior, but much of the variation in criminal behavior among people cannot be explained by any of the three, because these inhibiting effects apply only to people who are motivated to violate the law (Grasmick and Green, 1980). One criticism of this approach to the inhibition of criminal behavior suggests that data collected at only one point in time cannot lead to firm conclusions about the effect of these inhibiting factors on criminal behavior. Subjective appraisals of social disapproval and of the threat of punishment may influence criminal activity, but involvement in crime can also alter perceptions of social disapproval and the threat of punishment. Criminal activity may show an offender that the consequences of breaking the law are not serious, lead the offender to make a moral reassessment of norms, or provide the opportunity for an offender to learn an accomplice's values (D. Greenberg, 1981). Testing the effects of the three inhibiting factors thus requires a model like the one depicted in Figure 15.1.

One study that tried to test a model like this one found that internalized

Figure 15.1: A Model of Crime-Inhibiting Factors

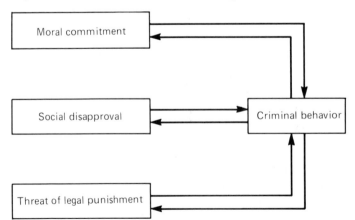

normative constraints, or moral commitment, was the best predictor of later delinquency by junior and senior high school students. Perceptions of the threat of both informal and formal sanctions added significantly to the model's ability to explain subsequent delinquency. There was also some evidence that the threat of sanctions might compensate for weak internalized constraints in inhibiting delinquency (Bishop, 1984).

Some research that has tried to disentangle the relationships shown in Figure 15.1 has found a difference between "deterrent effects"—which are measured by perceived sanctions a year before a self-report questionnaire is used to measure criminal behavior—and "experiential effects"—which are measured by perceived sanctions at the time the self-report questionnaire is filled out. Experiential effects are due to the influence of past criminal behavior on current perceptions of the risk of punishment. In other words, deterrence cannot be measured accurately by questions asked at the same time that a person reports his or her criminal activity, because current perceptions of risk reflect the individual's earlier experiences with the law. Some studies indicate that the deterrent effect—measured by the association between perceived threat a year before and current self-reported crime—is much weaker than researchers had thought it to be, and that the experiential effect is substantially stronger than once thought (Saltzman et al., 1982; Minor and Harry, 1982; Paternoster et al., 1983).

Specific and General Deterrence

Deterrence can be analyzed in terms of specific deterrence or general deterrence. *Specific deterrence* means that individuals who are punished for a particular crime will not commit that crime again because their risk-reward calculations have been altered by the punishment. They have learned that the risk is greater than they thought, and so the rewards become relatively less attractive, leading them to avoid crime in the future. Specific deterrence has not been explored to a great extent, partly because when offenders are punished, many things happen before they have the opportunity to commit another crime. Thus, upon release from prison, convicted robbers may refrain from robbery 1) because they fear further incarceration (specific deterrence), 2) because they have learned that robbery is wrong (a socializing effect), 3) because they have been changed by prison treatment programs (rehabilitation), or 4) because they are older than when they entered prison and are ready to retire from a criminal career (the exiting or maturing-out effect). Researchers have not yet succeeded in separating the specific deterrence effect from these other consequences of punishment.

General deterrence is the inhibition of the desire to engage in crime among the general population through the punishment of certain offenders. Most research focuses on the general deterrence effects of punishment rather than on specific deterrence. One report on deterrence even defines it only in terms of the inhibiting effects of sanctions on the criminal activity of people other than the punished offender (Blumstein, Cohen, and Nagin, 1978: 3).

Absolute, Restrictive, and Marginal Deterrence

The effects of punishment in deterring people from crime are rarely absolute. *Absolute deterrence* means that people refrain entirely from committing crime because of the perceived threat of a penalty. If a person never commits a crime, it is not necessarily due to absolute deterrence. For several reasons, that individual might never have committed a crime, even if the act were not punished at all, and thus the person cannot be said to have been deterred from the crime (Gibbs, 1975: 32–33).

Restrictive deterrence means that people limit their violation of the law in order to minimize the risk of punishment. They may continue to violate the law, but do so less frequently or less openly, in the belief that regular and overt violation of the law increases the chance of apprehension and punishment. People who engage in crime are not absolutely deterred by the threat of punishment, but the extent to which the threat of punishment leads them to restrict their criminal activity is not known (Gibbs, 1975: 33–34).

The *marginal deterrent effect* of punishment means the extent to which crime rates respond to incremental changes in the threat of sanctions (Nagin, 1978). Increasing the rate at which the police arrest offenders from 0 to 100 per cent would undoubtedly deter more criminals, but increasing the arrest rate from 20 to 22 per cent would probably have little or no impact on crime rates. Similarly, most research indicates that murder is not deterred by executing offenders rather than imprisoning them for life.

DETERRENCE AND THE CRIMINAL ACT

Some criminal behavior is apparently more easily deterred than other criminal behavior, either because of the nature of the offense itself or because of the way that certain crimes are planned.

A Typology of Crime Deterrence

William J. Chambliss (1969: 360–372) has developed a useful typology of the kinds of crimes that are more or less easily deterred by criminal sanctions. One dimension of the offense that Chambliss says is related to the ease with which a crime can be deterred is whether it is an instrumental or an expressive act. Instrumental or goal-oriented behavior, such as theft, is more easily deterred than expressive behavior that results from the inner needs of an offender, such as a violent outburst that leads to murder. This distinction between instrumental and expressive acts is not always easy to make. For instance, a juvenile gang member may steal in order to feel a sense of mastery over others (an expressive need), rather than to acquire property (an instrumental goal). Likewise, heroin addiction may result from the fulfillment of expressive needs such as the desire to fight despair or to suppress physical pain, but property crimes that provide the money with which to buy heroin are instrumental acts. Another difficulty with the instrumental-expressive distinction is that there is some evidence that expressive acts, such as homicide, can be deterred by increasing the risk of imprisonment, the length of prison sentences, and the penalty for carrying a firearm (Gibbs, 1968; Knight, 1979).

Chambliss also links the deterrence of crime to an offender's commitment to a life of crime. Offenders who are highly committed to a life of crime are more difficult to deter than offenders who are marginally committed to crime or not committed at all to crime as a way of life. Marginal offenders are those who are committed neither to a life of crime nor to a law-abiding way of life; they are perhaps the most easily influenced by the threat of punishment. People who are not committed to crime at all do not need to be deterred by the threat of punishment (Blumstein, Cohen, and Nagin, 1978: 53).

Table 15.1 presents Chambliss's typology of crime deterrence in terms of the expressive or instrumental nature of the act and the offender's degree of commitment to a life of crime. The type of offender who is least apt to be deterred is one with a high commitment to crime as a way of life and whose offenses result from expressive needs. Thus, most addicts and some murderers and sex offenders are not easily deterred. The expressive, high-commitment nature of drug addiction makes this crime difficult to deter; addicts have relapse rates that range from 50 to 97 per cent after they are withdrawn from heroin. Some violence is instrumental and can be deterred, as is the case with professional killers and kidnappers.

Table 15.1: Chambliss's Typology of Crime Deterrence

| | TYPE OF CRIMINAL ACT | |
COMMITMENT TO CRIME AS A WAY OF LIFE	*Instrumental*	*Expressive*
High	Professional thief Booster[a] Some check forgers Some murderers	Most drug addicts Some murderers Some sex offenders
Low	Snitch[b] Parking-law violator White-collar criminal Some murderers	Most murderers Some drug addicts Most sex offenders

[a] A booster is a professional shoplifter.

[b] A snitch is an amateur shoplifter.

SOURCE: From *Crime and the Legal Process* by William J. Chambliss. Copyright © 1969 McGraw-Hill Book Company. Used with the permission of McGraw-Hill Book Company.

Instrumental crimes by offenders who are not highly committed to a life of crime are probably the easiest to deter because those offenders are likely to reflect on the possible rewards and risks of committing a crime. If the costs of the crime outweigh its benefits, the offender may not commit the crime or may select a different kind of crime. A potential criminal is more likely to make such a decision if he or she has a low commitment to crime as a way of life.

Deterrence and Conventional Crime

Deterrence theory overlooks the fact that some conventional offenders, such as robbers and burglars, commit crime without carefully assessing the risks. Indeed, as we saw earlier in the book, risk may even make violation of the law exciting and thus rewarding to an offender. In addition, offenders may assess risks in quite a different way from the way that the general population does. For instance, one offender has described his feelings prior to his first mugging as follows: "I was scared, but it was exciting. You see, the whole thing, I was scared and excited. And I knew, you know, I had *a fifty-fifty chance* of either getting away or getting caught. But I figured *that was the chance I was going to take.* I wanted to get the money" (cited in Lejeune, 1977: 129; emphasis added here). This robber clearly overestimated the chance that he would be caught, for only about one-fourth of all reported robberies are solved by the police, and perhaps half of all robberies are not even reported, meaning that a mugger's real risk of being arrested is more like one in eight than one in two. Most people would probably not commit a robbery if they thought that the chance that they would be arrested was one in two, but some robbers are willing to run that risk.

Relatively few researchers have asked offenders what role the risk of arrest plays in their planning of particular crimes. Many offenders do not seem to consider the possible consequences of their crimes, because to do so would reduce their confidence in being able to perpetrate the crime or because they might not commit the crime if they seriously thought about the possibility of arrest (Conklin, 1972; Letkemann, 1973; Petersilia, Greenwood, and Lavin, 1977). Some offenders deliberately repress any thoughts of arrest before a crime; others use alcohol or drugs to help them to avoid thinking about the risks they are taking.

Conventional criminals sometimes think about the risks and rewards of their crimes. When they do, they probably tend to underestimate the risks more than do members of the general public, and they may place a greater emphasis on the rewards they expect from their crimes. This situation might result from the lack of educational and work opportunities, which makes crime seem relatively more rewarding than it would if there were alternative courses of action open to them. Offenders sometimes consider the following factors: the risk of being caught in one community rather than in another, the probability that the residents of one area rather than another will call the police, the emphasis that the police place on solving different kinds of crimes, and differences in penalties for various offenses (Merry, 1981; Wilson, 1983). However, we have little systematic research that offenders carefully weigh all of these factors before committing a crime, or that they plan their offenses in great detail in order to avoid arrest.

Deterrence and White-Collar Crime

White-collar crime usually involves instrumental acts by people with a low commitment to crime as a way of life, and thus this kind of offense is probably relatively easy to deter (Conklin, 1977; Braithwaite and Geis, 1982).

A realistic threat of detection and punishment can deter white-collar crime. Prison sentences for executives and stiff fines for corporations based on their assets or based on their illegal gains might force decision makers to consider the risk of punishment more seriously. The executives convicted of price fixing in the electrical equipment case in 1961 felt stigmatized and refused to allow their families or friends to visit them in prison. Lawyers who worked on that case believed that the prosecution, conviction, and incarceration of executives did deter price fixing:

> No one in direct contact with the living reality of business conduct in the United States is unaware of the effect the imprisonment of seven high officials in the electrical machinery industry . . . had on conspiratorial price fixing in many areas of our economy; similar sentences in a few cases each decade would almost completely cleanse our economy of the cancer of collusive price fixing, and the mere threat of such sentences is itself the strongest available deterrent to such activity (Spivack, 1963: 382).

One convicted executive said that the jail sentences in this case made other people in business reexamine their moral values. Some corporations established programs to reduce the chance of antitrust violations in the future, but the effectiveness of these programs was never evaluated (Whiting, 1962: 3).

When substantial sentences were handed out to violators of the Office of Price Administration's (OPA) regulations during and after World War II, compliance with the regulations seemed to increase (Clinard, 1952, 1969: 244–245). This compliance apparently resulted from the threat of punishment and the fear of injury to one's reputation. Prison sentences were effective deterrents to those who knew about the punishment of violators, but many people in the business world seemed to believe that few offenders were punished very severely.

A study of sixty-four retired middle-level executives found that several cited the threat of government sanctions as a major deterrent to illegal corporate behavior, singling out the effects of legal action against antitrust violators (Clinard, 1983). In one recent case, when the government filed a complaint for price fixing against bakery companies for colluding on prices, and when civil suits for treble damages were threatened, price fixing stopped and the price of bread dropped, even though no executives were actually convicted or sentenced to prison (Block, Nold, and Sidak, 1981).

In addition to imprisonment and fines, other sanctions might also deter white-collar crime. Convicted offenders might be suspended from a job or from a particular industry as a condition of probation or parole. They might be required to work at jobs that would increase their sympathy for the victims of their crimes; for instance, executives could be required to work in plants for which they had provided inadequate safety measures (Geis, 1974: 288). Companies convicted of fraud or false advertising might be made to spend their own money to inform the public of their violations. Firms that are repeatedly convicted of serious crimes might even be punished with a "corporate death penalty" by being forced into involuntary bankruptcy (Braithwaite and Geis, 1982).

One strategy to reduce corporate crime is to give adverse publicity to firms that violate the law. In a study of seventeen cases of corporate responses to negative publicity, Fisse and Braithwaite (1983) found that the impact was temporary, and that companies usually did not launch a counterattack, for fear that it would prolong the harmful publicity. Many companies introduced reforms as a result of the negative publicity, but none got as much public notice for their reforms as they had for their original offenses. The adverse publicity cost some companies sales, but others suffered little or no financial loss. It was the nonfinancial effects of the publicity—such as the loss of company and personal prestige, a decline in morale among the firm's workers, the distracting influence of media attention, and public humiliation—that led the companies to make reforms. In all seventeen cases, the reforms introduced as a result of the adverse publicity seemed designed to reduce the possibility of a recurrence of the offense, even though the actual effects of the reform might be minor.

Deterrence and Tax Evasion

Another offense that can apparently be deterred is tax evasion. The former head of the United States Bureau of Prisons has said, "The doctrine of deterrence, while it hasn't worked very well for some types of crime and offenders, has had a most benign effect on those who do not like to pay taxes" (Bennett, cited in Geis, 1974: 278).

In the mid-1970s the Internal Revenue Service in Idaho sought to get delinquents to pay their taxes through public embarrassment. Offices were pad-locked and cars were chained to telephone poles. A 1973 memorandum stated the following:

> A proven method of preventing delinquency has been through embarrassment to certain taxpayers. It has been my experience that seizures which result in "sensation-alism" tend to remain fixed in the public's mind and are a great deterrent to delin-quency" (cited in *The New York Times*, November 24, 1980, p. A24).

This policy was abandoned in 1977.

In recent years, tax cheating has become less risky for offenders, and there-fore more common. The number of IRS agents has declined, while the number of tax returns filed has increased. Even though computer audits are being used, the probability that any given tax return will be examined has fallen somewhat. Each IRS agent recovers six or seven times his or her salary in unpaid taxes, but efforts to reduce the size of the government bureaucracy have led to cutbacks in the IRS's staff since the mid-1970s. The reduction in deterrence from these cutbacks can be seen in the estimated increase in unpaid taxes from $26 billion in 1976 to $87 billion in 1981 (Quinn, 1981; Cowan, 1982). In 1983, the IRS began to use computerized information on the neigh-borhoods in which taxpayers live, the cars they drive, and the size of their telephone bills in order to identify people whose expenditures suggest that their incomes are higher than indicated by the taxes that they pay (Burnham, 1983).

Higher status taxpayers seem to be more influenced by the threat of punish-ment, and lower status taxpayers seem to be more affected by an appeal to their consciences and to the moral reasons for paying taxes (Schwartz and Orleans, 1967). The effectiveness of the threat of detection is suggested by the response to the federal government's requirement that banks and corpora-tions report to the IRS all interest and dividends paid to individuals, beginning in 1964. This change led to a 45 per cent increase in the amount of interest reported on individual tax returns, and to a 28 per cent increase in the taxes paid on that income (The President's Commission on Law Enforcement and Administration of Justice, 1967b: 103).

DETERRENCE AND THE SANCTIONING PROCESS

People have imperfect knowledge of the maximum penalties for various crimes, but they usually have some awareness of how the criminal justice system would punish them for committing a crime. People's perceptions of the severity of sanctions, the certainty with which they will be administered, and the promptness of punishment influence their choice of behavior.

Severity of Punishment

Lawmakers seem to assume that the severity of penalties has the greatest impact on behavior, for when confronted with a crime problem, they often increase penalties (Fishman, 1978). In fact, such changes in penalties seem to have little effect on crime rates. Stated in another way, the marginal deter-rent effect of harsher penalties seems limited, at least within the range of penalties used in any society at a given time. In some circumstances, harsh penalties can even backfire. For example, in early nineteenth-century Great Britain where over two hundred crimes could be punished with the death penalty, juries often acquitted defendants rather than send them to the gallows for relatively trivial offenses (Kalven and Zeisel, 1966).

The harshness of penalties clearly has some effect on behavior, but the limited range of penalties used for most offenses does not permit us to examine exactly how offenders react to increases or decreases in the severity of sanctions. For instance, a $50 fine for an expired parking meter would probably deter more drivers from overtime parking than would a $1 fine, and a fine less than the amount that had to be put in the meter would deter very few people. In a different context, one safecracker comments that "a law was passed which made using nitroglycerin on a safe a forty year prison term automatically. So everybody quit using it" (cited in King and Chambliss, 1984: 13–14). Alternative methods for breaking into safes were developed, but the harsher penalty did affect criminal behavior.

We do not have enough information on marginal deterrence effects to know how much crime will be deterred by a particular change in sanctions. There does seem to be a diminishing return from increased punishment at certain levels. Thus a twenty-year prison term probably deters more crime than a $10 fine, but it is not at all clear that a twenty-five-year sentence deters more crime than a twenty-year sentence.

A study in Chicago found that juvenile delinquents who were punished more harshly were arrested less often after they were punished. The "suppression effect"—that is, the drop in arrest rates after punishment—was greatest for juveniles who were treated most severely. For instance, offenders who were removed from their community and incarcerated for an indefinite time on an involuntary basis and with custodial supervision showed a greater drop in their rate of arrest after release than did juveniles who were removed from their community for a specified period and placed in a noncustodial and voluntary program. Moreover, the least harsh forms of treatment—supervision and probation—did not significantly reduce the rate at which juvenile offenders were rearrested. The researchers tentatively concluded that the juveniles reduced their involvement in delinquency because harsh punishment had altered the risk-reward ratio and deterred them from a continued high level of law-violating activity, even though their misbehavior did not cease altogether (Murray and Cox, 1979).

Certainty of Punishment

Probably more important than the maximum statutory penalty for a crime or the length of the sentences actually meted out by the courts is the certainty of some punishment for the crime. This was recognized two centuries ago by Cesare Beccaria (1764, 1963: 58), who stated the following: "The certainty of a punishment, even if it be moderate, will always make a stronger impression than the fear of another which is more terrible but combined with the hope of impunity." Thus, a 100 per cent chance of a one-year prison term may well deter more crime than a 5 per cent chance of a twenty-year sentence.

To determine the certainty of punishment, we must know how many crimes are actually committed, how many are reported to and recorded by the police, how many suspects are arrested, how many cases are prosecuted, how many defendants are found guilty, and how convicted offenders are punished. The United States has one of the harshest penalty structures of any Western society, but the certainty of punishment seems to be low compared to other countries. This probably reduces the deterrent effect of punishment and accounts in part for the comparatively high crime rate in the United States.

Increased certainty of punishment will probably have a greater effect in reducing crime rates than will increased maximum penalties, but the exact trade-off between certainty and severity is not known. A certain sentence of a $10 fine or one day in jail will probably deter few robbers, because they will think that "crime pays" if the costs are that low. Similarly, the low certainty of any punishment for white-collar crime probably limits the deterrent effect of even those laws that allow for harsh penalties; a convicted antitrust violator is, according to one estimate, less likely to be sentenced to prison than a violator of a migratory bird law (Yoder, 1978: 44). However, a 5 per cent chance of being executed would probably deter instrumental crimes by people who have little commitment to crime as a way of life; in these cases, the effect of a very severe penalty might offset the low certainty of punishment.

We have relatively little research on the exact combination of certainty and severity that maximizes the deterrence of particular crimes by various kinds of offenders. One study of felonies found an inverse relationship between certainty and severity; the greater the certainty of punishment, the less was its severity, and vice versa. Very severe penalties seemed to reduce the certainty of a conviction. At any given level of certainty, the severity of a penalty had only a weak-to-moderate relationship with the rate at which most felonies were committed. Perceived certainty of punishment had to be very high before increments in the severity of punishment would have a deterrent effect (Grasmick and McLaughlin, 1978).

It is not clear that certainty of punishment can easily be increased. Doing so would require better citizen reporting of crime, more complete recording of offenses by the police, higher arrest rates, higher rates of prosecution, or higher conviction rates. These changes cannot be made without greater expenditures, reorganization of law-enforcement agencies, or infringement on defendants' constitutional rights.

A high case attrition rate means a low certainty of punishment. Thus, the high case attrition rate in the United States accounts in part for its relatively high crime rate in comparison to other industrial societies. The chance that an arrested suspect in a robbery case will be convicted and sentenced to prison is more than three times as high in Great Britain as in the United States (Shinnar and Shinnar, 1975: 602). Certainty of arrest is also much higher in Japan, where the police in 1972 cleared 57 per cent of all serious crimes, in contrast to a clearance rate of only 22 per cent for index crimes in the United States in the same year (Clifford, 1976: 49–50). The conviction rate was also considerably higher in Japan than in the United States in 1972.

Certainty of punishment may deter some offenders but not others. This seems to be the case with bank robbery, which in the United States is frequently solved and typically leads to a conviction and a long prison sentence. The high probability of a severe sentence deters many professional thieves from bank robbery, but a "new breed" of bank robber has emerged in recent years: an amateur thief who does not plan the crime carefully, who is most often a black male in his early to mid-twenties, who is usually from a lower-class background, and who spends his money on luxuries. Punishment is probably about as certain and harsh as it can be for bank robbery, but this type of offender seems oblivious to the penalties or is willing to take substantial risks.

One study found that juveniles' perceptions of the certainty of punishment for particular crimes reflected the actual likelihood of punishment for those offenses. However, the relationship between their perceptions of the certainty of punishment and their involvement in self-reported crime was only moderate. Objective certainty of punishment was associated with perceived certainty, but perceived certainty did not seem to be linked to self-reported crime in a direct way. The researchers concluded that for the ten offenses and for the juveniles they studied, the deterrent effect of punishment was limited (Erickson and Gibbs, 1978).

One effort to deter drug sales and drug use was a New York state law that was implemented in 1973. This law increased the severity of penalties, especially for major drug dealers, who were to be sentenced to a minimum of fifteen years and a maximum of life in prison. An evaluation of this law found that it did not reduce heroin traffic in New York City and did not reduce property crimes associated with heroin addiction (Joint Committee on New York Drug Law Evaluation, 1978). The problem with the law was that while it increased the severity of sanctions, it left several ways for defendants to avoid these penalties. As a result, certainty of punishment after passage of the law was no greater than before, and many defendants avoided severe sanctions through plea bargaining. Indeed, the more severe penalties led those who were unable to plea bargain to their satisfaction to demand trials, causing a backlog in the courts that delayed punishment (another factor that may reduce the deterrent effect of punishment) (Wilson, 1983).

Certainty, Severity, and Informal Sanctions

Certainty and severity of punishment are only two of the factors influencing the decision to violate the law or abide by it. An understanding of the significance of certainty and severity requires attention to the importance of punishment relative to other costs of crime. An English study of fifteen-to-twenty-year-old males found that the shame of appearing in court and the possibility of being punished for a crime had some deterrent effect, but that this effect was less than the deterrent effect of losing the favor of one's family or losing a job (Willcock and Stokes, cited in Zimring and Hawkins, 1973: 103). The data in Table 15.2 indicate that formal sanctions are less important than informal ones in deterring crime, and that the shame that results from an appearance in court is a slightly more important deterrent than the actual punishment that is meted out.

This study asked the sample of 808 young males what would hold them

Table 15.2: Ranking of Deterrents to Crime and Delinquency

RANKING OF DETERRENTS	PERCENTAGES	MEAN RANK
What my family would think about it	49	2.38
The chances of losing my job	22	2.96
Publicity or shame of having to appear in court	12	3.88
The punishment I might get	10	4.40
What my girlfriend would think	6	4.72
Whether I should get fair treatment in court	2	6.07
What my mates would think	1	6.08
What might happen to me between being found out and appearing in court	2	6.20

SOURCE: Study by Willcock and Stokes, cited in Franklin E. Zimring and Gordon J. Hawkins, *Deterrence: The Legal Threat in Crime Control.* Chicago: University of Chicago Press, 1973, p. 192. Reprinted by permission of the University of Chicago Press. Copyright University of Chicago Press © 1973.

back or lead them to worry about engaging in a specific crime. When asked this question about car theft, 38.7 per cent answered that personal restraints—such as conscience, consideration for the injured party, and the lack of temptation in a particular situation—would keep them from committing that crime. Another 15.6 per cent said that they lacked the skill to steal a car. A total of 5.8 per cent gave vague answers or no answer at all, and 2.1 per cent said that nothing would deter them. Another 3.5 per cent said that they would be deterred by the opinions of their parents or other people, or by the possible impact of such behavior on their own future. The remaining 34.3 per cent of the boys said that they would be deterred by the possibility of arrest and punishment. Thus, about one-third of the young men said that they would be deterred by legal sanctions for auto theft.

The proportion of the young men who said that they would be kept from committing crime because of the threat of arrest, punishment, or sentence varied significantly from one offense to another. Relatively few said they would be deterred by the threat of punishment from starting a fight in a dance hall (15.6 per cent), from stealing a coat (19.8 per cent), or from throwing a stone at a street light (21.9 per cent). The deterrent effect of punishment was significantly greater for other offenses. About half of the boys said that the threat of arrest, punishment, or sentence would keep them from stealing from a large store; 39.8 per cent would be deterred from breaking into a private house; and 37.7 per cent would be deterred from breaking into a shop (Willcock and Stokes, cited in Zimring and Hawkins, 1973: 328–329).

One study that looked at the deterrent effects of sanctions outside the criminal justice system found that employee theft was related to a worker's perception of both the certainty and the severity of organizational sanctions. Perceived certainty of sanctions had a stronger effect than perceived severity, but both were important. Certainty and severity had additive effects; that is, each contributed to deterrence. Younger workers were not as easily deterred from theft as were older workers, even when both of them perceived high certainty and high severity of sanctions. Perhaps younger workers had a lower stake in conformity, and so were less affected by the potential costs of being fired or being socially ostracized by other workers (Hollinger and Clark, 1983a).

Promptness of Punishment

In addition to severity and certainty of punishment, the promptness with which sanctions are administered also seems to affect criminal behavior. However, there is little research on the impact that promptness of punishment has on violations of the law (Andenaes, 1975: 344). If an offender is punished soon after committing a crime, operant conditioning theory and learning theory suggest that both the specific deterrence of that individual from additional crime and the general deterrence of the public that knows of the punishment are likely to be greater than if the offender is punished years later. The closer in time a negative reinforcement (or legal sanction) is to the crime, the more likely it is that the behavior that elicited the negative reinforcement will be avoided. Punishment in the distant future may not be associated in people's minds with the offense that elicited the sanction. This was recognized years ago by Beccaria (1764, 1963: 56), who said that

> the promptness of punishments is more useful because when the length of time that passes between the punishment and the misdeed is less, so much the stronger and more lasting in the human mind is the association of these two ideas, *crime*

and punishment; they then come insensibly to be considered, one as the cause, the other as the necessary inevitable effect.

Types of Punishment

One aspect of punishment that has received relatively little attention from deterrence theorists and researchers is the type of punishment meted out to offenders. Little is known about the relative deterrent effects of imprisonment, restitution, fines, probation, and other sanctions. Marginal deterrence is often examined by focusing on the reduction of crime that results from using more of one type of penalty, rather than from using a different kind of penalty.

An experiment sponsored by the Police Foundation in Minneapolis in 1981 and 1982 tested the impact of different sanctions on men accused of domestic violence. The sanctions included arrest, mediation or advice, and ordering the violent man to leave the home for eight hours. Officers used one of these methods, chosen at random, to deal with "moderate" domestic violence, a simple assault that did not produce severe or life-threatening injury. Suspects were followed up for six months to determine if violence recurred; both official data and victims' reports were used. The results showed that arrests seemed to deter domestic assaults by male offenders. Only 10 per cent of the arrested men were involved in a new official report of domestic violence within six months. By contrast, 16 per cent of those receiving mediation or advice were involved in official reports of new incidents within that time, and 22 per cent of those who had been ordered from the home for eight hours were involved in a new domestic dispute within six months. Using victim self-reports, 35 per cent of cases in which no arrest was made led to new violence in the home within six months, but only 19 per cent of the victims of men who had been arrested reported new violence within six months. In addition, the deterrent effect was strongest in cases in which the police listened to the victim before making an arrest the first time, apparently because this led the victim to think that it was possible to get assistance from the police. This experiment involved men and women who were married or living together in low-income areas in the center of the city. The stigma of arrest for middle- or upper-class men might be even more effective in deterring domestic violence (Sherman and Berk, 1984; also, see Boffey, 1983a; Jacoby, 1983; *The New York Times*, May 30, 1984).

A legislative change to increase the sentence for rape in Pennsylvania had no measurable deterrent effect, in spite of the great publicity given to the change in the law. It is not clear that actual penalties meted out to rapists increased along with the statutory increase in penalties, but lengthening statutory penalties had no effect by itself in reducing the rate of rape (Schwartz, 1968). Rapists are probably not easily deterred because of the expressive nature of the crime, and because of the low certainty of punishment for the crime, even though penalties are severe when they are imposed. One suggestion for dealing with rapists is to alter radically the type of crime with which they are charged, thereby changing the kind of penalties that they receive. One unusual proposal would encourage rape victims to charge their assailants with indecent exposure rather than forcible rape. A man convicted of indecent exposure would get a shorter sentence than one convicted of rape, possibly offending the public's sense of justice, but the sentence would be more certain and probably more prompt than the sentence for a rapist. In some jurisdictions, the convicted offender would have to register with the local police as a sex offender after release from prison, and this would keep him under police surveillance. In addition, being labeled a sex offender because of indecent exposure might actually carry more of a social stigma, especially in prison, than being labeled a rapist (Williams, 1975: 877). Another proposal would define rapists as mentally ill; this might lead men who commit rape as a means of demonstrating their masculinity to avoid that crime out of fear of being labeled "crazy" (Toby, 1981).

Parents who fail to pay child support as ordered by the court have traditionally been forced to pay only when their former spouses persist in bringing them into court and demanding payment; even then compliance is erratic. Michigan sought to change this situation by charging the courts with initiating action against delinquent parents and by sentencing to jail those parents who continued not to pay. The proactive approach by the courts and the use of jail sentences for noncompliance significantly increased the overall rate of compliance with child support agreements (Lempert, 1981–82). In recent years, the federal government has also moved to increase the payment of child support through the development and use of national information systems and by withholding tax refunds from delinquent parents and paying that money directly to the parent to whom child support is owed. In 1984 a federal law was passed to have employers withhold wages earned by delinquent parents and pay them to the spouse to whom the child support is due.

Penalties different from those that have traditionally been used might increase the deterrent effect of punishment by increasing severity, certainty, or promptness. The exact combination of severity, certainty, promptness, and type of sanction that will maximize deterrence for different kinds of crimes is not yet known, but these factors strongly influence the effectiveness of punishment as a means of reducing crime.

DETERRENCE AND THE CRIMINAL JUSTICE SYSTEM

Until recently, most deterrence theorists and researchers focused on the circumstances under which the threat of punishment deters criminal behavior. Economists who have studied crime over the last few years have raised the problem of *simultaneity*: Sanctions may reduce crime, but the crime rate also affects the sanctions that are meted out by the criminal justice system. Thus an inverse relationship between crime rates and the severity or certainty of punishment—for example, higher crime rates when punishment is less certain, or lower crime rates when punishment is more certain—may exist because the threat of sanctions reduces crime, but this inverse relationship might also exist because a high crime rate reduces the certainty or severity of sanctions. For instance, a sudden increase in the crime rate might overburden the criminal justice system, reducing the ability of the police to arrest suspects or reducing the capacity of the prisons to incarcerate serious offenders. This would decrease the certainty and severity of punishment. Thus, the crime rate may affect the certainty and severity of penalties as much as the certainty and severity of penalties affect the crime rate (Blumstein, Cohen, and Nagin, 1978: 25–30). We need to be aware of this simultaneity of causation in looking at the role of the criminal justice system in deterring crime.

Deterrence and the Police

The question of simultaneity between crime rates and risk of apprehension by the police "remains unresolved at this time" (Blumstein, Cohen, and Nagin,

1978: 35). Increasing the resources of the police might increase the arrest rate and thus deter crime. However, a rising crime rate might lead to the appropriation of more resources for the police, which might increase the arrest rate and deter crime.

DETERRENCE AND SIZE OF THE POLICE FORCE

There is little evidence that increasing the resources or the numbers of the police will significantly alter crime rates. The President's Commission on Law Enforcement and Administration of Justice (1967a: 96, 106) found that for cities with populations of over 500,000, the ratio of police officers per 1,000 people ranged from 1.07 to 4.04, but there were no substantial differences among cities in reported crimes per capita. At least within the range of police per 1,000 people that exists in the United States, increasing or decreasing the number of officers will probably have no significant marginal deterrent effect on crime rates (Greenberg, Kessler, and Loftin, 1983). For instance, a study of Detroit found no systematic relationship between the level of that city's crime index and the size of its police force from 1926 to 1977 (Loftin and McDowall, 1982). Perhaps the variation in police strength over this time was not large enough to affect the crime rate.

It does seem that large variations in the number of police officers may affect crime rates. For instance, a ratio of one officer to every private citizen would clearly have some deterrent effect. Police saturation of certain areas sometimes occurs for a short time, but this policy is not feasible over the long run. At the other end of the spectrum, the presence of very few or no police officers would probably cause crime rates to rise. Several American cities have experienced widespread looting during blackouts, a time when the resources of the police are overtaxed. Montreal had disorder during a police strike in 1959, and in 1977 that city had a significant increase in crime during a police "slowdown." When the Nazis arrested the Danish police in 1944, rates of robbery, burglary, and larceny rose dramatically in spite of harsher penalties for people who were caught and convicted of crimes (Andenaes, 1974: 16–19). In contrast to these impressions about the impact of reduced police presence is the conclusion of a study of eleven cities that have had police strikes (Pfuhl, 1983). This study found very limited support for the idea that such strikes have any significant or systematic effect on rates of reported crime; this conclusion is consistent with the findings of other research that police presence has a minimal deterrent effect. Of course, during a police strike it may be difficult to get an accurate count of crimes, because there are fewer officers available to take citizen reports.

One problem with studies that look at the relationship between the number of police per capita in a city and that city's crime rate is that more crimes may be recorded if there are more police officers. One study that tried to avoid this problem correlated the number of officers per capita in twenty-six cities with the NCS victimization rates for those cities. The number of police per capita was inversely associated with victimization rates for household burglary, household larceny, personal larceny without contact, aggravated assault, simple assault, and rape; directly associated with victimization rates for robbery without injury and personal larceny with contact; and not significantly associated with rates of motor vehicle theft and robbery with injury (Decker, Shichor, and O'Brien, 1982). In other words, more police officers were associated with lower rates for some crimes, higher rates for some crimes, and made no difference for other offenses.

DETERRENCE AND RISK OF ARREST

The police may deter crime by increasing the risk of arrest. Even if the police are ineffective in arresting suspects, they may deter crime if people perceive the risk of arrest to be high. Some research has found an inverse relationship between clearance rates and crime rates; in other words, the more crime the police solve, the fewer crimes of that sort there are (Phillips and Votey, 1972; Tittle and Rowe, 1974; Logan, 1975; McPheters, 1976). A study that used victimization rates, rather than official crime rates, also found that crime rates were inversely related to arrest rates (Wilson and Boland, 1976). However, a study that used data from 1964 to 1970 for ninety-eight American cities found no consistent support for the idea that higher clearance rates cause lower crime rates. Perhaps the small changes in clearance rates over that time were not enough to affect crime rates, perhaps offenders did not perceive any change in clearance rates, or maybe clearance rates are not good indicators of the risk of arrest and conviction. Whatever the reason, the study did not find that higher clearance rates are likely to reduce crime, at least within the limits of clearance rates that characterize American police departments (Greenberg and Kessler, 1982).

The police, legislators, politicians, and the public commonly assume that the police deter crime through arrest or the threat of arrest, even though the rate at which the police solve crimes is quite low. Table 15.3 shows the percentage of index crimes cleared by arrest in 1983. These figures overestimate the chance that an offender will be arrested for any given crime, because many crimes are not reported to or recorded by the police.

Table 15.3: Clearance Rates of FBI Index Crimes, 1983

OFFENSE	PERCENTAGE CLEARED BY ARREST
Murder	75.9
Forcible rape	52.1
Robbery	26.0
Aggravated assault	60.9
Burglary	14.8
Larceny	19.5
Motor vehicle theft	14.7
Arson	17.3
Total index crimes	20.6

SOURCE: William H. Webster, *Crime in the United States, 1983: Uniform Crime Reports.* Washington, D.C.: U.S. Government Printing Office, 1984, p. 161.

Table 15.3 shows that crimes of violence are solved more easily than property crimes. This is because the offender and the victim in violent crimes are often acquainted with each other, and because face-to-face confrontations in violent crimes allow victims to identify offenders. Even though arrest rates are higher for violent crimes, these offenses are probably less easy to deter than property crimes. Violent offenses are often expressive in nature, and often occur in private settings to which the police have little access (Stinchcombe, 1963; Mawby, 1981). Crimes against property seem to involve planning and consideration of risks and rewards more often than crimes of violence do, but property crimes are solved infrequently and so may not easily be deterred.

DETERRENCE AND POLICE PATROL TACTICS

Police patrol cars increase the area that the police can cover, and increased mobility enhances the likelihood that officers will be at or near the scene of a crime when it occurs. However, patrol cars can isolate the police from the public and thus cut off a source of information that can be used to maintain order, prevent crime, and arrest suspects (Bittner, 1967).

There have been a few experimental studies to determine whether police patrol has a deterrent effect. Perhaps the best of these studies was conducted in Kansas City, Missouri, in 1972 and 1973 (Kelling et al., 1974). In this experiment, the number of patrol cars was doubled in five areas of the city, the number remained the same in five areas, and in five additional areas all patrol cars were taken off duty and reassigned to other areas (although they did answer calls for help). The fifteen areas were matched with each other by crime rate, characteristics of residents, and number of calls to the police. This study has been criticized because the areas that supposedly had no preventive police patrol did in fact have cars riding on the perimeter of the area, crossing the area to get to other parts of the city, and responding to calls (Larson, 1975; Pate, Kelling, and Brown, 1975). Thus the areas with no assigned patrol cars were not really entirely free of police presence.

The Kansas City experiment showed that changes in police patrol practices in the fifteen areas had "little value in preventing crime or making citizens feel safe" (McNamara, 1974: iii). There were no significant differences among the areas in the following measures of crime: rates of offenses reported to the police, rates of crime reported in victimization surveys, citizen fear of crime, and citizen satisfaction with the police.

The Kansas City experiment found no evidence of a *displacement effect*, a change in the pattern of crime without a reduction in the total amount of crime as a result of criminals' efforts to avoid punishment. Crime can be displaced from one target to another, from one area to another, or from one kind of offense to another (for instance, a burglary instead of a robbery). Displacement also refers to changes in a criminal's tactics or *modus operandi*, and to changes in the times at which crimes are committed (Hakim and Rengert, 1981a, 1981b). Visible police patrols might simply change patterns of crime by displacing crime rather than preventing it, but the Kansas City experiment found no evidence of such displacement as a result of variations in police patrol tactics.

There is, however, evidence from other studies that the police sometimes displace crime from one area to another where there are fewer officers or cars, or from a time when there are more officers and cars around to a time when the police are less likely to be present (Reppetto, 1974: 87–88). In a report on crime-reduction efforts in New York City, precinct captains and headquarters commanders claimed a drop in robbery rates as a result of police efforts, but officers on the street were more likely to believe that patrol tactics had merely displaced robbery. One community relations officer said, "As long as there are haves and have nots, we're never going to deter crime. We're just going to push it from one area to another" (cited in Farber, 1982a: B6). Displacement showed itself

> in the prostitutes whom the police have thrown off the north side of 86th Street but who parade, each night, along the south side; in the drug dealers and gamblers

Research in Kansas City found that police patrol cars did little to prevent crime or make people feel safe.

Photo © by Arthur Grace. Reprinted by permission of Stock, Boston. © by Stock, Boston, Inc., 1978.

who renew their operations in one store or on one corner almost as quickly as they are shut down on another, and in the youths who, with their beer and their blaring radios, annoy residents of one block after they have been chased from the last (Farber, 1982a: B6).

Even if an increase in the number of police officers could reduce the crime rate, we would have to weigh the cost of the additional officers against the number of crimes they prevent. For instance, a study of police patrols in subways found that it cost an estimated $35,000 for each felony that was prevented by increased patrol activity (Chaiken, Lawless, and Stevenson, 1974). Many people would think that such a program is too expensive, even if it does reduce crime.

Most research on the deterrent effects of the police has looked at the amount of money allocated to police departments, the number of officers on patrol, and clearance rates. Even more important than these factors may be what the police do while on patrol. An experiment in San Diego found that crimes such as robbery, burglary, theft, auto theft, assault, sex crimes, malicious mischief, and disturbances were reduced by an aggressive patrol strategy that included field interrogations or "street stops" (Boydstun, 1975). These street stops apparently changed perceived risks of apprehension, even though they had no significant impact on the actual number of arrests made by the police.

A survey of thirty-five large cities found that an aggressive patrol strategy or an increased number of patrol units produced higher arrest ratios and lower robbery rates. The researchers concluded that "citizens do not necessarily have to spend more money to get more law enforcement; they can get it by having police organizations capable of devising and maintaining a personnel, incentive, and management system that delivers more law enforcement" (Wilson and Boland, 1978: 378). This thirty-five-city study used cross-sectional data (data collected at one point in time) to test the relationship between police resources and tactics and robbery rates. Another study used time-series or longitudinal data (data collected at several points in time) and concluded that neither increased financial resources for the police nor more aggressive patrol practices deter robbery. Moreover, increased numbers of arrests for robbery did not seem to result in fewer reported robberies. Indeed, greater expenditures on the police seemed to increase citizen reporting and police recording of robberies (Jacob and Rich, 1981–82). The researchers in the original cross-sectional study replied to this criticism by saying that their evidence was consistent with a deterrent effect of aggressive police patrol, even if it did not prove that effect conclusively (Wilson and Boland, 1981–82).

Japanese experience is consistent with the idea that methods of police patrol can reduce the crime rate. The ratio of the police to the population is lower in Japan than in the United States, but the Japanese police patrol the streets in a way that apparently helps to keep the crime rate low. They spend much time getting acquainted with local residents, calling on them in their homes, and asking about suspicious persons and occurrences in the neighborhood. Cooperation between the police and the citizenry in Japan produces intensive surveillance of behavior. Such surveillance might be seen as oppressive by Americans, but it seems to contribute to Japan's low crime rate (Clifford, 1976; Bayley, 1976a; Whymant, 1979).

Deterrence and the Courts

Research on crime rates and the risk of conviction indicates that there is an inverse relationship between the two; lower crime rates are associated with higher conviction rates (Blumstein, Cohen, and Nagin, 1978: 42). Again the issue of simultaneity arises. A greater risk of conviction may deter offenders, but a lower crime rate may make convictions more likely. A high crime rate might reduce the risk of conviction if prosecutors drop cases because they lack the resources to bring all suspects to trial or if they lose cases because of hasty preparation. A high crime rate might also increase pressure for plea bargaining in order to ease the court's workload, and this might result in more guilty pleas but fewer convictions on the original, more serious charges. Because of the uncertainty raised by the problem of simultaneity, one report found that "no conclusion on the evidence of a deterrent effect of the conviction risk is yet warranted" (Blumstein, Cohen, and Nagin, 1978: 44).

One study that minimized the problem of simultaneity in looking at the relationship between certainty of conviction and draft evasion offenses compared the experiences of the various states, holding constant social characteristics and public opinion toward the Vietnam War. The researchers found that a higher certainty of punishment was linked to a lower rate of draft evasion. Draft evasion cases were a small part of the caseload of the federal courts, and these cases were given high priority by prosecutors. Consequently, the association between certainty of punishment and the rate of draft evasion did not seem to be due to a high rate of draft evasion causing an overload on the criminal justice system, which then reduced the certainty of punishment. Instead the research seemed to point to a deterrent effect of sanctions on draft evaders (Blumstein and Nagin, 1977; also, see Wilson, 1983).

A study of changes in crime rates in England and Wales from 1894 to 1967 suggests that changes in the certainty of punishment may cause changes in crime rates. Data of this sort are difficult to interpret, because other historical changes could have caused crime rates to rise and fall. However, the researcher provides several reasons to think that the association between certainty of punishment and crime rates was due to the deterrent effect of arrest, conviction, and punishment, rather than simply due to an overburdening of the criminal justice system (Wolpin, 1978; also, see Wilson, 1983).

One factor that often undermines the deterrent effect of conviction is the lack of promptness of punishment. The parties to criminal cases often want delay or have no particular interest in obtaining a speedy verdict. Defendants who are actually guilty seek delays so that witnesses will grow weary and refuse to come to court. Attorneys seek delays because they have taken on too many cases or because they require more time to prepare for a trial. Prosecutors go along with requests for delays because they assume that a defendant who is languishing in jail will feel pressured into pleading guilty, thus saving the court the inconvenience and expense of a trial and ensuring a conviction. Judges usually acquiesce to requests for postponements, because their refusal to grant delays could lead to cases being overturned on appeal if the defense had inadequate time to prepare for trial (Fleming, 1973). These factors cause delay, which may reduce the deterrent effect of convictions.

Deterrence and the Prisons

Researchers have generally found an inverse relationship between crime rates and the risk of imprisonment, but some of their studies have not found an inverse association between crime rates and the actual amount of time served in prison (Blumstein, Cohen, and Nagin, 1978: 37). One study found that higher crime rates seemed to reduce the risk of imprisonment, but did not find that a greater risk of imprisonment reduced crime rates (Nagin, 1978). However, another study found that higher rates of incarceration did seem to lead to lower crime rates, and that lower crime rates also led to lower rates of incarceration (McGuire and Sheehan, 1983). Another study found an inconsistent relationship between crime rates and imprisonment rates from 1941 to 1978, and concluded that evidence was lacking that crime could be reduced by the imprisonment of more offenders (Bowker, 1981). A research project that used data from Poland reached the conclusion that crime rates and imprisonment rates do not seem to respond consistently to each other, but instead seem to vary independently (Greenberg, 1980). One review of the research on this problem concluded that "no sound, empirically based conclusions can be drawn" about the existence of a deterrent effect of imprisonment on criminal behavior (Blumstein, Cohen, and Nagin, 1978: 42).

One strategy that has been tried as a deterrent to delinquency is a "shock sentence," with offenders being given "a taste of the bars" to keep them from further wrongdoing. For a time, the Massachusetts Department of Youth Services sentenced some juvenile offenders to thirty to sixty days of confinement, in the hope that their experience with "hard time" would break their pattern of delinquent activity (*The Boston Globe*, May 8, 1982). This would probably only work for people who have not already been incarcerated, and even for them it is not clear that it would be effective. For instance, one study found that a shock sentence and then probation had no apparent marginal deterrent effect over regular probation, if offenders with similar prior records were compared (Parisi, 1981).

A program similar to the shock sentence is the "Scared Straight" program. This program brings young people into prison to listen to a group of inmates talk about the unpleasantness of prison life; violence and homosexual rape are described in graphic terms to "scare straight" these young people. This program, called the Juvenile Awareness Project, was initiated at Rahway State Prison in New Jersey in 1976, and was the basis of a television documentary broadcast nationally in 1979. The show ended with the claim that the program was 80 to 90 per cent successful. However, a more systematic evaluation that used a six-month follow-up of delinquents who had and had not gone through the program found that those who had participated were actually arrested more often than those who had not (Finckenauer, 1979, 1982). This study had some methodological flaws, such as lack of random assignment of the juveniles to the treatment and control groups, but the researcher reanalyzed his data in response to methodological criticisms and still concluded that the Juvenile Awareness Project seemed more likely to set in motion a process by which those exposed to it became more rather than less delinquent. Another evaluation of the "Scared Straight" program reached a more optimistic conclusion, following up for twenty-two months a group of young men who had been arrested at least once. This study found that involvement in delinquent behavior by those who had participated in the Juvenile Awareness Project remained relatively constant after participation, but that the delinquent behavior of those who had not participated in the program increased significantly. This suggests that the program may keep delinquents from becoming more delinquent, which would have been their fate had they not been exposed to the program (Langer, 1979). This study too has been criticized for its methodology. In addition, though the participants in the Juvenile Awareness Project did better than the control group, still 85 per cent of those participants engaged in delinquent acts after exposure to the program (Finckenauer, 1982).

Deterrence and Capital Punishment

Much research has been done on the deterrent effect of capital punishment (e.g., see Schuessler, 1952; Sellin, 1967; Bedau and Pierce, 1976; Bedau, 1982; Lempert, 1983; Bowers, 1984). One strategy has been to compare the homicide rates of states that have the death penalty with the homicide rates of states that do not have the death penalty. Some researchers have studied the homicide rates in a state before and after its abolition of capital punishment to determine if that change affected murder rates. Another method has been to look at murder rates in an area just before and just after executions to see if those executions affected the homicide rate. These and other studies have consistently produced no evidence that either death penalty laws or actual executions deter homicide. One cross-national study even found that the abolition of the death penalty in a country was followed by a decline in the homicide rate more often than by the increase that deterrence theory would predict (Archer, Gartner, and Beittel, 1983). However, a review of the research on the death penalty concluded that although few studies have found a deterrent effect, "the current evidence on the deterrent effect of capital punishment is inadequate for drawing any substantive conclusions" (Blumstein, Cohen, and Nagin, 1978: 62).

A frequently cited study that used econometric methods did find a deterrent effect of the death penalty (Ehrlich, 1975). However, the methodological short-comings of this study are such as to invalidate its conclusions (Blumstein, Cohen, and Nagin, 1978: 59–62; Knorr, 1979). Another study that looked at twenty-two well-publicized executions in London from 1858 to 1921 found a 35.7 per cent drop in murders below the expected number in the two weeks after an offender was put to death. However, there was an increased number of murders a short time later, and by five weeks after the execution there was no net reduction in homicides (Phillips, 1980). One critic of this study says that it found a "delay effect" rather than a deterrent effect, ignored the impor-tant question of whether the death penalty has a marginal deterrent effect over life imprisonment, and used too much discretion in the choice of cases to study (Zeisel, 1982). Moreover, a study of the short-term effects of four recent American executions failed to find the pattern of deterrence found in the London study (McFarland, 1983).

There is some evidence that the administration of the death penalty may increase rather than decrease the homicide rate. One study found that an average of two additional homicides more than the normal number occurred in the month after an execution (Bowers and Pierce, 1980b; Bowers, 1984; Dietz, 1980). This *"brutalization effect"* seems to be due to the failure of most sane and rational citizens to identify with the kind of people who are executed, whereas unstable people who already have a victim, weapon, and motive in mind may be spurred to murder by seeing the state use lethal violence to take an offender's life (Bowers and Pierce, 1980b; Bowers, 1984). Evidence that contradicts the brutalization hypothesis comes from a study that examined actual executions and concluded that states that do not execute murderers do not have lower homicide rates than states that do (Lempert, 1983). One argument against the brutalization effect of executions is that peo-ple are able to distinguish between the state's use of force against serious criminals and their own use of violence in interpersonal disputes. Moreover, the ten-year moratorium on executions beginning in 1967 should have reduced the nation's homicide rate, according to the brutalization thesis; however, over that decade, the homicide rate increased by 44 per cent, from 6.1 per 100,000 people to 8.8 per 100,000 people (Yunker, 1982). Perhaps executions encourage some people to commit murder (the brutalization effect), and dis-suade others from lethal violence (the deterrent effect), but researchers have not yet been able to separate and measure these two effects (Bailey, 1983).

Most research is consistent with the conclusion that capital punishment does not deter those crimes for which it has been used in the United States—homicide and forcible rape (until 1977). There are several reasons to expect no deterrent effect from capital punishment for these crimes. Murderers and rapists usually do not reflect much on the future consequences of their behav-ior. Murder often occurs between people who are intimately associated with each other; such relationships are often charged with emotion, and this may interfere with a careful assessment of the risks of violating the law. Moreover, before an execution takes place, years may elapse while the case is appealed; this lack of promptness of punishment may reduce any general deterrent effect that the death penalty would have. Many capital punishment statutes apply only to specific kinds of murder, such as premeditated murders, ex-tremely brutal slayings, the killing of police or correctional officers, or assassina-

Figure 15.2: Number of Death-Row Inmates and Number of Executions at Yearend, 1953–1984

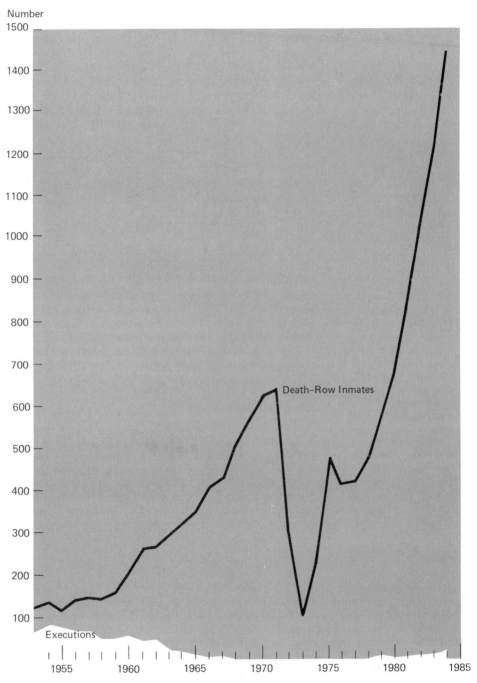

SOURCE: Bureau of Justice Statistics, *Capital Punishment 1982*. Washington, D.C.: U.S. Department of Justice, August 1984, cover page. (Updated with data from 1983 and 1984.)

tions; as a result, we would not expect these laws to have a general deterrent effect on all murders. In addition, capital punishment in the United States lacks certainty. Most murderers are not sentenced to death, and most of those who are given the death penalty are never executed (see Figure 15.2).

When the Supreme Court declared the states' death penalty statutes unconstitutional in 1972, no one had been put to death for five years. However, the public reacted to the Court's decision by demanding that the death penalty be put back on the law books; some of this outcry may have resulted from the large increase in official crime rates from 1963 to 1972. Today there is substantial public support for the death penalty; in 1985, 72 per cent of Americans favored it, according to the Gallup Poll (*The New York Times,* February 3, 1985).

Most people who support the death penalty believe that it deters crime, but many say they would support it even if it had no deterrent effect. Some have argued that the public's support for the death penalty is based more on expressive or symbolic grounds than on instrumental (deterrent) grounds, and that support for the death penalty is a value position learned through socialization (Tyler and Weber, 1982). There is a direct association between

---

A Cross-Cultural Perspective: Capital Punishment in China

Beginning a crackdown on crime in August 1983, the Chinese government started to execute criminals at an unprecedented rate and for crimes that are not usually punished by death in other countries. By some estimates, more than 5,000 offenders were executed by the end of 1983, and the campaign against crime continued beyond that point. There were even rumors that the government had set quotas for the number of criminals to be executed.

Offenders facing execution often must appear at public "sentencing rallies," where they carry banners telling of their crimes. They are paraded through the streets in trucks on their way to their execution, which is carried out by a bullet in the back of the head. These public displays are designed to create a general fear of punishment, and thus deter crime. According to Chinese sources, the nation's crime rate, which was already low by Western standards, declined significantly by the end of 1983 after this increase in executions.

Chinese law was changed at the beginning of this crackdown on crime. Public trials were suspended, and judicial review of death sentences for violent crimes was discontinued. The expansion of capital punishment to crimes other than murder can be seen in the offenses for which fifty-one people were put to death in Peking in mid-Oc-

tober 1983: fifteen for murder, fourteen for "hooliganism," six for rape, eight for burglary or robbery, four for kidnapping and selling girls or women, and four for other offenses. Chinese offenders have also been put to death for embezzlement; for instance, two accountants who had stolen funds to pay their gambling debts were executed.

The use of the death penalty is rooted in Chinese values that emphasize society's survival over the survival of the individual. There is a strong belief in the deterrent effect of capital punishment, and so there has been no public opposition to the recent increase in executions. One intellectual remarked, "If you don't execute someone who committed murder, other criminals will take a lesson from him." To instill widespread fear of the death penalty, the Chinese government has executed criminals who were descendants of national heroes and who were once Communist party leaders, and women as well as men have been put to death for their crimes.

SOURCES: Based on Christopher S. Wren, "Crime and Capital Punishment in China," *The New York Times,* November 20, 1983, p. E9; Jeff Sommer, "Chinese Execute 5000 since Start of Crime Crackdown," *The Boston Globe,* November 24, 1983, p. A42.

support for the death penalty and the belief that it is a deterrent, but it is not clear that people support the death penalty because they believe that it deters crime (Vidmar and Miller, 1980). A study of northern Californians found that most based their support or opposition to the death penalty on symbolic or ideological grounds, rather than on a set of reasoned beliefs. Nearly all of the 58.8 per cent of the sample who supported the death penalty believed that it was a better deterrent than life imprisonment, but two-thirds of those supporters said that they would favor capital punishment even if it had no deterrent effect. Nearly all of the 30.8 per cent of the sample who opposed the death penalty believed that it had no marginal deterrent effect over life imprisonment, but about three-fourths of them would continue to oppose the death penalty even if it proved to be a much better deterrent than life imprisonment (Ellsworth and Ross, 1983). One supporter of the death penalty presents this idea as follows:

> I have occasionally asked abolitionists if they would favor the death penalty were it shown that every execution deters, say, 500 murders. The answer to this admittedly hypothetical question, after some dodging, has always been no. This instructive answer demonstrates that abolitionists want to abolish the death penalty regardless of whether it deters (Van den Haag, 1983: A21).

Research by social scientists has focused on the deterrent effects of capital punishment, and the results of their work are consistent with the idea that executions do not deter crime, even though this proposition cannot be said to be proved. Still, people in the United States continue to support the death penalty, as do people in other societies such as China (see the Cross-Cultural Perspective). Public attitudes toward the death penalty seem to be based as much on ideas of retribution or just deserts as on ideas of deterrence. Issues such as the value of human life, the moral justification for the state taking the life of a convicted offender, and public outrage at certain criminals would exist even if there were definitive proof that the death penalty does or does not deter crime. We examine some of these issues in the next chapter.

INCAPACITATION

Incapacitation is the custodial control of convicted offenders so that they cannot commit crimes that affect the general public (Van Dine, Conrad, and Dinitz, 1979: 125). Incapacitation must be separated from specific and general deterrence and from rehabilitation as ways to reduce the crime rate. Incapacitation is based on the idea that offenders will commit a certain number of crimes if they remain in society, and that those crimes can be prevented by placing the offenders in prison for some time. Whether they reform during that time is not the issue; what is important is that they do not commit more crimes while in prison. The incapacitation rationale for punishment was succinctly stated by a Catholic priest as follows: "I am concerned that people who assault human lives should be safely contained like nuclear waste so their destruction in our midst will stop" (Byrne, 1979: A23).

According to James Q. Wilson (1983), incapacitation would work if three assumptions were correct:

1. Some offenders are repeaters.
2. Offenders who are taken off the street are not immediately and completely replaced by other offenders.

3. Prison does not increase crime by changing inmates in ways that offset the reduction in crime from incapacitation.

Wilson suggests that the first assumption is clearly correct. The second one is plausible for certain offenses. Replacement occurs in organized crime families, and probably among prostitutes, drug dealers, and white-collar offenders to some degree. Replacement is probably unimportant for crimes of family violence and for ordinary street crimes. Wilson acknowledges that the third assumption is debatable, but suggests that the "schooling" effect of prison probably does not outweigh its incapacitative effect.

Estimating the effect of incapacitation on crime rates is difficult. Because we lack good data on criminal careers—specifically on how many offenses different criminals will commit in a given period—it is difficult to determine how much crime is prevented by locking up offenders for a time. Offenders who are at the end of a criminal career might have stopped committing crime even if they had not been imprisoned, and so for them there would be little or no incapacitative effect.

Types of Incapacitation

Several approaches to the development of a policy of incapacitation have been proposed, with each approach differing in how to designate those offenders who should be held in prison for longer terms. Three approaches are *collective incapacitation, selective incapacitation,* and *criminal career incapacitation* (Greenberg, 1975; Cohen, 1983a, 1983b).

COLLECTIVE INCAPACITATION
One approach to incapacitating offenders is *collective incapacitation,* a policy of giving the same prison sentence to everyone convicted of a particular offense (Cohen, 1983a, 1983b). Estimates of how much a policy of collective incapacitation would reduce crime vary, depending on assumptions about how many crimes the average offender commits during a year on the street. Collective incapacitation would apparently reduce crime by about 10 to 20 per cent, a smaller effect than supporters of this policy sometimes claim. Even this much of a reduction would require a substantial increase in the prison population, and a corresponding investment of tax revenue to construct new prisons. It is not clear how much support there would be for higher taxes to build new prisons if people knew that to achieve a 10 to 20 per cent reduction in the crime rate would require a doubling, a tripling, or even more of an increase in the prison population (Cohen, 1983a, 1983b).

SELECTIVE INCAPACITATION
A more refined notion than collective incapacitation is predictive restraint or *selective incapacitation.* Instead of holding all offenders of a particular type in prison, only those who are the most likely to commit more crime if released would be held (Von Hirsch, 1976, 1984a, 1984b; Greenwood, 1982, 1984). This approach tries to separate high-risk offenders from low-risk offenders, and hold only those who are the most likely to be dangerous if released.

An important study of selective incapacitation by Peter Greenwood (1982, 1983, 1984) proposes a system that would help criminal justice practitioners to decide which offenders should get long, "incapacitating" prison sentences, and which ones might be released or placed in alternative programs. In this way, the limited amount of prison space might be allocated more efficiently and crime rates reduced. Greenwood claims that his plan could reduce robberies by adults in California by 20 per cent with only a 2.5 per cent increase in the prison population.

Using interviews with incarcerated robbers and burglars, Greenwood (1982, 1984) found that the offenders who perpetrated the most crimes in a given period had four or more of the following characteristics:

1. An earlier conviction for the same offense;
2. Imprisonment for more than half of the two years prior to the current arrest;
3. A conviction before the age of sixteen;
4. Previous commitment to a juvenile institution;
5. Use of heroin or barbiturates during the previous two years;
6. Use of heroin or barbiturates as a juvenile; and
7. Unemployment for half or more of the preceding two years.

Among imprisoned robbers, those who fit four or more of these criteria committed an average of thirty-one robberies per year while on the street, compared to an average of only two robberies per year for those who fit one or none of the criteria.

Greenwood's study of selective incapacitation has been subjected to criticism, some of it on methodological grounds. For instance, there is a problem in extrapolating from data gathered from a sample of incarcerated robbers and burglars to robbers and burglars who are still on the street. Offenders who are not locked up might commit less crime, or more crime, than inmates; not knowing which is the case makes it impossible to predict what impact a policy of selective incapacitation would have on offenders who are still at large. Greenwood's study relies on self-reported information, and this information would probably not be available at a hearing in which a judge decides how to sentence an offender. Moreover, some of the criteria listed by Greenwood to predict behavior would not be available to the judge; for instance, juvenile records are confidential. There is also some reluctance to use certain criteria—such as employment history—as a basis for incarcerating offenders for long periods. Critics also claim that the statistical association between the predictive criteria and subsequent criminal behavior might be good by some standards, but that it is weak enough that many errors of prediction would be made if the scale were used to predict behavior. Specifically, there is much concern with the high rate of "false positives," offenders who would be predicted to be likely to repeat their crimes and thus be incapacitated, even though they would in fact not have returned to crime if they had been released (Cohen, 1983a, 1983b; Blackmore and Welsh, 1983; Von Hirsch, 1984a, 1984b).

One response to these criticisms is that judges and parole boards now decide on sentences and release dates on the basis of their guesses about future behavior, and a selective incapacitation policy would simply allow them to use available data in the most efficient way possible to make their decisions. Statistical predictions may err, but even more mistakes are probably made when criminal justice practitioners operate on hunches about offenders' future behavior (Greenwood, 1982, 1984).

In addition to the methodological criticisms of selective incapacitation, there are also some moral objections. One is that offenders should get the punishment they deserve, based on the seriousness of the crime and their own blameworthiness; this is the policy of retribution or just deserts that we examine in the following chapter. Some of Greenwood's criteria fit a just deserts approach to punishment; indeed, a good case could be made that the only criterion that may not be an indicator of an offender's blameworthiness is unemployment for more than half of the preceding two years. However, critics argue that prior criminal history should play a less important role in determining a just penalty than does the harmfulness of the offense itself, and that none of Greenwood's predictive criteria base punishment on the amount of harm done (Von Hirsch, 1984a, 1984b). On the other hand, as we will see in the next chapter, retributivist models of punishment often make use of the blameworthiness of the offender as well as the harmfulness of the crime. Greenwood's approach would seem to be compatible with those just deserts models.

Most researchers, including both Greenwood and his critics, object to the use of predictive criteria over which offenders have no control, even if those criteria are associated with future criminal conduct. Thus, race, class, sex, and perhaps unemployment record might be excluded from predictive schemes; only unemployment is on Greenwood's list of criteria, and it might be argued that unemployment to some extent reflects voluntary behavior by the offender. One researcher found that home atmosphere when young and parental attitudes and behavior predicted later convictions of males for index crimes, but she concluded that people could not be punished on the basis of such predictors because they were not responsible for those factors in the way that they were responsible for their own criminal activity (McCord, 1981). Making predictions of future behavior is difficult, but not making predictions creates problems too, for it means that all offenders would be sentenced to the same term even though research shows that they are not equally dangerous (Greenwood, 1984).

CRIMINAL CAREER INCAPACITATION

In addition to collective and selective incapacitation, a third approach is *criminal career incapacitation* (Cohen, 1983a, 1983b). This approach would identify classes of criminals who seem to be the most likely to remain active in crime, and then incarcerate them. For instance, a study in Washington, D.C., found that convicted robbery and burglary defendants committed crimes at high rates during relatively short criminal careers; short prison sentences might significantly reduce robbery and burglary rates by locking the offenders up during the most active periods in their careers. For instance, a minimum two-year sentence for all adults convicted of robbery would have produced an 8 per cent drop in robberies by adults, while increasing the prison population by 7 per cent (Blumstein and Cohen, 1979; Cohen, 1983a, 1983b).

This criminal career incapacitation approach would use past and present criminal records to sentence offenders, thereby avoiding some of the problems of selective incapacitation models that use personal data to predict future behavior. In addition, criminal career incapacitation would be a form of "targeted collective incapacitation" and be applied in the same way to groups of similar offenders (Cohen, 1983a, 1983b).

Career criminal programs   With federal support, local district attorneys' offices around the country have established units to prosecute career criminals who repeatedly commit felonies. These programs concentrate resources on those suspects who have prior records of serious crimes in an effort to incapacitate them as quickly and for as long as possible. For instance, a New York state program focused on offenders with at least one prior felony conviction who were currently charged with a major crime. More than 95 per cent of these defendants were convicted, and nearly four-fifths of those who were convicted were sentenced on the highest charge they faced (Fowler, 1981).

One researcher who has looked closely at criminal careers says that existing data do not permit us to identify, with confidence, who will continue in a criminal career. We know that there is a group of offenders who commit much crime over time, but identifying them accurately has proved difficult so far (Petersilia, 1980).

Career criminal programs have managed to increase rates of conviction and incarceration and the length of sentences by only a small amount, although that amount is statistically meaningful (Phillips and Cartwright, 1981). These programs have achieved a slight reduction in crime rates, but their major importance seems to have been as a symbolic gesture to show the public that the criminal justice system can work effectively at times (Greenwood, 1980).

SUMMARY

Deterrence is the utilitarian philosophy that criminal activity can be inhibited by state-imposed punishment. This model assumes that offenders rationally consider the risks and rewards of crime before acting. Sometimes this assumption is correct, but not all offenders act with deliberation. Deterrence is but one of several effects of criminal sanctions, and separating it from the other effects has proved difficult.

Specific deterrence refers to the impact of a penalty on the offender who is punished; general deterrence refers to the effect that penalties have on the behavior of the general public. Penalties rarely deter crime absolutely, but sometimes they cause offenders to restrict their criminal activity. Marginal deterrence refers to the greater impact of one penalty rather than another on criminal behavior.

Instrumental acts are probably easier to deter than expressive crimes, and offenders who are not committed to crime as a way of life are easier to deter than those with a commitment to crime. A potential offender's assessment of the risks and rewards of crime, and the risks and rewards of alternative courses of action, also influences the deterrent effect of punishment. White-collar offenders are probably relatively easy to deter by the threat of punishment, because they commit instrumental crimes and have a low commitment to crime as a way of life.

Severity of punishment is probably less important in deterring crime than certainty of punishment. A high certainty of even a relatively minor penalty may reduce the amount of some kinds of crime. Punishment is probably a better deterrent if administered promptly than if delayed. In addition, the type of sanction makes a difference in determining the degree to which criminal behavior is deterred.

The impact of the police, the courts, and the prisons on crime rates is difficult to determine, because the problem of simultaneity arises; that is, crime rates affect the criminal justice system, just as the criminal justice system influences crime rates. Neither the size of the police force nor the rate at which the police make arrests seems to have much effect on a city's crime rate. There is little evidence that police patrol tactics have a major impact on the crime rate, although they may sometimes displace crime from one place to another or from one time to another. A higher probability of conviction can deter crime, but again the problem of simultaneity arises in interpreting the data. The same is true for the relationship between rates of imprisonment and crime rates. It is not clear whether programs that try to scare delinquents into going straight can deter young people from crime.

There is little or no evidence that capital punishment deters the crimes for which it has been used, but research has not yet definitively established the absence of a deterrent effect. Two studies that claimed to find a deterrent effect for the death penalty suffered from difficulties that cast doubt on that conclusion. There is some evidence that executions may "brutalize" a population and increase a society's homicide rate. The low certainty of this very severe penalty, and the lack of promptness in administering it, suggest that capital punishment is unlikely to deter crime.

Incapacitation is the policy of locking up offenders to prevent them from committing crimes that affect the general public. Collective incapacitation is a policy of sentencing everyone convicted of a particular crime in the same way; this policy would be expensive to implement and would reduce crime less than its supporters claim. Selective incapacitation would imprison those convicted offenders who are the most likely to commit more crime if released. This form of predictive restraint would use past behavior, including criminal activity, to determine who should be incarcerated. This approach has methodological and moral problems, but it would systematize decisions made by criminal justice practitioners, who now often rely on hunches in imprisoning and releasing offenders. A third policy is criminal career incapacitation, an approach that would incarcerate those kinds of criminals who seem to be the most likely to remain active in crime. Criminal career programs that concentrate the resources of district attorneys' offices on convicted felons have had a small impact on crime rates, but may show the public that the criminal justice system can work effectively at times.

IMPORTANT TERMS

absolute deterrence
"brutalization effect"
collective incapacitation
criminal career
   incapacitation

deterrence
displacement effect
general deterrence
incapacitation
marginal deterrent effect

restrictive deterrence
selective incapacitation
simultaneity
specific deterrence

SUGGESTED READINGS

ALFRED BLUMSTEIN, JACQUELINE COHEN, AND DANIEL NAGIN. *Deterrence and Incapacitation: Estimating the Effects of Criminal Sanctions on Crime Rates.* Washington, D.C.: National Academy of Sciences, 1978. An important review of the research on deterrence and incapacitation.

JACK P. GIBBS. *Crime, Punishment, and Deterrence.* New York: Elsevier, 1975. A detailed examination of the deterrence model of punishment.

PETER W. GREENWOOD, WITH ALLAN ABRAHAMSE. *Selective Incapacitation.* Santa Monica, Calif.: Rand, 1982. A report on an important study of selective incapacitation.

MARK H. MOORE ET AL. *Dangerous Offenders: The Elusive Target of Justice.* Cambridge, Mass.: Harvard University Press, 1984. An evaluation of proposals to deal selectively with dangerous offenders.

FRANKLIN E. ZIMRING AND GORDON J. HAWKINS. *Deterrence: The Legal Threat in Crime Control.* Chicago: University of Chicago Press, 1973. Another detailed exploration of the deterrence model and its implications for the reduction of the crime rate.

16

Retribution

In 1981, *The New York Times* and other newspapers carried editorials that strongly opposed parole for Sirhan Sirhan, the man who assassinated Senator Robert Kennedy in 1968. The editorials argued that an early parole, which was not granted, would have provided too lenient a sentence for a crime the magnitude of Sirhan's.

In another case that had received much media attention a few months earlier, William Rummel was sentenced to life in prison for his third felony conviction; the three crimes leading to this sentence under Texas's habitual offender law cost victims a total of $229.11 and involved no violence or threat of violence. The Supreme Court ruled by 5 to 4 that this sentence was not unconstitutionally "cruel and unusual," but Rummel eventually gained his release because of procedural irregularities (Mann, 1980).

These two cases raise the issue of how much punishment offenders deserve for their crimes. In the previous chapter, we looked at deterrence, a utilitarian rationale that requires sanctions to keep potential offenders from committing crime in the future. The next chapter examines the rehabilitation rationale, the idea that punishment should reform or change offenders so that they do not commit crime again. In contrast to deterrence and rehabilitation, *retribution* or *just deserts* reflects the idea that offenders should be punished because they deserve to suffer for the harm they have caused. Retribution is oriented toward behavior that the offender has already engaged in, rather than toward future conduct of the offender or other potential offenders.

THE RETRIBUTION MODEL

The retribution or just deserts rationale for punishment asserts that people who violate the law deserve punishment because they have intentionally hurt others. If there is no harm, a retributivist would claim that there should be no punishment. Retributivists argue that offenders deserve to be punished because they have gained an advantage over others by their crimes, and they must be punished in order to restore a balance among all citizens. The theory of retribution thus sees punishment as deserved and necessary "to restore an objective order rather than to satisfy a subjective craving for revenge" (Van den Haag, 1975: 11).

Retribution and Vengeance

Retribution differs from *vengeance,* which is "private and personal" and not imposed by an established authority such as the state. In contrast, retribution requires an authority with the acknowledged right to mete out sanctions to convicted offenders (Armstrong, 1971: 36). Whereas vengeance is typically motivated by the desire to be gratified or compensated for a loss, retribution is justified instead by the need to enforce the law and maintain social order (Van den Haag, 1975: 11).

The retribution rationale is commonly associated with *lex talionis,* the principle of "an eye for an eye, a tooth for a tooth," which was expressed in the Code of Hammurabi in the eighteenth century B.C. To take this rule literally, a person who blinded another person would be blinded in return. Being made to pay a small fine would be an unjustly lenient sentence, and execution would be an unjustly harsh penalty. Thus, retributivists claim that offenders should be punished because they deserve to suffer harm; moreover, offenders should be punished only in direct proportion to the harm that they have caused. The idea of making punishment proportional to the seriousness of the crime makes mercy possible, "because to be merciful is to let someone off for all or part of a penalty which he is recognized as having deserved" (Armstrong, 1971: 36).

Some critics argue that the principle of just deserts or retribution is simply a way to justify harsher criminal sanctions, perhaps to shore up a faltering capitalist economy (Reiman and Headlee, 1981; Reiman, 1982). Others point out that just deserts theorists have not supported harsh penalties in recent years, and that their work has not been directed at strengthening a troubled capitalist system (Greenberg and Humphries, 1982). In response to the criticism that a just deserts model inevitably leads to severe sanctions, one lawyer writes as follows:

> If one looks at the sentencing standards actually adopted in this country, one is struck by the fact that several of the more desert-oriented schemes (those of Minnesota and Oregon, for example) are moderate in their penalty levels, whereas some of the harshest systems (e.g., the sentencing standards adopted in New Mexico and Indiana) stress goals of incapacitation and deterrence (Von Hirsch, 1981: 778).

Retribution Compared to Deterrence and Rehabilitation

The principle of retribution suggests that people who violate the law are blameworthy and deserve moral disapproval for their acts. This reprobation is seen as the basis for punishment, even if that punishment does not serve a socially useful function such as deterring people from crime or rehabilitating offenders.

Retributivists assume that offenders are responsible and rational people who have freely chosen to violate the law. This implies that behavior is not determined by forces beyond people's conscious control, and that people are aware that punishment may result from their breaking the law. Retributivists sometimes assert that punishing people only because they deserve to suffer for having inflicted harm on others is treatment with dignity, because such an approach assumes that people who choose to break the law will pay the price in terms of punishment. This contrasts with the deterrence perspective, which has as its aim the social goal of crime control; offenders are punished so that they or other people will not commit crime in the future. The principle of retribution also differs from the rehabilitation perspective, which sees criminals as people who have made an incorrect decision to commit crime that they will not make again if they can be reformed. Some have claimed that the idea implicit in the rehabilitation perspective that offenders would not commit crime if they were the "right" kind of people undermines the dignity of those who break the law (Kittrie, 1971).

A retributive system of punishment would thus treat offenders as responsible people who have freely chosen to violate the law and who should be held accountable for their behavior. Unlike the theories of deterrence and rehabilitation, retribution does not require that punishment serve a larger social good. As one philosopher notes,

> It is too rarely noticed that retributivists in principle are fundamentally indifferent between the state of the world in which there is no crime, and the state of the world in which there is a wide variety of horrible crimes each of which is punished fully and exactly as retribution requires. Depressing the crime rate is of no concern to the retributivist; neither is avoiding recidivism; he willingly leaves these concerns to the utilitarian, thereby revealing just how narrow are his interests in the overall social problem of crime and punishment (Bedau, 1977: 69).

If the only goal of punishment were to deter people from crime, innocent people might be punished as long as the public believed that they were actually guilty. The punishment of individuals who were thought to be guilty might then deter others from criminal behavior. Similarly, a very severe penalty administered with certainty might have a strong deterrent effect; thus a thirty-year prison term for petty theft might deter stealing. The usual objection to punishing the innocent and to very harsh penalties is that those penalties are unjust. It is this idea of the "justness" of penalties that is the essence of a retribution rationale for punishment.

If rehabilitation were the only goal of punishment, people identified as potentially dangerous might be imprisoned and subjected to treatment even before they were convicted of a crime. If there were no effective treatment for a mass murderer, the rehabilitation rationale might require that such an offender not be imprisoned at all. If there were an effective treatment method that could fully reform a petty thief with a thirty-year prison sentence, such a penalty might be justified in terms of rehabilitation. The usual objection to penalties such as these is that they are fundamentally unjust. Indeed, it has been argued that if there were general agreement that a six-month prison term is a just penalty for petty theft, keeping a convicted petty thief locked up for even one month longer would be improper, even if that offender were rehabilitated by the extra month in prison and even if other people considering theft were deterred by that extra month (Von Hirsch, 1976).

Retributivists assert that deterrence and rehabilitation are secondary or derivative goals of punishment; the primary justification for punishment is that offenders deserve to be punished in proportion to the harm they have inflicted on the victim and on society. However, others suggest that deterrence and rehabilitation should play a part in determining sentences. Thus, one philosopher says that "a modified retributive theory is perfectly possible, one which only uses retributive considerations to fix some sort of upper limit to penalties and then looks to other factors to decide how much and what sort of pain shall be inflicted" (Armstrong, 1971: 38–39). A just deserts model might thus set an upper limit, a lower limit, or a range of penalties; considerations such as deterrence, incapacitation, or rehabilitation might then play a part in determining where within those limits the actual punishment falls (Morris,

1981; Wilson, 1983). For instance, a 1979 report by the American Bar Association called for a sentencing system in which just deserts would set broad limits but selective incapacitation would determine specific punishments. Some retributivists disagree with this approach, claiming that penalties should be proportional to the seriousness of the current offense, and that other considerations should not play a role in determining punishment (Von Hirsch, 1981).

A strict retributivist might argue about the appropriateness of the penalty meted out in a 1984 case in which a sixty-six-year-old man shot and killed his twenty-seven-year-old son, who had been suicidal and who had been disfigured after dousing himself with gasoline and setting himself on fire. The judge sentenced the father to 100 hours of community service a month for five years, saying that no punishment could be more severe than what the father had already suffered. The judge saw the crime as a mercy-killing that had caused the father great anguish, and believed that a relatively light sentence would not reduce the deterrent effect of the law for others because of the unusual circumstances of the case. The judge also apparently thought that the father was not in need of rehabilitation. Retributivists might claim that the harm done, the taking of a life, was worthy of harsher punishment, even though they might agree that the circumstances of the crime could be used to mitigate the father's penalty (*The New York Times*, May 12, 1984).

A SYSTEM OF JUST DESERTS

A workable system of retribution or just deserts would require the rank ordering of crimes by their relative seriousness and the rank ordering of punishments by their relative unpleasantness. Seriousness of crimes and unpleasantness of penalties are not objective facts about crime and punishment, so these rankings must be based upon subjective evaluations (Erickson and Gibbs, 1979). These scales must be carefully devised; attention must be given not only to the relative rank ordering of different crimes and different punishments, but also to the intervals between points on each scale (Hospers, 1977). For instance, a twenty-year prison term may be perceived as more unpleasant than a fifteen-year term, and a fifteen-year term may be seen as more unpleasant than a ten-year term. However, it is not obvious that people will regard a twenty-year term as being as much more unpleasant than a fifteen-year term as a fifteen-year term is in comparison to a ten-year term. After researchers develop scales of the seriousness of crimes and the severity of penalties, they then must find a way to link the two scales so that crimes of specific degrees of seriousness will be associated with penalties of certain levels of severity (Von Hirsch, 1976; Nevares-Muniz, 1984).

The Seriousness of Crimes

A scale that ranks offenses by seriousness might be based on the amount of harm caused by a crime and the blameworthiness of the offender, with harmfulness and blameworthiness being combined into a single measure of the seriousness of the crime (Bedau, 1977: 64). There has been some research to develop a scale of the harmfulness of different crimes, and also some research on how to rank offenders by degree of blameworthiness. There has, however, been little work to develop a measure of the seriousness of crimes that combines harmfulness and blameworthiness.

BLAMEWORTHINESS OF OFFENDERS

The issue of using the blameworthiness of an offender to judge the seriousness of a crime is a complex one. One form of retribution theory claims that penalties should be imposed only for the harm caused by the crime; this position would ignore the perpetrator of the offense. Another form of retribution theory holds that because offenders should be punished as they deserve, their blameworthiness must be considered in determining just sentences.

Blameworthiness can be measured in different ways. One way is to use the motivation or mental state of the offender to determine blameworthiness. There is some evidence that people's judgments of the seriousness of crimes are affected by the mental state they attribute to offenders, independently of the effect on those judgments of the harm done by offenders. When no mental state is specified, people tend to attribute intentionality to conventional street criminals, and recklessness or negligence to people who commit certain white-collar offenses (Sebba, 1980, 1984).

Blameworthiness may also be judged by the circumstances of a crime. Thus, an offender who is involved in a victim-precipitated crime or who is an unwilling or peripheral participant in a crime might be treated as less blameworthy than someone who plans and perpetrates a crime alone.

Perhaps the most common way to measure blameworthiness is by the number and seriousness of an individual's prior convictions. It is assumed that an offense is more serious if it is committed by a person who has committed other crimes in the past, rather than if it is committed by a first-time offender. There are, however, some problems with using prior record as an indicator of blameworthiness. One problem is that prior record can be measured in several ways, and each way seems to be related to sentence severity in a different way (Welch, Gruhl, and Spohn, 1984). Another problem is that the use of prior arrests or prior convictions to indicate blameworthiness might lead to "a cyclic reconfirmation of criminality" (Farrell and Swigert, 1978: 451). Because some research indicates that there is a bias in the criminal justice system against lower-class offenders—with such offenders being more likely than middle-class offenders to be arrested, convicted, and severely punished for the same crime—the use of prior records to indicate blameworthiness and determine penalties might have the effect of locking lower-class offenders into criminal careers.

HARMFULNESS OF CRIMES

More research has been done on developing a scale to measure the harmfulness of crimes than has been done on measuring the blameworthiness of offenders. Sellin and Wolfgang (1964) carried out a pioneering study on the perceived seriousness of offenses, and found widespread agreement about how crimes should be ranked. They showed that various components of a crime, such as amount of injury to the victim and amount of monetary loss, could be assigned scores, and a summary score could then be derived for the offense. This permitted Sellin and Wolfgang to rank crimes by their harmfulness and state how much more serious one crime was than another.

Table 16.1 shows the values assigned to the various elements of a crime incident. A robbery in which the victim suffered minor injuries and lost $300 when verbally threatened would have an overall score of 6: This is the sum of 1 point for minor injury, 3 for the theft of $300, and 2 for verbal intimidation in connection with a theft. A robbery in which there was no injury to the victim but a loss of $5 as a result of verbal intimidation would receive a score

Table 16.1: Seriousness Scores for Elements of Crimes

ELEMENT OF THE CRIME	SCORE VALUE
Minor injury to victim	1
Victim treated and discharged	4
Victim hospitalized	7
Victim killed	26
Victim of forcible sexual intercourse	10
Intimidated by weapon, add	2
Intimidation of persons in connection with theft, etc.	
(Other than in connection with forcible sex acts):	
Physical or verbal only	2
By weapon	4
Forcible entry of premises	1
Value of property stolen and/or damaged	
Under $10	1
$10–$250	2
$251–$2,000	3
$2,001–$9,000	4
$9,001–$30,000	5
$30,001–$80,000	6
Over $80,000	7
Theft of motor vehicle (recovered, undamaged)	2

SOURCE: Thorsten Sellin and Marvin E. Wolfgang, *The Measurement of Delinquency*. New York: John Wiley, 1964, p. 298. Copyright © John Wiley & Sons, Inc. Reprinted with permission.

of 3: This is the total of 0 points for no injury, 1 point for the loss of $5, and 2 points for verbal intimidation in connection with the theft. We could thus say that the first robbery was twice as serious as the second one.

Sellin and Wolfgang's scoring system allows for a more meaningful measurement of crime than is possible by just counting the number of incidents. The difference between a bank robbery in which a guard is seriously injured by an armed offender who steals $10,000, and a schoolyard robbery in which a child gives up his lunch money because of a verbal threat would not show up in the FBI's UCR statistics, because each event would be counted as one robbery. Sellin and Wolfgang's scoring system would emphasize the difference between the incidents. The bank robbery would be scored 16: This is the sum of 4 points for the use of a weapon in connection with the theft, 7 for injury to the guard, and 5 for the theft of $10,000. The schoolyard robbery would be scored 3: 1 point for the theft of less than $10 plus 2 points for verbal intimidation connected with the theft.

A national survey conducted in 1977 asked people to rank 204 illegal acts. Table 16.2 shows the average severity scores for some of these offenses. In general, different kinds of people agreed on the ranking of the crimes. However, victims tended to assign higher severity scores than nonvictims did. In addition, blacks and other minorities generally assigned lower severity scores than did whites, and older people ranked thefts with large losses as more severe than did younger respondents. In ranking a crime, people took into account factors such as the following:

• The ability of the victim to protect him/herself
• Extent of injury and loss

Table 16.2: Public Ranking of Severity of Crime

SEVERITY SCORE AND OFFENSE	SEVERITY SCORE AND OFFENSE	SEVERITY SCORE AND OFFENSE	SEVERITY SCORE AND OFFENSE
72.1—Planting a bomb in a public building. The bomb explodes and 20 people are killed.	13.9—A legislator takes a bribe from a company to vote for a law favoring the company.	illegally fix the retail prices of their products.	5.3—Loaning money at an illegally high interest rate.
52.8—A man forcibly rapes a woman. As a result of physical injuries, she dies.	13.0—A factory knowingly gets rid of its waste in a way that pollutes the water supply of a city.	8.6—Performing an illegal abortion.	5.1—A man runs his hands over the body of a female victim, then runs away.
43.2—Robbing a victim at gunpoint. The victim struggles and is shot to death.	12.2—Paying a witness to give false testimony in a criminal trial.	8.5—Selling marijuana to others for resale.	5.1—A person, using force, robs a victim of $10. No physical harm occurs.
39.2—A man stabs his wife. As a result, she dies.	12.0—A police officer takes a bribe not to interfere with an illegal gambling operation.	8.5—Intentionally injuring a victim. The victim is treated by a doctor but is not hospitalized.	4.9—Snatching a handbag containing $10 from a victim on the street.
35.7—Stabbing a victim to death.	12.0—Intentionally injuring a victim. The victim is treated by a doctor and hospitalized.	8.2—Knowing that a shipment of cooking oil is bad, a store owner decides to sell it anyway. Only one bottle is sold and the purchaser is treated by a doctor but not hospitalized.	4.8—A man exposes himself in public.
35.6—Intentionally injuring a victim. As a result, the victim dies.	11.8—A man beats a stranger with his fists. He requires hospitalization.	7.9—A teenage boy beats his father with his fists. The father requires hospitalization.	4.6—Carrying a gun illegally.
33.8—Running a narcotics ring.	11.4—Knowingly lying under oath during a trial.	7.7—Knowing that a shipment of cooking oil is bad, a store owner decides to sell it anyway.	4.5—Cheating on Federal income tax return.
27.9—A woman stabs her husband. As a result, he dies.	11.2—A company pays a bribe to a legislator to vote for a law favoring the company.	7.5—A person, armed with a lead pipe, robs a victim of $10. No physical harm occurs.	4.4—Picking a victim's pocket of $100.
26.3—An armed person skyjacks an airplane and demands to be flown to another country.	10.9—Stealing property worth $10,000 from outside a building.	7.4—Illegally getting monthly welfare checks.	4.2—Attempting to break into a home but running away when a police car approaches.
25.9—A man forcibly rapes a woman. No other physical injury occurs.	10.5—Smuggling marijuana into the country for resale.	7.3—Threatening a victim with a weapon unless the vic-	3.8—Turning in a false fire alarm.
24.9—Intentionally setting fire to a building causing $100,000 worth of damage.			3.7—A labor union official illegally threatens to organize a strike if an employer hires nonunion workers.
			3.6—Knowingly passing a bad check.

22.9—A parent beats his young child with his fists. The child requires hospitalization.

21.2—Kidnaping a victim.

20.7—Selling heroin to others for resale.

19.5—Smuggling heroin into the country.

19.5—Killing a victim by recklessly driving an automobile.

17.9—Robbing a victim of $10 at gunpoint. The victim is wounded and requires hospitalization.

16.9—A man drags a woman into an alley, tears her clothes, but flees before she is physically harmed or sexually attacked.

16.4—Attempting to kill a victim with a gun. The gun misfires and the victim escapes unharmed.

15.9—A teenage boy beats his mother with his fists. The mother requires hospitalization.

15.5—Breaking into a bank at night and stealing $100,000.

14.1—A doctor cheats on claims he makes to a Federal health insurance plan for patient services.

10.4—Intentionally hitting a victim with a lead pipe. The victim requires hospitalization.

10.3—Illegally selling barbiturates, such as prescription sleeping pills, to others for resale.

10.3—Operating a store that knowingly sells stolen property.

10.0—A government official intentionally hinders the investigation of a criminal offense.

9.7—Breaking into a school and stealing equipment worth $1,000.

9.7—Walking into a public museum and stealing a painting worth $1,000.

9.6—Breaking into a home and stealing $1,000.

9.6—A police officer knowingly makes a false arrest.

9.5—A public official takes $1,000 of public money for his own use.

9.4—Robbing a victim of $10 at gunpoint. No physical harm occurs.

9.3—Threatening to seriously injure a victim.

9.2—Several large companies [...]tim gives money. The victim gives $10 and is not harmed.

7.3—Breaking into a department store and stealing merchandise worth $1,000.

7.2—Signing someone else's name to a check and cashing it.

6.9—Stealing property worth $1,000 from outside a building.

6.5—Using heroin.

6.5—An employer refuses to hire a qualified person because of that person's race.

6.4—Getting customers for a prostitute.

6.3—A person, free on bail for committing a serious crime, purposefully fails to appear in court on the day of his trial.

6.2—An employee embezzles $1,000 from his employer.

5.4—Possessing some heroin for personal use.

5.4—A real estate agent refuses to sell a house to a person because of that person's race.

5.4—Threatening to harm a victim unless the victim gives money. The victim gives $10 and is not harmed.

3.6—Stealing property worth $100 from outside a building.

3.5—Running a place that permits gambling to occur illegally.

3.2—An employer illegally threatens to fire employees if they join a labor union.

2.4—Knowingly carrying an illegal knife.

2.2—Stealing $10 worth of merchandise from the counter of a department store.

2.1—A person is found firing a rifle for which he knows he has no permit.

2.1—A woman engages in prostitution.

1.9—Making an obscene phone call.

1.9—A store owner knowingly puts "large" eggs into containers marked "extra-large."

1.8—A youngster under 16 years old is drunk in public.

1.8—Knowingly being a customer in a place where gambling occurs illegally.

1.7—Stealing property worth $10 from outside a building.

1.6—Being a customer in a house of prostitution.

Table 16.2: (Continued)

SEVERITY SCORE AND OFFENSE	SEVERITY SCORE AND OFFENSE	SEVERITY SCORE AND OFFENSE
1.6—A male, over 16 years of age, has sexual relations with a willing female under 16.	1.3—Two persons willingly engage in a homosexual act.	ter the hour permitted by law.
1.5—Taking barbiturates, such as sleeping pills, without a legal prescription.	1.1—Disturbing the neighborhood with loud, noisy behavior.	0.6—Trespassing in the backyard of a private home.
1.5—Intentionally shoving or pushing a victim. No medical treatment is required.	1.1—Taking bets on the numbers.	0.3—A person is a vagrant. That is, he has no home and no visible means of support.
1.4—Smoking marijuana.	1.1—A group continues to hang around a corner after being told to break up by a police officer.	0.2—A youngster under 16 years old plays hooky from school.
	0.9—A youngster under 16 years old runs away from home.	
	0.8—Being drunk in public.	
	0.7—A youngster under 16 years old breaks a curfew law by being out on the street af-	

SOURCE: Study by Center for Studies in Criminology and Criminal Law, University of Pennsylvania. Table reproduced from Bureau of Justice Statistics, *Report to the Nation on Crime and Justice: The Data.* Washington, D.C.: U.S. Department of Justice, October 1983, pp. 4–5.

• For property crimes, the type of business or organization from which the property is stolen
• The relationship of the offender to the victim (Bureau of Justice Statistics, October 1983b: 5).

In addition to some evidence of consensus among various groups within the United States on the relative harmfulness of different crimes, there is some research that points to a cross-cultural consensus on the ranking of crimes. One study of India, Indonesia, Iran, Italy (Sardinia), Yugoslavia, and the United States found considerable agreement on the perceived harmfulness of various deviant acts and on the amount and type of punishment thought to be appropriate for each act. In this study, the effects of social-background variables on perceptions of deviance were minimal (Newman, 1976). Other research has found that the rankings of offenses are similar in the United States, Canada, Norway, Finland, Sweden, Denmark, the Netherlands, Great Britain, and Kuwait (Scott and Al-Thakeb, 1977; Kvålseth, 1980). A comparison of American and Kuwaiti students discovered much agreement on the ranking of offenses, with the exception of morals offenses, and revealed that religious fundamentalism affected rankings in both samples (Evans and Scott, 1984). However, not all researchers have found unanimity on how people in different societies rank crimes (Hsu, 1973).

A survey of 200 Baltimore residents conducted in 1972 found much agreement about the relative harmfulness of 140 offenses (Rossi et al., 1974). Crimes against the person and drug selling were regarded as more serious than crimes against property, which were regarded as more serious than various misdemeanors. Assaults against police officers were seen as more serious than assaults on private citizens. Crimes against victims who were known to the offenders were regarded as less serious than crimes against strangers. Offenses without complainants, such as prostitution, were not seen as very serious in comparison to other offenses. There was considerable agreement by people of different sexes, races, and educational levels about the relative ranking of crimes. A later study found much agreement between the rankings of this Baltimore sample and the rankings of 154 criminal justice bureaucrats, although the bureaucrats tended to use more of the characteristics of a crime to determine how to rank it (McCleary et al., 1981).

The Baltimore study found that people did not see white-collar crimes as particularly serious, but there was much variation in the ranking of different white-collar crimes. "Knowingly selling contaminated foods which results in a death" (ranked 26 out of 140 offenses) and "causing the death of an employee by neglecting to repair machinery" (ranked 51) were seen as quite harmful; other white-collar offenses were ranked lower on the scale. What seemed to be important was the nature of the crime and its harmful consequences. Thus, selling contaminated food that caused death was ranked as more serious than robbing a taxi driver, beating up a police officer, or killing a spouse's lover. A replication of the 1972 Baltimore survey carried out in a town in Illinois in 1979 found that white-collar crime had increased in relative ranking more than any other offense category, even though it was still seen as less harmful than most other kinds of crime. The change in the ranking was most notable for violent white-collar crime and corporate price fixing, and the highest scores for white-collar crime were given to offenses that involved physical harm (Cullen, Link, and Polanzi, 1982). Surveys that have focused on the seriously harmful physical effects of white-collar crime, rather than its diffuse economic consequences, have uncovered considerable public reprobation (Schrager and Short, 1978, 1980; Cullen et al., 1983).

The Unpleasantness of Penalties

A retributive system of punishment requires data on how people perceive the severity of penalties relative to each other. This means that we need to know how unpleasant one type of penalty is thought to be when compared with another type of penalty. For example, what is the relative unpleasantness of a sentence to a state prison, a sentence to a county jail, a fine, and probation? We also need to know the perceived unpleasantness of an increment of a particular kind of penalty; for instance, do people think that a ten-year prison term is twice as severe as a five-year sentence (Erickson and Gibbs, 1979; Buchner, 1979)?

There is probably general agreement on how unpleasant criminal sanctions are. Probation is seen as unpleasant because it imposes restrictions on offenders; they are required to report regularly to probation officers, and they have their mobility and privacy limited. Fines are unpleasant because they deprive offenders of property; they are a relatively lenient form of punishment because they do not disrupt ties to family and job as imprisonment does, but they do discriminate against people who cannot afford to pay. Imprisonment deprives offenders of freedom of movement and contacts with the outside world. Restraint on freedom of movement is subject to many gradations, with the amount of time and the institution to which an offender is confined indicating the severity of the penalty.

We have little research on the equivalence of different amounts of the various kinds of punishment. One study had people rate the severity of different penalties in comparison to a standard of one year in jail (Erickson and Gibbs, 1979). The researchers then developed a series of scales that allowed them to equate a particular jail sentence with a specific prison sentence, probationary period, or fine. For instance, one year in a local jail was perceived as equivalent to a six-month sentence to a state prison, 7.8 years on probation, or a fine of about $3,000. Similarly, a six-month jail sentence was equated to a three-month prison sentence, three years on probation, and a $1,000 fine. The researchers suggested that eventually it might be possible to convert different penalties into a common quantitative measure of perceived severity. Such a measure might be used to compare judges and jurisdictions in terms of the severity of penalties meted out. It might also be used to give convicted offenders a choice from a list of equivalent penalties, such as a choice of spending a year in jail, six months in prison, eight years on probation, or paying a $3,000 fine. One controversial effort to give offenders a choice of penalties has involved several judges who have offered convicted rapists a choice between a long prison sentence and castration (Monk, 1983).

A graded scale of penalties was developed by the Committee for the Study of Incarceration (Von Hirsch, 1976). The most lenient sentence suggested by the committee was a warning with unconditional release of the offender. Next was intermittent confinement, such as on weekends and during certain nights of the week; this would be more unpleasant than a warning and release, but less onerous than full-time incarceration. Incarceration, the most unpleasant of the recommended penalties, would be used for serious offenders. Fines were excluded from this system because of the difficulty of equalizing fines for people with different incomes.

Linking Penalties to Crimes

Developing a scale that measures the seriousness of crimes or the unpleasantness of penalties is easier than determining how unpleasant a penalty should be administered to a person who commits an offense of a certain degree of seriousness. The Eighth Amendment to the Constitution bars "cruel and unusual" punishment, but the Supreme Court has rarely overturned penalties for being excessively harsh. In a rare case of this sort, *Solem* v. *Helm* (1983), the Court ruled 5 to 4 that a sentence of life in prison without the possibility of parole was "significantly disproportionate" to the crime, which was the passing of a bad check for $100 by a man who had six previous convictions for nonviolent crimes. The Court saw this case as different from the one of the Texas man who received a life sentence for three property crimes, because in *Solem* v. *Helm* the offender would never have been eligible for parole. This decision reaffirmed the retributivist position that penalties must be proportional to the seriousness of the crime. According to the Court, a disproportionately long sentence would be one that exceeded the gravity of the crime and that was harsh when compared to the sentences meted out for similar crimes in other courts in the state (Greenhouse, 1983).

In an effort to establish standards that link crimes of differing degrees of seriousness with penalties of different magnitudes, the Committee for the Study of Incarceration recommended that a limited number of sentence levels should be used for offenders convicted of crimes of varying degrees of seriousness. The committee proposed that crimes be categorized by the harmfulness of the offense and by the number and seriousness of the offender's prior convictions. The committee suggested the following penalties:

1. *Minor offenses* should be punished least severely—by warning-and-release for the first offense, and by a light schedule of intermittent confinement (e.g., a loss of a few Saturdays) for repetitions. . . .
2. *Intermediate-level offenses* (from the slightly more than minor to the nearly serious) should be punished mainly by intermittent confinement, although warning-and-release should be used for first offenses in the lower range of this category. For offenses in the upper range, there would be stiff schedules of intermittent confinement involving substantial deprivations of offenders' leisure time. But incarceration should not be employed, since we are still speaking of crimes that do not qualify as serious. . . .
3. *Serious offenses* (*lower range*) might be punished by intermittent confinement for the first offense, reflecting our conception of a scaled-down penalty for first offenders. Repeated violations, however, should be punished by incarceration. . . .
4. *Serious offenses* (*upper range*) should receive sentences of incarceration in any event. Intentional and unprovoked crimes of violence that cause (or are extremely likely to cause) grave bodily injury to the victim fit here, as would the worst white-collar offenses such as those in which people's lives are knowingly endangered (Von Hirsch, 1976: 137–138).

The committee recommended that penalties for lower-range serious offenses be less than eighteen months, and that sentences for upper-range serious offenses fall between eighteen months and three years. There would be no sentences over five years, except for certain murders and a few cases involving exceptional circumstances.

This proposal for a system of punishment is based on the idea of just deserts. People might disagree over which crimes to place into which categories or disagree with the recommended penalties, but the committee's approach has several advantages over current practices. It would reduce penalties for first offenders and provide alternatives to incarceration for less serious offenders. It would limit the length of prison terms and standardize sentences. This proposal would also limit the discretion of judges and thus reduce sentence disparity.

The recommendations of the Committee for the Study of Incarceration are not derived from research on people's perceptions of how particular crimes should be punished. Research that first produces a scale of severity of penalties and a scale of seriousness of offenses, and then asks people to recommend specific penalties for different offenders, would be a better basis for a system of just deserts. Efforts to link crimes and penalties in this way have encountered obstacles, but there is some evidence that people use the principle of just deserts to prescribe penalties for crimes about which they are questioned; in other words, some research finds a close match between perceived seriousness of crimes and perceived severity of penalties (Hamilton and Rytina, 1980). However, other studies have found no straightforward relationship between a scale of seriousness of crimes and a scale of punishments, with a severe penalty being perceived as relatively much worse than a severe crime; this lack of proportionality in the two scales makes it hard to fit them together in a just deserts system (Hamilton and Rotkin, 1976). Another study found that people agreed on the relative severity of sentences for a group of offenses, but disagreed on the absolute magnitude of the sentences that were appropriate for each crime (Blumstein and Cohen, 1980). In other words, people may agree that a murderer should receive a harsher sentence than a rapist, but whether the murderer should be executed, get life in prison, or serve ten years in prison is a question that produces disagreement.

Research indicates that people view white-collar crimes as serious enough to warrant harsher sanctions than are now used, even though the criminal justice system would probably be unable to punish white-collar offenders more severely without a tremendous increase in the resources available to prosecutors (Braithwaite, 1982). A study at a southern university found that students favored lenient sentences for some white-collar criminals, but recommended relatively harsh penalties for a bank officer who embezzled a large sum of money, a landlord whose failure to repair a building caused a tenant's death, and a stockbroker who knowingly sold fraudulent securities (Reed and Reed, 1975). A survey in San Francisco found that about as many people wanted an antitrust violator imprisoned as called for the incarceration of a car thief, and about as many asked for the imprisonment of an advertiser who misrepresented a product as thought that someone who committed an assault should be sent to prison (Gibbons, 1969). In sum, there is evidence that a just deserts model of punishment would have to treat certain white-collar crimes as being more serious, and thus deserving of more punishment, than many people have thought them to be (Vidmar and Miller, 1980).

In general, people seem to call for the most severe penalties for offenders who violate laws that have the greatest social support. They are also most punitive toward offenders who appear to have committed their crimes intentionally and offenders who seem unrepentant; such offenders are thought to be more likely to repeat their crimes, because they do not acknowledge the moral validity of the law. Repeat offenders are also the targets of greater punitiveness, because continuing criminal behavior indicates a lack of commitment to the law. Offenders who show a commitment to group values are usually regarded with less punitiveness.

RETRIBUTION AND THE CRIMINAL JUSTICE SYSTEM

During the twentieth century, the criminal justice system in the United States has emphasized deterrence and rehabilitation. One sociologist has noted that the principle of retribution "does not appear to tell us how the law should be enforced, except to make the general requirement that a crime must never go unpunished." He goes on to say that the retribution model of criminal justice is "reactive and inert" and that the theories of deterrence and rehabilitation "have more to say about law enforcement" (Newman, 1978: 197).

Nevertheless, considerations of retribution and just deserts play an important part in the criminal justice system, and this role has increased in recent years as research has cast doubt on the effectiveness of rehabilitation. Today, as in the past, "doing justice" and giving offenders the penalties they deserve are major goals of the criminal justice system.

Retribution and the Police

One way to determine the goals of the police is to examine how they allocate their resources. Much of the time the police are not employed in the enforcement of the law or the maintenance of public order. They are called upon for public services such as driving an injured person to the hospital, searching for lost persons, or removing a fallen tree (Wilson, 1968: 18; *U.S. News & World Report,* November 1, 1982). Even though less than half of police patrol time involves law enforcement and order maintenance, the police probably consider these crime-control functions the essence of their work.

The structure of police departments gives us some idea of the attention that the police pay to serious crimes. Departments include detectives who specialize in the investigation of the most serious offenses. There may be a homicide squad or a narcotics squad to deal with crimes thought to be especially serious. A study of how police departments use their resources to investigate crime would find that more resources are spent on crimes that rank higher on the scale of seriousness, with the exception of white-collar crimes that cause physical harm.

There is some evidence that the way the police respond to apprehended suspects may be related to retributive considerations. The police are more likely to refer an apprehended juvenile to court for formal processing than to release that juvenile if the offense is a harmful one and if he or she appears blameworthy, something that might be indicated by prior contacts with the police (Goldman, 1963; Thornberry, 1973; Black, 1980). The harmfulness of the crime and the blameworthiness of the suspect probably affect police treatment of adult suspects as well. Retributive considerations thus influence the effort that the police expend on the investigation of unsolved cases and their disposition of suspects apprehended in the course of those investigations.

Retribution and the Courts

The principle of retribution is one consideration in district attorneys' decisions about how to prosecute defendants, and it is a factor in judges' decisions about how to sentence convicted offenders.

PROSECUTORS' DECISION MAKING

Prosecutors operate on the assumption that the defendants against whom they bring charges are guilty and should "receive their due" from the criminal justice system. They prefer that defendants plead guilty in order to save the court's time, and they pressure defendants to plead guilty. In negotiating a plea, prosecutors consider the harmfulness of the alleged offense and the prior criminal record of the defendant. As a result, defendants are usually punished according to the principle of just deserts (Sudnow, 1965; Rosett and Cressey, 1976). A formal system called the Prosecutor's Management Information System (PROMIS) has been developed to calculate a score (based on Sellin and Wolfgang's scale) for each crime and to use information on defendants to help prosecutors assign priority to cases (Roth, 1978).

One study of prosecutors' attitudes toward different offenses produced some unexpected results. Prosecutors thought that white-collar crime was very serious, equivalent to offenses such as kidnapping and rape and more serious than the theft of a similar amount of money by a conventional offender. The amount of money stolen in a crime was not seen as an important consideration in determining the seriousness of an offense, because the amount of money available to be stolen was often a matter of chance. In addition, whether the victim of an assault died was seen as partly due to chance, and so manslaughter was viewed as only slightly more serious than aggravated assault (Roth, 1978). These considerations are not written into the criminal code, but prosecutors depend on them to determine the penalty that they think is appropriate for a defendant in a particular case.

JUDGES' DECISION MAKING

Judges also consider how much punishment is deserved by defendants. Both judges and prosecutors typically assume guilt and are then faced with the problem of determining an appropriate penalty. Evidence from several studies indicates that the sentence is influenced primarily by the current charge and the prior record, when defendants of the same race, sex, or class are compared (Kleck, 1981; Spohn, Gruhl, and Welch, 1981–82; Pruitt and Wilson, 1983). However, other researchers have found that extralegal factors such as race, income, sex, and age sometimes do affect sentencing (Clarke and Koch, 1976; Cohen and Kluegel, 1978; Strasburg, 1978). One review of sentencing in the United States concluded that only 7 to 10 per cent of all sentences reflected "arbitrary or idiosyncratic judicial behavior," and that the rest of the sentences could be predicted from legal factors such as harmfulness of the crime and blameworthiness of the offender (Silberman, 1978: 292). As court personnel have become more professional and the courts more bureaucratized, these legal factors have become relatively more important in the sentencing of offenders (Pruitt and Wilson, 1983).

In spite of the strong relationship between penalties and the seriousness of offenses, there has been much concern with the consequences of judicial discretion. Until the 1970s, the *indeterminate sentence* was the most widely used penalty in the United States. Under this system, state legislators established long maximum sentences for different crimes. Judges could then impose any penalty up to the maximum. Sentences were often a range of years to be served in prison, such as five to ten years. Actual release dates were then set by parole boards, based on the board's opinion that an inmate had been rehabilitated.

In recent years, concern with the leeway that the indeterminate sentence allows judges, along with evidence that rehabilitation does not seem to work, has led to proposals for sentencing reform. The Committee for the Study of Incarceration's proposal that we examined includes a limited number of *presumptive sentences;* in other words, an offense of a certain degree of harmfulness committed by someone with a particular prior record would be presumed to carry a specified sentence, unless extraordinary circumstances justified a departure from that presumptive sentence. One way to establish such a system would be to have a sentencing commission write explicit and detailed sentencing guidelines that would reflect popular perceptions of appropriate sanctions for given offenses and offenders. Crimes would be defined as fitting into a given class, which would have a narrow range of prescribed prison sentences. A judge would then mete out a specific sentence from within that range, and the parole board could not release the inmate until that sentence had been served, except by giving some time off for good behavior in prison. Judges could give a sentence outside the prescribed range only if they carefully spelled out in writing the reasons for the unusual sentence. Defendants could appeal sentences above the upper limit, and prosecutors could appeal sentences below the range (White, 1981). In 1983, six states had presumptive sentencing systems of this sort; five other states had eliminated parole release for most prisoners, while retaining sentencing discretion for judges; and fourteen states had set standards to limit the discretion of parole boards but still retained early release (Taylor, 1983).

JUVENILE JUSTICE

In recent years there have been efforts to introduce retributive considerations into the juvenile justice system. Some states have proposed and even passed laws that lower the age at which defendants are to be tried as adults, and most states now allow some juveniles accused of serious crimes to be tried in criminal court rather than dealt with in juvenile court. These proposals and changes spring from the belief that there is a lack of proportionality between the harm caused by juvenile offenders and their degree of blameworthiness, on the one hand, and the way that they are treated by the juvenile courts, on the other hand.

One proposal to deal with juveniles would require states to pass laws that use current charge and prior record to determine which juveniles must be tried as adults in criminal court (Feld, 1983). However, there is some evidence that even in states where "dangerous" juvenile offenders are singled out for treatment as adults, the criteria adopted by legislators to identify such offenders "single out many juveniles whose records do not appear to be very serious and fail to identify many juveniles whose records are characterized by violent, frequent, and persistent delinquent activity" (Osbun and Rode, 1984: 199).

Some proposals to deal with offenders suggest that records of juvenile offenses, which have traditionally been kept "sealed" or secret, should be used to assess the blameworthiness of either juvenile or adult offenders so as to set penalties that fit with the principle of retribution (U.S. Department of Justice, 1981). The United States today has a "two-track" system in which juvenile records are not available to judges in dealing with juveniles or in sentencing adults. Thus, frequent juvenile offenders may receive a light sentence for their first few adult offenses, because they seem to be first-time offenders (Boland and Wilson, 1978). In 1981, the Attorney General's Task Force on Violent Crime recommended a "one-track" system similar to that of England, where juvenile records are routinely used in criminal court proceedings involving adults (U.S. Department of Justice, 1981). One longitudinal study in England found that prior convictions as a juvenile influenced sentence severity for adults on their first conviction, independently of the harmfulness of the offense or the age of the defendant. The harsher penalties for adults who had been juvenile offenders made sense in light of the finding that there was a close relationship between appearances in court as a juvenile and convictions for crime as an adult (Langan and Farrington, 1983).

Retribution and the Prisons

State and federal correctional systems include prisons that differ in their amount of control over inmates. Maximum-, medium-, and minimum-security institutions limit inmates' freedom of movement and isolate them from the outside world to varying degrees. The blameworthiness of the offender and the harmfulness of the crime largely determine the kind of institution to which an offender is sent.

Because sentences in most states cover a range of years—for example, five to ten years for a robbery—the decision about how long an inmate actually stays in prison is made by the parole board rather than the court. Some studies indicate that parole boards may reduce sentence disparity among inmates, but this research is not yet conclusive (Gottfredson, 1979a, 1979b; Petersilia, 1983).

Decisions about when inmates are to be released from prison are predictable to a large degree from the harmfulness of the offense for which they have been imprisoned, their prior criminal record, and their conduct while in prison (Silberman, 1978: 290). In other words, the decision about how much of a court-imposed sentence is actually served is based largely on retributive considerations, even when this decision is theoretically determined by whether an inmate has been rehabilitated. Because parole boards have not been subjected to judicial review in the way that judges have been, and because parole board decisions often seem arbitrary, some states have restricted the use of parole.

Retribution and Capital Punishment

As we saw in the previous chapter, public support for the death penalty is based partly on the belief that it is a deterrent, but many supporters say they would favor it even if it had no deterrent effect. Rather than focusing on the utility of the death penalty, many people believe that justice requires that people who commit certain heinous crimes be deprived of their own lives. This belief is reflected in the Soviet Union's legal system, as well as in the American system, as we can see in the Cross-Cultural Perspective.

The death penalty has been both supported and opposed on religious grounds. One minister suggests that "capital punishment must stand as a silent but powerful witness to the sacredness of God-given life"; he bases this argument on "the authority of Scripture" (Vellenga, 1959: 7–9). Traditionally, the Catholic Church has accepted the right of the state to execute people convicted of serious crimes. However, in recent years the death penalty has been redefined as inconsistent with Catholic theology because execution lacks utility and dignity, fails to contribute to the common good and the well-being of citizens who are directly affected by the punishment, and discriminates against the poor and minorities (Beristain, 1977). In 1983, Pope John Paul II asked for clemency or pardon for people under the sentence of death; this was the first time that a pope has criticized capital punishment. In recent years, Catholic bishops in the United States have also voiced opposition to the death penalty, linking their rejection of capital punishment to a "right to life" philosophy that includes opposition to abortion (Franklin, 1983). Protestant religious leaders in the United States have opposed capital punishment since 1957,

A Cross-Cultural Perspective: Capital Punishment in the Soviet Union

The Soviet Union has had capital punishment since 1918, the year after the Bolshevik Revolution. Since 1961, it has been used for economic crimes such as bribery, corruption, and embezzlement. The death penalty can also be administered for murder, rape, treason, sabotage, espionage, the killing of a police officer, and air hijacking.

In 1982, a former deputy minister in the Ministry of Fisheries was put to death for illegal involvement in the sale of caviar to a Western company. An article in Pravda by the public prosecutor suggested that just deserts was the basis for this harsh penalty: "Bribery is a particular social danger. This forces us to apply the most severe measures of punishment. . . . There can be no indulgence here whatsoever." The idea that punishment should be proportional to the harm caused by an offense is clear from the way that executions are usually reported in the Soviet press: "In connection with the exceptional scope of the crime, [the defendant] has been sentenced to the supreme measure of punishment, execution by shooting."

In recent years, the Soviet legal system has been inflexible in administering punishment to people who cause "irreparable suffering in the lives of individual Soviet citizens." Flexibility and humanitarian considerations are used only when dealing with minor offenders.

SOURCE: Serge Schmemann, "In Soviet, No Debates Rage around Capital Punishment," *The New York Times*, August 3, 1983, pp. A1, A4; Harry Trimborn, "Soviet Official Executed," *The Boston Globe*, April 29, 1982, p. 3.

denying that the state has any right to execute offenders and seeing capital punishment as "a contradiction of both the values of our Christian traditions and the principles of humane government" (cited in Franklin, 1982: 30).

Some opponents of the death penalty claim that even if certain offenders deserve to die, a civilized society should not execute them. They argue that it is immoral for the state to take a human life as a form of punishment, and that by doing so the state "cheapens the value of human life" and may even encourage others to kill (Johnson, 1982).

Even people who support capital punishment do not always agree about when it is appropriate for this penalty to be administered. Thus, few Americans today would support capital punishment for thieves, but thieves were executed in eighteenth- and nineteenth-century England. However, many Americans now would favor the death penalty for someone who brutally murdered several children or someone who assassinated the president.

The Supreme Court has changed its view over time as to what crimes can appropriately be punished with death. The Eighth Amendment to the Constitution prohibits "cruel and unusual punishment," and although the Court has never ruled that capital punishment by itself is cruel and unusual, it has ruled that the death penalty is cruel and unusual punishment for some crimes—specifically, crimes of forcible rape (*Coker* v. *Georgia* [1977]).

In 1972, the Supreme Court, in *Furman* v. *Georgia*, struck down the states' death penalty statutes because they had been administered in an excessively arbitrary way. Four years later the Court approved a new kind of law that it thought would be administered more fairly. In a criminal trial, a defendant's guilt or innocence is determined, and then in a second and separate proceeding a judge or a jury considers the death penalty as a possible sentence. Looking at the harmfulness of the offense and the blameworthiness of the defendant, the judge or the jury can choose the death penalty only if there are aggravating circumstances that are defined by state law, and if there are no mitigating circumstances that counteract those aggravating factors. The introduction of

Support for capital punishment is sometimes based on grounds of retribution or just deserts, rather than on a belief in the deterrent effect of the death penalty.

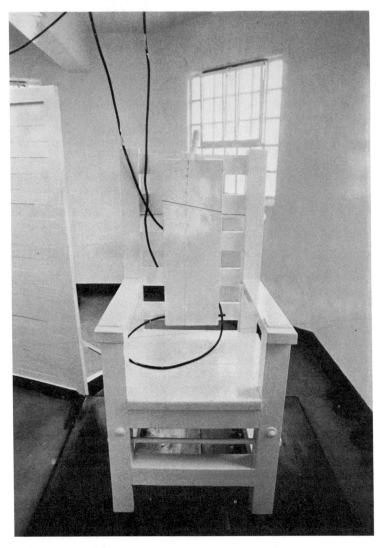

Photo by Owen Franken. Reprinted by permission of Stock, Boston. © by Stock, Boston, Inc., 1977.

specified aggravating and mitigating factors was the result of an attempt to be fair to defendants while still using the principle of retribution.

Since the 1960s, a majority of Americans have supported capital punishment. It is not clear that a majority would actually favor the execution of any specific offender, or would support the immediate execution of all prisoners on Death Row, but there is at the very least considerable support for having the death penalty available for use (Bedau, 1982).

Even though the American public supports capital punishment, there is not much articulate support for the death penalty in the intellectual community. Two exceptions are Walter Berns (1979) and Ernest Van den Haag (1975, 1983), both of whom have argued that the death penalty is a deserved and appropriate penalty for some crimes. They believe that justice requires capital punishment, and that this penalty is a reasonable expression of community outrage at the violation of important values. They argue that executions can reinforce the moral order. Critics of this position point out that retribution simply requires a punishment proportional to the crime, not any specific kind of penalty such as the death penalty (Bedau, 1980).

A report on the families of murder victims provides some support for Berns's and Van den Haag's argument that punishment may be functional in expressing community outrage. Some people report a sense of satisfaction after the killer of their relative has been executed, and express frustration when appeals delay the execution for years and keep the memory of the murder alive. One execution took place nine years after the murder, and led the brother of the victim to remark that the execution "was an extraordinary relief. I don't know how to explain it. It relieved the grief. This has been an overriding obsession for all of us" (cited in Joyce, 1984b: A18).

One argument against the death penalty is that when an error is made in the criminal justice system and an innocent person is executed, there is no way to rectify the error as there is with other penalties. One survey found seventy-four cases between 1893 and 1962 that could have led to an execution and that seemed to involve errors. There were eight cases in which innocent people were actually put to death (Bedau, 1982: 234–241). Because it is difficult to reconstruct cases years later, there may have been even more innocent people executed. Some abolitionists would suggest that the execution of even one innocent person is reason enough to get rid of the death penalty; proponents might argue that only a handful of mistakes in the nearly 4,000 executions over this period indicates that the criminal justice system is quite reliable. Moreover, because the most recent error that was detected occurred in the 1930s, supporters of the death penalty might claim that recent developments in the procedural rights of defendants have made similar errors very unlikely today.

Support for and opposition to the death penalty are based to a large extent on considerations of just deserts. Even if there were irrefutable evidence that the death penalty does or does not deter crime, the ultimate decision about its use would probably be based on values concerning the sanctity of human life and the requirements of justice. However, evidence that many people do not see capital punishment as a much more severe penalty than life imprisonment without parole suggests that the public's sense of justice might be satisfied if the most serious offenders were incarcerated for life rather than put to death (Hamilton and Rotkin, 1976).

SUMMARY

Most criminal justice systems use the principle of retribution or just deserts: Only the guilty should be punished, and penalties should be proportional to the harmfulness of the crime and the blameworthiness of the offender. In contrast to the theories of deterrence and rehabilitation, the principle of retribution does not try to contribute to the social good, but simply aims to do justice by punishing offenders. Retribution does not require harsher penalties than exist under other systems of punishment.

A system of just deserts that is based on empirical data would include a scale to measure the seriousness of crimes and a scale to rank the severity of punishments. The seriousness of a crime is determined both by the harmfulness of the act and the blameworthiness of the offender. There is much agreement on the ranking of crimes by seriousness, and there is some evidence that people rank penalties by degree of severity in a similar way. However, there is little research that links the two scales, and this is needed for a system of just deserts. Some white-collar crimes, especially those in which physical harm is done to victims, rank relatively high on the scale of seriousness of crimes, and seem to warrant more punishment than they usually receive.

Retribution plays an important part in the criminal justice system, and its role has probably increased in the United States in recent years. The police show that they consider some offenses to be more serious than others in the way that they allocate their resources and in the special attention they pay to crimes such as murder and rape. The courts also use the principle of just deserts. Prosecutors take into consideration the harmfulness of the crime and the blameworthiness of the defendant in negotiating guilty pleas, and in deciding which cases to prosecute with the greatest vigor. Judges use just deserts considerations in deciding how to sentence offenders. The exercise of judicial discretion in imposing indeterminate sentences has led to reforms in recent years, including presumptive sentencing systems that limit the discretion of judges. The idea of just deserts has been introduced into the juvenile justice system in recent years, with efforts being made to reduce the age at which people are treated as adults and to allow juveniles accused of certain kinds of crimes to be tried in adult court. Retribution also plays a part in the incarceration of inmates; length of sentence and kind of prison are determined in large part by the harmfulness of the crime and the blameworthiness of the offender.

The death penalty is often supported or opposed on grounds of just deserts. Religious beliefs have been used both to support and to oppose the death penalty. Some people do not think that the state should execute anyone, and others disagree about which crimes warrant capital punishment. Only a few intellectuals support the death penalty, but a majority of the American public does. The Supreme Court has not yet ruled that capital punishment itself is cruel and unusual, but it has ruled that capital punishment is a cruel and unusual punishment for forcible rape. Support for or opposition to the death penalty is often based to a large degree on the principle of just deserts.

IMPORTANT TERMS

indeterminate sentence	*lex talionis*	retribution
just deserts	presumptive sentence	vengeance

SUGGESTED READINGS

ERNEST VAN DEN HAAG AND JOHN P. CONRAD. *The Death Penalty: A Debate*. New York: Plenum, 1983. A good introduction to the arguments supporting and opposing capital punishment.

ANDREW VON HIRSCH. *Doing Justice: The Choice of Punishments*. New York: Hill and Wang, 1976. A lucid presentation of the just deserts model of punishment.

_____. "Utilitarian Sentencing Resuscitated: The American Bar Association's Second Report on Criminal Sentencing," *Rutgers Law Review* 33 (Spring 1981), 772–789. A critique of the ABA's report, which tried to combine selective incapacitation with just deserts.

17

Rehabilitation

Rehabilitation is the restoration of criminals to a law-abiding way of life through treatment. More specifically, rehabilitation is the result of any planned intervention focused on the offender that reduces criminal activity, whether that reduction is achieved by changes in personality, abilities, attitudes, values, or behavior. Excluded from rehabilitation are the effects of fear and intimidation—or specific deterrence—and the maturational effects that cause older offenders to leave a life of crime (Sechrest, White, and Brown, 1979: 20–21).

THE REHABILITATION MODEL

The rehabilitation model had its origins in the eighteenth and nineteenth centuries, but it was probably most influential in the United States between the 1920s and the 1970s. The assumptions of this model, and the policies that are derived from it, are quite different from those of the deterrence model and the retribution or just deserts model.

Historical Background

In Colonial America, punishment was not designed to rehabilitate offenders. Instead, physical pain was publicly inflicted on convicted criminals in order to humiliate them and to deter other people from crime. Imprisonment was rarely used for punishment.

During the late eighteenth century, theories of punishment began to change. The ideas of the Enlightenment and the work of European philosophers, most notably Cesare Beccaria, led Americans to see people as rational beings who could control their own behavior, rather than as sinful beings. This view led to a reevaluation of punishment and the beginning of a search for the causes of criminal behavior. Prison was increasingly seen as a way to punish offenders, but not yet as a way to rehabilitate them (Cullen and Gilbert, 1982). In 1787, Dr. Benjamin Rush urged that a prison be established to cure offenders, rather than simply to punish them. This pioneering effort relied on the work of the English prison reformer, John Howard, who a few years earlier had suggested that reflection on the errors of their ways would lead inmates to repent.

The belief that offenders could be rehabilitated began to take hold in the

1820s and 1830s. Reforms were aimed at creating orderly prisons, enforcing discipline among inmates, separating offenders from criminal influences, requiring hard work, and training inmates in religion. Geographic and social mobility, urban growth, and economic development disrupted American society during this time, and many people began to see crime as a symptom of the breakdown of social order. People started to believe that offenders should be placed in "an orderly environment that would effect their reform by furnishing them with the strong moral fiber needed to resist the corrupting influences that were rampant in the wider community" (Cullen and Gilbert, 1982: 61; also, see Rothman, 1971, 1980).

During the 1820s, two approaches to rehabilitation emerged, but both shared the belief that "the purpose of the criminal justice system should be to rehabilitate offenders and not merely to subject them to the irrationality of aimless punishment" (Cullen and Gilbert, 1982: 64). The Quakers recommended silence and reflection, and the isolation of inmates in their own cells, where they worked, ate, and read the Bible by themselves. This approach was implemented in a prison established at Cherry Hill in Philadelphia in 1829. A different approach was used at the New York state prison at Auburn in the 1820s. There inmates slept alone in their cells, but they worked, ate, and worshipped together during the day, although they were to remain silent while in each other's presence.

American prisons had not succeeded in establishing rehabilitation as their primary goal by the time of the Civil War. Because offenders served sentences that were fixed by the courts, there was little to motivate them to change. Post-Civil War reformers suggested giving offenders the incentive of early release as a way to motivate them to reform, and so the indeterminate sentence was introduced. A "new penology" that was developed at the National Congress on Penitentiary and Reformatory Discipline in 1870 advocated industrial labor and training, education, religious instruction, better living conditions in prison, assistance to ex-convicts in becoming reintegrated into society, separate institutions for women and juveniles, and the training of correctional officers. Two ideas guided these recommendations: "a firm belief in the curative powers of the indeterminate sentence and a fundamental conviction that the 'supreme aim' of American criminal justice should be 'the reformation of criminals, not the infliction of vindictive suffering' " (Cullen and Gilbert, 1982: 72). These recommendations were first implemented in a reformatory at Elmira, New York; other states followed this model, though they were more likely to use it for younger, less hardened offenders than for older career criminals.

The Progressive Era of the early twentieth century was characterized by faith in the state's ability to improve society through liberal reform. Progressives used the ideas of the new penology articulated in the 1870s as the basis of their approach to crime: rehabilitation rather than retribution. They relied on the indeterminate sentence to effect rehabilitation, advocated treatment within the community rather than in prison, favored parole boards to release offenders who seemed likely to stay away from crime, argued for probation or supervised release of convicted offenders, and suggested that probation officers examine the backgrounds of convicted offenders and provide judges with presentence reports to be used to individualize sentences (Cullen and Gilbert, 1982). The positivist approach of the newly developing behavioral sciences, especially sociology and psychology, supported this therapeutic approach by focusing on the causes of crime. These developments gave rise to a medical model that saw law breaking as a kind of disease that could be diagnosed, treated, and cured (Conrad and Schneider, 1980; Cullen and Gilbert, 1982).

The Progressives had a major impact on the American system of criminal justice. The number of states with indeterminate sentence systems increased from five in 1900 to thirty-seven about two decades later. By the mid-1920s, almost every state had parole, though few did in 1900. In 1897, only two states had probation, but by 1920 two-thirds of the states had it for adults and all had it for juveniles (Cullen and Gilbert, 1982). The philosophy of rehabilitation espoused by the Progressives probably had its greatest effect on the juvenile justice system. The first juvenile court was created in 1899 in Illinois as a result of the "child saving movement"; by 1920, all but three states had juvenile courts (Platt, 1977).

In spite of its important consequences for American criminal justice, the rehabilitation model was never fully implemented. Crime was never treated solely as a medical problem that could be cured. No state had sentencing that was fully indeterminate; all states set upper limits on the time to be served. Probationers and parolees never received the intensive supervision and help in becoming reintegrated into society that the Progressives had envisioned. Community corrections did not replace incarceration, and parole and probation seemed to be ways for states to expand their control over law breakers rather than ways to take inmates out of prisons and put them on the streets (Cullen and Gilbert, 1982). In spite of these shortcomings, the ideology of rehabilitation was the dominant perspective, indeed almost an unchallenged one, in the criminal justice system from the 1920s to the 1970s, when attacks on the therapeutic model led to a search for alternative ways of dealing with offenders.

Assumptions Underlying Rehabilitation

One of the best statements of the rehabilitation model of punishment is Francis A. Allen's (1971: 318):

> It is assumed, first, that human behavior is the product of antecedent causes. These causes can be identified as part of the physical universe, and it is the obligation of the scientist to discover and to describe them with all possible exactitude. Knowledge of the antecedents of human behavior makes possible an approach to the scientific control of human behavior. Finally, and of primary significance for the purposes at hand, it is assumed that measures employed to treat the convicted offender should serve a therapeutic function, that such measures should be designed to effect changes in the behavior of the convicted person in the interests of his own happiness, health, and satisfaction and in the interest of social defense.

This position assumes that offenders can be changed by treatment, even though prisons emphasize custody more than treatment. The principle underlying these treatment programs is to return "the offender to society not with the negative vacuum of punishment-induced fear but with the affirmative and constructive equipment—physical, mental and moral—for law-abidingness" (Wiehofen, 1971: 261).

Inmates are not required to join treatment programs, but these programs are not truly voluntary. Prisoners are deprived of their liberty while incarcerated, so they are in prison against their will. To gain their release, inmates must either serve the full sentence or convince a parole board that they are sufficiently rehabilitated to be released without posing a threat to the community. To be released by a parole board requires inmates to be relatively free of disciplinary reports while in prison and to demonstrate that they have tried to change. This usually means that inmates feel under pressure to join prison treatment programs that will help them to change. Inmates may join these programs more to gain early release than to change, for they know that participation is viewed favorably by the parole board. In a sense, then, treatment programs are not really voluntary, because freedom depends on participation in those programs. Joining too few treatment programs may be taken as evidence that the inmate has not changed and does not wish to, but joining too many programs may suggest to the parole board that the inmate is trying to win over the parole board rather than to change. As a result, inmates must try to figure out how many programs to join and which programs are favored by those who have the power to release prisoners.

Court decisions have guaranteed inmates the right to have access to treatment programs that can help them. The law thus sees rehabilitation as a required function of punishment. A different view is that inmates may suffer from having treatment forced on them and should thus be guaranteed the right to refuse treatment (Kittrie, 1971). We must remember that "measures depriving persons of their liberty against their will are essentially punitive in nature no matter how well-intentioned the authorities administering those measures" (Wiehofen, 1971: 259). Treatment may be dehumanizing and de-

Criminals and delinquents do not always agree with the view that they are defective and in need of treatment. Here a detained youth argues with a counselor.

Photo by Vicki Lawrence. Reprinted by permission of Stock, Boston. © by Stock, Boston, Inc., 1977.

structive of human dignity. Many criminals are rational rather than ill, and to tell them that they are defective and in need of treatment is degrading as well as inaccurate. The idea of rehabilitation implies not only that the behavior that led to punishment was legally wrong, but also that it was the result of personal defects. One ex-convict has reacted to this assumption as follows:

> The whole point of the psychological diagnosis is to get [the inmate] to go for the fact that he's "sick," yet the statement he's sick deprives him of his integrity as a person.
>
> Most prisoners I know would rather be thought bad than mad. They say society may have a right to punish them, but not a hunting license to remold them in its own sick image (cited in Mitford, 1973: 104).

Offenders who consciously choose to violate the law and are willing to accept their punishment if caught resent treatment programs based on the premise that they are "sick." For example, one man imprisoned for robbery was a bookie who went badly into debt when several of his customers unexpectedly won large bets. He borrowed a large sum of money from a loan shark to get his bet-taking operation back in order. To recover more quickly, he bet this borrowed money, but lost. The loan shark then threatened to kill the bookie's wife and children unless the bookie repaid the debt immediately. At this point, the bookie robbed a bank, escaped with a large sum of money, and paid off the loan shark. He was eventually caught and given a long prison sentence for the robbery (Conklin, 1972: 66). Some might claim that this man needs rehabilitation, but it would be difficult to attribute his decision to rob the bank to deep-seated psychological problems that require intensive therapy. From his perspective, the decision to hold up the bank was rational, given the situation in which he found himself. He received a long prison sentence, but said that he would do the same thing again if faced with the same situation. He believed that he had chosen wisely in trading a long prison term for the safety of his family. Many inmates see their crimes as rational and conscious efforts to solve problems confronting them at a particular time, and they often deny that they need to be rehabilitated.

Rehabilitation Compared to Retribution and Deterrence

The rehabilitation perspective is quite different from the retribution and deterrence perspectives. Retributivists claim that penalties should be specific and just, thus allowing punished offenders to retain their dignity by paying for their crimes. C. S. Lewis (1971: 306) has contrasted rehabilitation with retribution as follows:

> To be "cured" against one's will and cured of states which we may not regard as disease is to be put on a level with those who have not yet reached the age of reason or those who never will; to be classed with infants, imbeciles, and domestic animals. But to be punished, however severely, because we have deserved it, because we "ought to have known better," is to be treated as a human person made in God's image.

Retribution does not necessarily lead to more severe penalties than rehabilitation; indeed, as we will see later in this chapter, the rehabilitation model may actually produce longer sentences that are justified by the need to cure inmates.

The deterrence perspective sees offenders and potential offenders as rational decision makers who will stay away from crime if the threat of punishment is great enough; those who commit crime presumably think that the threat of punishment is outweighed by the rewards of crime. The rehabilitation perspective, on the other hand, regards people who violate the law as defective and in need of treatment, not as rational decision makers who knowingly take risks when they break the law.

REHABILITATION AND THE CRIMINAL JUSTICE SYSTEM

The rehabilitation perspective has had a significant impact on the American criminal justice system, especially in the three decades following World War II. The behavior of the police, prosecutors, judges, and especially correctional administrators has been influenced in important ways by the belief that offenders can and should be changed.

Rehabilitation and the Police

Rehabilitation is not generally considered a police function, because the police deal with people suspected, rather than convicted, of breaking the law, and it would seem to violate the legal principle that suspects are to be presumed innocent until proved guilty if the police tried to rehabilitate suspects. However, the rehabilitation perspective does influence the way that the police deal with suspects.

The police claim that they only enforce the law, but in fact they exercise considerable discretion in doing so (Skolnick, 1975). The idea of rehabilitation may influence a police officer's decision to charge a suspect with a crime or to release that suspect with a warning. An officer may think that a particular suspect will avoid crime in the future if subjected to the shock of arrest and a court appearance, or believe that another suspect will be most likely to stay away from crime if sent home to his or her parents. If the police do not think that correctional programs work, or believe that the negative effects of a court appearance will outweigh its beneficial effects, they may formally charge a suspect with crime only as a last resort.

Police officers are especially likely to consider the possibility of rehabilitation for juvenile suspects. Some cities have *police diversion* programs that allow the police to recommend to juvenile suspects that they enroll in a program that offers counseling or training. Some police departments provide treatment through an informal *police probation* program that requires juvenile troublemakers to report to the police regularly, attend school, make restitution, and maintain a neat personal appearance (Lemert, 1971). Police probation usually results from informal agreements among officers, juveniles, and the juveniles' parents or guardians. Police probation and police diversion programs may avoid the legal stigma of court appearance and institutionalization, but these programs do involve the police in the treatment of individuals who have not been proved guilty or found delinquent. Because these programs channel individuals into formal programs, they may have the unanticipated consequence of labeling young people who would not have been labeled at all had these programs not existed (Cressey and McDermott, 1973).

Rehabilitation and the Courts

The rehabilitative ideal plays an important part in the courts, both in the decision to prosecute and in the decision about how to sentence offenders.

PRETRIAL DIVERSION

Many jurisdictions have *pretrial diversion* programs that allow district attorneys to recommend to judges that a criminal proceeding be suspended while a suspect participates in a treatment program. Pretrial diversion may keep suspects from acquiring criminal records and criminal identities, although one study concluded that there was not enough evidence that court appearances had labeling effects to justify the creation of diversion programs on those grounds (Mahoney, 1974).

Pretrial diversion programs for suspected drug offenders include halfway houses, methadone treatment, group therapy, education, and job training. Similar programs exist for people charged with other crimes. If a suspect is not arrested again while enrolled in a diversion program, and seems to profit from that program, the judge at the suggestion of the district attorney may "file" the case—that is, not charge the suspect and eventually dismiss the case.

Juvenile courts have adopted pretrial diversion on the assumption that the labeling effects of a court appearance may do more harm than good. One study that looked at status offenders—those juveniles charged with acts that would not be crimes if committed by adults—found no difference in the likelihood of rearrest for those processed formally by the juvenile courts and those placed in diversion programs. The researcher concluded that the data neither supported labeling theory's contention that diversion is better, nor deterrence theory's claim that court processing will keep status offenders from getting into trouble again (Rausch, 1983). Another study also concluded that the diversion of status offenders had no significant effects on their behavior or attitudes, but found that there was competition for diverted juveniles among various community-based programs and warned that this might "widen the net" of the juvenile justice system and lead to the processing of more juveniles (Rojek and Erickson, 1981–82).

Pretrial diversion is based on the idea that rehabilitation may be more likely for some suspects if they are not formally processed by the criminal justice system or the juvenile justice system. One problem with pretrial diversion is that suspects may feel pressured to enter such programs rather than face the charges against them in court. However, they are given the option of facing charges rather than participating in diversion programs.

PLEA BARGAINING

The sentences to which district attorneys and judges agree in exchange for guilty pleas from defendants may be influenced to some degree by district attorneys' and judges' ideas about what kinds of sentences are most likely to lead to rehabilitation. However, considerations of just deserts probably play a more important role in determining the kinds of penalties to which prosecutors and judges will agree. Critics of plea bargaining sometimes claim that it creates cynicism toward the criminal justice system among defendants and thereby impedes their rehabilitation; others see plea bargaining as an essential first step in the rehabilitation process, because it forces defendants to take responsibility for their own behavior (Casper, 1978).

SENTENCING

Once a defendant is convicted, a judge's decision about the length and type of sentence may depend on the idea of rehabilitation as well as on the principle of just deserts. Judges consider the possible benefits of the various treatment programs available in the community and in correctional institutions. They may consider the rehabilitative effects of paying a fine or making restitution, or place offenders on probation if they think that this is the best method to keep them away from a life of crime (Langley, 1972). Other offenders may be sent to prisons that have treatment programs appropriate to their needs. In reality, judges usually have few sentencing alternatives from which to choose. State prisons rarely differ much in their treatment programs, and many offenders cannot be fined or placed on probation because the law prohibits it or because the judge's or the public's sense of just deserts would not permit it.

Rehabilitation and the Prisons

The major way that the correctional system has been influenced by the idea of rehabilitation is in its use of the indeterminate sentence and the parole board.

THE INDETERMINATE SENTENCE

Introduced at the end of the nineteenth century in the United States, the indeterminate sentence is a penalty meted out by a judge that requires an offender to serve an inexact period of time in custody. For example, an offender may receive a sentence of one year to life in prison, or a sentence of five to ten years. The offender will be released from custody when he or she is deemed rehabilitated by a parole board. The offender may serve the maximum sentence, the minimum sentence, some time between the two, or be paroled after serving a fixed proportion of the minimum sentence. If rehabilitation programs are ineffective, offenders may be kept in prison for periods closer to the maximum than to the minimum.

The rationale for the indeterminate sentence was a humanitarian one: Inmates should be released as soon as they are cured. However, the actual impact of the indeterminate sentence has been to lengthen sentences for offenders. For instance, in 1900 the inmates at Indiana State Prison, sentenced under the recently introduced indeterminate sentence system, served an average of six months and twenty-three days longer than inmates committed to the same institution for the same crimes in 1890, when a system of definite sentences was in effect (Mitford, 1973: 84). The length of time served by inmates also increased when the California correctional system introduced the idea of rehabilitation (American Friends Service Committee, 1971: 91). Indeterminate sentences can also lead to the incarceration of more offenders, as well as to longer sentences for those who are imprisoned, because the underlying assumption of the indeterminate sentence is that people who are imprisoned are being helped. The principle of rehabilitation thus acts as a "highly efficient control mechanism," even though its original justification was humanitarian (Irwin, 1974: 975).

PAROLE

Parole boards determine when an offender serving an indeterminate sentence is ready to be released. Parole boards determine how much of a sentence is to be served behind bars, and how much if any is to be served under the supervision of a parole officer on the street. In deciding when to release an inmate, the parole board considers the offense for which the offender was sent to prison, the inmate's prior criminal record, the number of disciplinary reports filed against the inmate while incarcerated, and the treatment programs in which the inmate has participated. Participation in treatment programs and number of disciplinary reports are used to indicate the extent to which an offender is rehabilitated and ready for release; the original offense and prior criminal history are retributive considerations in deciding on the length of incarceration.

The conditions that the state places on paroled offenders are designed to aid in the rehabilitation process: staying away from known criminals, establishing ties to a job, supporting a family, and avoiding the use of alcohol and drugs. However, some parole conditions—such as restrictions on having a driver's license or on driving a great distance from home—can impede rehabilitation by making it more difficult to live a normal life and get a good job. Moreover, the heavy caseload of most parole officers means that ex-convicts receive little counseling that might help them to avoid a return to crime. Critics have thus suggested that parole is "surveillance and control, not casework and counseling" (Kassebaum, Ward, and Wilner, 1971: 3).

DOES REHABILITATION WORK?

The goal of treatment programs is the rehabilitation of inmates, but it would be surprising if these programs had significant effects. Most of them are poorly funded, inadequately staffed, and available to a limited number of inmates. For example, a 1978 survey of one Massachusetts prison found that only 41 of 396 state jobs at the institution dealt with treatment, counseling, or other social services. Only 6 per cent of the $11,200 that it cost to house each inmate in that prison for one year was spent for treatment and social services (Karagianis, 1978). Most of the resources available to prisons are spent on custody and maintenance.

Even when treatment and social services are available, they are often of little use in rehabilitating offenders. Skills learned in prison industries are often inapplicable to the outside world; for example, there is little demand for the skill of manufacturing license plates, because many states manufacture all license plates in their prisons. One study found that only 36 per cent of all parolees in California had received any training at a trade while in prison, and only 12 per cent of that group later found a job in a field related to the training (American Friends Service Committee, 1971: 90). The survey of the Massachusetts prison found that on one particular Monday there were 657 inmates, of whom fewer than half (261) spent the morning working at the manufacture of license plates, brooms, road signs, manhole covers, or stationery embossed with the state seal. On that day, only twenty-seven inmates received some vocational training, and only thirty saw psychiatric counselors. Treatment and training are limited in most prisons, and where they are available they may be irrelevant to what offenders will need to adjust satisfactorily to society after release.

Measuring the Success of Treatment Programs

The effectiveness of a particular method of treatment can be assessed by the reduction in the likelihood of getting into trouble with the law again, or by various indicators of improved social functioning such as holding a job or supporting a family.

RECIDIVISM RATES

The usual way to measure whether offenders are helped by the treatment they receive in prisons, on probation, or on parole is by a *recidivism rate*. This rate is typically calculated by taking the percentage of offenders who, during a specific period after their treatment has ended, are arrested and convicted of new offenses or have their punishment made more restrictive because they have failed to meet the conditions of a less restrictive sentence. The recidivism rate of inmates released from prison is often calculated by adding the number of releasees who are arrested for new crimes and the number who are sent back to prison because their parole is revoked, and dividing that number of "failures" by the total number of released inmates. Thus, if 100 inmates are released from prison, and within three years eighteen of them are back in prison because they have been convicted of new crimes, and another thirty-three are back in prison because their parole has been revoked for a suspected new crime or for violation of parole conditions, the recidivism rate would be 51 per cent for the three-year period (Kassebaum, Ward, and Wilner, 1971).

Recidivism rates vary from one study to another. In some jurisdictions, parole is revoked quickly, and so those communities have high recidivism rates. Where parole officers are more tolerant of violations of parole conditions, recidivism rates are lower. The length of the follow-up period also affects the recidivism rate; the longer the period after release, the higher is the recidivism rate. For instance, one study (Kitchener, Schmidt, and Glaser, 1977) found the following percentages of federal ex-convicts returned to prison as parole violators or for new sentences for felonies or felony-like offenses:

Years after Release	Recidivism Rate
1	15%
2	34%
5	51%
10	59%
18	63%

A more recent study that used data from fourteen states found that 14.9 per cent of inmates were back in prison within a year of their release, 26.1 per cent were back within two years, and 31.5 per cent were back within three years. Half or more of the ex-convicts who were returned to prison were sent back for new crimes rather than because their parole had been revoked (*The Boston Globe*, December 3, 1984).

A major problem in using rearrest data to measure recidivism is that many crimes that ex-convicts commit are not reported to the police or do not lead to an arrest if they are reported. For instance, a study of eighty-three convicted rapists and fifty-four convicted child molesters found that they admitted to two to five times as many sex offenses as they had been arrested for. Because of the low visibility of sex offenses—that is, their low rate of being reported to the police and the difficulty of making arrests in such crimes—recidivism rates may be especially poor measures of the degree to which sex offenders have been rehabilitated (Groth, Longo, and McFadin, 1982).

OTHER MEASURES OF TREATMENT EFFECTIVENESS

Recidivism rates are not the only way to determine the effectiveness of treatment. Another way is to measure self-reported crime by offenders. This might produce a more accurate indicator of the rate at which inmates have returned to crime, because many crimes are not reported and recorded and many are not solved. However, it would be difficult to get valid results from such self-report studies, because inmates who have recently been paroled or released after "wrapping up" a sentence would fear that revealing undiscovered offenses might lead to arrest or to the revocation of parole.

The effectiveness of rehabilitation programs could also be measured by changes in personality, attitude, or behavior that are produced by treatment. The impact of drug and alcohol treatment programs might be measured by the rate of relapse by inmates who have drug and alcohol problems. The outcome of treatment programs can also be measured by how released inmates function in the community, on the job, in school, and within the family (Lipton, Martinson, and Wilks, 1975: 12–14). A treatment program that improves the ability of ex-convicts to support a family or hold a legitimate job, even if those ex-convicts occasionally engage in petty crime, might be considered more successful than a program whose graduates also commit petty crimes but lack the ability to support a family or hold a job.

Rather than designate ex-convicts as "successes" or "failures" on the basis of whether they remain crime-free after release, it might be better to measure differences in criminal behavior before and after treatment. Thus, the success of a treatment program could be measured by the degree to which it reduced or suppressed the rate of arrest of its participants. A program might also be considered a partial success if it lengthened the time from release until the time that ex-convicts committed new crimes. For instance, a program whose graduates were crime-free for two years but then returned to crime might be seen as more successful than a program whose graduates returned to crime within a month of their release. A reasonable goal for a rehabilitation program is to reduce the number and the seriousness of the crimes that its participants commit, even if they are not kept from criminal activity altogether. Treatment programs that have such beneficial effects may eventually make it possible for offenders to leave a life of crime.

Measures of diminished criminal activity and personal adjustment are used to evaluate treatment programs less often than is the rate at which releasees return to prison. As the American Friends Service Committee (1971: 44) says:

> Surely it is ironic that although treatment ideology purports to look beyond the criminal's crime to the whole personality, and bases its claims to sweeping discretionary power on this rationale, it measures its success against the single factor of an absence of reconviction for a criminal act.

EXPERIMENTAL DESIGN AND TREATMENT EFFECTIVENESS

Inmates who are released from prison may not return to crime because they are deterred by the fear of more punishment, because they have matured while in prison, or because they have been rehabilitated. The proper way to isolate the effect of treatment from the other effects of imprisonment is to assign inmates randomly to a group that receives treatment (experimental group) or to a group that does not receive treatment (control group). If the treatment is effective, inmates in the experimental group will show a lower recidivism rate (or some other kind of improvement) in comparison to the control group. The difference between the experimental and control groups in recidivism rates or some other measure of improvement can then be attributed to the effects of treatment, because chance determined the group to which an inmate was assigned, and the inmates in each group presumably had similar experiences in prison except for their exposure or lack of exposure to treatment.

Efforts to evaluate treatment programs by experimental studies often encounter problems in implementing a research design in an institutional setting. Because these studies sometimes take years to complete, results may not be available when policy makers need them to develop intervention strategies. Forces outside the prison also make it difficult to evaluate treatment programs; for instance, the effects of labeling by family, friends, and employers may vary from one ex-convict to another and make it difficult to assess the impact that the treatment program itself has on its participants. Properly conducted experiments are expensive, and it may be difficult to find the funds to evaluate programs, but the failure to carry out such experiments means that treatment programs that are both expensive and ineffective will continue (Sechrest, White, and Brown, 1979).

THE AMENABILITY ISSUE

One issue that complicates research on rehabilitation is the possibility that certain kinds of offenders are amenable to treatment of a particular sort, with other kinds of offenders not gaining from exposure to the same treatment. This *amenability issue* might arise in evaluating a treatment program in which 50 per cent of the participants avoided recidivism and 50 per cent returned to prison. In this case, it is possible that those who were not recidivists were amenable to the treatment they received, and those who returned to prison were not amenable to that treatment. Randomization in the evaluation of treatment methods avoids some of this difficulty, but still leaves unanswered the question of whether inmates with specific characteristics might be matched to particular treatment methods in ways to achieve higher rates of success. One review of evaluations of rehabilitation programs concluded that we do not yet really know anything about the suitability of certain kinds of offenders for different forms of treatment, and that more research is needed on this issue (Sechrest, White, and Brown, 1979).

Types of Treatment

Treatment programs take many forms. Some deal with individuals and others with groups. Some seek to alter personality and others only to change behavior. Some equip offenders with vocational skills or educational credentials and others try to cure drug addiction or alcoholism.

EDUCATION AND WORK PROGRAMS

Since World War II, several states have established prerelease programs such as work-release and education-release. These programs emphasize the problem of reentry into society and help inmates to gain access to jobs and educational opportunities outside prison walls (Moeller, 1974). Furlough programs serve similar functions, but the release of inmates for a few hours or days during their prison term has generated public opposition and probably has little value as a method of rehabilitation.

In an effort to provide work experience for inmates to help them to find jobs after they are released and also to give private firms a source of inexpensive labor, Congress in 1979 passed a law to allow products made by inmates to be sold and distributed in interstate commerce, something that had been prohibited since 1940. Since 1979, many states have also passed legislation to expand work opportunities for inmates. In seven pilot projects, inmates were hired by private firms to work within prison walls at a minimum wage, considerably more than the fifty cents to one dollar per day that inmates typically earn at prison work. There was strong opposition to this program from labor unions, who criticized businesses for hiring cheap inmate labor rather than union members who could do the same work (Gargan, 1983).

One analysis of employment and crime concluded that the only effective long-term strategy is to provide job training and education for inmates, because there are few indications that job-placement or income-supplement programs affect crime rates in the short run. For instance, recent income-supplement programs have had disappointing results; income subsidies for released inmates reduce their need to steal and thus cut down on crime, but they also create a work disincentive that leads to unemployment and greater involvement in crime (Berk, Lenihan, and Rossi, 1980). The only offenders on whom such programs might have significant effects are those whose potential economic status is improved enough to replace criminal activity with legitimate behavior. If these marginally committed offenders are a small proportion of all offenders, job-placement and income-supplement programs will have little impact on the crime rate. Those who are most likely to give up crime for a legitimate job seem to be offenders who are older, married, educated, have no major drug or alcohol problems, have shown a willingness to work, have committed crimes for monetary gain, and are of relatively low economic status (Orsagh and Witte, 1981).

METHADONE PROGRAMS

One treatment program that was introduced in the United States in the late 1960s and early 1970s is *methadone maintenance* for heroin addicts. Methadone is an addictive drug that does not produce euphoria if taken orally in regulated doses, but does block the euphoric effects of any heroin that is used. Methadone is inexpensive, has effects that last for a full day, and its oral administration avoids the risk of contracting a disease from an infected needle.

One premise behind methadone treatment programs is that much crime that addicts commit to support their expensive habits could be eliminated if they were taken off heroin and put on methadone. Methadone maintenance programs have attracted many heroin addicts, but the majority of addicts do not try to enter such programs. Researchers have found that these programs have a limited impact on crime rates. Drug offenses become less common among those who stay in the program, but many participants continue to engage in crime even after they have stopped using heroin (Epstein, 1974). In addition, methadone programs that allow participants to take their doses home rather than come to the clinic every day have found much illegal resale of methadone on the streets and high rates of overdoses among those who buy and use methadone illegally (Barbanel, 1982).

BEHAVIOR MODIFICATION

One treatment program that has been tried in some prisons is *behavior modification* or behavior therapy. This approach tries to change behavior, rather than personality, by rewarding desirable actions and punishing undesirable ones. This approach sees criminal behavior as learned, and is built on the principles of classical and operant conditioning. Criminal behavior is not regarded as a symptom of underlying personality problems that must be dealt with, as it is by psychotherapists and counselors; instead, criminal behavior is seen as the problem that must be dealt with directly.

Behavior modification is "the systematic application of proven principles of conditioning and learning in the remediation of human problems" (Milan and McKee, 1974: 746). Classical conditioning pairs an undesired behavior with an unpleasant event; for instance, alcoholism may be treated by administering electrical shocks when a person drinks alcoholic beverages. Operant conditioning allows the effects of a person's behavior on the environment to produce consequences for that individual and thus shape his or her behavior; giving money for desired behavior is one method that has been tried with juvenile offenders.

A major question regarding behavior modification is whether changes produced in inmates will persist after they are released. Behavior modification methods also raise ethical issues. Some claim that such methods must be voluntary to be ethical, but as we previously suggested, no treatment program in prison is truly voluntary if inmates can be released earlier for participation in such a program.

INDIVIDUAL THERAPY

A method of treatment commonly used in prison is *individual therapy* carried out by psychiatrists, psychologists, or psychiatric social workers. This approach assumes that offenders are emotionally troubled people who need to solve the psychological problems that cause them to commit crime. We would not expect therapy to work unless inmates did have psychological problems, and, though offenders have behavior problems, there is not much evidence that they have psychological problems (Halleck and Witte, 1977). Another reason that we might not expect psychotherapy to work is that therapists manipulate and control verbal behavior rather than change overt actions directly. One inmate claims that offenders sometimes manipulate therapists, pretending to be "crazy" in the early sessions by presenting a "good case" and then acting increasingly normal and showing "insight" as time passes. This may convince the therapist that the inmate is being helped, and the therapist may then recommend to the parole board that the inmate is ready to be released (Rettig, Torres, and Garrett, 1977: 167–168).

A major problem with psychotherapy is that it tries to deal with offenders within institutional walls, rather than in the environment in which criminal behavior actually occurs. There is thus a question about the extent to which any beneficial effects that therapy appears to have on inmates will carry over to behavior in the outside world. Moreover, very few prisons provide therapy that is intensive enough to have much impact on inmates.

CASEWORK

In many prisons, social workers provide inmates with individual counseling that is intended less to help them to understand their motivations than to help them to cope with specific problems they face. This *casework* approach is oriented toward getting inmates to realize their own capacities for change, advising them on how to solve problems of daily living, teaching them how to adapt to reality, and informing them of community resources that might aid them in their rehabilitation (Lipton, Martinson, and Wilks, 1975: 10).

MILIEU THERAPY

Milieu therapy is a treatment method that introduces the idea of rehabilitation into all aspects of an institution, including relations between inmates and staff members. Milieu therapy employs casework and group counseling, stresses inmate responsibility and self-determination, and creates a warm and supportive climate for change.

GROUP COUNSELING

Another treatment method is *group counseling,* which allows several inmates to be treated at the same time and at a low cost, especially if correctional officers are used as group leaders. Other group counseling programs use as leaders either psychotherapists or people who have been trained in guided-group interaction (Lipton, Martinson, and Wilks, 1975). In these groups, where inmates discuss their feelings and attitudes, the goal is to create mutual acceptance and a supportive environment. However, in a correctional system that uses parole, inmates may conceal their true feelings rather than risk having the feelings they reveal in the group be used against them later in a parole hearing.

Group counseling may emphasize either the change of an individual with the support of the group, or the change of the group as a whole. Alcoholics Anonymous has been used as a prototype for some group counseling programs. These programs seek to change an individual deviant to conform to the nondeviant values of other group members, and then to have group members reinforce their own commitment to nondeviant values by working to convince newer members to conform to those values.

Testing the Effects of a Group Counseling Program

One of the best studies of the effectiveness of a prison treatment program is reported in Kassebaum, Ward, and Wilner's *Prison Treatment and Parole Survival* (1971). This study measured the effects of group counseling in a medium-security California prison for men. Group counseling was supposed to reduce conflicts among inmates and between inmates and the prison staff, encourage participation in treatment programs, and reduce recidivism rates. The study tested three hypotheses about changes that might result from group counseling:

1. Group counseling would lessen endorsement of the inmate code;
2. Group counseling would reduce the number of prison disciplinary reports; and
3. Group counseling would reduce the rate at which inmates were returned to prison (Kassebaum, Ward, and Wilner, 1971: 71).

The group counseling program used correctional officers rather than clinically trained personnel to lead the groups; this was to minimize the cost of the treatment. Groups ranged in size from ten to twelve, had one leader, and met for one or two hours each week.

EVALUATING GROUP COUNSELING

The evaluation of the effectiveness of this program used an experimental design. Because a new prison was being opened, the researchers were able to get the administration's permission to assign inmates randomly to experimental groups (with group counseling) and control groups (without group counseling). Inmates were assigned to one of the following: a voluntary small group, a mandatory small group, a mandatory large group, a mandatory control not assigned to any group, or a voluntary control who chose to join no group. The leaders of some counseling groups received extra training in running groups to determine whether inmates were affected differently by the expertise of the leader. Inmates were followed for three years after their release to see if they were arrested for new crimes or had their parole revoked.

RESULTS OF THE EXPERIMENT
Kassebaum, Ward, and Wilner found that group counseling had little impact on inmates. It did not reduce their endorsement of the values and beliefs of the inmate code, did not influence social solidarity among inmates, and did not reduce their opposition to the prison staff.

Prior to release, inmates who had been in group counseling were found not to differ from inmates in the control groups in terms of parole prognosis (how well they were expected to do after release on the basis of traditional predictors of parole success), in prison experiences, or in parole conditions. The experimental and control groups differed only in their exposure to group counseling. The researchers found no difference between ex-convicts who had been in group counseling and those who had not been in group counseling in employment record while on parole. No significant differences between the groups were found in parole citations for drug or alcohol abuse. These findings on employment and on drug and alcohol abuse suggest that group counseling did not help ex-convicts adjust to society.

The traditional measure of success, the recidivism rate, also did not indicate that group counseling had been effective. About half (51 per cent) of all inmates were back in prison within three years of their release; 18 per cent were convicted of new offenses and 33 per cent were returned for parole violations. Experimental and control groups did not differ significantly in felony or misdemeanor arrests while ex-convicts were on parole, nor did they differ in the number of weeks spent in jail after release. There was also no difference between the experimental group and the control group in the seriousness of parole violations. In other words, group counseling did not significantly affect recidivism rates; "parole performance . . . was no different for the participants in group counseling than it was for nonparticipants" (Kassebaum, Ward, and Wilner, 1971: 242).

There were no differences between the experimental group and the control group that were due to the amount of training received by the group leader. The size of the group made no difference in parole success either, nor did the initial attitudes of the inmates toward the staff or toward the value of counseling. Regularity of attendance at group meetings and changes in leaders also did not influence parole success.

WHY DID GROUP COUNSELING FAIL?
What is important about this study is its finding that group counseling failed to have any significant impact on recidivism rates or other outcome measures. Group counseling probably failed because it took place in a context that emphasized custody rather than treatment. Even inmates who joined groups voluntarily probably joined with at least some hope that doing so would be viewed favorably by the parole board.

Group counseling also failed because most released inmates returned to the same social environment that led them into crime in the first place. They associated with the same friends, probably had more trouble finding a good job, and encountered the same temptations and pressures to commit crime. A correctional system that pulls offenders out of their social environment, "warehouses" them for a time, and then returns them to the same social setting can be expected to have a high recidivism rate.

The social causes of crime are hardly touched by group counseling in prison, but this treatment method nevertheless continues to be used throughout the nation, including at the California prison where it was found ineffective. The program does not work, but it apparently does no harm to inmates, and it is inexpensive to run. The program may help the administration to control inmates, especially if the leaders of the groups are correctional officers.

The Effectiveness of Treatment Methods

Thousands of treatment programs have been tried in prison and in the community, but only a few hundred programs have been designed so that they can be evaluated according to the standards of social science research. Many obstacles stand in the way of people who try to evaluate rehabilitation programs. Some programs have no control group. Others fail to follow participants after they leave the program. Programs may also not be established or maintained according to their stated goals. Researchers sometimes face the problem that even programs that have been properly designed and evaluated are difficult to assess because information about those programs is not widely disseminated and not published in professional journals that rely on professional peer review.

EVALUATIONS OF TREATMENT EFFECTIVENESS

The most comprehensive examination of treatment programs is Lipton, Martinson, and Wilks's (1975) review of 231 programs conducted between 1945 and 1967. Each of the programs yielded data that made it possible to evaluate the effectiveness of treatment by the conventional methods used by social science researchers. In other words, each program produced an independent measure of the improvement of participants and a comparison of an experimental group of treated offenders with a control group of untreated ones. However, no more than 35 per cent of these programs randomly assigned inmates to experimental and control groups (Sechrest, White, and Brown, 1979).

Martinson (1974: 25) has summarized the impact of treatment on recidivism as follows: "With few and isolated exceptions, the rehabilitative efforts that have been reported so far have had no appreciable effect on recidivism." He goes on to say that the data reviewed

> are the best available and give us very little reason to hope that we have in fact found a sure way of reducing recidivism through rehabilitation. This is not to say that we found no instances of success or partial success; it is only to say that these instances have been isolated, producing no clear pattern to indicate the efficacy of any particular method of treatment. And neither is this to say that factors *outside* the realm of rehabilitation may not be working to reduce recidivism—factors such as the tendency for recidivism to be lower in offenders over the age of 30; it is only to say that such factors seem to have little connection with any of the treatment methods now at our disposal (Martinson, 1974: 49).

Lipton, Martinson, and Wilks uncovered little evidence that even those prison treatment programs that prepared inmates for life outside prison through education, vocational training, or the development of social skills had any appreciable impact on recidivism rates. There was little evidence that individual counseling or group counseling reduced recidivism rates, nor did Lipton, Martinson, and Wilks find any evidence that milieu therapy worked. They said that existing evidence did not permit them to conclude that the length of a sentence or the type of institution where a sentence was served affected recidivism rates. Apparently, shorter sentences would not increase recidivism rates much; they would, however, reduce the burden on convicted offenders, and minimize the expense of maintaining and staffing prisons, the cost of welfare assistance to the inmates' dependents, and the loss of productivity during periods of incarceration.

Lipton, Martinson, and Wilks found that programs tried outside prison walls also seemed to have little impact on recidivism rates. Intensive supervision on probation in lieu of prison seemed to improve behavior, but this was apparently due to deterrence rather than rehabilitation. Probationers threatened by the severe sanctions that might result from intensive supervision by probation officers seemed to stay away from crime.

Several other reviews of treatment programs have reached conclusions consistent with those of Lipton, Martinson, and Wilks. An examination of 100 programs found that the rehabilitative effects were "slight, inconsistent, and of questionable reliability" (Bailey, 1966: 157). A survey of programs a few years later also concluded that treatment programs did not have important beneficial effects (Robison and Smith, 1971). Yet another survey of evaluations of treatment programs found that "many correctional dispositions are failing to reduce recidivism" (Greenberg, 1977a: 140). The author went on to say the following:

> Much of what is now done in the name of "corrections" may serve other functions, but the prevention of return to crime is not one of them. Here and there a few favorable results alleviate the monotony, but most of these results are modest and obtained through evaluations seriously lacking in rigor. The blanket assertion that "nothing works" is an exaggeration, but not by very much (Greenberg, 1977a: 140–141).

A updating of Lipton, Martinson, and Wilks's review of treatment programs that was carried out for the National Academy of Sciences found that the conclusion that nothing yet tried has been proved effective was still essentially correct, and that the earlier survey may even have been too generous toward treatment programs in assessing their benefits. Programs evaluated since 1967—the cut-off date for Lipton, Martinson, and Wilks's review—provided little evidence that any form of rehabilitation works (Sechrest, White, and Brown, 1979).

Even the Swedish correctional system, one of the world's most progressive, has not succeeded in curbing recidivism. A review of treatment programs in Sweden concluded as follows: "Despite shorter terms of confinement, more open institutions, and more treatment resources given both during and after institutionalization, the Swedish correctional institutions seem to produce recidivism rates as high as the American" (Ulla Bondeson, cited in Ward, 1979: 135). One reason that has been given for Sweden's lack of success is that rejection by other Swedes makes it difficult for offenders to become reintegrated into society. Some have also suggested that the relatively good conditions in Sweden's prisons lead to "prisonization," with some parolees not being especially upset at the prospect of having to return to prison.

Why rehabilitation is ineffective Defenders of the rehabilitation perspective sometimes claim that the apparent ineffectiveness of rehabilitation efforts is simply a result of the failure to implement treatment programs properly, but critics suggest that the rehabilitative ideal has intrinsic flaws that may make it unworkable. For instance, Martinson (1974: 49) suggests that treatment programs may not work because

> there is a . . . radical flaw in our present strategies—that education at its best, or that psychotherapy at its best, cannot overcome, or even appreciably reduce, the powerful tendency for offenders to continue in criminal behavior. Our present treatment programs are based on a theory of crime as a "disease"—that is to say, as something foreign and abnormal in the individual which can presumably be cured. This theory may well be flawed, in that it overlooks—indeed, denies—both the normality of crime in society and the personal normality of a very large proportion of offenders, criminals who are merely responding to the facts and conditions of our society.

An effective method of rehabilitation requires an empirically supported theory of crime causation; today's treatment methods are often based instead on vague or untested assumptions about why individuals commit crimes. One review of treatment programs makes this statement: "Where the theoretical assumptions of programs are made explicit, they tend to border on the preposterous. More often they are never made explicit, and we should be little surprised if hit-or-miss efforts fail" (Greenberg, 1977a: 141). In a similar vein, Kassebaum, Ward, and Wilner (1971: 320) say the following:

> The most fundamental requirement for further research on the effectiveness of prison and parole programs would seem to us to be a frank recognition that psychological treatment programs involve assumptions about the causes of crime, the informal and formal organization of the prison and parole, and the nature of the postrelease experience, all of *which may be quite unrealistic when applied to actual existing conditions.* (Emphasis in the original.)

Enrico Ferri (1901, 1971: 231) recognized this long ago when he said that punishment is "directed against effects, but it does not touch the causes, the roots, of the evil." Only if the causes of crime are clearly identified can effective strategies to reduce crime be devised. For instance, strengthening the conventional bonds of offenders and minimizing their ties to other criminals is a correctional strategy that can be derived from control theory and differential association theory (Glaser, 1979).

REAFFIRMING REHABILITATION

Not everyone accepts the conclusion that rehabilitation is ineffective. Some criminologists reject the conventional wisdom that nothing works, pointing out that there is mixed evidence about the impact of treatment and that "treatment destruction techniques" have been used to cast doubt on the positive results that some programs have had (Palmer, 1975; Gottfredson, 1979c; Cullen and Gilbert, 1982).

The effort to reaffirm the rehabilitation perspective points out that even those reviews of the research that conclude that treatment programs have not been proved effective often find that many programs do have positive results. For instance, Lipton, Martinson, and Wilks found that about half of the sixty-five programs in their sample that had used the most scientifically acceptable research designs had achieved positive results (Palmer, 1975). Other reviews of evaluations of treatment programs also indicate that many had positive results (Gottfredson, 1979c). Even Martinson (1979), in a follow-up study of more recent treatment programs, concludes that some treatment programs can lower recidivism rates under certain circumstances. A review that assessed ninety-five correctional programs carried out and evaluated between 1973 and 1978 also found that some programs had beneficial results under certain conditions; family intervention strategies were found to be especially effective. Several reasons that some criminologists have concluded that "nothing works" are cited by the authors:

1. Treatment programs are sometimes evaluated singly, rather than in combination with other correctional methods.
2. Evaluators often look at a single outcome measure, rather than at several measures of improvement.
3. The amenability issue has been ignored.
4. Program participants often get insufficient treatment.
5. Lack of cooperation among different agencies sometimes impedes treatment (Gendreau and Ross, 1979).

Those who seek to reaffirm the effectiveness of rehabilitation argue that critics of the rehabilitation perspective often apply especially rigorous methodological standards to their evaluation of treatment programs, and thus are led to conclude that nothing has yet been proved to be effective (Gottfredson, 1979c). One treatment destruction technique, or way of making even positive results seem questionable, is to raise possible alternative explanations for the positive findings, thereby casting doubt on the conclusion that the program itself has had a beneficial effect. Another method of attacking positive results is to show that the criterion of success is inadequate; thus, parole revocation might be criticized as a criterion of success if one argues that the decision to revoke parole is highly arbitrary and unreliable as a measure of an ex-convict's readjustment to society. Likewise, arrest rates might be questioned as a criterion by the claim that most crimes do not lead to arrests. Another treatment destruction technique is to claim that even if a program seems to work, it may not work for everyone, or at least has not been proved to work for everyone. These methodological criticisms are valid, but those seeking to reaffirm the effectiveness of rehabilitation claim that the application of such high standards means that it is unlikely that any treatment program will ever be declared an unqualified success. They argue that these methodological criticisms serve to minimize the beneficial effects that some treatment programs have on certain offenders.

Another argument for the rehabilitation perspective is that even if the impact of treatment on recidivism rates is unclear, rehabilitation programs do seem to have some positive effects on adjustment in prison, attitude and personality change, educational achievement, and vocational adjustment (Cullen and Gilbert, 1982: 172). Rehabilitation has also been supported as "the only justification of criminal sanctioning that obligates the state to care for an offender's needs or welfare" (Cullen and Gilbert, 1982: 247). Thus, it is claimed, we should not abandon the rehabilitative ideal because it contributes in an important way to the humanity of the correctional system.

"DOING LESS"

Even if treatment programs have not been proved to be effective in reducing offenders' chances of returning to crime, these programs do not seem to make offenders any worse. This has led some to the conclusion that "if we can't do more for (and to) offenders, at least we can safely do less" (Martinson, 1974: 48). Alternatives to imprisonment are less expensive; for instance, it costs about ten times as much to imprison offenders as to have them on parole or probation. Alternatives to imprisonment are also less onerous for offenders and may even benefit society. Thus, punishing convicted offenders by requiring them to work for a time—say, one eight-hour day a week for six months—for a public or charitable agency would allow them to atone for their crimes, subject them to a regular work routine, satisfy the public's demand for just deserts, provide society with a useful service, permit surveillance by probation or parole officers, and be less expensive than imprisonment (Brown, 1977).

In order to reduce prison overcrowding and the high cost of incarceration, some states have introduced community corrections or expanded their use of probation and parole. In the early 1970s, Massachusetts replaced its reform schools for delinquents with community-based work and educational programs, specialized foster care, and group homes. The juveniles in these programs were no more likely to be arrested than were juveniles previously sentenced to reform schools, according to an assessment a decade later (Rawls, 1982a). In the Cross-Cultural Perspective, we see how China deals with its youthful offenders.

According to one estimate, in 1982 there were more than one hundred programs in the United States that sentenced offenders to community service rather than imprison them; community service includes activities such as cleaning parks and helping the elderly (Leland, 1982a). In order to alleviate prison overcrowding, states have explored alternative sentencing programs, such as permitting convicted offenders to pay back their victims and rehabilitate themselves outside prison walls. Intermittent imprisonment and intensive supervision on probation and parole are other alternatives that may work no worse and perhaps even better than treatment in prison.

Critics have attacked community corrections and alternative sentencing programs for failing to fulfill their promise of reducing the prison population, and for perhaps even contributing to recent increases in the prison population (Irwin, 1980; Austin and Krisberg, 1982; Hylton, 1982). These programs have

A Cross-Cultural Perspective: Dealing with Juvenile Delinquency in China

The Chinese have dealt with their rising rate of juvenile delinquency by adopting a program "aimed at restoring self-respect in the youngsters and showing them love in cases where love is lacking." Youths who commit minor infractions are placed in a situation with "a high ratio of concerned adults to each offender." Party committees organize teams of pensioners, teachers, police officers, and parents to help delinquents. When young workers break the law, they are assigned to the best worker in their factory so that they can learn appropriate attitudes toward work and society.

In China, no one under eighteen can be imprisoned, except for the most serious crimes, but there are "work-study schools" or reformatories where delinquents between fourteen and sixteen are sent for one to three years. These reform schools are run by the Ministry of Education. The day is spent on moral instruction, academic work, manual labor, and political study. The youths are taught self-discipline and how to be a law-abiding citizen. They are allowed to visit home one day a week, and their parents usually visit them once a week in the reform school. In general, the Chinese aim to rehabilitate the less serious juvenile offenders in the community, but when this fails they turn to a system much like traditional reformatories in the United States.

SOURCES: Based on James P. Sterba, "China Says Its Rising Juvenile Crime Stems from Cultural Revolution," *The New York Times*, December 26, 1979, p. A12; Tom Ashbrook, "In China, Juvenile Delinquents Are Redirected with a Soft Touch," *The Boston Globe*, April 14, 1984, p. 3.

also been criticized for extending the criminal justice system's control over a larger number of offenders, without effectively reducing their recidivism rate. One critic of prison treatment programs has characterized rehabilitation as "liberal totalitarianism," because it is used to maintain control over prisoners while purporting to help them (Wright, 1973). Critics of community corrections and alternative sentencing programs suggest that liberal totalitarianism may also characterize those programs.

REINTEGRATING THE OFFENDER INTO SOCIETY

The idea that offenders need to be reintegrated into the community is at best part of the answer to the crime problem. The important issue is the kind of community into which an offender is being reintegrated. Community-based correctional institutions, work-release, and education-release may all help offenders to maintain ties to a community that is characterized by crime-generating conditions as well as by more positive social conditions. What is needed are programs in the community that help offenders to develop a stake in conformity and to form conventional social bonds.

More attention must be given to the adjustment problems faced by ex-convicts. On leaving prison, they must support themselves financially, cope with parole restrictions, and stay away from the "old bag" (their former life of crime) (Irwin, 1970). Many inmates want to gratify their desires and meet certain goals when they leave prison, but lack of resources and unfamiliarity with the outside world make this difficult. Providing ex-convicts with a place to live and new clothing could ease their transition from prison to the outside world. One important aspect of this transition is finding and keeping a job that offers some hope for future advancement. One thief describes a predicament faced by many ex-convicts as follows: "During the last month [since release from prison] I have had at least forty invitations from thieves to go out stealing with them, but I have not had a single suggestion from a legitimate person about how I could make some money honestly" (cited in Sutherland, 1937: 188). Providing ex-convicts with good jobs in times of high unemployment rates can be difficult, particularly if honest, unemployed workers think that ex-convicts have an advantage over them. Sometimes it is difficult to motivate ex-convicts to search for work and keep a job, because their lack of job skills often means that only the most mundane jobs are open to them and because they may have unrealistically high expectations.

The effectiveness of programs that ease the "post-release trauma" for ex-convicts is unclear. A program in Iowa and Illinois claims a recidivism rate only one-third the national average for its clients, who are given food, shelter, clothing, counseling, education, and assistance in finding housing and medical care (*The New York Times*, October 2, 1983). However, another look at the post-release trauma concludes that its impact on ex-convicts is exaggerated. This study questions the "role discontinuity" for released inmates, suggesting that for many of them a criminal life style existed before they were imprisoned, affected their behavior while in prison, and continues to influence their actions after release. This study finds that programs that try to ease the transition from prison to the outside world have not yet been shown to be effective in reducing the recidivism rate (Minor and Courlander, 1979).

The Future of Rehabilitation

Today the rehabilitative ideal has been abandoned by some of its former advocates, while others seek to reaffirm it. Critics argue that treatment programs have not been proved effective, but defenders of those programs point to some that have had beneficial results. Critics claim that the indeterminate sentence and the ineffectiveness of treatment programs have combined to lengthen sentences and extend the criminal justice system's control over offenders; defenders of the rehabilitative ideal claim that it has been a force for greater humanity in the correctional system.

Diminished faith in the rehabilitative ideal has led some criminologists, lawmakers, and citizens to argue that until treatment is shown to be effective, punishment should be based on the principle of just deserts (Von Hirsch, 1976). Offenders found guilty of crimes serious enough to warrant imprisonment would be incarcerated for fixed terms under humane conditions. Voluntary treatment programs might then be provided for inmates, with the clear understanding that participation would not affect the length of the sentence or the conditions of release. Because treatment up to now has been provided under a system of indeterminate sentences and because participation in programs has affected the time and terms of release, we cannot know whether treatment under such a just deserts system would be more effective than it seems to have been so far. Treatment might be more effective under such a system because programs would presumably be populated only with inmates who sincerely wanted to change (Goodstein, 1980).

In spite of efforts by some criminologists to reaffirm the rehabilitative ideal, it has become less dominant in the American criminal justice system since the mid-1970s. Lawmakers have introduced sentencing reforms that are based on the theories of just deserts, incapacitation, and deterrence, rather than on the rehabilitative ideal. For instance, parole has been restricted, weakening inmates' motivation to participate in treatment programs. Rehabilitation efforts will continue, but they are now given relatively less attention by the correctional system than they were just a few years ago.

SUMMARY

The idea that punishment should rehabilitate or reform offenders so that they do not commit additional crimes had its origins in the ideas of the Enlightenment and in the work of prison reformers during the eighteenth and nineteenth centuries. This rehabilitation model was dominant in the American criminal justice system from the 1920s until the mid-1970s, when considerations of just deserts, incapacitation, and deterrence became relatively more important. This rehabilitation model assumes that offenders can be changed, although prisons usually emphasize custody rather than treatment. Rehabilitation can be demeaning to offenders, who are treated as defective people in need of change, rather than as rational decision makers or as people who should pay the price for having broken the law.

The criminal justice system is influenced in many ways by the rehabilitation rationale for punishment. The police exercise their discretion in part on the basis of ideas about what kind of response is most likely to keep a suspect away from crime in the future; sometimes suspects are kept out of court and prison by police diversion or police probation programs. In court, pretrial diversion is sometimes used to prevent labeling, which might push defendants into a life of crime. Plea bargaining may be influenced by prosecutors' and judges' ideas about what kind of punishment is most likely to reform an offender. Judges are influenced by their ideas about rehabilitation when they sentence offenders. Indeterminate sentences and parole are products of the idea that offenders should be sentenced to indefinite periods and released only when they are rehabilitated. Because treatment in prison is usually secondary to the goal of custody, rehabilitation programs have not usually been given priority by prison administrators.

Efforts to measure the success of treatment programs usually employ recidivism rates, but other measures of improvement have also been used. Treatment may be considered effective if it causes ex-convicts to reduce the rate at which they commit crime or if it helps them to function better in the community, in their family, or at a job. Research on rehabilitation has been complicated by the amenability issue, the idea that some kinds of offenders may be suited only to certain types of treatment.

Among the many forms of treatment are education and work programs, methadone treatment for heroin addicts, behavior modification, individual therapy, casework, milieu therapy, and group counseling. An experimental study that evaluated group counseling in a California prison found that it did not reduce the inmates' recidivism rate, nor did it change attitudes toward the inmate code or toward the prison staff. This program probably failed because it took place in a custodial setting and because it did not deal with the causes of crime.

Evaluations of treatment programs that have used experimental and control groups have not proved that any kind of treatment consistently and significantly reduces involvement in criminal behavior, even though some programs seem to show positive results. Even if the impact of treatment on recidivism rates is unclear, we might do less to and for offenders than we now do without changing the crime rate significantly. Using alternatives to prison might reduce the financial cost of punishment and lessen the burden on offenders. However, critics claim that alternative sentencing programs and community corrections have not reduced the recidivism rate and may even have increased the prison population and the extent of control over offenders by the criminal justice system. Reintegration of offenders into the community is an important aspect of correctional policies, but careful attention must be paid to the kind of community into which offenders are being reintegrated. Rehabilitation will continue to be an important part of the American criminal justice system, but it is now a less influential perspective on punishment than it once was.

IMPORTANT TERMS

amenability issue	individual therapy	police probation
behavior modification	methadone maintenance	pretrial diversion
casework	milieu therapy	recidivism rate
group counseling	police diversion	rehabilitation

SUGGESTED READINGS

Francis T. Cullen and Karen E. Gilbert. *Reaffirming Rehabilitation.* Cincinnati, Ohio: Anderson, 1982. An eloquent argument for keeping the rehabilitation perspective central to the American criminal justice system; includes a thorough history of rehabilitation in the United States.

Gene Kassebaum, David A. Ward, and Daniel M. Wilner. *Prison Treatment and Parole Survival: An Empirical Assessment.* New York: Wiley, 1971. A meticulous experimental study that finds a lack of impact of group counseling on prison inmates.

DOUGLAS LIPTON, ROBERT MARTINSON, AND JUDITH WILKS. *The Effectiveness of Correctional Treatment: A Survey of Treatment Evaluation Studies.* New York: Praeger, 1975. A comprehensive assessment of 231 treatment programs carried out between 1945 and 1967.

ROBERT MARTINSON. "What Works?—Questions and Answers about Prison Reform," *The Public Interest* No. 35 (Spring 1974), 22–54. A widely cited and controversial paper that summarizes the results of the study by Lipton, Martinson, and Wilks.

LEE SECHREST, SUSAN O. WHITE, AND ELIZABETH D. BROWN, EDS. *The Rehabilitation of Criminal Offenders: Problems and Prospects.* Washington, D.C.: National Academy of Sciences, 1979. An evaluation of research on treatment programs that updates the Lipton, Martinson, and Wilks study, but with much the same conclusion.

18

Solving the Crime Problem

M any solutions to the crime problem have been proposed, but few have reduced crime in any significant way. As a result, there is widespread pessimism about the possibility of solving the problem. We may know too little about the causes of crime to design crime-reduction programs, or we may simply not yet have developed and implemented the correct policies. In this chapter, we look at three ideological positions and their proposals for reducing crime. We then trace the politics of crime in the United States since the mid-1960s. Finally, we look at three strategies for solving the crime problem: reforming the criminal justice system, minimizing the opportunities for crime, and dealing with the causes of crime.

IDEOLOGICAL APPROACHES TO SOLVING THE CRIME PROBLEM

Three general ideological orientations toward the crime problem can be delineated: a conservative approach, a liberal approach, and a radical approach. Each position includes a set of general beliefs and assumptions about the causes of crime and the appropriate ways to reduce it. The assumptions of each position underlie the policies proposed by its adherents, even though those assumptions may not always be made explicit (Miller, 1973).

The Conservative Approach

The *conservative approach* seeks to preserve the status quo from criminals, who are seen as challengers to the existing social order. Conservatives focus on the high costs of crime and the criminal justice system. They emphasize conventional crimes such as the FBI's index offenses; white-collar crime and government corruption are ignored, denied, or even justified.

Conventional crime is attributed to the lower and working classes, who are thought to be improperly socialized or irresponsible. Crime is said to be caused by the defective family structure of the poor and by the failure of those families to inculcate in children the values appropriate to a law-abiding life. Conservatives' concern with the permissiveness and immorality of groups that have high rates of conventional crime has a long history, going back at least as far as nineteenth-century Paris where crime was attributed to the "dangerous classes," a term synonymous with the lower and working classes (Chevalier, 1973).

The conservative solution to the crime problem is to encourage "adherence to the legitimate directives of constituted authority" (Miller, 1973: 144). The means to do this include the improvement of family life, better discipline, more self-control, and harsher and more certain penalties. Because conservatives are ideologically opposed to the intrusion of the government into the home, even into homes that produce criminals, they rarely give much attention to programs to strengthen the family or to teach parents better ways to instill law-abiding values in their children. Instead, conservatives emphasize deterrence, incapacitation, and just deserts, and rely on the criminal justice system to mete out certain, severe, prompt, and just penalties. Conservatives call for a larger, more efficient, and less restrained police force; a higher conviction rate in court; and longer prison sentences. Conservatives are often willing to sacrifice or abridge the procedural rights of defendants, and indeed the rights of the entire population, in order to increase the chances of arrest, conviction, and punishment.

The Liberal Approach

The *liberal approach* holds that crime can be reduced by policies that attack its underlying causes. Liberals claim that people are the products of the social and economic system in which they live. Inequality of income and power and the lack of opportunities for certain groups increase the probability that more members of disadvantaged groups will engage in behavior defined as criminal by those who hold power.

Liberals believe that society can be reformed in ways that will reduce the crime rate, but they reject the idea that a full-scale revolution is required. They tend to focus on conventional crimes, which they see as a lower-class and working-class phenomenon that results from poverty, discrimination, and oppression. As a consequence, they propose that educational and vocational training, welfare assistance, job opportunities, antidiscrimination laws, and community organization and change can reduce the crime rate. Liberals have traditionally argued that the primary function of criminal penalties should be the rehabilitation of convicted offenders, but with growing evidence that many treatment programs do not work, some liberals have shifted to a theory of punishment that stresses just deserts to a greater degree (Bayer, 1981).

The Radical Approach

A third perspective on the crime problem is the *radical approach.* This viewpoint focuses on crime by both the underprivileged and the privileged, and attributes crime by both groups to the conditions of a capitalist society. Radicals point to evidence—such as some self-report studies—that indicates that crime is more evenly distributed among the classes than is suggested by official crime statistics. Differences in crime rates among various groups are then attributed to the differential handling of groups by the criminal justice system, rather than to actual differences in their criminal behavior. The crime problem is regarded as a socially defined product of selective crime reporting and recording, media attention, and differential treatment by the criminal justice system.

The radical approach places greater emphasis on white-collar crime and political corruption than do the conservative and liberal approaches. Conventional criminals are seen as victims of a capitalist system, rather than as offenders against society. Radicals shift attention from the criminal offender to the social and economic system that defines certain behavior as criminal and pushes people into crime by failing to meet their needs. The radical perspective emphasizes justice rather than crime, and looks at the negative implications of values such as competition and material success. The criminal law is seen as a tool of the capitalist class, even though there is evidence that crimes such as murder, rape, and robbery are abhorred by members of all classes in all kinds of societies (Brown, 1952; Newman, 1976; Thomas, Cage, and Foster, 1976).

The radical perspective offers few specific solutions to the crime problem, other than calling for the construction of a new and basically different social system, one that is vaguely described as communist or socialist. Whether such a society now exists anywhere or can be created in the future is open to question; radicals rarely describe in detail the alternative society that might keep crime to a minimum.

THE POLITICS OF CRIME

Since the 1960s, crime has sometimes been a major issue for politicians at the national, state, and local levels. Generally, those who have made the most use of the crime issue have been "law and order" politicians who have adopted a conservative approach, although in the 1984 election the more liberal Democratic party developed policies to deal with the problem of crime.

The President's Commission on Law Enforcement and Administration of Justice

The rates of index crimes began to rise dramatically in the mid-1960s. One of the earliest political reactions to this increase was President Johnson's appointment in 1965 of the President's Commission on Law Enforcement and Administration of Justice. President Johnson asked the commission to "deepen our understanding of the causes of crime and of how society should respond to the challenge of the present levels of crime" (The President's Commission on Law Enforcement and Administration of Justice, 1967a: 2). The seventeen volumes published by the commission in 1967 included many proposals to deal with crime, but little new information about the causes of crime. Because the commission was comprised primarily of lawyers, police administrators, judges, and correctional officials, it is not too surprising that the commission's recommendations emphasized reform of the criminal justice system.

The conservative approach to crime reduction was stressed by the commission. The very first sentence of the summary chapter of its final report stated that "America can *control* crime" (The President's Commission on Law Enforcement and Administration of Justice, 1967a: 279; emphasis added here). The commission did give passing attention to the liberal approach:

[C]rime flourishes where the conditions of life are the worst, and . . . therefore the foundation of a national strategy against crime is an unremitting national effort for social justice. Reducing poverty, discrimination, ignorance, disease and urban blight, and the anger, cynicism or despair those conditions can inspire, is one great step toward reducing crime. *It is not the task, indeed it is not within the competence, of a Commission on Law Enforcement and Administration of Justice to make detailed proposals about housing or education or civil rights, unemployment or welfare or health.* However, it is the Commission's clear and urgent duty to stress that forceful action in these fields is essential to crime prevention, and to adjure the officials of every agency of criminal justice—policemen, prosecutors, judges, correctional authorities—to associate themselves with and labor for the success of programs that will improve the quality of American life (The President's Commission on Law Enforcement and Administration of Justice, 1967a: 279; emphasis added here).

Why the commission thought that their broad mandate from the president to devise a national policy to reduce crime allowed them to avoid detailed proposals about the social causes of crime is a puzzle.

To reduce crime in America, the commission recommended federal support to meet eight major goals:

1. State and local planning.
2. Education and training of criminal justice personnel.
3. Surveys and advisory services concerning organization and operation of criminal justice agencies.
4. Development of coordinated national information systems.
5. Development of a limited number of demonstration programs in agencies of justice.
6. Scientific and technological research and development.
7. Institutes for research and training personnel.
8. Grants-in-aid for operational innovation (The President's Commission on Law Enforcement and Administration of Justice, 1967a: 285).

The implementation of these proposals might have produced a more streamlined and better-funded system of criminal justice, but there is little evidence from criminological research that such changes would have reduced the crime rate.

The Law Enforcement Assistance Administration

The work of the commission led to a 1968 law, the Omnibus Crime Control and Safe Streets Act, which established the Law Enforcement Assistance Administration (LEAA) in the United States Department of Justice. This agency funneled money appropriated by Congress to the states to fund various crime-control programs. The budget of LEAA rose dramatically from $63 million in 1968 to $880 million in 1975, but declined to $486 million in 1980. The agency was disbanded in 1982, but during its existence it spent $7.7 billion.

Some of LEAA's funds were used for controversial purposes, such as establishing a computerized file of "suspected subversives" and purchasing tanks for local police departments to use during riots. LEAA did not have an overall guiding philosophy behind its disbursement of funds; indeed, the development of such a rationale was inhibited by the requirement that most funds be given to the states in block grants that were to be used as the states wished. Over the years, LEAA funds were increasingly used for correctional programs rather than for police crime-control measures.

LEAA may have improved the efficiency and professionalism of local law-enforcement agencies, but it failed to meet its goal of reducing the crime rate. An analysis of the impact of LEAA that was based on interviews with federal officials concluded that the agency's impact was primarily negative: It helped to weaken the belief that capital punishment was a deterrent; it undermined faith in rehabilitation as a solution to the crime problem; and it showed that changes in police methods—such as saturation patrolling, faster response time, and more education for officers—would not reduce the crime rate (Cronin, Cronin, and Milakovich, 1981).

The 1968 and 1972 Presidential Elections

In the 1968 presidential election, the major domestic issue was crime, with the Vietnam War being the major foreign policy issue. Two of the candidates, Richard M. Nixon and George C. Wallace, were ardent and vocal advocates of a "law-and-order" approach to crime that was based on the conservative belief that the crime rate could be reduced by strengthening the criminal justice system (Epstein, 1975). Nixon and Wallace claimed that the Democrats, incumbents for eight years, had been "soft" on street crime, ghetto rioting, and campus violence. The Democratic candidate, Hubert H. Humphrey, did not speak out in favor of such violence, but Nixon and Wallace were able to parlay the issue of "crime in the streets" into millions of votes in November. Many voters switched their traditionally Democratic votes to the Republican party or the American Independent party because of the crime issue.

The burglary at the Watergate complex occurred in 1972, the year of another presidential election. The power of the office of the presidency was great enough to allow President Nixon to cover up this crime until he was reelected. Ironically, surveys show that a major reason for his victory in 1972, as well as in 1968, was the "law-and-order" vote (Gallup, 1972). People who would otherwise have voted for the Democratic candidate, Senator George Mc-Govern, voted for President Nixon because of his opposition to crime in the streets.

Crime is still a political issue, but its significance has waned since the 1972 election. One reason is that official crime rates continued to climb during the 1970s in spite of the election of law-and-order politicians, and so it became difficult for them to claim that they had solved the crime problem. Another reason for the decline in crime as a political issue after 1972 was that economic issues such as inflation and unemployment began to occupy voters' attention. Finally, the fact that several law-and-order candidates were shown to be hypocritical and involved in criminal activities themselves reduced their credibility. Vice President Spiro Agnew, an outspoken advocate of harsh punishment for criminals, resigned under pressure because he had violated laws on taxation and bribery. President Nixon resigned in 1974 after a congressional committee voted bills of impeachment against him for obstruction of justice and other illegal acts. Some claim that these and other law-and-order politicians who violated the law were no more dishonest than other politicians, but the fact that they had adopted a holier-than-thou attitude undermined their law-and-order approach to crime reduction and lessened the political impact of the crime issue. We can see in the Cross-Cultural Perspective that crime has also been a political issue in France in recent years.

The National Advisory Commission on Criminal Justice Standards and Goals

In 1971, the National Advisory Commission on Criminal Justice Standards and Goals was established to formulate policies to reduce crime. The recommendations of this commission were similar to those of the 1967 President's Commission on Law Enforcement and Administration of Justice, for they also emphasized criminal justice reforms as the way to reduce crime (The National

A Cross-Cultural Perspective: The Politics of Crime in France

In the 1970s, street crime in France began to increase steadily, and by the late 1970s public concern with crime had become an important issue that conservative politicians exploited. The rightist government of President Valéry Giscard D'Estaing blamed crime on immigrants and on lenient judges. In 1980, Giscard D'Estaing introduced a "Security and Liberty" law that proposed harsher penalties, eliminated much judicial discretion, and allowed the police to make unlimited checks on people's identities. Judges opposed this law, but Parliament passed it in 1980. An immediate effect was a substantial increase in the size of the prison population.

In spite of these changes in the criminal justice system, crime rates continued to rise. In May 1981, Giscard D'Estaing lost office to François Mitterand and the Socialists, who had criticized the incumbent for contributing to the public's fear of crime and for threatening civil liberties. Mitterand's minister of justice, Robert Badinter, led an assault on Giscard D'Estaing's policies. He abolished capital punishment, urged the use of alternative sentences such as restitution and community service, sought harsher penalties for white-collar crime, and made prison life less stringent.

These reforms ran into strong opposition. French judges and the "penitentiary lobby," which is composed of prison guards and administrators, attacked Badinter's prison reforms. This lobby, which is closely linked to conservative political parties, claimed that the Socialists' policies contributed to the crime rate by emptying the prisons. Extreme right-wing groups, such as the National Front, criticized Mitterand's government for exacerbating the crime problem, pointing to immigrants and lax judges as the sources of that problem. Mitterand resisted pressure for a more conservative approach to crime, but even the Socialist-dominated Parliament supported some conservative measures, such as the right of the police to make identity checks, and there was little evidence among government officials of support for Badinter's efforts to liberalize the criminal justice system.

SOURCE: Based on Daniel Cohen, "Problems of Punishment," *Atlantic Monthly* 253 (January 1984), 28–32.

Advisory Commission on Criminal Justice Standards and Goals, 1973). Neither commission approached the problem of crime reduction by looking for the underlying causes of crime and then proposing ways to eradicate those causes. Both assumed that the existing criminal justice system was the appropriate apparatus for dealing with crime and that this system only needed improvement to solve the crime problem.

The Crime Issue during the Reagan Administration

Crime was not the major issue in either the 1980 or the 1984 presidential election, but President Reagan has made occasional use of the issue during his time in office. In a speech before the International Association of Chiefs of Police in 1981, he incorporated several recommendations made by the Attorney General's Task Force on Violent Crime in its report issued earlier in that year (U.S. Department of Justice, 1981; Raines, 1981; *The New York Times*, September 29, 1981). The Task Force focused on the criminal justice system as the solution to the crime problem, and Reagan followed suit, except that he did comment on the causes of crime. In his speech, President Reagan did not mention the Task Force's recommendation for $2 billion in federal assistance to the states for the construction of prisons. He called for the denial of bail under certain conditions for defendants who seemed likely to commit more crime if released, even though this system of preventive detention had been ineffective in Washington, D.C., during the previous decade. The president supported reform of the exclusionary rule, which disallows the use in court of evidence illegally seized by the police. This is a popular position with the police, but seems unlikely to affect the crime rate much because relatively few defendants have cases dismissed due to violations of the exclusionary rule. Reagan also called for capital punishment, the use of the military to develop information to be used in curbing drug importation, mandatory prison terms for people convicted of using handguns during felonies, and the use of IRS records to prosecute gangsters and drug dealers. Most of these proposals involved changes in the law, rather than any increase in federal expenditures.

This speech reflected a conservative, law-and-order approach to the crime problem. In it, the president called crime "ultimately a moral dilemma," rather than simply a question of more funds for the criminal justice system. He claimed that the "war on crime will only be won when an attitude of mind and a change of heart take place in America," and when truths such as right and wrong, individual responsibility, and swift and certain punishment for wrongdoing take hold. He criticized social scientists, social workers, and psychiatrists who assert that poverty, disadvantaged childhoods, and a bad environment lead to crime. Instead, he claimed that crime is a way of life that some people consciously choose, not usually because they are "seeking bread for their families," but because they "are driven crazy with desire for stuff they'll never be able to afford." He saw criminals as people who commit crime because it is easy and not very risky, and who believe that they are entitled to what they steal. President Reagan did not propose to treat the causes of crime directly by changing people's values—for example, by restricting advertising that stimulates materialism—but instead focused on the criminal justice system to mete out penalties based on the ideas of deterrence, incapacitation, and just deserts (*The New York Times*, September 29, 1981).

In October 1984, President Reagan signed into law the Comprehensive Crime Control Act, which he had recommended and pushed but which was also the product of bipartisan efforts in Congress. This law was wide-ranging in its reforms, but because it applied just to federal law, under which only 5 per cent of all criminal defendants are tried, it will probably have limited impact on the nation's crime problem. The law introduced preventive detention on the federal level in order to reduce bail crime. It abolished parole for federal prisoners and established a committee to design presumptive sentences that would limit judicial discretion and reduce sentence disparity. The law limited the insanity defense to people who were unable to appreciate the wrongfulness of their acts. It also created a victim-compensation program, expanded federal jurisdiction over credit-card fraud, made it easier for the government to seize the illegal profits of drug dealers and organized criminals, and lengthened penalties for drug dealers and repeat offenders (Taylor, 1984).

CRIME AND THE CRIMINAL JUSTICE SYSTEM

In this section we look at several proposals for reducing crime by reforming the criminal justice system. These proposals deal with the kinds of behavior over which the law should or should not have jurisdiction and with the operation of the police, the courts, and the prisons.

Overreach of the Criminal Law

Some critics propose that the criminal justice system might be more effective if it gave up jurisdiction over certain kinds of behavior. This claim that efficiency is hindered by the "overreach" of the criminal law is often applied to *victimless crimes*, those offenses that are consensual and lack a complaining participant. One argument for this change is that the principle of retribution requires that acts that harm no one should not be punished. Another argument is that the limited resources of the criminal justice system could better be applied to conventional crimes than to victimless crimes such as public drunkenness and gambling (Morris and Hawkins, 1970: 3–25).

From time to time the proposal has been made to reduce the overreach of the criminal law by legalizing heroin. Because drug enforcement overburdens the police, the courts, and the prisons, one way to free resources for other criminal investigations is to make heroin legally available to addicts in clinics. Free or inexpensive heroin would reduce addicts' need to commit property crimes to support their habit, although many of them would probably continue to commit some crime anyway. Legalization might increase the number of addicts by making heroin more easily available; a counterargument is that legal heroin would have less of the mystique that now leads some people to use it. For years, Great Britain has made heroin legally available to addicts who are registered with the government and treated by a physician (Trebach, 1982; Burstein, 1982). Whether this system would be effective in the United States is questionable. Indeed, there is even some question about the effectiveness of this approach in Great Britain, where the estimated number of heroin addicts quadrupled from 1980 to 1985, and where officials state that only about 12 per cent of the country's addicts were registered for treatment in 1985 (*The New York Times*, April 11, 1985, p. A15).

The Police

Suggested reforms in the criminal justice system often focus on how the police might combat crime more effectively, even though there is little evidence that the police make much difference in crime rates. As we saw earlier in the book, within the range that now exists for the size of police forces in American cities, the number of officers per capita makes little or no difference in crime rates, even though the public seems to believe that more officers on the street is a major part of the solution to the crime problem.

Even if more police officers were available, there is little reason to expect that crime would be reduced. There is a nearly unlimited number of targets for crime, and offenders have little difficulty finding targets in spite of the presence of the police. The Kansas City police patrol experiment found that the number of officers in an area did not affect the amount of crime in the area (Kelling et al., 1974). Even if the presence of the police did deter an offender from committing a crime against a particular target, the offender could easily wait until the police leave or could search out another target. Street patrols might change the type of crime that an offender commits; for instance, a criminal might avoid robbery in favor of burglary. We cannot say with certainty that the police never prevent crime, but there is little evidence that they can have a major impact on the crime rate.

If more police officers do not make any obvious difference in the crime rate, it is still possible that the kind of action that the police take will affect criminal behavior. For instance, we saw earlier that a study of police response to domestic violence in Minneapolis showed that arrest was a more effective deterrent than was police mediation of disputes, which in turn worked better than having the police tell members of the household to separate for eight hours. On the basis of this study, in 1984 the New York City Police Department implemented a policy of making immediate arrests in domestic dispute cases in which the victim wanted to bring charges, rather than have officers issue desk summonses as they had previously done. Domestic disputes were defined to include married couples as well as any other people who lived together in a "family-type relationship" or who had previously lived in such a relationship. Homosexuals and unwed heterosexuals were included in this definition, and attention was paid to complaints from children as well as from adult partners (LeMoyne, 1984).

There might be a reduction in crime rates over the long run if the police established better relationships with the community and increased public trust so that more crimes were reported. Offenders might then realize that the chance that their crimes would be reported was greater, and that the probability of arrest and conviction was higher. However, it is not clear that the public's reporting of crime can be increased enough so that potential offenders will realize that they face a significantly greater threat of punishment.

FEDERAL LAW ENFORCEMENT

The federal government has usually adopted a policy of dealing with drug use that relies on policing the borders of the country to prevent drug importation. These efforts apparently have increased the amount of drugs confiscated at the borders, but even this increased amount appears to be only a small proportion of all of the drugs that importers try to get into the country. Importers may simply increase their activity to compensate for the larger amounts lost to law enforcers. Estimates of the proportion of all heroin, cocaine, and other dangerous drugs seized while coming into the country range from 2 to 13 per cent, but these figures are only guesses (Maitland, 1983). In 1983, a report by the General Accounting Office said that rivalry among various federal law-enforcement agencies and the failure to prosecute many arrested suspects in drug trafficking cases had limited the impact of recent efforts to curb drug importation (*The New York Times*, January 9, 1983).

In 1967 the National Crime Information Center (NCIC) was established under the jurisdiction of the FBI. The NCIC has expanded its computerized records in recent years, in spite of concern about the accuracy of those records and their threat to privacy. A study at the Office of Technology Assessment, for instance, found that nearly half of a group of criminal history records sent by the FBI to local law-enforcement agencies and other institutions were incomplete or inaccurate (cited in Michaels, 1983). After criticism about the threat to privacy, the FBI shelved a plan to expand the NCIC to cover people considered suspicious but not wanted for crimes (Burnham, 1984b). In spite of problems with this system, a national clearinghouse for information on crime is an important tool for law enforcement. Local police departments can get rapid responses to their inquiries about whether a car is stolen or whether suspects they are questioning are wanted outside their state. The importance of a nationally coordinated system can be seen in the results of an FBI study that concluded that half of all offenders are arrested in more than one state during their criminal career, and that 17.8 per cent are arrested in three or more states (Kelley, 1976: 43). Serial murderers wander from state to state killing their victims, and a centralized system of records is needed to uncover patterns of similar crimes in different parts of the country. In response to this problem, the FBI in 1984 established the Violent Criminal Apprehension Program (VICAP) to collect and analyze standardized reports on violent crimes and missing persons (Lindsey, 1984b).

The Courts

The primary way that the courts can attempt to reduce crime is by increasing the certainty of punishment. Countries with comparatively low crime rates, such as Japan and Great Britain, have criminal justice systems that punish offenders with much greater certainty than does the American system, even though the severity of penalties in those countries is less than in the United States. However, it is not obvious that certainty of punishment can be increased significantly in this country without infringing on the constitutional rights of defendants or greatly expanding the resources of the criminal justice system. One observer remarks that "given American traditions, it is questionable whether law enforcement agencies can be much more effective in curbing criminality than they are now" (Bayley, 1976b: 68).

SENTENCING STRATEGIES

One proposal to reduce crime rates is to change sentencing procedures. Rather than providing indeterminate sentences, lawmakers might create a system of fixed sentences and thus increase the uniformity of sentences meted out to offenders. This would not necessarily increase the severity of sentences, but it would implement the principle of just deserts better than the current sentencing system does. It might also reduce the bitterness that now exists among inmates because of sentence disparity and parole board arbitrariness; this bitterness can impede rehabilitation. More uniform sentences might also be more certain in their application, and this could increase the deterrent effect of punishment.

Several strategies have been adopted to punish offenders differently than in the past. For example, Pennsylvania has implemented a package of reforms that combine various approaches: mandatory minimum sentences, the abolition of the parole board, the reduction of sentences for good behavior in prison, longer sentences for some crimes, a stronger department of corrections, and the construction of new prison cells. To increase the deterrent effect of these policies, television and radio advertisements have been used to educate the public about the increased risks of criminal activity (Rawls, 1982b).

MAKING PROSECUTION EASIER

Laws against sex offenses, such as forcible rape and child molestation, have traditionally included impediments to prosecution. One way to increase certainty of punishment would be to reform those laws to make prosecution easier and conviction more likely. For instance, in 1984 New York, Nebraska, and Washington, D.C., required evidence to support a child's testimony in a case of child molestation (Holtzman, 1984). Because this offense usually occurs in private, the unwillingness of the courts to believe young victims has made prosecution very difficult in those jurisdictions and has thus made the certainty of punishment very low, thereby reducing the law's deterrent effect. Abolition of this corroboration requirement might reduce child molestation in those places.

Some states have also required corroboration in cases of forcible rape, which has made prosecution of this crime difficult. Moreover, the testimony of a rape victim could be examined in court by asking her about her past sexual conduct, often making it seem that she, rather than the accused rapist, was on trial. Some states have now passed "shield laws" that protect rape victims from this kind of cross examination, even though critics claim that this effort to protect victims has restricted the rights of rape defendants (Minsky, 1984b). Another legal reform that has made the prosecution of rape defendants easier is the division of this crime into several degrees of rape and sexual assault, with different penalties specified for each of the three or four degrees of the offense. This might make it easier to get a conviction for rape from a jury that thinks that mitigating circumstances do not warrant the severe penalty that was previously attached to the single type of forcible rape.

PROSECUTING ORGANIZED CRIME

New legislation and increased resources have made it possible for the federal government and local district attorneys to prosecute the leaders of organized crime more successfully. The FBI began to devote more of its resources to the prosecution of organized crime beginning in the mid-1970s. The Racketeer-Influenced Corrupt Organization law (RICO) now makes it possible for the federal government to prosecute defendants who engage in a series of crimes. More use of undercover agents and informers, the pooling of resources by law-enforcement agencies, and more FBI concentration on narcotics crimes have increased the prosecution and conviction of organized crime leaders. Witnesses have been given immunity and new identities in different parts of the country in return for testifying against suspects, and this has made prosecution easier (Werner, 1983).

Even though critics of these policies contend that imprisoned gangsters are replaced from within the organized crime "family," and that organized crime is not much affected by law-enforcement efforts, an intensive effort to prosecute leaders that is carried out over time might reduce this kind of criminal activity. One United States Attorney claims the following:

> The old-timers are not easily replaceable. The founders are now dying off, and we're dealing with the second, third and fourth level. They are not able to replenish themselves the way they could before. The ones they would have recruited are now in college and law school (Rudolph W. Giuliani, cited in Werner, 1983: D18).

PROSECUTING WHITE-COLLAR CRIME

The rational nature of much white-collar crime suggests that it might be deterred by penalties that are more severe, more certain, and more promptly applied (Conklin, 1977; Clinard and Yeager, 1980). Federal and state agencies now lack the resources to prosecute very many cases, and those that they select for prosecution sometimes require years of investigation. Consequently, certainty of punishment is low and even those offenders who are punished do not suffer any penalty for years.

Many people believe that the penalties for corporate offenders are too lenient to deter white-collar crime. Fines levied against corporations are often minuscule compared to the company's total assets, and executives who are fined may be paid back by the company. Few corporate officers are imprisoned, and when they are it is usually for a short term in a minimum-security prison. Penalties could be made more harsh by requiring guilty corporations to take remedial action, by levying heavier fines, by prohibiting corporate recidivists from securing government contracts, and by sentencing more corporate officers to prison (Clinard and Yeager, 1980). Negative publicity might also affect corporate behavior, because firms are concerned with their public reputations and may make changes in response to adverse publicity (Fisse and Braithwaite, 1983). In extreme cases, an offending corporation might even be taken over by the federal government or prohibited from doing business.

JUVENILE COURTS

Earlier in the book, we saw that many arrested suspects are juveniles. Juvenile crimes may have declined somewhat as a part of the overall crime problem because young people have become a smaller proportion of the total population, but there is some evidence that juveniles have become increasingly prone to violence and that they are beginning to commit crime at an earlier age (Boffey, 1982). In addition, juvenile delinquents are more likely to go on to adult criminal careers than are nondelinquents. For these reasons, the search for solutions to the crime problem often focuses on young people.

One proposed reform would end the secrecy of juvenile court records, so that young adults with long records of serious offenses as juveniles could be sentenced as long-term criminals rather than as first-time offenders when they first appear in criminal court. This policy is in effect in Great Britain, in contrast to the "two-track" system in the United States. Another proposal would lower the age at which adolescents are legally prosecuted as adults. For instance, in 1982 New Jersey passed a law that allowed defendants fourteen or older to be tried as adults when they were charged with certain serious crimes (Sullivan, 1982).

Some have proposed that alternative sentences for juveniles should replace incarceration in reformatories, which might be reserved for those who repeatedly commit serious offenses. Placement in a group home, especially one in a different community, might have a greater impact in reducing criminal activity than does returning youths to their family's home. Group homes might provide a surrogate family, especially for juveniles from families that generate crime. Another innovative proposal is to treat the entire family of the youthful offender, rather than isolate the juvenile for treatment. The problems of juvenile delinquents frequently stem from poor relationships within the family, and as long as that problem remains untreated it is unlikely that the juvenile's behavior will change.

The Prisons

Some criminologists support the idea that prisons are "schools for crime"— that is, that inmates learn to commit crimes from others while incarcerated. We have no solid evidence that inmates later engage in crimes that they would not otherwise have committed because of what they have learned from other prisoners, but some information and skills that are useful in the pursuit of a life in crime may be exchanged among inmates.

Because there is no clear and consistent evidence that incarceration reduces crime through rehabilitation, some have suggested that the imprisonment of offenders should be based on the principle of just deserts. Treatment could be made optional during a fixed period of confinement. Whenever possible, pretrial diversion and sanctions of warnings or probation could be substituted for imprisonment, which is both expensive and ineffective in curbing crime.

Some criminologists have suggested that offenders who seem unlikely to commit additional dangerous crimes should be left in the community where they can maintain ties to families and jobs. This recommendation has several problems. First, leaving offenders in the community may continue to expose them to the influences that led them to violate the law in the first place. Second, predicting which offenders are likely to commit more crimes is difficult; research shows that we cannot accurately distinguish potentially dangerous offenders from those who are not potentially dangerous.

SITUATIONAL CRIME PREVENTION

A second general strategy for solving the crime problem—in addition to relying on the criminal justice system to deter, incapacitate, and rehabilitate—is *situational crime prevention*. This involves measures "(1) directed at highly specific forms of crime (2) that involve the management, design, or manipulation of the immediate environment in as systematic and permanent a way as possible (3) so as to reduce the opportunities for crime and increase its risks as perceived by a wide range of offenders" (Clarke, 1983: 225). This strategy involves "target hardening," self-protective measures, informal social control, and community crime prevention.

Target Hardening

One approach to reducing opportunities for crime is to make it more difficult for an offender to carry out a crime against a particular target. This policy is often referred to as *target hardening*. Included here are the installation of bars and locks on doors and windows, the use of spotlights, the purchase of guard dogs, and the use of alarms. These measures might reduce the chance that the target-hardened building will be burglarized, but it is likely that a burglar who is motivated to steal and who perceives a low risk of arrest will simply move to another, less well-protected target.

One instance of target hardening that seemed to curb bank robbery was the installation in New York City banks during the early 1980s of bulletproof Plexiglass shields to protect tellers, who could press an alarm button and ignore the robber's demands. These barriers were in use in about half of the city's banks by early 1983, and were partly responsible for the decline in bank robberies in the city from 848 in 1979 to 447 in 1982. The robbery rate at banks with the protective shields was only one-fourth as high as the robbery rate at banks without the barriers (Buder, 1983b).

A variation on target hardening is to remove from the home property that might be stolen by a burglar. In recent years, increasing prices of gold and silver and more investment in gems and artwork have led many people to place their valuables in safe-deposit boxes. In some cities, private depositories that store property have developed. These private firms meet a growing demand for the safe-keeping of goods that banks either cannot fulfill, because all safe-deposit boxes have been rented, or are unwilling to fulfill, because of the inconvenience to the bank caused by depositors who make weekly or even daily trips to the box to get silverware or jewelry (*The New York Times*, May 2, 1982). Private depositories probably reduce the risk of a major loss in a burglary, but they do so at the cost of much inconvenience and expense to the property owner. Moreover, it is likely that burglars are simply displaced to less well-protected targets. If everyone used these depositories, some mar-

Target-hardening policies try to reduce opportunities for crime by making it more difficult to carry out offenses against particular targets. Here chains are used to prevent the shoplifting of jackets.

Photo by Cary Wolinsky. Reprinted by permission of Stock, Boston. © by Stock, Boston, Inc., 1983.

ginal offenders might be deterred from crime altogether, but other thieves might develop methods to burglarize the depositories or rob people on their way to them.

Target-hardening measures have been proposed as a method to reduce computer crime. Traditional safeguards against unauthorized access to computerized information have been passwords and other electronic "locks," but these efforts to protect information have been neutralized by "hackers" and by more experienced professional computer operators who guess or steal passwords to gain access to the information. Passwords as a method of target hardening against computer crime have not been very successful, especially as the number of personal computers has grown. A new technique to make the computer more impermeable is being developed: encryption. This method translates information into code so that even someone who gains access to the information in the computer cannot interpret its meaning. So far, this method has not been widely used, because executives are often nonchalant about the possibility of computer crime and because it is expensive to code and decode information for use within a company. Some companies have chosen less burdensome methods to protect their computerized information, such as passwords that are more difficult to guess and systems in which a user is called back before being allowed access to the computer (Dolnick, 1983).

Self-Protective Measures

Some self-protective measures are much like target hardening, for they are designed to make it more difficult for offenders to perpetrate a crime successfully against an individual. The sale of firearms after urban riots and during crime waves is based on the belief that gun owners will be less likely to be victimized, or more likely to be able to resist successfully if they are attacked or robbed. People also buy dogs and take karate lessons to reduce their risk of victimization.

In the early 1980s, following several robbery-murders, many Californians enrolled in programs to train them how to use tear gas sprays against robbers, rapists, and assailants. However, tear gas may be ineffective in great heat, when the attacker is drunk or under the influence of drugs, or when the victim has difficulty getting the spray out and using it. The use of a tear gas spray may be dangerous to a victim if it does not work, because an offender may be more likely to use violence against a resisting victim. However, the widespread use of tear gas sprays may increase the public's sense of security and lead some people to go out when they otherwise would have feared to do so (Willens, 1981; Lindsey, 1981).

Informal Social Control

One way to reduce opportunities for crime is to increase informal social control over criminal behavior. This might be done through defensible space architecture, although we have seen that this method may be of limited value. Another proposal is to improve street lighting, which makes public places more visible and draws to those places more people, who in turn enhance informal control. In 1981, Miami Beach installed television cameras to monitor the behavior of potential offenders and give them the idea that they were being watched, even though some of those cameras were dummies that merely created the impression of surveillance (*The New York Times*, November 16, 1981). This measure was abandoned in 1984 as ineffective in reducing the crime rate.

To prevent robbery and shoplifting, the 7-Eleven chain of convenience stores developed a security system that relies in part on informal social control. Cashiers are told to look their customers in the eye when waiting on them, thus giving potential thieves the idea that they may be identified to the police by the cashier; this could, however, increase a robber's motivation to kill the cashier to prevent identification. Lighting has been improved outside 7-Eleven stores, and display racks have been lowered so that thieves will not have the idea that they are hidden from passersby on the street and from other customers. These and other changes—such as a special cash register that makes it impossible to rob large sums of money—were responsible for a 26 per cent reduction in robbery in 7-Eleven stores from 1976 to 1982, as well as for a decline in the average amount of money stolen in each crime (*The New York Times,* May 7, 1982).

Another way to increase surveillance is to increase people's perception that the streets are safe and that incivil behavior in their community is rare. One unsuccessful attempt to do this was a controversial program in the South Bronx that stuck vinyl decals on burned-out buildings to improve community morale by making the area more attractive. Oakland, California, has adopted a more extensive program of this sort, seeking to erase signs of decay that create the impression of a dangerous community, including graffiti, broken windows, open prostitution and panhandling, and loitering on street corners (Kurtz, 1983). The long-run impact of this strategy is uncertain, but if these changes draw more people to the streets, they might reduce crime by enhancing informal social control.

Community Crime Prevention

Another strategy of situational crime prevention involves the organization of the community. In 1976 a project was undertaken to reduce robbery and burglary in an area of Hartford, Connecticut, with the hope that changes in the community would reduce fear of crime and thereby enhance informal social control. This project altered the physical features of the community by changing roads to cul-de-sacs and one-way streets in order to reduce motorist traffic and in order to define the neighborhood more clearly in a visual sense. A neighborhood police team was organized, and better communication between the community and the local police was created. In addition, a formal neighborhood organization was established to deal with local problems. In an evaluation of this project published six years later, the researchers concluded that environmental design can strengthen a neighborhood. By making a neighborhood more residential, the degree to which people exercise informal control over the area and the way they feel about their neighbors can be changed. By strengthening informal control, fear and concern about crime can be reduced. The evaluators of the Hartford project concluded that increased informal control in a neighborhood does not, by itself, necessarily reduce robbery and burglary, but in combination with aggressive and effective police practices it can help to curb crime (Fowler and Mangione, 1982).

As we pointed out earlier in the book, informal control only helps to reduce crime if people can be counted on to take action against criminals by intervening in a crime or reporting the crime to the police. The city of Houston has recently implemented a program to encourage people to act on their knowledge of crime. Unsolved crimes are dramatized for television, radio, and the newspapers. Rewards, which are donated by private businesses and individuals, are offered to anyone—including criminal accomplices—who provides information leading to an arrest and an indictment for an unsolved crime. This program, which was initiated in Albuquerque, New Mexico, in 1976, now exists in hundreds of communities in the United States and Canada. Crime Stoppers U.S.A., Inc., a national organization that acts as a clearinghouse for these programs, reports that by early 1984 these programs had led to the solution of about 40,000 felonies, the recovery of $150 million in stolen property and illegal drugs, and the indictment of 10,000 felons. Most crimes that are solved are not those that are shown in advertisements in the mass media, but the promise of a reward for helping to arrest and indict a suspect has drawn much public response. In Houston, informants who call in a tip are given identification numbers so as to protect their anonymity; an informant collects cash by presenting that number at a prearranged place if the crime is solved. Many tips come from other offenders, and in this way the program may disrupt relationships among criminals, who fear that their accomplices will turn them in for a reward (King, 1984).

DEALING WITH THE CAUSES OF CRIME

Trying to reduce crime by relying on the criminal justice system is like relying on therapeutic or curative medicine rather than preventive medicine to deal with disease. Sick people do need help, but research into the causes of disease can lead to more effective treatment methods and may even suggest ways to prevent the disease from occurring in the first place. A search for the causes of a disease may in the short run be more costly than using traditional methods of treatment, but the long-term benefits of a successful search for the causes of a disease will be greater. Similarly, finding the causes of crime and attacking them is a more efficient way to reduce crime than waiting for crimes to occur and then using traditional methods to deal with offenders. The ineffectiveness of the criminal justice system in dealing with crime is suggested by James Q. Wilson, a political scientist who is an authority on crime and criminal justice; he says, "I doubt that a criminal justice system which I designed and I ran would have more than a small impact on the total crime rate" (cited in McCain, 1984: 2).

The causes of crime are not easily eradicated. As Gabriel Tarde said years ago, "If the tree of crime, with all its roots and rootlets, could ever be torn out of our society, it would leave a vast abyss" (cited in Radzinowicz and King, 1977: 84). Social conditions are not easily changed, but the solution to the crime problem seems to lie in policies that deal with the underlying causes of crime. One critic of this approach advises against this emphasis on causative factors such as "poverty, low education, youthful bravado, relative deprivation, social isolation, peer-group influence, family disorganizaiton, habitual drug use, and so on," claiming that this approach would require "massive (and unlikely) social transformations" (Wilson, 1974: xvi). However, it is factors such as these that distinguish societies with high crime rates from those that have low crime rates. Consequently, making countries with high crime rates more like those with low crime rates would seem to be a useful strategy for reducing the crime rate. Doing this requires attention to the causes of crime and the development of policies that directly affect those causes.

Economic Factors

Countries undergoing economic development usually experience significant increases in crime rates, but neither China nor Japan seems to have had that experience. China has apparently avoided rising crime rates through careful social planning that has been implemented by an authoritarian regime. This has provided a full employment economy in which people are trained and given rewarding jobs (Chiu, 1977; Cohen, 1977). In Japan, workers are typically employed by the same company for life; that company takes a great interest in the welfare of its employees. In recent years, job mobility has increased in Japan, but employee turnover is still only half as common as in the United States (Clifford, 1976; Bayley, 1976a, 1976b).

In the United States, there is a need for policies that reduce unemployment, stabilize the economy, and provide technical skills and job counseling. We have seen that at the national level there is no clear relationship between the unemployment rate and the crime rate, but many people who commit conventional crimes are without job skills and are unemployed. Perhaps even more importantly, they lack the social bond to the conventional order that work provides. Income subsidies to ex-convicts have not directly reduced crime rates; they reduce the incentive to steal, but they also reduce the need to find a job that would provide an attachment to the conventional order and lead them out of a criminal career. Income subsidies that maintain an ex-convict's incentive to find full-time employment might help to reduce crime by creating such an attachment (Berk, Lenihan, and Rossi, 1980; Rossi, Berk, and Lenihan, 1980). To provide this bond to the social order, job training must include socialization in job-related skills as well as in the techniques of the work; these skills include promptness, an ability to cooperate with other workers, and a willingness to take orders from supervisors (Cook, 1975). Policies that reduce job turnover and encourage loyalty to an employer might also help to reduce the crime rate by creating a stake in conformity for workers. Even more important than getting a job for an ex-convict is keeping a job over time and becoming habituated to a work routine.

Economic changes might also reduce white-collar crime. One strategy would be to require the federal chartering of corporations; this might make them more responsive to public needs. However, federal regulation of corporations in the twentieth century has not been very successful in reducing corporate crime, and so more regulation might have little impact on crime. The divestiture of some large companies might reduce white-collar crime, at least insofar as large size is a factor conducive to such crime, but this change might increase prices and lead to the laying off of workers, thereby severing people's bonds to the conventional order and increasing conventional crime. Various corporate organizational changes have been suggested, such as greater stockholder control of the company, but changes in the way that corporate decisions are made would be hard to achieve and might create new problems (Conklin, 1977; Clinard and Yeager, 1980). Conflict theorists claim that it is the capitalist system itself that is the source of white-collar crime, as well as conventional crime, and that only the elimination of privately held means of production can solve the problem of corporate crime. In a sense this may be true, but socialist alternatives create economic crimes of their own. The Soviet Union, in particular, has difficulties with crimes against socialist property, counterfeiting, and bribery that result from its efforts to eliminate capitalism (Chalidze, 1977; Simis, 1982).

Nations that have low crime rates commonly have less relative deprivation than nations with high crime rates. In China, control of the mass media limits access to information about the standard of living of the rest of the world and thus minimizes the "demonstration effect," which can increase expectations beyond the current level of well-being. The absolute level of economic well-being in a nation may be a less important influence on crime rates than relative deprivation, the gap between current economic well-being and economic expectations. The Chinese are absolutely deprived compared to Americans, but they are largely unaware of this because their expectations have not been increased by constant exposure to higher standards of living.

In contrast to China, Americans at all economic levels are exposed to great wealth and are exhorted to work hard to achieve material success, which is seen as an indicator of individual worth. Thus, Americans who have higher absolute standards of living than most Chinese often see themselves as relatively disadvantaged compared to other Americans. These perceptions can lead to both conventional property crimes and white-collar crimes. Policies that reduce the emphasis of American culture on material well-being as a sign of personal worth might reduce crime. However, these policies could reduce the motivation to pursue material success through legitimate channels and could adversely affect the economy by lowering the demand for consumer goods.

One examination of inequality and crime predicted that "gross economic measures to reduce the gap between the poor and the rest of the population will reduce crime" (Braithwaite, 1979: 231). However, focusing only on the alleviation of poverty will not necessarily reduce inequality, because of problems with antipoverty programs:

1. They will not normally succeed in lifting people out of poverty.
2. They foster cynicism and disappointment by raising expectations which they cannot fulfill.
3. They label people as disreputable and inferior.
4. Even if they do succeed in lifting people out of poverty, in a capitalist economy they typically do so at the expense of other people who are thrust into poverty.
5. Even if they do reduce the total number of poor people in a city, this is unlikely to reduce crime because cities with smaller numbers of poor people do not have lower crime rates (Braithwaite, 1979: 232).

In sum, relative deprivation and people's expectations seem to motivate them to break the law to a greater extent than does absolute poverty, and policies to reduce poverty, while beneficial in other ways, may not curb the crime rate in any dramatic way. Indeed, official crime rates in the United States increased significantly during and just after the War on Poverty in the 1960s, even though this federal effort did substantially reduce the proportion of Americans living in poverty.

The Process of Social Change

Crime might be reduced by policies that minimize the disruptive effects of social change. In recent decades, both China and Japan have experienced internal migration and urbanization, trends commonly associated with rising crime rates. In China, migration from rural areas to large cities is carefully planned so that those who move are provided with jobs in their new communities. Japan has experienced urbanization without increased crime rates, apparently because group influence in inducing conformity continues to exist, and is perhaps even enhanced, in large cities. Switzerland has also avoided a high crime rate through a slow process of urbanization that has minimized the disruption of individual lives (Clinard, 1978).

Countries that have experienced social change without increased crime rates seem to have maintained groups that have traditionally provided people with bonds to relatives, friends, neighbors, and others who encourage conformity to the law. This is consistent with control theory, which proposes that crime and delinquency will be less common when people have a stake in conformity and are concerned with the good opinion of those who are close to them. China, Japan, and Switzerland have all avoided high crime rates by maintaining people's ties to groups that induce conformity.

Political Factors

The political ideology of China seems conducive to low crime rates. Prior to the Communist Revolution in 1949, China was a country composed of relatively autonomous regions; today it is a more integrated nation that commands its citizens' loyalty. People thus have an attachment to an institution with authority—the state—and this attachment reduces their motivation to engage in crime for selfish reasons.

The situation in Japan is similar in some ways, even though the political ideology is quite different. As in China, individuals in Japan are subordinated to the nation, the family, the community, and the company for which they work. The Japanese are greatly concerned with the good opinion of other nations and censure behavior that brings shame upon the country in the eyes of the rest of the world.

Because crimes are often committed to improve the situation of the individual perpetrator, crime rates seem to be low in nations where people learn supraindividual goals and high where people learn to pursue individual goals. It is difficult to suggest policies that might reduce the American culture's emphasis on individualism and increase its emphasis on national goals, but it is important to recognize that one cost of individualism may be a high crime rate.

Community Ties

Nations with low crime rates often have neighborhoods that are socially integrated, thereby increasing the attachment of individuals to each other and reducing crime by increasing their stake in conformity. Socially integrated neighborhoods make the surveillance of behavior more likely and can reduce crime through the fear of being observed, reported, and arrested. Local communities in Japan are closely knit, and attachment to community is also strong in Switzerland. Programs that strengthen community ties might reduce crime rates, but it could be difficult to implement such policies in a nation such as the United States where the value of individualism is so strongly held and where geographic mobility is so common. A report on criminal violence in the United States suggested that crime might be reduced by implementing a program tried in Puerto Rico that created a sense of community in a slum by allowing poor people to take charge of their own lives and by requiring offenders to work to improve the local community (Silberman, 1978: 429–466).

The Family

Another group that is usually strong in nations that have low crime rates is the family. Chinese and Japanese families have traditionally stressed close attachments between children and their parents, whose "psychological presence" curbs the children's tendency toward delinquency. The Chinese family is organized on a hierarchical basis, emphasizing respect for elders while providing parental affection for children. As a result, the Chinese usually have low crime rates, whether they live in China or in other nations (Count-Van

Manen, 1971). The Japanese family has similar characteristics. Japanese children learn to be concerned about the good opinion of their family and to avoid bringing shame on it; this creates an investment in conformity and keeps children from delinquency. Swiss children also learn to be concerned with the good opinion of others and to avoid law-violating behavior that would bring public censure on themselves and their families.

In the United States, people who violate the law typically come from families that differ from the Chinese, Japanese, and Swiss families that are conducive to low crime rates. Policies might be devised and implemented to strengthen the ability of American families to prevent children's involvement in delinquency and crime. The closeness of adolescents and their elders in Switzerland suggests the possibility of creating programs that integrate young people and adults in common activities (Clinard, 1978: 132–133). Family treatment programs could focus on child and spouse abuse, which are crimes in themselves and which also seem to lead to crimes by people who are abused as children. Laws that require police officers to take criminal complaints from the victims of child and spouse abuse, and to arrest abusing individuals, might prevent crime. The treatment of entire families when one member gets into trouble with the law might be more effective than programs that single out the offender for treatment. There is some evidence that family intervention strategies can reduce delinquency if they treat children when they first get into trouble, focus on the child's family and school experiences, and keep the child in the community. These methods teach family members to communicate better with each other and to resolve conflicts. However, these methods do not seem to work very well with children whose behavior is extremely disruptive or with severely disturbed families, and it may be those families that are most likely to produce delinquents and criminals (Gendreau and Ross, 1979: 470–472).

The family can also be changed through reforms of the welfare system and the income tax system. Crime might be reduced if the welfare system encouraged families to stay together, rather than taking a neutral stance toward family breakups or even encouraging family dissolution in order to become eligible for certain kinds of public assistance. A guaranteed minimum income might increase family stability and harmony. The income tax system could be redesigned to encourage family stability, which in turn would reduce crime. Currently, the tax system allows parents to deduct the same amount for each dependent child before paying taxes. This policy might lead people to have more children; at least it does not provide an economic incentive not to have more children. This tax-deduction policy might thus contribute indirectly to the crime problem, because delinquents and criminals tend to come from larger families than do nonoffenders, even when offenders and nonoffenders from the same class are compared. Policies that encourage people to have fewer children might thus reduce crime in the long run. In addition, more flexible work hours and inexpensive day care centers—and tax incentives to encourage these programs—might provide better supervision of children and instill the "psychological presence" of adults that can inhibit violation of the law.

One view of the family is that child-rearing is so important a correlate of crime and delinquency that

> when we consider the potential effects of any governmental action on crime and delinquency, we should specifically consider its impact on the ability of parents to

monitor, recognize, and punish the misbehavior of their children. When we conclude that the action would have an adverse impact on the family, we should be extremely reluctant to endorse it *as a crime prevention measure* (Hirschi, 1983: 55–56; emphasis in original).

One possible policy is to provide instruction on child-rearing to high school students or to prospective or new parents. Teachers and school administrators might also teach child-rearing by example, because they interact with school children on a daily basis, monitor their behavior, and mete out punishment for misconduct. More research on the differences between parents who rear delinquents and those who rear law-abiding children might point the way to policies that can influence child-rearing in ways that curb delinquency and crime (Hirschi, 1983).

The School

In China, the family's influence is reinforced by schools and government-run play centers, which tie children to adults who have authority. Schools and play centers also reduce the time available for children to engage in delinquency and minimize the boredom that has been cited as a cause of delinquency in the United States. In Japan, the tremendous academic pressure on students to succeed and not disappoint their families has been cited as a cause of recent increases in delinquency, although Japanese schools also provide control over students' deviant behavior.

Rates of crime and delinquency might be reduced through changes in the school system. The school is an institution that cuts across all communities, classes, and racial and ethnic groups, and it is often a center of social activity for community residents. Because young people are economically superfluous and isolated in school, it is a particularly good place to provide them with a legitimate identity (Empey, 1974).

Most schools need smaller classes so that students can be dealt with on an individual basis by teachers (Rubel, 1978). Reforms that tie students more closely to the school and its teachers may create a "psychological presence" that keeps young people from violating the law. Revision of school curricula could also help to reduce crime and delinquency. Courses might be made more relevant to the interests and needs of students in order to strengthen their attachment to the school. School curricula should provide students with the skills to achieve legitimate success, and should be designed to fit the needs, values, and institutions of the specific community.

Nonacademic programs might also help to reduce the crime problem. For instance, experiences such as survival training in the wilderness or contact with elderly people in the community might broaden students' perspectives and develop their self-confidence. Programs that strengthen a sense of personal responsibility and create empathy with others could reduce crime and delinquency by undermining the ability to use techniques of neutralization to justify violations of the law.

Juveniles might also be provided with access to the goods and services that they now seek through criminal behavior. For example, "car libraries" might allow adolescents to rent cars, reducing their incentive to steal cars and possibly teaching them to drive and to repair cars (Morris and Hawkins, 1970: 171). Much delinquency is a search for "rep" or prestige among peers, and efforts to change the basis on which prestige is awarded might reduce violations of the law. This might be done by expanding athletic programs or by creating programs that offer different kinds of rewards to those who rely on delinquent peers for prestige.

Discrimination

Efforts to eliminate the racial and ethnic discrimination that denies minority groups equal access to valued opportunities can help to solve the crime problem, because these minority groups sometimes contribute disproportionately to a society's crime rate. Discrimination weakens a group's attachment to the conventional social order, increasing the chance that it will have a high crime rate. Disenfranchisement or obstacles placed in the way of the right to vote deny political power to a minority group and thus weaken its ties to the political system. Schools that are segregated or poorly funded provide minorities with an inadequate education and leave them unprepared for good jobs; this reduces their attachment to teachers and schools, and makes it less likely that they will find jobs to which they can form strong ties. Job discrimination that means that minority-group members are the "last hired and the first fired" may keep them from developing loyalty to an employer. Housing discrimination that relegates minorities to the most run-down areas of the city may weaken their ties to the community. Discrimination in education, work, and housing are sources of high rates of poverty among minority groups. When this poverty is combined with a cultural emphasis on material success, as it is in the United States, there is a strong motivation for committing property crimes. Eliminating discrimination would open legitimate opportunities and create bonds to the conventional order among groups that have traditionally had high crime rates, and thus help to reduce the overall crime rate.

Conclusion

Eliminating the motivation to commit crime may be the most effective way to reduce crime in the long run. In the short run, the expression of this motivation may be minimized by developing informal control mechanisms that induce people to conform to the law (Toby, 1974). By creating a legitimate identity, a sense of competence and personal responsibility, and links to school and work, social policies can create a stake in conformity that makes the rewards of a law-abiding way of life and the risks of criminal behavior great enough to reduce violations of the law (Schrag, 1974: 726). Increasingly harsh or certain punishment seems less likely to reduce crime than policies that make it more rewarding to abide by the law. Policies that strengthen the institutions that tie people to others whose good opinion matters to them are likely to be especially effective in reducing the crime rate in the long run.

SUMMARY

Three approaches to solving the crime problem differ in their ideas about crime causation and their recommendations for reducing the crime rate. The conservative approach focuses on index crimes, which are attributed to the poor and to people who have been improperly socialized. Its solution focuses on the criminal justice system to deter and incapacitate criminals, rather than on eliminating poverty or strengthening the family. The liberal approach emphasizes conventional crime, suggesting that it can be reduced by policies that alleviate poverty and provide legitimate opportunities for everyone. The radical approach looks at both conventional crime and white-collar crime, which are attributed to the structure of a capitalist system. Only the elimination of privately held property can solve the crime problem, according to this perspective.

Since the 1960s, several national commissions have studied crime and recommended changes in the criminal justice system, rather than changes in the larger society, as the way to reduce crime. The Law Enforcement Assistance Administration failed in its attempt to reduce crime by changing the criminal justice system; it was disbanded in 1982. Crime was a major issue in the 1968 and 1972 presidential campaigns, contributing in an important way to the victory of Richard Nixon in both elections. Since 1972, crime has faded as a major political issue for several reasons, including the involvement of some law-and-order politicians in crimes of their own. President Reagan has occasionally raised the crime issue, and in 1984 he signed into law a sweeping set of reforms aimed at curbing crime.

The first of three general recommendations for reducing the crime rate is to change the criminal justice system. One way to do this would be to cut back on the overreach of the criminal law, so that limited resources could be concentrated on the most serious crimes. The number of police officers in a city does not seem to make a difference in its crime rate, but the kind of action that the police take might make a difference; for instance, arrest can deter domestic disputes, and better communication with the public may increase crime reporting. The federal government has tried to curb drug importation for years, but it is not clear that the amount of drugs entering the country has decreased as a result. The federal government has developed computerized record systems to assist local law-enforcement agencies in their investigations. The courts might try to curb crime by increasing the certainty of punishment, but it is not clear that this can be done within the constraints of existing constitutional rights. Prosecution might be made easier by legislative changes that make it more likely that victims and witnesses will testify in court. According to some sources, concentrated efforts to imprison organized crime leaders have had an impact on gangsters' activities in recent years. Reforms of the legal system might make it easier to prosecute white-collar crime and thus deter it. There have been proposals to prevent crime by opening the juvenile court's records for use by criminal court judges and by lowering the age at which offenders are prosecuted as adults. The impact of prisons on reducing crime seems limited; rehabilitation has not been shown to be very effective in prison settings.

A second strategy is situational crime prevention. This involves target hardening to make buildings and property less vulnerable to theft. Self-protective measures may reduce the chance that an individual will be victimized; the carrying of tear gas sprays is an example. Strategies to increase informal social control can reduce crime, and community crime prevention has had some effect in curbing crime, especially when it is used in conjunction with aggressive police practices.

The third strategy is to deal with the causes of crime. This may involve economic policies that provide offenders with work, and thus with a bond to the conventional social order. It may mean changing the role of the corporation in the economy to prevent white-collar crime. Crime can also be curbed by policies that minimize the disruptive effects of social change. Attachment to the nation might help to keep a country's crime rate low, as it has in China and Japan, and strong ties to the local community may have the same effect. Policies that strengthen the family and teach parents how to raise law-abiding children can reduce crime. Policies that encourage small families and help parents to keep their families intact could have the same result. Schools can reduce delinquency and crime by helping young people to establish close ties to their teachers and by providing them with the skills to succeed in legitimate careers. Eliminating discrimination can reduce the crime rate by strengthening the attachment to the conventional order of minority groups that have traditionally had high crime rates. In general, providing stronger ties to conventional people and institutions seems to be an effective strategy for solving the crime problem.

IMPORTANT TERMS

conservative approach

liberal approach

radical approach

situational crime prevention

target hardening

victimless crime

SUGGESTED READINGS

WILLIAM CLIFFORD. *Crime Control in Japan.* Lexington, Mass.: D. C. Heath, 1976. A detailed examination of a society that has crime rates much lower than those of the United States.

THOMAS E. CRONIN, TANIA Z. CRONIN, AND MICHAEL E. MILAKOVICH. *U.S. v. Crime in the Streets.* Bloomington, Ind.: Indiana University Press, 1981. A comprehensive study of federal crime-reduction efforts since the 1960s.

DAVID M. GORDON. "Capitalism, Class, and Crime in America," *Crime and Delinquency* 19 (April 1973), 163–186. A succinct statement of the radical perspective on crime.

WALTER B. MILLER. "Ideology and Criminal Justice Policy: Some Current Issues," *Journal of Criminal Law and Criminology* 64 (June 1973), 141–162. A useful investigation of perspectives on crime and criminal justice held by the left and the right.

JAMES Q. WILSON. *Thinking about Crime,* rev. ed. New York: Basic Books, 1983. An exploration of crime in the United States that focuses on the criminal justice system and its capacity to deal with crime.

Important Terms

Absolute deterrence The effect of punishment that leads people to refrain entirely from committing crime because of the perceived threat of a penalty.

Age-specific arrest rate The number of arrests per 100,000 people in a given age category.

Amenability issue The possibility that certain kinds of offenders are amenable or suited to a particular type of treatment.

Analytic induction A research strategy that involves the repeated testing and reformulating of a hypothesis, with the goal of developing a general explanation of a phenomenon.

Anomie Normlessness, or a disjunction between institutionalized means and culturally approved goals.

Appeal to higher loyalties A technique of neutralization that justifies a violation of the law by the demands of a group that is smaller than the whole society but which requires of its members conformity to standards that may be incompatible with the law.

Argot A specialized language that differentiates offenders from others and creates solidarity among offenders.

Atavism A person "born out of time" and similar to primitive people or lower animals in his or her biological makeup; the basis of Lombroso's theory of the "born criminal."

Bail A system of pretrial release designed to ensure that defendants will show up to face charges when the trial is scheduled, while allowing them to remain free until the trial takes place.

Behavior modification A treatment program that tries to change behavior, rather than personality, by rewarding desirable actions and punishing undesirable ones.

Biographical method A research strategy in which the experiences of a single individual are examined in detail.

Brawner rule The legal rule that a person will be found not guilty by reason of insanity "if at the time of such conduct as a result of mental disease or mental defect, he lacks substantial capacity either to appreciate the criminality of his conduct or to conform his conduct to the requirements of the law."

"Brutalization effect" An increase in the homicide rate as a result of the administration of the death penalty.

Cartography An approach to the study of crime that uses official data to map or chart patterns of crime.

Case attrition A funnel or sieve effect that characterizes the criminal justice system, with cases being sorted out as they proceed through the system and with relatively few crimes that occur ending up with a perpetrator being convicted and imprisoned.

Casework A treatment program designed to help offenders to cope with specific problems they face.

Certification The social verification by the criminal justice system or by conventional people that an offender is rehabilitated.

Child savers A late nineteenth-century movement of people committed to providing delinquent adolescents with help rather than punishment.

Class Social standing based on economic resources, occupational prestige, political power, or life style.

Classical conditioning Conditioning that is a result of the contiguity of stimuli.

Classical school An approach to crime that emphasizes free will and the deterrence of criminal behavior by the fear of punishment.

Clearance rate The proportion of cases that the police solve to their satisfaction.

Cohort A carefully defined group of people who are in a common situation at one time.

Collective incapacitation A policy of giving the same prison sentence to everyone convicted of a particular offense, in order to reduce the crime rate.

Community-based corrections An approach to punishment that includes a reduced emphasis on the "warehousing" of offenders in large prisons far from their homes and an increased emphasis on keeping offenders within their own community.

Comparative research A research strategy that looks at crime in societies with different cultures and social structures.

Compensation A system in which the state repays crime victims for their financial losses or physical injuries.

Computer crime Any violation of the law in which a computer is the target or the means.

Concentric-zone model A model of metropolitan areas that identifies concentric rings that have distinctive characteristics.

Concern with crime A political position that may form the basis of support for "law-and-order" politicians.

Concordance rate A measure of the similarity of criminal behavior that is used in studies of twins.

Condemnation of the condemners A technique of neutralization that asserts that it is the motives and behavior of the people who are condemning the offender, rather than the motives and behavior of the offender, that should be condemned.

Conflict gang A gang that provides a way for adolescents to achieve prestige in the eyes of their peers through fighting.

Conflict perspective An approach that sees the criminal law as closely intertwined with the distribution of political power and economic resources in a society.

Conformity A mode of adaptation in which both cultural goals and the institutional means to reach those goals are accepted.

Consensus perspective An approach that claims that the criminal law in any society represents social consensus or agreement about what kinds of behavior should be punished by the state.

Conservative approach An approach that seeks to preserve the status quo from criminals, who are seen as challengers to the existing social order.

Containment theory The theory that people are insulated to various degrees against pressures to commit deviant acts by external and internal factors.

Contingency A factor that determines movement from one criminal role to another, or from one crime to another.

Control theory The theory that people who engage in crime or delinquency are relatively free of intimate attachments, aspirations, and moral beliefs that bind them to a conventional and law-abiding way of life.

Costs related to criminal violence The financial losses that result from violent crimes in which victims are physically hurt.

Crime An act that violates the criminal law and is punishable by the state.

Crime index The total number of eight serious crimes, which are defined by the FBI.

Crime rate The number of reported crimes divided by the number of people in an area, often expressed as a rate of crimes per 100,000 people.

Criminal career A sequence of criminal acts over time by one person.

Criminal career incapacitation An approach that would reduce crime by identifying and incarcerating classes of offenders who seem to be especially likely to remain active in crime.

Criminal gang A gang that seeks material gain, power, and prestige through illegitimate means such as theft.

Criminal intent The willed or conscious desire to commit an act that violates a criminal law.

Criminology A discipline that gathers and analyzes empirical data to explain violations of the criminal law and societal reactions to those violations.

Dark figure The number of crimes that actually occur but are not recorded by the police.

Defensible space The subdivision and design of housing to allow residents to distinguish stranger from neighbor and thus elicit a sense of territoriality, which can reduce crime by informal social control.

"The deluxe ratio" The amount of heroin used in excess of the amount needed to prevent withdrawal.

Denial of injury The technique of neutralization that claims that no one is hurt by an offender's crime, even if it technically violates the law.

Denial of responsibility The technique of neutralization that involves the denial of personal responsibility for actions that violate the criminal law.

Denial of the victim The technique of neutralization that claims that a crime is justified as a rightful retaliation against the victim.

Deterrence The inhibition of criminal activity by state-imposed penalties.

Deviance The violation of a norm.

Differential association-reinforcement theory A theory of crime and delinquency that states that learning occurs through operant conditioning in both nonsocial and social situations, even though most learning results from interaction with others.

Differential association theory A theory that proposes that crime and delinquency are learned in face-to-face interaction and occur when there is an excess of definitions favorable to violation of the law over definitions unfavorable to violation of the law.

Differential identification theory The theory that people engage in criminal or delinquent behavior because they identify with real or imaginary persons from whose perspective their crime or delinquency seems acceptable.

Differential opportunity theory A theory of delinquency that focuses on the discrepancy between aspirations and access to both legitimate and illegitimate means to reach those goals.

Diffusion of responsibility The situation that exists among groups of witnesses to an emergency or a crime, when people say that someone should act but that it need not be themselves because other potential helpers are present.

Direct loss The result of a crime in which the stock of useful things is reduced, as in arson or vandalism.

Discretion The use of judgment to decide what action to take.

Displacement effect A change in the pattern of crime without a reduction in the total amount of crime that results from criminals' efforts to avoid punishment; displacement may be from one target to another, from one area to another, or from one kind of offense to another.

Drift A condition of limbo between a conventional life style and a criminal life style with no strong attachment to either.

Economist's model A model of criminal behavior that focuses on instrumental rather than expressive offenses, and sees crime as purposefully chosen by offenders to achieve certain ends.

EFT crime Any violation of the law that would not have occurred except for the presence of an electronic fund transfer system.

"Empty shell" family A family in which both parents are physically present in the home, but in which there is limited or conflict-ridden interaction between parents and between parents and children.

Enforcement costs The kind of financial cost of crime that results from the money spent on various criminal justice agencies.

Exiting A successful disengagement from a previous pattern of criminal behavior.

Experiment A controlled study in which people are treated in different ways to determine the effects of that treatment on their attitudes and behavior.

Expressive crime An offense in which the act itself fulfills an emotional need for the offender.

Fear of victimization The perception of a high risk of becoming involved in a crime.

Focal concern A value or area of interest that elicits widespread, persistent attention and emotional involvement.

Formal social control An effort to bring about conformity to the law by agents of the criminal justice system such as the police, the courts, and correctional institutions.

General deterrence The inhibition of the desire to engage in crime among the general population through the punishment of certain offenders.

Good Samaritan problem The issue of how bystanders respond to emergencies such as crimes.

Group counseling A treatment program that allows several inmates to be treated at the same time and at a low cost; it involves the discussion of feelings and attitudes in an effort to create mutual acceptance and a supportive environment.

Halfway house A community-based correctional program in which offenders who have been released from prison live with other ex-convicts in a situation with little or no security.

Historical research A research strategy that examines the same society at different times and looks at the way that crime has changed with economic and social development.

Illegal expenditures The costs of crimes that divert money from the legitimate economy and represent a loss of potential revenue for people who produce and supply legal goods and services.

Incapacitation The custodial control of convicted offenders so that they cannot commit crimes that affect the general public.

Indeterminate sentence A penalty imposed under a system that establishes long maximum sentences for different crimes and allows judges to impose any penalty up to the maximum; sentences are often a range of years to be served in prison.

Individual therapy A method of treatment commonly used in prison in which psychiatrists, psychologists, or psychiatric social workers help offenders to solve psychological problems that are thought to be the cause of criminal behavior.

Informal social control The reactions of individuals and groups that bring about conformity to norms and laws; it includes peer and community pressure, bystander intervention in a crime, and collective responses such as citizen patrol groups.

Innovation The mode of adaptation in which cultural goals are accepted, but means are used that society regards as unacceptable.

Instrumental crime A crime in which the offender gets satisfaction from the product of the crime.

Intensive offender A person who engages in criminal activity that begins at an early age and is sustained over time, consciously planned, persistent, skilled, and frequent.

Interest group People who organize to further their shared economic, political, or moral goals.

Intermittent offender A person who engages in irregular and opportunistic crimes with low payoffs and great risks, and does not think of himself or herself as a professional criminal.

Just deserts The idea that offenders should be punished because they deserve to suffer for the harm they have caused.

Juvenile delinquent A person below a legally specified age who has been adjudged by a juvenile court to have violated the law or committed a juvenile status offense.

The labeling perspective The perspective on deviant behavior that emphasizes the effects that a socially imposed label has on a person who breaks a social rule.

Law A kind of norm that is written down and formalized by the political system.

Learning disabilities An impairment in sensory and motor functioning that leads to deviant classroom performance, and is the result of an abnormal physical condition.

Lex talionis The principle of "an eye for an eye, a tooth for a tooth."

Liberal approach The perspective that crime can be reduced by attacking its underlying causes through social reforms.

Machismo The demonstration of masculinity through the manipulation and exploitation of women.

Marginal deterrent effect The extent to which crime rates respond to incremental changes in the threat of sanctions.

Master status The situation in which other aspects of a person's behavior become submerged in a particular social identity, such as that of a deviant.

M'Naghten rule The legal rule that a person will be found not guilty by reason of insanity if at the time of the crime the person was under a defect of reason so as to be unable to know the nature and the quality of the act, or if the person was aware of the nature of the act, he or she did not know that wrong was being done.

Mechanical solidarity A unity based on shared values and norms and on the similarity of functions performed by all members of the society.

Methadone maintenance A treatment program for heroin addicts that uses an addictive drug (methadone) that does not produce euphoria if taken orally in regulated doses, but that does block the euphoric effects of any heroin that is used.

Milieu therapy A treatment method that introduces the idea of rehabilitation into all aspects of an institution, including relations between inmates and staff members.

Mode of adaptation A way that individuals who occupy a particular social position adapt to cultural goals and the institutionalized means to reach those goals.

Moral entrepreneurs People who promote the idea that certain behavior is harmful and should be punished.

Norm A rule that makes explicit certain social expectations about what is appropriate behavior for a particular person in a specific situation.

Obscene material Material, often pornographic in nature, that has been declared illegal because it poses a threat to the state or to organized religion, violates common morality, has no redeeming social value, or appeals to the prurient or lascivious interest.

Observation A research strategy that involves the careful and systematic watching of behavior.

Operant conditioning theory A theory that emphasizes the interaction of the person and the environment, and sees people's behavior as affecting the world around them in ways that in turn influence their future behavior.

Organic solidarity A unity based on an interdependence of functions, much as in a complex biological organism.

Parole A system under which inmates are released before they complete their full sentences, and are then supervised on the street and sent back to prison if they violate the conditions of their release.

Patterns-of-crime approach A research strategy that involves the use of data to determine where crime is committed, who commits crime, who is victimized, and what are the major dimensions of the criminal act.

Plea bargaining An informal but structured process of negotiation in which the prosecutor and the defense attorney agree about a guilty plea and the sentence that the prosecutor will recommend to the judge.

Pluralistic ignorance A situation in which witnesses in a group fail to help the victim of an emergency or a crime because they interpret the failure of other witnesses to help as a sign that no help is needed.

Police diversion A program that allows the police to recommend to juvenile suspects that they enroll in a program that offers counseling or training.

Police probation A program that requires juvenile troublemakers to report to the police regularly, attend school, make restitution, and maintain a neat personal appearance.

Population density The number of people per unit of space; for instance, the number of people per square mile, or the number of people per room in a housing unit.

Pornography Material that is intended to arouse people sexually by portraying sexual matters in visual or verbal terms.

Positivism A perspective that relies on the scientific method to quantify and measure behavior and the social conditions associated with behavior.

Premenstrual syndrome (PMS) A set of symptoms associated with the onset of menstruation, including tension, nervousness, irritability, fatigue, headaches, cramps, and depressed moods.

Presumptive sentence A specified sentence that is presumed for someone with a particular criminal record who is convicted of an offense of a certain degree of harmfulness.

Pretrial diversion A program that allows a district attorney to recommend to a judge that a criminal proceeding be suspended while a suspect participates in a treatment program.

Prevention and protection costs The financial costs of crimes that result from expenditures on alarm systems, spotlights, locks, bars, and other "target-hardening" devices, as well as the money that people spend on insurance premiums to cover their losses through theft.

Preventive detention A system in which some defendants are held without bail while awaiting trial.

Primary deviation A initial act of deviance that has not been socially labeled as deviant.

Prisoners' rights movement A social movement led by ex-convicts and attorneys on behalf of people still in prison.

Proactive police work Efforts by the police to discover and deal with crime on their own initiative.

Probation A form of supervised release imposed on convicted offenders by judges, without any time being served in jail or prison.

Protective neighboring A combination of cooperative surveillance and willingness to intervene in a crime by the residents of a community.

Psychoanalytic perspective A psychological approach to crime causation that sees crime as the behavior of people who are inadequately socialized.

Psychopath A person who has a specific cluster of personality traits and who is asocial, aggressive, highly impulsive, unable to form lasting bonds of affection with others, and feels little or no guilt for antisocial activities.

Radical approach A perspective that focuses on crime by both the underprivileged and the privileged, and attributes crime by both groups to the conditions of a capitalist society.

Radical nonintervention A policy to minimize official reaction to delinquency in order to prevent the labeling of adolescents that could drive them into criminal careers.

Reaction-formation A repudiation of goals to which a person is emotionally attached but unable to attain, such as a reversal of middle-class goals by lower- or working-class delinquents.

Reactive police work Efforts in which the police respond to a citizen's report of a crime.

Rebellion A mode of adaptation in which people reject cultural goals and develop a new set of goals, and reject institutionalized means to reach cultural goals and develop a new set of means; behavior in which a person seeks to create a new social structure that will more effectively allow people to meet what the rebel considers appropriate goals.

Recidivism rate The percentage of offenders who, during a specific period after their treatment has ended, are arrested and convicted of new offenses or have their punishment made more restrictive because they have failed to meet the conditions of a less restrictive sentence.

Rehabilitation The restoration of criminals to a law-abiding way of life through treatment; the result of any planned intervention focused on the offender that reduces criminal activity.

Relative deprivation The discrepancy between people's expectations about the goods and conditions of life to which they are rightfully entitled, and their capabilities, or the goods and conditions of life they believe they can attain and maintain under the current social system.

Restitution A system that requires offenders to make monetary payments or provide services, either to the victim or to the community at large.

Restrictive deterrence The effect of a penalty that causes people to limit their violations of the law in order to minimize the risk of punishment.

Retreatism A mode of adaptation in which cultural goals are abandoned and institutionalized means are also rejected.

Retreatist gang A gang formed by juveniles who have failed to use both legitimate and illegitimate means to achieve success, and which usually engages in the use of drugs or alcohol.

Retribution The idea that offenders should be punished because they deserve to suffer for the harm they have caused.

Ritualism A mode of adaptation in which cultural goals are scaled down or given up, while norms about the institutionalized means to reach cultural goals are accepted.

Routine activities approach A perspective that sees crime as a function of people's everyday behavior, and stresses motivated offenders, target suitability, and guardianship.

Sanction An effort to ensure future conformity to a norm and punish past nonconformity.

Schizophrenia A psychosis that involves disordered thought patterns characterized by fantasy, delusion, and incoherence.

Secondary deviation Deviant behavior that is the result of the labeling process.

Selective incapacitation A system of predictive restraint in which only those offenders who are the most likely to commit more crime if released are held.

Self-report study Research that measures crime by having respondents report their own violations in confidential interviews or on anonymous self-administered questionnaires.

Sentence disparity The difference between criminal sanctions that are meted out to people who are convicted of similar offenses and who have similar criminal records.

Simultaneity A reciprocal cause-and-effect relationship between two variables; for instance, sanctions by the criminal justice system may affect the crime rate, but the crime rate may also affect the sanctions that are meted out by the criminal justice system.

Situational crime prevention Measures that involve the management, design, or manipulation of the environment in order to reduce opportunities for crime and increase the perceived risks of crime.

Social control A process that brings about conformity to society's norms and laws.

Somatotype A body type that results from embryonic development and that is thought to be associated with a particular temperament and propensity to crime and delinquency.

Specific deterrence The effect of a penalty that causes an individual who is punished for a crime not to commit that crime again because his or her risk-reward calculations have been altered by the punishment.

Status offense An act defined as unacceptable for people below a given age and used as a basis for juvenile court proceedings; included are underage drinking, running away from home, and truancy.

Subculture A patterned way of life similar in some ways but different in others from the dominant culture of a society.

Subculture-of-violence theory The theory that the norms shared by a group of people may define violence as an appropriate response to certain circumstances and lead members of the group to engage in violent crime in order to conform to others' expectations.

Subterranean value A value or ideal that is subordinate or below the surface in the dominant value system, and is sought by most people only occasionally and in appropriate circumstances.

Survey A research strategy in which a sample of people who are representative of a larger population are asked a series of prepared questions.

Target hardening A policy of reducing opportunities for crime by making it more difficult for offenders to carry out crimes against particular targets.

Technique of neutralization A justification used prior to a crime by an offender to render inoperative the social controls that would otherwise check law-violating behavior.

Tort A civil wrong in which a plaintiff, or complaining party, can sue a defendant who is alleged to have caused the plaintiff harm.

Transfer of property The cost of crimes in which property is transferred from one person to another, such as from the victim of a theft to the thief.

Tutelage Instruction or socialization in criminal motives and skills, including how to spot opportunities for theft, how to plan thefts, and how to carry out thefts.

Typology A set of categories of crimes or criminal careers.

Value Something that is considered worthy, desirable, or proper.

Vengeance A private and personal response to a wrong; it does not involve an established authority such as the state.

Victim precipitation The situation that exists when a person who suffers eventual harm from a crime plays a direct role in causing the crime to be perpetrated.

Victim proneness The tendency for certain people to be victimized repeatedly.

Victimization survey A systematic effort to measure the experiences of the victims of crime by interviewing a cross section of a population.

Victimless crimes Offenses that are consensual and lack a complaining participant.

White-collar crime An illegal act, punishable by a criminal sanction, that is committed in the course of a legitimate pursuit or occupation by a corporation or by an otherwise respectable individual of high social status.

Working personality The police officer's distinctive approach to the situations and events that are encountered on the job.

XYY chromosome A rare biological trait of some men that has been linked to a tendency to violate the law, or at least to be arrested for such violations.

Bibliography

ABT ASSOCIATES, INC. *American Prisons and Jails,* Vol. II: *Population Trends and Projections.* Washington, D.C.: U.S. Government Printing Office, 1980.

ADAMS, VIRGINIA. "Studies Relate Physical Causes to Delinquency," *The New York Times,* June 26, 1979, pp. C1, C3.

ADLER, FREDA. *Nations Not Obsessed with Crime.* Littleton, Colo.: Fred B. Rothman, 1983.

ADLER, PATRICIA A., AND PETER ADLER. "Shifts and Oscillations in Deviant Careers: The Case of Upper-Level Drug Dealers and Smugglers," *Social Problems* 31 (December 1983), 195–207.

AGETON, SUZANNE S. "The Dynamics of Female Delinquency, 1976–1980," *Criminology* 21 (November 1983), 555–584.

————, AND DELBERT S. ELLIOTT. "The Effects of Legal Processing on Self-Concept." Boulder, Colo.: Institute of Behavioral Science, University of Colorado, 1973.

AICHHORN, AUGUST. *Wayward Youth.* New York: Viking, 1935, 1951.

AKERS, RONALD L. *Deviant Behavior: A Social Learning Approach,* 3rd ed. Belmont, Calif.: Wadsworth, 1985.

————. "Socioeconomic Status and Delinquent Behavior: A Re-Test," *Journal of Research in Crime and Delinquency* (January 1964), 38–46.

————, ET AL. "Social Learning and Deviant Behavior: A Specific Test of a General Theory," *American Sociological Review* 44 (August 1979), 635–655.

AL-THAKEB, FAHAD. "Crime Trends in Kuwait," International Criminological Symposium, Stockholm, Sweden, 1978.

ALBANESE, JAY S. "God and the Mafia Revisited: From Valachi to Fratianno," in Gordon P. Waldo, ed., *Career Criminals.* Beverly Hills, Calif.: Sage Publications, 1983, pp. 43–58.

ALBINI, JOSEPH L. *The American Mafia: Genesis of a Legend.* New York: Appleton-Century-Crofts, 1971.

ALBRECHT, PETER-ALEXIS, CHRISTIAN PFEIFFER, AND KLAUS ZAPKA. "Reactions of the Agencies of Social Control to Crimes of Young Foreigners in the Federal Republic of Germany," *International Summaries.* Washington, D.C.: U.S. Department of Justice, 1978.

ALBRECHT, STAN L., BRUCE A. CHADWICK, AND DAVID S. ALCORN. "Religiosity and Deviance: Application of an Attitude-Behavior Contingent Consistency Model," *Journal for the Scientific Study of Religion* 16 (September 1977), 263–274.

ALLEN, FRANCIS A. "Criminal Justice, Legal Values and the Rehabilitative Ideal," in Stanley E. Grupp, ed., *Theories of Punishment.* Bloomington, Ind.: Indiana University Press, 1971, pp. 317–330.

ALLEN, VERNON L., AND DAVID B. GREENBERGER. "An Aesthetic Theory of Vandalism," *Crime and Delinquency* 24 (July 1978), 309–321.

ALTHEIDE, DAVID L., ET AL. "The Social Meanings of Employee Theft," in John M. Johnson and Jack D. Douglas, eds., *Crime at the Top: Deviance in Business and the Professions.* Philadelphia: Lippincott, 1978, pp. 90–124.

ALTMAN, LAWRENCE K. "Drug Abuse Found in Medical Training," *The New York Times,* August 19, 1983a, p. A8.

_____. "The Private Agony of an Addicted Physician," *The New York Times,* June 7, 1983b, pp. C1, C8.

AMERICAN FRIENDS SERVICE COMMITTEE. *Struggle for Justice: A Report on Crime and Punishment in America.* New York: Hill and Wang, 1971.

AMERICAN LAW INSTITUTE. *Model Penal Code.* Philadelphia: American Law Institute, 1971.

AMIR, MENACHEM. *Patterns in Forcible Rape.* Chicago: University of Chicago Press, 1971.

ANDELMAN, DAVID A. "City Crime Wave Spreading to Suburbs," *The New York Times,* January 30, 1972, p. 49.

ANDENAES, JOHANNES. "General Prevention—Illusion or Reality," *Journal of Criminal Law, Criminology and Police Science* 43 (July–August 1952), 176–198.

_____. "General Prevention Revisited: Research and Policy Implications," *Journal of Criminal Law and Criminology* 66 (September 1975), 338–365.

_____. *Punishment and Deterrence.* Ann Arbor, Mich.: University of Michigan Press, 1974.

ANDERSON, LINDA S., THEODORE G. CHIRICOS AND GORDON P. WALDO. "Formal and Informal Sanctions: A Comparison of Deterrent Effects," *Social Problems* 25 (October 1977), 103–114.

ANDERSON, OSCAR E. *The Health of a Nation: Harvey E. Wiley's Fight For Pure Food.* Chicago: University of Chicago Press, 1958.

ANDERSON, SUSAN HELLER. "The Big Couture Rip-Off," *The New York Times Magazine,* March 1, 1981, pp. 62–78.

ANGEL, ARTHUR, ET AL. "Preventive Detention: An Empirical Analysis," *Harvard Civil Rights Civil Liberties Law Review* 6 (March 1971), 300–396.

ARCHER, DANE, AND ROSEMARY GARTNER. *Violence and Crime in Cross-National Perspective.* New Haven, Conn.: Yale University Press, 1984.

_____, AND ROSEMARY GARTNER. "Violent Acts and Violent Times: A Comparative Approach to Postwar Homicide Rates," *American Sociological Review* 41 (December 1976), 937–963.

_____, ROSEMARY GARTNER, AND MARC BEITTEL. "Homicide and the Death Penalty: A Cross-National Test of a Deterrence Hypothesis," *Journal of Criminal Law and Criminology* 74 (Fall 1983), 991–1013.

ARMSTRONG, K. G. "The Retributivist Hits Back," in Stanley E. Grupp, ed., *Theories of Punishment.* Bloomington, Ind.: Indiana University Press, 1971, pp. 19–40.

ASHBROOK, TOM. "In China, Juvenile Delinquents Are Redirected with a Soft Touch," *The Boston Globe,* April 14, 1984, p. 3.

AUSTIN, JAMES, AND BARRY KRISBERG. "The Unmet Promise of Alternatives to Incarceration," *Crime and Delinquency* 28 (July 1982), 374–409.

AUSTIN, ROY L. "Race, Father-Absence, and Female Delinquency," *Criminology* 15 (February 1978), 487–504.

_____. "Women's Liberation and Increases in Minor, Major, and Occupational Offenses," *Criminology* 20 (November 1982), 407–430.

AUSTIN, WILLIAM. "Sex Differences in Bystander Intervention in a Theft," *Journal of Personality and Social Psychology* 37 (November 1979), 2110–2120.

AXENROTH, JOSEPH B. "Social Class and Delinquency in Cross-Cultural Perspective," *Journal of Research in Crime and Delinquency* 20 (July 1983), 164–182.

BACON, MARGARET K., IRVIN L. CHILD, AND HERBERT BARRY, III. "A Cross-Cultural Study of Correlates of Crime," *Journal of Abnormal and Social Psychology* 66 (April 1963), 291–300.

BAILEY, WALTER C. "An Evaluation of 100 Studies of Correctional Outcome," *Journal of Criminal Law, Criminology and Police Science* 57 (June 1966), 153–160.

BAILEY, WILLIAM C. "Disaggregation in Deterrence and Death Penalty Research: The Case of Murder in Chicago," *Journal of Criminal Law and Criminology* 74 (Fall 1983), 827–859.

BAKER, MARY HOLLAND, ET AL. "The Impact of a Crime Wave: Perceptions, Fear, and Confidence in the Police," *Law and Society Review* 17 (1983), 319–335.

BALDWIN, JOHN. "Ecological and Areal Studies in Great Britain and the United States," in Norval Morris and Michael Tonry, eds., *Crime and Justice: An Annual Review of Research*, Vol. 1. Chicago: University of Chicago Press, 1979, pp. 29–66.

————, AND MICHAEL MCCONVILLE. "Criminal Juries," in Norval Morris and Michael Tonry, eds., *Crime and Justice: An Annual Review of Research*, Vol. 2. Chicago: University of Chicago Press, 1980, pp. 269–319.

BALKAN, SHEILA, RONALD J. BERGER, AND JANET SCHMIDT. *Crime and Deviance in America: A Critical Approach*. Belmont, Calif.: Wadsworth, 1980.

BALL-ROKEACH, SANDRA J. "Values and Violence: A Test of the Subculture of Violence Thesis," *American Sociological Review* 38 (December 1973), 736–749.

BANDURA, ALBERT, DOROTHEA ROSS, AND SHEILA A. ROSS. "Transmission of Aggression through Imitation of Aggressive Models," *Journal of Abnormal and Social Psychology* 62 (1961), 575–582.

BARBANEL, JOSH. "Half Guilty under Gun Law Get Mandated Term," *The New York Times*, November 11, 1984, p. B4.

————. "Methadone Linked to Addict Deaths," *The New York Times*, February 2, 1982, pp. A1, D4.

BARIDON, PHILIP C. *Addiction, Crime, and Social Policy*. Lexington, Mass.: D.C. Heath, 1976.

BARMASH, ISADORE. "Retailers Losing Theft Battle," *The New York Times*, May 27, 1981, pp. D1, D18.

BARNETT, RANDY E. "Restitution: A New Paradigm of Criminal Justice," in Randy E. Barnett and John Hagel, III, eds., *Assessing the Criminal: Restitution, Retribution, and the Legal Process*. Cambridge, Mass.: Ballinger, 1977, pp. 349–383.

BARTH, ALAN. "The Vanishing Samaritan," in James M. Ratcliffe, ed., *The Good Samaritan and the Law*. Garden City, N.Y.: Doubleday, 1966, pp. 159–169.

BASLER, BARBARA. "State's Gun Law: Impact and Intent Uncertain," *The New York Times*, April 11, 1982, pp. 1, 41.

BAYER, RONALD. "Crime, Punishment, and the Decline of Liberal Optimism," *Crime and Delinquency* 27 (April 1981), 169–190.

BAYLEY, DAVID H. *Forces of Order: Police Behavior in Japan and the United States*. Berkeley, Calif.: University of California Press, 1976a.

————. "Learning about Crime—The Japanese Experience," *The Public Interest* No. 44 (Summer 1976b), 55–68.

————. "Police: History," in Sanford H. Kadish, ed., *Encyclopedia of Crime and Justice*, Vol. 3. New York: Free Press, 1983, pp. 1120–1125.

BEASLEY, RONALD W., AND GEORGE ANTUNES. "The Etiology of Urban Crime: An Ecological Analysis," *Criminology* 11 (February 1974), 439–461.

BECCARIA, CESARE. *On Crimes and Punishments*. Indianapolis, Ind.: Bobbs-Merrill, 1764, 1963.

BECKER, HOWARD S. *Outsiders: Studies in the Sociology of Deviance.* New York: Free Press, 1973.

BEDAU, HUGO ADAM. "Concessions to Retribution in Punishment," in J. B. Cederblom and William L. Blizek, eds., *Justice and Punishment.* Cambridge, Mass.: Ballinger, 1977, pp. 51–73.

_____. *The Death Penalty in America,* 3rd ed. New York: Oxford University Press, 1982.

_____. "Review of Walter Berns, *For Capital Punishment: Crime and the Morality of the Death Penalty,*" *Ethics* 90 (April 1980), 457–466.

_____, AND CHESTER M. PIERCE, EDS. *Capital Punishment in the United States.* New York: AMS Press, 1976.

BEHN, NOEL. *Big Stick-Up at Brink's!* New York: G. P. Putnam's Sons, 1977.

BEIRNE, PIERS. "Generalization and Its Discontents: The Comparative Study of Crime," in Israel L. Barak-Glantz and Elmer H. Johnson, eds., *Comparative Criminology.* Beverly Hills, Calif.: Sage Publications, 1983, pp. 19–38.

BELL, DANIEL. "Crime as an American Way of Life: A Queer Ladder of Social Mobility," in *The End of Ideology: On the Exhaustion of Political Ideas in the Fifties,* rev. ed. New York: Free Press, 1962, pp. 127–150.

BELSON, WILLIAM A. *Juvenile Theft: The Causal Factors.* London: Harper & Row, 1975.

BENNETT, RICHARD R. "Constructing Cross-Cultural Theories in Criminology: Application of the Generative Approach," *Criminology* 18 (August 1980), 252–268.

BENNETTS, LESLIE. "Do the Arts Inspire Violence in Real Life?" *The New York Times,* April 26, 1981, pp. H1, H25.

BERISTAIN, ANTONIO. "Capital Punishment and Catholicism," *International Journal of Criminology and Penology* 5 (November 1977), 321–335.

BERK, RICHARD A., KENNETH J. LENIHAN AND PETER H. ROSSI. "Crime and Poverty: Some Experimental Evidence from Ex-Offenders," *American Sociological Review* 45 (October 1980), 766–786.

BERKOWITZ, LEONARD. "Some Determinants of Impulsive Aggression: Role of Mediated Associations with Reinforcements for Aggression," *Psychological Review* 81 (March 1974), 165–176.

_____, AND JACQUELINE MACAULAY. "The Contagion of Criminal Violence," *Sociometry* 34 (June 1971), 238–260.

BERNARD, THOMAS J. "The Distinction between Conflict and Radical Criminology," *Journal of Criminal Law and Criminology* 72 (Spring 1981), 362–379.

BERNS, WALTER C. *For Capital Punishment: Crime and the Morality of the Death Penalty.* New York: Basic Books, 1979.

BIDERMAN, ALBERT D. "Sources of Data for Victimology," *Journal of Criminal Law and Criminology* 72 (Summer 1981), 789–817.

BISHOP, DONNA M. "Legal and Extralegal Barriers to Delinquency: A Panel Analysis," *Criminology* 22 (August 1984), 403–419.

BITTNER, EGON. "The Police on Skid-Row: A Study of Peace Keeping" *American Sociological Review* 32 (October 1967), 699–715.

BLACK, DONALD J. *The Behavior of Law.* New York: Academic Press, 1976.

_____. "Crime as Social Control," *American Sociological Review* 48 (February 1983), 34–35.

_____. *The Manners and Customs of the Police.* New York: Academic Press, 1980.

_____. "Production of Crime Rates," *American Sociological Review* 35 (August 1970), 733–748.

——————, AND ALBERT J. REISS, JR. "Police Control of Juveniles," *American Sociological Review* 35 (February 1970), 63–78.

BLACKMORE, JOHN, AND JANE WELSH. "Selective Incapacitation: Sentencing According to Risk," *Crime and Delinquency* 29 (October 1983), 504–528.

BLOCH, HERBERT A., AND ARTHUR NIEDERHOFFER. *The Gang: A Study in Adolescent Behavior.* New York: Philosophical Library, 1958.

BLOCK, ALAN A., AND FRANK R. SCARPITTI. *Poisoning for Profit: The Mafia and Toxic Waste in America.* New York: Morrow, 1985.

BLOCK, ELIZABETH J. "Bandits Wielding Plastic," *The New York Times,* May 22, 1983, pp. F12, F13.

BLOCK, MICHAEL KENT, FREDERICK CARL NOLD, AND JOSEPH GREGORY SIDAK. "The Deterrent Effect of Antitrust Enforcement," *Journal of Political Economy* 89 (June 1981), 429–445.

BLOCK, RICHARD. "Victim-Offender Dynamics in Violent Crime," *Journal of Criminal Law and Criminology* 72 (Summer 1981), 743–761.

——————. *Violent Crime: Environment, Interaction, and Death.* Lexington, Mass.: D. C. Heath, 1977.

——————, AND CAROLYN R. BLOCK. "Decisions and Data: The Transformation of Robbery Incidents into Official Robbery Statistics," *Journal of Criminal Law and Criminology* 71 (Winter 1980), 622–636.

BLUMBERG, ABRAHAM S. "Crime and the Social Order," in Abraham S. Blumberg, ed., *Current Perspectives on Criminal Behavior: Original Essays on Criminology.* New York: Knopf, 1974, pp. 3–34.

——————. *Criminal Justice: Issues & Ironies,* 2nd ed. New York: New Viewpoints, 1979.

BLUMENTHAL, MONICA, ET AL. *Justifying Violence: Attitudes of American Men.* Ann Arbor, Mich.: Institute for Social Research, 1972.

BLUMENTHAL, RALPH. "Illegal Dumping of Toxins Laid to Organized Crime," *The New York Times,* June 5, 1983, pp. 1, 44.

BLUMSTEIN, ALFRED. "On the Racial Disproportionality of United States' Prison Populations," *Journal of Criminal Law and Criminology* 73 (Fall 1982), 1259–1281.

——————. "Prisons: Population, Capacity, and Alternatives," in James Q. Wilson, ed., *Crime and Public Policy.* San Francisco: ICS Press, 1983, pp. 229–250.

——————, AND JACQUELINE COHEN. "Estimation of Individual Crime Rates from Arrest Records," *Journal of Criminal Law and Criminology* 70 (Winter 1979), 561–585.

——————, AND JACQUELINE COHEN. "Sentencing of Convicted Offenders: An Analysis of the Public's View," *Law and Society Review* 14 (Winter 1980), 223–261.

——————, JACQUELINE COHEN, AND WILLIAM GOODING. "The Influence of Capacity on Prison Population: A Critical Review of Some Recent Evidence," *Crime and Delinquency* 29 (January 1983), 1–51.

——————, JACQUELINE COHEN, AND DANIEL NAGIN. *Deterrence and Incapacitation: Estimating the Effects of Criminal Sanctions on Crime Rates.* Washington, D.C.: National Academy of Sciences, 1978.

——————, AND ELIZABETH GRADDY. "Prevalence and Recidivism in Index Arrests: A Feedback Model," *Law and Society Review* 16 (1981–82), 265–290.

——————, AND DANIEL NAGIN. "The Deterrent Effect of Legal Sanctions on Draft Evasion," *Stanford Law Review* 29 (January 1977), 241–276.

BLUNDELL, WILLIAM E. "Equity Funding: 'I Did It for the Jollies,'" in Donald Moffitt, ed., *Swindled! Classic Business Frauds of the Seventies.* Princeton, N.J.: Dow Jones Books, 1976, pp. 42–89.

BOFFEY, PHILIP M. "Domestic Violence: Study Favors Arrest," *The New York Times,* April 5, 1983a, pp. C1, C4.

_____. "Psychiatric Group Urges Stiffer Rules for Insanity Plea," *The New York Times,* January 20, 1983b, p. A18.

_____. "Youth Crime Puzzle Defies a Solution," *The New York Times,* March 5, 1982, pp. B1, B4.

BOGGS, SARAH L. "Formal and Informal Crime Control: An Exploratory Study of Urban, Suburban, and Rural Orientations," *Sociological Quarterly* 12 (Summer 1971), 319–327.

BOHANNAN, PAUL, ED. *African Homicide and Suicide.* Princeton, N.J.: Princeton University Press, 1960.

BOLAND, BARBARA, AND JAMES Q. WILSON. "Age, Crime, and Punishment," *The Public Interest* No. 51 (Spring 1978), 22–34.

BOOKIN-WEINER, HEDY, AND RUTH HOROWITZ. "The End of the Youth Gang: Fad or Fact?", *Criminology* 21 (November 1983), 585–602.

BOOTH, ALAN. "The Built Environment as a Crime Deterrent: A Reexamination of Defensible Space," *Criminology* 18 (February 1981), 557–570.

_____, DAVID R. JOHNSON, AND HARVEY M. CHOLDIN. "Correlates of City Crime Rates: Victimization Surveys versus Official Statistics," *Social Problems* 25 (December 1977), 187–197.

_____, SUSAN WELCH, AND DAVID RICHARD JOHNSON. "Crowding and Urban Crime Rates," *Urban Affairs Quarterly* 11 (March 1976), 291–307.

[*The Boston Globe*]. "Ask the Globe," *The Boston Globe,* May 7, 1980, p. 86.

_____. "Childhood Aggressiveness, Adult Criminality Linked," *The Boston Globe,* August 28, 1983, p. 7.

_____. "Crime Rates Are Inadequate Gauge of Police Efficiency, Chief Contends," *The Boston Globe,* February 14, 1983, p. 6.

_____. "Family Accused in Slaying of Daughter's Boyfriend," *The Boston Globe,* June 19, 1980, p. 8.

_____. "Hyperactivity Tied to Crime," *The Boston Globe,* November 26, 1982, p. 11.

_____. "Psychiatrists Back Insanity Plea," *The Boston Globe,* July 1, 1982, p. 6.

_____. "Senate Panel Told Gang Problem Is Spreading," *The Boston Globe,* July 10, 1981, p. 11.

_____. "Shock Sentence for DYS," *The Boston Globe,* May 8, 1982, p. 10.

_____. "Study: Pornography Affects Attitude on Rape," *The Boston Globe,* November 21, 1982, p. 5.

_____. "Study Shows 25% back in Prison within 2 Years," *The Boston Globe,* December 3, 1984, p. 9.

_____. "20% of Americans in Study Said to Admit Tax-Cheating," *The Boston Globe,* March 25, 1985, p. 12.

_____. "Vermont's Tougher Treatment of Juveniles," *The Boston Globe,* July 12, 1982, p. 13.

BOWERS, WILLIAM J. "The Pervasiveness of Arbitrariness and Discrimination under Post-*Furman* Capital Statutes," *Journal of Criminal Law and Criminology* 74 (Winter 1983), 1067–1100.

_____, AND GLENN L. PIERCE. "Arbitrariness and Discrimination under Post-*Furman* Capital Statutes," *Crime and Delinquency* 26 (October 1980a), 563–635.

_____, AND GLENN L. PIERCE. "Deterrence or Brutalization: What Is the Effect of Executions?", *Crime and Delinquency* 26 (October 1980b), 453–484.

_____, WITH GLENN L. PIERCE AND JOHN F. MCDEVITT. *Legal Homicide: Death as Punishment in America, 1864–1982*. Boston: Northeastern University Press, 1984.

BOWKER, LEE H. "Crime and the Use of Prisons in the United States: A Time Series Analysis," *Crime and Delinquency* 27 (April 1981), 206–212.

BOYDSTUN, JOHN E. *San Diego Field Interrogation: Final Report*. Washington, D.C.: Police Foundation, 1975.

BRADY, JAMES P. "Arson, Fiscal Crisis, and Community Action: Dialectics of an Urban Crime and Popular Response," *Crime and Delinquency* 28 (April 1982), 247–270.

_____. "Arson, Urban Economy, and Organized Crime: The Case of Boston," *Social Problems* 31 (October 1983a), 1–27.

_____. "Behind the Burning of Boston," *The Boston Globe Magazine*, October 23, 1983b, pp. 9–11, 49–66.

BRAITHWAITE, JOHN. "Challenging Just Deserts: Punishing White-Collar Criminals," *Journal of Criminal Law and Criminology* 73 (Summer 1982), 723–763.

_____. *Inequality, Crime, and Public Policy*. London: Routledge and Kegan Paul, 1979.

_____. "*The Myth of Social Class and Criminality* Reconsidered," *American Sociological Review* 46 (February 1981), 36–57.

_____, AND GILBERT GEIS. "On Theory and Action for Corporate Crime Control," *Crime and Delinquency* 28 (April 1982), 292–314.

BRANTINGHAM, PAUL, AND PATRICIA BRANTINGHAM. *Patterns in Crime*. New York: Macmillan, 1984.

BRERETON, DAVID, AND JONATHAN D. CASPER. "Does It Pay to Plead Guilty? Differential Sentencing and the Functioning of Criminal Courts," *Law and Society Review* 16 (1981–82), 45–70.

BRIAR, SCOTT, AND IRVING PILIAVIN. "Delinquency, Situational Inducements, and Commitment to Conformity," *Social Problems* 13 (Summer 1965), 35–45.

BRIDGES, JAMES H., JOHN T. GANDY, AND JAMES D. JORGENSEN. "The Case for Creative Restitution in Corrections," *Federal Probation* 43 (September 1979), 28–35.

British Journal of Criminology 22 (July 1982), Special Issue on Dangerousness.

BROAD, WILLIAM J. "Every Computer 'Whispers' Its Secrets," *The New York Times*, April 5, 1983, pp. C1, C8.

BRODY, JANE E. "Researchers Trace Key Factors in Profiles of Assassins on the American Scene," *The New York Times*, April 1, 1981, p. A26.

BROOKE, JIM. "Feminism in Foreign Lands: Two Perspectives: Macho Killing in Brazil Spurs Protesters," *The Boston Globe*, January 3, 1982, pp. A23, A24.

BROWN, BAILEY. "Community Service as a Condition of Probation," *Federal Probation* 41 (December 1977), 7–9.

BROWN, JULIA S. "A Comparative Study of Deviations from Sexual Mores," *American Sociological Review* 17 (April 1952), 135–146.

BROWN, RICHARD MAXWELL. "The American Vigilante Tradition," in Hugh Davis Graham and Ted Robert Gurr, eds., *Violence in America: Historical and Comparative Perspectives*. Staff Report to the National Commission on the Causes and Prevention of Violence, Vol. 1. Washington, D.C.: U.S. Government Printing Office, 1969, pp. 121–169.

_____. *The South Carolina Regulators*. Cambridge, Mass.: Belknap Press of Harvard University Press, 1963.

BROWN, STEPHEN E. "Social Class, Child Maltreatment, and Delinquent Behavior," *Criminology* 22 (May 1984), 259–278.

BROWNMILLER, SUSAN. *Against Our Will: Men, Women and Rape*. New York: Simon and Schuster, 1975.

BUCHNER, DEBORAH. "Scale of Sentence Severity," *Journal of Criminal Law and Criminology* 70 (Summer 1979), 182–187.

BUDER, LEONARD. "Almost 25% of Homicides in City in '81 Tied to Drugs," *The New York Times*, February 18, 1983a, p. B1.

_____. "Sharp Drop in Bank Robberies Cited by New York City Police," *The New York Times*, January 30, 1983b, p. A22.

BUREAU OF JUSTICE STATISTICS. *The American Response to Crime.* Washington, D.C.: U.S. Department of Justice, December 1983.

_____. *Capital Punishment 1982.* Washington, D.C.: U.S. Department of Justice, August 1984a.

_____. *Crime and Seasonality: National Crime Survey Report.* Washington, D.C.: U.S. Department of Justice, May 1980.

_____. *Criminal Victimization in the United States, 1981.* Washington, D.C.: U.S. Department of Justice, November 1983a.

_____. *Criminal Victimization 1983.* Washington, D.C.: U.S. Department of Justice, June 1984.

_____. *The Economic Cost of Crime to Victims.* Washington, D.C.: U.S. Department of Justice, April 1984.

_____. *Electronic Fund Transfer and Crime.* Washington, D.C.: U.S. Department of Justice, February 1984.

_____. *Households Touched by Crime, 1983.* Washington, D.C.: U.S. Department of Justice, May 1984.

_____. *Justice Expenditure and Employment in the U.S., 1979.* Washington, D.C.: U.S. Department of Justice, June 1983.

_____. *Prisoners and Alcohol.* Washington, D.C.: U.S. Department of Justice, January 1983.

_____. *Prisoners and Drugs.* Washington, D.C.: U.S. Department of Justice, March 1983.

_____. *Prisoners at Midyear 1983.* Washington, D.C.: U.S. Department of Justice, October 1983a.

_____. *Prisoners in 1983.* Washington, D.C.: U.S. Department of Justice, April 1984b.

_____. *Prisoners in State and Federal Institutions on December 31, 1982.* Washington, D.C.: U.S. Department of Justice, August 1984b.

_____. *Probation and Parole 1982.* Washington, D.C.: U.S. Department of Justice, September 1983.

_____. *Report to the Nation on Crime and Justice: The Data.* Washington, D.C.: U.S. Department of Justice, October 1983b.

_____. *Tracking Offenders.* Washington, D.C.: U.S. Department of Justice, November 1983b.

_____. *Violent Crime by Strangers.* Washington, D.C.: U.S. Department of Justice, April 1982.

BURGESS, ANN WOLBERT, AND LYNDA LYTLE HOLMSTROM. "Rape: Its Effect on Task Performance at Varying Stages in the Life Cycle," in Marcia J. Walker and Stanley L. Brodsky, eds., *Sexual Assault.* Lexington, Mass.: D. C. Heath, 1976, pp. 23–33.

BURGESS, ROBERT L., AND RONALD L. AKERS. "A Differential Association-Reinforcement Theory of Criminal Behavior," *Social Problems* 14 (Fall 1966), 128–147.

BURNHAM, DAVID. "F.B.I. Arrest Data Found Inaccurate," *The New York Times*, July 29, 1984a, p. 17.

_____. "F.B.I. Shelves Plan to Expand Its Computer Files," *The New York Times*, April 29, 1984b, p. 21.

_____. "Fear of Muggers Looms Large in Public Concern over Crime," *The New York Times,* May 20, 1968, p. 52.

_____. "Private Computers' Income Data to Aid I.R.S. in Hunt for Evaders," *The New York Times,* August 29, 1983, pp. A1, B8.

_____. "Some Criminal Records Sent out by F.B.I. Are Found to Be Inaccurate or Incomplete," *The New York Times,* October 25, 1982, p. A10.

BURSIK, ROBERT J., JR., AND JIM WEBB. "Community Change and Patterns of Delinquency," *American Journal of Sociology* 88 (July 1982), 24–42.

BURSTEIN, JUDD. "Decriminalizing Heroin," *The New York Times,* October 6, 1982, p. A27.

BUTTERFIELD, FOX. "Crime-Conscious Peking Has First Bank Robbery," *The New York Times,* February 10, 1980, p. 9.

_____. "How the Chinese Police Themselves," *The New York Times Magazine,* April 18, 1982, pp. 32, 36–40, 50–56.

BYNUM, TIM S., GARY W. CORDNER, AND JACK R. GREENE. "Victim and Offense Characteristics: Impact on Police Investigative Decision-Making," *Criminology* 20 (November 1982), 301–318.

BYRNE, HARRY J. " 'Society Needs Draconian Justice,' " *The New York Times,* November 20, 1979, p. A23.

CAHALAN, MARGARET. "Trends in Incarceration in the United States since 1880: A Summary of Reported Rates and the Distribution of Offenses," *Crime and Delinquency* 25 (January 1979), 9–41.

CAMERON, MARY OWEN. *The Booster and the Snitch: Department Store Shoplifting.* New York: Free Press, 1964.

CANTER, RACHELLE. "Family Correlates of Male and Female Delinquency," *Criminology* 20 (August 1982), 149–167.

CAPLAN, LINCOLN. "Annals of Law: The Insanity Defense," *The New Yorker,* July 2, 1984, pp. 45–78.

CAPOTE, TRUMAN. *In Cold Blood: A True Account of a Multiple Murder and Its Consequences.* New York: Random House, 1965.

CARMODY, DEIRDRE. "Law Graduate Held in $607,000 Fraud," *The New York Times,* February 20, 1974, pp. 1, 45.

CARROLL, LEO, AND PAMELA IRVING JACKSON. "Inequality, Opportunity, and Crime Rates in Central Cities," *Criminology* 21 (May 1983), 178–194.

_____, AND MARGARET E. MONDRICK. "Racial Bias in the Decision to Grant Parole," *Law and Society Review* 11 (Fall 1976), 93–107.

CASPER, JONATHAN D. "Having Their Day in Court: Defendant Evaluations of the Fairness of Their Treatment," *Law and Society Review* 12 (Winter 1978), 237–249.

CATER, DOUGLASS, AND STEPHEN STRICKLAND. *TV Violence and the Child: The Evolution and Fate of the Surgeon General's Report.* New York: Russell Sage Foundation, 1975.

CERNKOVICH, STEPHEN A. "Conceptual and Empirical Ambiguity in Class-Oriented Theories of Crime and Delinquency," *International Journal of Criminology and Penology* 6 (May 1978a), 105–120.

_____. "Evaluating Two Models of Delinquency Causation: Structural Theory and Control Theory," *Criminology* 16 (November 1978b), 335–352.

_____. "Value Orientations and Delinquency Involvement," *Criminology* 15 (February 1978c), 443–458.

CHAIKEN, JAN M., AND MARCIA R. CHAIKEN. "Crime Rates and the Active Criminal," in James Q. Wilson, ed., *Crime and Public Policy.* San Francisco: ICS Press, 1983, pp. 11–29.

_____, AND MARCIA R. CHAIKEN. *Varieties of Criminal Behavior.* Santa Monica, Calif.: Rand, 1982a.

_____, AND MARCIA R. CHAIKEN, WITH JOYCE E. PETERSON. *Varieties of Criminal Behavior: Summary and Policy Implications.* Santa Monica, Calif.: Rand, 1982b.

_____, MICHAEL W. LAWLESS, AND KEITH A. STEVENSON. *The Impact of Police Activity on Crime: Robberies in the New York City Subway System.* New York: Rand, 1974.

CHAIKEN, MARCIA R., AND JAN M. CHAIKEN, "Offender Types and Public Policy," *Crime and Delinquency* 30 (April 1984), 195–226.

CHALIDZE, VALERY. *Criminal Russia: Crime in the Soviet Union.* New York: Random House, 1977.

CHAMBER OF COMMERCE OF THE UNITED STATES. *A Handbook on White Collar Crime: Everyone's Problem, Everyone's Loss.* Washington, D.C.: Chamber of Commerce of the United States, 1974.

CHAMBERS, CARL D., AND JAMES A. INCIARDI. "Deviant Behavior in the Middle East: A Study of Delinquency in Iraq," *Criminology* 9 (August–November 1971), 291–315.

CHAMBERS, MARCIA. "Life in City's Gangs: Some Things Have Changed, but It's Still a Dead End," *The New York Times,* September 27, 1983, pp. B1, B4.

CHAMBLISS, WILLIAM J., ED. *Crime and the Legal Process.* New York: McGraw-Hill, 1969, pp. 360–378.

_____. *On the Table: From Petty Crooks to Presidents.* Bloomington, Ind.: Indiana University Press, 1978.

_____. "The State, the Law, and the Definition of Behavior as Criminal or Delinquent," in Daniel Glaser, ed., *Handbook of Criminology.* Chicago: Rand McNally, 1974, pp. 20–25.

_____. "Vice, Corruption, Bureaucracy, and Power," *Wisconsin Law Review* No. 4 (1971), 1130–1155.

CHAPMAN, WILLIAM. "In Japan, a Problem with Loan Sharks," *The Boston Globe,* May 15, 1983a, p. 140.

_____. "Rising Delinquency in Japanese Junior High Schools," *The Boston Globe,* April 5, 1983b, p. 3.

CHEIN, ISIDOR, ET AL. *The Road to H: Narcotics, Delinquency, and Social Policy.* New York: Basic Books, 1964.

CHESNEY-LIND, MEDA. "Judicial Enforcement of the Female Sex Role: The Family Court and the Female Delinquent," *Issues in Criminology* 8 (Fall 1973), 51–69.

CHEVALIER, LOUIS. *Laboring Classes and Dangerous Classes in Paris during the First Half of the Nineteenth Century.* New York: Howard Fertig, 1973.

CHIBNALL, STEVE. *Law-and-Order News: An Analysis of Crime Reporting in the British Press.* London: Tavistock, 1977.

CHILTON, ROLAND J. "Delinquency Area Research in Baltimore, Detroit and Indianapolis," *American Sociological Review* 29 (February 1964), 71–83.

_____. "Persistent Problems of Crime Statistics," in Simon Dinitz and Walter C. Reckless, eds., *Critical Issues in the Study of Crime: A Book of Readings.* Boston: Little, Brown, 1968, pp. 89–95.

_____, AND JIM GALVIN, EDS. "Special Issue: Race, Crime, and Criminal Justice," *Crime and Delinquency* 31 (January 1985).

CHIRA, SUSAN. "What Children 'See' When Watching TV," *The New York Times,* January 6, 1983, pp. C1, C6.

CHIU, HUNGDAH. "Criminal Punishment in Mainland China: A Study of Some Yunnan Province Documents," *Journal of Criminal Law and Criminology* 68 (September 1977), 374–398.

CHRISTIANSEN, KARL O. "A Preliminary Study of Criminality among Twins," in Sarnoff A. Mednick and Karl O. Christiansen, eds., *Biosocial Bases of Criminal Behavior.* New York: Gardner Press, 1977, pp. 89–108.

_____. "Seriousness of Criminality and Concordance among Danish Twins," in Roger Hood, ed., *Crime, Criminology, and Public Policy: Essays in Honour of Sir Leon Radzinowicz.* New York: Free Press, 1974, pp. 63–77.

CHRISTIANSON, SCOTT. "Our Black Prisons," *Crime and Delinquency* 27 (July 1981), 364–375.

CLARK, JOHN P., AND EDWARD W. HAUREK. "Age and Sex Roles of Adolescents and Their Involvement in Misconduct: A Reappraisal," *Sociology and Social Research* 50 (July 1966), 496–508.

_____, AND LARRY L. TIFFT. "Polygraph and Interview Validation of Self-Reported Deviant Behavior," *American Sociological Review* 31 (August 1966), 516–523.

CLARK, RAMSEY. *Crime in America: Observations on Its Nature, Causes, Prevention and Control.* New York: Simon and Schuster, 1970.

CLARKE, RONALD V. "Situational Crime Prevention: Its Theoretical Basis and Practical Scope," in Michael Tonry and Norval Morris, eds., *Crime and Justice: An Annual Review of Research,* Vol. 4. Chicago: University of Chicago Press, 1983, pp. 225–256.

CLARKE, STEVENS H., AND GARY G. KOCH. "The Influence of Income and Other Factors on Whether Criminal Defendants Go to Prison," *Law and Society Review* 11 (Fall 1976), 57–92.

CLEAVER, ELDRIDGE. *Soul On Ice.* New York: Dell, 1968.

CLECKLEY, HERVEY. *The Mask of Sanity,* 4th ed. St. Louis: C. V. Mosby, 1964.

CLELLAND, DONALD, AND TIMOTHY J. CARTER. "The New Myth of Class and Crime," *Criminology* 18 (November 1980), 319–336.

CLIFFORD, WILLIAM. *Crime Control in Japan.* Lexington, Mass.: D. C. Heath, 1976.

_____. "Culture and Crime—In Global Perspective," *International Journal of Criminology and Penology* 6 (February 1978), 61–80.

CLINARD, MARSHALL B. *The Black Market: A Study of White Collar Crime.* Montclair, N.J.: Patterson Smith, 1952, 1969.

_____. *Cities with Little Crime: The Case of Switzerland.* Cambridge, Engl.: Cambridge University Press, 1978.

_____. *Corporate Ethics and Crime: The Role of Middle Management.* Beverly Hills, Calif.: Sage Publications, 1983.

_____. "The Process of Urbanization and Criminal Behavior," *American Journal of Sociology* 48 (September 1942), 202–213.

_____. "Rural Criminal Offenders," *American Journal of Sociology* 50 (July 1944), 38–45.

_____, AND DANIEL J. ABBOTT. *Crime in Developing Countries: A Comparative Perspective.* New York: Wiley, 1973.

_____, AND PETER C. YEAGER. *Corporate Crime.* New York: Free Press, 1980.

CLOWARD, RICHARD A., AND LLOYD E. OHLIN. *Delinquency and Opportunity: A Theory of Delinquent Gangs.* New York: Free Press, 1960.

COATES, ROBERT B., AND ALDEN D. MILLER. "Neutralization of Community Resistance to Group Homes," in Yitzhak Bakal, ed., *Closing Correctional Institutions.* Lexington, Mass.: D. C. Heath, 1973, pp. 67–84.

COCOZZA, JOSEPH J., AND HENRY J. STEADMAN. "Prediction in Psychiatry: An Example of Misplaced Confidence in Experts," *Social Problems* 25 (February 1979), 265–276.

COHEN, ALBERT K. *Delinquent Boys: The Culture of the Gang.* New York: Free Press, 1955.

COHEN, DANIEL. "Problems of Punishment," *Atlantic Monthly* 253 (January 1984), 28–32.

COHEN, JACQUELINE. *Incapacitating Criminals: Recent Research Findings.* Washington, D.C.: National Institute of Justice, U.S. Department of Justice, December 1983a.

_____. "Incapacitation as a Strategy for Crime Control: Possibilities and Pitfalls," in Michael Tonry and Norval Morris, eds., *Crime and Justice: An Annual Review of Research,* Vol. 5. Chicago: University of Chicago Press, 1983b, pp. 1–84.

COHEN, JEROME ALAN. "Reflections on the Criminal Process in China," *Journal of Criminal Law and Criminology* 68 (September 1977), 323–355.

COHEN, LAWRENCE E. "Modeling Crime Trends: A Criminal Opportunity Perspective," *Journal of Research in Crime and Delinquency* 18 (January 1981), 138–162.

_____, AND DAVID CANTOR. "The Determinants of Larceny: An Empirical and Theoretical Study," *Journal of Research in Crime and Delinquency* 17 (July 1980), 140–159.

_____, AND DAVID CANTOR. "Residential Burglary in the United States: Life-Style and Demographic Factors Associated with the Probability of Victimization," *Journal of Research in Crime and Delinquency* 18 (January 1981), 113–127.

_____, AND MARCUS FELSON. "Social Change and Crime Rate Trends: A Routine Activity Approach," *American Sociological Review* 44 (August 1979), 588–608.

_____, AND JAMES R. KLUEGEL. "Determinants of Juvenile Court Disposition: Ascriptive and Achieved Factors in Two Metropolitan Courts," *American Sociological Review* 43 (April 1978), 162–176.

_____, JAMES R. KLUEGEL, AND KENNETH C. LAND. "Social Inequality and Predatory Criminal Victimization: An Exposition and Test of a Formal Theory," *American Sociological Review* 46 (October 1981), 505–524.

COLLINS, GLENN. "The Violent Child: Some Patterns Emerge," *The New York Times,* September 27, 1982, p. B10.

COLLINS, JAMES J., JR. *Alcohol Use and Criminal Behavior: An Executive Summary.* Washington, D.C.: U.S. Department of Justice, National Institute of Justice, 1981a.

_____, ED. *Drinking and Crime: Perspectives on the Relationships between Alcohol Consumption and Criminal Behavior.* New York: Guilford Press, 1981b.

COLTON, KENT W., ET AL. *Computer Crime: Electronic Fund Transfer Systems and Crime.* Washington, D.C.: U.S. Government Printing Office, 1982.

COLVIN, MARK. "The 1980 New Mexico Prison Riot," *Social Problems* 29 (June 1982), 449–463.

CONKLIN, JOHN E., ED. *The Crime Establishment: Organized Crime and American Society.* Englewood Cliffs, N.J.: Prentice-Hall, 1973.

_____. "Explaining Changes in Crime Rates," 1973, unpublished paper.

_____. *"Illegal but Not Criminal": Business Crime in America.* Englewood Cliffs, N.J.: Prentice-Hall, 1977.

_____. *The Impact of Crime.* New York: Macmillan, 1975.

_____. *Robbery and the Criminal Justice System.* Philadelphia: Lippincott, 1972.

_____, AND EGON BITTNER. "Burglary in a Suburb," *Criminology* 11 (August 1973), 206–232.

_____, AND DERMOT MEAGHER. "The Percentage Deposit Bail System: An Alternative to the Professional Bondsman," *Journal of Criminal Justice* 1 (Winter 1973), 299–317.

CONNOR, WALTER D. "Juvenile Delinquency in the U.S.S.R.: Some Quantitative and Qualitative Indicators," *American Sociological Review* 35 (April 1970), 283–297.

CONRAD, PETER, AND JOSEPH W. SCHNEIDER. *Deviance and Medicalization: From Badness to Sickness.* St. Louis: C. V. Mosby, 1980.

COOK, PHILIP J. "The Correctional Carrot: Better Jobs for Parolees," *Policy Analysis* 1 (1975), 11–54.

_____. "The Influence of Gun Availability on Violent Crime Patterns," in Michael Tonry and Norval Morris, eds., *Crime and Justice: An Annual Review of Research,* Vol. 4. Chicago: University of Chicago Press, 1983, pp. 49–89.

_____. "Research in Criminal Deterrence: Laying the Groundwork for the Second Decade," in Norval Morris and Michael Tonry, eds., *Crime and Justice: An Annual Review of Research,* Vol. 2. Chicago: University of Chicago Press, 1980, pp. 211–268.

COOK, R. F., AND J. A. ROEHL. *Preventing Crime and Arson—A Review of Community-Based Strategies.* Reston, Va.: Institute for Social Analysis, 1983.

CORDILIA, ANN. *The Making of an Inmate: Prison as a Way of Life.* Cambridge, Mass.: Schenkman, 1983.

COUNT-VAN MANEN, GLORIA. "A Deviant Case of Deviance: Singapore," *Law and Society Review* 5 (February 1971), 389–406.

COVINGTON, JEANETTE. "Insulation from Labeling: Deviant Defenses in Treatment," *Criminology* 22 (November 1984), 619–643.

COWAN, EDWARD. "Your Honest Taxpayer Bears Watching," *The New York Times,* April 11, 1982, p. E4.

CRESSEY, DONALD R. *Criminal Organization.* New York: Harper & Row, 1972.

_____. *Other People's Money: A Study in the Social Psychology of Embezzlement.* Belmont, Calif.: Wadsworth, 1953, 1971.

_____. *Theft of the Nation: The Structure and Operations of Organized Crime in America.* New York: Harper & Row, 1969.

_____, AND ROBERT A. MCDERMOTT. *Diversion from the Juvenile Justice System.* Washington, D.C.: U.S. Government Printing Office, 1973.

CRIMINAL DIVISION, U.S. DEPARTMENT OF JUSTICE. Cited in *Congressional Record—Senate* 114 (July 18, 1968), 21986.

CRONIN, THOMAS E., TANIA Z. CRONIN, AND MICHAEL E. MILAKOVICH. *U.S. v. Crime in the Streets.* Bloomington, Ind.: Indiana University Press, 1981.

CRUTCHFIELD, ROBERT D., MICHAEL R. GEERKEN, AND WALTER R. GOVE. "Crime Rate and Social Integration: The Impact of Metropolitan Mobility," *Criminology* 20 (November 1982), 467–478.

CSIKSZENTMIHALYI, MIHALY, AND REED LARSON. "Intrinsic Rewards in School Crime," *Crime and Delinquency* 24 (July 1978), 322–335.

CULLEN, FRANCIS T., AND KAREN E. GILBERT. *Reaffirming Rehabilitation.* Cincinnati, Ohio: Anderson, 1982.

_____, BRUCE G. LINK, AND CRAIG W. POLANZI. "The Seriousness of Crime Revisited: Have Attitudes toward White-Collar Crime Changed?" *Criminology* 20 (May 1982), 83–102.

_____, WILLIAM J. MAAKESTAD, AND GRAY CAVENDER. "The Ford Pinto Case and Beyond: Corporate Crime, Moral Boundaries, and the Criminal Sanction," in Ellen Hochstedler, ed., *Corporations as Criminals*. Beverly Hills, Calif.: Sage Publications, 1984, pp. 107–130.

_____, ET AL. "Public Support for Punishing White-Collar Crime: Blaming the Victim Revisited?" *Journal of Criminal Justice* 11 (1983), 481–493.

CULLEN, TOM A. *When London Walked in Terror*. New York: Avon, 1965.

CUMMINGS, JUDITH. "Increase in Gang Killings on Coast Is Traced to Narcotics Trafficking," *The New York Times*, October 29, 1984, pp. A1, A10.

CURRAN, DEBRA A. "Judicial Discretion and Defendant's Sex," *Criminology* 21 (February 1983), 41–58.

CURTIS, LYNN A. *Criminal Violence: National Patterns and Behavior*. Lexington, Mass.: D. C. Heath, 1974.

_____. *Violence, Race and Culture*. Lexington, Mass.: D. C. Heath, 1975.

CUSHMAN, PAUL, JR. "Relationship Between Narcotic Addiction and Crime," *Federal Probation* 38 (September 1974), 38–43.

DALGARD, ODD STEFFEN, AND EINAR KRINGLEN. "A Norwegian Twin Study of Criminality," *British Journal of Criminology* 16 (June 1976), 213–232.

DANNEFER, DALE, AND RUSSELL K. SCHUTT. "Race and Juvenile Justice Processing in Court and Police Agencies," *American Journal of Sociology* 87 (March 1982), 1113–1132.

DANZIGER, SHELDON, AND DAVID WHEELER. "The Economics of Crime: Punishment or Income Redistribution," *Review of Social Economy* 33 (October 1975), 113–131.

DARLEY, JOHN M., AND C. DANIEL BATSON. " 'From Jerusalem to Jericho': A Study of Situational and Dispositional Variables in Helping Behavior," *Journal of Personality and Social Psychology* 27 (July 1973), 100–108.

DAVIES, CHRISTIE. "Crime, Bureaucracy, and Equality," *Policy Review* 23 (Winter 1983), 89–105.

DAVIS, JOHN A. "Justification for No Obligation: Views of Black Males toward Crime and the Criminal Law," *Issues in Criminology* 9 (Fall 1974), 69–87.

DECKER, DAVID L., DAVID SHICHOR, AND ROBERT M. O'BRIEN. *Urban Structure and Victimization*. Lexington, Mass.: D. C. Heath, 1982.

DeFLEUR, LOIS B. "Biasing Influences on Drug Arrest Records: Implications for Deviance Research," *American Sociological Review* 40 (February 1975), 88–103.

_____. *Delinquency in Argentina: A Study of Córdoba's Youth*. Pullman, Wash.: Washington State University Press, 1970.

DeFLEUR, MELVIN L., AND RICHARD QUINNEY. "A Reformulation of Sutherland's Differential Association Theory and a Strategy for Empirical Verification," *Journal of Research in Crime and Delinquency* 3 (January 1966), 1–22.

DeFRANCO, EDWARD J. *Anatomy of a Scam: A Case Study of a Planned Bankruptcy by Organized Crime*. Washington, D.C.: U.S. Government Printing Office, 1973.

DeFRONZO, JAMES. "Economic Assistance to Impoverished Americans: Relationship to Incidence of Crime," *Criminology* 21 (February 1983), 119–136.

DELLA FAVE, L. RICHARD. "The Culture of Poverty Revisited: A Strategy for Research," *Social Problems* 21 (June 1974), 609–621.

DEMING, ROMINE R. "Correctional Restitution: A Strategy for Correctional Conflict Management," *Federal Probation* 40 (September 1976), 27–32.

DENTLER, ROBERT A., AND LAWRENCE J. MONROE. "Social Correlates of Early Adolescent Theft," *American Sociological Review* 26 (October 1961), 733–743.

DIETZ, JEAN. "Executions Seen Spiraling into Violence," *The Boston Globe*, August 13, 1980, p. 40.

_____. "Study: 1 in 4,000 Acquitted by Insanity," *The Boston Globe*, April 29, 1984, p. 32.

DIETZ, MARY LORENZ. *Killing for Profit: The Social Organization of Felony Homicide*. Chicago: Nelson-Hall, 1983.

DINITZ, SIMON, FRANK R. SCARPITTI, AND WALTER C. RECKLESS. "Delinquency Vulnerability: A Cross Group and Longitudinal Analysis," *American Sociological Review* 27 (August 1962), 515–517.

DINNERSTEIN, LEONARD. *The Leo Frank Case*. New York: Columbia University Press, 1968.

DIRKS, RAYMOND L., AND LEONARD GROSS. *The Great Wall Street Scandal*. New York: McGraw-Hill, 1974.

DOERNER, WILLIAM G. "The Index of Southernness Revisited: The Influence of Wherefrom upon Whodunnit," *Criminology* 16 (May 1978), 47–56.

DOLESCHAL, EUGENE. "Crime—Some Popular Beliefs," *Crime and Delinquency* 25 (January 1979), 1–8.

DOLNICK, EDWARD. "Codes May Stop Computer Theft," *The Boston Globe*, December 12, 1983, pp. 45, 48.

DOWD, MAUREEN. "20 Years after Kitty Genovese's Murder, Experts Study Bad Samaritanism," *The New York Times*, March 12, 1984, pp. B1, B4.

DUBOW, FRED, EDWARD MCCABE, AND GAIL KAPLAN. *Reactions to Crime: A Critical Review of the Literature*. Evanston, Ill.: Northwestern University, 1979.

DUFFY, MIKE. "The Medium's Message: Call It Distorted," *The Boston Globe*, December 13, 1982, p. 35.

DULL, R. THOMAS. "Friends' Use and Adult Drug and Drinking Behavior: A Further Test of Differential Association Theory," *Journal of Criminal Law and Criminology* 74 (Winter 1983), 1608–1619.

DURKHEIM, EMILE. *The Division of Labor in Society*, trans. by George Simpson. Glencoe, Ill.: Free Press, 1895, 1933.

_____. *The Rules of the Sociological Method*, trans. by Sarah A. Solovay and John H. Mueller; ed. by George E. G. Catlin. New York: Free Press, 1895, 1938.

EBERTS, PAUL, AND KENT P. SCHWIRIAN. "Metropolitan Crime Rates and Relative Deprivation," *Criminologica* 5 (February 1968), 43–52.

ECK, JOHN. "Solving Crimes," *NIJ Reports*. Washington, D.C.: U.S. Department of Justice, March 1984, pp. 4–8.

EDELHERTZ, HERBERT. *The Nature, Impact and Prosecution of White-Collar Crime*. Washington, D.C.: U.S. Government Printing Office, 1970.

EDWARDS, ANNE. "Sex and Area Variations in Delinquency Rates in an English City," *British Journal of Criminology* 13 (April 1973), 121–137.

EGAN, JOHN W. "The Internal Revenue Service and Corporate Slush Funds: Some Fifth Amendment Problems," *Journal of Criminal Law and Criminology* 69 (Spring 1978), 59–74.

EHRLICH, ISAAC. "The Deterrent Effect of Capital Punishment: A Question of Life and Death," *American Economic Review* 65 (June 1975), 397–417.

ELIAS, ROBERT. "Alienating the Victim: Compensation and Victim Attitudes," *Journal of Social Issues* 40 (1984), 103–116.

_____. *Victims of the System: Crime Victims and Compensation in American Politics and Criminal Justice*. New Brunswick, N.J.: Transaction Books, 1983.

ELIFSON, KIRK W., DAVID M. PETERSEN, AND C. KIRK HADAWAY. "Religiosity and Delinquency: A Contextual Analysis," *Criminology* 21 (November 1983), 505–527.

ELLIOTT, DELBERT S., AND SUZANNE S. AGETON. "Reconciling Race and Class Differences in Self-Reported and Official Estimates of Delinquency," *American Sociological Review* 45 (February 1980), 95–110.

_____, AND DAVID HUIZINGA. "Social Class and Delinquent Behavior in a National Youth Panel: 1976–1980," *Criminology* 21 (May 1983) 149–177.

_____, AND HARWIN L. VOSS. *Delinquency and Dropout*. Lexington, Mass.: D. C. Heath, 1974.

ELLIS, LEE. "Genetics and Criminal Behavior: Evidence through the End of the 1970s," *Criminology* 20 (May 1982), 43–66.

ELLSWORTH, PHOEBE C., AND LEE ROSS. "Public Opinion and Capital Punishment: A Close Examination of the Views of Abolitionists and Retentionists," *Crime and Delinquency* 29 (January 1983), 116–169.

ELMHORN, KERSTIN. "Study in Self-Reported Delinquency among Schoolchildren in Stockholm," in Karl O. Christiansen, ed., *Scandinavian Studies in Criminology*, Vol. 1. London: Tavistock, 1965, pp. 117–146.

EMPEY, LAMAR T. "Crime Prevention: The Fugitive Utopia," in Daniel Glaser, ed., *Handbook of Criminology*. Chicago: Rand McNally, 1974, pp. 1095–1123.

_____, AND MAYNARD L. ERICKSON. "Hidden Delinquency and Social Status," *Social Forces* 44 (June 1966), 546–554.

_____, AND STEVEN G. LUBECK. *Explaining Delinquency: Construction, Test, and Reformulation of a Sociological Theory*. Lexington, Mass.: D. C. Heath, 1971.

ENNIS, PHILIP H. *Criminal Victimization in the United States: A Report of a National Survey*. Field Surveys II of the President's Commission on Law Enforcement and the Administration of Justice. Washington, D.C.: U.S. Government Printing Office, 1967.

EPSTEIN, EDWARD JAY. "The Krogh File—The Politics of 'Law and Order'," *The Public Interest* No. 39 (Spring 1975), 99–124.

_____. "Methadone: The Forlorn Hope," *The Public Interest* No. 36 (Summer 1974), 3–24.

EREZ, EDNA. "Planning of Crime and the Criminal Career: Official and Hidden Offenses," *Journal of Criminal Law and Criminology* 71 (Spring 1980), 73–76.

ERICKSON, MAYNARD L., AND LAMAR T. EMPEY. "Court Records, Undetected Delinquency and Decision Making," *Journal of Criminal Law, Criminology and Police Science* 54 (December 1963), 456–469.

_____, AND JACK P. GIBBS. "Objective and Perceptual Properties of Legal Punishment and the Deterrence Doctrine," *Social Problems* 25 (February 1978), 253–264.

_____, AND JACK P. GIBBS. "On the Perceived Severity of Legal Penalties," *Journal of Criminal Law and Criminology* 70 (Spring 1979), 102–116.

_____, JACK P. GIBBS, AND GARY F. JENSEN. "Conventional and Special Crime and Delinquency Rates," *Journal of Criminal Law and Criminology* 68 (September 1977), 440–453.

_____, AND GARY F. JENSEN. " 'Delinquency Is Still Group Behavior!': Toward Revitalizing the Group Premise in the Sociology of Deviance," *Journal of Criminal Law and Criminology* 68 (June 1977), 262–273.

ERICKSON, PATRICIA G., AND MICHAEL S. GOODSTADT. "Legal Stigma for Marijuana Possession," *Criminology* 17 (August 1979), 208–216.

ERIKSON, KAI T. *Wayward Puritans: A Study in the Sociology of Deviance*. New York: Wiley, 1966.

ERLANGER, HOWARD S. "The Empirical Status of the Subculture of Violence Thesis," *Social Problems* 22 (December 1974), 280–292.

_____. "Is There a 'Subculture of Violence' in the South?," *Journal of Criminal Law and Criminology* 66 (December 1975), 483–490.

ERMANN, M. DAVID, AND RICHARD J. LUNDMAN. *Corporate Deviance.* New York: Holt, Rinehart and Winston, 1982.

ERVIN, SAM J., JR. "Foreword: Preventive Detention—A Step Backward for Criminal Justice," *Harvard Civil Rights Civil Liberties Law Review* 6 (March 1971), 291–299.

EVANS, SANDRA S., AND RICHARD J. LUNDMAN. "Newspaper Coverage of Corporate Price-Fixing: A Replication," *Criminology* 21 (November 1983), 529–541.

_____, AND JOSEPH E. SCOTT. "The Seriousness of Crime Cross-Culturally: The Impact of Religiosity," *Criminology* 22 (February 1984), 39–59.

EVE, RAYMOND A. "A Study of the Efficacy and Interactions of Several Theories for Explaining Rebelliousness among High School Students," *Journal of Criminal Law and Criminology* 69 (Spring 1978), 115–125.

EYSENCK, HANS. *Crime and Personality.* London: Routledge and Kegan Paul, 1977.

FARBER, M. A. "Big Push on Crime Merely Pushes It Elsewhere, Many Officers Feel," *The New York Times,* June 1, 1982a, pp. B1, B6.

_____. "Decade after Knapp Inquiry, a Sense of 'Revolution' Pervades Police Dept.," *The New York Times,* November 29, 1982b, pp. B1, B5.

FARNSWORTH, CLYDE H. "Imitation Goods Costly to the U.S.," *The New York Times,* February 5, 1984, p. 4.

FARRELL, RONALD A., AND JAMES F. NELSON. "A Sequential Analysis of Delinquency," *International Journal of Criminology and Penology* 6 (August 1978), 255–268.

_____, AND VICTORIA LYNN SWIGERT. "Prior Offense Record as a Self-Fulfilling Prophecy," *Law and Society Review* 12 (Spring 1978), 437–453.

FARRINGTON, DAVID P. "Longitudinal Research on Crime and Delinquency," in Norval Morris and Michael Tonry, eds., *Crime and Justice: An Annual Review of Research,* Vol. 1. Chicago: University of Chicago Press, 1979, pp. 289–348.

_____. "Self-Reports of Deviant Behavior: Predictive and Stable?" *Journal of Criminal Law and Criminology* 64 (March 1973), 99–110.

FEENEY, FLOYD, AND ADRIANNE WEIR, EDS. *The Prevention and Control of Robbery.* Davis, Calif.: Center on Administration of Criminal Justice, University of California at Davis, 1973.

FELD, BARRY C. "Delinquent Careers and Criminal Policy: Just Deserts and the Waiver Decision," *Criminology* 21 (May 1983), 195–212.

FELSON, RICHARD B., AND HENRY J. STEADMAN. "Situational Factors in Disputes Leading to Criminal Violence," *Criminology* 21 (February 1983), 59–74.

FERDINAND, THEODORE. "Reported Index Crime Increases between 1950 and 1965 Due to Urbanization and Changes in the Age Structure of the Population Alone," in Donald J. Mulvihill, Melvin M. Tumin, and Lynn A. Curtis, eds., *Crimes of Violence,* Staff Report to the National Commission on the Causes and Prevention of Violence, Vol. 11. Washington, D.C.: U.S. Government Printing Office, 1969, pp. 145–152.

FERRACUTI, FRANCO. "European Migration and Crime," in Marvin E. Wolfgang, ed., *Crime and Culture: Essays in Honor of Thorsten Sellin.* New York: Wiley, 1968, pp. 189–219.

_____, SIMON DINITZ, AND ESPERANZA ACOSTA DE BRENES. *Delinquents and Nondelinquents in the Puerto Rican Slum Culture.* Columbus, Ohio: Ohio State University Press, 1975.

FERRERO, GINA LOMBROSO. *Criminal Man according to the Classification of Cesare Lombroso.* New York: G. P. Putnam, 1911.

FERRI, ENRICO. "The Positive School of Criminology," in Stanley E. Grupp, ed., *Theories of Punishment.* Bloomington, Ind.: Indiana University Press, 1901, 1971, pp. 229–242.

FIGUEIRA-MCDONOUGH, JOSEFINA, AND ELAINE SELO. "A Reformulation of the 'Equal Opportunity' Explanation of Female Delinquency," *Crime and Delinquency* 26 (July 1980), 333–343.

FINCKENAUER, JAMES O. "Scared Crooked," *Psychology Today* 13 (August 1979), 6, 10–11.

_____. *Scared Straight! and the Panacea Phenomenon.* Englewood Cliffs, N.J.: Prentice-Hall, 1982.

FINESTONE, HAROLD. "Cats, Kicks and Color," in Howard S. Becker, ed., *The Other Side: Perspectives on Deviance.* New York: Free Press, 1964, pp. 281–297.

FISHER, JOSEPH C. "Homicide in Detroit: The Role of Firearms," *Criminology* 14 (November 1976), 387–400.

FISHMAN, MARK. "Crime Waves as Ideology," *Social Problems* 25 (June 1978), 531–543.

FISSE, BRENT, AND JOHN BRAITHWAITE. *The Impact of Publicity on Corporate Offenders.* Albany, N.Y.: State University of New York Press, 1983.

FLEMING, MACKLIN. "The Law's Delay: The Dragon Slain Friday Breathes Fire Again Monday," *The Public Interest* No. 32 (Summer 1973), 13–33.

FLOUD, JEAN, AND WARREN YOUNG. *Dangerousness and Criminal Justice.* Totowa, N.J.: Barnes and Noble, 1981.

FOREMAN, JUDY. "How to Tell If You Are 'Muggable'," *The Boston Globe,* January 20, 1981, pp. 20, 21.

FOSTER, JACK D., SIMON DINITZ, AND WALTER C. RECKLESS. "Perceptions of Stigma Following Public Intervention for Delinquent Behavior," *Social Problems* 20 (Fall 1972), 202–209.

FOUCAULT, MICHEL. *Discipline and Punish,* trans. by Alan Sheridan. New York: Pantheon, 1978.

FOWLER, FLOYD J., JR., AND THOMAS W. MANGIONE. *Neighborhood Crime, Fear and Social Control: A Second Look at the Hartford Program.* Washington, D.C.: National Institute of Justice, U.S. Department of Justice, 1982.

FOWLER, GLENN. "More 'Career Criminals' Convicted in State Effort," *The New York Times,* January 8, 1981, p. B7.

FOX, JAMES ALAN, ED. *Methods in Quantitative Criminology.* New York: Academic Press, 1981a.

_____. *Models in Quantitative Criminology.* New York: Academic Press, 1981b.

FRANKLIN, ALICE. "Criminality in the Work Place: A Comparison of Male and Female Offenders," in Freda Adler and Rita James Simon, eds., *The Criminology of Deviant Women.* Boston: Houghton Mifflin, 1979, pp. 167–170.

FRANKLIN, JAMES L. "The Churches and the Death Penalty," *The Boston Globe,* March 14, 1982, p. 30.

_____. "Why Bishops Are Trying to Halt Execution of Sullivan," *The Boston Globe,* November 30, 1983, p. 18.

FRAZIER, CHARLES E. *Theoretical Approaches to Deviance: An Evaluation.* Columbus, Ohio: Charles E. Merrill, 1976.

FREEDMAN, JONATHAN L. *Crowding and Behavior.* New York: Viking, 1975.

FREEDMAN, LAWRENCE ZELIC. "No Response to the Cry for Help," in James M. Ratcliffe, ed., *The Good Samaritan and the Law.* Garden City, N.Y.: Doubleday, 1966, pp. 171–182.

_____. "Presidential Assassins Strike out More at the Symbol Than the Man," *The Boston Globe*, April 5, 1981, p. A3.

FREEDMAN, RICHARD B. "Crime and Unemployment," in James Q. Wilson, ed., *Crime and Public Policy*. San Francisco: ICS Press, 1983, pp. 89–106.

FREUD, SIGMUND. *Civilization and Its Discontents*, trans. by James Strachey. New York: Norton, 1930, 1962.

_____. *New Introductory Lectures on Psycho-analysis*, ed. and trans. by James Strachey. New York: Norton, 1933.

FRIENDLY, JONATHAN. "Do TV's Lights Illuminate Justice," *The New York Times*, April 29, 1984, p. E22.

FURSTENBERG, FRANK F., JR. "Public Reaction to Crime in the Streets," *American Scholar* 40 (Autumn 1971), 601–610.

FYFE, JAMES J. "Observations on Police Deadly Force," *Crime and Delinquency* 27 (July 1981), 376–389.

GAGNON, JOHN H. "Sexual Conduct and Crime," in Daniel Glaser, ed., *Handbook of Criminology*. Chicago: Rand McNally, 1974, pp. 233–272.

GALAWAY, BURT. "The Use of Restitution," *Crime and Delinquency* 23 (January 1977), 57–67.

_____, AND JOE HUDSON, EDS. *Perspectives on Crime Victims*. St. Louis: C. V. Mosby, 1981.

GALLE, OMER R., WALTER R. GOVE, AND J. MILLER McPHERSON. "Population Density and Pathology: What Are the Relations for Man?," *Science* 176 (April 7, 1972), 23–30.

GALLUP, GEORGE. "Safety Fears Swelled Nixon Vote," *The Boston Globe*, November 11, 1972, p. 7.

GALVIN, JIM. "Introduction: Special Issue: Prisons and Sentencing Reform: Prison Policy Reform Ten Years Later," *Crime and Delinquency* 29 (October 1983), 495–503.

GANSBERG, MARTIN. "Jersey City's Corruption Spawns Fear That Makes People Reluctant to Talk," *The New York Times*, November 17, 1970, p. 27.

GARFINKEL, HAROLD. "Conditions of Successful Degradation Ceremonies," *American Journal of Sociology* 61 (March 1956), 420–424.

GARGAN, EDWARD A. "The Nation's Prisoners Join the Labor Force," *The New York Times*, August 28, 1983, pp. F6–F7.

GAROFALO, JAMES. "Crime and the Mass Media—A Selective Review of Research," *Journal of Research in Crime and Delinquency* 18 (July 1981), 319–350.

GARTNER, ALLAN, COLIN GREER, AND FRANK REISSMAN, EDS. *The New Assault on Equality*. New York: Harper & Row, 1973.

GASTIL, RAYMOND D. "Homicide and a Regional Culture of Violence," *American Sociological Review* 36 (June 1971), 412–427.

GEBHARD, PAUL H., ET AL. *Sex Offenders*. New York: Harper & Row, 1965.

GEIS, GILBERT. "Avocational Crime," in Daniel Glaser, ed., *Handbook of Criminology*. Chicago: Rand McNally, 1974, pp. 273–298.

_____. "The Crime Intervenor: Samaritan or Superman?" Lecture presented February 5, 1981 at University of California, Irvine.

_____. "White Collar Crime: The Heavy Electrical Equipment Antitrust Cases of 1961," in Marshall B. Clinard and Richard Quinney, eds., *Criminal Behavior Systems: A Typology*. New York: Holt, Rinehart and Winston, 1967, pp. 139–151.

GEIST, WILLIAM E. "Residents Give a Bronx Cheer to Decal Plan," *The New York Times*, November 12, 1983, pp. 1, 26.

GELFAND, DONNA M., ET AL. "Who Reports Shoplifters?," *Journal of Personality and Social Psychology* 25 (February 1973), 276–283.

GELLER, WILLIAM, AND KEVIN J. KARALES. "Shootings of and by Chicago Police: Uncommon Crises. Part I: Shootings by Chicago Police," *Journal of Criminal Law and Criminology* 72 (Winter 1981), 1813–1866.

GELLES, RICHARD J. "Domestic Criminal Violence," in Marvin E. Wolfgang and Neil Alan Weiner, eds., *Criminal Violence*. Beverly Hills, Calif.: Sage Publications, 1982, pp. 201–235.

GENDREAU, PAUL, AND BOB ROSS. "Effective Correctional Treatment: Bibliotherapy for Cynics," *Crime and Delinquency* 25 (October 1979), 463–489.

GEORGES-ABEYIE, DANIEL E., AND KEITH D. HARRIES, EDS. *Crime: A Spatial Perspective*. New York: Columbia University Press, 1980.

GERBNER, GEORGE, AND LARRY GROSS. "Living with Television: The Violence Profile," *Journal of Communication* 26 (Spring 1976), 173–199.

GERETY, PIERCE, JR. "A French Program to Reduce Pretrial Detention: Contrôle Judiciare," *Crime and Delinquency* 26 (January 1980), 22–34.

GIBBONS, DON C. "Crime and Punishment: A Study of Social Attitudes," *Social Forces* 47 (June 1969), 391–397.

_____. *Society, Crime, and Criminal Careers*, 4th ed. Englewood Cliffs, N.J.: Prentice-Hall, 1982.

GIBBS, JACK P. "Crime, Punishment, and Deterrence," *Social Science Quarterly* 48 (March 1968), 515–530.

_____. *Crime, Punishment, and Deterrence*. New York: Elsevier, 1975.

GIBBS, JOHN J., AND PEGGY L. SHELLY. "Life in the Fast Lane: A Retrospective View by Commercial Thieves," *Journal of Research in Crime and Delinquency* 19 (July 1982), 299–330.

GILBERT, SARI. "Tax Cheating a Way of Life for the Italian," *The Boston Globe*, April 19, 1984, p. 54.

GILLESPIE, ROBERT W. *Economic Factors in Crime and Delinquency: A Critical Review of the Empirical Evidence*. Washington, D.C.: National Institute of Law Enforcement and Criminal Justice, Department of Justice, 1975.

GILLIS, A. R., AND JOHN HAGAN. "Density, Delinquency, and Design: Formal and Informal Control and the Built Environment," *Criminology* 19 (February 1982), 514–529.

GIORDANO, PEGGY C. "Girls, Guys and Gangs: The Changing Social Context of Female Delinquency," *Journal of Criminal Law and Criminology* 69 (Spring 1978), 126–132.

GLASER, DANIEL. "The Classification of Offenses and Offenders," in Daniel Glaser, ed., *Handbook of Criminology*. Chicago: Rand McNally, 1974, pp. 45–83.

_____. *Crime in Our Changing Society*. New York: Holt, Rinehart and Winston, 1978.

_____. "Criminal Theories and Behavioral Images," *American Journal of Sociology* 61 (March 1956), 433–444.

_____. "A Review of Crime-Causation Theory and Its Application," in Norval Morris and Michael Tonry, eds., *Crime and Justice: An Annual Review of Research*, Vol. 1. Chicago: University of Chicago Press, 1979, pp. 203–237.

_____. *Social Deviance*. Chicago: Markham, 1971.

GLUECK, SHELDON, AND ELEANOR GLUECK. *Family Environment and Delinquency*. Boston: Houghton Mifflin, 1962.

_____, AND ELEANOR GLUECK. *Physique and Delinquency*. New York: Harper & Brothers, 1956.

_____, AND ELEANOR GLUECK. *Unraveling Juvenile Delinquency.* Cambridge, Mass.: Harvard University Press, 1950.

GOLD, MARTIN. *Delinquent Behavior in an American City.* Belmont, Calif.: Brooks/Cole, 1970.

GOLDKAMP, JOHN S. "Questioning the Practice of Pretrial Detention: Some Empirical Evidence from Philadelphia," *Journal of Criminal Law and Criminology* 74 (Winter 1983), 1556–1588.

GOLDMAN, NATHAN. *The Differential Selection of Juvenile Offenders for Court Appearance.* New York: National Council on Crime and Delinquency, 1963.

GOLDSTEIN, MICHAEL J., AND HAROLD S. KANT. *Pornography and Sexual Deviance.* Berkeley, Calif.: University of California Press, 1973.

GOLEMAN, DANIEL. "Violence against Women in Films," *The New York Times,* August 28, 1984, pp. C1, C5.

GOODE, ERICH. "The Criminology of Drugs and Drug Use," in Abraham S. Blumberg, ed., *Current Perspectives on Criminal Behavior: Original Essays on Criminology.* New York: Knopf, 1974, pp. 165–191.

GOODSTADT, MICHAEL S. "Legal Stigma for Marijuana Possession," *Criminology* 17 (August 1979), 208–216.

GOODSTEIN, LYNNE. "Psychological Effects of the Predictability of Prison Release: Implications for the Sentencing Debate," *Criminology* 18 (November 1980), 363–384.

GORA, JOANN GENNARO. *The New Female Criminal: Empirical Reality or Social Myth?* New York: Praeger, 1982.

GORANSON, RICHARD E. "A Review of Recent Literature on Psychological Effects of Media Portrayals of Violence," in Robert K. Baker and Sandra J. Ball, eds., *Mass Media and Violence.* Staff Report to the National Commission on the Causes and Prevention of Violence, Vol. 9. Washington, D.C.: U.S. Government Printing Office, 1969, pp. 395–413.

GORDON, DAVID M. "Capitalism, Class, and Crime in America," *Crime and Delinquency* 19 (April 1973), 163–186.

GORDON, ROBERT A. "Issues in the Ecological Study of Delinquency," *American Sociological Review* 32 (December 1967), 927–944.

GORING, CHARLES. *The English Convict: A Statistical Study.* London: His Majesty's Stationery Office, 1913.

GOTTFREDSON, DON M. "Probation and Parole: Release and Revocation," in Sanford H. Kadish, ed., *Encyclopedia of Crime and Justice,* Vol. 3. New York: Free Press, 1983, pp. 1247–1255.

GOTTFREDSON, MICHAEL R. "Parole Board Decision Making: A Study of Disparity Reduction and the Impact of Institutional Behavior," *Journal of Criminal Law and Criminology* 70 (Spring 1979a), 77–88.

_____. "Parole Guidelines and the Reduction of Sentencing Disparity: A Preliminary Study," *Journal of Research in Crime and Delinquency* 16 (July 1979b), 218–231.

_____. "Treatment Destruction Techniques," *Journal of Research in Crime and Delinquency* 16 (January 1979c), 39–54.

GOULD, LEROY, ET AL. *Crime as a Profession.* Washington, D.C.: U.S. Department of Justice, 1966.

GRASMICK, HAROLD G., AND DONALD E. GREEN. "Legal Punishment, Social Disapproval and Internalization as Inhibitors of Illegal Behavior," *Journal of Criminal Law and Criminology* 71 (Fall 1980), 325–335.

_____, AND STEVEN D. MCLAUGHLIN. "Comment: Deterrence and Social Control," *American Sociological Review* 43 (April 1978), 272–278.

GRAY, CHARLES M., ED. *The Costs of Crime.* Beverly Hills, Calif.: Sage Publications, 1979.

GRAY, SUSAN H. "Exposure to Pornography and Aggression toward Women: The Case of the Angry Male," *Social Problems* 29 (April 1982), 387–398.

GREEN, EDWARD. "Race, Social Status, and Criminal Arrest," *American Sociological Review* 35 (June 1970), 476–490.

GREEN, JEFFREY P. "How to Fend Off Computer Culprits," *The New York Times,* January 29, 1984, p. F3.

GREEN, PENNY A., AND H. DAVID ALLEN. "Severity of Societal Response to Crime: A Synthesis of Models," *Law and Society Review* 16 (1981–82), 181–205.

GREENBERG, DAVID F. "The Correctional Effects of Corrections: A Survey of Evaluations," in David F. Greenberg, ed., *Corrections and Punishment.* Beverly Hills, Calif.: Sage Publications, 1977a, pp. 111–148.

_____. "Delinquency and the Age Structure of Society," *Contemporary Crises* 1 (April 1977b), 189–223.

_____. "The Incapacitative Effect of Imprisonment: Some Estimates," *Law and Society Review* 9 (Summer 1975), 541–580.

_____. "Methodological Issues in Survey Research on the Inhibition of Crime," *Journal of Criminal Law and Criminology* 72 (Fall 1981), 1094–1101.

_____. "Penal Sanctions in Poland: A Test of Alternative Models," *Social Problems* 28 (December 1980), 194–204.

_____, AND DREW HUMPHRIES. "Economic Crisis and the Justice Model: A Skeptical View," *Crime and Delinquency* 28 (October 1982), 601–609.

_____, AND RONALD C. KESSLER. "The Effects of Arrests on Crime: A Multivariate Panel Analysis," *Social Problems* 60 (March 1982), 771–790.

_____, RONALD C. KESSLER, AND COLIN LOFTIN. "The Effects of Police Employment on Crime," *Criminology* 21 (August 1983), 375–394.

GREENBERG, JOEL. "Why Do Some People Turn away from Others in Trouble?," *The New York Times,* July 14, 1981, pp. C1, C3.

GREENBERG, STEPHANIE W. "Alcohol and Crime: A Methodological Critique of the Literature," in James J. Collins, Jr., ed., *Drinking and Crime: Perspectives on the Relationships between Alcohol Consumption and Criminal Behavior.* New York: Guilford Press, 1981, pp. 71–109.

_____, AND FREDA ADLER. "Crime and Addiction: An Empirical Analysis of the Literature, 1920–1973," *Contemporary Drug Problems* 3 (Summer 1974), 221–269.

GREENHOUSE, LINDA. "Justices, 5–4, Void Life Term As Too Long for Minor Crime," *The New York Times,* June 29, 1983, pp. A1, A23.

GREENWOOD, PETER W. "Career Criminal Prosecution: Potential Objectives," *Journal of Criminal Law and Criminology* 71 (Summer 1980), 85–88.

_____. "Controlling the Crime Rate through Imprisonment," in James Q. Wilson, ed., *Crime and Public Policy.* San Francisco: ICS Press, 1983, pp. 251–269.

_____. "Selective Incapacitation: A Method of Using Our Prisons More Effectively," *NIJ Reports,* January 1984, pp. 4–7.

_____, WITH ALLAN ABRAHAMSE. *Selective Incapacitation.* Santa Monica, Calif.: Rand, 1982.

GRILLO, E. G. *Delincuencia en Caracas.* Caracas, Venezuela: Universidad del Zulia, 1970.

GRINNELL, RICHARD M., JR., AND CHERYL A. CHAMBERS. "Broken Homes and Middle-Class Delinquency: A Comparison," *Criminology* 17 (November 1979), 395–400.

GROPPER, BERNARD A. "Probing the Links between Drugs and Crime," *NIJ Reports*, November 1984, pp. 4–8.

GROTH, A. NICHOLAS. *Men Who Rape: The Psychology of the Offender*. New York: Plenum Press, 1979.

_____, ROBERT E. LONGO, AND J. BRADLEY MCFADIN. "Undetected Recidivism among Rapists and Child Molesters," *Crime and Delinquency* 28 (July 1982), 450–458.

GRUTZNER, CHARLES. "How to Lock out the Mafia," *Harvard Business Review* 48 (March–April 1972), 45–58.

GURR, TED ROBERT. "Historical Trends in Violent Crime: A Critical Review of the Evidence," in Michael Tonry and Norval Morris, eds., *Crime and Justice: An Annual Review of Research*, Vol. 3. Chicago: University of Chicago, 1981, pp. 295–353.

_____. *Why Men Rebel*. Princeton, N.J.: Princeton University Press, 1970.

GUSFIELD, JOSEPH R. *Symbolic Crusade: Status Politics and the American Temperance Movement*. Urbana, Ill.: University of Illinois Press, 1963.

HABERMAN, CLYDE. "In Japan, A Crime Wave Is Measured in Drops," *The New York Times*, August 2, 1983, p. 2.

HACKNEY, SHELDON. "Southern Violence," in Hugh Davis Graham and Ted Robert Gurr, eds., *Violence in America: Historical and Comparative Perspectives*. Staff Report to the National Commission on the Causes and Prevention of Violence, Vol. 2. Washington, D.C.: U.S. Government Printing Office, 1969, pp. 387–404.

HAGAN, JOHN, ED. *Deterrence Reconsidered: Methodological Innovations*. Beverly Hills, Calif.: Sage Publications, 1982.

_____, AND KRISTEN BUMILLER. "Making Sense of Sentencing: A Review and Critique of Sentencing Research," in Alfred Blumstein et al., eds., *Research on Sentencing: The Search for Reform*, Vol. 2. Washington, D.C.: National Academy Press, 1983, pp. 1–54.

HAKIM, SIMON, AND GEORGE F. RENGERT, EDS. *Crime Spillover*. Beverly Hills, Calif.: Sage Publications, 1981a.

_____, AND GEORGE F. RENGERT. "Introduction," in Simon Hakim and George F. Rengert, eds., *Crime Spillover*. Beverly Hills, Calif.: Sage Publications, 1981b, pp. 7–19.

HALLECK, SEYMOUR L., AND ANN D. WITTE. "Is Rehabilitation Dead?" *Crime and Delinquency* 23 (October 1977), 372–382.

HAMILTON, V. LEE, AND LAURENCE ROTKIN. "Interpreting the Eighth Amendment: Perceived Seriousness of Crime and Severity of Punishment," in Hugo Adam Bedau and Chester M. Pierce, eds., *Capital Punishment in the United States*. New York: AMS Press, 1976, pp. 502–524.

_____, AND STEVE RYTINA. "Social Consensus on Norms of Justice: Should the Punishment Fit the Crime?" *American Journal of Sociology* 85 (March 1980), 1117–1144.

HANEY, CRAIG, CURTIS BANKS, AND PHILIP ZIMBARDO. "Interpersonal Dynamics in a Simulated Prison," *International Journal of Criminology and Penology* 1 (February 1973), 69–97.

HARMETZ, ALJEAN. " 'Jedi' Prints Stolen for Cassette Piracy, Movie Industry Says," *The New York Times*, July 9, 1983, pp. 1, 10.

HARRING, SIDNEY L. "Policing a Class Society: The Expansion of the Urban Police in the Late Nineteenth and Early Twentieth Centuries," in David F. Greenberg, ed., *Crime & Capitalism*. Palo Alto, Calif.: Mayfield, 1981, pp. 292–313.

_____. *Policing a Class Society: The Experience of American Cities, 1865–1915*. New Brunswick, N.J.: Rutgers University Press, 1983.

HARRIS, CHAUNCY D., AND EDWARD L. ULLMAN. "The Nature of Cities," *Annals of the American Academy of Political and Social Science* 242 (November 1945), 7–17.

HARTJEN, CLAYTON A., AND DON C. GIBBONS. "An Empirical Investigation of a Criminal Typology," *Sociology and Social Research* 54 (October 1969), 56–62.

_____, AND S. PRIYADARSINI. *Delinquency in India: A Comparative Analysis.* New Brunswick, N.J.: Rutgers University Press, 1983.

HAWKINS, GORDON. "God and the Mafia," *The Public Interest* No. 14 (Winter 1969), 24–51.

HEINZ, ANNE M., AND WAYNE A. KERSTETTER. "Pretrial Settlement Conference: Evaluation of a Reform in Plea Bargaining," in Burt Galaway and Joe Hudson, eds., *Perspectives on Crime Victims.* St. Louis: C. V. Mosby, 1981, pp. 266–276.

HEINZELMANN, FRED. "Crime Prevention and the Physical Environment," in Dan A. Lewis, ed., *Reactions to Crime.* Beverly Hills, Calif.: Sage Publications, 1981, pp. 87–101.

HELLMAN, DARYL A. *The Economics of Crime.* New York: St. Martin's Press, 1980.

HENNESSY, MICHAEL, PAMELA J. RICHARDS, AND RICHARD A. BERK. "Broken Homes and Middle Class Delinquency," *Criminology* 15 (February 1978), 505–528.

HENRY, ANDREW F., AND JAMES F. SHORT, JR. *Suicide and Homicide: Some Economic, Sociological, and Psychological Aspects of Aggression.* New York: Free Press, 1954.

HEPBURN, JOHN R. "The Impact of Police Intervention upon Juvenile Delinquents," *Criminology* 15 (August 1977), 225–262.

HERBERS, JOHN. "Fear of Crime Leads in Survey of Reasons to Leave Big Cities," *The New York Times*, May 16, 1981, p. 8.

HERBERT, DAVID T. *The Geography of Urban Crime.* New York: Longman, 1982.

HEYL, BARBARA. "Prostitution: An Extreme Case of Sex Stratification," in Freda Adler and Rita James Simon, eds., *The Criminology of Deviant Women.* Boston: Houghton Mifflin, 1979, pp. 196–210.

HILLS, STUART L. *Demystifying Social Deviance.* New York: McGraw-Hill, 1980.

HINDELANG, MICHAEL J. "Causes of Delinquency: A Partial Replication and Extension," *Social Problems* 20 (Spring 1973), 471–487.

_____. "Class and Crime," in Sanford H. Kadish, ed., *Encyclopedia of Crime and Justice*, Vol. 1. New York: Free Press, 1983, pp. 175–181.

_____. *Criminal Victimization in Eight American Cities: A Descriptive Analysis of Common Theft and Assault.* Cambridge, Mass.: Ballinger, 1976.

_____. "Race and Involvement in Common Law Personal Crimes," *American Sociological Review* 43 (February 1978), 93–109.

_____, MICHAEL R. GOTTFREDSON, AND JAMES GAROFALO. *Victims of Personal Crime: An Empirical Foundation for a Theory of Personal Victimization.* Cambridge, Mass.: Ballinger, 1978.

_____, TRAVIS HIRSCHI, AND JOSEPH G. WEIS. "Correlates of Delinquency: The Illusion of Discrepancy between Self-Report and Official Measures," *American Sociological Review* 44 (December 1979), 995–1014.

HIRSCHI, TRAVIS. *Causes of Delinquency.* Berkeley, Calif.: University of California Press, 1969.

_____. "Crime and the Family," in James Q. Wilson, ed., *Crime and Public Policy.* San Francisco: ICS Press, 1983, pp. 53–68.

_____, AND MICHAEL J. HINDELANG. "Intelligence and Delinquency: A Revisionist Review," *American Sociological Review* 42 (August 1977): 571–587.

_____, AND HANAN C. SELVIN. *Principles of Survey Analysis.* New York: Free Press, 1973.

HOCHSTEDLER, ELLEN. *Crime against the Elderly in 26 Cities.* Washington, D.C.: Department of Justice, Bureau of Justice Statistics, 1981.

HOFFMAN-BUSTAMANTE, DALE. "The Nature of Female Criminality," *Issues in Criminology* 8 (Fall 1973), 117–136.

HOLLIE, PAMELA G. "Apple Fights Counterfeits in Asia," *The New York Times,* August 11, 1982, pp. D1, D4.

HOLLINGER, RICHARD C., AND JOHN P. CLARK. "Deterrence in the Workplace: Perceived Certainty, Perceived Severity, and Employee Theft," *Social Forces* 62 (December 1983a), 398–418.

_____, AND JOHN P. CLARK. *Theft By Employees.* Lexington, Mass.: D. C. Heath, 1983b.

HOLTZMAN, ELIZABETH. "To Help Prosecute Child Molesters," *The New York Times,* March 28, 1984, p. A27.

HOLZMAN, HAROLD R. "Learning Disabilities and Juvenile Delinquency: Biological and Sociological Theories," in C. R. Jeffery, ed., *Biology and Crime.* Beverly Hills, Calif.: Sage Publications, 1979, pp. 77–86.

_____. "The Rationalistic Opportunity Perspective on Criminal Behavior: Toward a Reformulation of the Theoretical Basis for the Notion of Property Crime as Work," *Crime and Delinquency* 28 (April 1982), 233–246.

HOOTON, ERNEST A. *The American Criminal: An Anthropological Study.* Cambridge, Mass.: Harvard University Press, 1939.

HOOVER, J. EDGAR. *Crime in the United States, 1963: Uniform Crime Reports.* Washington, D.C.: U.S. Government Printing Office, 1964.

_____. *Crime in the United States, 1970: Uniform Crime Reports.* Washington, D.C.: U.S. Government Printing Office, 1971.

HOPKINS, ANDREW. "Controlling Corporate Deviance," *Criminology* 18 (August 1980), 198–214.

HORN, PATRICE, AND THE EDITORS OF *Psychology Today.* "Newsline," *Psychology Today* 7 (September 1973), 17.

HORNING, DONALD N. M. "Blue-Collar Theft: Conceptions of Property, Attitudes toward Pilfering, and Work Group Norms in a Modern Industrial Plant," in Erwin O. Smigel and H. Laurence Ross, eds., *Crimes against Bureaucracy.* New York: Van Nostrand Reinhold, 1970, pp. 46–64.

HOROWITZ, RUTH. *Honor and the American Dream: Culture and Social Identity in a Chicano Community.* New Brunswick, N.J.: Rutgers University Press, 1983.

_____, AND GARY SCHWARTZ. "Honor, Normative Ambiguity and Gang Violence," *American Sociological Review* 39 (April 1974), 238–251.

HOSPERS, JOHN. "Retribution: The Ethics of Punishment," in Randy E. Barnett and John Hagel, III, eds., *Assessing the Criminal: Restitution, Retribution, and the Legal Process.* Cambridge, Mass.: Ballinger, 1977, pp. 181–209.

HOWARD, JAN, AND PHILLIP BORGES. "Needle-Sharing in the Haight: Some Social and Psychological Functions," in David E. Smith and George R. Gay, eds., *"It's So Good, Don't Even Try It Once": Heroin in Perspective.* Englewood Cliffs, N.J.: Prentice-Hall, 1972, pp. 125–136.

HSU, MARLENE. "Cultural and Sexual Differences in the Judgment of Criminal Offenses: A Replication Study of the Measurement of Delinquency," *Journal of Criminal Law and Criminology* 64 (September 1973), 348–353.

HUMPHREYS, LAUD. *Tearoom Trade: Impersonal Sex in Public Places,* enlarged ed. Chicago: Aldine, 1975.

HUNT, LEON GIBSON, AND CARL D. CHAMBERS. *The Heroin Epidemics: A Study of Heroin Use in the U.S., 1965–75.* New York: Spectrum, 1976.

HUTCHISON, ROBERT A. *Vesco.* New York: Praeger, 1974.

HYLTON, JOHN H. "Rhetoric and Reality: A Critical Appraisal of Community Correctional Programs," *Crime and Delinquency* 28 (July 1982), 341–373.

HYMAN, HERBERT A. "The Value Systems of Different Classes," in Reinhard Bendix and Seymour Martin Lipset, eds., *Class, Status and Power: Social Stratification in Comparative Perspective*, 2nd ed. New York: Free Press, 1966, pp. 488–499.

IANNI, FRANCIS A. J. "New Mafia: Black, Hispanic and Italian Styles," in Francis A. J. Ianni and Elizabeth Reuss-Ianni, eds., *The Crime Society: Organized Crime and Corruption in America*. New York: New American Library, 1976, pp. 127–148.

——————, WITH ELIZABETH REUSS–IANNI. *A Family Business: Kinship and Social Control in Organized Crime*. New York: Russell Sage Foundation, 1972.

IGNATIEFF, MICHAEL. *A Just Measure of Pain: The Penitentiary in the Industrial Revolution, 1750–1850*. New York: Pantheon, 1978.

——————. "State, Civil Society, and Total Institutions: A Critique of Recent Social Histories of Punishment," in Michael Tonry and Norval Morris, eds., *Crime and Justice: An Annual Review of Research*, Vol. 3. Chicago: University of Chicago Press, 1981, pp. 153–192.

INCIARDI, JAMES A. *Careers in Crime*. Chicago: Rand McNally, 1975.

——————. "Heroin Use and Street Crime," *Crime and Delinquency* 25 (July 1979), 335–346.

——————. "Problems in the Measurement of Criminal Behavior," in Delos H. Kelly, ed., *Criminal Behavior: Readings in Criminology*. New York: St. Martin's Press, 1980a, pp. 59–68.

——————, ED. *Radical Criminology: The Coming Crises*. Beverly Hills, Calif.: Sage Publications, 1980b.

——————. "Women, Heroin, and Property Crime," in Susan K. Datesman and Frank R. Scarpitti, eds., *Women, Crime, and Justice*. New York: Oxford University Press, 1980c, pp. 214–222.

IRWIN, JOHN. "Adaptation to Being Corrected: Corrections from the Convict's Perspective," in Daniel Glaser, ed., *Handbook of Criminology*. Chicago: Rand McNally, 1974, pp. 971–993.

——————. *The Felon*. Englewood Cliffs, N.J.: Prentice-Hall, 1970.

——————. *Prisons in Turmoil*. Boston: Little, Brown, 1980.

JACKSON, BRUCE. *A Thief's Primer*. New York: Macmillan, 1969.

JACKSON, PAMELA IRVING, AND LEO CARROLL. "Race and the War on Crime: The Sociopolitical Determinants of Municipal Police Expenditures in 90 Non-Southern U.S. Cities," *American Sociological Review* 46 (June 1981), 290–305.

JACKSON, ROBERT L. "Tax Cheats Cost U.S. $80b Yearly, Unit Told," *The Boston Globe*, March 18, 1982, p. 8.

JACOB, HERBERT, AND MICHAEL J. RICH. "The Effects of the Police on Crime: A Rejoinder," *Law and Society Review* 16 (1981–82), 171–172.

JACOBS, JANE. *The Death and Life of Great American Cities*. N.Y.: Vintage, 1961.

JACOBY, SUSAN. "Hers: Arrests May Be the Best Deterrent to Family Violence," *The New York Times*, May 5, 1983, p. C2.

JAMES, JENNIFER. "Motivations for Entrance into Prostitution," in Laura Crites, ed., *The Female Offender*. Lexington, Mass.: D. C. Heath, 1976, pp. 177–205.

——————, AND WILLIAM THORNTON. "Women's Liberation and the Female Delinquent," *Journal of Research in Crime and Delinquency* 17 (July 1980), 230–244.

JAQUITH, SUSAN M. "Adolescent Marijuana Use: An Empirical Test of Differential Association Theory," *Criminology* 19 (August 1981), 271–280.

JARVIS, G. K., AND H. B. MESSINGER. "Social and Economic Correlates of Juvenile Delinquency Rates: A Canadian Case," *Canadian Journal of Criminology and Corrections* 16 (1974), 361–372.

JASPAN, NORMAN. *Mind Your Own Business.* Englewood Cliffs, N.J.: Prentice-Hall, 1974.

JEFFERY, C. R. "Biology and Crime: The New Neo-Lombrosians," in C. R. Jeffery, ed., *Biology and Crime.* Beverly Hills, Calif.: Sage Publications, 1979, pp. 7–18.

_____. *Crime Prevention through Environmental Design,* rev. ed. Beverly Hills, Calif.: Sage Publications, 1977.

JENKINS, RICHARD L. "Adaptive and Maladaptive Delinquency," *Nervous Child* 2 (October 1955), 9–11.

JENSEN, GARY F. "Inner Containment and Delinquency," *Journal of Criminal Law and Criminology* 64 (December 1973), 464–470.

_____. "Race, Achievement, and Delinquency: A Further Look at *Delinquency in a Birth Cohort,*" *American Journal of Sociology* 82 (September 1976), 379–387.

_____, AND DAVID BROWNFIELD. "Parents and Drugs: Specifying the Consequences of Attachment," *Criminology* 21 (November 1983), 543–554.

_____, AND MAYNARD L. ERICKSON. "The Religious Factor and Delinquency: Another Look at the Hellfire Hypotheses," in Robert Wuthnow, ed., *The Religious Dimension: New Directions in Quantitative Research.* New York: Academic Press, 1979, pp. 157–177.

JENSEN, MICHAEL C. "Business Students Disagree on Bribes," *The New York Times,* March 27, 1976, p. 37.

JOE, DELBERT, AND NORMAN ROBINSON. "Chinatown's Immigrant Gangs: The New Young Warrior Class," *Criminology* 18 (November 1980), 337–345.

JOHNSON, ELMER H., AND ISRAEL L. BARAK-GLANTZ. "Introduction," in Israel L. Barak-Glantz and Elmer H. Johnson, eds., *Comparative Criminology.* Beverly Hills, Calif.: Sage Publications, 1983, pp. 7–17.

JOHNSON, KIRK ALAN, AND PATRICIA L. WASIELEWSKI. "A Commentary on Victimization Research and the Importance of Meaning Structures," *Criminology* 20 (August 1982), 205–222.

JOHNSON, PERRY M. "A Prison Chief Says 'No' to Death Penalty," *The Boston Globe,* October 17, 1982, p. A7.

JOHNSON, RICHARD E. "Social Class and Delinquent Behavior: A New Test," *Criminology* 18 (May 1980), 86–93.

JOINT COMMISSION ON CORRECTIONAL MANPOWER AND TRAINING. *The Public Looks at Crime and Corrections.* Washington, D.C.: Joint Commission on Correctional Manpower and Training, 1968.

JOINT COMMITTEE ON NEW YORK DRUG LAW EVALUATION. *The Nation's Toughest Drug Law: Evaluating The New York Experience.* Washington, D.C.: U.S. Government Printing Office, 1978.

JONES, ALFRED WINSLOW. *Life, Liberty and Property.* New York: Octagon, 1941, 1964.

JOYCE, FAY S. "Courts Study Link between Victim's Race and Imposition of Death Penalty," *The New York Times,* January 5, 1984a, p. A18.

_____. "Some Victims' Families Find Relief in Executions," *The New York Times,* January 19, 1984b, p. A18.

JUDSON, HORACE FREELAND. *Heroin Addiction in Britain: What Americans Can*

Learn from the English Experience. New York: Harcourt Brace Jovanovich, 1974.

KAISER, GUENTHER. "The Comparative Method in Criminology," trans. by Sybille Jobin. *International Summaries.* Washington, D.C.: U.S. Department of Justice, National Institute of Justice, 1978.

KALVEN, HARRY, JR., AND HANS ZEISEL. *The American Jury.* Boston: Little, Brown, 1966.

KANDEL, DENISE B., AND ISRAEL ADLER. "Socialization into Marijuana Use among French Adolescents: A Cross-Cultural Comparison with the United States," *Journal of Health and Social Behavior* 23 (December 1982), 295–309.

KARACKI, LARRY, AND JACKSON TOBY. "The Uncommitted Adolescent: Candidate for Gang Socialization," *Sociological Inquiry* 32 (Spring 1962), 203–215.

KARAGIANIS, MARIA. "Rehabilitation Is Low on Walpole's List," *The Boston Globe,* July 23, 1978, pp. 29, 32.

KASSEBAUM, GENE, DAVID A. WARD, AND DANIEL M. WILNER. *Prison Treatment and Parole Survival: An Empirical Assessment.* New York: Wiley, 1971.

KATES, DON B., JR., ED. *Firearms and Violence: Issues of Public Policy.* Cambridge, Mass.: Ballinger, 1984.

KAUFMAN, IRVING R. "The Insanity Plea on Trial," *The New York Times Magazine,* August 8, 1982, pp. 16–20.

KELLEY, CLARENCE M. *Crime in the United States, 1975: Uniform Crime Reports.* Washington, D.C.: U.S. Government Printing Office, 1976.

KELLEY, THOMAS M. "Status Offenders Can Be Different: A Comparative Study of Delinquent Careers," *Crime and Delinquency* 29 (July 1983), 365–380.

KELLING, GEORGE L., ET AL. *The Kansas City Preventive Patrol Experiment.* Washington, D.C.: Police Foundation, 1974.

KELLY, CHARLES. "The Bolles Case: Where Does It Go from Here?" *The Boston Globe,* November 13, 1977, p. 48.

KESSLER, RONALD. "Heroin Deaths on the Increase," *The Boston Globe,* July 6, 1983, p. 10.

KIHSS, PETER. "Limited Heroin Use Is Urged by Expert," *The New York Times,* September 26, 1982, p. 36.

KING, HARRY, AND WILLIAM J. CHAMBLISS. *Harry King: A Professional Thief's Journey.* New York: Wiley, 1984.

KING, WAYNE. "Gang Strife on Rise among California Vietnamese," *The New York Times,* May 29, 1982, p. 6.

_____. "Houston Finds That Dramatizing Crime Does Pay," *The New York Times,* January 23, 1984, p. A8.

KITCHENER, HOWARD, ANNESLEY K. SCHMIDT, AND DANIEL GLASER. "How Persistent Is Post-Prison Success?" *Federal Probation* 41 (March 1977), 9–15.

KITSUSE, JOHN I., AND AARON V. CICOUREL. "A Note on the Use of Official Statistics," *Social Problems* 11 (Fall 1963), 131–138.

KITTRIE, NICHOLAS N. *The Right to Be Different: Deviance and Enforced Therapy.* Baltimore, Md.: Johns Hopkins University Press, 1971.

KLECK, GARY. "Racial Discrimination in Criminal Sentencing: A Critical Evaluation of the Evidence with Additional Evidence on the Death Penalty," *American Sociological Review* 46 (December 1981), 783–805.

KLEMKE, LLOYD W. "Does Apprehension for Shoplifting Amplify or Terminate Shoplifting Activity?" *Law and Society Review* 12 (Spring 1978), 391–403.

KLOCKARS, CARL B. *The Professional Fence.* New York: Free Press, 1974.

The Knapp Commission Report on Police Corruption. New York: George Braziller, 1972.

KNIGHT, MICHAEL. "Boston Study Finds Gun Law Is Working," *The New York Times,* June 18, 1979, p. D14.

KNORR, STEPHEN J. "Deterrence and the Death Penalty: A Temporal Cross-Sectional Approach," *Journal of Criminal Law and Criminology* 70 (Summer 1979), 235–254.

KOBRIN, SOLOMON. "The Conflict of Values in Delinquency Areas," *American Sociological Review* 16 (October 1951), 653–661.

KOHLMEIER, LOUIS M. "The Bribe Busters," *The New York Times Magazine,* September 26, 1976, pp. 47–60.

KRAJICK, KEVIN. "The Growing Crisis in Prison Crowding," *The Boston Globe,* June 13, 1982, p. A3.

KRAMER, RONALD C. "Corporate Crime: An Organizational Perspective," in Peter Wickman and Timothy Dailey, eds., *White-Collar and Economic Crime.* Lexington, Mass.: D. C. Heath, 1982, pp. 75–94.

KRANTZ, SHELDON. "Prisoners, Legal Rights Of," in Sanford H. Kadish, ed., *Encyclopedia of Crime and Justice,* Vol. 3. New York: Free Press, 1983, pp. 1190–1197.

KREBS, ALBIN. "Willie Sutton, 79, Dead; Notorious Bank Robber," *The New York Times,* November 19, 1980, p. A31.

KRISBERG, BARRY. *Crime and Privilege: Toward a New Criminology.* Englewood Cliffs, N.J.: Prentice-Hall, 1975.

KROHM, GREGORY. "The Pecuniary Incentives of Property Crime," in Simon Rotenberg, ed., *The Economics of Crime and Punishment.* Washington, D.C.: American Enterprise Institute for Public Policy Research, 1973, pp. 31–34.

KROHN, MARVIN D., ET AL. "Social Status and Deviance: Class Context of School, Social Status, and Delinquent Behavior," *Criminology* 18 (November 1980), 303–318.

——————, JAMES P. CURRY, AND SHIRLEY NELSON-KILGER. "Is Chivalry Dead? An Analysis of Changes in Police Dispositions of Males and Females," *Criminology* 21 (August 1983), 417–437.

KROST, JACK. "He Tries to Determine What Makes Criminals Tick," *The Boston Globe,* October 24, 1982, p. 8.

KRUTTSCHNITT, CANDACE. "Women, Crime, and Dependency: An Application of the Theory of Law," *Criminology* 19 (February 1982), 495–513.

KURTZ, HOWARD. "In Oakland, New Tactics Are Helping to Cut Crime," *The Boston Globe,* October 10, 1983, p. 20.

KVÅLSETH, TARALD O. "Seriousness of Offenses: An Experimental Study Based on a Psychological Scaling Technique," *Criminology* 18 (August 1980), 237–244.

LAB, STEVEN P. "Patterns in Juvenile Misbehavior," *Crime and Delinquency* 30 (April 1984), 293–308.

LAFREE, GARY D. "The Effect of Sexual Stratification by Race on Official Reactions to Rape," *American Sociological Review* 45 (October 1980), 842–854.

——————. "Official Reactions to Social Problems: Police Decisions in Sexual Assault Cases," *Social Problems* 28 (June 1981), 582–594.

LANDIS, DYLAN. "Insurance Fraud: Billions in Losses," *The New York Times,* July 6, 1982, pp. D1, D2.

LANE, ROBERT E. *The Regulation of Businessmen: Social Conditions of Government Economic Control.* New Haven, Conn.: Yale University Press, 1954.

LANE, ROGER. *Policing the City: Boston 1822–1885.* Cambridge, Mass.: Harvard University Press, 1967.

LANGAN, PATRICK A., AND DAVID P. FARRINGTON. "Two-Track or One-Track Justice? Some Evidence from an English Longitudinal Survey," *Journal of Criminal Law and Criminology* 74 (Summer 1983), 519–546.

LANGER, SIDNEY. *The Rahway State Prison Lifers' Group: A Critical Analysis.* New Jersey: Kean College Department of Sociology, October 1979.

LANGLEY, MICHAEL H. "The Juvenile Court: The Making of a Delinquent," *Law and Society Review* 7 (Winter 1972), 273–298.

LARSON, RICHARD C. "What Happened to Patrol Operations in Kansas City? A Review of the Kansas City Preventive Patrol Experiment," *Journal of Criminal Justice* 3 (Winter 1975), 267–297.

LATANÉ, BIBB, AND JOHN M. DARLEY. *The Unresponsive Bystander: Why Doesn't He Help?* New York: Appleton-Century-Crofts, 1970.

LAUDON, KENNETH. "A Risky Index of Crime," *The New York Times*, July 24, 1981, p. A27.

LAVRAKAS, PAUL J., AND ELICIA J. HERZ. "Citizen Participation in Neighborhood Crime Prevention," *Criminology* 20 (November 1982), 479–498.

LEBLANC, MARC, AND LOUISE BIRON. "Status Offenses: A Legal Term without Meaning: An Empirical Demonstration," *Journal of Research in Crime and Delinquency* 17 (January 1980), 114–125.

LEDERMAN, LEON M. "To Reduce Crime, Eliminate Cash," *The New York Times*, April 27, 1981, p. A23.

LEFKOWITZ, MONROE M., ET AL. *Growing up to Be Violent: A Longitudinal Study of the Development of Aggression.* New York: Pergamon, 1977.

LEJEUNE, ROBERT. "The Management of a Mugging," *Urban Life* 6 (July 1977), 123–148.

LEJINS, PETER P. "Uniform Crime Reports," *Michigan Law Review* 64 (April 1966), 1011–1030.

LELAND, TIMOTHY. "Alternatives to a Jail Sentence," *The Boston Globe*, November 17, 1982a, pp. 1, 24.

————. "Sentencing Philosophy Examined," *The Boston Globe*, November 17, 1982b, p. 24.

LEMERT, EDWIN M. *Instead of Court: Diversion in Juvenile Justice.* Washington, D.C.: U.S. Government Printing Office, 1971.

————. "Isolation and Closure Theory of Naive Check Forgery," *Journal of Criminal Law, Criminology and Police Science* 44 (September–October 1953), 293–307.

————. *Social Pathology.* New York: McGraw-Hill, 1951.

LEMOYNE, JAMES. "A Firmer Response to Family Strife," *The New York Times*, April 15, 1984, p. E7.

LEMPERT, RICHARD. "The Effect of Executions on Homicides: A New Look in an Old Light," *Crime and Delinquency* 29 (January 1983), 88–115.

————. "Organizing for Deterrence: Lessons from a Study of Child Support," *Law and Society Review* 16 (1981–82), 513–568.

LEONARD, EILEEN B. *Women, Crime, and Society: A Critique of Criminology Theory.* New York: Longman, 1982.

LEONARD, WILLIAM N., AND MARVIN GLENN WEBER. "Automakers and Dealers: A Study of Criminogenic Market Forces," *Law and Society Review* 4 (February 1970), 407–424.

LERMAN, PAUL. "Argot, Symbolic Deviance and Subcultural Delinquency," *American Sociological Review* 32 (April 1967), 209–224.

LETKEMANN, PETER. *Crime as Work.* Englewood Cliffs, N.J.: Prentice-Hall, 1973.

LEVEY, ROBERT. "Inmate Race Ratio Concerns Him," *The Boston Globe*, October 29, 1979, p. 2.

LEVI, MICHAEL. *The Phantom Capitalists—The Organization and Control of Long-Firm Fraud.* London: Heinemann, 1981.

LEVIN, JACK, AND JAMES ALAN FOX. *Mass Murder: America's Growing Menace.* New York: Plenum, 1985.

LEVINE, JAMES P. "Jury Toughness: The Impact of Conservatism on Criminal Court Verdicts," *Crime and Delinquency* 29 (January 1983), 71–87.

_____. "The Potential for Crime Overreporting in Criminal Victimization Surveys," *Criminology* 14 (November 1976), 307–330.

_____. "Reply to Singer," *Criminology* 16 (May 1978), 99–103.

LEWIS, C. S. "The Humanitarian Theory of Punishment," in Stanley E. Grupp, ed., *Theories of Punishment.* Bloomington, Ind.: Indiana University Press, 1971, pp. 301–308.

LEWIS, DAN A., ED. *Reactions to Crime.* Beverly Hills, Calif.: Sage Publications, 1981.

_____, AND MICHAEL G. MAXFIELD. "Fear in the Neighborhoods: An Investigation of the Impact of Crime," *Journal of Research in Crime and Delinquency* 17 (July 1980), 160–189.

_____, AND GRETA SALEM. "Community Crime Prevention: An Analysis of a Developing Strategy," *Crime and Delinquency* 27 (July 1981), 405–421.

LEWIS, ROY, AND ROSEMARY STEWART. *The Managers: A New Examination of the English, German and American Executive.* New York: New American Library, 1961.

LICHTER, LINDA S., AND S. ROBERT LICHTER. *Prime Time Crime: Criminals and Law Enforcers in TV Entertainment.* Washington, D.C.: Media Institute, 1983.

LIEBER, JAMES. "The American Prison: A Tinderbox," *The New York Times Magazine,* March 8, 1981, pp. 26–35, 56–61.

LIEBERT, ROBERT M., AND ROBERT A. BARON. "Some Immediate Effects of Televised Violence on Children's Behavior," *Developmental Psychology* 6 (1972), 469–475.

LIND, ANDREW W. "Some Ecological Patterns of Community Disorganization in Honolulu," *American Journal of Sociology* 36 (September 1930), 206–220.

LINDESMITH, ALFRED R. *Addiction and Opiates.* Chicago: Aldine, 1968.

_____. *Opiate Addiction.* Bloomington, Ind.: Principia Press, 1947.

_____. "Problems in the Social Psychology of Addiction," in Daniel M. Wilner and Gene C. Kassebaum, eds., *Narcotics.* New York: McGraw-Hill, 1965, pp. 118–139.

_____. "A Reply to McAuliffe and Gordon's 'A Test of Lindesmith's Theory of Addiction,'" *American Journal of Sociology* 81 (July 1975), 147–153.

_____. "A Sociological Theory of Drug Addiction," *American Journal of Sociology* 43 (January 1938), 593–613.

LINDSEY, ROBERT. "Cocaine Trafficking and Its Huge Profits Luring Middle Class," *The New York Times,* October 24, 1982, pp. 1, 26.

_____. "Fear of Crime Is Creating Tear Gas Boom on Coast," *The New York Times,* February 8, 1981, p. 24.

_____. "Officials Cite a Rise in Killers Who Roam U.S. for Victims," *The New York Times,* January 21, 1984a, pp. 1, 7.

_____. "Stopping Them before They Kill Again and Again and Again," *The New York Times,* April 22, 1984b, p. E4.

LIPTON, DOUGLAS, ROBERT MARTINSON, AND JUDITH WILKS. *The Effectiveness of Correctional Treatment: A Survey of Treatment Evaluation Studies.* N.Y.: Praeger, 1975.

LITTLE, CRAIG B., AND CHRISTOPHER P. SHEFFIELD. "Frontiers and Criminal Justice: English Private Prosecution Societies and American Vigilantism in the Eighteenth and Nineteenth Centuries," *American Sociological Review* 48 (December 1983), 796–808.

LIZOTTE, ALAN J., AND DAVID J. BORDUA. "Firearms Ownership for Sport and Protection: Two Divergent Models," *American Sociological Review* 45 (April 1980), 229–244.

LOFTIN, COLIN, MILTON HEUMANN, AND DAVID MCDOWALL. "Mandatory Sentencing and Firearms Violence: Evaluating an Alternative to Gun Control," *Law and Society Review* 17 (1983), 287–318.

―――――, AND ROBERT H. HILL. "Regional Subculture and Homicide: An Examination of the Gastil-Hackney Thesis," *American Sociological Review* 39 (October 1974), 714–724.

―――――, AND DAVID MCDOWALL. "The Deterrent Effects of the Florida Felony Firearm Law," *Journal of Criminal Law and Criminology* 75 (Spring 1984), 250–259.

―――――, AND DAVID MCDOWALL. " 'One with a Gun Gets You Two': Mandatory Sentencing and Firearms Violence in Detroit," *Annals of the American Academy of Political and Social Science* 455 (May 1981), 150–167.

―――――, AND DAVID MCDOWALL. "The Police, Crime, and Economic Theory: An Assessment," *American Sociological Review* 47 (June 1982), 393–401.

LOGAN, CHARLES H. "Arrest Rates and Deterrence," *Social Science Quarterly* 56 (December 1975), 376–389.

LOHR, STEVE. "Crackdown on Counterfeiting," *The New York Times*, May 7, 1984, p. 12.

LUBASCH, ARNOLD H. "Police Report Rise in Mob Infiltration of Businesses," *The New York Times*, July 17, 1983, p. 28.

LUCKENBILL, DAVID F. "Criminal Homicide as a Situated Transaction," *Social Problems* 25 (December 1977), 176–186.

―――――, AND JOEL BEST. "Careers in Deviance and Respectability: The Analogy's Limitations," *Social Problems* 29 (December 1981), 197–206.

LUNDMAN, RICHARD J. "Shoplifting and Police Referral: A Reexamination," *Journal of Criminal Law and Criminology* 69 (Fall 1978), 395–401.

LUNDQUIST, JOHN H., AND JANICE M. DUKE. "The Elderly Victim at Risk: Explaining the Fear-Victimization Paradox," *Criminology* 29 (May 1982), 115–126.

LUNDSGAARDE, HENRY P. *Murder in Space City: A Cultural Analysis of Houston Homicide Patterns.* New York: Oxford University Press, 1977.

LUPSHA, PETER A. "Individual Choice, Material Culture, and Organized Crime," *Criminology* 19 (May 1981), 3–24.

MACANDREW, CRAIG, AND ROBERT B. EDGERTON. *Drunken Comportment: A Social Explanation.* Chicago: Aldine, 1969.

MACCOBY, ELEANOR E., AND CAROL NAGY JACKLIN. "Sex Differences in Aggression: A Rejoinder and a Reprise," *Child Development* 51 (December 1980), 964–980.

―――――, JOSEPH P. JOHNSON, AND RUSSELL M. CHURCH. "Community Integration and the Social Control of Juvenile Delinquency," *Journal of Social Issues* 14 (June 1958), 38–51.

MAHONEY, ANNE RANKIN. "The Effect of Labeling upon Youths in the Juvenile Justice System: A Review of the Evidence," *Law and Society Review* 8 (Summer 1974), 583–614.

MAITLAND, LESLIE. "Arson Destroying New York Housing at a Record Rate," *The New York Times*, November 10, 1980, pp. A1, B4.

_____. "U.S. Tries New Tack in Drug Fight as Global Supply and Use Mount," *The New York Times,* January 30, 1983, pp. 1, 18.

MALTZ, MICHAEL D. "Crime Statistics: A Historical Perspective," *Crime and Delinquency* 23 (January 1977), 32–40.

MANN, DAVID W. "Age and Differential Predictability of Delinquent Behavior," *Social Forces* 60 (September 1981), 97–113.

MANN, JIM. "Locked Up, Let Out and Messed Up," *The Boston Globe,* November 18, 1980, p. 3.

MANNHEIM, HERMANN. *Comparative Criminology.* Boston: Houghton Mifflin, 1965.

MARGOLICK, DAVID. "Changes Endorsed on Insanity Pleas," *The New York Times,* February 10, 1983, p. A18.

_____. "Marital Rape Is Legal Issue in an Appeal," *The New York Times,* December 18, 1984, pp. B1, B2.

MARKHAM, JAMES M. "Soaring Urban Crime Troubling Spaniards," *The New York Times,* December 18, 1977, p. 16.

MARTIN, ROBERT G., JR., AND RAND D. CONGER. "A Comparison of Delinquency Trends: Japan and the United States," *Criminology* 18 (May 1980), 53–61.

MARTINSON, ROBERT. "New Findings, New Views: A Note of Caution Regarding Sentencing Reform," *Hofstra Law Review* 7 (Winter 1979), 243–258.

_____. "What Works?—Questions and Answers about Prison Reform," *The Public Interest* No. 35 (Spring 1974), 22–54.

MARX, GARY T., AND DANE ARCHER. "Citizen Involvement in the Law Enforcement Process: The Case of Community Police Patrols," *American Behavioral Scientist* 15 (September–October 1971), 52–72.

_____, AND DANE ARCHER. "Picking up the Gun: Some Organizational and Survey Data on Community Police Patrols." A paper presented at the Symposium on Studies of Public Experience, Knowledge and Opinion of Crime and Justice. Washington, D.C.: Bureau of Social Science Research, Inc., March 1972.

_____, AND DANE ARCHER. "The Urban Vigilante," *Psychology Today* 6 (January 1973), 45–50.

MATSUEDA, ROSS L. "Testing Control Theory and Differential Association: A Causal Modeling Approach," *American Sociological Review* 47 (August 1982), 489–504.

MATZA, DAVID. *Delinquency and Drift.* New York: Wiley, 1964.

_____, AND GRESHAM M. SYKES. "Juvenile Delinquency and Subterranean Values," *American Sociological Review* 26 (October 1961), 712–719.

MAURER, DAVID W. *The American Confidence Man.* Springfield, Ill.: Charles C. Thomas, 1974.

_____. *Whiz Mob: A Correlation of the Technical Argot of Pickpockets with Their Behavior Pattern.* New Haven, Conn.: College & University Press, 1955, 1964.

MAWBY, R. I. "Overcoming the Barriers of Privacy: Police Strategies against Nonvisible Crime," *Criminology* 18 (February 1981), 501–521.

MAYNARD, DOUGLAS W. "The Structure of Discourse in Misdemeanor Plea Bargaining," *Law and Society Review* 18 (1984), 75–104.

MAYO, PATRICIA ELTON. *The Making of a Criminal: A Comparative Study of Two Delinquency Areas.* London: Weidenfeld and Nicolson, 1969.

MCAULIFFE, WILLIAM E., AND ROBERT A. GORDON. "Issues in Testing Lindesmith's Theory," *American Journal of Sociology* 81 (July 1975), 154–163.

_____, AND ROBERT A. GORDON. "A Test of Lindesmith's Theory of Addiction: The Frequency of Euphoria among Long-Term Addicts," *American Journal of Sociology* 79 (January 1974), 795–840.

MCBRIDE, DUANE C., AND CLYDE B. MCCOY. "Crime and Drug-Using Behavior: An Areal Analysis," *Criminology* 19 (August 1981), 281–302.

McCaghy, Charles H. "Child Molesters: A Study of Their Careers as Deviants," in Marshall B. Clinard and Richard Quinney, eds., *Criminal Behavior Systems: A Typology*. New York: Holt, Rinehart and Winston, 1967, pp. 75–88.

——. *Deviant Behavior: Crime, Conflict, and Interest Groups*. New York: Macmillan, 1976.

——. "Drinking and Deviance Disavowal: The Case of Child Molesters," *Social Problems* 16 (Summer 1968), 43–49.

——, Peggy C. Giordano and Trudy Knicely Henson. "Auto Theft: Offender and Offense Characteristics," *Criminology* 15 (November 1977), 367–385.

McCain, Nina. "James Q. Wilson Talks about Crime and Punishment in the U.S.," *The Boston Globe*, August 11, 1984, p. 2.

McCarthy, John D., and Dean R. Hoge. "The Dynamics of Self-Esteem and Delinquency," *American Journal of Sociology* 90 (September 1984), 396–410.

McCleary, Richard, Barbara C. Nienstedt, and James M. Erven. "Uniform Crime Reports as Organizational Outcomes: Three Time Series Experiments," *Social Problems* 29 (April 1982), 361–372.

——, et al. "Effects of Legal Education and Work Experience on Perceptions of Crime Seriousness," *Social Problems* 28 (February 1981), 276–289.

McClintock, F. H., and Evelyn Gibson. *Robbery in London*. London: Macmillan & Co., Ltd., 1961.

McCord, Joan. "A Longitudinal Perspective on Patterns of Crime," *Criminology* 19 (August 1981), 211–218.

——. "Some Child-Rearing Antecedents of Criminal Behavior in Adult Men," *Journal of Personality and Social Psychology* 37 (1979), 1477–1486.

——. "A Thirty-Year Followup of Treatment Effects," *American Psychologist* 33 (March 1978), 284–289.

McCord, William. "Psychopathy," in Sanford H. Kadish, ed., *Encyclopedia of Crime and Justice*, Vol. 4. New York: Free Press, 1983, pp. 1315–1318.

——, and Joan McCord. *Origins of Crime: A New Evaluation of the Cambridge-Somerville Youth Study*. New York: Columbia University Press, 1959.

——, and Joan McCord. *The Psychopath: An Essay on the Criminal Mind*. Princeton, N.J.: D. Van Nostrand, 1964.

McDonald, Lynn. *Social Class and Delinquency*. Hamden, Conn.: Archon, 1969.

McFadden, Robert D. "Ruins in South Bronx to Get Make-Believe Lived-in Look," *The New York Times*, November 7, 1983, pp. A1, B5.

McFarland, Sam G. "Is Capital Punishment a Short-Term Deterrent to Homicide? A Study of the Effects of Four Recent American Executions," *Journal of Criminal Law and Criminology* 74 (Winter 1983), 1014–1032.

McGlothin, William H., M. Douglas Anglin, and Bruce D. Wilson. "Narcotic Addiction and Crime," *Criminology* 16 (November 1978), 293–315.

McGuire, William J., and Richard G. Sheehan. "Relationships between Crime Rates and Incarceration Rates: Further Analysis," *Journal of Research in Crime and Delinquency* 20 (January 1983), 73–85.

McIntosh, Mary. *The Organisation of Crime*. London: The Macmillan Press, Ltd., 1975.

McKay, Robert. "Riots: Prison Riots," in Sanford H. Kadish, ed., *Encyclopedia of Crime and Justice*, Vol. 4. New York: Free Press, 1983, pp. 1394–1398.

McLellan, Vin. "Computer 'Hacking' Crackdown," *The Boston Globe*, October 24, 1983, pp. 41, 43.

McNamara, Eileen. "Crime Victims Gain Rights in State Law," *The Boston Globe*, December 18, 1983, pp. 1, 21.

McNamara, John H. "Uncertainty in Police Work: The Relevance of Police Recruits'

Backgrounds and Training," in David J. Bordua, ed., *The Police: Six Sociological Essays*. New York: Wiley, 1967, pp. 163–252.

MCNAMARA, JOSEPH D. "Preface," in George L. Kelling et al., *The Kansas City Preventive Patrol Experiment*. Washington, D.C.: Police Foundation, 1974, pp. iii–iv.

MCPHETERS, LEE R. "Criminal Behavior and the Gains from Crime," *Criminology* 14 (May 1976), 137–152.

MCVISK, WILLIAM. "Toward a Rational Theory of Criminal Liability for the Corporate Executive," *Journal of Criminal Law and Criminology* 69 (Spring 1978), 75–91.

MEADOW, ARNOLD, ET AL. "Self-Concept, Negative Family Affect, and Delinquency: A Comparison across Mexican Social Classes," *Criminology* 19 (November 1981), 434–448.

MEDINNUS, GENE R. "Delinquents' Perceptions of Their Parents," *Journal of Consulting Psychology* 29 (December 1965), 592–593.

MEDNICK, SARNOFF A., AND JAN VOLAVKA. "Biology and Crime," in Norval Morris and Michael Tonry, eds., *Crime and Justice: An Annual Review of Research*, Vol. 2. Chicago: University of Chicago Press, 1980, pp. 85–158.

_____, ET AL. "Biology and Violence," in Marvin E. Wolfgang and Neil Alan Weiner, eds., *Criminal Violence*. Beverly Hills, Calif.: Sage Publications, 1982, pp. 21–80.

_____, ET AL. "EEG as a Predictor of Antisocial Behavior," *Criminology* 19 (August 1981), 219–229.

MEGARGEE, EDWIN I. "Psychological Determinants and Correlates of Criminal Violence," in Marvin E. Wolfgang and Neil Alan Weiner, eds., *Criminal Violence*. Beverly Hills, Calif.: Sage Publications, 1982, pp. 81–170.

MEISENHELDER, THOMAS. "An Exploratory Study of Exiting from Criminal Careers," *Criminology* 15 (November 1977), 319–334.

MEISLER, STANLEY. "The Mounties Went Forth," *The Boston Globe*, June 20, 1981, p. 3.

MENARD, SCOTT, AND BARBARA J. MORSE. "A Structuralist Critique of the IQ-Delinquency Hypothesis: Theory and Evidence," *American Journal of Sociology* 89 (May 1984), 1347–1378.

MERRY, SALLY ENGLE. *Urban Danger: Life in a Neighborhood of Strangers*. Philadelphia: Temple University Press, 1981.

MERTON, ROBERT K. "Social Structure and Anomie," in *Social Theory and Social Structure*, 1968 enlarged ed. New York: Free Press, 1968, pp. 185–214.

MESSNER, STEVEN F. "Poverty, Inequality, and the Urban Homicide Rate: Some Unexpected Findings," *Criminology* 20 (May 1982), 103–114.

_____. "Regional and Racial Effects on the Urban Homicide Rate: The Subculture of Violence Revisited," *American Journal of Sociology* 88 (March 1983a), 997–1007.

_____. "Regional Differences in the Economic Correlates of the Urban Homicide Rate: Some Evidence on the Importance of Cultural Context," *Criminology* 21 (November 1983b), 477–488.

MICHAELS, JULIE. "The Underground Angels," *The Boston Globe Magazine*, May 24, 1981, pp. 8–9, 19–28.

MICHAELS, MARGUERITE. "F.B.I.: What Does It Mean Today?", *Parade Magazine*, February 27, 1983, pp. 4–6.

MILAN, MICHAEL A., AND JOHN M. MCKEE. "Behavior Modification: Principles and Applications in Corrections," in Daniel Glaser, ed., *Handbook of Criminology*. Chicago: Rand McNally, 1974, pp. 745–776.

MILAVSKY, J. RONALD, ET AL. *Television and Aggression: A Panel Study.* New York: Academic Press, 1983.

MILGRAM, STANLEY. "The Experience of Living in Cities: A Psychological Analysis," *Science* 167 (March 13, 1970), 1461–1468.

——————, AND PAUL HOLLANDER. "The Murder They Heard," in Renatus Hartogs and Eric Artzt, eds., *Violence: Causes & Solutions.* New York: Dell, 1970, pp. 206–212.

MILLER, NORMAN C. *The Great Salad Oil Swindle.* New York: Coward-McCann, 1965.

MILLER, STUART J., SIMON DINITZ, AND JOHN P. CONRAD. *Careers of the Violent: The Dangerous Offender and Criminal Justice.* Lexington, Mass.: D. C. Heath, 1982.

MILLER, WALTER B. "American Youth Gangs: Past and Present," in Abraham S. Blumberg, ed., *Current Perspectives on Criminal Behavior: Original Essays in Criminology.* New York: Knopf, 1974, pp. 210–239.

——————. "Ideology and Criminal Justice Policy: Some Current Issues," *Journal of Criminal Law and Criminology* 64 (June 1973), 141–162.

——————. "Lower Class Culture as a Generating Milieu of Gang Delinquency," *Journal of Social Issues* 14 (No. 3, 1958), 5–19.

MILLS, C. WRIGHT. *The Power Elite.* N.Y.: Oxford University Press, 1956.

MINOR, W. WILLIAM. "Techniques of Neutralization: A Reconceptualization and Empirical Examination," *Journal of Research in Crime and Delinquency* 18 (July 1981), 295–318.

——————, AND MICHAEL COURLANDER. "The Postrelease Trauma Thesis: A Reconsideration of the Risk of Early Parole Failure," *Journal of Research in Crime and Delinquency* 16 (July 1979), 273–293.

——————, AND JOSEPH HARRY. "Deterrent and Experiential Effects in Perceptual Deterrence Research: A Replication and Extension," *Journal of Research in Crime and Delinquency* 19 (July 1982), 190–203.

MINSKY, TERRI. "The Odds on Being Slain—Worse for Young Black Males," *The Boston Globe,* February 23, 1984a, pp. 1, 47.

——————. "Shield Law: Gang-Rape Trials Spur Controversy," *The Boston Globe,* April 7, 1984b, pp. 1, 16.

MITFORD, JESSICA. *Kind & Usual Punishment: The Prison Business.* New York: Knopf, 1973.

MLADENKA, KENNETH R., AND KIM QUAILE HILL. "A Reexamination of the Etiology of Urban Crime," *Criminology* 13 (February 1976), 491–506.

MOELLER, H. G. "Community-Based Correctional Services," in Daniel Glaser, ed., *Handbook of Criminology.* Chicago: Rand McNally, 1974, pp. 895–907.

MOLOTSKY, IRVIN. "The Hidden Costs of the Cashless Society," *The New York Times,* March 4, 1984, p. E3.

MONK, JOHN. "Sentence Giving Rapists Choice of Castration Creates Controversy," *The Boston Globe,* December 11, 1983, p. 14–15.

MOORE, MARK H., ET AL. *Dangerous Offenders: The Elusive Target of Justice.* Cambridge, Mass.: Harvard University Press, 1984.

MORASH, MERRY. "Establishment of a Juvenile Police Record: The Influence of Individual and Peer Group Characteristics," *Criminology* 22 (February 1984), 97–111.

MORRIS, NORVAL. *Madness and the Criminal Law.* Chicago: University of Chicago Press, 1982.

——————. "Punishment, Desert, and Rehabilitation," in Hyman Gross and Andrew

Von Hirsch, eds., *Sentencing.* New York: Oxford University Press, 1981, pp. 257–271.

————, AND GORDON HAWKINS. *The Honest Politician's Guide to Crime Control.* Chicago: University of Chicago Press, 1970.

MURRAY, CHARLES A. "The Physical Environment and Community Control of Crime," in James Q. Wilson, ed., *Crime and Public Policy.* San Francisco: ICS Press, 1983, pp. 107–122.

————, AND LOUIS A. COX, JR. *Beyond Probation: Juvenile Corrections and the Chronic Delinquent.* Beverly Hills, Calif.: Sage Publications, 1979.

MUSON, HOWARD. "Teenage Violence and the Telly," *Psychology Today* 11 (March 1978), 50–54.

NAGEL, ILENE H., AND JOHN HAGAN. "Gender and Crime: Offense Patterns and Criminal Court Sanctions," in Michael Tonry and Norval Morris, eds., *Crime and Justice: An Annual Review of Research,* Vol. 4. Chicago: University of Chicago, 1983, pp. 91–144.

NAGIN, DANIEL. "Crime Rates, Sanction Levels, and Constraints on Prison Population," *Law and Society Review* 12 (Spring 1978), 341–366.

NATIONAL ADVISORY COMMISSION ON CRIMINAL JUSTICE STANDARDS AND GOALS. *A National Strategy to Reduce Crime.* Washington, D.C.: U.S. Government Printing Office, 1973.

NATIONAL CENTER FOR HEALTH STATISTICS, U.S. DEPARTMENT OF HEALTH AND HUMAN SERVICES. *Monthly Vital Statistics Report: Provisional Statistics, Annual Summary for the United States, 1983.* Washington, D.C.: U.S. Department of Health and Human Services, 1984.

NELSON, BRYCE. "Children Who Kill: Personality Patterns Are Identified," *The New York Times,* October 11, 1983a, pp. C1, C8.

————. "Psychologists Determine Best Ways to Talk to Assailants," *The New York Times,* August 16, 1983b, pp. C1, C11.

NELSON, JAMES F. "Multiple Victimization in American Cities: A Statistical Analysis of Rare Events," *American Journal of Sociology* 85 (January 1980), 870–891.

NESSON, CHARLES. "A Needed Verdict: Guilty but Insane," *The New York Times,* July 1, 1982, p. A19.

NETTLER, GWYNN. "Embezzlement without Problems," *British Journal of Criminology* 14 (January 1974), 70–77.

————. *Explaining Crime,* 2nd ed. New York: McGraw-Hill, 1978.

————. *Explaining Crime,* 3rd ed. New York: McGraw-Hill, 1984.

————. *Lying, Cheating, Stealing.* Cincinnati, Ohio: Anderson, 1982.

NEUBAUER, DAVID W. *Criminal Justice in Middle America.* Morristown, N.J.: General Learning Press, 1974.

NEVARES-MUNIZ, DORA. "The Eighth Amendment Revisited: A Model of Weighted Punishments," *Journal of Criminal Law and Criminology* 75 (Spring 1984), 272–289.

[*The New York Times*]. "Abolition of the Insanity Defense Is Backed by Medical Association," *The New York Times,* December 7, 1983, p. B8.

————. "Adults Charged with Training Youths to Rob," *The New York Times,* November 2, 1980, p. 63.

————. "Arrest May Be Deterrent in Domestic Violence, Study Shows," *The New York Times,* May 30, 1984, p. C4.

————. "Battling the Computer Pirates," *The New York Times,* January 5, 1983, pp. D1, D7.

_____. "British Clinics Are Struggling as Heroin Addiction Climbs," *The New York Times*, April 11, 1985, p. A15.

_____."British Legal Debate: Premenstrual Tension and Criminal Behavior," *The New York Times*, December 29, 1981, p. C3.

_____. "Coast Survey of Students Links Rise in TV Use to Poorer Grades," *The New York Times*, November 9, 1980, p. 66.

_____. "Controls on Guns Supported in Poll," *The New York Times*, June 20, 1983, p. A16.

_____. "Crime Panels Reassessed as U.S. Unit Nears End," *The New York Times*, April 12, 1982, p. B7.

_____. "Crime 'Quite a Problem,' Peking Official Says," *The New York Times*, June 24, 1983, p. A5.

_____. " 'Crimes of Honor' Still the Pattern in Rural Greece," *The New York Times*, February 10, 1982, p. 22.

_____. "Cuban Refugee Crime Troubles Police across U.S.," *The New York Times*, March 31, 1985, p. 30.

_____. "Excerpts from President's Address on Program for Fighting Crime in U.S.," *The New York Times*, September 29, 1981, p. A18.

_____. "Fast-Rising Crime in Israel Tests Ingenuity of Police," *The New York Times*, November 22, 1980, p. 2.

_____. "Father Sentenced to Perform Public Service for Killing Son," *The New York Times*, May 12, 1984, p. 8.

_____. "Group Finds Gain in Rehabilitation," *The New York Times*, October 2, 1983, p. 30.

_____. "I.R.S. Once Used Embarrassment as Delinquents' Penalty in Idaho," *The New York Times*, November 24, 1980, p. A24.

_____. "Impact of Fight to Halt Drug Flow Called Negligible," January 9, 1983, p. 19.

_____. "Miami Beach to Use Cameras to Deter Crime," *The New York Times*, November 16, 1981, p. A17.

_____. "Morgenthau Says Data Link a Third of Crimes to the Career Criminal," *The New York Times*, April 9, 1981, p. B3.

_____. "Official Laxity Threatens Crime Fund in Tennessee," *The New York Times*, October 28, 1979, p. 53.

_____. "Panel Assails Justice-System Attitude on Minorities," *The New York Times*, October 18, 1980, p. 26.

_____. "Poll Says 72% of Americans Favor Death Penalty for Murder," *The New York Times*, February 3, 1985, p. 23.

_____. "Private Security Patrols on Rise in City's Middle-Class Areas," *The New York Times*, September 18, 1983, p. 50.

_____. "Professionals Blamed for Vehicle Theft Rise," *The New York Times*, November 26, 1984, p. A13.

_____. "Round-the-Clock Private Vaults Grow with the Crime Rate," *The New York Times*, May 2, 1982, p. 39.

_____. "The 7-Elevens' Battle to Curb Crime," *The New York Times*, May 7, 1982, p. D4.

_____. "Sharp Rise in Rustling Hurts Bee Industry on Coast," *The New York Times*, August 22, 1982, p. 23.

_____. "Shooting of a 'Prowler' Shocks Prosperous Suburb of Capital," *The New York Times*, October 18, 1970, p. 74.

_____. "Study Cites Lack of Programs for Retarded Inmates in U.S.," *The New York Times*, June 14, 1982, p. A17.

_____. "Study Says Hedges May Stop Burglars," *The New York Times*, November 17, 1983, p. C11.

_____. "Study Stresses Link between Heroin Dependence and Incidence of Crime," *The New York Times*, March 22, 1981, p. 22.

_____. "That Costly White-Collar Mob," *The New York Times*, January 2, 1977, Section 3, p. 15.

_____. "2 Found Guilty in '76 Bomb Killing of Phoenix Investigative Reporter," *The New York Times*, November 7, 1977, pp. 1, 21.

_____. "U.S. Studies Trials of Juveniles," *The New York Times*, December 6, 1982, p. B8.

_____. "Youth Arrested in Teacher's Killing," *The New York Times*, May 19, 1978, p. A12.

NEWMAN, GRAEME. *Comparative Deviance: Perception and Law in Six Cultures.* New York: Elsevier, 1976.

_____. *The Punishment Response.* Philadelphia: Lippincott, 1978.

NEWMAN, OSCAR. *Architectural Design for Crime Prevention.* Washington, D.C.: U.S. Government Printing Office, 1973.

_____. *Defensible Space: Crime Prevention through Urban Design.* New York: Macmillan, 1972.

[*Newsweek*]. "Justice: The Woman's Touch," *Newsweek*, January 6, 1975, p. 35.

NIXON, RICHARD M. *RN: The Memoirs of Richard Nixon.* New York: Grosset and Dunlap, 1978.

NORMANDEAU, ANDRÉ. *Trends and Patterns in Crimes of Robbery*, Ph.D. dissertation. Philadelphia: University of Pennsylvania, 1968.

NYE, F. IVAN. *Family Relationships and Delinquent Behavior.* Westport, Conn.: Greenwood Press, 1958.

_____, JAMES F. SHORT, JR., AND VIRGIL L. OLSON. "Socioeconomic Status and Delinquent Behavior," *American Journal of Sociology* 63 (January 1958), 381–389.

O'CONNOR, JAMES F., AND ALAN LIZOTTE. "The 'Southern Subculture of Violence' Thesis and Patterns of Gun Ownership," *Social Problems* 25 (April 1978), 420–429.

OFFICE OF YOUTH DEVELOPMENT. *Juvenile Court Statistics, 1972.* Washington, D.C.: U.S. Department of Health, Education, and Welfare, 1974.

OPPENHEIM, CAROL. "Breaking a Deadly Family Tradition: Los Angeles Wages War on Street Gangs," *The Boston Globe*, April 18, 1983, p. 3.

OPPENLANDER, NAN. "Coping or Copping out: Police Service Delivery in Domestic Disputes," *Criminology* 20 (November 1982), 449–465.

ORESKES, MICHAEL. "Witness Says Crime Figures Rule Disposal of Toxic Waste," *The New York Times*, September 20, 1984, p. B10.

ORSAGH, THOMAS, AND ANN DRYDEN WITTE. "Economic Status and Crime: Implications for Offender Rehabilitation," *Journal of Criminal Law and Criminology* 72 (Fall 1981), 1055–1071.

OSBUN, LEE ANN, AND PETER A. RODE. "Prosecuting Juveniles as Adults: The Quest for 'Objective' Decisions," *Criminology* 22 (May 1984), 187–202.

PACE, DENNIE F., AND JIMMIE C. STYLES. *Organized Crime—Concepts and Controls*, 2nd ed. Englewood Cliffs, N.J.: Prentice-Hall, 1983.

PACE, ERIC. "Crime's Lingering Allure," *The New York Times*, June 6, 1982, p. F9.

PALMER, TED. "Martinson Revisited," *Journal of Research in Crime and Delinquency* 12 (July 1975), 133–152.

PARISI, NICOLETTE. "Are Females Treated Differently? A Review of the Theories and Evidence on Sentencing and Parole Decisions," in Nicole Hahn Rafter and Elizabeth Anne Stanko, eds., *Judge, Lawyer, Victim, Thief: Women, Gender Roles, and Criminal Justice*. Boston: Northeastern University Press, 1982, pp. 205–220.

_____. "A Taste of the Bars?" *Journal of Criminal Law and Criminology* 72 (Fall 1981), 1109–1123.

PARKER, DONN B. *Crime By Computer*. New York: Scribner's, 1976.

_____. *Fighting Computer Crime*. New York: Scribner's, 1983.

PATE, TONY, GEORGE L. KELLING, AND CHARLES BROWN. "A Response to 'What Happened to Patrol Operations in Kansas City?'" *Journal of Criminal Justice* 3 (Winter 1975), 299–320.

PATERNOSTER, RAYMOND. "Race of Victim and Location of Crime: The Decision to Seek the Death Penalty in South Carolina," *Journal of Criminal Law and Criminology* 74 (Winter 1983), 754–785.

_____, ET AL. "Perceived Risk and Social Control: Do Sanctions Really Deter?," *Law and Society Review* 17 (1983), 457–479.

PATTERSON, G. R. "Children Who Steal," in Travis Hirschi and Michael Gottfredson, eds., *Understanding Crime: Current Theory and Research*. Beverly Hills, Calif.: Sage Publications, 1980, pp. 73–90.

PEAR, ROBERT. "Anticrime Agency Is U.S. Budget Victim," *The New York Times*, October 12, 1980, p. 26.

PEPINSKY, HAROLD E. *Crime Control Strategies: An Introduction to the Study of Crime*. New York: Oxford University Press, 1980.

PERRY, JOSEPH B., JR., AND ERDWIN H. PFUHL, JR. "Adjustment of Children in 'Solo' and 'Remarriage' Homes," *Marriage and Family Living* 25 (May 1963), 221–223.

PETERSILIA, JOAN. "Criminal Career Research: A Review of Recent Evidence," in Norval Morris and Michael Tonry, eds., *Crime and Justice: An Annual Review of Research*, Vol. 2. Chicago: University of Chicago Press, 1980, pp. 321–379.

_____. *Racial Disparities in the Criminal Justice System*. Santa Monica, Calif.: Rand, 1983.

_____, PETER W. GREENWOOD, AND MARVIN LAVIN. *Criminal Careers of Habitual Felons*. Santa Monica, Calif.: Rand, 1977.

PETERSON, IVER. "Gold and Silver Prices Cause Rash of Thefts throughout Country," *The New York Times*, February 1, 1980, p. A1, A10.

PETERSON, MARK A., AND HARRIET BRAIKER, WITH SUZANNE M. POLICH. *Who Commits Crimes: A Survey of Prison Inmates*. Boston: Oelgeschlager, Gunn & Hain, 1981.

PETERSON, RUTH D., AND JOHN HAGAN. "Changing Conceptions of Race: Towards an Account of Anomalous Findings of Sentencing Research," *American Sociological Review* 49 (February 1984), 56–70.

PETTIGREW, THOMAS F., AND ROSALIND B. SPIER. "The Ecological Structure of Negro Homicide," *American Journal of Sociology* 67 (May 1962), 621–629.

PFUHL, ERDWIN H., JR. "Police Strikes and Conventional Crime: A Look at the Data," *Criminology* 21 (November 1983), 489–503.

PHILLIPS, DAVID P. "The Deterrent Effect of Capital Punishment: New Evidence on an Old Controversy," *American Journal of Sociology* 86 (July 1980), 139–148.

—————. "The Impact of Mass Media Violence on U.S. Homicides," *American Sociological Review* 48 (August 1983), 560–568.

—————, AND JOHN E. HENSLEY. "When Violence Is Rewarded or Punished: The Impact of Mass Media Stories on Homicide," *Journal of Communication* 34 (Summer 1984), 101–116.

PHILLIPS, JOEL, AND CHARLSEY CARTWRIGHT. "The California Career Criminal Prosecution Program One Year Later," *Journal of Criminal Law and Criminology* 71 (Summer 1980), 107–112.

PHILLIPS, LLAD, AND HAROLD L. VOTEY, JR. "An Economic Analysis of the Deterrent Effect of Law Enforcement on Criminal Activity," *Journal of Criminal Law, Criminology and Police Science* 63 (September 1972), 330–342.

—————, AND HAROLD L. VOTEY, JR. *The Economics of Crime Control.* Beverly Hills, Calif.: Sage Publications, 1981.

PHILLIPS, PHILLIP D. "Characteristics and Typology of the Journey to Crime," in Daniel E. Georges-Abeyie and Keith D. Harries, eds., *Crime: A Spatial Perspective.* New York: Columbia University Press, 1980, pp. 167–180.

PIERCE, GLENN, AND WILLIAM J. BOWERS. "The Bartley-Fox Gun Law's Short-Term Impact on Crime in Boston," *Annals of the American Academy of Political and Social Science* 455 (May 1981), 120–137.

PILIAVIN, IRVING, AND SCOTT BRIAR. "Police Encounters with Juveniles," *American Journal of Sociology* 70 (September 1964), 206–214.

PINES, MAYA. "Violence Termed Hard to Foretell," *The New York Times,* June 27, 1982, p. 25.

PITTMAN, DAVID J. "Drugs, Addiction, and Crime," in Daniel Glaser, ed., *Handbook of Criminology.* Chicago: Rand McNally, 1974, pp. 209–232.

PLATT, ANTHONY M. *The Child Savers: The Invention of Delinquency,* 2nd ed. Chicago: University of Chicago Press, 1977.

—————. "Prospects for a Radical Criminology in the USA," in Ian Taylor, Paul Walton, and Jock Young, eds., *Critical Criminology.* London: Routledge and Kegan Paul, 1975, pp. 95–112.

—————, AND PAUL TAKAGI, EDS. *Crime and Social Justice.* London: The Macmillan Press, Ltd., 1981.

PODOLEFSKY, AARON, AND FREDRIC DuBOW. *Strategies for Community Crime Prevention: Collective Responses to Crime in Urban America.* Springfield, Ill.: Charles C. Thomas Publisher, 1981.

POLK, KENNETH. "Delinquency and Adult Criminal Careers," in Delos H. Kelly, eds., *Criminal Behavior: Readings in Criminology.* New York: St. Martin's Press, 1980, pp. 143–150.

POLLOCK, VICKI, SARNOFF A. MEDNICK, AND WILLIAM F. GABRIELLI, JR. "Crime Causation: Biological Theories," in Sanford H. Kadish, ed., *Encyclopedia of Crime and Justice,* Vol. 1. New York: Free Press, 1983, pp. 308–315.

POOLE, ERIC D., AND ROBERT M. REGOLI. "Parental Support, Delinquent Friends, and Delinquency: A Test of Interaction Effects," *Journal of Criminal Law and Criminology* 70 (Summer 1979), 188–193.

—————, AND ROBERT M. REGOLI. "Race, Institutional Rule Breaking, and Disciplinary Response: A Study of Discretionary Decision Making in Prison," *Law and Society Review* 14 (Summer 1980), 931–946.

PORTERFIELD, AUSTIN L. *Youth in Trouble: Studies in Delinquency and Despair, with Plans for Prevention.* Fort Worth, Tex.: Leo Potishman Foundation, 1946.

POUND, ROSCOE. "The Future of Criminal Law," *Columbia Law Review* 21 (January 1921), 1–16.

POWERS, EDWIN, AND HELEN L. WITMER. *An Experiment in the Prevention of*

Delinquency: The Cambridge-Somerville Youth Study. New York: Columbia University Press, 1951.

PREBLE, EDWARD, AND JOHN J. CASEY, JR. "Taking Care of Business: The Heroin User's Life on the Street," in David E. Smith and George R. Gay, eds., *"It's So Good, Don't Even Try It Once": Heroin in Perspective.* Englewood Cliffs, N.J.: Prentice-Hall, 1972, pp. 97–118.

THE PRESIDENT'S COMMISSION ON LAW ENFORCEMENT AND ADMINISTRATION OF JUSTICE. *The Challenge of Crime in a Free Society.* Washington, D.C.: U.S. Government Printing Office, 1967a.

_____. *Crime and Its Impact—An Assessment.* Washington, D.C.: U.S. Government Printing Office, 1967b.

_____. *Organized Crime.* Washington, D.C.: U.S. Government Printing Office, 1967c.

THE PRESIDENT'S COMMISSION ON OBSCENITY AND PORNOGRAPHY. *Report.* Washington, D.C.: U.S. Government Printing Office, 1970.

PRUGH, JEFF. "In Atlanta, a Pall of Fear," *The Boston Globe,* February 14, 1981, p. 3.

PRUITT, CHARLES R., AND JAMES Q. WILSON. "A Longitudinal Study of the Effect of Race on Sentencing," *Law and Society Review* 17 (1983), 613–635.

QUINN, JANE BRYANT. "The Income-Tax Cheat May Be Finding It Easier," *The Boston Globe,* April 6, 1981, p. 19.

QUINNEY, RICHARD. *The Social Reality of Crime.* Boston: Little, Brown, 1970.

RAAB, SELWYN. "Asia Crime Groups Spreading in U.S., Smith Tells Panel," *The New York Times,* October 24, 1984a, pp. A1, B4.

_____. "Witness Asserts Ky Heads Vietnamese Gangs in U.S.," *The New York Times,* October 26, 1984b, p. B5.

RADELET, MICHAEL L. "Racial Characteristics and the Imposition of the Death Penalty," *American Sociological Review* 46 (December 1981), 918–927.

RADZINOWICZ, SIR LEON, AND JOAN KING. *The Growth of Crime: The International Experience.* New York: Basic Books, 1977.

RAINES, HOWELL. "Reagan Proposes Revision of Laws to Combat Crime," *The New York Times,* September 29, 1981, pp. A1, A19.

RANKIN, JOSEPH H. "The Family Context of Delinquency," *Social Problems* 30 (April 1983), 466–479.

RATCLIFFE, JAMES M., ED. *The Good Samaritan and the Law.* Garden City, N.Y.: Doubleday, 1966.

RAUSCH, SHARLA. "Court Processing versus Diversion of Status Offenders: A Test of Deterrence and Labeling Theories," *Journal of Research in Crime and Delinquency* 20 (January 1983), 39–54.

RAWLS, WENDELL, JR. "Fear Linked to Killings Rises among Atlanta Youths," *The New York Times,* March 22, 1981, p. 24.

_____. "Juvenile Justice Stirs New Debate," *The New York Times,* January 24, 1982a, p. 23.

_____. "Pennsylvania Shapes Prison Law to Cut Crime," *The New York Times,* July 8, 1982b, pp. A1, B10.

RECKLESS, WALTER C. "Containment Theory," in Barry Krisberg and James Austin, eds., *The Children of Ishmael: Critical Perspectives on Juvenile Justice.* Palo Alto, Calif.: Mayfield, 1978, pp. 187–193.

_____. *The Crime Problem,* 5th ed. New York: Appleton-Century-Crofts, 1973.

REED, JOHN P., AND ROBIN S. REED. " 'Doctor, Lawyer, Indian Chief': Old Rhymes and New on White Collar Crime," *International Journal of Criminology and Penology* 3 (August 1975), 279–293.

REED, JOHN SHELTON. "To Live—and Die—in Dixie: A Contribution to the Study of Southern Violence," *Political Science Quarterly* 86 (September 1971), 429–443.

REIMAN, JEFFREY H. "Marxist Explanations and Radical Misinterpretations: A Reply to Greenberg and Humphries," *Crime and Delinquency* 28 (October 1982), 610–617.

_____. *The Rich Get Richer and the Poor Get Prison: Ideology, Class, and Criminal Justice*, 2nd ed. New York: Wiley, 1984.

_____, AND SUE HEADLEE. "Marxism and Criminal Justice Policy," *Crime and Delinquency* 27 (January 1981), 24–47.

REINHOLD, ROBERT. "An 'Overwhelming' Violence—TV Tie," *The New York Times*, May 6, 1982a, p. C27.

_____. "Shortages Spur Illicit Traffic in Silicon Chips," *The New York Times*, March 11, 1984, pp. 1, 24.

_____. "Study Says Criminal Tendencies May Be Inherited," *The New York Times*, January 8, 1982b, p. B5.

REISS, ALBERT J., JR. "Foreword: Towards a Revitalization of Theory and Research on Victimization by Crime," *Journal of Criminal Law and Criminology* 72 (Summer 1981), 704–713.

_____. "Inappropriate Theories and Inadequate Methods as Policy Plagues: Self-Reported Delinquency and the Law," in N. J. Demerath, III, Otto Larsen, and Karl F. Schuessler, eds., *Social Policy and Sociology*. New York: Academic Press, 1975, pp. 211–222.

_____. *The Police and the Public*. New Haven, Conn.: Yale University Press, 1971.

_____. "Police Brutality—Answers to Key Questions," *Trans-Action* 5 (July/August 1968), 10–19.

_____, AND DAVID J. BORDUA. "Environment and Organization: A Perspective on the Police," in David J. Bordua, ed., *The Police: Six Sociological Essays*. New York: Wiley, 1968, pp. 25–55.

_____, AND ALBERT LEWIS RHODES. "The Distribution of Juvenile Delinquency in the Social Class Structure," *American Sociological Review* 26 (October 1961), 720–732.

REPPETTO, THOMAS A. *Residential Crime*. Cambridge, Mass.: Ballinger, 1974.

RETTIG, RICHARD P., MANUAL J. TORRES, AND GERALD R. GARRETT. *Manny: A Criminal-Addict's Story*. Boston: Houghton Mifflin, 1977.

REUSS-IANNI, ELIZABETH. *Two Cultures of Policing: Street Cops and Management Cops*. New Brunswick, N.J.: Transaction Books, 1983.

REUTER, PETER. *Disorganized Crime: The Economics of the Visible Hand*. Cambridge, Mass.: MIT Press, 1983.

_____, AND JONATHAN B. RUBINSTEIN. "Fact, Fancy, and Organized Crime," *The Public Interest* No. 53 (Fall 1978), 45–67.

RHODES, WILLIAM C. *Behavioral Threat and Community Response*. New York: Behavioral Publications, 1972.

RICHARDS, PAMELA. "Quantitative and Qualitative Sex Differences in Middle-Class Delinquency," *Criminology* 18 (February 1981), 453–470.

_____, RICHARD A. BERK, AND BRENDA FOSTER. *Crime as Play: Delinquency in a Middle Class Suburb*. Cambridge, Mass.: Ballinger, 1979.

RIDING, ALAN. "Brazilians Turn to Lynchings to Fight Soaring Crime Rate," *The New York Times*, April 15, 1984, pp. 1, 12.

_____. "Criminals in Mexico: How Many Are Policemen?" *The New York Times*, February 13, 1983, p. 12.

ROBBINS, WILLIAM. "Anticrime Patrols Grow in Number and Effect," *The New York Times*, August 30, 1982, pp. A1, A15.

_____. "Effectiveness of Guardian Angels Called Uncertain," *The New York Times*, August 7, 1981, p. A8.

ROBIN, GERALD D. "The Corporate and Judicial Disposition of Employee Thieves," in Erwin O. Smigel and H. Laurence Ross, eds., *Crimes against Bureaucracy*. New York: Van Nostrand Reinhold, 1970, pp. 119–142.

_____. "Patterns of Department Store Shoplifting," *Crime and Delinquency* 9 (April 1963), 163–172.

ROBISON, JAMES, AND GERALD SMITH. "The Effectiveness of Correctional Programs," *Crime and Delinquency* 17 (January 1971), 67–80.

ROGERS, JOSEPH W. *Why Are You Not a Criminal?* Englewood Cliffs, N.J.: Prentice-Hall, 1977.

ROHRLICH, TED. "Study Finds Racial Bias in Sentencing," *The Boston Globe*, July 5, 1983, p. 5.

ROJEK, DEAN G., AND MAYNARD L. ERICKSON. "Delinquent Careers: A Test of the Career Escalation Model," *Criminology* 20 (May 1982), 5–28.

_____, AND MAYNARD L. ERICKSON. "Reforming the Juvenile Justice System: The Diversion of Status Offenders," *Law and Society Review* 16 (1981–82), 241–264.

ROSE, BILL. "Bully Went Too Far for This Little Town," *The Boston Globe*, July 26, 1981, pp. 41, 42.

ROSENBAUM, MARSHA. *Women on Heroin*. New Brunswick, N.J.: Rutgers University Press, 1981.

_____. "Work and the Addicted Prostitute," in Nicole Hahn Rafter and Elizabeth Anne Stanko, eds., *Judge, Lawyer, Victim, Thief: Women, Gender Roles, and Criminal Justice*. Boston: Northeastern University Press, 1982, pp. 131–150.

ROSENQUIST, CARL M., AND EDWIN I. MEGARGEE. *Delinquency in Three Cultures*. Austin, Tex.: University of Texas Press, 1969.

ROSETT, ARTHUR, AND DONALD R. CRESSEY. *Justice by Consent: Plea Bargains in the American Courthouse*. Philadelphia: Lippincott, 1976.

ROSSI, PETER H., RICHARD A. BERK, AND KENNETH J. LENIHAN. *Money, Work, and Crime: Experimental Evidence*. New York: Academic Press, 1980.

_____, ET AL. "The Seriousness of Crimes: Normative Structure and Individual Differences," *American Sociological Review* 39 (April 1974), 224–237.

ROTH, JEFFREY A. "Prosecutor Perceptions of Crime Seriousness," *Journal of Criminal Law and Criminology* 69 (Summer 1978), 232–242.

ROTHENBERG, FRED. "Glued to the Tube: Americans Set Record for Hours in Front of the TV Set," *The Boston Globe*, January 25, 1984, pp. 1, 10.

ROTHMAN, DAVID J. *Conscience and Convenience: The Asylum and Its Alternatives in Progressive America*. Boston: Little, Brown, 1980.

_____. *The Discovery of the Asylum*. Boston: Little, Brown, 1971.

ROWE, DAVID C., AND D. WAYNE OSGOOD. "Heredity and Sociological Theories of Delinquency: A Reconsideration," *American Sociological Review* 49 (August 1984), 526–540.

RUBEL, ROBERT J. "Analysis and Critique of HEW's *Safe School Study Report to the Congress*," *Crime and Delinquency* 24 (July 1978), 257–265.

RUBENSTEIN, LEONARD S. "Against 'Guilty but Mentally Ill'," *The New York Times*, August 5, 1982, p. A19.

RUSSELL, DIANA E. H. *The Politics of Rape: The Victim's Perspective.* New York: Stein and Day, 1975.

_____. *Rape in Marriage.* New York: Macmillan, 1982.

RUSSELL, DONALD H., AND G. P. HARPER. "Who Are Our Assaultive Juveniles? A Study of 100 Cases," *Journal of Forensic Sciences* 18 (October 1973), 387–393.

SALAS, LUIS, AND WILLIAM WILBANKS. "Latin American Homicide Statistics: A Critique of Available Statistics." A paper presented at the American Society of Criminology Meeting. Washington, D.C., November 1981.

SALTZMAN, LINDA, ET AL. "Deterrent and Experiential Effects: The Problem of Casual Order in Perceptual Deterrence Research," *Journal of Research in Crime and Delinquency* 19 (July 1982), 172–189.

SAMENOW, STANTON E. *Inside the Criminal Mind.* New York: Times Books, 1984.

SAMPSON, ROBERT J. "Structural Density and Criminal Victimization," *Criminology* 21 (May 1983), 276–293.

SANDERS, WILLIAM B. *Detective Work.* New York: Free Press, 1977.

SANGER, DAVID E. "The Gavel Comes down on Computer Copycats," *The New York Times,* October 23, 1983, p. F8.

SAVITZ, LEONARD D. *Delinquency and Migration,* Ph.D. dissertation. Philadelphia: University of Pennsylvania, 1960.

SCHAFER, STEPHEN. *The Political Criminal: The Problem of Morality and Crime.* New York: Free Press, 1974.

_____. *The Victim and His Criminal: A Study in Functional Responsibility.* Englewood Cliffs, N.J.: Prentice-Hall, 1968.

SCHMEMANN, SERGE. "In Soviet, No Debates Rage around Capital Punishment," *The New York Times,* August 3, 1983, pp. A1, A4.

SCHMITT, ROBERT C. "Density, Delinquency and Crime in Honolulu," *Sociology and Social Research* 41 (March–April 1957), 274–276.

_____. "Density, Health, and Social Disorganization," *Journal of American Institute of Planners* 32 (1966), 38–40.

SCHNEIDER, ANNE L. "Victimization Surveys and Criminal Justice System Evaluation," in Wesley G. Skogan, ed., *Sample Surveys of the Victims of Crime.* Cambridge, Mass.: Ballinger, 1976, pp. 135–150.

_____, AND PETER R. SCHNEIDER. *Private and Public Minded Citizen Responses to a Neighborhood-Based Crime Prevention Strategy.* Eugene, Oreg.: Institute of Policy Analysis, 1978.

SCHRAG, CLARENCE. "Theoretical Foundations for a Social Science of Corrections," in Daniel Glaser, ed., *Handbook of Criminology.* Chicago: Rand McNally, 1974, pp. 705–743.

SCHRAGER, LAURA SHILL, AND JAMES F. SHORT, JR. "How Serious a Crime? Perceptions of Organizational and Common Crimes," in Gilbert Geis and Ezra Stotland, eds., *White-Collar Crime: Theory and Research.* Beverly Hills, Calif.: Sage Publications, 1980, pp. 14–31.

_____, AND JAMES F. SHORT, JR. "Toward a Sociology of Organizational Crime," *Social Problems* 25 (April 1978), 407–419.

SCHUESSLER, KARL F. "The Deterrent Influence of the Death Penalty," *Annals of the American Academy of Political and Social Science* 284 (November 1952), 54–62.

_____, AND DONALD R. CRESSEY. "Personality Characteristics of Criminals," *American Journal of Sociology* 55 (July–August 1953), 166–176.

SCHULTZ, LEROY G. "Why the Negro Carries Weapons," *Journal of Criminal Law, Criminology and Police Science* 53 (December 1962), 476–483.

SCHUR, EDWIN M. *Crimes without Victims: Deviant Behavior and Public Policy.* Englewood Cliffs, N.J.: Prentice-Hall, 1965.

_____. *Interpreting Deviance: A Sociological Introduction.* New York: Harper & Row, 1979.

_____. *Labeling Deviant Behavior: Its Sociological Implications.* New York: Harper & Row, 1971.

_____. *Narcotic Addiction in Britain & America.* London: Tavistock, 1962.

_____. *Our Criminal Society: The Social and Legal Sources of Crime in America.* Englewood Cliffs, N.J.: Prentice-Hall, 1969.

_____. *Radical Nonintervention: Rethinking the Delinquency Problem.* Englewood Cliffs, N.J.: Prentice-Hall, 1973.

SCHWARTZ, BARRY. "The Effect in Philadelphia of Pennsylvania's Increased Penalties for Rape," *Journal of Criminal Law, Criminology and Police Science* 59 (December 1968), 509–515.

SCHWARTZ, RICHARD D. "Law in the Kibbutz: A Response to Professor Shapiro," *Law and Society Review* 10 (Spring 1976), 439–442.

_____. "Social Factors in the Development of Legal Controls: A Case Study of Two Israeli Settlements," *Yale Law Journal* 63 (February 1954), 471–491.

_____, AND SONYA ORLEANS. "On Legal Sanctions," *University of Chicago Law Review* 34 (Winter 1967), 283–300.

_____, AND JEROME H. SKOLNICK. "Two Studies of Legal Stigma," *Social Problems* 10 (Fall 1962), 133–142.

SCHWENDINGER, HERMAN, AND JULIA SCHWENDINGER. "Defenders of Order or Guardians of Human Rights?" in Ian Taylor, Paul Walton, and Jock Young, eds., *Critical Criminology.* London: Routledge and Kegan Paul, 1975, pp. 113–146.

SCHWENDINGER, JULIA R., AND HERMAN SCHWENDINGER. *Rape and Inequality.* Beverly Hills, Calif.: Sage Publications, 1983.

SCIMECCA, JOSEPH A. "Labeling Theory and Personal Construct Theory: Toward the Measurement of Individual Variation," *Journal of Criminal Law and Criminology* 68 (December 1977), 652–659.

SCOTT, JOSEPH E., AND FAHAD AL-THAKEB. "The Public's Perceptions of Crime: Scandinavia, Western Europe, the Middle East, and the United States," in C. Ronald Huff, ed., *Contemporary Corrections: Social Control and Conflict.* Beverly Hills, Calif.: Sage Publications, 1977, pp. 77–88.

SEBBA, LESLIE. "Crime Seriousness and Criminal Intent," *Criminology* 30 (April 1984), 227–244.

_____. "Is Mens Rea a Component of Perceived Offense Seriousness?" *Journal of Criminal Law and Criminology* 71 (Summer 1980), 124–135.

SECHREST, LEE, SUSAN O. WHITE, AND ELIZABETH D. BROWN, EDS. *The Rehabilitation of Criminal Offenders: Problems and Prospects.* Washington, D.C.: National Academy of Sciences, 1979.

SEIDMAN, DAVID, AND MICHAEL COUZENS. "Getting the Crime Rate Down: Political Pressure and Crime Reporting," *Law and Society Review* 8 (Spring 1974), 457–493.

SEIDMAN, ROBERT B. "Witch Murder and *Mens Rea:* A Problem of Society under Radical Social Change," *Modern Law Review* 28 (January 1965), 46–61.

SEITZ, STEVEN THOMAS. "Firearms, Homicides, and Gun Control Effectiveness," *Law and Society Review* 6 (May 1972), 595–613.

SELLIN, THORSTEN. "The Basis of a Crime Index," *Journal of Criminal Law and Criminology* 22 (September 1931), 335–356.

_____, ED. *Capital Punishment.* New York: Harper & Row, 1967.

_____. *Culture Conflict and Crime.* New York: Social Science Research Council, 1938.

_____, AND MARVIN E. WOLFGANG. *The Measurement of Delinquency.* New York: Wiley, 1964.

SELZNICK, PHILIP. *Law, Society, and Industrial Justice.* New York: Russell Sage Foundation, 1969.

SERRILL, MICHAEL S. "A Cold New Look at the Criminal Mind," *Psychology Today* 11 (February 1978), 86–92, 106.

SHAH, SALEEM A., AND LOREN H. ROTH. "Biological and Psychophysiological Factors in Criminality," in Daniel Glaser, ed., *Handbook of Criminology.* Chicago: Rand McNally, 1974, pp. 101–173.

SHANLEY, FRED J. "Middle-Class Delinquency as a Social Problem," *Sociology and Social Research* 51 (January 1967), 185–198.

SHANNON, LYLE W. *Assessing the Relationship of Adult Criminal Careers to Juvenile Careers: A Summary.* Washington, D.C.: U.S. Government Printing Office, June 1982.

SHAW, CLIFFORD R., AND HENRY D. McKAY. *Juvenile Delinquency and Urban Areas,* rev. ed. Chicago: University of Chicago Press, 1942, 1969.

SHEARING, CLIFFORD D., AND PHILIP C. STENNING. "Private Security: Implications for Social Control," *Social Problems* 30 (June 1983), 493–506.

SHELDON, WILLIAM H. *Varieties of Delinquent Youth: An Introduction to Constitutional Psychiatry.* New York: Harper & Brothers, 1949.

SHELEFF, LEON SHASKOLSKY, AND DAVID SHICHOR. "Victimological Aspects of Bystander Involvement," *Crime and Delinquency* 26 (April 1980), 193–201.

SHELLEY, LOUISE I. *Crime and Modernization: The Impact of Industrialization and Urbanization on Crime.* Carbondale, Ill.: Southern Illinois University Press, 1981a.

_____. "Urbanization and Crime: The Soviet Case in Cross-Cultural Perspective," in Louise I. Shelley, ed., *Readings in Comparative Criminology.* Carbondale, Ill.: Southern Illinois University Press, 1981b, pp. 141–152.

SHENON, PHILIP. "One Price of High Bail: Overcrowded City Prisons," *The New York Times,* November 13, 1983, p. E6.

SHEPPARD, NATHANIEL, JR. "Atlanta Children Bloom in New Climate of Calm," *The New York Times,* April 10, 1982, p. 8.

_____. "Kentucky Bail Plan Cuts Defendants' Time in Jail," *The New York Times,* December 17, 1979, p. A22.

SHERMAN, LAWRENCE W., AND RICHARD A. BERK. "The Specific Deterrent Effects of Arrest for Domestic Assault," *American Sociological Review* 49 (April 1984), 261–272.

SHICHOR, DAVID, DAVID L. DECKER, AND ROBERT M. O'BRIEN. "Population Density and Criminal Victimization: Some Unexpected Findings in Central Cities," *Criminology* 17 (August 1979), 184–193.

SHILS, EDWARD. "The Sanctity of Life," *Encounter* 28 (January 1967), 39–49.

SHINNAR, SHLOMO, AND REUEL SHINNAR. "The Effects of the Criminal Justice System on the Control of Crime: A Quantitative Approach," *Law and Society Review* 9 (Summer 1975), 581–611.

SHIPLER, DAVID K. "Rising Youth Crime in Soviet Troubles Regime and Public," *The New York Times,* March 5, 1978a, pp. 1, 16.

_____. "Soviet Crime Problem Tied to City Life and Social Ills," *The New York Times,* March 6, 1978b, pp. A1, A10.

_____. "To Pistol-Packing Israelis, A Gun Is a Patriotic Badge," *The New York Times,* April 13, 1981, p. A2.

SHIPP, E. R. "99% of Felony Arrests in the City Fail to Bring Terms in State Prison," *The New York Times*, January 4, 1981, pp. 1, 28.

SHORT, JAMES F., JR. "Collective Behavior, Crime, and Delinquency," in Daniel Glaser, ed., *Handbook of Criminology*. Chicago: Rand McNally, 1974, pp. 403–449.

_____. "Introduction to the Revised Edition," Clifford R. Shaw and Henry D. McKay, *Juvenile Delinquency and Urban Areas*, rev. ed. Chicago: University of Chicago Press, 1942, 1969, pp. xxv–liv.

_____, AND F. IVAN NYE. "Extent of Unrecorded Juvenile Delinquency: Tentative Conclusions," *Journal of Criminal Law, Criminology and Police Science* 49 (December 1958), 296–302.

_____, AND F. IVAN NYE. "Reported Behavior as a Criterion of Deviant Behavior," *Social Problems* 5 (Winter 1957), 207–213.

_____, AND FRED L. STRODTBECK. *Group Process and Gang Delinquency*. Chicago: University of Chicago Press, 1965.

SHOVER, NEAL. "The Later Stages of Ordinary Property Offender Careers," *Social Problems* 31 (December 1983), 208–218.

_____. "The Social Organization of Burglary," *Social Problems* 20 (Spring 1973), 499–514.

SIBLEY, JOHN. "Student Says a Policeman Tried to Falsify Her Report of Holdup," *The New York Times*, November 23, 1972, pp. 1, 40.

SILBERMAN, CHARLES E. *Criminal Violence, Criminal Justice*. New York: Random House, 1978.

SILVER, ALLAN. "The Demand for Order in Civil Society: A Review of Some Themes in the History of Urban Crime, Police, and Riot," in David J. Bordua, ed., *The Police: Six Sociological Essays*. New York: Wiley, 1967, pp. 1–24.

SIMIS, KONSTANTIN M. *USSR: The Corrupt Society*. New York: Simon and Schuster, 1982.

SIMON, RITA JAMES. *The Jury and the Defense of Insanity*. Boston: Little, Brown, 1967.

SINCLAIR, UPTON. *The Jungle*. New York: New American Library, 1906, 1960.

SINGER, RICHARD. "In Favor of 'Presumptive Sentences' Set by a Sentencing Commission," *Crime and Delinquency* 24 (October 1978), 401–427.

SKOGAN, WESLEY G. "Citizen Reporting of Crime: Some National Panel Data," *Criminology* 13 (February 1976a), 535–549.

_____. "Crime and Crime Rates," in Wesley G. Skogan, ed., *Sample Surveys of the Victims of Crime*. Cambridge, Mass.: Ballinger, 1976b, pp. 105–119.

_____. "On Attitudes and Behaviors," in Dan A. Lewis, ed., *Reactions to Crime*. Beverly Hills, Calif.: Sage Publications, 1981, pp. 19–45.

_____. "Reporting Crimes to the Police: The Status of World Research," *Journal of Research in Crime and Delinquency* 21 (May 1984), 113–137.

_____, AND MICHAEL G. MAXFIELD. *Coping with Crime: Individual and Neighborhood Reactions*. Beverly Hills, Calif.: Sage Publications, 1981.

SKOLNICK, JEROME H. *Justice without Trial: Law Enforcement in Democratic Society*, 2nd ed. New York: Wiley, 1975.

SMIGEL, ERWIN O. "Public Attitudes toward Stealing as Related to the Size of the Victim Organization," *American Sociological Review* 21 (June 1956), 320–327.

_____, AND H. LAURENCE ROSS, "Introduction," in *Crimes against Bureaucracy*. New York: Van Nostrand Reinhold, 1970, pp. 1–14.

SMITH, ANSON. "Ripoffs without Violence: White Collar Crime Costlier than Armed Robberies," *The Boston Globe*, January 13, 1981, p. 40.

SMITH, DAVID E., AND GEORGE R. GAY, EDS. *"It's So Good, Don't Even Try It Once": Heroin in Perspective.* Englewood Cliffs, N.J.: Prentice-Hall, 1972.

SMITH, DOUGLAS A., AND JODY R. KLEIN. "Police Control of Interpersonal Disputes," *Social Problems* 31 (April 1984), 468–481.

—————, AND CHRISTY A. VISHER. "Street-Level Justice: Situational Determinants of Police Arrest Decisions," *Social Problems* 29 (December 1981), 167–177.

—————, CHRISTY A. VISHER, AND LAURA A. DAVIDSON. "Equity and Discretionary Justice: The Influence of Race on Police Arrest Decisions," *Journal of Criminal Law and Criminology* 75 (Spring 1984), 234–249.

SOMMER, JEFF. "Chinese Execute 5000 since Start of Crime Crackdown," *The Boston Globe,* November 24, 1983, p. A42.

SORIN, MARTIN D. "How to Make Bail Safer," *The Public Interest* No. 76 (Summer 1984), 102–110.

SOROKIN, PITIRIM A. "An Experimental Study of Efficiency of Work under Various Specified Conditions," *American Journal of Sociology* 35 (March 1930), 765–782.

SPARKS, RICHARD F. "Criminal Opportunities and Crime Rates," in Stephen E. Fienberg and Albert J. Reiss, Jr., eds., *Indicators of Crime and Criminal Justice: Quantitative Studies.* Washington, D.C.: Bureau of Justice Statistics, U.S. Department of Justice, 1980a, pp. 18–28.

—————. "A Critique of Marxist Criminology," in Norval Morris and Michael Tonry, eds., *Crime and Justice: An Annual Review of Research,* Vol. 2. Chicago: University of Chicago Press, 1980b, pp. 159–210.

—————. "Multiple Victimization: Evidence, Theory, and Future Research," *Journal of Criminal Law and Criminology* 72 (Summer 1981a), 762–778.

—————. *Research on Victims of Crime: Accomplishments, Issues, and New Directions.* Washington, D.C.: U.S. Government Printing Office, 1982.

—————. "Surveys of Victimization—An Optimistic Assessment," in Michael Tonry and Norval Morris, eds., *Crime and Justice: An Annual Review of Research,* Vol. 3. Chicago: University of Chicago Press, 1981b, pp. 1–60.

SPITZER, STEVEN. "The Political Economy of Policing," in David E. Greenberg, ed., *Crime & Capitalism.* Palo Alto, Calif.: Mayfield, 1981, pp. 314–340.

SPIVACK, GORDON B. "Antitrust Enforcement in the United States: A Primer," *Connecticut Bar Journal* 37 (September 1963), 375–389.

SPOHN, CASSIA, JOHN GRUHL, AND SUSAN WELCH. "The Effect of Race on Sentencing: A Reexamination of an Unsettled Question," *Law and Society Review* 16 (1981–82), 71–88.

STACK, STEVEN. "Income Inequality and Property Crime: A Cross-National Analysis of Relative Deprivation Theory," *Criminology* 22 (May 1984), 229–257.

—————. "Social Structure and Swedish Crime Rates: A Time-Series Analysis, 1950–1979," *Criminology* 20 (November 1982), 499–513.

STAFFORD, MARK C., AND OMER R. GALLE. "Victimization Rates, Exposure to Risk, and Fear of Crime," *Criminology* 22 (May 1984), 173–185.

STANKO, ELIZABETH ANNE. "The Impact of Victim Assessment on Prosecutors' Screening Decisions: The Case of the New York County District Attorney's Office," *Law and Society Review* 16 (1981–82), 225–239.

STARK, RODNEY. "Whose Status Counts?" *American Sociological Review* 44 (August 1979), 668–669.

—————, DANIEL P. DOYLE, AND LORI KENT. "Rediscovering Moral Communities: Church Membership and Crime," in Travis Hirschi and Michael Gottfredson, eds., *Understanding Crime: Current Theory and Research.* Beverly Hills, Calif.: Sage Publications, 1980, pp. 43–52.

————, Lori Kent, and Daniel P. Doyle. "Religion and Delinquency: The Ecology of a 'Lost' Relationship," *Journal of Research in Crime and Delinquency* 19 (January 1982), 4–24.

————, et al. "Crime and Delinquency in the Roaring Twenties," *Journal of Research in Crime and Delinquency* 20 (January 1983), 4–23.

Stebbins, Robert A. *Commitment to Deviance: The Nonprofessional Criminal in the Community*. Westport, Conn.: Greenwood, 1971.

Steffensmeier, Darrell J. "Assessing the Impact of the Women's Movement on Sex-Based Differences in the Handling of Adult Criminal Defendants," *Crime and Delinquency* 26 (July 1980), 344–357.

————. "Organization Properties and Sex-Segregation in the Underworld: Building a Sociological Theory of Sex Differences in Crime," *Social Forces* 61 (June 1983), 1010–1032.

————, and Michael J. Cobb. "Sex Differences in Urban Arrest Patterns," *Social Problems* 29 (October 1981), 37–50.

————, and Renee Hoffman Steffensmeier. "Trends in Female Delinquency: An Examination of Arrest, Juvenile Court, Self-Report, and Field Data," *Criminology* 18 (May 1980), 62–85.

Stein, M. L. "Citizens of Suburban Los Angeles Fight Back as Crime Hits Home," *The Boston Globe*, October 28, 1981, p. 2.

Steinmetz, Suzanne K., and Murray A. Straus. "The Family as a Cradle of Violence," in Delos H. Kelly, ed., *Criminal Behavior: Readings in Criminology*. New York: St. Martin's Press, 1980, pp. 130–142.

Stenross, Barbara. "Police Response to Residential Burglaries: Dusting for Prints as a Negative Rite," *Criminology* 22 (August 1984), 389–402.

Stephens, Richard C., and Rosalind D. Ellis. "Narcotic Addicts and Crime: Analysis of Recent Trends," *Criminology* 12 (February 1975), 474–488.

Sterba, James P. "China Says Its Rising Juvenile Crime Stems from Cultural Revolution," *The New York Times*, December 26, 1979, p. A12.

Stinchcombe, Arthur L. "Institutions of Privacy in the Determination of Police Administration," *American Journal of Sociology* 69 (September 1963), 150–160.

Stone, Christopher D. *Where the Law Ends*. New York: Harper & Row, 1974.

Stookey, John Alan. "A Cost Theory of Victim Justice," in Burt Galaway and Joe Hudson, eds., *Perspectives on Crime Victims*. St. Louis: C. V. Mosby, 1981, pp. 80–89.

Strasburg, Paul A. *Violent Delinquents: A Report to the Ford Foundation from the Vera Institute of Justice*. New York: Monarch, 1978.

Stuart, Reginald. "Atlanta Deaths: Fear Felt by Young," *The New York Times*, January 26, 1981, pp. A1, A12.

Sudnow, David. "Normal Crimes: Sociological Features of the Penal Code in a Public Defender Office," *Social Problems* 12 (Winter 1965), 255–276.

Sullivan, Joseph F. "Strict New Rules on Juvenile Crime Adopted in Jersey," *The New York Times*, July 24, 1982, pp. 1, 28.

Sullivan, Walter. "Violent Pornography Elevates Aggression, Researchers Say," *The New York Times*, September 30, 1980, pp. C1, C3.

Sutherland, Edwin H. "The Diffusion of Sexual Psychopath Laws," *American Journal of Sociology* 56 (September 1950), 142–148.

————. *The Professional Thief*. Chicago: University of Chicago Press, 1937.

————. *White Collar Crime: The Uncut Version*. New Haven, Conn.: Yale University Press, 1949, 1983.

————, and Donald R. Cressey. *Criminology*, 10th ed. Philadelphia: Lippincott, 1978.

SUTTLES, GERALD D. *The Social Order of the Slum: Ethnicity and Territory in the Inner City.* Chicago: University of Chicago Press, 1968.

SVIRIDOFF, MICHELLE, AND JAMES W. THOMPSON. "Links between Employment and Crime: A Qualitative Study of Rikers Island Releasees," *Crime and Delinquency* 29 (April 1983), 195–212.

SWIGERT, VICTORIA LYNN, AND RONALD A. FARRELL. "Corporate Homicide: Definitional Processes in the Creation of Deviance," *Law and Society Review* 15 (1980–1981), 161–182.

_____, AND RONALD A. FARRELL. *Murder, Inequality, and the Law.* Lexington, Mass.: D. C. Heath, 1976.

_____, AND RONALD A. FARRELL. "Normal Homicides and the Law," *American Sociological Review* 42 (February 1977), 16–32.

SYKES, GRESHAM M. *The Society of Captives: A Study of a Maximum Security Prison.* Princeton, N.J.: Princeton University Press, 1958.

_____, AND DAVID MATZA. "Techniques of Neutralization: A Theory of Delinquency," *American Sociological Review* 22 (December 1957), 664–670.

TAYLOR, IAN, PAUL WALTON, AND JOCK YOUNG, EDS. *Critical Criminology.* London: Routledge and Kegan Paul, 1975a.

_____, PAUL WALTON, AND JOCK YOUNG. "Critical Criminology in Britain: Review and Prospects," in Ian Taylor, Paul Walton, and Jock Young, eds., *Critical Criminology.* London: Routledge and Kegan Paul, 1975b, pp. 6–62.

_____, PAUL WALTON, AND JOCK YOUNG. *The New Criminology: For a Social Theory of Deviance.* London: Routledge and Kegan Paul, 1973.

TAYLOR, RALPH B., STEPHEN D. GOTTFREDSON, AND SIDNEY BROWER. "Block Crime and Fear: Defensible Space, Local Social Ties, and Territorial Functioning," *Journal of Research in Crime and Delinquency* 21 (November 1984), 303–331.

_____, STEPHEN D. GOTTFREDSON, AND SIDNEY BROWER. "The Defensibility of Defensible Space: A Critical Review and a Synthetic Framework for Future Research," in Travis Hirschi and Michael Gottfredson, eds., *Understanding Crime: Current Theory and Research.* Beverly Hills, Calif.: Sage Publications, 1980, pp. 53–71.

TAYLOR, STUART, JR. "New Crime Act a Vast Change, Experts Assert," *The New York Times,* October 15, 1984, pp. A1, B6.

_____. "The Plea of Insanity and Its Use in Criminal Cases," *The New York Times,* July 27, 1981, p. A9.

_____. "Strict Penalties for Criminals: Pendulum of Feeling Swings," *The New York Times,* December 13, 1983, pp. A1, B6.

TELTSCH, KATHLEEN. "Private Guard Forces Feared as Drain on Money for Police," *The New York Times,* January 29, 1984, p. 33.

THOMAS, CHARLES W., ROBIN J. CAGE, AND SAMUEL C. FOSTER. "Public Opinion on Criminal Law and Legal Sanctions: An Examination of Two Conceptual Models," *Journal of Criminal Law and Criminology* 67 (March 1976), 110–116.

THOMAS, JO. "For Britain, New Debate on Firearms," *The New York Times,* June 17, 1984, p. 11.

THOMPSON, JAMES W., ET AL. *Employment and Crime: A Review of Theories and Research.* Washington, D.C.: National Institute of Justice, U.S. Department of Justice, 1981.

THORNBERRY, TERENCE P. "Race, Socioeconomic Status and Sentencing in the Juvenile Justice System," *Journal of Criminal Law and Criminology* 64 (March 1973), 90–98.

_____. "Sentencing Disparities in the Juvenile Justice System," *Journal of Criminal Law and Criminology* 70 (Summer 1979), 164–171.

_____, AND R. L. CHRISTENSON. "Unemployment and Criminal Involvement: An Investigation of Reciprocal Causal Structures," *American Sociological Review* 49 (June 1984), 398–411.

_____, AND MARGARET FARNWORTH. "Social Correlates of Criminal Involvement: Further Evidence on the Relationship between Social Status and Criminal Behavior," *American Sociological Review* 47 (August 1982), 505–518.

THORSELL, BERNARD A., AND LLOYD W. KLEMKE. "The Labeling Process: Reinforcement and Deterrent?" *Law and Society Review* 6 (February 1972), 393–403.

THRASHER, FREDERIC M. *The Gang: A Study of 1,313 Gangs in Chicago,* abridged ed. Chicago: University of Chicago Press, 1927, 1963.

TIMNICK, LOIS. "Psychic Trauma Follows Chowchilla Kidnaping," *The Boston Globe,* January 24, 1981, p. 3.

TITTLE, CHARLES R. "Social Class and Criminal Behavior: A Critique of the Theoretical Foundation," *Social Forces* 62 (December 1983), 334–358.

_____, AND ALAN R. ROWE. "Certainty of Arrest and Crime Rates: A Further Test of the Deterrence Hypothesis," *Social Forces* 52 (June 1974), 455–462.

_____, WAYNE J. VILLEMEZ, AND DOUGLAS A. SMITH. "The Myth of Social Class and Criminality: An Empirical Assessment of the Empirical Evidence," *American Sociological Review* 43 (October 1978), 643–656.

_____, AND MICHAEL R. WELCH. "Religiosity and Deviance: Toward a Contingency Theory of Constraining Effects," *Social Forces* 61 (March 1983), 653–682.

TOBIAS, J. J. *Crime and Industrial Society in the 19th Century.* New York: Schocken, 1967.

TOBY, JACKSON. "Affluence and Adolescent Crime," in The President's Commission on Law Enforcement and Administration of Justice. *Task Force Report: Juvenile Delinquency and Youth Crime.* Washington, D.C.: U.S. Government Printing Office, 1967, pp. 132–144.

_____. "Deterrence without Punishment," *Criminology* 19 (August 1981), 195–209.

_____. "The Differential Impact of Family Disorganization," *American Sociological Review* 22 (October 1957), 505–512.

_____. "The Socialization and Control of Deviant Motivation," in Daniel Glaser, ed., *Handbook of Criminology.* Chicago: Rand McNally, 1974, pp. 85–100.

TREBACH, ARNOLD S. *The Heroin Solution.* New Haven, Conn.: Yale University Press, 1982.

TRIMBORN, HARRY. "Soviet Official Executed," *The Boston Globe,* April 29, 1982, p. 3.

TURK, AUSTIN T. *Political Criminality: The Defiance and Defense of Authority.* Beverly Hills, Calif.: Sage Publications, 1982.

TURNER, STANLEY. "The Ecology of Delinquency," in Thorsten Sellin and Marvin E. Wolfgang, eds., *Delinquency: Selected Studies.* New York: Wiley, 1969, pp. 27–60.

TWOMEY, STEVE. "Timber Theft Becomes Big Problem," *The New York Times,* September 14, 1982, p. 11.

TYLER, TOM R., AND RENEE WEBER. "Support for the Death Penalty: Instrumental Response to Crime, or Symbolic Attitude?" *Law and Society Review* 17 (1982), 21–45.

UHLMAN, THOMAS M., AND N. DARLENE WALKER. " 'He Takes Some of My Time; I Take Some of His': An Analysis of Sentencing Patterns in Jury Cases," *Law and Society Review* 14 (Winter 1980), 323–341.

UNITED NATIONS. *Demographic Yearbook 1981.* New York: United Nations, 1983.

_____. *Demographic Yearbook 1982.* New York: United Nations, 1984.

"United Nations Crime Survey (1977)," in Louise I. Shelley, ed., *Readings in Comparative Criminology.* Carbondale, Ill.: Southern Illinois University Press, 1981, pp. 153–174.

UNNEVER, JAMES D. "Direct and Organizational Discrimination in the Sentencing of Drug Offenders," *Social Problems* 30 (December 1982), 212–225.

U.S. DEPARTMENT OF COMMERCE, BUREAU OF THE CENSUS. *General Population Characteristics: United States Summary, 1970.* Washington, D.C.: U.S. Government Printing Office, 1972.

_____. *General Population Characteristics: United States Summary, 1980.* Washington, D.C.: U.S. Government Printing Office, 1983.

U.S. DEPARTMENT OF JUSTICE, ATTORNEY GENERAL'S TASK FORCE ON VIOLENT CRIME, *Final Report.* Washington, D.C.: U.S. Government Printing Office, 1981.

[*U.S. News & World Report*]. "American Justice: ABC's of How It Really Works," *U.S. News & World Report,* November 1, 1982, pp. 35–58.

_____. "Crime Expense: Now Up to $51 Billion a Year," *U.S. News & World Report,* October 26, 1970, p. 33.

_____. "More Punch for Antitrust—Moves You Can Expect," *U.S. News & World Report,* November 25, 1974, p. 47.

VAN DEN HAAG, ERNEST. "For the Death Penalty," *The New York Times,* October 17, 1983, p. A21.

_____. *Punishing Criminals: Concerning a Very Old and Painful Question.* New York: Basic Books, 1975.

_____, AND JOHN P. CONRAD. *The Death Penalty: A Debate.* New York: Plenum, 1983.

VAN DINE, STEVE, JOHN P. CONRAD, AND SIMON DINITZ. "The Incapacitation of the Chronic Thug," *Journal of Criminal Law and Criminology* 70 (Spring 1979), 125–135.

VELLENGA, JACOB J. "Is Capital Punishment Wrong?" *Christianity Today* 4 (October 12, 1959), 7–9.

VERA INSTITUTE OF JUSTICE. *Felony Arrests,* rev. ed. New York: Vera Institute of Justice and Longman, 1981.

VIDMAR, NEIL, AND DALE T. MILLER. "Socialpsychological Processes Underlying Attitudes toward Legal Punishment," *Law and Society Review* 14 (Spring 1980), 565–602.

VOLAVKA, JAN, ET AL. "EEGs of XYY and XXY Men Found in a Large Birth Cohort," in Sarnoff A. Mednick and Karl O. Christiansen, eds., *Biosocial Bases of Criminal Behavior.* New York: Gardner Press, 1977, pp. 189–198.

VOLD, GEORGE B. *Theoretical Criminology,* 2nd ed., prepared by Thomas J. Bernard. New York: Oxford University Press, 1979.

VON HENTIG, HANS. *The Criminal and His Victim.* Hamden, Conn.: Archon Books, 1948, 1967.

VON HIRSCH, ANDREW. *Doing Justice: The Choice of Punishments.* New York: Hill and Wang, 1976.

_____. "The Ethics of Selective Incapacitation: Observations on the Contemporary Debate," *Crime and Delinquency* 30 (April 1984a), 175–194.

_____. "Selective Incapacitation: A Critique," *NIJ Reports*, January 1984b, pp. 5–8.

_____. "Utilitarian Sentencing Resuscitated: The American Bar Association's Second Report on Criminal Sentencing," *Rutgers Law Review* 33 (Spring 1981), 772–789.

_____, AND KATHLEEN HANRAHAN. *Abolish Parole?* Washington, D.C.: U.S. Government Printing Office, 1978.

VORENBERG, JAMES, AND IRVING F. LUKOFF. "Addiction, Crime, and the Criminal Justice System," *Federal Probation* 37 (December 1973), 3–7.

VOSS, HARWIN L. "Ethnic Differentials in Delinquency in Honolulu," *Journal of Criminal Law, Criminology and Police Science* 54 (September 1963), 322–327.

_____, AND JOHN R. HEPBURN. "Patterns in Criminal Homicide in Chicago," *Journal of Criminal Law, Criminology and Police Science* 59 (December 1968), 499–508.

VOTEY, HAROLD L., JR., AND LLAD PHILLIPS. "The Control of Criminal Activity: An Economic Analysis," in Daniel Glaser, ed., *Handbook of Criminology.* Chicago: Rand McNally, 1974, pp. 1055–1093.

WAEGEL, WILLIAM B. "The Use of Lethal Force by Police: The Effect of Statutory Change," *Crime and Delinquency* 30 (January 1984), 121–140.

WALDO, GORDON P., AND SIMON DINITZ. "Personality Attributes of the Criminal: An Analysis of Research Studies, 1950–1965," *Journal of Research in Crime and Delinquency* 4 (July 1967), 185–201.

WALKER, NIGEL. *Crimes, Courts and Figures: An Introduction to Criminal Statistics.* Harmondsworth, Engl.: Penguin, 1971.

_____. "Lost Causes in Criminology," in Roger Hood, ed., *Crime, Criminology and Public Policy: Essays in Honour of Sir Leon Radzinowicz.* New York: Free Press, 1974, pp. 47–62.

WALLACE, CHRISTOPHER. "Atkins Announces Drive against Black-Area Crime," *The Boston Globe*, August 19, 1971, p. 3.

WALLERSTEIN, JAMES S., AND CLEMENT J. WYLE. "Our Law-Abiding Law-Breakers," *Probation* 35 (April 1947), 107–112.

WALLIS, C. P., AND R. MALIPHANT. "Delinquent Areas in the County of London: Ecological Factors," *British Journal of Criminology* 7 (July 1967), 250–284.

WALSH, MARILYN E. *The Fence: A New Look at the World of Property Theft.* Westport, Conn.: Greenwood, 1977.

WARD, DAVID A. "Sweden: The Middle Way to Prison Reform?" in Marvin E. Wolfgang, ed., *Prisons: Present and Possible.* Lexington, Mass.: D. C. Heath, 1979, pp. 89–167.

WARR, MARK, AND MARK STAFFORD. "Fear of Victimization: A Look at the Proximate Causes," *Social Forces* 61 (June 1983), 1033–1043.

WARREN, DONALD I. "Neighborhood Structure and Riot Behavior in Detroit: Some Exploratory Findings," *Social Problems* 16 (Spring 1969), 464–484.

WEBSTER, WILLIAM H. *Crime in the United States, 1980: Uniform Crime Reports.* Washington D.C.: U.S. Government Printing Office, 1981.

_____. *Crime in the United States, 1983: Uniform Crime Reports.* Washington, D.C.: U.S. Government Printing Office, 1984.

WEINER, NORMAN L. "The Teen-Age Shoplifter: A Microcosmic View of Middle-Class Delinquency," in Jack O. Douglas, ed., *Observations of Deviance.* N.Y.: Random House, 1970, pp. 213–217.

WEIS, JOSEPH G. "Crime Statistics: Reporting Systems and Methods," in Sanford

H. Kadish, ed., *Encyclopedia of Crime and Justice*, Vol. 1. New York: Free Press, 1983, pp. 378–392.

WEIS, KURT, AND SANDRA S. BORGES. "Victimology and Rape: The Case of the Legitimate Victim," *Issues in Criminology* 8 (Fall 1973), 71–115.

WELCH, SUSAN, JOHN GRUHL, AND CASSIA SPOHN. "Sentencing: The Influence of Alternative Measures of Prior Record," *Criminology* 22 (May 1984), 215–227.

WELSH, RALPH S. "Delinquency, Corporal Punishment, and the Schools," *Crime and Delinquency* 24 (July 1978), 336–354.

WERNER, LESLIE MAITLAND. "U.S. Officials Cite Key Successes in War against Organized Crime," *The New York Times*, November 7, 1983, pp. A1, D18.

_____. "U.S. Parole Unit to Seek Testimony from Victim," *The New York Times*, June 1, 1984, p. A22.

WEST, D. J. *Delinquency: Its Roots, Careers and Prospects*. Cambridge, Mass.: Harvard University Press, 1982.

_____. *Present Conduct and Future Delinquency*. London: Heinemann, 1969.

_____, AND D. P. FARRINGTON. *The Delinquent Way of Life*. London: Heinemann, 1977.

_____, AND D. P. FARRINGTON. *Who Becomes Delinquent?* London: Heinemann, 1973.

WHITE, W. PAUL. "Punishing Criminals," *The Boston Globe*, April 9, 1981, p. 13.

WHITING, RICHARD A. "Antitrust Enforcement and the Corporate Executive II," *Virginia Law Review* 48 (January 1962), 1–49.

WHYMANT, ROBERT. "Tokyo's Safe but at What Price?" *The Boston Globe*, June 11, 1979, p. 2.

WIATROWSKI, MICHAEL D., DAVID B. GRISWOLD, AND MARY K. ROBERTS. "Social Control Theory and Delinquency," *American Sociological Review* 46 (October 1981), 525–541.

WICKER, TOM. "After the Hinckley Case," *The New York Times*, June 25, 1982, p. A31.

WIEBE, G. D. "Responses to the Televised Kefauver Hearings: Social Psychological Implications," *Public Opinion Quarterly* 16 (Summer 1962), 181–200.

WIEHOFEN, HENRY. "Punishment and Treatment: Rehabilitation," in Stanley E. Grupp, ed., *Theories of Punishment*. Bloomington, Ind.: Indiana University Press, 1971, pp. 255–263.

WILBANKS, WILLIAM. "Does Alcohol Cause Homicide?" *Journal of Crime and Justice* 4 (1981), 149–170.

_____. *Murder in Miami*. Lanham, Md.: University Press of America, 1984.

WILEY, NORBERT. "The Ethnic Mobility Trap and Stratification Theory," *Social Problems* 15 (Fall 1967), 147–159.

WILKINSON, KAREN. "The Broken Home and Delinquent Behavior: An Alternative Interpretation of Contradictory Findings," in Travis Hirschi and Michael Gottfredson, eds., *Understanding Crime: Current Theory and Research*. Beverly Hills, Calif.: Sage Publications, 1980, pp. 21–42.

_____, B. GRANT STITT, AND MAYNARD L. ERICKSON. "Siblings and Delinquent Behavior: An Exploratory Study of a Neglected Family Variable," *Criminology* 20 (August 1982), 223–239.

WILLENS, MICHELE. "Movie Stars Fighting Crime with Tear Gas," *The New York Times*, May 10, 1981, p. A26.

WILLIAMS, JAY R., AND MARTIN GOLD. "From Delinquent Behavior to Official Delinquency," *Social Problems* 20 (Fall 1972), 209–229.

WILLIAMS, KIRK R. "Economic Sources of Homicide: Reestimating the Effects of Poverty and Inequality," *American Sociological Review* 49 (April 1984), 283–289.

WILLIAMS, WILLIE (PSEUDONYM). "A Street Man's Answer to Rape: Humiliate the Raper," in Barbara Allen Babcock et al., *Sex Discrimination and the Law: Causes and Remedies*. Boston: Little, Brown, 1975, p. 877.

WILSON, JAMES Q. "Foreword," in Thomas A. Reppetto, *Residential Crime*. Cambridge, Mass.: Ballinger, 1974, pp. xv–xvi.

_____. *Thinking About Crime*, rev. ed. New York: Basic Books, 1983.

_____. *Varieties of Police Behavior: The Management of Law and Order in Eight Communities*. Cambridge, Mass.: Harvard University Press, 1968.

_____, AND BARBARA BOLAND. "Crime," in William Gorham and Nathan Glazer, eds., *The Urban Predicament*. Washington, D.C.: Urban Institute, 1976, pp. 179–230.

_____, AND BARBARA BOLAND. "The Effect of the Police on Crime," *Law and Society Review* 12 (Spring 1978), 367–390.

_____, AND BARBARA BOLAND. "The Effects of the Police on Crime: A Response to Jacob and Rich," *Law and Society Review* 16 (1981–82), 163–169.

_____, AND GEORGE L. KELLING. "Broken Windows," *Atlantic Monthly* 249 (March 1982), 29–38.

WINICK, CHARLES. "Physician Narcotic Addicts," in Howard S. Becker, ed., *The Other Side: Perspectives on Deviance*. New York: Free Press, 1964, pp. 261–279.

WISE, NANCY BARTON. "Juvenile Delinquency among Middle-Class Girls," in Edmund W. Vaz, ed., *Middle-Class Juvenile Delinquency*. New York: Harper & Row, 1967, pp. 179–188.

WITKIN, HERMAN A., ET AL. "Criminality in XYY and XXY Men," *Science* 193 (August 13, 1976), 547–555.

WOLFGANG, MARVIN E. "Crime in a Birth Cohort," in Roger Hood, ed., *Crime, Criminology and Public Policy: Essays in Honour of Sir Leon Radzinowicz*. New York: Free Press, 1974, pp. 79–92.

_____. *Patterns in Criminal Homicide*. Philadelphia: University of Pennsylvania Press, 1958.

_____. "Urban Crime," in James Q. Wilson, ed., *The Metropolitan Enigma*. Garden City, N.Y.: Doubleday, 1968, pp. 270–311.

_____, AND FRANCO FERRACUTI. *The Subculture of Violence: Towards an Integrated Theory in Criminology*. Beverly Hills, Calif.: Sage Publications, 1967, 1982.

_____, ROBERT M. FIGLIO, AND THORSTEN SELLIN. *Delinquency in a Birth Cohort*. Chicago: University of Chicago Press, 1972.

_____, AND SIMON I. SINGER. "Victim Categories of Crime," *Journal of Criminal Law and Criminology* 69 (Fall 1978), 379–394.

WOLPIN, KENNETH I. "An Economic Analysis of Crime and Punishment in England and Wales, 1894–1967," *Journal of Political Economy* 86 (October 1978), 815–840.

WOOTTON, BARBARA. *Social Science and Social Pathology*. London: George Allen and Unwin, 1959.

WREN, CHRISTOPHER S. "Crime and Capital Punishment in China," *The New York Times*, November 20, 1983, p. E9.

WRIGHT, ERIK OLIN. *The Politics of Punishment: A Critical Analysis of Prisons in America*. New York: Harper & Row, 1973.

WRIGHT, JAMES D., PETER H. ROSSI, AND KATHLEEN DALY. *Under the Gun: Weapons, Crime, and Violence in America*. New York: Aldine, 1983.

YIN, PETER. "Fear of Crime as a Problem for the Elderly," *Social Problems* 30 (December 1982), 240–245.

YOCHELSON, SAMUEL, AND STANTON E. SAMENOW. *The Criminal Personality,* Vol. 1: *A Profile for Change.* New York: Jason Aronson, 1976.

————, AND STANTON E. SAMENOW. *The Criminal Personality,* Vol. II: *The Change Process.* New York: Jason Aronson, 1977.

YODER, STEPHEN A. "Criminal Sanctions for Corporate Illegality," *Journal of Criminal Law and Criminology* 69 (Spring 1978), 40–58.

YUNKER, JAMES A. "The Relevance of the Identification Problem to Statistical Research on Capital Punishment," *Crime and Delinquency* 28 (January 1982), 96–124.

ZARR, GERALD H. "Liberia," in Alan Milner, ed., *African Penal Systems.* London: Routledge and Kegan Paul, 1969.

ZATZ, MARJORIE S. "Race, Ethnicity, and Determinate Sentencing: A New Dimension to an Old Controversy," *Criminology* 22 (May 1984), 147–171.

ZEISEL, HANS. "A Comment on 'The Deterrent Effect of Capital Punishment' by Phillips," *American Journal of Sociology* 88 (July 1982), 167–169.

————. "An International Experiment on the Effects of the Good Samaritan Law," in James M. Ratcliffe, ed., *The Good Samaritan and the Law.* Garden City, N.Y.: Doubleday, 1966, pp. 209–212.

————. "Race Bias in the Administration of the Death Penalty: The Florida Experience," *Harvard Law Review* 95 (December 1981), 456–468.

ZEITLIN, LAWRENCE R. "A Little Larceny Can Do a Lot for Employee Morale," *Psychology Today* 5 (June 1971), 22–26, 64.

ZIMBARDO, PHILIP G. "Pathology of Imprisonment," *Society* 9 (April 1972), 4–8.

————. "The Prison Game," Hearings before Subcommittee #3 of the Committee on the Judiciary, House of Representatives, 92nd Congress, 1st Session, Part II, Serial No. 15, October 25, 1971, pp. 110–113. Reprinted in Norman Johnston and Leonard D. Savitz, eds., *Legal Process and Corrections.* New York: Wiley, 1982, pp. 195–198.

————, ET AL., "A Pirandellian Prison," *The New York Times Magazine,* April 8, 1973, pp. 38–60.

ZIMRING, FRANKLIN E., "Kids, Groups and Crime: Some Implications of a Well-Known Secret," *Journal of Criminal Law and Criminology* 72 (Fall 1981), 867–885.

————, AND GORDON J. HAWKINS. *Deterrence: The Legal Threat in Crime Control.* Chicago: University of Chicago Press, 1973.

NAME INDEX

SUBJECT INDEX